THE FLOWERING OF THE MIDDLE AGES

THE FLOWERING OF **THE**

TEXTS BY

EDITED BY JOAN EVANS

THAMES AND HUDSON · LONDON

MIDDLE AGES

CHRISTOPHER BROOKE

GEORGE ZARNECKI

JOHN HARVEY

CHRISTOPHER HOHLER

RICHARD HUNT

T. S. R. BOASE

DONALD KING

ANDREW MARTINDALE

JOAN EVANS

631 illustrations
192 in colour
439 photographs, drawings,
maps, plans
and chronological tables

Designed and produced by THAMES AND HUDSON, London

MANAGING EDITOR: Ian Sutton BA

ART EDITOR: Ian Mackenzie Kerr ARCA

EDITORIAL: Clarissa Cairns BA

RESEARCH: R. Davidson-Houston BA, FRAI;
Emily Lane BA

MAPS: John Woodcock ARCA, MSIA

PLANS AND DRAWINGS: P. A. Faulkner ARIBA;
M. E. Weaver AA DIP, Jon D. Wilsher

SPECIAL PHOTOGRAPHY: Peter Cannon Brookes,
Jean Roubier, John Webb

BLOCKS: Klischeewerkstätten der Industriedienst, Wiesbaden,
Germany

PRINTED in Western Germany by DuMont Presse, Cologne

PAPER: Woodfree White Art and Apex Smooth Grey
supplied by Frank Grunfeld Ltd., London

BOUND by Van Rijmenam N.V., The Hague, Holland

© THAMES AND HUDSON 1966, LONDON

CONTENTS

CONTENTS

CONTENTS

FOREWORD

FIFTY YEARS AGO history was mainly studied in school and university, and as a consequence by the educated reader, in terms of wars, political alliances and constitutional developments. Its base was properly in written documents, and even social history was not envisaged in other than documentary terms. Eight half-tone illustrations were enough for any historical work and most were not illustrated at all.

Now, at least for the general reader, all is changed. Schoolmasters attempt to give some visual background to their history lessons; occasionally even a Professor of History may show a few slides. Professional historians and archivists rightly continue to study every facet of their subject in documented detail, but for most people 'history' has become a much more general matter, that provides them with a background to what they see and what they read. For them, at least, historians must so interpret the documents as to make them reveal the life of the past rather than its battles and its political machinations.

This change is due less to the professional historians themselves than to a change of view in the reading public: a change that can only be paralleled in the second half of the nineteenth century when trains and steamers made it easy to travel and everyone began to know their Europe. That time produced its Ruskin and its Viollet-le-Duc, its Lasteyrie and its Henry Adams; but we forget that Ruskin had to draw, or to engage others to draw for him, the things he wrote and talked about, and that Viollet-le-Duc was never able to reproduce a photograph.

In our own day a new wave of travel by car and plane has been accompanied by incredible developments in photography and in reproduction. Black and white photographs and half-tone blocks revolutionized the study of architecture and art at the end of the 19th century, and the great archaeological discoveries of the day made the general public willing to accept an object or a building *pari passu* with a written document. In our own time colour photographs and colour plates have enriched these studies in a way that would have seemed miraculous to Ruskin.

Moreover, though education remains astonishingly bookish, our recreations have trained our eyes. An experienced and successful lecturer of 1900 said that a slide must remain on the screen for at least a minute to give the audience time to take it in. Now, the cinema screen and the television set have trained us in visual nimbleness, and we 'see' much more quickly.

All these trends have combined to create a need for a new kind of historical book, that is more concerned with the social background than with political events, and that by a rich illustration makes that background live. This volume is one in a series that attempts to meet the need. Nine authors have each written a chapter on an aspect of the social life of the Middle Ages. The inevitable documentary bases of their work have not been forgotten but it is their *interpretation* which is attempted here.

Alongside the written text runs another, a visual interpretation of the same themes. Each double-page spread has a unity of its own, closely related to the written text but attempting to do more than illustrate it. The smaller illustrations are brought into the complex scheme by individual captions. We have felt free to illustrate *ideas* as well as the literary chapters. In certain instances one picture-section may be equally relevant to another chapter than that with which it has been bound in.

Somewhere about 1100 it seems as if Europe settled on an even keel. In England the Norman dynasty had established itself militarily and administratively. In France Philip I had established a rival kingdom, the Cluniac reform had revivified religious life, and the Crusades had started on their way. In Germany Henry IV was establishing the Empire on a firmer basis. In Italy Pope Gregory VII had lost his fight against the Emperor, but had gained new spiritual force for Rome. In Spain Alfonso VI of Castile had made Toledo the capital of Christian Spain, and the Cid had conquered Valencia. In the Eastern Empire the Comneni had suffered the inroads first of the Normans and then of the Crusaders; the weight of power was shifting westward. In Europe it is fair to say that a measure of stability had been achieved, in which the forces of feudalism, monasticism, scholastic philosophy and civic growth could work together to make the history of the Middle Ages.

To make that history more real to the ordinary reader is the purpose of this book. Its authors have not here published unknown documents, unknown monuments or unknown works of art, but have tried by the interpretation of what is known to make the Christian civilization of Europe in the Middle Ages more significant and more comprehensible to the readers of today. The keyword to our conception of history is civilization.

JOAN EVANS

9

Acknowledgments

In preparing this book the editor and publishers have received
generous help from many quarters. The authors themselves have
patiently answered a multitude of queries and given advice on
the choice of pictures and the wording of the captions, though
the final responsibility for these rests with the publishers. Of the
many other institutions and individuals all over the world who
have assisted us we should like specially to thank the following:

The late Dr Eric G. Millar; Dr J. K. St Joseph; The Walters
Art Gallery, Baltimore; Kupferstichkabinett and Gemäldegalerie
der Staatlichen Museen, Berlin; Bibliothèque Publique, Boulogne;
Bibliothèque Royale de Belgique and Institut Royal du Patrimoine
Artistique, Brussels; Bibliothèque Municipale Classée, Cambrai;
Corpus Christi College, Fitzwilliam Museum, Gonville and Caius
College, Magdalene College, Trinity College, University Archives
and University Library, Cambridge; Fogg Art Museum, Harvard
University, Cambridge, Mass.; Musée Condé, Chantilly; Cleve-
land Museum of Art, Ohio; Wallraf-Richartz-Museum, Cologne;
Bibliothèque Municipale and Musée de Dijon; Dean and Chapter
of Durham Cathedral; Faculty of Advocates and National
Library of Scotland, Edinburgh; Biblioteca Riccardiana, Florence;
Universitätsbibliothek, Freiburg im Breisgau; Centrale Biblio-
theek der Rijksuniversiteit, Ghent; Koninklijke Bibliotheek and

Rijksmuseum Meermanno-Westreenianum, The Hague; Belgian
National Tourist Office, British Museum (Departments of
British and Medieval Antiquities, of Coins and Medals and of
Manuscripts), British Travel Association, Courtauld Institute of
Art, National Buildings Record, National Gallery, Royal Com-
mission on Historical Monuments and Victoria and Albert
Museum, London; John Rylands Library, Manchester; Bayeri-
sches Landesamt für Denkmalpflege and Bayerische Verwaltung
der Staatlichen Schlösser, Gärten und Seen, Munich; Metropoli-
tan Museum of Art and the Pierpont Morgan Library, New York;
Bodleian Library (Departments of Oriental Books and of Western
Manuscripts), Corpus Christi College, Merton College and New
College, Oxford; Biblioteca del Seminario, Padua; Bibliothèque
Nationale, Ministère des Affaires Culturelles, Musée Carnavalet
and Musée du Louvre, Paris; Musée de l'Oeuvre Notre-Dame,
Strasbourg; Württembergische Landesbibliothek, Stuttgart;
Münsterbauamt, Ulm; Biblioteca Apostolica Vaticana, Vatican
City; Kupferstichkabinett, Akademie der bildenden Künste,
Kunsthistorisches Museum and Österreichische Nationalbiblio-
thek, Vienna; National Gallery of Art, Washington, D. C.; Dean
and Chapter of York Minster, and Graphische Sammlung der
Zentralbibliothek, Zürich.

1 INTRODUCTION

The Structure of Mediaeval Society

CHRISTOPHER BROOKE

'I looked up at the East at the high sun,

And saw a tower on a toft artfully fashioned.

A deep dale was beneath with a dungeon in it,

And deep ditches and dark, dreadful to see.

A fair field full of folk I found between them,

With all manner of men, the meanest and the richest,

Working and wandering as the world demanded.'

WILLIAM LANGLAND, 'THE VISION OF PIERS PLOWMAN'

What made a King?

and how was his authority conceived? The answer would take us to the heart of mediaeval society, for it is a characteristic mixture of idealism and power, of religion and economics. On the one hand, a king was God's anointed, and to rebel against him was to commit sacrilege as well as treason. On the other, a king could be unjust, or weak . . . or poor; his nobles could lose faith in him; the common good might demand that he be replaced. Every monarch knew that the sacred bond, however strong, needed an army, firm government and money, to keep it in being.

The sacred rite of coronation is the theme of this manuscript illumination (opposite) from an English Coronation *ordo* (text of the ceremony) written between 1272 and 1325. The king may be Edward II, but more probably it is not so much the representation of an actual event as a sort of general view of a coronation with the various courtiers and priests who took part in it.

The king sits on a throne that is almost certainly copied from the Coronation Chair in Westminster Abbey (see overleaf). He is dressed in four ceremonial vestments: first, a white robe, the *colobium sindonis*, touching the feet, with sleeves reaching to the wrists; over that, a red tunic with tight sleeves and rows of buttons along the forearms; then a rich dalmatic, horizontally striped in yellow and pale mauve; and lastly a brown cloak lined on the inside with miniver and fastened across the chest by a sexfoil gold brooch. He is crowned, and holds a gold rod surmounted by a finial

of leaves in his right hand, and an orb with a white cross in his left.

The other personages can be identified with reasonable confidence. In the background, starting from the left, are a judge, or some dignitary of the law, with a white coif over his head and a furred hood; then the Bishop of Rochester holding a gold cross with a green staff; and next to the throne the Archbishop of Canterbury, his left hand on the king's crown, his right opening a gold vessel held by the figure below. On the other side of the king are, first the Abbot of Westminster (clean-shaven); then the Archbishop of York, also touching the crown with one hand and holding a cross with the other; then the Sacrist of Westminster; and finally a bearded, bare-headed man holding a round piece of gold—he may be the Great Chamberlain.

In the foreground, again starting from the left, are a layman with head uncovered, holding a pair of white gloves which he will present to the king; then—on each side—two mitred figures about whom there is still some controversy: they each hold a golden cup with open lid, though nothing can be seen inside; and on the far right is another judge or lawyer.

Behind the whole group runs a trellis-pattern of squares, and inside each square, if one looks closely, are crudely drawn but unmistakable human faces—a symbolic picture of the mob, the common people, watching the crowning of their sovereign from afar, secluded by the bars of an iron grill. (1)

super mternu̅ ⁊ coutulbat̅ e̅ nalde ⁊
laxate sunt o̅s aie̅ q̅ ciurut i isturod̅ ⁊
clamalat uoce magna diſētes uɿ̅
dicimus te rp̅ɿ ſu̅ di inu̅ q̅ dignat̅

es nob iɿ fugeru̅i daɿe h̅ diei ⁊ h̅ no̅
tis quam totu̅ tempꝰ q̅ urumus
ſrtia̅. bi ergo q̅u tudo du̅it diē d̅d̅a̅
q̅u n̅pi lje̅bi̅t ꝓtē ai ſcā̅ i ſcā̅ ſcloɿ.

A settled capital, a court, a coronation church, a dynastic burial place—these were all signs of a stable monarchy and were first achieved in mediaeval Europe by France. A detail from the *Très Riches Heures* (right) shows the Ile de la Cité in the 15th century, with the old royal palace and La Sainte Chapelle.

St-Denis had been the burial place of French kings from the 6th century. England had no corresponding royal mausoleum until Edward the Confessor (1042–66) refounded Westminster Abbey. Below right: the Confessor's shrine (draped) surrounded by Plantagenet tombs—Henry V (centre), Queen Philippa, and Edward III (right foreground). (4, 5)

A king's anointing, in the presence of his lords, spiritual and temporal, took place at Rheims in France and Westminster in England. Above: a 13th-century English coronation; and the Coronation Chair, made in 1300, as it still stands in the Abbey. (2, 3)

A king's nightmare: that the three estates would rise up and destroy him. John of Worcester tells how Henry I of England dreamed that a band of peasants with scythes and pitchforks stood by his bed 'gnashing their teeth' (top); then a group of soldiers armed with swords and lances, 'looking as if they wanted to kill him' (centre); and then bishops and abbots 'pointing their staves at him'. That these were no idle fantasies is proved by the peasants' revolts, by the fatal quarrel of Henry II with Becket, and by the endless struggle between kings and barons. (7)

The German crown still carried with it the mystical authority of the Holy Roman Empire. But its ideals were seldom translated into practice and Germany never reaped the benefits of strong, unchallenged central government. The career of Henry VI, one of the greatest emperors, illustrates both its immense possibilities and its inherent flaws. Born in 1165, he inherited Germany from his father, Frederick I, and Sicily (which included southern Italy) from his wife's family. He attempted to rule both, but his position was rendered hazardous by the petty princes and bishops of the north (who could refuse to ratify his policy at the Diets) and by the Pope and the Italian princes in the south. Yet he claimed far more territory than any other monarch in Europe—Germany, Italy and almost the whole Mediterranean world. (6)

The hierarchy of power

in church and state is vividly displayed by Andrea da Firenze in his great fresco in the Spanish Chapel, Florence, painted to glorify the Dominican Order. The backcloth is the Church itself. Before it, in the centre, stand the two Vicars of Christ on Earth, Pope and Emperor, with the various levels of their delegated authority: cardinal, archbishop and abbot on one side, king and count palatine on the other. At their feet lie Christ's sheep, the Christian community, guarded from heretical wolves by black and white

'Papal monarchy', though absolute, is elective. Early popes were appointed by a variety of means, but since 1059 the choice of the pope has lain with the cardinals. The 14th-century miniature (above), from the Decretals of Boniface VIII, shows the pope presiding over the Sacred College. (9)

The Conclave makes its choice (above) and the new pope, holding the keys, is crowned with the tiara in St Peter's: two illuminations from the *Cronaca Villani*. (10, 11)

dogs, the Dominicans (*Domini canes*, 'dogs of the Lord'). The foreground is filled with representatives of all the grades of society: bishops, monks, friars, nuns and hermits on the ecclesiastical side; noblemen, townsfolk, peasants and beggars on the secular. (8)

Good government brings prosperity and the blessings of peace; wisdom, concord and justice are its guides; arts and learning flourish and the citizens rejoice. Bad government, rooted in avarice, pride and vainglory, leads only to discord, war, treason and death.

Such is the message of Ambrogio Lorenzetti's allegorical frescoes that decorate the Palazzo Pubblico at Siena, a detail of which is shown here. The painter's own native city forms the scene. On the right is the city wall and gate, surmounted by the emblem of the wolf and twins, adopted by the Sienese from Rome. In the foreground, peasants and merchants carry on their trades in peace. Laden asses, a goatherd with his flock, countrywomen with poultry and baskets pass to and fro. There is a shoe-shop, a spice-dealer, a tailor cutting his cloth at a sloping table and (in the centre) a teacher with his class of children. In the background masons are at work on the roof of a house. The city itself is portrayed with a wealth of detail—streets, churches, alleys, balconies, towers and windows crowd together in a confusion that brings vividly to life the busy tempo of a 14th-century Italian town. (13)

Siena personified as an old man appears in another part of the allegory. Over him hover *Fides* (Faith), *Caritas* (Charity) and *Spes* (Hope) and by his side sit *Prudentia* and *Magnanimitas*. Round his head are the letters C. S. C. C. V. (but the second C is an interpolation) standing for *Communa Senarum Civitatis Virginis*. (12)

18

'**There was a certain rich man,** which was clothed in purple and fine linen, and fared sumptuously every day: And there was a certain beggar named Lazarus, which was laid at his gate, full of sores. And desiring to be fed with the crumbs which fell from the rich man's table: moreover the dogs came and licked his sores'—Luke, XVI. Below: the story of Dives and Lazarus at Moissac—Dives at table, Lazarus dying and his soul being gathered up to heaven by an angel. Poverty in the Middle Ages was accepted as inevitable, though the rich had a duty to give alms and the poor were consoled by hopes of everlasting life. St Martin of Tours (left) divided his cloak with a beggar, the type of Christ—'Inasmuch as ye have done it unto one of the least of these my brethren, ye have done it unto me.' (14, 19)

Avarice was a deadly sin, and that included both the inordinate love of money and parsimony in parting with it. Hence not only the condemnation of usury and the commission of large-scale works of charity but also the (to us) almost incredibly lavish spending on pure display. The 12th-century carving of a tormented miser (above) is in a Burgundian church. (15)

The ultimate misery was to be a cripple or a leper. Leprosy, for reasons still not fully understood, became extremely widespread in Europe during the Middle Ages and every large town had its leperhouse. In the 15th and 16th centuries, equally inexplicably, it diminished and in places died out altogether. Below left: a leper with bowl and rattle, and a man with deformed foot. Below right: a leprous beggar woman with her pathetic cry, 'Sum good my gentyll mayster for God sake.' (16, 17)

The rich man's hopes, however, were not so easily dashed, and provided he gave generously in charity the church did not labour the point about the eye of the needle. Above: the duc de Berry being received by St Peter with the respect due to his rank. (18)

'**A little poor man,** of mean stature and humble aspect, propped it up with his own back, and thus saved it from falling'—Pope Innocent III's dream of the collapsing Lateran Basilica and its preservation by St Francis, shown here in Giotto's fresco at Assisi. St Francis's Christ-like devotion to poverty expresses one side of the mediaeval attitude to worldly riches. (20)

'**Forty-two marks of gold,** a multifarious wealth of precious gems, jacinths, rubies, sapphires, emeralds and topazes, and an array of large pearls.' Abbot Suger's proud description of the high altar of St-Denis no less completely reveals the opposite approach. This detail (right) shows one of Suger's altars as it was in the 15th century still surmounted by the cross of St Eloi. (25)

Fold out ▶

'**Command** that a great fire be kindled and I will enter the fire with your priests, that even thus you may learn which faith is the surer...' St Francis's challenge to the Sultan of Egypt is the subject of another of Giotto's frescoes(above).Opposite: the portrait of St Francis attributed to Cimabue in the Lower Church of Assisi. (21, 22)

St Francis died in 1226, aged forty-four, happy that 'he had kept faith with the Lady Poverty to the end'. His body was carried back to Assisi and on the way 'they passed by the church of S. Damiano where at that time the noble virgin Clare, now glorified in heaven, lived cloistered with her Sisters; and there for a space they stayed, and set down the holy body'. Giotto's picture (left) makes S. Damiano an ornate Gothic church. The real building (above) is low, humble and unadorned. (23, 24)

Abbot Suger, portrayed (left) in a stained glass window at St-Denis, entered the monastery there as a child in 1090, and served it all his life. Several of the treasures that he acquired for it and described so lovingly still survive. Below left: 'We also procured for the services at the aforesaid altar a precious chalice out of one solid sardonyx.' Below: 'And further we adapted for the service of the altar, with the aid of gold and silver, a porphyry vase, made admirable by the hand of the sculptor and polisher, after it had lain idly in a chest for many years, converting it from a flagon into the shape of an eagle.' (26, 27, 28)

On the Feast of Relics churches possessing relics held (in some cases still hold) a mass in commemoration of the saints venerated there. The reliquaries, upon which some of the most exquisite materials and artistry of the Middle Ages were lavished, were exposed to the veneration of the faithful. This page (right) from a 15th-century breviary shows scenes from that day. In the large picture Mass is being celebrated; the reliquaries stand on a table to the left; in the foreground, a sermon. The text is the beginning of the Office *Reliquiarum Sacrarum*, the smaller pictures illustrating, with quotations, particular stages in it. (29)

mie. Iusti in perpetuu. Scd
mentis.
Letamini in dno. fulgebut iusti
+ tanqin sentille in arundineto discur
rent iudicabunt naciones + nacra
bunt ineternum. Magnificat.

resta quesumus
omnipotens deus
ut sancte dei geni
tricis semp virginis marie
+ sanctoꝛ tuoꝛ quoꝛ relique
in hac continentur ecclesia
nos protegant menta quatin

Pilgrimage was an act of penance, a proof of devotion and (for many) a holiday. It united rich and poor—the world of Suger and the world of St Francis. The pilgrim himself renounced worldly comforts, but the shrines that he passed shone with precious reliquaries and splendid works of art. In the cloister of Santo Domingo de Silos, on the road to Compostela, Christ is shown in the guise of a pilgrim (above) with scrip and scallop shell emblem. (30)

St James (above)—*Santiago*—became the warrior patron-saint of Spain in her long battle with the Moors. In the 9th century bones reputed to be his were discovered at Compostela, on the north-western tip of Spain. It soon became one of the revered pilgrimage places of Europe; the great cathedral (above right) was built in the 12th century. In the popular mind St James took his place beside the other great folk-hero of the war against Islam— Roland, slain at Roncevaux during the reign of Charlemagne. Right centre: the saint as *matamoros*, 'slayer of Moors', a tympanum of the cathedral; and (bottom) Roland charging an enemy knight, from a capital at Estrella. (33-36)

◀ **The rewards of the journey** were not exclusively spiritual. Mediaeval writers (above all Chaucer) make it clear that pilgrims expected to enjoy themselves. Above left: the return from a pilgrimage, playing games to make the way shorter. Below left: the evening meal at a hostelry on the road. (31, 32)

The holy war

against the infidel was waged on many fronts—in Spain against the Moors, in Palestine against the Saracens, in eastern Europe against the Magyars and pagan Slavs. These wars were all aspects of an expanding Christendom, a sign that mediaeval Europe had found new unity and strength.

Jerusalem (left) was both a real place conquered by Crusaders, and the city of God promised after Christ's Second Coming. Both meanings are combined in this schematic representation from a Venetian miniature of the late 13th century. Its style is Byzantine, Venice always being open to strong Byzantine influence. Under a golden sky warriors attack and defend the sacred city. Christ raises his hand in blessing from a trefoil canopy in the centre. (37)

'I think' that they honoured him insufficiently who did not place him among the martyrs, seeing the great pains that he endured on the pilgrimage of the cross . . . For if God died on the cross, so did he, for he was a Crusader wearing the cross when he died at Tunis.' St Louis, King of France, set out on his second Crusade in July 1270 and died of the plague eight weeks later. In this manuscript (below) he leaves Paris with his knights, followed by a procession of monks. (38)

The Structure
of Mediaeval Society

CHRISTOPHER BROOKE

The Pope and the Beggar

IN THE SUMMER OF 1210 a ragged band of a dozen beggars waited on the greatest potentate in Christendom, Pope Innocent III. They demanded permission to live according to a religious Rule which committed them to obedience and chastity and a poverty more total than any officially accepted Rule had hitherto enforced. They won from the Pope some measure of verbal approval. The Pope had been prepared for this concession by a dream, if the story made famous by Giotto's fresco in the Upper Church at Assisi is true: the Lateran Palace, the headquarters of the papacy since the days of the Emperor Constantine, was falling down, and was saved from destruction by a poor, despised beggar.

p 22 (20)

The contrast of rich and poor in this story struck contemporaries as it strikes us. We are not unfamiliar with the problems of want and poverty; but our attitude is fundamentally different from that of St Francis and Pope Innocent, because we no longer accept poverty as an inevitable part of the order of things. An affluent society can contemplate the abolition of poverty, at least as a conceivable ideal. In an undeveloped or developing society, like those of western Europe in the Middle Ages, full employment is impossible and a high proportion of the population must resign themselves to seasonal employment—to long hours of labour at time of harvest or when the retinue of a great man has to be transported through their villages, to long hours of idleness in winter, and perhaps to famine if the harvest is poor. Many people had their plots of land to till; for them poverty meant a low standard of living and something worse in a bad year. Many more were landless, and for these poverty could be a harsher and more constant companion. All had their compensations: the need for mutual aid is a natural assumption in such societies, and the Church constantly preached to the wealthy their duty to be generous in charity to the poor and provided at least a theoretical framework of poor relief.

p 23 (21)

'Then he took off his shoes from his feet, laid down his staff, threw away his purse and his money, contented himself with one scanty tunic, and putting aside his belt took a rope for girdle.' Here St Francis in a 14th-century miniature, cuts out the coarse garment that became the standard Franciscan habit. It has changed little since then: at first grey, it is now dark brown; a rosary of seventy beads hangs from the cord; and there are some modifications according to the climate. (1)

Under these conditions it is understandable that poverty should be taken for granted—'the poor you have always with you'. We are often tempted to think that this acceptance was too easy: to suggest, for example, that it would have been better to pay higher wages than for so many folk to depend on charity and largesse. This is in part because we are not accustomed to the workings of such societies, though many similar ones exist in the world today. In practice higher wages would often have meant that fewer men were employed, that more were totally unemployed; and for many the hope of lavish charity was the only barrier between them and the threat of disaster. In a similar way the tendency of mediaeval churchmen to idealize poverty jars on the modern student. There was indeed little that was sentimental in this: the story of Dives and Lazarus, the constant source of hope for the Christian poor, paints a picture of Lazarus's sufferings in this world which was harsh and vivid and true to the experience of mediaeval life. Poverty was a constant and tragic fact of experience; one of the great problems of the Church was to make the facts of life palatable while alleviating their consequences.

p 21 (14–17)

p 21 (19)

Wealth, Charity and Hopes of Heaven

Nor was the lot of the rich entirely enviable. Wealth was insecure; disaster could come swiftly and unforeseen, and churchmen were inclined to find it their duty from time to time to remind their hearers that 'it is easier for a camel to go through the eye of a needle, than for a rich man to enter into the kingdom of God'. There was indeed, on this as on every topic, much diversity of view; but in most men's eyes the force of this text was mitigated by two circumstances. First of all, particularly in the early Middle Ages, it was reckoned that in any case very few would be saved—Lazarus was almost as sure of torment as Dives. From the 12th century onwards the prospects of mankind in the after-life brightened, at the same time as they were brightening in the present; and the social value of wealth, as well as its traditional secular enjoyment, was too engrained for the fate of Dives constantly to disturb the rich man's sleep. It was appreciated in any case that the saying of Jesus was related essentially to what a man did with his wealth; and it was universally assumed in theory at least that a man's resources were a trust of which he was the steward rather than the owner. So long as a man spent lavishly on charity —used his money and did not hoard it—the Church was happy. A diplomatic English bishop of the 12th century could write a letter to a great and wealthy earl, in which he slipped in a reference to the needle's eye merely as prelude to commending the earl for his large and systematic almsgiving, and other pious works.

p 21 (18)

The real sin, in mediaeval eyes, was avarice, and its close companion, usury. Money was there to be spent, not to be hoarded or invested. The Church preached charity, the world preached lavish display and splendid hospitality; a good man was expected to live beyond his income. With certain differences and qualifications, this applied to churchmen as well as to laymen. At its crudest display could be taken as a sign of divine favour. The heathen of Pomerania in the early 12th century repudiated a group of ascetic missionaries who came to preach the Gospel in rags; but chased each other into the baptistery when they saw the splendid vestments and magnificent retinue of Bishop Otto of Bamberg; nor were there lacking men in Christendom itself who took the wealth and outward show of the Church to be a sign of divine favour. Most men assumed that the rich and powerful lived up to their wealth; and although Rome's love of gold was a constant and favourite theme with satirists from the 11th century onwards, it was normally taken for granted that the princes of the Church should live surrounded by magnificence. When Francis appeared before Pope Innocent in rags, he meant no criticism of the Pope: his life and writings reveal at every turn implicit acceptance and respect for the papacy as he knew it, in an age in which pope and Curia had many critics. The world had its palaces and its hovels; and the Church, as Francis saw it, must to this extent be the mirror of the world, in that it too had its princes and its beggars.

p 20 (15)

'In one of the frescoes of the Upper Church of Assisi', wrote Paul Sabatier in his *Life of St Francis of Assisi*, 'Giotto has represented St Clare and her companions coming out from S. Damiano

p 24 (23)

all in tears, to kiss their spiritual father's corpse as it is being carried to its last home. With an artist's liberty he has made the chapel a rich church built of precious marbles.

p 24 (24)
'Happily the real S. Damiano is still there, nestled under some olive-trees like a lark under the heather; it still has its ill-made walls of irregular stones, like those which bound the neighbouring fields. Which is the more beautiful, the ideal temple of the artist's fancy, or the poor chapel of reality? No heart will be in doubt.'

The decoration of churches offers a different, but not wholly dissimilar contrast to that between the way of life of beggars and princes. In the early 12th century there arose the heresy of the Petrobrusians, who in many respects anticipated the doctrines of the more puritanical of the Protestant Reformers. They disapproved of richly ornate churches root and branch, and put their disapproval to practical effect by sacking churches and making bonfires of crucifixes. The attack on ornament was not confined to the un-p 56 (47)orthodox. No one was stricter in Catholic orthodoxy in the age of the Petrobrusians than St Bernard of Clairvaux; yet in a famous p 46-47 (8-12) diatribe Bernard lavished all the arts of Latin rhetoric on a denunciation of the glories of the abbey of Cluny in his day. Clairvaux—and all the churches of the Cistercian Order while Bernard lived and reigned—had bare walls, windows of plain glass, wooden altars: no images, no stained glass windows, no wall-paintings, no silver or gold or precious stones; all these were regarded as distractions. The minds of the monks must be turned away from earthly glories to those of Heaven. This view was doubtless accepted by Bernard's very numerous followers; but there were many more in the same age who believed the exact opposite. Thus Abbot p 26 (26) Suger, in one of the books in which he described his labours for his abbey of St-Denis, near Paris, openly and directly defended the opposite opinion. As he put it, 'the increase which almighty God of His beneficence had granted to this church in the time of our prelacy, both in the acquisition of new lands and in the recovery of what had been lost…, in the construction of buildings and in the gathering of gold, silver and most precious jewels and splendid tapestries'. We are given a vivid impression of the aging abbot contemplating with complacent affection the glories of the church he had done so much to beautify, and dwelling with particular delight on the precious stones in the great cross and reliquaries on and above the High Altar. He quoted the prophet Ezekiel: 'Every precious stone was thy covering, the sardius, the topaz, and the jasper, the chrysolite, and the onyx, and the beryl, the sapphire, and the carbuncle, and the emerald.' He noted with satisfaction that all these stones were there, save only the carbuncle, and then went on to describe how contemplation of their earthly beauty drew his mind away from the cares of the world to contemplate the heavenly virtues which the jewels represented; how they helped directly to transport his mind to a higher world. And he argued that the most precious and expensive things should be p 26 (27,28) used for the administration of the Holy Eucharist. Those who take a different view object that a 'holy, pure mind and faithful intention' are what count; these are of first importance, admits Suger, but 'we assert that we should do service in the outward ornaments of the vessels we use' as well as in purity of heart.

Anointed Kings

Suger was a business man and a man of taste as well as an abbot, and it will not have escaped notice how closely he associates the economic improvement of his abbey's properties—as he would have said, the properties of Denis, patron saint of his abbey and of the kingdom of France—with the adornment of the church. He was several other things besides: author, diplomat and statesman. Francis and Innocent have served to illustrate some of the fundamental social contrasts in the Church and the world in the Middle Ages; Suger and his jewels may now serve to draw our minds to the range of interest which a monk-statesman could have, and so to some of the contrasts in mediaeval government.

Abbot Suger was a man of exceptional talent. It perhaps seems strange to us today that the interests and experience of a mediaeval monk should fit him to rule a kingdom; yet Suger was one of the leading statesmen of France and effective ruler of the French kingdom in the late 1140s, when King Louis VII (1137–80) was absent

The mediaeval view of poverty, kingship and the divine will are all illustrated in a story from the 12th-century Life of King Edward the Confessor. *It tells how 'Gilla Michael', an Irish cripple, went to Rome in search of a cure, only to be told by St Peter this could be granted if King Edward of England would carry him on his back from Westminster Hall to the Abbey. The saintly King consented. On the way the cripple felt his 'nerves loosen and his legs stretch out.' Blood from his sores ran on to the royal clothes, but the King carried him to the altar of the Abbey. There he was cured, departed on foot and hung up his crutches in memory of the miracle. The drawing is from the atelier of Matthew Paris. (2)*

on the Second Crusade. Any abbot had in some degree the responsibilities of a landowner, but the Cistercians tried to combine these with as complete a withdrawal from the world as was feasible. This was in part a deliberate reaction from the involvement of the old Benedictine houses in secular affairs. The monks of St-Denis lived in their cloister and worshipped in the abbey choir, both of them, in the main, reserved to their sole use. Yet the abbey was in some ways very much in the world. The nave of the abbey church was open to laymen and women, who came in throngs as pilgrims on the festivals of St Denis; one of Suger's motives in rebuilding was to give these throngs more space and to open the church's vistas, so that pilgrims could admire and enjoy its beauties and look through the choir to the High Altar and the reliquaries.

The domain over which the French kings had effective control between the establishment of the dynasty of Hugh Capet in 987 and the end of the 12th century was narrow; and the result was that they wandered less and had a more stable headquarters than the English kings of the same period. Thus Paris, long the greatest city of the kingdom, was the undisputed capital of the French kings. For centuries kings and abbots had co-operated to tighten the knots which attached the abbey to the monarchy and to spread the cult of St Denis, patron of both. When Suger had finished his work pilgrims from all over the kingdom could look up the vista to the apse, and in the apse, between altar and vault, surrounded by the ornaments which sparkled with Suger's favourite jewels, see the shrine of St Denis; and before and behind lay the tombs of p 25 (25 Frankish kings of every century from the 6th to their own.

Down to the mid-11th century the English kings had no capital like Paris, no patron saint, and no mausoleum comparable p 14 (4) with St-Denis. The chief seat of government lay perhaps in Winchester; the leading city of the kingdom was London. It was no doubt in direct imitation of St-Denis that Edward the Confessor (1042–66) revived and substantially enlarged Westminster p 14 (2, 3, 5) Abbey and made it for the English kings what St-Denis was for the French. Like St-Denis it collected royal tombs, and, also like St-Denis, it fabricated legends and privileges, so that it presently became established that a king must be anointed and crowned in the abbey. In the mid-12th century the monks of Westminster successfully petitioned the pope for Edward's canonization, and his shrine assumed the place in the abbey that the shrine of Denis occupied in the French abbey, though Edward never became a national patron saint. In the mid-13th century King

Henry III, like Suger a great connoisseur, though, unlike Suger, no statesman, dedicated his best energies to rebuilding the abbey to the honour of God, the English monarchy and Edward the Confessor; and he showed his devotion to one source of English royal legend by calling his eldest son Edward, just as Henry VII was to show his interest in another by calling his eldest son Arthur. The ranks of royal tombs from the chapel of King Edward to the chapel of King Henry VII in Westminster Abbey today are the result of this fostering of the links of king and abbey in imitation of the French kings and St-Denis.

p 105
(79)

Portrait of Louis VI

In his later years, Suger was given to reminiscence; and the young monks of the abbey, who had often stayed up late out of respect for his 'narrative old age', urged him to put on parchment the account of his administration of the abbey. He also took time off to write an account of the reign of his first royal patron, King Louis VI (1108–37). A king could not live by legends alone.

It was not Westminster Abbey which made London the capital of England: already the greatest city, its position at the centre of communications in the south-east of the country when England was ruled (as it had been in Roman times) by a dynasty whose older established interests lay on the continent, made it a natural centre of government in the 12th and 13th centuries when government was growing more stable and administration coming to need (for the first time in the Middle Ages) a permanent headquarters. The arrival of London as a capital is marked, not by the revival of the abbey in the 11th century, still less by the establishment of Parliament, which could meet in Oxford as late as 1681, but by the final establishment of the royal treasury there in the late 12th century. Strategy and finance were the making of London, and Suger was well aware of the importance of these commodities to his own kings. His *Life of Louis VI* is full of wars and rumours of wars. Louis was a strenuous, conscientious and chivalrous man, and none of these qualities lost anything in the telling. His summers were filled with warfare, especially with efforts to repress lawlessness and piracy by the disobedient lords of his own domain. He also found time for the personal exercise of royal justice; and his justice was widely admired, so that the semi-independent princes (dukes and counts) who ruled the rest of France occasionally submitted their disputes to him. But on the whole he was one among a group of princes, in most of his affairs no more than *primus inter pares*. Yet he held in reserve the legend of a great past and he was an anointed king. He was successor to Charlemagne, who had ruled over most of western Europe. The other princes, in some measure, acknowledged that he was their feudal overlord. Against a king you could rebel, if you thought your cause just (as rebels easily do); but in some sense it was widely thought impossible, or very difficult, to wash the balm from an anointed king; and it was very unusual for a king to be deposed or to die a violent death. The feudal bond, the traditional aura of kingship and pious legend had their uses; and this too was well known to Suger. In 1124 he was able to act as stage manager to a little drama.

A crude form of crutch is shown in this small drawing from a manuscript of Gerald of Wales. The man has deformed feet; he drags himself along on his knees, keeping half-upright by leaning on wooden supports. (3)

Henry V, King of Germany and, like nearly all the kings of Germany of these centuries, Holy Roman Emperor, formed an alliance with Henry I, King of England and Duke of Normandy, who as Duke was formally a vassal of Louis, and as father of the Empress Matilda was father-in-law to the Emperor. The Emperor Henry V put a large army into the field and made a sudden attack on Rheims.

'When King Louis had received reports from his friends of this attack, he vigorously and boldly set in motion a levy which he had not looked to hold, gathered his nobles and explained what was afoot. He knew from many folks' report and his own frequent experience that St Denis is the special patron and unique protector after God of the kingdom. So he hastened to him, and urged him from his heart, with prayers and gifts, to defend the kingdom, preserve his person, and resist his enemies as was his custom. The blessed and wondrous defender and his companions (i.e. their relics)..., if another kingdom dares invade the kingdom of the French, are placed on Denis's altar to conduct the defence; and so this was done with splendour and devotion in the King's presence. Then the King took from the altar the standard (the Oriflamme) of the county of the Vexin—as Count, Louis was a vassal of the Church; he took it under oath as from his overlord; and he flew against the enemy with a small force on his own account, strongly urging the whole of France meanwhile to follow him. The accustomed ardour of France was roused by the unaccustomed audacity of her enemies; it spread everywhere and gathered a military levy, a strong force of men, their minds full of ancient courage and former victories.'

The combined generalship of King and relics proved irresistible. Levies came to Rheims from many parts of northern France. The Duke of Aquitaine made a gesture of interest. The Count of Blois, nephew to the King of England and his ally, and so officially at war with Louis, appeared in person to join his host. The German army melted rapidly away, and Louis returned to Paris in triumph.

'During all the time of the host's gathering the silver caskets, holy and venerable, containing the most holy relics, lay on the high altar. The monks celebrated office there constantly day and night, and flocks of devoted people and pious women came to pray for the army. And so (on his return) the pious King with filial devotion and copious tears, on his own shoulders carried his lords and patrons back to their place, and rewarded them for these and other good works with numerous gifts of land and other benefits.'

Earthly Crowns: the Secular Monarch

It is a nice point whether the relics of Denis, memory of their feudal oaths or common interest had more effect on the princes who assembled at Rheims to confound the invader; but each in its way played its part, and the effect was a notable victory for the one of the three kings whom any ordinary calculation would have reckoned the least powerful. The Emperor's invasion was part of a strategy concerted with his father-in-law, Henry I of England. Henry of England attributed the débâcle to the inadequacy of the Emperor's army and its method of recruitment, and he advised his son-in-law to levy a tax and hire mercenaries, over whom he would have more control than over the levies from his domains and those of his bishops and leading nobles, who came to his banner according to a traditional contract, none too well-defined. But the German kingdom, though the largest and traditionally the most powerful in western Europe, was comparatively poor in economic resources, and Henry V lacked the freedom of manoeuvre of his father-in-law. Henry I of England was a man of the world, which helps to explain why he was successful in some of his endeavours, and unsuccessful in his wars against Louis VI. His father, William the Conqueror, had ruled Normandy by inheritance, England, whatever he might claim, by conquest; and he had made his conquest effective by building royal castles, by using the financial and administrative resources of the kingdom to the full, and by developing the bonds which linked him to his leading subjects, the 'feudal' bonds as they are commonly called. He developed the doctrine that great barons and bishops held all their lands of him, in return for a specified amount of military service. He and his successors recruited their armies of 'knights' and archers by a judicious mixture of laying out money on mercenaries and of exploiting their subjects' obligation to serve. Yet there was much more in the bonds of king and barons than this. The barons swore oaths to the king and thereby became his personal followers; and all the Conqueror's barons owed their possessions in England to his personal patronage. So large and successful a conquest can happen only at rare intervals, and Henry I had to deal with a baronage which owed nothing to him. The Conqueror's eldest son inherited Normandy; William, the second son, became King of England; and it was only when William was killed in the New Forest in August 1100, that Henry could take any substantial part of his father's inheritance. He claimed England by inheritance, and in 1106 took Normandy by conquest, consigning his eldest brother to prison for life. Whenever opportunity offered he formed new baronies, raised new barons who would owe their wealth and power to him and not to his father or one of his brothers, and so by an extensive use of patronage made his court what his father's had been, a personal reflection of the reigning king's glory. Castles, knights, archers, landed wealth, silver coins, and the personal bonds and personal relations which tied the barons to him and kept them loyal—these were the pillars of Henry I's strength.

In different proportions all these items figured in the list of properties of the monarchies of the genial Louis VI of France and the ruthless Emperor Henry V. Both had less command of money; and so both were more dependent on their relations with their subjects to recruit their armies. In Louis's case these relations were close only with the lands and men of his own royal domain, the Ile de France; Henry's domains were wider, and he exercised more control over the dukes, archbishops, and bishops of Germany at large than Louis could command outside the Ile de France. But the dukes were not Henry's creations, nor did they owe him precisely defined services; and in his later years one of the greatest of them, Lothar of Saxony, held wholly aloof. Earls who held aloof from the court of Henry I were liable to find themselves rapidly extinguished.

Louis VI had, nonetheless, some remarkable successes, although he was a man of mediocre resources and very ordinary attainments. These he owed to strenuous activity (sustained till very near the end of his life, when obesity and illness finally made it impossible for him to be lifted into the saddle), to good fortune, to the fact that he was the kind of man who was implicitly trusted, and to his good relations with the Church. The 11th century had witnessed a dramatic transformation in the papacy, followed by the creation of the papal monarchy: the attempt to make actual in the life of Christendom the papacy's ancient claims to primacy and leadership. One pillar of this was the attempt to reduce lay influence in the appointment of bishops, an influence particularly symbolized by the act of investiture, by which the king presented a new bishop with ring and pastoral staff, which were commonly reckoned the spiritual symbols of his office. In the opening years of the 12th century the kings of England, France and Germany were all in different ways trying to defend themselves against the popes' condemnation of this practice. Their methods were characteristic of the men. Louis VI, who was effective ruler even before his father's death in 1108, had influence over a narrow circle of bishoprics outside his domain, and was fearful of losing it; and he had little understanding of the new-fangled papal pretensions. But he was a pious man and in no position to resist strong pressure; in due course he began to understand a little of the papacy's views, and rather more of the value of its alliance to him; and in later years the influence of Suger and St Bernard made his relations with Church and papacy close, greatly to the practical benefit of both parties. Henry I of England carried his defence of lay investiture to the point of an open breach with his archbishop, St Anselm, and the Pope. But Henry needed all the support he could get for the conquest of Normandy; and once he had grasped that he could surrender the ceremony of investiture while retaining control over appointments, the way was open for the compromise negotiated in 1106–7. The Emperor Henry V tried to enforce his will by violence: he captured the Pope and extracted a full concession from him, a concession that the Pope was bound to repudiate as soon as the Alps divided him from

Henry. The Emperor's violence only embittered the dispute and uselessly prolonged it. In the end, in 1122, after his enemies in Germany had exploited the long dispute—already thirty years old when Henry succeeded to the throne—to weaken royal influence in the German bishoprics and abbeys, Henry agreed to a compromise like that enjoyed by his father-in-law for the past fifteen years.

Papal Monarchy

What is the meaning of the phrase 'the papal monarchy'? In the 11th century the structure of government began to develop which gave the papacy and the hierarchy of the Church, between the 13th century and the Reformation, a coercive power unique in the history of Christendom. This coercive power presupposed a machinery of government and groups of people in need of coercion. Throughout the early Middle Ages the Church had been strongly authoritarian. At various times the exigencies of a missionary Church had compelled the toleration of paganism; but this was dropped as soon as conveniently possible, and the same tolerance was rarely extended to Christian heretics. Bishops and secular rulers worked closely together for the control of men's souls as well as their bodies. Muslim traders were accepted, Jewish inhabitants of Christendom tolerated and even protected; but apostasy was condemned, and when heresy first began seriously to reappear in the 11th century, lay rulers and lay mobs took the initiative in consigning the heretics to the flames, the traditional punishment for witchcraft. In the late 11th century the papal reformers seem to have canalized into orthodox channels the hidden popular religious zeal which had led to the spread of heresy; but this alliance of the hierarchy and popular movements did not last, and in the course of the 12th century heresy of various kinds became widespread and deeply-rooted. It took two main forms: that of the Petrobrusians and Waldensians, essentially an anticipation of Protestant and Puritan doctrines, and that of the Cathars or Albigensians, a dualist or Gnostic group of heresies, fed by missionaries from the East. The dualists preached that the material world was evil, the creation of a wicked angel or god of evil; that goodness could only exist in spirit. They had many adherents in western Germany, the Low Countries and northern France, but it was in southern France and northern Italy that their main strength was concentrated; and in these lands they formed a hierarchy of their own, which was for a time an open and powerful rival to the hierarchy of the Catholic Church. It was these circumstances which led an authoritarian Church to become coercive, and induced among the leaders of the Catholic Church the siege mentality which lasted from the days of Innocent III to those of Pius XII. Innocent's nephew and ultimate successor, Hugolino, Pope Gregory IX (1227–41), curiously combined the roles of patron of St Francis and St Dominic and founder of the Holy Inquisition.

Innocent and Gregory were autocrats, but not despots. Their claims to authority were in principle unlimited; but they knew that in practice they needed earthly allies, colleagues and associates. Especially crucial to both of them were their relations with their cardinals and bishops and with the kings of Germany, by p 16 (8) tradition also Holy Roman Emperors. The traditional authority of bishops was strong; and even if this had not been respected by such sticklers for legal respectability as Innocent and Gregory, it was quite impracticable to govern the Church without their co-operation. In a world without modern means of transport and communication, all government had in some sense to be local government, and kings and popes could only govern effectively if they could count on the co-operation of their local officers and colleagues. On this the popes could never entirely count, and papal monarchy in the Middle Ages never in practice attained the authority which it claimed. Theory and practice were always far apart. The authority of popes and bishops was based on similar premises; and although the bishops always had their own local loyalties, and often links with local secular potentates more potent than their loyalty to Rome, bishops and popes were united by their orders, by their education, by their Latin speech, the universal language of the mediaeval Church, and by some measure of acceptance of the Church's law. At the end of the Middle Ages, espe-

Under Philip the Fair the Parlement of Paris became a more stable and responsible body, meeting twice a year for a session of two months. It consisted of the lords spiritual and temporal, and acted both as an advisory body to the king and as a court of law. In this miniature of about 1322 the King, dressed in a fleur-de-lys robe presides over his bishops on one side, laity on the other. Each has his coat-of-arms above him. (4)

cially in the 14th and 15th centuries, the most remarkable exercise of power in which the popes engaged was the attempt to appoint to bishoprics and benefices, under certain conditions, all over western Christendom, the practice of 'papal provision'. In the 12th and 13th centuries in particular—and in some measure throughout the later Middle Ages—the most stable external manifestation of papal authority was the papal Curia's standing as the supreme appeal tribunal in spiritual cases in Christendom; to it a river of appeals flowed, on cases both serious and absurd.

They came from the courts of archdeacons and bishops, and the effective exercise of papal authority depended on the pope's relations with bishops, and other members of the higher clergy. When the tangled matrimonial affairs of an Essex squire came before the pope, or rival claims to a vicarage, or an interminable argument between two schoolmasters, who loved litigation, as to which of them had the right to teach grammar in Winchester, it was scarcely possible for him to elucidate the evidence at a distance of six weeks' or two months' journey from the scene of the dispute. So he laid down the law on the issue involved and left the question of fact to be decided by papal judges-delegate—bishops, abbots, archdeacons; even, in time, rural deans, the N.C.O.s of the mediaeval hierarchy.

Thus the peasantry of Essex might witness a case of marriage and inheritance being argued in their midst in two courts, royal and papal, according to two sets of law; and it was very frequently a nice problem of argument or diplomacy how the relations between these systems of law and rival courts should be adjudicated. This was only one aspect of the complex relations between clergy and lay folk. In some respects the division between clergyman and layman was one of the most fundamental of social

barriers: clerical education, the vow of celibacy and holy orders set the clergy apart. As time went on, more and more laymen acquired some degree of education; it is doubtful if celibacy was ever very effective among the rank and file of the parish clergy in the Middle Ages. And at all times the clergy had ties of every kind with the lay society in which they mingled. Thus Chaucer's parson had a ploughman for brother, and two bishops of Winchester, Henry of Blois (1129–71) and Henry Beaufort (1404–47), were brothers of kings. Thomas Becket, as royal chancellor, had hunted and jousted with king and barons; as Archbishop he justified resistance to royal demands by sophisticated clerical arguments. The loyalty of many of King Henry II's barons and knights had something in it of the feeling which had inspired the warriors in the poem on the battle of Maldon (991) to fight and die with their leader. Words spoken in haste by the King in a violent passion could stir this feeling and lead to murder in Canterbury Cathedral. The feeling was natural and instinctive; yet Christendom was not only shocked by a public act of murder and sacrilege; it was also very much surprised by this treatment of the King's former friend.

Bishop-princes

The paradoxes of a bishop's position come out strikingly in Henry *f 5* of Blois, the prince-bishop of Winchester. The son of the Count of Blois, and grandson (through his mother) of William the Conqueror, he early joined the great French abbey of Cluny in which he combined training in the monastic routine and preparation, among other young men of noble birth, for a distinguished career in the Church. He never quite ceased to be either monk or prince. From 1129 he held in plurality the offices of abbot of Glastonbury, England's oldest and one of its richest abbeys, and Bishop of Winchester, a see which gave its mediaeval bishops the income of multi-millionaires. He thus became a great landowner and financier; he loved to see a good field of waving corn, and he had a genius for finance. He was a splendid patron, and the list of great treasures he gave or redeemed from pawn for Winchester Cathedral shows that he had an eye akin to Suger's. When his favourite schemes collapsed in the Roman Curia, he consoled himself by buying antique statues and transporting them to Winchester. His affection for Cluny never died, and whenever he found England too hot for him, he retreated to Cluny, characteristically combining enjoyment of the monastic routine that it offered with energetic measures to restore the abbey's finances. He was a great builder, and his cathedral has still some evidences of this; but his most striking monuments are his castles—Wolvesey, Merdon, Farnham, Bishop's Waltham— as much of them as has survived King Henry II's slighting and the ravages of time.

Henry of Blois was younger brother of King Stephen (1135–54). Under Stephen's rule the country subsided into civil war. In these circumstances the Bishop of Winchester might have been expected to act as mediator between his brother and his cousin Matilda; or he might have expected to be Stephen's closest supporter. At various times he tried both lines, and thereby discredited himself as a bishop and a statesman. In Stephen's early years Henry was the most forceful and brilliant figure among the English bishops, but for some reason now obscure Stephen would not let him be Archbishop of Canterbury; and although he ruled the English Church for a time as papal 'legate' or representative in England, he suffered for a number of years from thwarted ambition. This combined with a genuine sense of what was due to the Church to make him resist Stephen to the face when he gave some of Henry's fellow bishops cavalier treatment. Henry then tried to sit in judgment on Stephen and Matilda, and even supported Matilda for a time. Thus he became directly involved in the civil war, in siege and countersiege in his own episcopal city; and it was not soon forgotten that flaming bolts fired from the battlements of Wolvesey started a fire which wasted much of Winchester. To us it seems obvious that Henry had gone too far. Yet for two reasons it was more difficult for Henry to understand this before the outcome made it only too clear to him. First of all, a bishop was an official both of Church and kingdom: he could not stand aloof. Attempts were being made —never wholly successfully—to distinguish more clearly between a bishop's spiritual and secular functions. This might have affected even the Conqueror's grandson, but for the circumstance that a conscientious bishop was also liable to regard himself as acting, like the prophets of the Old Testament, with divine authority, interpreting and enforcing divine sanctions.

Henry's authority as bishop was based on Old Testament precedents, and was also intimately linked with the saints whose reliquaries he enriched and refurbished in his cathedral, notably that of his obscure but celebrated predecessor, St Swithun. In the same period a humble community in Cornwall was providing a yet more obscure saint with a new shrine. In two ways the reliquary of St Petroc is more remarkable than the far grander one of St Swithun: it still survives, and can be seen in the parish church of Bodmin, Petroc's home; and we can see from its character that it was made and adorned by Arab craftsmen in Norman Sicily. It is one of a number of striking tributes to the close links between the two most highly organized kingdoms of 12th-century Europe—the kingdom which the Normans had developed on the solid foundations of the Old English monarchy, and that other kingdom, in south Italy and Sicily, which the Normans forged in the same period from Muslim, Greek and native elements.

The Norman principalities in Italy and Sicily were established at the same time as the papal reform; and in the long run the Norman rulers became valuable allies to the popes in their conflicts with the Emperors. In the late 12th century this alliance was p 15 (6) threatened when the Emperor Henry VI married the heiress of the Norman kingdom. Henry died young, leaving a disputed succession both in Germany and in Sicily. The immediate threat

of encirclement was lifted from the papacy; but when, in the next year (1198), Innocent III mounted the papal throne, he was determined to play an effective and dignified part in settling these difficulties, and especially those in Germany. To state a complex case briefly, Innocent claimed that because the pope crowned the Emperor, he had the right to sit in judgment on the person of the emperor-elect; and any king of Germany was an emperor-elect. For two years he waited, hoping that the disputants would submit to judgment. When they failed to do so, he proceeded to make his decision. In a secret consistory he argued the case of the two disputants—to whom he added a third, Henry's young son, hitherto too young to be regarded as a serious candidate; and he laid out the case in terms of what was legally right, of what was morally fitting, of what was politically expedient. The third element showed that Innocent realized that it was useless to declare for a theoretically sound candidate if there was no hope of his winning sufficient support. Yet in this lay the weakness of Innocent's position: once he had made his choice, it should have been final, but a change in circumstances could and did alter 'what was expedient', and Innocent found himself committed, with the best of intentions, to fomenting civil war in Germany and changing sides three times. He had ended by committing on the grand scale the error of Henry of Blois.

Papacy by Election

His final choice proved successful; but Frederick II of Hohenstaufen, Henry VI's son, grew up to combine the kingdoms of Sicily and Germany, and however morally fitting his success may have been, it was politically dangerous for the papacy. Nor did Frederick show any gratitude to his maker. Thus it came to pass that in 1241, Pope Gregory IX, as he lay dying, was fiercely resolved to ensure that his successor should carry on the struggle which had been developing throughout his pontificate between pope and Emperor. The pope might be an autocrat; he might even over-ride (as Gregory had done) some measure of opposition among the cardinals to his policies. But when he died it was the cardinals, not he, who chose his successor, and until that successor was chosen they acted corporately as the rulers of the Church. There are now about eighty cardinals. In the Middle Ages there could be as many as fifty-three; but in practice the number often fell below that figure, and in 1241 there were only twelve. They were much divided, and Gregory feared that they would fail to elect a successor to carry on his war against the Emperor with sufficient dispatch, and perhaps even fail to elect a successor at all. So he summoned the Senator of Rome, Matteo Orsini, and gave him certain instructions. When the Pope died, the Senator gathered all the cardinals within reach and hustled them into a Roman palace which he had fitted out as a prison; there they remained his prisoners until they had elected a pope. After weeks of suffering, the cardinals found a means of escape. One of their number had died; a second was on his death-bed. They hastily elected him pope, and in the brief interval before he also went his way, they had escaped. A few remained in Orsini's power, but their summons to their colleagues to return fell on deaf ears.

'We have turned over among us the innumerable sufferings, the continual heat, the stench, the misery of our confinement, the insults, hunger, famine, sickness by which we were assaulted until life was scarce worth living...'—and also the death of two colleagues and the shadow of death hanging over them all. 'We have turned over all this; and we can find no canon which could lead you to summon us for the election in that very place' where the senior cardinal was still held prisoner, 'an insult to the church, a spectacle to the world, to men and angels', and so forth.

'Do you think we have forgotten how we were dragged to prison, bound hand and foot, and beaten like thieves?'; and they proceeded to describe in lurid detail the sufferings of one venerable cardinal who, after assault and battery, was 'hustled through the main streets of the city in a carpet'; also their own sufferings owing to the sanitary arrangements in their prison; and those of another cardinal who was shut in a charnel house, where his warders spat on him and sang comic songs at his expense, not to mention poking their cross-bows at him from under the bed. Finally, the *Duchess of Malfi* touch: 'Nor must it be forgotten that

Henry of Blois, Bishop of Winchester and Abbot of Glastonbury, typifies the secular power wielded by the great officers of the Church. He was King Stephen's brother and a grandson of William the Conqueror, a great landowner, financier and patron of the arts. His so-called 'mirror' is really an enamel plaque from a reliquary probably given by Bishop Henry ('Henricus Episcopus') to his own Cathedral. There would originally have been three whole roundels, as in the box that he is shown holding. The impression of humility conveyed by Henry's posture is somewhat belied by the inscription round the rim which hails him as 'equal to the muses in intellect and greater in eloquence than Marcus (Cicero)'. (5)

the senator tortured us with terrifying threats, and thundered at us instantly to reveal the new pope when we had elected him, and to speed us on our way he dug up the corpse of the late pope and planted it in our midst...'

In the event, after two years' wrangling, they agreed to the election of Cardinal Sinibaldo Fieschi, who took the name of Innocent IV (1243); and Innocent proceeded at once to show what was the difference between a cardinal and a pope by being converted from a moderate to as implacable an enemy of the Emperor as Gregory IX himself.

Cardinals: the 'Senate' of the Holy See

Thus was the papal conclave born; and in spite of its origins the conclave soon became an established part of the electoral law. The cardinals have ever since had supreme power during a vacancy, but have been effectively prevented from exercising it. The growth of their power was a natural accompaniment to the development of the papal monarchy. The office of cardinal was ancient; but only when the papal reform got under way did the cardinals become a body of papal advisers, of men recruited from all over Europe, able to give the pope aid and counsel, to act as his representatives on embassies. Above all, the revived papacy could not avoid the consequences of being an elective monarchy. If it were to remain powerful and independent, the popes had to be elected by a powerful and independent body. And so the cardinals became the papal chapter, the 'Senate' of the Holy See. In 1059 Pope Nicholas II (whose election had been anything but orderly) passed the first election decree, which placed essential power in the hands of the cardinals. But it was still possible for the cardinals to elect two different men as popes, and there was no clear criterion by which the candidates could be judged. It was common for two men to claim to be popes between 1059 and 1179; in that year the danger of a dual election was effectively abolished by the introduction, for the first time in any mediaeval election, of a majority principle: a vote of two-thirds of the cardinals makes a man pope. The fact that this rule could be made, and could be effective, presupposed that the body of cardinals had achieved sufficient coherence and independence to act as a body, independently (in a measure at least) of the pressures of secular potentates. When they came to be called the 'college' of cardinals, and when (in the mid-13th century) they assumed the red hat, which has ever since been their mark of distinction, the cardinals finally became established as the permanent papal council and body of electors.

Their very independence, however, involved a new danger: they might wish to be independent of the pope himself. This might lead, as in 1241-43, to their refusal to elect a pope at all; or it might

lead to their rebelling against the pope. In the 14th century, when the papacy was settled for two generations at Avignon, a comparatively small body of cardinals acquired habits of authority and a princely standard of living which led them to regard the pope as *primus inter pares*. In 1378, after their return to Rome, a body of cardinals as small as that of 1241 elected a curial official, who they believed would continue to accept their direction, as Pope Urban VI. But the worm turned, and Urban proved violent, tactless and dictatorial. Most of the cardinals fled, and on the pretext that they had elected Urban under pressure, declared his election invalid; they proceeded to elect one of their own number as a rival pope, who settled with his cardinals at Avignon. The Great Schism lasted from 1378 to 1415; before it was finished there were three popes, three colleges of cardinals, and a Church in chaos. The schism was resolved by a General Council, which had always been acknowledged as a possible safeguard if papal authority collapsed, but had only met in recent centuries to confirm papal authority at its height. Since the Council of Constance no pope has resigned or been deposed.

The decree of 1059, broadly speaking, placed the election of the pope in the hands of the cardinals. More precisely, it gave the first voice in the election to the cardinal bishops, who were then joined in the election itself by the other cardinal clergy; and the elect was then acclaimed by the whole clergy and people of Rome and the event notified to the Emperor. What is the meaning of this rigmarole? First and foremost, that a modern notion of election, in which a free decision lies with the majority of a specified body of electors, was quite foreign to the ideas of the early Middle Ages. It was customary to say that popes, bishops and kings were 'elected', 'chosen', in Latin *electi*; but the process of choice belonged to that dream-world of common assumptions which everyone understands and no one can explain. It was often said that the people chose their king; this never happened, in any modern sense of these words. It was often said that God chose popes, bishops and kings; however one may view this notion, it throws little light on the techniques by which God's wishes were interpreted by mortal and fallible men. The word very commonly means 'accepted', and refers to a formal process by which a king was acclaimed by his leading followers. But how did they know whom to acclaim?

King-making

King-making was a very formal matter, though behind the forms must have lurked all manner of informal discussions and intrigues. A mediaeval 'election' survives in fossilized form in the opening ceremony in a modern British coronation, when the Archbishop of Canterbury presents the new sovereign to the people for their acceptance and acknowledgment. This goes back at least to the 11th century, when the English acclaimed William the Conqueror so vociferously that the Norman guards thought it was a riot. Ideally, the people acclaimed whomsoever the leading dignitary presented to them; the leading dignitary presented whoever had been previously designated by the former king; and the old king designated his eldest son or closest suitable relation. In France the Capetian dynasty produced male heirs with astonishing regularity, and it was normal practice to ensure the succession by 'electing', anointing and crowning the heir in his father's lifetime. This did not usually involve the displacement of the old king, unless (like Louis VI's father) he happened to be in his dotage. It simply underlined the desperate care—only too intelligible to those who have studied kingship in other societies—to avoid a bloody succession and the abolition of the reigning dynasty. In England lip service was paid to the hereditary principle even in 1066; it became strictly accepted in theory in the 12th century, but hardly in practice till the 13th, when in 1216 the boy-king Henry III succeeded even in conditions of civil war. But the old medley of principles and practices survived for many centuries. When Henry IV usurped the throne in 1399, it was given out that Richard II had voluntarily resigned the throne and designated Henry as his successor, that he had proved unsatisfactory as king and had to be removed, that Henry had been elected by the magnates of the realm, and that he was in any case king by hereditary right. Most of this was probably fiction, but it is all the more

p 17 (9)

p 17 (10-11)

p 13 (1)

revealing for that—revealing of what custom asserted ought to happen in such cases, and of the care which had to be exercised by an insecure king in the late 14th century to hide the fact that he had won his throne by war and the people's choice.

The English succession was firmly hereditary, though only fully clarified by statute in the 18th century. The French rules were already tolerably fixed, and only differed from the English because the long succession of male heirs between the 10th and the early 14th centuries enabled the French lawyers to keep the English Edward III off the French throne by inventing the Salic law, which barred from the throne an heir whose title came through a woman. Of the major European monarchies only the German had become elective. Down to 1077 the normal process of king-making in Germany was much as in France and England: the old king designated, the Archbishop of Mainz designated again, the princes accepted, the people acclaimed, the Archbishop anointed and crowned. What was special to the German kings (from the 10th century onwards) was their right to go to Rome to be anointed and crowned Emperors. But in 1077 there was civil war; and Henry IV was also at loggerheads with the papacy. In spite of a temporary submission to the pope, Henry was declared deposed by the rebel princes, who proceeded to elect one of their own number as his successor. This was not quite a modern election; the body of electors was not clearly defined, and so there could be no strict majority principle; and this piece of king-making was hardly a success. After a few years Henry IV was left in possession of the field. But its memory survived, and when male heirs failed, or archbishops and princes felt disinclined to listen to the old king's voice, something like an election could take place. The growing power of the German dynastic princes, the occasional failure of heirs and conflict with the papacy produced a situation in the late 13th century in which the king-emperor was in practice elected by the princes. Inheritance played its part; but the Emperors had to accept the consequences of being the creations of the electors, and of owing them some consideration. The process was canonized by Charles IV in 1356, when by the Golden Bull he laid down who the electors were and their rights before the Crown. For the first time a strict electoral principle entered the politics of a secular kingdom. Elsewhere it was held at bay much longer. In the sense that Charles IV's successors were elected, no English king has ever been elected; and the majority principle did not even apply in practice to Members of Parliament—though it crept into the Statute Book in theory in the early 15th century—until the 19th century.

The Politics of Marriage

Hereditary succession was thus a principle firmly entrenched in most European kingdoms in the later Middle Ages. To choose a king who must rule as well as reign by an accident of birth is a curious proceeding; but the human affection of those in power combined with the urgent need to avoid doubt and disputation to give it a remarkable strength; and custom has never hesitated to consecrate absurdities. It was the inevitable ambition of kings and barons to consolidate and enlarge their domains by successful warfare and judicious marriages; and so marriage in high society became a kind of dynastic game. But just as primogeniture had its compensating advantages, so the subordination of marriage to estate management brought at least one blessing in its wake. The Church had preached monogamy for centuries; but William the Conqueror's great-grandfather had had two wives and his father had none. He was himself the first of his line to be conspicuously faithful to a single wife; piety, affection and the memory of his own fearful childhood played their part in this, but he must also have known that the children he begot were heirs to great and vital possessions. On the whole it seems likely that it was the last of these factors which made (for example) English lay society as strict as the Church on monogamy and stricter than the Church in enforcing the principle that only a legitimate heir could inherit. No doubt the play of human affection, human need and common sense frequently overcame the obstacles to domestic felicity imposed by custom and ambition, but the history of mediaeval marriage has many ludicrous passages. One of the sensational results of the marriage market was the empire of Henry II who was King

of England and Duke of Normandy by inheritance from his mother's father, Count of Anjou by inheritance from his father, and Duke of Aquitaine by his wife's right. This helped to strengthen the marital attitudes of his courtiers. In 1163 Henry fought an unsuccessful campaign in Wales. His Constable was accused by a fellow-baron of cowardice, fought a duel to prove his innocence, and lost. The result was forfeiture and disgrace; and the Earl of Oxford, who had recently married the Constable's daughter, immediately felt compelled to repudiate his disastrous marriage. When it had been arranged the girl was too young to marry, so she was delivered to the Earl's brother for safe-keeping. The Earl alleged that his brother and fiancée had cohabited; if true, this established a barrier of affinity between them which would be a bar to marriage—a similar allegation was used by King Richard I twenty-five years later to excuse him from marrying the French king's daughter. The girl was locked up and subjected to contumely, but she managed to get her case heard in the Church courts, which handled matrimonial causes. For political reasons, however, her case proceeded slowly; nearly nine years elapsed before the pope finally insisted that the Earl restore to her the rights of a wife. The Earl complied, and they reared a family together. Of the inwardness of their married life we know nothing; but this preposterous story was the prelude to an outwardly successful marriage.

Nearly three centuries later a girl of twelve, as the result of a vision, accepted a man almost three times her age as her second husband; a few months later he died leaving her pregnant. She married twice more, yet had no more children. It was a strange chance that she had any, stranger still that a single child should have survived the illnesses of childhood and the dangers of a great inheritance. The young Margaret Beaufort had been an eligible widow because the blood of kings flowed in her veins; and her son was the future King Henry VII.

Landlords and Townsmen

In most parts of mediaeval Europe, the possession of land was the basis of livelihood, wealth, social status and government. The peasant lived by what he tilled; the warrior-aristocrat fed on the produce of his land, owed his income to its surplus or its rents, his standing to the breadth of his acres and the numbers of his tenantry and followers. A feudal society was a society in which social bonds and legal status were inextricably entangled with land tenure. Yet every country had its cities, and in some parts of Europe town predominated over village as a social centre, a centre p 18 of government, of population and of wealth. This was especially (12, 13) true of north and central Italy and the Low Countries, but in very different ways; and the contrast between the relations of landlords and burghers north and south of the Alps is very instructive.

Before the 11th century Italy had been ruled, under its king, by a number of great nobles, dukes and marquises. In the 11th century the southern duchies were conquered by the Normans and became in due course part of the Norman kingdom. The area round Rome was the papal patrimony. Further north, in Tuscany and Lombardy, higher authority tended to disappear. The marquises died out; the King of Italy was also King of Germany, and was an occasional visitor. Authority tended to devolve upon the bishops, who found themselves having to treat with the growing power and pretensions of townsmen. Power gradually passed into the hands of oligarchies within the greater cities; oligarchies formed by an alliance between the richer merchants within and the stronger country barons and knights without the walls. The alliance in early days was often made easier by the fact that many members of both parties sprang from the same families, and more intimate by the practice of the military (still dramatically revealed by the buildings of Siena and S. Gimignano) of building their castles within the city walls. This intimacy, however, often led to faction and war; and in the long run the interests of merchants, artisans and landowners came increasingly to diverge. The city oligarchies tended to find themselves at loggerheads with the warrior nobles on whom the city's security depended. These problems were solved in different places in different ways; meanwhile the cities succeeded in forming governments independent of their ultimate overlord. The league of Lombard cities asserted, with intermittent success, their independence of the Hohenstaufen Emperors; and the name of the city of Alessandria still commemorates their alliance with Pope Alexander III against the Emperor Frederick Barbarossa (1152–90). In the long run they became wholly independent of outside authority, though the greater cities, such as Venice, Florence and Genoa, built up their own little empires; and they were thus enabled to develop their widely spread mercantile policies without interference from the local ambitions and petty piracy of a feudal aristocracy.

Feudal warriors and peaceful burghers always found it difficult to understand one another; but north of the Alps their common interests were more frequently appreciated, and their alliances more lasting than in Italy. Town-building became a favourite occupation of kings and great landlords. Southern France contains hundreds of towns deliberately planted by the Counts of Provence and the Dukes of Aquitaine (also kings of England) and by St Louis and his successors. When Edward I of England, who well knew the new towns of Gascony, conquered Wales, he reckoned to overawe his new subjects by building great castles and to convert them to the arts of peace by surrounding them with towns. One can still trace the neat grid patterns of streets of several Edwardian towns in the modern street-plans; and even if re-paving and rebuilding have hopelessly obscured this continuity as one walks in the streets, a photograph taken from the air can make it plain.

A great landlord valued his land for the number of tenants it could hold, whom he could summon to his standard in time of war, and for the silver it brought into his money-chests. In the early Middle Ages, on the whole, he was more interested in providing himself with warriors; as the centuries passed his tastes became more expensive, more varied and more sophisticated; and even for his wars money, which could hire men and buy supplies, might be more useful than tenants. He or his tenants needed to find good markets for the produce of their fields—corn, wool, meat and so forth; markets which would attract merchants from near and far to carry such of their produce as was not consumed nearby to places where it could be used, and also to bring to the local markets metal for his weapons, cloth for his liveries, carpets and tapestries to adorn his castles, silks for his wife, spices for his kitchen and (in southern Europe at least) slaves to serve in his household.

Between the 11th and the 13th centuries the need for money rose sharply. The standard of living and of civilization of the nobility rose; but their chief extravagances continued to be in building and warfare. In the golden age of castle-building these activities were often not distinct; and some of the reasons for the growing need for money can be brought home vividly to us if we compare the simple earth mound, shown in the Bayeux Tapestry, which formed the basis of the motte-and-bailey castle of the 11th century, with the more elaborate stone structures of the same age, such as the Tower of London; or again, with the growing elaboration of ring walls, towers and living-quarters of the castles of Henry of Blois or those the Crusaders built in Palestine and Syria; or with the final development of the mediaeval castle in those of Edward I, with their elaborate rings of walls, and their intricate devices to give the defenders command of every line of fire, and to counter every move of the besiegers. These were royal castles, and the immense sums spent by Edward I in castle-building help to explain the chronic financial difficulties of his later years, which embroiled even so strong and effective a king with his subjects. If the king was in constant financial trouble, one can understand why even the wealthiest of lesser men were concerned to make the most of their resources. Hence their patronage of towns, behind whose walls permanent markets could convert their produce into silver, and their silver into the needs and luxuries of the age.

Ways to Salvation: Pilgrims and Crusades

Building and war were combined in the most powerful of mediaeval weapons, the castle. Extravagant building, however, was not only indulged in to provide a lord with domestic and military equipment; it catered also for the salvation of his soul. Immense sums were lavished on the building of monasteries and churches, monuments to the piety or troubled conscience of their patrons, in

which the most fervent prayers available could ceaselessly argue their case at the gate of Heaven. For a short period temporal and spiritual ends were joined together in the notion of the Crusade— a short period, that is, if one considers the real vogue and practical effectiveness of the Crusades, which lasted only from 1096 to the early 13th century. The fashion, however, did not die quickly; even in the 15th century a conscientious pope might still think it one of his primary tasks to launch a Crusade.

Next to church-building the most popular traditional technique for mediaeval laymen actively to pursue the path to Heaven was by going on pilgrimage. The spiritual treasury of mediaeval Europe was inexhaustible. Every church had its relics; most great churches had the shrine of a local saint who attracted pilgrims from his own country. Richest in saints and relics was Rome itself, which in the early Middle Ages had been viewed more as the home of the saints, a centre of pilgrimage, than as a seat of government. Second only to Rome in popularity and efficacy was the pilgrimage to St James, Santiago de Compostela in north-western Spain; and the pilgrim routes through southern France and northern Spain carried the pilgrim past the shrines of numerous saints less eminent than St James the Apostle, but far from negligible. For those who loved adventure, or whose sins were desperate, there was also the pilgrimage to the Holy Land itself.

A barbarian king of an earlier century, in the process of receiving instruction in the Christian faith, was supposed to have said that if he and his warriors had been present at Calvary, things would have turned out differently. As the centuries passed the need to consecrate the warlike activities of a warrior aristocracy was increasingly felt; and at many different levels the idea was current that lance and sword could be used to do God's work. The popes of the late 11th century developed the idea of a holy war in defence of Christendom, for the 'defence' or recovery of lands which had once been Christian, and especially of Jerusalem and Palestine; a war which God would bless since it served His purposes, and which would lead Him also to give His blessing, and salvation, to those who engaged in it: a noble idea in its way, if one ignores its consequences. More immediately reflected in action was the popular idea which gave it violent and widespread effect: that a special climacteric was at hand when men should arise with God's blessing to slaughter His enemies, be they Jews (never before massacred in western Europe) or Muslims. In fairness, one must remember that the Church's leaders were trying to chisel a very stony problem: how to curb the violence of a society bred to war and to draw out its potential idealism. The popes themselves not only had a reasonable fear of the consequences of Turkish military success, but also an excessive trust in the capacity of earthly weapons to fulfil what they believed to be God's purposes. The First Crusade was remarkably successful: Jerusalem was captured and remained in Christian hands for nearly a century; a large throng of the most violent elements in western society were removed to a safe distance. It is probable that the Crusades played a large part in helping to make western Europe a somewhat more peaceable area than it had been hitherto. They also played a part in the expansion of Christendom in the 12th and 13th centuries, as growing population led to a period of colonization, within and without the established frontiers of western Europe. In some measure these factors were known and appreciated by the Church's leaders; they were aware too that the Crusades brought out the depths of human squalor as well as notable and devoted heroism. Yet they were primarily concerned with the defence of Jerusalem and the conquest or reconquest of lands from Islam.

The Beggar and the Pope

There was another way of pursuing these aims. Most of the famous stories about St Francis come from biographers writing after his death and canonization. One of them, however, was narrated by a French bishop in Syria in a letter written a few days, or at most a few weeks, after the event. 'Master Reiner, prior of St Michael, has entered the order of the Brothers Minor, an order which is multiplying rapidly on all sides, because it imitates the primitive Church and follows the life of the Apostles in everything. The master of these brothers is named Brother Francis; he is so lovable that he is venerated by everyone. Having come into

136 (2)
138 (8)
p 140
(13)

p 141
(20)

p 28, 29
(30–36)

p 30 (37)

our army, he has not been afraid, in his zeal for the faith, to go to that of our enemies. For days together he announced the word of God to the Saracens, but with little success; then the Sultan, king of Egypt, asked him in secret to entreat God to reveal to him, by some miracle, which is the best religion.' Later legend asserted that Francis offered to walk through a fire to prove the truth of his faith; but the Sultan prudently refused, and Francis's missionary work among the Muslims came to a speedy end.

p 24 (22)

Missionary work went on hand in hand with the Crusades: the 11th century had seen the conversion of Scandinavia completed, together with that of Hungary and Poland; in the 12th century large tracts of northern and central Europe were the scene of missionary enterprise. In the 13th century news began to trickle through of the Mongol empire of Jenghiz Khan, and the popes dreamed of a great act of missionary strategy which would encircle Islam. In the event this failed, and the Crusades and missionary enterprise tended to decay together, until the latter was revived in the days of the Counter-Reformation.

The meeting of St Francis and the Sultan is one of many ways in which the *poverello* can be seen to reflect and summarize the themes of this chapter. It is sometimes the most exceptional figures which help to bring a past age most vividly to life. We must not look to Francis for the actions or reactions of an ordinary man; but he will show us the interests and assumptions of his age softened and deepened by a rare humanity and illuminated by a brilliant imagination. His father was a merchant in a small Italian city; but a merchant with connections which took him into France, where he was travelling when Francis, 'Francesco', the Frank or Frenchman, was born in Assisi. Mercantile activity was developing the prosperity of Europe, and developing the capacity of cities small and large to cultivate the arts of war and peace. The rich young ruler in the Gospel went away sorrowing. Francis joyfully gave up all the wealth to which he had been brought up—joyfully, but not easily; his acute sense of what money could mean comes out in his almost violent insistence that his friars, vowed to poverty, should not touch or handle coins: the brother who pressed him to accept money to further some highly laudable cause was made to carry it in his teeth and drop it in a pile of manure, so that coins should always retain this association in his mind. Francis knew the subtlety of human temptation, and had a brilliant gift for direct teaching through the senses of smell and hearing and above all of sight: he acted many little parables before his friars. He also knew, from his father and probably from his own feelings as a boy, the power of money to attract and captivate. But his early ambitions had not lain in the market place. He had heard stories of chivalry and dreamed of being a knight; he had engaged in the petty warfare of the Italian cities and had been imprisoned in Perugia for his pains. He had used his father's money to buy arms and the trappings of chivalry, and had planned to join a band of *condottieri*. From this he was saved by a revulsion of feeling and a sudden illness, and by a growing sense that his call was to another of the many ideals of the age.

f 1

It was Francis's practice in later years, when he met a worm on the path or road on which he was walking, to pick it up carefully and place it on one side. A horror of seeing creatures trampled on and squashed was a conventional attribute of a mediaeval saint; but this was hardly the point in Francis's mind. The worm was a traditional symbol of the Saviour: 'I am a worm and no man' was interpreted as referring to Jesus Himself. Francis enforced the meaning of this paradox of humility by taking what would have been regarded as absurd pains to save a mere worm from its fate. When he instructed the birds to sing God's praises he was not indulging in sentimental fantasy, but forcing on his hearers his conviction that the world was God's world, a part of the wonder of His creation. This was in tune with the beginning of a new tendency to look straight at nature and a new capacity to reproduce it with precision, which reaches its first perfection in the middle of the 13th century.

God's world—and so good, however perverted by the consequences of the Fall. The notion that the world was good needed some emphasis in an age and a land accustomed to the preaching of the Cathars, who taught that the world was irremediably evil. Cathar doctrine grew and flourished in western Europe in the 12th and 13th centuries partly because it was attuned to a profound traditional attitude to God and the world: God was seen as a judge, the wickedness of the world was so far removed from his goodness that every human activity was tainted with sin and Jesus was thought of also as a judge—it was all but forgotten that he had once been a man. The Cathars, indeed, denied that he had been a man: the Incarnation had only been an appearance, Jesus was a spirit in human form. But even while this doctrine enjoyed its greatest power, an interest in the human Jesus was also coming to appeal—and with it a renewed interest in the divine capacities of human nature, and (at the theological level) in human qualities. In a famous midnight gathering in Greccio, Francis united two of the most vital elements in his experience when he arranged for the Christmas Mass to be celebrated with all solemnity in an improvised stable with real donkeys and oxen standing by.

Communities of men dedicated to poverty were a familiar sight in France and Italy in Francis's childhood. Many of them, like the groups which gathered round Waldo (the Waldensians), the merchant of Lyons who had abandoned his wealth for a life of preaching and poverty, had started in orthodoxy and ended in heresy. But the principle of obedience to the Church's hierarchy was deep and strong in Francis, and this explains why he visited pope and Curia as soon as his community began to form, and why he looked constantly in later years to Pope and Cardinal Protector, not to grant him privileges or special protection, but to help him to sustain the ideal of his Order within the established hierarchy of the Church. He made of obedience the central pillar of his Order; but it was no negative, passive obedience, but joyful submission.

'Holy obedience . . . makes a man subject to all men on this earth, and not to men only, but to the beasts of the field, to do with him—so far as is given to them from the Lord on high— what they will.'

Thus Francis added a new dimension to one of the most conventional and traditional principles of the society in which he lived. Similarly, there was nothing new in dedicating one's life to poverty; nor in the perception that there could be little direct contact between the hierarchy of the Church, authoritarian, powerful, rich, educated, and the ignorant poor masses of the people. But Francis found new methods of forming links between them, and made a new effort to give some unity or coherence to Christian society. The history of his Order and of the Church in the centuries after his death constantly gives evidence of his failure. But to say that Francis failed is, in the end, no more sensible than to say that Rembrandt failed as a painter because he died bankrupt.

'The brothers should rejoice', wrote Francis in one version of his *Rule*, 'when they are living among humble, despised folk, among the poor and weak, sick, lepers, beggars.' It needed emphasis: any success the friars might enjoy depended on their being accepted by the poor as of their own kind. Nor was it easy even for Francis. 'The Lord granted me to begin to do penance because, when I lived among my sins, it seemed to me too horrible even to look at lepers: and the Lord himself led me among them and I did a work of mercy with them . . . And so what seemed horrible was transformed to sweetness both of mind and body. And after a little delay I left the life of the world. And the Lord gave me great faith in churches . . . and in priests . . . . And I wish above all that the most holy mysteries [of Christ's body and blood] shall be honoured, revered and kept in precious places . . . . And after the Lord gave me some brothers, no one showed me what I ought to do; but the Highest himself revealed to me that I ought to live according to the pattern of the Holy Gospel. And in few words and simply I had it written down, and the Lord Pope confirmed it to me . . . .'

II THE MONASTIC WORLD

The Contribution of the Orders

GEORGE ZARNECKI

'In living our life ... the path of God's commandments is run

with unspeakable loving sweetness; so that never leaving His school,

but persevering in the monastery until death in His teaching,

we share by our patience the sufferings of Christ,

and so merit to be partakers in His Kingdom.'

ST BENEDICT, PROLOGUE TO THE RULE

'There was once a man

of venerable life whose name was Benedict ... He was born of good family in the province of Nursia, and from there was sent to the schools of Rome. But ... he despised his studies, abandoned his home and his father's wealth, and desiring to please God alone sought for the habit of holy religion.'

St Benedict was not the first monk, but he was the first to see the monastery not as a collection of hermits, each privately dedicated to his own personal salvation, but as a community with a united way of life and a united purpose. He was born in 480, at a time when the Roman Empire in the West had totally collapsed and Italy was divided between the Ostrogoths in the north and the precarious rule of the Eastern (Byzantine) Emperor in the south. It was a desolate age and Benedict's new monasticism was one of the measures to meet it. It consolidated the Church, preserved culture, and trained missionaries who might eventually push forward the borders of Christendom.

Benedict's first period as a monk was on the 'Egyptian' pattern —solitude, self-punishment and prayer in a cave at Subiaco. Then for 18 years he supervised a colony of monks at Vicovaro, rationalizing the harsh precepts of the Desert Fathers and systematizing his own ideas for a balanced, self-supporting community. About 529 he moved to Monte Cassino and wrote his *Regula* for the guidance of future generations. Its provisions are severe but practical, and it has survived without essential change as the foundation of monastic life until the present day.

St Gregory the Great, a Benedictine monk who became Pope, wrote the *Life of St Benedict* (or rather the Second Book of his *Dialogues*, which contains it) probably in 593 or 594. Its opening sentences have been quoted above, and its closing page is illustrated here from an 11th-century manuscript made at Monte Cassino. The six scenes may be described in St Gregory's own words:

Top left: the writing of the Rule. 'For he wrote a Rule for monks, which is remarkable both for its discretion and for the lucidity of its style.'

Top right: 'Presently a fever attacked him, exhausting him with its burning heat, and he grew weaker every day ... Then supporting his feeble limbs by the help of his disciples, he stood with his hands raised to Heaven and gave forth his last breath in words of prayer.'

Centre left: 'He was buried in the Chapel of St John the Baptist, which he himself had built after destroying the altar of Apollo.'

Centre right: 'On that same day two of his monks, the one in the monastery, the other far away, saw the selfsame vision. They saw a path, strewn with rich coverings and flashing with innumerable lamps, stretching eastwards from his monastery to the sky. And beside it above stood a man in venerable garments, who asked them whose path it was that they saw. When they confessed that they knew not, "This", said he, "is the path by which Benedict, the beloved of the Lord, ascended to heaven."'

Bottom left: 'A certain woman became affected in her mind and reached such a degree of madness that she went wandering day and night over hill and by dale, through field and forest, never resting except when compelled by sheer exhaustion. One day, having strayed farther than usual, she came to the cave of this blessed father [i.e. the cave where he had lived as a hermit at Subiaco], entered it unwittingly and spent the night there. Next morning she left it as completely cured as if she had never suffered from any madness; and she preserved for the rest of her life the good health which she had thus received.'

Bottom right: St Gregory finishes his Life of St Benedict: 'I must now cease talking for a while, so that by silence I may repair my strength and be able to narrate the miracles of others.' (1)

Sebtur quid sptnator. Suidamtur
uac ardtrchetur etridentr.

Ulnars he perndicr. hmnr ulnars. Asttarg; scmdtr.

Tesse cetrdeatur. chotus ofmu
trl lachmratur...

Sic pact arstfa pttgtr. hisptr turnr. angtf
tdra.

Her subttr. hnc decoss. marntr. hic Atmtrsrbg;
fr scos...

Sic Benedicctar' tspmr. Smo plurtmar. lingua
quttscatr...

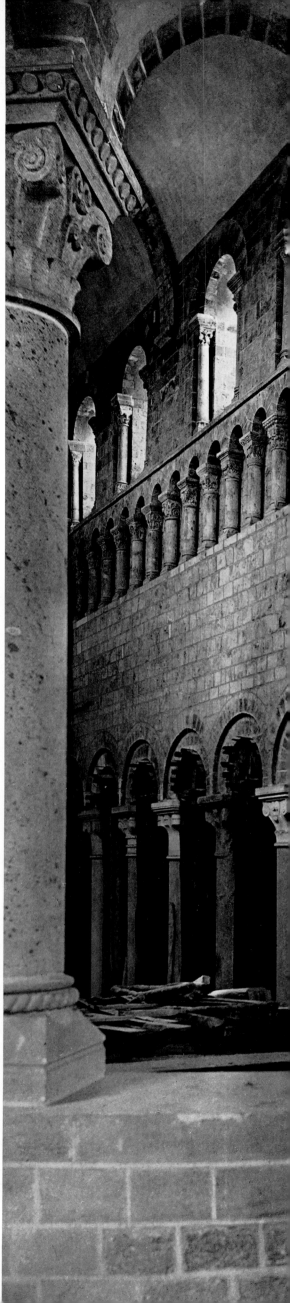

'It was as if the whole earth, having cast off the old by shaking itself, were clothing itself anew in a white robe of churches', wrote Raoul Glaber, a Cluniac monk, about 1003. Architecturally this was the period known as 'First Romanesque'. S. Pedro de Roda (above left) in Spain, consecrated in 1022 but finished later, has a barrel-vault and capitals of classical inspiration. The special distinction of the roughly contemporary St-Philibert at Tournus in France (above right) is the variety of its vaults; here are shown transverse tunnel-vaults in the nave and groin-vaults in the aisle. Below: the west wall of S. Pietro, Civate (c.1040) with its later fresco of God's victory over the forces of Evil. (2, 3, 4)

The relics of St Benedict were rescued from the monastery of Monte Cassino when it was sacked by the Lombards in 585 and brought to Fleury. As 'St-Benoît-sur-Loire', Fleury became a famous centre of pilgrimage; the east end of the church (left) dates from 1070–80. Top: the atrium of the monastery of S. Ambrogio at Milan (c. 1100), an early version of the monastic cloister. Above: Paray-le-Monial, a daughter-house of Cluny, and a 'Cluny in miniature'—see overleaf. (5, 6, 7)

'Among all the abbeys

beyond the Alps, there shines first and foremost that of Cluny . . . without doubt it surpasses all other monasteries, even the most ancient.' So spoke Gregory VII at the Council of Rome in 1077. Cluny had been founded 170 years earlier in 910 and under a series of exceptionally able, pious and long-lived Abbots—Odo (926–42), Odilo (994–1049) and Hugh (1049–1109)—became the leader of a strongly centralized reform movement that eventually, in the 12th century, included nearly 1,500 monasteries. The third and greatest of the abbey churches of Cluny was begun by St Hugh in 1088. By 1095 the east end was finished and it was consecrated by

Pope Urban II, himself a former Cluniac monk. The ceremony is depicted below; the church, seen from the south, is shown schematically but on the right, where Abbot Hugh stands with his monks, the east end with its apse and circle of chapels can be recognized. In the centre, under the crossing, is the altar; and on the left the nave (then unbuilt) with the Pope and members of the Papal Court. Right: two sides of one of the surviving capitals from the choir. The figures, which are unique in Romanesque art, represent two of the 'tones' of plainsong—a reminder of the important part played by music in the Cluniac liturgy. (8, 9, 10)

Christ enthroned gazed down from the great east apse of Cluny. Of that fresco nothing remains, but a smaller one, identical in subject and contemporary in date, still exists at the Cluniac grange of Berzé-la-Ville (above), a favourite retreat of St Hugh in his old age. (11)

The abbey was destroyed during the French Revolution and little beside the ruins of one transept still stands (left). There were originally towers over both transepts and over the crossing. 'It took twenty years to build,' we read in the old *Life of St Hugh*, 'was so spacious that thousands of monks could assemble there, so magnificent that an emperor could have built nothing finer, and surpassed all known churches in construction and beauty.' (12)

47

A bitter attack

on the worldliness and luxury of Cluniac life was launched by the great reformer St Bernard of Clairvaux (see pp. 56–7). By the 12th century the Cluniacs had in many ways compromised their early ideals. Instead of representing austerity they were among the richest orders in Europe; instead of withdrawing from the world, the Abbot of Cluny was a potentate hardly inferior to the Pope. 'Tell me, ye poor,' asked St Bernard, 'if indeed ye be poor, what doth this gold in your sanctuary?'

Harpies, from the cloister of Silos, would have come under St Bernard's condemnation—like 'those monstrous centaurs, those half-men'. (13)

Cluniac politics: Abbot Ulric of Payerne took sides with Pope Gregory against the Emperor—hence St Peter's prominence on this capital. (14)

A spirited lion—on a capital from the crypt of Canterbury Cathedral. Monastic carving (*pace* St Bernard) provides a wonderful Bestiary. (15)

'The church is adorned with gemmed crowns of light—nay, with lustres like cart-wheels, girt round with lamps, but no less brilliant with the precious stones that stud them.' The chandelier (above) is at St Michael's, Hildesheim. Nearly 30 feet in diameter, it symbolizes the Heavenly Jerusalem. (18)

'Moreover we see candelabra standing like trees of massive bronze fashioned with marvellous subtlety of art, and glistening no less brightly with gems than with the lights they carry. What, think you, is the purpose of all this? The compunction of penitents or the admiration of the beholders?' Only the foot of this huge candelabrum from St-Remi at Rheims survives (right). Complete, it stood four times the height of a man. (19,20)

◀ The first attempts at reviving monumental sculpture in marble had been made only a century earlier in such works as the lintel of St-Genis-des-Fontaines, 1020 (left) closely based on a manuscript illumination. Sophistication came with surprising speed. (16)

◀ 'To what purpose are those unclean apes?... Many bodies are seen under one head, or again, many heads to a single body... In short, so many and so marvellous are the varieties of diverse shapes on every hand, that we are more tempted to read in the marble than in our books.' Left: another capital from Silos, showing grotesque animals. (17)

'Let us take our part in the psalmody, that mind and voice accord together,' wrote St Benedict. Much of the monk's day was spent in choir (above). There were seven regular services, from 2.30 in the morning to 7.30 at night: Lauds, Prime, Tierce, Sext, None, Evensong and Compline. (25)

The number of Orders grew throughout the Middle Ages, and in the 13th century was augmented by the revolutionary new Orders of friars, who lived not in the cloister but in the world. Each Order had its distinguishing dress: the roundels on the left show four of them—Carmelite friars, Franciscans, Dominicans and Benedictines. Right: a novice receiving his habit and casting out the devil of this world. (21–24, 26)

Communities of nuns go back as far as those of monks and there were almost as many different Orders. St Benedict's Rule was early adapted for the religious life of women, and St Francis and St Dominic instituted Mendicant Orders of nuns as well as of friars. The Franciscan nuns were called 'Poor Clares' after their foundress, St Clare. Below: Poor Clares at table. The nun reading (as was prescribed by their Rule) is Beata Umiltà and is therefore shown haloed. (27)

The ideal convent is portrayed in this French manuscript of about 1300 (above). In the top row Mass is being celebrated; behind the priest and his assistants stands the abbess with her crozier and the sacristan, pulling the bell-ropes. One of the other nuns, with a bunch of large keys at her wrist, is the cellarer. Three novices look out from upper windows. The lower scene shows a procession going through the cloister; the abbess with crozier is again present with five nuns carrying music books. (28)

Poor Clares in choir: nuns were not expected to be as learned as the men. They have their missals for reference, where the monks know the liturgy by heart. (29)

'The monastery itself', wrote St Benedict, 'ought if possible to be so constructed as to contain within it all necessaries . . . so that there be no occasion for monks to wander abroad, since this is in no wise expedient for their souls.'

The gatehouse (Thornton Abbey, Lincolnshire): 'Let there be stationed at the gate of the monastery some wise old man who knows how to give and receive an answer, and whose age will not allow him to wander from his post.' (30)

The abbot (Durandus of Moissac): 'Let the abbot have equal love for all, and let all, according to their deserts, be under the same discipline.' (31)

The chapter-house (Bristol): 'Whenever any weighty matters have to be transacted in the monastery, let the abbot call together all the community and himself propose the matter for discussion.' (32)

The kitchen (Fontevrault, far right): 'The brethren are so to serve each other that no one be excused from work in the kitchen unless on the score of health.' (34)

The barn (Great Coxwell): 'Idleness is the enemy of the soul. Because this is so the brethren ought to be occupied at specific times in manual labour.' (33)

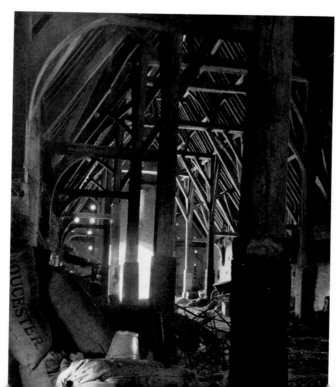

The ground-plans of monasteries were standardized and remained essentially unchanged from the 9th century onwards. This aerial view of the Cistercian house at Rievaulx shows some of the most important parts: (a) and (b), the nave and chancel of the church; (c) chapterhouse; (d) cloister; (e) undercroft of the dormitory; (f) refectory; (g) infirmary cloister. (35)

The cloister was the centre of the common life of the monastery. That of Mont-St-Michel (below) has been exceptionally well preserved and restored, though the monastic buildings themselves, perched on a narrow rock, could not follow the normal plan. (36)

The refectory (Royaumont; note the reader's pulpit in the wall): 'Two dishes of cooked food must suffice for all the brethren, and if there be any fruit or young vegetables these may be added to the meal as a third dish. Let a pound weight of bread suffice for each day ... We think that a pint of wine a day is sufficient for anyone ... There ought always to be reading while the brethren eat at table.' (37)

The night-stairs, i.e. stairs connecting the dormitory to the church as a kind of short-cut for nocturnal services (right: Hexham): 'In the winter the brethren shall get up at the eighth hour of the night, so that having rested till a little after midnight they may rise refreshed.' (38)

Labourers in the fields: early Cistercian communities were entirely self-supporting. These three miniatures (above and right) from an early 12th-century manuscript made at Cîteaux show their ragged brown habits; later, at the miraculous suggestion of Our Lady, they changed to white. (39, 40, 42)

The confessor (below): a Franciscan friar hears confession from a Poor Clare; note behind him, the penitential birch-rod. (41)

A multitude of services now regarded as the business of the state were in the Middle Ages performed by the monasteries. They were charitable institutions, hospitals, inns; their schools supplied the civil servants who administered the country; their libraries were the only places where the literature of the past—pagan as well as Christian—was preserved. Hardly any aspect of secular life was untouched by their presence.

The scribe (below): Eadwine, monk of Christchurch, Canterbury—a self-portrait from his own Psalter of about 1150. His use of colour is vivid though eccentric, and he has given himself blue hair and a green face. The copying of books in the 12th century was largely in the hands of monks, and a large and famous *scriptorium* like Canterbury's would have been known all over Europe. (44)

The cellarer (left): monasteries were never without guests, from the poorest pilgrims to knights and barons who sat at the abbot's table. The cellarer had charge of supplies; he kept the keys, and sometimes his portrait, as here, seems tinged with envy. (43)

The penitents (right): satires on the monks grow more frequent in the later Middle Ages. This miniature of a monk and his mistress in the stocks occurs in the margin of a book painted for Augustinian canons. (46)

A living monastery of the mid-12th century is recorded in this unique diagram of Canterbury. It was made by (or for) the engineer installing a new water-system, but it shows the cathedral and all the monastic buildings in exact and still verifiable detail. Elevations are drawn at right angles to one of their base lines, so that the plan has to be turned in different directions to be read.

We are looking south. At the top is the church, with two cloisters built against it. That on the right is bordered by the *cellarium*, refectory, dormitory and chapter-house (below the refectory is the kitchen with a vine growing up the wall). In the second cloister, on the other side of the dormitory, stands a water-tower, the centre of the new water-system. East of this cloister (which is divided in two by a fence, half of it being used as a *herbarium*) is the infirmary and to the north the *necessarium*, or monks' latrines. (45)

55

The first Cistercians were a band of monks from Molesme in Burgundy, who in 1098 left their monastery where the observance of the Rule had become lax, and built themselves a church in a wild spot called Cîteaux (in Latin *Cistercium*). Under Abbot Stephen Harding (1109–34) the characteristic Cistercian pattern of life was established: a strict return to the Rule, the complete rejection of riches and display. In 1113 Harding was joined by St Bernard (left), one of the greatest preachers of the Middle Ages whose denunciation of Cluniac luxury has already been quoted (p. 49). Two years later St Bernard founded Clairvaux. The reform movement spread rapidly, and the Cistercians soon rivalled the power and influence of Cluny itself. (47)

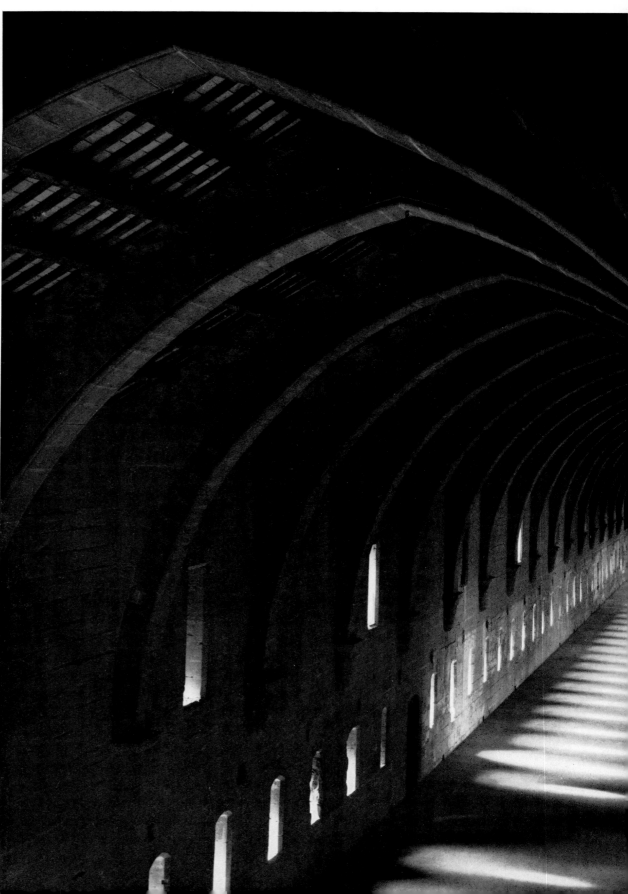

Strong links bound every Cistercian abbey to its founding house and so to Cîteaux, though in a more familial relationship than that of Cluny. Above: Alcobaça, in Portugal shows Cistercian functionalism unaffected by local styles. Right: the great dormitory of Poblet, in Spain. 'All shall sleep in separate beds,' says the Rule, 'and each shall receive, according to the appointment of his abbot, bedclothes fitted to the condition of his life. If it be possible let them all sleep in a common dormitory . . . Let a candle be constantly burning in the room until morning, and let the monks sleep clothed and girt with girdles or cords.' (49, 50)

56

In their search for total seclusion the Cistercians chose the loneliest and wildest places. Their buildings are always remote from towns, a fact which today only adds to the grandeur of their ruins. Ornament is reduced to a minimum; they are like the lives that were led in them—dedicated, simple and strong. Left: Fossanova, near Rome, begun 1187, a French Gothic church transplanted to Italy. Right: Pontigny, the second 'daughter' of Cîteaux, founded in 1114. A new east end was added in 1186 and, though plain, already marks a relaxation of Cistercian strictness. Below right: Fontenay, in Burgundy. Built during the lifetime of St Bernard (about 1140) it embodies all his austere ideals in terms of Burgundian architecture. (48, 51, 52)

Cistercian art (almost a contradiction in terms to St Bernard) flourished even from the beginning. Scribes were excused work in the fields, and many rules were relaxed for their benefit. Below: part of Stephen Harding's Bible (c.1110). To the left, a fantastic initial 'H'; to the right the 'I' of *In principio*, formed by St John (in the white habit of a Cistercian) and his eagle, which digs its talons into his eyes, nose, mouth and ears, symbolizing the word of God being imprinted upon his senses. (54)

The Order grew in numbers, in power and in wealth. Great patrons enriched their favourite abbeys and gradually the reforming zeal and dedicated principles of Cîteaux and Clairvaux went the way of Cluny. By the 15th century the old prohibitions were being completely disregarded and just as many expensive works of art were being commissioned by the Cistercians as by any other order. Left: a 14th-century stained glass window probably made for the abbey of Amelungsborn in Lower Saxony. (53)

English embroidery – *opus Anglicanum* — was an art in which the nunneries may claim some share. The only signed example from the Middle Ages was made by a nun, Joanna of Beverley. More usually, however, it seems to have been produced by professional craftsmen for churches and religious houses. The Syon Cope (opposite) dates in its original form, a chasuble, to between 1300 and 1320. It later belonged to the Brigittine convent of Syon, near London. This detail, about a twentieth of the whole, shows the Dormition of the Virgin. (55)

The knightly Orders owed their origin to the Crusades. Their members took monastic vows but lived the lives of soldiers, guarding the Holy Places, protecting pilgrims and resisting the infidel. When the Kingdom of Jerusalem was lost the Hospitallers retreated first to Cyprus and then to Rhodes, where their fortified town (right, the hall of the Infirmary) still stands. (58)

The Templars were founded in 1118, reached their peak in the early 13th century, and declined when Palestine had to be evacuated in 1291. They had become rich and envied. Their rivals, the Hospitallers, and King Philip of France caused them to be accused of heresy and blasphemy, convicted on forced confessions, and suppressed. These two miniatures show them being arraigned before the Pope and the King, and the Grand Master, Jacques de Moley, being burned at the stake in 1312. (56, 57)

The strange Templars' Church of Vera Cruz has a polygonal exterior (above right) and an interior built round a raised sanctuary. (59, 60)

60

The Holy Sepulchre at Jerusalem was round, and many of the Templars' Churches (often with that dedication) were given the same shape. Their two principal churches in Europe—in Paris and London—were both circular. That of London still survives (below), though much altered and badly damaged in the Second World War. (61)

Krak des Chevaliers, Krak of the Knights (above), was among the strongest Crusader castles. Built by the Hospitallers in the early 12th century, its function was to guard the vital passes between the East and the Mediterranean coast. Its construction was massive, with two rings of mighty walls and bastions and an approach through corridors safe from attack. This view is from the south-west, with the old aqueduct on the right. Krak was held, amid continual battle and bloodshed, for 150 years; it was never captured, but had to be abandoned by the Knights in 1271. (62)

The Teutonic Knights began, like the others, as defenders of the Holy Land, but in 1225 they were invited to Poland to help fight the heathen Prussians. Here the Order acquired large estates on the Baltic coast and soon became a wealthy and powerful state, a ruthless oppressor of its subjects and neighbours. The headquarters were at Marienburg, on the Vistula, where during the 14th century they built themselves the huge castle (left) which stood until the Second World War. The 'middle castle', inside the walls, contained the apartments of the Grand Master. (63)

61

St Dominic

founded the second Order of Friars in 1215. St Francis had founded the first in 1210. These two, Franciscans and Dominicans, were the last radical movement of reform within mediaeval monasticism. St Francis has already been treated on pp. 22–4. St Dominic was a very different character—a scholar, an organizer, a fighter (often a merciless fighter) against heresy—qualities that he bequeathed to his Order, especially in his native Spain. The portrait (left) is attributed to Guido da Siena and was painted within a generation after his death. Dominican art rises to greatness in the work of Fra Angelico, a friar of the Convent of San Marco in Florence, who in the early 15th century painted the bare cells of his brethren with scenes of the Passion and the saints. The cell shown below (note the low ceiling and door on the right) contains the Transfiguration with St Dominic and the Virgin Mary as witnesses. (64, 66)

Bitter resentment was provoked when the wandering friars seemed to be usurping the functions of the local clergy. This marginal painting (below), from a treatise by the Archbishop of Armagh, shows a Dominican and a Franciscan—the latter with a devil on his back. (65)

The Contribution of the Orders

GEORGE ZARNECKI

UNDER CHARLEMAGNE and his successors, the monasteries had achieved a unique position of leadership—intellectual, spiritual and artistic. They alone provided teachers, scribes and diplomats; they alone nourished scholarship, preserving intact not only the text of the Bible and the early Fathers, but also much of the culture of the classical world.

The break-up of the Carolingian Empire brought a period of political and economic anarchy, during which these values could barely survive. The repeated invasions, the savage and ruthless behaviour of rulers and the wretchedness of everyday existence were hardly conditions in which the contemplative life could flourish. Monasteries were sacked and burnt; monks often became fugitives, concerned only to save their lives, their few possessions and their sacred relics. In such circumstances, it was difficult—even impossible—to observe the monastic rule. That monastic life, and with it Europe's civilization, was saved from complete disintegration was due to a few men of great faith and courage, who set themselves the task of restoring moral values by first reforming the monasteries.

The work before them was enormous and not without personal danger. Raffredus, the Abbot of Farfa in Lazio, was poisoned in 936 by two of his monks because he attempted to enforce the Benedictine rule there. One of his murderers, Campo, became abbot and he and his accomplice lived in the monastery with their wives and children. Another attempt at reform resulted in the expulsion of Campo from the monastery, but the new abbot was also poisoned. Not until the end of the century was Farfa successfully reformed by an abbot, who, however, in order to carry out this task, had to use simony to be elected.

One of the most famous monasteries in Gaul was Fleury (now St-Benoît-sur-Loire), which owed its great reputation to the relics of the founder of Western monasticism, St Benedict, which the monks of Fleury claimed to have rescued from Monte Cassino. Even this monastery was in need of reform, and when in the 10th century Odo, abbot of Cluny, went there in order to enforce the rule, he was met by armed monks ready to resist the unwanted interference. It is a measure of Odo's courage and saintliness that in an age when only brute force was understood, he gained entry, as testified by his contemporary and biographer, John of Salerno, with the disarming words: 'I come peacefully—to hurt no one, injure no one, but that I may correct those who are not living according to rule'.

He was of course referring to the *Regula* of St Benedict (c. 480–c. 550), a set of rules for the monks of Monte Cassino, which was gradually adopted by all the monasteries of Western Europe. Although based essentially on the customs practised by Eastern monasticism, the rule of St Benedict adapted those customs to the character of the people and the conditions of life in Western Europe. Instead of the eremitical way of life in complete isolation, St Benedict recommended a communal life within the precincts of the monastery, under the rule of the elected abbot, whose authority was absolute.

The life of the monastery was centred around the *opus Dei*, the performing of the divine services, but there was much time devoted to reading and manual work. Possessions were to be held in common. Prayer, work and charity as a group were the aims, in

'We have written this Rule,' wrote St Benedict, 'that by observing it in monasteries, we may show ourselves to have some degree of goodness in life and a beginning of holiness.' The picture of St Benedict handing his book (the Rule) to a group of monks symbolizes the foundation of Western monasticism, and is often included at the beginning of texts of the Rule. This manuscript dates from the 12th century. (1)

contrast to the Eastern stress on eremitical isolation, the contemplative life and bodily austerity. Thus, although St Benedict derived many of his ideas from the East and especially from St Pachomius and St Basil, he modified them in such a way that they proved to be ideal for the peoples of the West.

If the monasteries of Europe were in such a deplorable condition in the 10th century, it was not exclusively the result of warfare and anarchy. The Benedictine rule, when transplanted from Monte Cassino to other countries, proved to have certain weak points. Since every monastery was autonomous, each existed in great isolation. Furthermore, one of the requirements of the rule was the *stabilitas loci*, the obligation of each monk to remain all his life in the monastery he originally entered. This was an excellent rule so far as discipline was concerned, but it also led to a lack of contact among monasteries, and this rendered them an easy prey to outside interference and control.

Within the monastery, the rule of the abbot was absolute, and thus the conduct of the monks and the business of the abbey depended on the quality of the abbot. According to the rule, the monks elected their abbot, who was then nominated by the bishop. Realizing the importance of free monastic elections, Pope Gregory the Great had already forbidden bishops to interfere with them, but unfortunately this prohibition was soon disregarded. Lay benefactors interfered even more than the bishops, especially when they were powerful rulers. In many cases the abbot became merely the tool of a layman, and consequently the discipline and moral standards of his monastery suffered a decline.

Cluny: the Spirit of Reform

The reform of the monastic rule at Farfa and at Fleury, the two monasteries mentioned previously, was due to the activities of Cluny, the monastery to which European civilization owes an enormous debt.

This Burgundian monastery, founded in 910 by William the Pious, Duke of Aquitaine, was placed under the direct control of

A novice receives the tonsure. Shaving the head ('tondere' means 'to shear') was in Roman times a mark of slavery and for this very reason was adopted by the early monks. It became a separate ceremony in the Western Church in the 7th century, taking place when parents offered their young sons to the service of God. This drawing, from the late 12th century, shows Guthlac, an early English saint, receiving the tonsure from his bishop. Behind the bishop stands his clerk with a book, and on the other side an abbess with two nuns. (2)

Rome, and thus it was exempted from any future local interference. This, combined with a series of exceptionally wise, energetic and saintly abbots, assured Cluny's importance. The early abbots devoted themselves to reform, and this they carried out not only in France but also in the Empire, Italy, Spain and England. Though at first the reformed abbeys retained their autonomy, gradually a close link was established between them and Cluny. The Benedictine independence was replaced by an organization of a feudal character. Thus the Cluniac Order was born and, during the abbacy of St Hugh (1049–1109), granted official recognition by Pope Urban II. By then a number of important abbeys belonged to the Cluniac Order—La Charité-sur-Loire, Moissac, St-Martial at Limoges, St-Martin-des-Champs in Paris, and also the first nunnery, that of Marcigny in Burgundy, which was founded in 1056.

The Cluniac Order was essentially aristocratic, since the monks came chiefly from the nobility. Manual work was no longer considered a suitable occupation and was replaced by an elaborate liturgy, which took up most of the monks' time. Cluny's organization was based on the feudal idea of hierarchy. The abbot of Cluny was an absolute ruler who often nominated his own successor. All Cluniac monasteries were subject to him and they were not allowed the status of abbeys, but were priories. Only a few very ancient foundations, reformed by Cluny, were allowed to retain their former title. Not all priories were equal. As in contemporary society where the king was at the apex, with barons, knights, lesser nobility and the rest in a descending scale of importance, so was the abbot of the Cluniac Order the head of the whole hierarchy of subordinate members. The five privileged priories, known as the five daughters of Cluny, including Lewes, the mother-house of the English Cluniacs, had dependencies of their own. The abbot appointed the priors, but the priors of the five privileged priories appointed the priors of their dependencies. The link with Cluny was close, and every monk had to come to Cluny at least once in his lifetime, for all novices had to be admitted to the order at Cluny.

The Cluniac Order expanded with a phenomenal speed from the middle of the 10th century onwards, and at the height of its popularity, early in the 12th century, it consisted of nearly fifteen hundred monasteries. The popes were great champions of the Order and several of them were formerly Cluniac monks. The secular clergy was, generally speaking, less well-disposed to Cluny, and some bishops particularly resented its exemption from their control. One extreme case is that of Adalberon, Bishop of Laon (d. 1030), who gave expression to his disapproval of Cluny in a satirical poem, in which he ridiculed Cluniac customs.

There can be no doubt that these customs were excessively ritualistic. Joan Evans has said: 'The chanting of psalms and liturgical prayers, together with hymns, canticles, responses and anthems on feast-days . . . took up a great part of the Cluniac day.' Even St Peter Damian (d. 1072), a severe reformer, found the Cluniac time-table too full and exacting. In fact, this excess of ceremonial is considered to be the main reason for the decline of the Cluniacs in the latter half of the 12th century. However, this decline followed two hundred years of expansion, and the achievements of the order during that time were truly remarkable. p 50 (25)

The Cluniac reform inspired, sometimes indirectly, reforms in other countries. The English reform of St Dunstan, St Oswald and St Ethelwold, inspired by Fleury, itself reformed by Cluny, was short-lived, and it was only after 1066, under Norman influence, that great monastic reorganization was carried out in England by Archbishop Lanfranc.

The 10th-century spirit of reform and the problems of secular influence in monastic affairs are both illustrated in the story of the establishment of the Benedictine Rule at Mont-St-Michel. Here a group of notoriously lax monks had been in possession for many years when, in 966, Duke Richard of Normandy decided to make over the site to the Benedictines. The occupants resisted and were only ejected by force. In this drawing from the 12th-century Cartulary of the abbey the new abbot, Maynard, sits enthroned with Duke Richard beside him. The Rule of St Benedict is symbolically handed down to the assembled monks below, while the three figures being shut out on the left may well represent their unworthy and now dispossessed predecessors. But it was such cases, where the abbey owed everything to a rich lay patron, that led later to difficult conflicts of authority between Church and state. (3)

Monastic sites mentioned in this chapter; those marked as Cluniac include not only those under the supervision of Cluny but also those who adopted the Cluniac reforms. The extent of territory controlled by the Teutonic Knights fluctuated; that shown here is an average for the 14th century. (4)

More lasting than the 10th-century reform of the Anglo-Saxon monasteries was the reform carried out in Flanders and Lotharingia. The Lotharingian movement started at Gorzé, near Metz, and led to the reform of some seventy abbeys.

Amongst the great reformers of the age, the man who stands out most particularly, because of his extraordinary achievement, is William of Volpiano. This monk from Piedmont, who followed Abbot Mayeul to Cluny, became the abbot of St-Bénigne at Dijon, founded the abbey of Fruttuaria near Volpiano, reformed Fécamp and a string of other abbeys in Normandy, and before his death ruled over twelve hundred monks in forty abbeys. It was due to him that Normandy and Italy established the close links which gave to Normandy and England such men as Lanfranc and Anselm. From Fruttuaria the reform spread to the Empire.

To the Limits of Christendom

The Cluniac reform also spread to Rome and other Italian centres, but did not take lasting root there. Italy, with its extraordinary mingling of races and cultures, had some monasteries of an unusual character. For instance, the famous abbey of St Boniface and St Alexis, on the Aventine in Rome, was founded for both Greek and Latin communities. From this house many missionaries went to Eastern Europe and it was here that St Adalbert of Prague was a monk before his martyrdom (997) while converting the Prussians.

In those parts of Italy where Byzantine rule or influence persisted, Basilian monasteries existed side by side with Latin, at least until the middle of the 13th century.

The Normans who, in the course of the 11th century, conquered southern Italy and Sicily, were not supporters of Cluny,

and only one Cluniac priory, that at Sciacca in Sicily, existed in their dominions. However, an order which imitated the Cluniac customs was established at Cava dei Tirreni near Salerno. This *Ordo Cavensis* ruled forty abbeys, thirty-five priories and sixty churches with a monastic community of three thousand. Amongst the monasteries of the Order were the celebrated S. Paolo fuori le mura in Rome, and Monreale, the foundation of King William II, as well as a number of Greek monasteries in Calabria, such as Rossano. The Order established a foothold in the Holy Land in 1070, founding Sta Maria Latina with the hospital of St John at Jerusalem.

The *Ordo Cavensis*, supported by the Norman rulers, dominated Sicily and the south, while the region north of Naples and up to Rome was under the influence of Monte Cassino. Restored in the 10th century on the model of Cluny, this cradle of Western monasticism became a flourishing centre of religious and artistic life. Favoured by the popes and the emperors, it grew in power, wealth and influence. Odo of Cluny visited Monte Cassino in 940 and established cordial relations, which were to last throughout the period of Cluny's greatness.

The reform movement started by Cluny was gathering momentum and in the 11th century embraced the whole of Western Europe. In no other country outside France was the Cluniac influence stronger than in Spain. During the 11th century, some of the most important Spanish abbeys became Cluniac, and many new ones were founded as Cluniac priories. S. Juan de la Peña became Cluniac in 1022, and was followed by S. Millan de la Cogolla, Leyre and Sahagun. Silos and Ripoll adopted Cluniac customs without, however, joining the Order.

Of all the monarchs of the age, Alfonso VI was the most

p 48

(13, 17)

(5)

The chief pilgrimage routes across France to Santiago de Compostela. The routes are known in considerable detail from the 12th-century Pilgrim's Guide in the so-called 'Codex Callixtinus,' which gives information on roads, hostelries and shrines worth visiting on the way. These shrines were housed in 'pilgrimage churches,' some of great repute, as for instance that of Ste-Foy at Conques (see p. 90).

Pilgrims were a familiar sight on the roads of Europe. The rich were lavish in their offerings, and many pilgrimage-centres became extremely wealthy, but poorer travellers existed on the charity of the towns and monasteries through which they passed, carrying only a few belongings and a staff, and wearing in their broad hats badges from the shrines they had already visited. This German woodcut (right) was printed in 1499. (6)

enthusiastic admirer of Cluny, and the greatest benefactor of this Burgundian abbey. It was during his rule and under the influence of St Hugh of Cluny, that the ancient Mozarabic Rite was replaced by the Roman in his realm.

The reform movement in the Empire was, at least in part, due to the activities of such abbeys as Gorzé or others in Flanders. The Cluniac reform came by various routes. The direct influence was seen in the group of monasteries headed by Hirsau, but the Cluniac customs also reached Germany by way of Italy, from Fruttuaria. The Emperors, especially the Ottos and Henry II were great supporters of reform, not only of monastic but also of all forms of religious life, but when the quarrel with the papacy developed over the question of the investiture, they adopted an attitude of open hostility.

In the countries newly converted to Christianity the work of the monasteries was of the greatest importance. In fact the conversion of the Scandinavian countries was due to monastic missionaries from Germany and England. In spite of the early successes of Slav missions amongst the Czechs and Poles, it was Rome that finally succeeded in converting them. The first Benedictine monasteries in Bohemia date from the end of the 10th century. Those in Poland were swept away by the pagan reaction of 1034 and only from the middle of the 11th century onwards did well-endowed monasteries begin to appear in large numbers. Tyniec, near Cracow, where recent excavations have revealed the foundations of the church and the well-preserved tombs of some of its abbots, is one of the oldest.

King Stephen of Hungary was in contact with Cluny and the reforming centres in Lorraine, for he was a warm supporter of monks and monasteries. Monasteries were the essential means of bringing to the newly converted countries not only Christianity but also learning and various crafts and skills.

Art for the New Age

Romanesque art was born in monasteries. The earliest architectural experiments, which are known by the convenient label of First Romanesque, were conducted chiefly in Benedictine monasteries in northern Italy. These buildings, often quite crude, were built not by monks but by secular masons, the *magistri comacini*, who were organized in gilds and carried on their profession throughout the darkest period of the Middle Ages. S. Pietro at Agliate (c. 875) p 44 (4) and S. Pietro at Civate (c. 1040) are examples of the early and late

development of this First Romanesque style. The abbey of Civate, built on a high mountain peak in an ideally defensible and secluded position, is an ambitious structure with two apses and a crypt and is decorated with stucco reliefs and wall-paintings.

The First Romanesque style spread east to Dalmatia and west to France, and even further to Catalonia where, in contact with Mozarabic architecture, great innovations were made, especially in improving the vaulting of churches. These vital experiments were carried out in Benedictine monasteries, of which St-Martin-du-Canigou, Sta Maria de Ripoll, St Michel de Cuxa, S. Vicente de Cardona and S. Pedro de Roda are a few of the most famous. p 44 (2)

It was also in the part-Spanish, part-French region of Roussillon and in Catalonia that the first ambitious attempts at monumental sculpture in marble were made. The lintel of St-Genis-des-Fontaines (1020–21) and related sculpture in the nearby monasteries, though modest in every way, together form an important landmark in the history of sculpture. After many centuries of neglect, architectural sculpture once more gained recognition at St-Genis-des-Fontaines, by being placed over the entrance to the church. Here again, as in the case of contemporary buildings, the monks presumably acted as patrons and advisers, or influenced the design by lending illuminated manuscripts. Most important, by providing the opportunities, they gave the arts a new and much needed impetus. p 49 (16)

The First Romanesque style penetrated north along the rivers Rhône and Rhine, and some of the most spectacular buildings of this early age are the abbey churches of St-Philibert at Tournus p 44 (3) (where all possible forms of vaulting were experimented with) and St-Bénigne at Dijon; the latter was built by William of Volpiano in the first years of the 11th century; only the crypt survives.

A contemporary architectural development, based on quite different traditions, was taking place in Ottonian Germany. Modelled partly on Early Christian basilicas and influenced by Byzantine structures and their decoration, Ottonian buildings have a monumental character of their own. Owing to the power of bishops and to imperial patronage, German monastic cathedrals are particularly grand buildings. The *Kaiserdome* at Mainz, Worms and Speyer were all begun in the Ottonian period, but were finished or enlarged in the Romanesque style. Their impressive size, the peculiarities of their plans and the use of towers exceeding in size and number anything elsewhere, put these buildings in a class by themselves. St Michael of Hildesheim, built by Bishop Bernward for the Benedictine monks in the first years of the 11th century, has two choirs, two transepts and four towers and is an imposing building, which had few rivals in the West at that time.

In 1912 the French art historian Lefèvre-Pontalis introduced the term 'the Benedictine plan', which is used to describe a church with a central apse and a choir flanked by side-aisles terminating in apses; the plan included further apses in each arm of the transept and a tower over the crossing, and usually but not always, two western towers at the beginning of the aisled nave. Although many Benedictine churches are of this type, this plan does not seem to be exclusively Benedictine, nor does it apply, for instance, to such Benedictine churches as Hildesheim.

The 'Benedictine plan' was used in the 10th century (before 981) at Cluny, for the building which, because it replaced the original structure, was called by Professor Conant Cluny II. This plan, introduced into Normandy from Burgundy by William of Volpiano, eventually reached England, where it had a great vogue throughout the Romanesque period.

The Benedictine plan of Cluny II was imitated in other countries as well. The most important Romanesque church in Switzerland is Payerne, the church where, at that time, the Emperors were crowned as kings of Burgundy. (The Kingdom of Burgundy, which included Switzerland, the region along the Rhône from Lyons to the sea and Provence, belonged at that time to the Empire, and should not be confused with the Duchy of Burgundy, which owed its allegiance to the French kingdom. Cluny was in the Duchy, though practically on its border with the Empire.) Payerne was founded in 967 as a Cluniac priory and was much favoured by Abbot Odilo, under whose patronage the rebuilding was started. It was usual to begin building a church at its east end, but in the case of Payerne the work was done piecemeal, in order to preserve the old 10th-century abbey-church for services as long as possible. The apse was the last part to be built, about 1080, and incorporates a particularly interesting twin capital showing Christ in Majesty and St Peter on His right. To be properly understood, this composition must be viewed in the context of contemporary events. Abbot Ulric of Payerne (later St Ulric) was deeply involved in the controversy over the investiture, siding with Pope Gregory against the Emperor Henry IV. In this controversy the arguments of the Pope were based on the claim that his power was derived from St Peter. The extraordinary place allocated to St Peter in the apse at Payerne must thus be seen as propaganda for the Pope's party.

p 48 (14)

A plan based on that of Cluny II was adopted by the German abbey of Hirsau and by its dependencies. From 1079 Hirsau followed the Cluniac customs, though in a somewhat modified form, and within less than twenty years, it ruled over thirty new monasteries, while more than a hundred old ones adopted the Cluniac customs. The Hirsau Congregation was particularly popular in the south, but the period of expansion and prosperity was short, and during the 12th century it declined.

p 88 (16)

The plan of Cluny II is also reflected in some Spanish churches, but unfortunately many important monasteries which adopted Cluniac customs there have been destroyed.

The Road to Compostela

While the 'Benedictine plan' was being adopted all over Europe, another spectacular type of monastic church came into being. This was the pilgrimage church, of which the most outstanding examples are the abbeys on the route to the most romantic of mediaeval pilgrimage centres, Santiago de Compostela.

The claim that the body of St James had been discovered there gradually made Santiago a pilgrimage place of some importance, but it was only in the 11th century that it acquired international repute and became as important a place of pilgrimage as Rome and Jerusalem. For a long time scholars claimed that this sudden popularity of Santiago was the work of Cluny. Cluny was supposed to have encouraged the movement of pilgrims, for, having built a network of Cluniac priories along the route, it was making huge financial profits from this enterprise. The truth is that although Cluny undoubtedly encouraged the pilgrimages to Santiago, as it encouraged pilgrimages to Jerusalem and Rome, it was not responsible for them. The *Codex Callixtinus*, which includes the famous Pilgrims' Guide, was not Cluniac-inspired.

p 29 (33)

The enormous popularity of Santiago was due not to any monastic conspiracy but to the spirit of the age. The *Chansons de Geste*, which were born in the 11th century on the pilgrimage routes of Santiago, fired the imagination with stories of heroes, especially that of Roland.

Roland's valiant exploits and death while fighting the Moors must have been the inspiration for many pilgrimages to Santiago. The Moors were still in possession of the greater part of the Peninsula, as in the time of Charlemagne when Roland died. Encouraged by the Church, the desire to free Spain from the rule of the infidel became the driving force of the pilgrimage movement. A pilgrimage led in many cases to the joining of the Crusade against the Arabs. It is not a coincidence that the re-conquest of Spain was contemporary with the greatest popularity of Santiago. The pilgrimage and the holy war became in many minds the same thing. The image of St James on a white horse slaying the Moors, appearing miraculously at the Battle of Clavijo, became the symbol of both. He is shown as the Moor-slayer, the *Matamoros*, on many church tympana, including one at Santiago itself.

p 29 (36)

p 29 (35)

The movement of pilgrims meant that not only objects of art and souvenirs travelled long distances, thus spreading artistic styles from country to country, but also that churches had to be built in such a manner as to allow the smooth circulation of large crowds of pilgrims. For the pilgrims were not satisfied with simply travelling to Santiago, but visited *en route* many of those churches which were famous for their relics. The Pilgrims' Guide lists and describes many such churches which were worthy of a visit. Among them are the Romanesque abbeys of St-Martin at Tours, St-Martial at Limoges, Ste-Foy at Conques and St-Sernin at Toulouse. All these buildings, together with the Cathedral of Santiago, are architecturally related, having wide aisles around the whole church, including the choir, thus allowing the faithful to proceed past the shrine with relics, exhibited in the choir, behind the main altar. These 'pilgrimage churches' differ in details of structure or decoration, but they clearly follow a plan based on the same principle. The connection between these churches becomes even more evident when (e.g., Conques and Toulouse with Santiago) they are closely related in sculptural decoration. But although most of these churches are monastic, there is nothing that would prevent this type of church being used for a non-monastic purpose. It was not monastic association but the possession of important relics that dictated the choice.

f 5

p 90 (28)

p 29 (34)

Cluny: the Consummation

However impressive the pilgrimage churches are, it was the third successive building of the abbey church of Cluny, the so-called Cluny III, begun in 1088 by Abbot Hugh, that was one of the greatest churches of mediaeval times. Financed chiefly by Alfonso VI of Spain, and later by Henry I of England, it represented, as Professor Conant has said, 'the monastic achievement in building better than any other edifice'. Unfortunately the church and monastic buildings have largely disappeared, but, thanks to Conant's excavations and to old descriptions and drawings, they

p 46 (8) are well-known. By 1095 the east end with five altars was ready for dedication; by 1100 the transepts were ready, by 1115 the west front, and by 1121 the nave was vaulted. The great Abbot Hugh did not see his enterprise finished, for he died in 1109. (He was canonized eleven years later at Cluny by Pope Callixtus II). As so often happened with these ambitious mediaeval buildings, the vaulting of the nave collapsed soon after completion, but was repaired and the building was consecrated in 1130.

It was a five-aisled basilica with two transepts, an ambulatory with radiating chapels to the east and a narthex to the west. The church was, of course, vaulted throughout and was one of the first in the West to use pointed arches, which have been claimed, on insufficient evidence, to have been introduced from Monte Cassino. The church at Cluny presented the extraordinary sight of a string of apses, not only clustered around the curved east end but also along the east walls of the transepts, of which each had

p 47 (12) a crossing tower; and there were also towers over the arms of the western transept. Later a pair of western towers was added and the whole mass of harmoniously arranged forms must have been breathtaking.

The church was decorated with wall-paintings, dominated by a Christ in Majesty in the main apse. Some idea of their quality can perhaps be gained from the superb contemporary paintings

p 47 (11) which still survive in the chapel at Berzé-la-Ville, a grange which belonged to Cluny and was a favourite place of retreat for Abbot Hugh. Nearly five hundred capitals decorated the interior of the abbey, and those of the ambulatory are still preserved. For their time (c.1095, the date of the consecration of the choir) they are extremely sophisticated in their subject-matter and style. Most of

p 46 (9, 10) their subjects are allegories such as the Seasons, the Tones of the Gregorian chant and the Virtues. The façade was decorated with a carved portal (before 1115), executed in a more mature style than that of the choir capitals; fragments of this portal were excavated recently by Professor Conant and the lintel survives.

When Cluny had recovered after a severe epidemic in 1144, and had further expanded under its last great abbot, Peter the Venerable, the number of monks was 460. It is no wonder that

f 8 the buildings required for such a large community were extensive. Novices had their own cloister and their own living-quarters

around it. The lay brothers' quarters were close to the workshops and stables. The monks' cloister was on the south adjoining the abbey church. This was the centre of the monks' activities outside the choir and all their living-quarters and meeting places were placed around it: the chapter-house, the refectory, the dorter, the library. Separate groups of buildings were devoted to guests and to the sick. The first was near the main gate, the other at the opposite end of the building complex, south-east of the abbey church and ominously next to the cemetery.

The general layout was essentially traditional, as is suggested by the similarity of this plan to the celebrated Carolingian plan of an ideal abbey preserved at St Gall.

The plan of Cluny III was not imitated in France, though the Cluniac priory at Paray-le-Monial is in a number of ways a smaller version of the great abbey. La Charité-sur-Loire, Souvigny and St-Etienne at Nevers are also buildings which were closely related to Cluny III without attempting to imitate its grandiose plan. However, Cluny III was the model for the mother-house of the English Cluniacs, the priory of Lewes.

There is an account of the circumstances of its founding. An English couple, William de Warenne and his wife Gundrada (perhaps daughter of William the Conqueror), stopped at Cluny while on a pilgrimage to Rome in 1077. They were so much impressed with what they saw that they resolved to introduce the Order in England. Lewes was colonized from Cluny and obviously the monks brought with them the plan of the great abbey, for Lewes (known from excavations and scanty remains) repeats the two-transept arrangement of Cluny as well as the disposition of the monastic buildings, though on a more modest scale, including the characteristic Infirmary Chapel.

All English Cluniac priories were lavish in their decoration but on the whole, so far as one can judge from their ruins, they were built in the Anglo-Norman style, with only an occasional detail derived from the Burgundian mother-house.

Two royal foundations, Reading (founded by Henry I, a great benefactor of Cluny) and Faversham (by Stephen), were abbeys colonized from Cluny and following the Cluniac customs, but which never joined the Order.

Cluniac influences in England can be seen not only in Cluniac priories and in abbeys founded with Cluniac help, but also in Benedictine churches which had no obvious link with Cluny. This is particularly true of Canterbury, the metropolitan church of England. Here at Christchurch, which was rebuilt at the time when the famous Anselm was Archbishop of this cathedral-abbey, the plan of the choir follows the double-transept arrangement of p 48 (15)
Cluny. Some parts of Anselm's church survive today, but the p 55 (45)
buildings as a whole can be seen in the famous mid-12th-century drawing, now in the library of Trinity College, Cambridge. This plan had a far-reaching effect on later English architecture of the Gothic period, when most cathedral churches imitated the two-transept plan.

Except in England, the effect of Cluny III was not great. By the time the building was completed, the great age of Cluny had passed. The artistic initiative passed from Burgundy to the French royal domain, to Paris and the Ile-de-France. It is to the Benedictine abbey of St-Denis, and above all to its Abbot Suger, that we owe the first Gothic edifice.

Suger (d. 1151) was one of the most outstanding statesmen of p 25-7 (25-28)
the age and well deserved the title of 'Father of his Country' given to him by Louis VII. He was, however, also an abbot devoted to his monks and abbey. St-Denis was the burial place of the French kings and the abbey had a privileged position amongst all French monasteries. Suger's *Libellus de Consecratione Ecclesiae S. Dionysii* is a priceless document describing the rebuilding of the church, which involved the façade (dedicated in 1140) and the choir (dedicated in 1144). Both works are of the greatest importance to the subsequent history of architecture and sculpture. The façade introduced the 'royal portals' with their column-figures, which were to change the appearance of churches for many centuries to come. The choir of St-Denis is Gothic and was even p 92 (31)
more revolutionary in its influence than the façade. No single man effected greater artistic changes in the 12th century than Abbot Suger. Although he was anxious to be remembered by his

When Abbot Hugh of Cluny began his great new church, we are told in the old 'Chronicon Cluniacense' (late 12th century), one of his monks, Gunzo, lay sick in bed and had a dream. St Peter and St Paul appeared to him and showed him by means of ropes the size and shape of the church to be built. (7)

The monastery of Cluny at the height of its prosperity in the mid-12th century. It consisted of a medley of buildings of various dates going back to the beginning of the previous century. The church (a) had been begun in 1088 and finished in 1130. The third church on the site (hence the name by which it is known in architectural history, Cluny III), it was the most ambitious building of its date in Christendom, with double aisles, two transepts each with eastern chapels, and five radiating chapels at the east end. The narthex at the west end was not finished until the 13th century. Of the previous church, Cluny II, the fragmentary east end still remained (b), but the rest had been demolished to make room for an enlarged cloister (c). Round this were grouped the monastic buildings in accordance with the standard Benedictine plan—chapter-house (d), dormitory (e) and refectory (f). The infirmary (g) was to the east with its own cloister. The Abbot of Cluny occupied palatial quarters (h) to the south of the church, with his own courtyard (j) and chapel (k). Other buildings included kitchen (l), latrines (m), stables (n) and guest-house (o). (8)

gifts to the abbey treasury of objects made from precious stones and metals, his architectural and sculptural innovations are of far greater importance.

The rebuilding of St-Denis marks the end of an era. The initiative was passing from monasteries to cities. The monastic school was being gradually replaced by a new scholastic institution, the university. The abbey, once the chief patron of the arts, lost its leadership. Now the city cathedral became the place for experiment and innovation. The itinerant artists had by now settled in the town and had started to organize themselves into professional gilds. Life became more settled, better organized and more prosperous, and art became technically more accomplished but also more stereotyped. With the decline of the importance of monasteries came the end of Romanesque art.

Return to Simplicity

Cistercium is the Latin name of Cîteaux, a place in wild and remote country south of Dijon in Burgundy, where the mother-house of a new Order was founded in 1098. A group of monks, hoping for a more secluded and stricter life than in their Benedictine abbey at Molesme, settled there under Robert, the Abbot of Molesme. He, however, returned to his former abbey, but the community at Cîteaux stayed on first under Abbot Alberic (d. 1109) and then under Stephen Harding (d. 1134), an English monk from Sherborne. The idea of founding an Order separate from the Benedic-

tine and in some ways in opposition to it, was crystallized under Abbot Stephen, who became the new Order's able legislator. The *Carta Caritatis* of 1119 is the constitution of the Cistercians, the White Monks as they were to be called because of their robes, dealing not only with the internal structure of each abbey but also with the relationships that were to exist between all the houses belonging to the Order.

In contrast to the Benedictine and even more to the autocratic Cluniac organizations, the Cistercians aimed, at least in theory, at something more democratic. The abbot of Cîteaux was to be the head of the Order, but his power was limited and though he could visit and supervise the daughter-houses, the abbots of these could, in turn, inspect Cîteaux. The abbey from which a new foundation was made had the right to supervise its daughter-house. Each abbey was to be represented at the annual meeting of the General Chapter at Cîteaux and this Chapter was to be the supreme authority of the Order.

The ascetic aims of the founders demanded that the monks should live as far away as possible from the centres of wealth and power. The abbeys were to be built far from cities and settlements, and the monks and lay brothers were themselves to cultivate the land. This meant a return to the earlier Benedictine ideal, which had been abandoned by the Cluniacs. The White Monks, however, went even further, and by shortening and simplifying the liturgy, obtained more time for work in the fields and workshops. It is not surprising that, with their excellent organization and their dedication, they soon became pioneers of agricultural progress throughout Europe.

The four earliest foundations from Cîteaux, the four elder daughters, as they were called, were all in Burgundy: La Ferté founded in 1113, Pontigny in 1114, Clairvaux and Morimond both in 1115. Five years later a dozen Cistercian abbeys were already in existence. In 1128 the first English house, at Waverley in Surrey, was founded; it was the thirty-sixth Cistercian abbey. Further expansion was even more spectacular and by the end of the 12th century, that is, a hundred years after its foundation, the Order had 530 houses; the number rose in the next century to 742. To this impressive total must be added some 900 nunneries, some admittedly very small and not all under the strict Cistercian discipline.

Gradually poverty and simplicity were abandoned, for agricultural exploitation was very profitable with the cheap labour of

The Cistercians broke with Cluniac practice not only in their internal regulations and manner of living but also in the relationship between one abbey and another. Instead of all being under the direction of one house and one abbot (the abbot of Cluny), the supreme authority of the Cistercian Order was a General Chapter which met once a year and at which every abbey was represented. Abbots visited other monasteries, and the abbot of Cîteaux his daughter-houses. It was to be a universal spiritual confraternity, symbolized in this illustration from a manuscript of St Jerome. In 1125 Stephen Harding, abbot of Cîteaux, visited the monastery of St-Vaast at Arras, and it was on his orders that the book was produced. He stands with the abbot of St-Vaast; both carry models of their churches which they offer to the Virgin. Osbert, the scribe, presents the volume to Harding. (9)

70

the lay brothers. Moreover, the expansion of the Order to such distant countries as the Holy Land, Hungary, Portugal and Norway, resulted in their exemption from the visitations and attendances of the General Chapter. As a result, discipline was greatly relaxed.

The Cistercian Pope Benedict XII attempted, in 1335, the reform of the Order, but with little success. As riches accumulated, lay rulers resorted to the practice of appointing abbots *in commendam*, that is, the granting of revenues to bishops or even laymen who did not live in the abbey or fulfil the duties of true abbots. A decline set in and the Reformation finally extinguished the Order in many countries. In France, where they were most numerous, the Cistercians had two reforms, leading to the establishment of the Feuillants and the Trappists, but the original Order exists to our day, and in a number of cases the White Monks have returned to the sites of former abbeys to refound communities there.

What the Reformation did to the Cistercian abbeys in England, the Revolution did in France. Most Cistercian abbeys in these two countries are ruins, but in Germany, Italy, Spain and many other countries, Cistercian buildings can still be studied, often in their original mediaeval form.

The Severities of St Bernard

The great age of the White Monks was unquestionably the 12th century. The need for an Order where prayer and work could be practised in equal measure for the benefit of both soul and body must have been very genuine. However, the prodigious expansion and influence the Order attained in so short a time were due to the leadership of one man, St Bernard. He joined Cîteaux with a group of followers in 1112 and three years later, at the command of Stephen Harding, selected a site for a new abbey, of which he became the first abbot. This was Clairvaux, the abbey which, at the time of Bernard's death in 1153, had no less than sixty-eight dependent abbeys. St Bernard, supported by the popes and especially by the Cistercian Eugenius III, had great power and influence on the religious life of his time. He was a man of action, incessantly travelling across Europe, fighting heresies and preaching the Second Crusade. He was also a reformer, critic and founder of religious orders, a champion of the papacy, a profound thinker and a writer—he left 350 sermons, well over 500 letters and a number of tracts. He was doing all this while at the same time ruling his abbey of 700 monks.

The Cistercian Order was born out of dissatisfaction with the state of other religious orders, especially the Benedictines and the Cluniacs. It was therefore inevitable that there should be rivalry and tension between them, especially since both the Cluniacs and the Cistercians had their principal houses in Burgundy. St Bernard was not a tolerant nor a tactful man and he soon came out into the open with an attack on the Black Monks.

The celebrated *Apologia*, written by St Bernard in 1127, is an indictment of Cluny for its alleged betrayal of the Benedictine ideal. No doubt much of the criticism was justified, especially when applied to Cluny under the misrule of Abbot Pons. Yet, for all their faults, the less austere Cluniacs are more sympathetic than the Cistercians because of their greater humanity and warmth. It was in a Cluniac and not a Cistercian house that Abailard found refuge, and it was Peter the Venerable and not Bernard who comforted him and gave him absolution.

The statutes of the White Monks prohibited painting and sculpture, the employment of colours, precious metals and fine fabrics in their churches. Crucifixes were to be of wood only, chalices of silver and not gold, and elaborate liturgical vestments were to be avoided. Bell-towers of stone were forbidden. The aim of all this was a return to the simplicity of monastic life such as was intended by St Benedict. But St Bernard was not satisfied with such a limited objective. Since monastic simplicity was desirable, all monastic orders should follow the example of the Cistercians. Thus in his *Apologia* he makes a violent attack on the monastic art of the Benedictine churches. He makes it clear that he was not against the use of art in non-monastic churches, since secular clergy, 'unable to excite the devotion of carnal folk by spiritual things, do so by bodily adornments'. But in monastic

The Cistercian plan was the same as the Benedictine with minor variations. On this plan of Rievaulx, founded in 1131, the letters correspond with those on the aerial photograph on p. 53: the church (ab), chapter-house (c), cloister (d), dormitory (e), refectory (f) and infirmary cloister (g). The main peculiarity of the Cistercians was that their refectories were placed at right angles to the cloister walk instead of along it. All abbeys of the order were dedicated to the Virgin. (10)

churches the situation is different. Here, lavish adornments are designed not to invite a prayer but to excite vanity and provoke generous offerings. *O vanitas vanitatum, sed non vanior quam insanior*—he exclaims. ('O vanity of vanities, yet no more vain than insane.') St Bernard was ready to overlook the relics cased in gold, saints 'gaudily painted', crowns of light 'like cartwheels' studded with precious stones, candelabra like 'trees of massive bronze' and other church adornments for the sake of the simple and devout congregation. However, in the seclusion of the cloister, which is the monks' exclusive domain, the situation is different. Here the Benedictine and Cluniac monk is supposed to pray and to study. Yet in St Bernard's day the cloister was the most lavishly decorated structure of the whole monastic complex of buildings. It is enough to recall the Benedictine cloister of Silos in Spain, of Arles in Provence and of St-Aubin at Angers, or the Cluniac marvels such as the cloister at Moissac. Each capital of the arcades is superbly carved and, as if this were not enough, some capitals are doubled, thus multiplying the available surface for carving. And here the tormented imagination and fantasy of the Romanesque sculptor seemed to run wild, unrestrained by any consideration for the sanctity of the site. No wonder that a puritan such as St Bernard could no longer tolerate this: 'What profit is there in those ridiculous monsters, in that marvellous and deformed comeliness, that comely deformity?' In the conclusion of his *Apologia*, St Bernard points out the danger to which the monks are exposed, for 'we are more tempted to read in the marble than in our books'.

St Bernard was expressing not only his own opinions, but also the official attitude of his Order. The Cistercian church buildings were, from the start, simple in plan and elevation, and plain in detail. The only dull Romanesque capitals are those in Cistercian buildings. Very early in the history of the Order a standard church-plan was devised with the result that Cistercian abbeys in England, Portugal or Poland look remarkably similar; similar, that is, in the general form of their design, which was supplied from Burgundy. This 'Bernardine plan' is characterized by its square-ended choir and a pair or more of barrel-vaulted rectangular chapels on each arm of the transept. The local builders, however, could not or would not ignore the local style of building and they always managed to introduce some elements that were foreign to the Burgundian mother-houses. For instance, the nave of Fountains Abbey in Yorkshire (after 1135) was not vaulted with the usual barrel but was covered with a flat wooden ceiling; it had a crossing tower, forbidden by the Cistercians after 1157, but a characteristic

of Anglo-Norman churches. As time went on, Burgundian directives were less and less binding, and if local forms were used without excessive ornamentation there was no discrimination against them.

Since the destruction of Cîteaux and Clairvaux during the French Revolution, Fontenay (c. 1140) is the best-preserved Cistercian abbey in Burgundy. St Bernard must have been well-pleased with this abbey constructed with an almost forbidding austerity. The monastic buildings are beautifully grouped around the cloister, which contains only plain capitals so that nothing would distract the monks from prayer and contemplation. The fine workmanship and the rational planning of the whole complex is very striking. The site, like that of almost all Cistercian abbeys, is enchanting, and it incorporates a stream, for it was common practice for the sites of these abbeys to have either a stream or a pond. The natural beauty of Fontenay, Fountains, Fossanova, Bebenhausen and so many other abbeys is unforgettable.

Although some early Cistercian buildings have a half-Gothic appearance, the Cistercians were not architectural innovators. Roche Abbey in Yorkshire may be the first Gothic building in England (c. 1160), but it is not entirely original, for it is derived from north-east French non-Cistercian churches.

Rib-vaulting was adopted by the Cistercians about 1150, and was common to all Cistercian buildings throughout Europe erected after this date. But the rib was only one step in the direction of Gothic architecture, and the character of Cistercian churches often remained largely Romanesque, in some instances until the early years of the 13th century.

No sooner had St Bernard died (1153) than the monks set about the task of enlarging the east end of his abbey of Clairvaux. Ready by 1174, the new chevet, with an ambulatory and nine radiating chapels in the most up-to-date north French Gothic style, replaced the modest Bernardine structure. Other Burgundian abbeys soon followed suit. The chevet of Pontigny (c. 1186) still survives; it is a beautifully simple and yet elegant structure, in which the Gothic style was admirably adapted to the demands, or rather restrictions, of the Cistercian Rule.

The Cistercians are sometimes credited with the introduction of brick architecture from Italy into Germany, and thence to other parts of eastern and northern Europe. It is true that some of the Cistercian buildings in Lombardy, for example Chiaravalle di Milano, founded by St Bernard in 1135, were built of brick, the material that was natural to the place. It is equally true that many Cistercian abbeys north of the Alps were built of brick, for

p 28 (30)

f 10

p 57 (52)

p 57 (51)

The close ties between Cîteaux and England during the early 12th century were probably due to the personal taste of the Abbot Stephen Harding, himself an Englishman. This sculptured capital and two illuminated initials, for instance, all share a dragon of peculiar distinction. His ears are pointed, his spine generally ridged, his feet have three claws and a spur, his tail ends in a bunch of leaves and along his back and wings run rows of beading. The sources are as follows: Top left: capital from the crypt of Canterbury Cathedral, c.1120. Lower left: initial A from a Josephus manuscript made at Canterbury between 1120 and 1140. Below: initial G from Augustine's 'De Civitate Dei', Cîteaux, 1100–1120. (11, 12, 13)

of the century, was a more ambitious decoration of books once again sponsored by some Cistercian abbeys, notably Pontigny. This time the inspiration was again probably English and was due to Archbishop Thomas Becket's stay at Pontigny during his exile from England. The illuminations of Pontigny and Canterbury are at this time indistinguishable, and the lack of narrative scenes in these illuminations may mean that, in this respect, the inspiration was Cistercian rather than English and that the style was transplanted through the gifts of books sent by Thomas and his secretary, Hubert Bosham, from France to Canterbury.

The art of illumination was never practised by the Cistercian monks on any large scale and such books as were produced for Cîteaux or Pontigny were presumably made by commercial secular artists. When the discipline of the Order was relaxed in the later Middle Ages, illuminations again appeared in Cistercian books, but then also commercial illuminators had to be employed, as in the documented instance of the abbey at Clairmarais in the 15th century, whose abbot had to send to Troyes for an illuminator. Yet there are exceptions to this rule, as in the case of the painter Stanislaus. The original simplicity and severity of the Order and its buildings were difficult to reconcile with the lavish gifts accepted from powerful and rich patrons. Las Huelgas outside Burgos, a Cistercian convent founded by Alfonso VIII of Castile as his burial place, or Royaumont Abbey founded in 1228 by St Louis and Alfonso's sister, Blanche of Castile, as the family mausoleum, would have scandalized St Bernard. Royaumont had a cathedral-like plan with an ambulatory and radiating chapels, and a beautifully proportioned elevation typical of the best Parisian buildings in the most up-to-date High Gothic style.

As time went on, not only the buildings but also the furnishings became lavish. In the Abbey of Obazine (Corrèze), the tomb of

instance, Chorin in Germany, Sorø in Denmark and Pelplin in the territory of the Teutonic Knights. They were, however, not the only brick buildings there and they were also not the earliest. The question whether in fact the Cistercians were influential in spreading the use of brick outside Italy must remain open.

Cistercian Prosperity—the Ideal Fades

p 54
(39, 40, 42)
p 58
(54)
f 12, 13

Unlike the austere Cistercian churches, the early manuscripts produced at Cîteaux are lavishly illuminated. This must have been due to the personal taste of Abbot Stephen Harding, especially as his Bible shows numerous traces of English influence. The so-called inhabited initials (i.e., initials occupied by figures) in this Bible, completed before 1109, have the vigour associated with the illuminations produced at Canterbury, Rochester and elsewhere in England, and it has in common with other contemporary Cîteaux books a feature which is quite unexpected in this serious and humourless order: satirical representations of monks in their occupations. Towards the middle of the 12th century, Cîteaux produced some striking illuminated books in which Byzantine elements are predominant, but by then the Order's uncompromising attitude to figurative art made itself felt even in the field of book decoration, and Cistercian books ceased to receive any but the simplest of ornament. Only for a short time, in the seventies the founder, St Etienne (d. 1159), must have been originally quite simple, but by the third quarter of the 13th century, it was replaced by a magnificently carved shrine, with an effigy of the saint and scenes from his life. During the first hundred years after the foundation of the Order, the Cistercians were extremely strict in prohibiting any burials in their abbeys except for kings, queens and bishops. The penalties for the rare abuses were very severe such as the deposition of the abbot and the transfer of the prior and other officials to another abbey. The restrictions became gradually less stringent and when, in 1215, the abbot of Font-froide was accused by the General Chapter of permitting the burial of a woman in his church, his defence that her name was Reine was accepted and his penalty was only nominal: two days on bread and water and prohibition from using his seat in the stalls for forty days.

Royal tombs were allowed, and in churches built especially as mausolea, for example, Royaumont, they were of particular magnificence. Not only was St Louis buried there, but also his p 217 (28) brother Philippe de France and his children, Louis de France (d. 1260), Blanche and Jean. The founders of Cistercian abbeys were at first not allowed to be buried within the churches and at Cîteaux the Dukes of Burgundy, as founders, had to be buried in a specially built chapel at the entrance. When the restrictions were later disregarded, the abbey became crowded with splendid p 211 (15) tombs, including that of Philippe Pot, which was excuted c. 1480, during his lifetime, and is now in the Louvre.

The tombs of the monks were quite plain but sometimes exceptions were made. For instance, by special permission of the General Chapter in 1253, the monks of Longpont were allowed to erect a tomb in the choir of the abbey into which the body of Jean de Montmirail (d. 1217) was translated. This tomb is known from a watercolour: it represented Jean as a monk and underneath, partly hidden by the arcading, there was another effigy of Jean as a knight, for he had taken the habit of a White Monk late in life. This splendid canopied tomb, richly painted, would certainly have horrified St Bernard.

He would have disapproved also of the lax attitude to other p 58 (53) prohibitions. The superb series of 14th-century glass windows from the Cistercian abbey of Amelungsborn in Saxony illustrates the refined taste of the monks, and suggests that they were prepared to spend large sums of money on decorating their church.

At the end of the Middle Ages the disregard for the earlier prohibitions was complete. The story of the Polish painter, Stanislaus Samostrzelnik, illustrates the Cistercian mode of life at the end of the 15th and beginning of the 16th centuries. Born in the mid-1480s he was, in 1506, a monk at the Cistercian Abbey of Mogila near Cracow. At that time he is referred to as *religiosus Stanislaus pictor de Mogila*. Not finding enough interesting work in his abbey, he obtained leave of absence in 1511 and became chaplain to a powerful magnate, who was widely known as a patron of the arts. While in his service, the Cistercian illuminated a number of luxurious books of which examples survive in Books of Hours in the British Museum and the Bodleian Library, Oxford. But the art of book illumination was becoming obsolete and Brother Stanislaus eventually returned to the monastic life. Before his death in 1541 he provided a series of wall-paintings for his abbey at Mogila, many of which still survive.

It is difficult to imagine a greater contrast than that between the life of this man who left his abbey for the more exciting life of a chaplain and the ideals that prompted the monks of Molesme to seek the solitude of Cîteaux.

Monasteries for Men and Women

Colleges of clergy serving a cathedral and living under a common discipline existed even before the foundation of the Benedictine Order. As a result of the reform movement of the 10th and 11th centuries these colleges or Regular Canons (*canonici regulares*) followed a common code known as the Rule of St Augustine, from which they derived their name, the Austin (Augustinian) Canons. (Because of their robes they were also called the 'Black Canons'.) The Rule was based on a letter from St Augustine to a convent of nuns in North Africa in which he discussed the spirit of monastic life.

Hugh of St-Victor, seen here in a French manuscript of the 12th century, was one of the outstanding teachers of his time. He was born in 1096 and in 1133 became head of the Parisian school of St-Victor, a house following a modified form of the Augustinian rule known as the 'Victorine'. Besides being a scholar, theologian and philosopher ('the second Augustine') he is also important as a mystical writer. (14)

Recommended by Rome in 1059, the Augustinian Canons became especially popular in the 12th century, for quasi-monastic community life, without the rigours of strict monastic discipline, assured for the clergy a more dignified existence than hitherto and won them general respect and support.

Their earliest establishment in England was at Colchester (c. 1095), but the real popularity of the Rule occurred during the reign of Henry I, when many new foundations were made that were to rise to eminence.

The Black Canons inspired numerous reforms from which new orders were born. The Canons Regular of St-Victor in Paris, or the Victorines, were founded in 1113 by William of Champeaux, the teacher of Abailard, and numbered amongst their ranks some of the best scholars and writers of the 12th century, including Hugh of St-Victor, originally from the Augustinian *f 1.* abbey of Hamersleben near Halberstadt, and Richard of St-Victor, a Scot. This Order was never very large. An English knight, Oliver de Merlimond, built for them a church at Shobdon about 1135, but disturbances during the civil war forced them to leave Shobdon for Wigmore, where they founded an abbey. Even here the scholastic tradition of the Order was observed and Wigmore could boast a celebrated commentator on the Old Testament, Abbot Andrew (d. 1175).

An order of canons, inspired by Cîteaux, was founded by St Norbert, a German preacher active in France and a future Archbishop of Magdeburg. This was the Premonstratensian Order (White Canons, Norbertines) so called after Prémontré in Champagne, where in 1120 they established their first house. Their Rule was far more austere than that of the Regular Canons and included, for instance, the prohibition of meat. In addition to the occupations such as were usual in the Cistercian Order, the White Canons were engaged in parochial duties and missionary work and that is the reason why they had a particularly large number of houses in central and eastern Europe. The first of thirty-four English houses, of which two were for women, was founded in 1143 at Newhouse in Lincolnshire.

The only religious order which originated in England was founded in 1131 by St Gilbert, the Rector of Sempringham in Lincolnshire. The Order was for both men and women. The nuns were governed by the Rule of St Benedict, the men were Augustinian Canons and acted as chaplains to the nuns. The lay brothers were under the Cistercian discipline. St Gilbert was the first Master of this Order, which enjoyed a considerable reputation. Of the twenty-six houses of the Order, eleven were for both men and women. Such double monasteries, in which the monk-priests attended to the needs of nuns, originated in Egypt and were introduced to Western Europe in the 6th century. There were a number of such monasteries in Gaul: for instance, Jouarre. In Spain there existed in the early Middle Ages two hundred double monasteries. St Columbanus (d. 615) was a great supporter of this institution, though there was only one such monastery in Ireland, at Kildare. Introduced into England either from Ireland or Gaul, double monasteries had tremendous popularity there but they vanished after the Danish invasions.

Founded about 1100 for nuns, lay sisters and their chaplains, and ruled by an abbess, the Order of Fontevrault (near Angers) was a successor to these earlier double monasteries; it had an immediate success and in less than twenty years it had a community of three thousand nuns, housed at Fontevrault and its dependencies. It was an aristocratic community, with abbesses who were usually daughters of the royal family, while the nuns came from the high nobility. The English daughter-house of Fontevrault, which existed at Amesbury, had the same character. The abbey of Fontevrault is a distinguished Romanesque building, its nave covered with four domes (reconstructed in this century) related to the domed churches in Aquitaine. This impressive structure was imitated by the monks of Leominster priory in England, which shows traces of an intention to cover the nave with domes—the only instance of this method in England.

p 52 (34) Fontevrault is known for yet two other reasons. The monastic kitchen there is the most spectacular structure of its kind surviving from the Romanesque period; it is very much larger and more elaborate than the other mediaeval kitchen, that at Glastonbury Abbey. The other outstanding feature of Fontevrault is a series of Plantagenet tombs preserved there, including those of Henry II and Richard the Lion Heart.

Double monasteries were tolerated by the Church but never encouraged, for fear of scandal. That is why this system never became universal.

In the later Middle Ages, about 1346, there was a last attempt to revive double communities under the rule of St Bridget of Sweden. This order had a famous house in England, that of Syon, founded by Henry V in 1415.

The Contemplative Life

The eremitical or contemplative life, which was frequently practised in Italy in the 5th and 6th centuries, was inspired by the example of Eastern Christendom. It is not surprising that the revival of the eremitical movement, which spread throughout Western Europe in various forms, started in Italy and more especially in the Byzantine South. St Nilus (d. 1005), a Calabrian, who was at first active among Basilian monasteries, later moved north and in 1004 founded the Basilian monastery at Grottaferrata near Rome. In spite of Latin influences, this monastery remained the centre of Greek life and learning in Italy, and it had as one of its abbots the famous Greek scholar, John Bessarion

(d. 1472). Soon after its foundation, Grottaferrata became the centre from which Greek monastic and eremitical traditions spread north.

The Western eremitical movement started, if not as a reaction to Cluny, at least in contrast to its way of life, which was full of ceremonial. It was not an accident that St Romuald, the man who founded an order based on the example of the Egyptian hermits, was for a time a Cluniac and abbot of S. Apollinare in Classe, outside his native city of Ravenna. Dissatisfied with Cluniac life, he resigned the abbacy to lead a more ascetic life. Eventually, he founded a community of hermits at Fonte Avellana in the Apennines, and later a monastery at Camaldoli near Arezzo (c. 1012), which gave birth to the Camaldolese Order. Another order, even more severe, was founded by St John Gualbert in 1039. This was the Vallombrosan Order (from Vallombrosa, near Florence) in which perpetual silence, absolute poverty and enclosure were strictly observed. Manual work was prohibited and the administration f the monastery was entrusted to lay brothers, the *conversi*, a development which practically all other monastic orders were to imitate sooner or later.

A rather severe advocate of the eremitical life was Romuald's disciple, Peter Damian. The movement soon spread outside Italy

The Carthusian plan is at once seen to be basically different from any other monastic layout. The reason is that the monks of this order lived solitary rather than communal lives and instead of one dormitory and refectory there are a series of individual cells (or rather quite roomy apartments, often of two storeys). Mount Grace in Yorkshire is typical. Round a large cloister (a), part of which served as a cemetery, run fifteen cells, each with its house (b) and garden (c). The church (d) where the brethren met three times a day for Mass, is comparatively insignificant, as is the room (e) where on feast days they ate together, though still in silence. An outer court (f) accommodates a few more cells and gardens, a guest-house (g), granary (h) and stables (j). The prior's lodging (k), hardly larger than any other monk's, was west of the church. (15)

and hermits appeared in France, for instance the group led by Robert of La Chaise-Dieu (d. 1067), and in England and Germany.

The desire for a stricter life than that offered by the existing monastic orders continued throughout the Middle Ages, either resulting in reforms of the established orders or new foundations. Tiron, founded in 1109 by a monk called Bernard and inspired by the early Cistercians, developed into a separate order with numerous dependencies. Its aim was simplicity of liturgy and the performing of manual work, especially through the practice of various crafts.

Another order known for its strictness was that of Grandmont, founded about 1100, where the vows of poverty and silence were observed. To achieve this more completely, the lay brothers were given more initiative in running the administration than in any other order. Grandmont had a comparatively small following and in England, for instance, only three houses were established.

Among the numerous foundations of an eremitical character that came into being in this period was the Norman abbey of Savigny, which began in 1105 as a hermitage and which eventually adopted a modified Benedictine rule and the distinctive grey habit. Before long, daughter-houses sprang up in France and the British Isles, but in 1147 these joined the Cistercian Order.

Hermitages frequently grew into monasteries. On the other hand, hermits were often attracted into the vicinity of monasteries, under whose protection they could live in seclusion. Sometimes monks were allowed to live in hermitages outside their monastery. This seems to have been the case of Roger, a 12th-century monk of the Benedictine house of St Albans, who lived in a hermitage near St Albans, still remaining under the discipline of his abbot. He was joined by a wealthy girl named Christina, who, forced by her parents into marriage, escaped to lead the life of an anchoress. She lived in a cell next to Roger's, under his protection and guidance. She had a great reputation for sanctity and miraculous powers and she eventually became the Prioress of Markyate.

Another example can be quoted of a monastery which began as a hermitage. St Godric, a one-time pirate, made two pilgrimages to Jerusalem, one to Santiago and three to Rome. He eventually settled at Finchale near Durham about 1115 under the spiritual guidance of the priors of Durham. He lived there for sixty years with his servants and a priest, next to a church he built in honour of the Holy Sepulchre and St John the Baptist. On the site of his hermitage was founded, at the very end of the 12th century, the priory of Finchale, of which the early Gothic church, and the cloister which was rebuilt in the 14th century, still survive. In the period of the decline of monastic discipline, towards the end of the Middle Ages, the priory was used as a holiday place for the monks of Durham, who would come in groups of four for three weeks' stay in this enchanting spot on the River Wear.

The most successful and lasting of the orders inspired by the Egyptian hermits was that of the Carthusians.

Hermits of the Chartreuse

When Philip le Hardi, Duke of Burgundy, anticipating the huge fortune which the inheritance of his wife Margaret was to bring him, resolved in 1379 to build a mausoleum for the dukes of the Valois dynasty at Champmol outside his capital, Dijon, he selected the Carthusian monks to live there as guardians. That a worldly man like Philip should give preference to this Order is a testimony of the high reputation for strict observance which the Carthusian monks enjoyed.

He built the church and to the south of it the chapter-house, the refectory and other monastic buildings grouped around a small cloister, while the cells of the twenty-five monks and their prior, which were in fact small separate houses with little enclosed gardens, formed a large quadrangle with a cloister walk and a well in the centre, which was enriched by the famous *Calvary* of Claus Sluter. Each of the cells had a painting of the Crucifixion, painted by a team of Flemish and Dutch artists.

At the time when the Chartreuse was built at Champmol, the Carthusian order was three hundred years old, but it was still as strict in following the Rule as it had been at the time of its foundation.

The Order was founded by St Bruno of Cologne. He relin-

The Templars of the 13th century became a byword for wealth and pride, but when originally founded in 1118 they adopted the austere Cistercian Rule of St Bernard. In this drawing by Matthew Paris their poverty is pointedly conveyed by showing two of the founders mounted on one horse—a motiv later used on the seal of the Order. (16)

quished the post of teacher in the cathedral school at Rheims, and settled in 1084 with some disciples in the wild mountainous region near Grenoble, called the Chartreuse. After a few years he left France for Italy, never to return, but the community of hermits which he left behind grew in number and their customs were codified in the early 12th century. Many of these were borrowed from the Cistercians: for example, the dress and the external organization centred on the mother-house, the Grande Chartreuse. The life of the monks was solitary, spent in individual cells, which could be left only three times a day for Mass and prayers in the church. Only on feast-days did the monks eat together, but even then in silence. The monks who were craftsmen were allowed to practise their art in the cell, and many did. We learn about a Carthusian goldsmith from Ghiberti's *Commentaries*. He was 'a very old Carthusian named Fra Jacopo, a goldsmith like his father before him. Fra Jacopo was a draughtsman and took great pleasure in the art of sculpture'. Like Vallombrosan monks, the Carthusians had the help of the lay brothers, the *conversi*, whose buildings ('lower house') were separate from those of the monks ('upper house').

Because of its austerity, the Order never became very popular, but on the other hand, its discipline was always observed; consequently the Carthusians were never in need of reform (*numquam reformata quia numquam difformata*).

The Order was introduced into England by Henry II, it is said in expiation for the murder of Becket. Their first house was at Witham in Somerset, where, after initial difficulties, they settled down well under the prior, Hugh, a nobleman from Avalon near Grenoble, who was Bishop of Lincoln from 1186 and was canonized in 1220. Little is left of the monastery, save the chapel of the lay brothers. Better preserved is the second (1227) Carthusian foundation in England, at Hinton, where the layout of the quadrangle and the cells is visible and where there is a good, well-preserved 13th-century building, said to have been the library.

Seven Charterhouses, as they were called in England, were built in the 14th and 15th centuries. Not all were in remote places, and one was built in London in 1349 over the mass-grave of the citizens who died during an epidemic of the plague. Of these seven, only the buildings of the Charterhouse of Mount Grace, *f 15* in Yorkshire, survive.

After a slow start, Charterhouses became, in the 14th century, even more popular in Italy than in England, and almost every large town had in its neighbourhood a *Certosa*. The famous Certosa di Pavia was founded in 1396 and owes its repute to the superb buildings and works of art, the majority of which, however, are already in the Renaissance style.

Warrior Monks

The success of the First Crusade, crowned by the capture of Jerusalem in 1099, presented the Christian authorities there with a number of difficult problems. One of these was caused by the pilgrims who, encouraged by the victory, were arriving in large numbers by sea and land. The strenuous and dangerous journey, the climate and disease, were some of the perils which threatened all westerners who came to the Holy Land. The greatest danger was, however, the journey through the long, exposed roads of Asia Minor, where the Muslims could strike at will.

p 291
(20)

The headquarters of the Templars in the East influenced not only the characteristic round plan of their churches (based on the church of the Holy Sepulchre at Jerusalem) but sometimes even their decoration. A detail from the Templars' church at Garway, in Herefordshire, clearly betrays its Islamic origin. (17)

It was to deal with this situation, to provide safety, hospitality and medical care for those who came to the Latin Kingdom of Jerusalem as pilgrims, that military orders were founded.

The Knights of the Order of the Hospital of St John of Jerusalem, commonly known as Hospitallers, were established about 1110 as a military order following a modified Rule of St Augustine. While in Jerusalem they were attached to the church of St John the Baptist, but after Saladin's victory in 1187 they moved their headquarters to Acre, then to Cyprus (1291–1309), Rhodes (1310–1523) and after 1530 to Malta. Their robes were black with a white cross. The Hospitallers established their houses not only in the Holy Land but also, during the 12th century, they extended their activities to practically all the countries of Europe.

p 60 (58)

Their rivals, the Knights Templar—or, for short, Templars—started modestly in 1118 as a confraternity in a house near the Dome of the Rock, the beautiful mosque built on the site of the Temple of Solomon, whence the name of the Order. Ten years later, persuaded by St Bernard, they adopted the Cistercian Rule. Their robes were white with a red cross on the front. The Templars rose to power with astonishing speed and amassed considerable wealth in all the countries of Europe, settling there to administer their properties. During the 13th century they owned nine thousand castles and manors and it was necessary to divide the Order into nine provinces. Their organization was complex, consisting of different ranks from knights to craftsmen. The expressed purpose of the Order was to defend Jerusalem from the Muslims, but when Jerusalem fell in 1187 the Templars could claim that they were needed to defend those parts of the Holy Land still left in Christian hands. In fact they fought with fanatical courage and in the final battle at Acre in 1291 the Master of the Order was killed. The Templars had many enemies; not only their rivals the Hospitallers, but also those who resented their power and wealth. Their end came when King Philip the Fair, accusing them of immorality and heresy, obtained confessions of guilt by torture. Sixty-eight Templars were burnt at Paris and Senlis and the possessions of the Order passed to the Hospitallers, that is, what was left of them after the King of France had taken his share. Since the Order of the Temple was dissolved by the pope, it ceased to exist in other countries as well.

p 60 (56, 57)

These two military orders were responsible for a great deal of building throughout Europe. In the Holy Land their most important buildings were castles, and some of the most spectacular creations of military architecture are due to them. Krak des Chevaliers, Tortosa and Safita are among the most famous. The popular belief is that all the churches built by these orders are based either on the church of the Holy Sepulchre, the *Anastasis*,

p 61 (62)

a round Constantinian structure (twice burnt and rebuilt) or on the polygonal Dome of the Rock, the Muslim mosque used by the Templars as their main church. It is quite true that many of their churches, including the Temples in Paris and London, were circular. This is understandable, and the Hospitallers and Templars were not isolated in their desire to build their churches in imitation of the Holy Sepulchre. In mediaeval times, however, it was often thought a sufficient imitation simply to include the name 'Holy Sepulchre' in the dedication of a church, without going to the length of imitating the structure of the church in Jerusalem.

p 61 (61)

All the known English churches of the Templars are circular, but not all their churches and chapels in the Holy Land were of that shape; for example, the chapel at Safita is fitted into a rectangular keep and, in consequence, is also rectangular.

The two principal churches of this Order in the West, in Paris and in London, were both originally circular, but both proved to be too small and had rectangular choirs added later. The Paris rotunda, of a mid-12th-century date, perished during the French Revolution, but is known from drawings. The London structure was consecrated in 1185 by Heraclius, Patriarch of Jerusalem, in the presence of King Henry II, while the choir was added in 1240. This 'New Temple' was erected on the site of the first church, the 'Old Temple', built c.1135, which was also circular. One of the small English Templar churches, at Garway, is of additional interest, for not only had it a circular nave, but the carving of the chancel arch consists of geometric patterns of purely Islamic origin and was evidently the result of the Order's Eastern connections.

f 17

The military orders in countries such as Germany, England and France, had little justification, save to administer their properties and to recruit members. In Spain and Portugal the situation was different. These countries were in course of being freed from Muslim rule and it is not surprising that the military orders took a particular interest in them. In fact it has been suggested that the *Codex Callixtinus*, which contained the Pilgrims' Guide, was inspired by the Templars.

The churches of the military orders on the Peninsula are usually within formidable fortresses. The castle at Thomar in Portugal was begun in 1160 by the Templars under their Master, Gualdim Paës, and in 1190 it successfully repulsed a Muslim attack. Within its walls is a circular church of ambitious proportions. The Templars' church of Vera Cruz near Segovia, dedicated in 1208, is circular within and polygonal without. It contained the relics of the True Cross sent from Rome in 1224.

p 60 (59, 60)

'Brother William, Englishman and companion of St Francis', drawn by Matthew Paris—his feet bare, hands covered in a gesture of humility and an ordinary coarse rope round his waist. (18)

The Hospitallers' architecture can best be studied on the island of Rhodes, which the Order occupied during the 14th and 15th centuries. The city of Rhodes, which contained the various buildings of the Hospitallers, was protected by walls and massive gateways. The Gothic buildings, chiefly southern French in character, included the Great Hospice, for throughout its existence the Order never ceased to take seriously the task for which it was founded.

p 60
(58)

The memory of the topography of the various holy sites in Jerusalem was reflected in the arrangement of the buildings in many places. For instance, in Cambridge, the present St John's College occupies the site where the buildings of the Hospitallers originally stood. As if to preserve the familar topography of the Order's headquarters in Jerusalem, a round church was built (c.1130) nearby, imitating and bearing the name of the church of the Holy Sepulchre.

The Hospitallers, and especially the Templars, because of their connection with the Cistercians, were not great patrons of the arts. Their buildings were utilitarian, and any enrichment (as for instance, the doorways of the Temple, London) very modest. The celebrated tombs in the London Temple are of secular people, not Templars, and thus presumably reflected the taste of the people who paid for them.

The Teutonic Knights

Amongst the military orders of the Middle Ages, one attained extraordinary power, and was to influence the political scene in Europe to such an extent that the effects are felt to this day. This was the Teutonic Order. It developed into an order out of the Hospital of St Mary of the Germans in Jerusalem and the temporary hospital which the German merchants established in Acre in 1190. The attendants of this hospital adopted the rule of the Knights Hospitallers and were recognized by the pope in 1191. Shortly afterwards, with the pope's approval, this charitable Order changed into a military one with the aim of tending the sick and fighting the heathen. Their robes were white with a black cross on the front.

Very soon, about 1200, the Order had possessions in Germany and shortly afterwards in Greece, Sicily, Apulia, Moravia and Bohemia. Invited to help defend Hungary in 1211, their members came into conflict with King Andrew II and were promptly expelled. By an act of incalculable folly, the Polish Duke Conrad of Mazovia invited them to his province in 1225 to help to fight the Prussians, who remained heathen in spite of the various attempts to convert them to Christianity, starting with the mission of St Adalbert, who had lost his life there in 997.

The Knights arrived in Poland in 1230 and three years later entered Prussia. Within fifty years, by ruthless conquest, they held the whole country and the southern coast of the Baltic from Esthonia to Pomerellen, settling Germans in the newly-founded towns such as Memel and Königsberg, or in existing ones such as Gdansk (Danzig), which they annexed. Before long the Order was a powerful and wealthy political state under the nominal suzerainty of Rome and of the German Emperor. When Lithuania accepted Christianity in 1386 and became united with Poland, there were no more heathens left to convert and to conquer. The 14th century was the period of the Order's greatest prosperity, which ended, however, in the disastrous defeat inflicted in 1410 on the Knights by the Poles and Lithuanians. The Order continued to exist until the Reformation, when it was secularized.

The Order kept the Baltic lands in submission by superior organization based on superb military architecture. All their castles, here as elsewhere, were of brick. The headquarters of the Order was established in Marienburg on the Vistula, and the Grand Master moved there from Venice in 1309. The fortress of Marienburg consisted at that time of a quadrangle of buildings for twelve knights, erected about 1280, and a chapel, the whole complex being defended by strong walls. After 1309 these buildings, the 'upper castle', were no longer sufficient; they were extensively rebuilt and enlarged, and a vast 'middle castle' and 'lower castle' were built. This last was for stores and stables. The 'middle castle' contained the palatial quarters of the Grand Master and the high officials of the Order. The Grand Master had two

p 61
(63)

A thumbnail sketch of the great Franciscan philosopher William of Ockham, in the margin of a contemporary copy of one of his works. Both Dominican and Franciscan Orders produced outstanding thinkers. William of Ockham (1290–1349) subjected the whole structure of traditional theology to incisive criticism, drawing a radical distinction between revealed faith and natural knowledge. He came into conflict with the Pope over (among other things) the question of clerical poverty and was excommunicated in 1328. (19)

refectories—one for use in the winter and another for summer, which had two rows of windows in three of its walls. These buildings, some of the most luxurious at that time in Europe, in which monastic and military architecture were blended, suffered severely in the last war. There can be little doubt that few mediaeval bodies exploited religion for their own ends with more cynicism than the Teutonic Knights.

There were many minor military orders, especially in Spain, besides these three, but they were of local rather than general interest.

Grey Friars and Black Friars

With the end of the 12th century, the mediaeval flowering of the monasteries was over. Individual monasteries and even monastic orders continued to maintain high standards, but the spirit which had inspired their founders was lacking. Their wealth did not encourage strict discipline. The custom of obtaining monasteries *in commendam*, in order to use their revenues, brought the final decline. The Fourth Lateran Council of 1215 tried to improve standards by introducing the system of general chapters for all orders on the model of the Cistercians, but this attempt was largely ignored.

The founding of the Mendicant Orders nearly coincided with this Council. The Franciscans were recognized by Innocent III in 1210, the Dominicans came into being between 1206 and 1216 and held their first General Chapter in 1220. The age of the Friars was to replace that of the monks.

p 22–3
(20, 21)

The Franciscan Order or Friars Minor (*fratres minores*), also called the Grey Friars, was, when founded by St Francis, based on the ideal of absolute poverty, not only individual but corporate as well. Begging was preferred to owning money. This ideal was soon found difficult to observe in an Order that increased with great rapidity. Even during St Francis's life the majority of Friars wanted to modify the restrictions on property, but a small group, the 'Spirituals', opposed any changes. The conflict between these two parties continued throughout the Middle Ages, the popes consistently siding against the stricter party. The bitterness of feeling on both sides is well illustrated by the case of William of Ockham, the celebrated Franciscan philosopher who was excom-

ƒ 18

p 50 (22)

ƒ 19

municated in 1328 for attacking the pope over the question of poverty.

He was not the only Franciscan scholar of fame. Duns Scotus, and earlier still St Bonaventure, were amongst the most celebrated in an Order which was founded not to cultivate learning, but for preaching and missionary work.

Nothing illustrates better the difference between the earlier enclosed monasteries and the innovations of the Friars than the Tertiaries, instituted by St Francis for ordinary people living in the world, who wished to practise some of the Franciscan ideals without actually joining the Order: a new spirit of greater humanity and gentleness even in the secular world was the result of the life of St Francis.

p 50   The Dominicans, or the Black Friars (actually their habits are
(23) white, but the cloaks over them black), were founded as an order of preachers (*Ordo Praedicatorum*) with the aim of converting the Albigensian heretics; but even in St Dominic's lifetime the Order spread far beyond the regions of heresy in southern France. Like the Franciscans, the Black Friars rejected all property, personal and corporate, except the buildings needed to house them. When, however, this prohibition was revoked by Rome in 1465, it was only the official recognition of a state of affairs which had existed for a long time.

p 62   St Dominic was a canon of Osma, in his native Spain, and that
(64) is why he based his rule on that of the Augustinian Canons. The organization of the Order was founded on a series of Chapters. The Conventual Chapters sent two representatives to the annual Provincial Chapters, and these, in turn, elected delegates to the supreme body of the Order, the Chapter General. This system of rule by elected bodies, so different from, for instance, the autocratic rule at Cluny, had an influence on the subsequent history of representative institutions, including the English
p 51 parliament. On the model of the Franciscans, the Black Friars
(27–29) introduced orders which were under their care, one for contemplative nuns, another for nuns who lived outside a nunnery, and another of Tertiaries.

Founded to combat heresy, the Dominicans remained the guardians of orthodoxy, frequently through the dreaded Inquisition. However, the field in which the Dominicans achieved the most lasting results was learning and education.

The two Mendicant Orders were joined by a third in the middle
p 50 of the 13th century. This was the Carmelite Order, which had to
(21) retreat, after the collapse of the Crusades, from Mount Carmel in the Holy Land, where it was originally established, to the West. Here it was reorganized as an order of friars, differing from the other two orders in greater strictness of discipline and self-imposed hardships.

St Francis specifically stated: 'Let the Brothers take great care not to receive churches, habitations, and all that men build for them.' When it became clear to all that the saint was going to die at any moment, armed men from Assisi were sent to Siena, where Francis happened to be, to make sure that the body would be brought back safely for use as a relic in the future. Francis died shortly afterwards (1226), having returned to his beloved Portiuncula outside Assisi. Nobody has ever been canonized with greater speed. He was declared a saint in 1228 and work was begun promptly on the magnificent basilica of S. Francesco (dedicated in 1253) and on another church at Portiuncula. This disregard of the saint's wishes started the long but not very distinguished history of Franciscan architecture. The church at Assisi was built on a simple, aisleless plan; it is attributed by Vasari to Jacopo da Alemania. Stylistic connections of this Gothic structure are with Anjou rather than Germany, and it has been suggested that the architect was not from Germany proper but from the French territories within the Empire, such as Provence or Franche-Comté. It is interesting, however, that the earliest stained glass windows in S. Francesco (from before 1253) were by German artists. The simple plan of the mother-church was imitated elsewhere, but neither Franciscans nor Dominicans evolved a single type of church, as did the Cistercians. In France the Dominican churches were frequently of the double nave plan (as at Toulouse). Similar plans were used by friars in Poland and Bohemia, but no single plan predominated

At Vignory an illiterate sculptor carved the word LEO ('lion') both forwards and backwards, evidently copying a model without understanding what it meant. (20)

there either, and the earliest Franciscan church in Poland was built of brick about 1240 in Cracow on a Greek cross plan. One common characteristic that distinguishes all friaries is the spaciousness, and the slimness of columns, if any were used, no doubt in order not to obstruct the view of the altar and to provide the most suitable conditions for preaching.

There was no sculpture and painting which can be called Franciscan, Dominican or Carmelite, though all three Orders employed lay painters and sculptors, sometimes the greatest masters of the day, such as Giotto, who painted in Sta Croce   p 24
in Florence. Occasionally a friar was an artist and was allowed   (22)
to practise his art without hindrance. The Dominican, Fra Angelico, not only painted the altarpiece for the church, and devotional pictures on the walls of each cell, in his own monastery   p 62
of S. Marco in Florence, but was permitted to go to Rome and   (66)
elsewhere to paint churches. He was allowed to train pupils. The same freedom was given to another famous painter of the same monastery, Fra Bartolommeo. Fra Filippo Lippi entered the Carmelite monastery of Sta Maria del Carmine in Florence when he was fifteen years old. He must have learnt his art while in the monastery, perhaps from Masaccio and Masolino. Filippo's fresco in the cloister of his monastery, showing the *Reform of the Carmelite Rule*, is stylistically indebted to these artists. One could cite many more such examples, but in every case the artist belonged to the local stylistic school and is indistinguishable from secular artists.

A Franciscan artist of extraordinary talent is mentioned by Matthew Paris, who owned a large, exquisite drawing of Christ as the *Son of Man of the Apocalypse* and inscribed it as follows: *Hoc opus fecit Fr. Willelmus de ordine minorum socius beati Francisci secundus in ordine ipso conversacione sanctus nacione Anglicus.* ('This work was made by Brother William, a Minor, the companion of   f 18
St Francis, second to join the Order, holy in life, English by nationality.') This English companion of St Francis, known not only from Paris, but also from early Franciscan sources, probably abandoned his art on joining the Order.

Amongst the rare cases of sculptors who were friars, one stands out particularly. He was the Dominican Fra Guglielmo, the pupil of Niccolò Pisano and creator of the pulpit in the church of S. Giovanni Fuorcivitas at Pistoia, and co-sculptor of the celebrated shrine of St Dominic in S. Domenico Maggiore in Bologna.

The contribution of the friars to art and architecture was not comparable with that of the earlier orders. This is understandable. The emphasis in their activities lies elsewhere: in preaching, education and missionary work.

Monastic Art and Artists

There are no reasons to think that the sculpture in abbeys and priories, any more than their buildings, was the work of monastic craftsmen. This does not mean that there were never any monk-sculptors. Some signatures prove that there were. For instance, *Guinamundus monachus* executed the tomb of the patron saint of St-Front at Périgueux, and *Martinus monachus* signed the now partly destroyed tomb of St Lazarus at Autun. There are other similar inscriptions and also documentary evidence for the existence of monastic sculptors. However, one can assume that in the majority of cases these men were trained in their art before taking the vow. The romantic idea that all monastic art was created by monks is totally discredited. But it really matters little whether any given sculpture or other work of art was made by a monk or a layman. The important thing is that the sculpture which decorates a monastic building, a church or a cloister, testifies to the taste of the monks who commissioned the work and paid for it.

Monks were no doubt interested in the iconography of the sculpture decorating their buildings, and it is very probable that they specified what they wanted before the work started. In this sense, they influenced the designs of all important works of monastic sculpture.

It is inconceivable that the enormous tympanum of Moissac could have been carved without the monks' instructions and probably also sketches. The extraordinary similarity of quite simple motifs carved on the capitals in the crypt of Canterbury Cathedral, to the initials in the books illuminated in the monastic *scriptorium* at Canterbury, strongly suggest that the designs for the capitals came from the same *scriptorium*. This is rather an exceptional case, and one must not assume that the mediaeval sculptor was merely executing in stone what the monks had designed for him in his pattern-book.

Sculptors must often have been illiterate. At Vignory, which was a priory of St Bénigne at Dijon, a capital carved with a lion is inscribed in reverse: OƎ⅃ LEO, probably the result of copying a pattern against the light. They naturally needed guidance from the monks in theological matters. The tympanum at Conques, one of the largest carved in the 12th century, with its crowd of figures and elaborate Latin inscriptions, is even more unthinkable, without the learned help of the monks, than that at Moissac.

Most wall-paintings were presumably done by lay artists, who had to be mobile, moving from place to place as commissions required. It would have been difficult for a monk to spend his life in this way. Occasionally monumental paintings were the work of monks. William, the favourite painter of Henry III of England, was a monk of Westminster. But, not surprisingly, he had been a practising painter before becoming a monk.

Much the same situation existed in painting as in sculpture: the monasteries provided ideas, especially the subject matter, but the monks seldom did the work themselves. The monasteries were also the most important patrons for many centuries. The best Romanesque wall-paintings are always to be found in monastic churches. St-Savin-sur-Gartempe, Berzé-la-Ville, S. Clemente in Rome, S. Angelo in Formis, Tahul, León, Winchester, Reichenau and hundreds of other famous cycles of wall-paintings are all in monastic churches.

There is very seldom any mention in documents of a nun who was a painter, such as Clara Gatterstedt from the convent of St James at Kreuzberg, who, in the 14th century, painted portraits of the abbots of Fulda. It was, however, needlework in all its forms which was the art practised most frequently by the nuns. In the lives of female saints there is often reference to embroidery made in nunneries. The celebrated 12th-century English anchoress, Christina, later Prioress of Markyate, made embroidered mitres and sandals for the pope. The Abbess Cunegunde of Göss in Austria and her nuns embroidered, in the 13th century, the antependium for their altar and a whole range of liturgical vestments. Sometimes the work was less serious and in the same century Archbishop Rigaud of Rouen had to forbid repeatedly the nuns of St-Amand to embroider their own purses and veils.

English Gothic embroidery, the *opus anglicanum*, was highly valued all over Europe and many beautiful examples are preserved in Continental churches. The Syon Cope, now in the Victoria and Albert Museum, made in the early 14th century, is a superb example of this type of embroidery, being worked with numerous Biblical subjects and heraldic devices. This cope is not only of artistic but also of historical interest, for it belonged to, though it was not made for, the Brigittine convent of Syon, the foundation of Henry V in 1415. The nuns went into exile during the reign of Queen Elizabeth I, but when the convent was reborn in 1810, the cope was brought back.

Another English embroidery, also worked in the early 14th century and in the same museum, an antependium or altar frontal, is unique, for it is the only signed *opus anglicanum*. It was made by a nun, Joanna of Beverley. However, it appears that the greater part of the high quality embroidery done during the Middle Ages was not the work of nuns but of professional workshops under the direction of men, in which both men and women were employed.

The Making of Books

It can be said, without much exaggeration, that until the development of the universities the intellectual life of Europe was based on the monasteries. The Benedictine Rule, because of its balance between prayer, work and study, provided very suitable conditions for the pursuit of learning. The Cluniacs were too occupied with liturgical duties and the Cistercians with manual work, to be able to devote much time to study and thus they produced only a comparatively small number of writers and thinkers of distinction. Some orders established traditions for learning. For instance, in the 12th century the Victorines were outstanding for the number of distinguished theologians amongst their members, but the order that was most particularly devoted to study so as to be able to preach effectively and above all to defend orthodoxy against the heretics, was that of the Dominicans. However, their learning is more part of the history of the universities than of the monasteries.

For intellectual pursuits not only time but also books were needed, and in this field, the old Benedictine houses, in which books had accumulated for centuries, had a great advantage. But books were, of course, being copied continously in the *scriptoria* attached to every monastery. In them, letters were written, documents prepared and books for the choir and cloister copied.

In big monasteries in the 11th and 12th centuries, there would be up to a dozen copyists, but during the 12th century more and more professional lay scribes were available, and thus monasteries could now buy books. It has been calculated that an average

Part of a 13th-century catalogue of the jewels in the treasury of St Albans Abbey. Each item is illustrated and described, with a note on the donor who presented it. The ring at the top has a sapphire in the centre, surrounded by four pearls and four garnets. The stone below is especially interesting, since it is clearly an antique Roman cameo fairly accurately portrayed. It was given to the abbey by King Ethelred and was reputed to be of great use to women in childbirth. (21)

copyist would produce three to six folios a day and that to copy the Bible one whole year was required. Sometimes monks from other monasteries would come to copy a precious text. In other cases books were lent for copying. The *Magna Vita* of St Hugh of Lincoln tells of one such loan, though a rather exceptional one. On hearing of a very splendid Bible just completed by the Benedictine monks of Winchester cathedral-monastery, Henry II persuaded them to lend the book to the newly founded Carthusian house at Witham. This book was presumably the celebrated Winchester Bible.

The number of books in some monastic libraries is known from catalogues, or rather book-lists, which the librarians kept. Cluny had, in the 12th century, about 570 books, Reichenau about 1,000, Christchurch at Canterbury 600. This last library contained 4,000 books at the time of the Dissolution. It must be remembered, however, that mediaeval volumes usually contained at least three books bound together.

Many of the books were illustrated by initials or pictures. The scribe and the illuminator were usually different people and frequently one book was the work of several scribes and illuminators. The Winchester Bible, mentioned above, is a striking example of a splendid work on which several artists were engaged, each employing a style of his own. This exceptionally rich manuscript must have taken many years to complete.

The question of the extent to which the art of illumination was practised by monks is impossible to answer. There were many monk-illuminators. We have their signatures and even their portraits. One such artist of c.1100 not only painted his self-portrait, but also signed his name *Hugo Pictor*. There is no doubt that he was a monk, for he painted himself with a tonsure.

p 296 (29)

Matthew Paris (d. c.1259), a Benedictine monk of St Albans, is probably the most celebrated of English monastic artists and historians. The outline drawings illustrating his *Chronica Majora* and others of his historical writings, are perhaps not great works of art, but they have great liveliness and freedom. His enormous output required assistants who absorbed his style quite well. On the whole it is safe to assume that if manuscripts associated with an abbey show stylistic continuity, or at least a relationship with each other, they were painted in the monastic *scriptorium* of that abbey. For instance, the manuscripts of the 11th and 12th centuries from Monte Cassino have such an unmistakable stylistic similarity that it is clear they were decorated in one *scriptorium* even if many years separate them. The same is true of manuscripts from many other centres, including Canterbury, Limoges and Regensburg.

f 16

The difficulty in deciding whether any particular book was made commercially for the use of a monastery or in that monastery by its own monks is very great. As time went on, the chance that the work might have been made in the monastic *scriptorium* diminishes. Yet even in the early 15th century there were serious monastic painters such as Don Simone (d. c.1426) and above all Lorenzo Monaco (d. 1425), both natives of Siena and both Camaldolese monks. In the later Middle Ages it is easier to find a manuscript in which a monk is ridiculed than one in which he displays his skill. In a book painted for the Augustinian Canons at St Bartholomew's, Smithfield, in London, a comic marginal painting shows a monk and a woman in the stocks, for a sin too obvious to require a caption. In another famous manuscript, the Queen Mary Psalter, nuns and monks are shown playing musical instruments and dancing together. This is truly a world far removed from the saintly reformers of an earlier age.

p 54 (46)

'Fashioned with Marvellous Subtlety'

The author of the well-known manual of art entitled *Schedula Diversarum Artium*, who wrote under the name of Theophilus, is frequently identified as Roger, a monk of Helmarshausen. Roger was a monk-goldsmith in a monastery which was, in the 12th century, an important art centre. Whether Theophilus and Roger of Helmarshausen were one and the same person cannot be proved, but what is important is the fact that Theophilus was a monk and a man who knew very intimately every artistic craft practised in the Middle Ages.

This evidence, together with many accounts of metalwork which was done by monks means that this art was practised in *some* monasteries. Metalwork was obviously considered a noble craft since so many chroniclers attribute the practice of it to important saints, not only St Eligius (Eloi), Bishop of Noyon, who was the patron saint of metalworkers, but also, at a much later date, St Bernward of Hildesheim, whose candlesticks were said to have been found in his coffin when it was opened in the 12th century.

p 302

Many of these accounts, however, seem to contain a considerable element of fiction. For instance, in the middle of the 11th century there was a monk at Bury St Edmunds so skilled in his art that, when he later became abbot of Abingdon, we are told that he was commissioned by the German Emperor to make him a crown. Apart from the improbable story that he ran away with the jewels supplied for this work, it is most unlikely that any German would order a metal object to be made abroad, for it is precisely in this art that the Germans of the Middle Ages excelled. An English chronicler of the middle of the 11th century, describing a metal screen at Beverley, calls it *opus teutonicum*—'German work'—meaning metalwork. When in 1198, the shrine of St Edmund was slightly damaged by fire at Bury St Edmunds, and the monks wanted to repair it during the night, before the arrival of the pilgrims next morning 'to avoid the scandal of the matter', they had to send for a goldsmith, which shows that there was nobody in that large and rich monastery who could do this work.

Whatever the truth is about metalwork as a monastic craft, there can be no doubt that metal objects were the most valued of all artistic works, and this was not only on account of the precious metals, stones and gems used. Shrines, which were usually made of gold, were venerated because of their contents. The naive yet majestic figure of Ste Foy at Conques was found, when recently restored, to have additions made at eight different periods, as if almost every generation of monks had been anxious to contribute something to the precious statue-reliquary.

f 21

The altar-frontals of gold, the altar candlesticks and crosses, the gold covers studded with precious stones on liturgical books, the chalices and patens, the reliquaries and later the monstrances, —these were all objects of cult or connected with Divine Service and, by virtue of this connection, they were especially precious. The material value was not, however, without its importance and such objects were in times of need pawned and even melted down. The wonderful skill in fashioning these objects was obviously greatly admired. Abbot Suger, when describing additions to the golden altar at St-Denis, talks of the chased relief work equally admirable for its form as for its material. Even St Bernard, that severe critic of the arts, when talking of metal objects, uses such expressions as 'fashioned with marvellous subtlety of art, and glistening brightly with gems', for even he could not hide his admiration for their beauty and artistry.

p 25 (25)

III THE MASON'S SKILL

The Development of Architecture

JOHN HARVEY

'Masters of masons, holding a rod and glove in their hands,

say to others "Cut it for me this way" and do

no labour; and yet they receive a higher fee.'

NICOLAS DE BIARD, SERMON

The Great Architect of the Universe

is an image of God the Father that goes back into the Middle Ages. It is often represented in illustrated Bibles, like this 13th-century example painted in France, and apart from its theological implications provides good evidence for the high status enjoyed by architects. From the very beginning they were regarded as practising a liberal art, not merely a useful skill. The career, which was open only to free men, demanded a long apprenticeship plus some knowledge of mathematics and geometry. The gild of the masons was one of the best organized and most exclusive of the Middle Ages, and to become a royal master mason was to be one of the leading figures of the country.

'Here God creates the heavens, the earth, the sun, the moon and all the elements,' runs the caption along the top of this miniature. It is a careful illustration of the First Book of Genesis: 'In the beginning God created the heaven and the earth, and the earth was without form and void' (this is the shapeless mass in the middle of the circle) . . . 'And God said, Let there be a firmament in the midst of the waters . . . and God called the firmament heaven' (the wavy blue shape represents 'the waters which were above the firmament') . . . 'And God made two great lights, the greater light to rule the day, and the lesser light to rule the night: he made the stars also.'

The compass with which God traces out the limit of the Universe is a typical mediaeval instrument, and not, as might at first be thought, exaggeratedly large (one is illustrated overleaf). With it the master-mason could transfer the design from a small working-drawing to actual size on a plaster floor. The idea that the great abbeys and cathedrals were erected by priests or monks has long been shown to be absurd. Every mediaeval building of any size must have had detailed plans and drawings, and been supervised by a professional. A few of these drawings have survived, and the names of the architects can sometimes be recovered from the records. Even so, the length of time needed for any large project in the Middle Ages, as well as the number of separate skills that had to be brought together for its completion, make it impossible to ascribe any building solely to the genius of one man. Romanesque and Gothic architecture were not anonymous, as was once believed; neither were they exaggeratedly individualistic. In these styles the contributions of many personal talents combined to express the spirit of a whole age and faith. (1)

Dynasties of architects were common in the Middle Ages, when trades were passed from father to son. The Parler family (from *Parlier*, 'foreman') was prominent in Central Europe in the 14th century. Peter Parler, born about 1325, took over the building of Prague Cathedral in 1353 and placed his own portrait (below) in the triforium of the choir. Below right: one of his drawings for a tower window. (2, 3)

The most complete set of architectural drawings to have survived from the Middle Ages relate to the Cathedral of Strasbourg. The Parler family, among others, worked on the west front, and the drawing below is by Michael, Peter's brother, for the arcade containing statues of the Apostles (about 1385). The photograph shows it as built. (4, 5)

The soaring spire of Ulm Minster—another place where the Parler family was active—was designed by Ulrich von Ensingen; the western steeple was carried up by Matthäus Böblinger in 1474–92. After nearly 400 years it was finished (above right) according to Böblinger's drawing of 1482 in the late 19th century. (6, 7)

'I have been to many lands', wrote Villard de Honnecourt about 1235, 'but I never saw a tower like that at Laon.' His drawing (above), to which he added an accurate plan, was probably made as a useful model for his own architectural work. Laon's use of open canopies placed diagonally with their peering oxen clearly intrigued him. (8, 9)

On the gravestone of the architect of Notre-Dame at Caudebec, Guillaume Letellier (far right), is carved his plan of the church, mallet, level and trowel. His skeleton holds a pair of compasses similar to those still preserved at York (right), which are of relatively the same dimensions. (10, 11)

The immense labour of building a cathedral with only the simplest mechanical aids is difficult to realize and only faintly suggested by contemporary illuminations. The miniature below is by Jean Fouquet. Its subject is the building of Solomon's Temple, but the artist imagines it as a great cathedral porch. In the foreground workmen are mixing mortar, fetching water, making a mortise-joint in the surface of one block of stone and carving mouldings on others. The finished work is being gilded—the newly-built upper portion is still white. (13)

Hoisting engines consisted of cranes attached to great wheels worked either like a capstan or like a treadmill. Left: miniature from a French Old Testament of the 13th century showing the treadmill type, masons laying chequered masonry and a man carrying the mortar up a ladder. Below: a Flemish Book of Hours, late 15th century. On the left can be seen the mason's 'lodge', originally simply a shelter for those cutting the stones. The crane here is hand-operated; note the mechanical grip, the scaffolding tied together with thongs and fixed into the wall, and the wooden centering for the arch. (12, 14)

Twelve churches in honour of the ▶ twelve Apostles were founded by Girart de Roussillon and his wife Berthe after they had lost all their children. A French manuscript of 1448 (opposite) gives a composite picture of their achievement, illustrating many aspects of mediaeval building. The big church in the foreground has been begun at the east end, as was almost invariable, and the chancel is already finished, consecrated and in use. Work is going forward on the transept and nave, which seem to be built of brick with stone facing (as, for instance, in Bell Harry tower at Canterbury), with the mouldings of doors and windows in a darker stone. The other churches are complete or nearly so—that on the left has a strange trefoil ogee vault of wood, presumably covered with lead. The elaborate steeples, the last parts to be built, are still under scaffolding. (15)

The style called Romanesque

emerged in the 11th century. Social and political stability led to buildings on a larger scale than had previously been attempted. New structural problems had to be solved and it was ultimately to Roman models, which must at that time have been plentiful, that the masons looked: hence the name. The basic elements of Romanesque are the arcade of round arches resting on masonry piers, massive walls held together with lavish use of cement, and the tunnel- and groin-vaults. These had all been achieved by the beginning of our period (late 11th century), and until the coming of Gothic in the latter part of the 12th century there was no essential change. Development was mainly in the more confident handling of the same principles and in more sophisticated use of ornament. On this page we illustrate three aspects—the capital, the vault and sculptural decoration.

The capital: the simple cushion capital (top left) and the crudely imitated Ionic motif with foliage (second) show early and relatively inexpert use of Romanesque forms. Both these are from the 11th century, the first at Hirsau, the second at Durham Castle. A hundred years later an endless profusion of shapes was being created, including exquisite leaf-patterns (third, at Königslutter) and a wholly original variant, the figure-capital, which reached its perfection in France. This example (bottom left) is at Vienne and represents Samson rending the lion. (16–19)

The vault: groin-vaulting (right: the crypt at Canterbury, about 1105) which results when two barrel-vaults meet at right angles, had been used by the Romans and was easy to do on a small scale. Romanesque experiments with large-scale vaults on this pattern led to the evolution of ribs. The earliest (for instance at Bayeux, above, about 1075) were inevitably crude, but were destined to have revolutionary consequences. (20, 22)

The first high rib-vault in Europe is now generally agreed to be that of Durham Cathedral. The vaults of the choir were complete by 1104, those of the nave (left) by 1133. The proportions and decoration, for instance the zigzag on the subsidiary ribs, are still typically Romanesque, but the way was now open for important structural advances. Durham has another sign of things to come—the slightly pointed transverse arches separating the square vaulting compartments. (21)

Decoration was prolific and varied widely from country to country. Above: the west door of Iffley, in Oxfordshire, has signs of the zodiac, beak-heads (a motif inherited from the Anglo-Saxons) and zigzag. Above right: the west door of St-Trophîme at Arles. Here the Romans are still remembered: a pediment above, straight entablature on columns below, and large classical statues of Apostles like Roman senators. Right: Saintes, in the Charente, with tiny figures, foliage, animals and angels. (23, 24, 25)

Variations on a theme:

regional styles within Romanesque are extremely diverse, probably more so than in Gothic. Even within a single country pronounced local forms often clearly distinguish one province from its neighbour.

The Baptistery, Cathedral and Campanile at Pisa (below) exemplify one variety of Central Italian Romanesque; note the use of marble and the rows of tiny arches running across the front of the Cathedral and round the Leaning Tower (the upper parts of the Baptistery are later). Right: Worms Cathedral—Rhineland Romanesque, with characteristic western apse and tall flanking towers. Different as they are in plan and proportions, both are built up from elements that are basically the same. (26, 27)

The rich soil of Burgundy nourished some of the most fertile architectural experiments of the Romanesque period. Right: the nave and (later) choir of La Madeleine at Vézelay. The abbey church is one of the treasure-houses of mediaeval sculpture, and the opulent effect is increased by the banded brown and white stonework. It is groin-vaulted and already has a suggestion of Gothic verticality. (30)

In England the Romanesque style after the Conquest was based largely on that of Normandy. In parts of the West Country, however, a local style took root which looks rather towards Burgundy and which is probably due to monastic contacts. Its speciality is very tall cylindrical piers, seen at their most striking in Gloucester Cathedral (above). Triforium and clerestory are dwarfed by the giant arcade. The stone vault is much later (1242–45); originally Gloucester, like the majority of Romanesque buildings, had a wooden roof. (29)

◀ **Nestling round its church,** the small town of Conques in southern France (left) can still evoke something of Europe in the 12th century. Conques was on the pilgrimage route to Compostela (see p. 28–29) and the church belongs to a small group, including St-Sernin at Toulouse and Santiago de Compostela itself, all built to a distinctive pattern created for the needs of occasional crowds of pilgrims. In this view of the east end of Conques one can see the apsed chancel with its ambulatory, aisled transept and octagonal crossing tower. (28)

Two of the keys to what happened in France after 1140 are the rib-vault and the pointed arch. Both had appeared already in Romanesque architecture, but they were now used together with a clear structural purpose. Below: the first truly 'Gothic' vault, in the narthex of St-Denis. (31)

With the skeleton vault late Gothic reached its ultimate freedom and fantasy. Its source was the English Decorated style. Above: the Berkeley Chapel vestibule and the south aisle of Bristol Cathedral, c. 1311–40. Below: two examples of developments in Germany—Langenstein (probably after 1500) and Schwäbisch Hall (late 15th century). (36–39)

Growing strength and growing complexity mark the development of the vault, ending in elaboration divorced from logic. Above: at Sens—as elsewhere in the 12th century—masons favoured the sexpartite vault, an extra transverse arch dividing the bay into six instead of four. Right: three examples from the 13th and 14th centuries. The classic French design was one simple quadripartite compartment per bay, as at Le Mans (choir 1217–54) (top). Soon, especially in England, subsidiary ribs were added—first 'tiercerons' (ribs fanning out from the wall-shaft to meet a ridge-rib running along the crown) as at Lincoln, c. 1235–40 (centre), and then 'liernes' also (small ribs connecting the main ones, added purely for decoration,) e.g. Ely presbytery (bottom) built about 1335. (32–35)

The birth of Gothic has been fixed by common agreement at 1132, when Abbot Suger began to rebuild the church of St-Denis. The new style can be seen in two ways—as an advance in technique, systematically exploiting the possibilities of the pointed arch, the rib-vault and the flying buttress, and as a change in aesthetic feeling, a desire for greater lightness, height and emphatic upward movement. There is no doubt that the Middle Ages did find in this style an expression of its intense Christian worship, but at the same time it knew, in the words of one of the masons of Milan Cathedral, that *ars sine scientia nihil est* ('skill without knowledge is worthless').

The pointed arch, an eastern idea probably transmitted by Crusaders, sometimes occurs in Romanesque, for instance at Autun Cathedral (above), dating from 1120–32. (40)

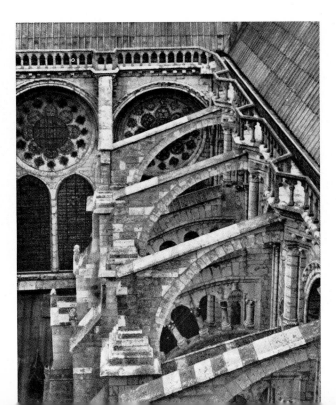

'Who was the sublime madman who dared launch such a monument into the air?' asked Vauban, the 17th-century engineer, of the central tower of Coutances (above). Coutances shows the tendencies of early Gothic particularly clearly since it was built within a single generation (1220–50) and is therefore almost uniquely consistent in style. This view from the east shows the elaborate exterior support for the choir vault. Flying-buttresses had grown from simple half-arches (e.g. the lower row at Chartres, left) to these wider, more dynamic curves (Chartres upper row and Coutances) and finally into leaping, angular lines of traceried stone. The detail (right) is of Amiens. (41, 42, 43)

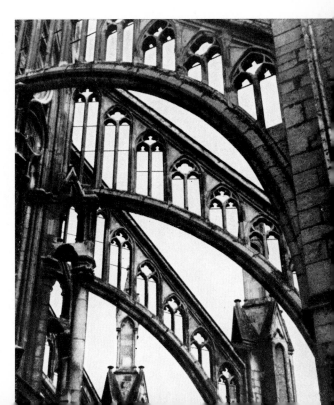

'**Beauty consists** in a certain consonance of diverging elements,' wrote St Thomas Aquinas. It is a definition that seems especially to fit the great cathedrals of the first mature Gothic style in France. From St-Denis in 1140 to Beauvais a century later they are informed by a constant purpose, aiming at height, slenderness of members, balance and unity. Arcade, triforium, clerestory and vault seem to grow from a single irresistible impulse. On the exterior, towers, pinnacles, spires, tracery and flying buttresses are all—again in St Thomas's words—'ordered towards God'.

The master of Bourges was perhaps the most individual architect of them all. The cathedral was begun before 1195 and the nave was complete by 1265. The piers are 56 feet high—so tall that the aisles behind them have their own arcade, triforium and clerestory as tall as the main elevation of most cathedrals (right). The vertical emphasis is further increased by carrying the vaulting shafts right up from floor to ceiling. The whole of the east end retains its original 13th-century glass (left, detail of the masons' window showing building and a scene from the story of Dives). The west front (below) was never finished but is still on a vast scale, lavishly adorned with sculpture of the highest quality. (44, 45, 46)

Tracery,
the network of stone

that held the ever-growing areas of stained glass, offers an endless variety of Gothic forms. In Romanesque architecture the only tracery had been the wheel window in the gable wall (above left: S. Rufino, Assisi), and the first phase of Gothic used only long windows without tracery (e.g. Coutances, pl. 42). Then came plate-tracery, in which the shapes are simply cut out of the wall, the plane surface remaining between them, as at Chartres (above centre; see also pl. 41). In about 1210 bar-tracery was invented at Rheims. Its earliest phase ('Geometrical' in England, *rayonnant* in France) is seen for instance at Bourges (pl. 45), Paris and Rheims (opposite). The second phase began in England as 'Curvilinear,' producing an amazing abundance of beautiful designs, for instance the 'Bishop's Eye' window at Lincoln, about 1330 (above right); and led to the last French style, *flamboyant*, represented here by the south transept of Amiens (right). (47–50)

National character is easier to recognize in late than in earlier Gothic. Tracery in particular grew more and more distinctive. Far left: a bay from the south walk of the cloister of Norwich Cathedral. Built about 1324, the straight lines of the lights in the middle are the first sign of the austere Perpendicular style that was soon to replace Curvilinear (see p. 104–105). Left: the monastery of Batalha, in Portugal. Batalha owes much to English ideas (English or Irish masons worked there late in the 14th century), but the 'Manueline' style, with its vegetable and even sub-marine motifs is an exotic product of Portugal alone. (51, 52)

The triumphant entrance to the great French cathedrals of the 'classic century' is by way of a portal lined with figure sculpture and forming part of a monumental two-tower west front. The source of this splendid plan was Normandy. Below: the 11th-century church of La Trinité at Caen, founded by the wife of William the Conqueror; the lines of the blind arcading are still arbitrary and the elevation of the towers not closely related to that of the end wall of the nave. By about 1210, at Notre-Dame, Paris (bottom), these elements have been tied into a firm unity. The whole design fits inside a perfect square, but is still flat and somewhat static. At Amiens (bottom right) in about 1220 the porches are deeper, the niches and pinnacles modelled in sharper relief and the porch gables beginning to thrust through the horizontal lines in an exultant upward movement. (53, 54, 56)

Rheims, the coronation church of the French kings, was begun in 1211 and most of the west front (above), designed by Bernard de Soissons, was built between 1255 and 1290. The towers were left unfinished in 1427. Here the dynamic qualities of Amiens are achieved with even greater confidence and power. There is more glazing (e.g. the tympana over the doors and the areas above and below the great rose window) and every available space—portals, gables, buttresses and the 'gallery of kings'—is filled with figure sculpture that seems, flame-like, to strive upwards, like the restless crockets and pinnacles of the towers themselves. (55)

97

Gothic came to England in 1174, when a French architect, William of Sens, was commissioned to rebuild the choir of Canterbury Cathedral after it had been destroyed by fire. It marked the beginning of the style known as 'Early English', which lasted to the middle of the 13th century and which is perhaps best represented by the Cathedral of Salisbury. From a distance (right) it is now dominated by its superb central tower and spire, added in the 14th century by Richard of Farleigh to piers never intended to carry them. But the interior (below) has the cool clarity of Early English—deep mouldings, plain capitals, the lines of shaft and column emphasized by the use of black Purbeck marble (a fashion that started at Canterbury). Except for the tower and spire Salisbury, like Coutances, was built within a single lifetime, from 1220 to 1266. (57, 58)

Lincoln's 'Angel Choir' (above) stands at the end of the Early English style, when increasing richness and complexity had brought it to the threshold of Curvilinear. Superficially it looks the same as the choir of Salisbury (left), but a closer scrutiny reveals significant changes: the multiplication of shafts against the piers and next to the large window at the end; the addition of tierceron ribs to the vault (see pl. 34); the introduction of tracery—still geometrical, but cusped and in the clerestory *doubled;* above all, the profusion of sculpture—foliage on the capitals and on the corbels supporting the vaulting shafts and figures of angels in the spandrels of the triforium, giving the choir its name. (59)

In a brief surge of creative energy at the turn of the 13th century English architects invented a new style—Cur-vilinear (or 'Decorated')—that was to have repercussions all over Europe. Members are no longer kept separate; tracery escapes from geometrical dis-cipline; vistas are interrupted; light, volume and space manipulated with a new freedom. Among its triumphs is the octagon of Ely—a huge wooden lantern built over the crossing in 1322. The real construction is con-cealed, and the upper section seems to float weightlessly on the soaring tiercerons beneath. Its builder was William Hurley, the King's master-carpenter. (60)

England's answer to the classic west front of France was the screen-front with towers outside the aisles, first attempted at Old St Paul's about 1130. At Salisbury and at Wells (below) the fronts mask the structure behind. The lower part of Wells, with the ranks of sculpture, dates from about 1230–60, the towers from 1365–1435. (61)

To Spain, some time about 1440, came a German architect from the Rhineland, Hans of Cologne. As 'Juan de Colonia' he settled in Burgos, designing the light openwork spires of the western towers (right). The Cathedral (begun in 1222 in a style derived mainly from France) was completed by Hans's son Simón, builder of the rich octagonal Chapel of the Constable (below) in 1482–94, and by his grandson Francisco, who designed the central tower as late as 1540. (62, 63)

Extreme width is as characteristic of developed Spanish Gothic as height is of French and length of English. Below: the Tinell, at Barcelona; 56 feet wide, it was built between 1359 and 1370. Below right: Gerona Cathedral. Here in 1416 it was decided to throw the whole width of the earlier chancel and aisles into one vast space, 75 feet wide, for the nave. (64, 65)

When Germany's greatest cathedral, Cologne (right), was finally completed in 1880, six hundred years after it had been begun, it suddenly became clear where 'Juan de Colonia' had found his inspiration—in the drawings for the cathedral of his own native city. During the Middle Ages, and for long after, Cologne stood as a huge gaunt fragment made up of the east end and the lower stages of one tower. The original drawings, however, survived and were rediscovered by Georg Moller in 1817, enabling it to be finished with complete authenticity. (68)

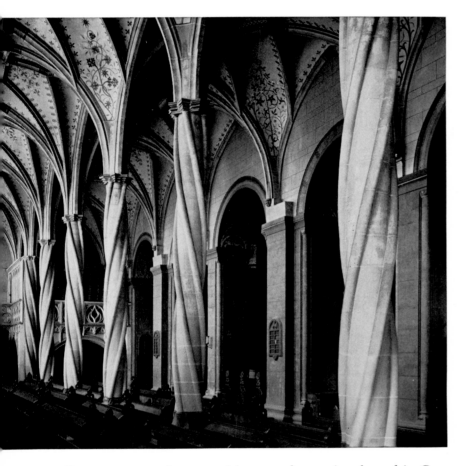

Sharp contrasts between richness and austerity abound in German Gothic. Above: Brunswick, about 1469. Note the arbitrary ribbing of the vault, the spiral shafts and the strange jagged capitals. Below: the Frauenkirche at Munich, of 1468–88, a brick cathedral in a country lacking stone. (66, 67)

Italian Gothic stands apart from the rest of Europe, unconcerned with height and verticality, uninterested in the complexities of shaft, pinnacle and vault. There is nevertheless a calm spaciousness that recalls Romanesque —even Roman—proportions, and has its own beauty, as in the Dominican church of SS. Giovanni e Paolo at Venice (right). Instead of exterior flying buttresses, interior tie-beams hold the brick vault rigid. (70)

The city-states of northern and central Italy could boast municipal buildings which often surpassed those of the Church or Empire. At Siena the Palazzo Pubblico (below) was begun in 1289, but the only reminder of northern Gothic is in the windows, which have simple plate-tracery. (69)

Memories of France clearly influenced Niccolò and Giovanni Pisano in their design for Siena's west front (above right), but with its banded marble, bright polychrome decoration and use of mosaic it is unmistakably Italian. The 'Chapel of the Thorn' at Pisa (left) also looks north of the Alps, though its miniature scale suggests a reliquary as much as a church. (71, 72)

The serene republic of Venice produced an architecture entirely its own—light, colourful and rich, a union of Gothic, Islamic and Byzantine. Both the Doge's Palace and the Ca' d'Oro (right) show the typical loggias and rows of ogee arches. (73, 74)

A golden age

of English culture began with the evolution of the Perpendicular style in the 1330s, reaching its climax under the enlightened patronage of Richard II in the last decade of the century. Poets like Chaucer and Langland, composers like Dunstable, artists like the painter of the Wilton Diptych made this a period of unsurpassed achievement. In architecture it was no less creative—the age of splendid church towers, of hammer-beam roofs, fan-vaults and vast walls of glass held in a straight mesh of tracery.

Fan-vaulting can first be seen in the cloister of Gloucester Cathedral (left) of about 1370. Its distinction consists in having all the ribs of the same length and the same curvature, producing a series of half-funnel shapes. (75)

Hammer-beams are the horizontal members which project from the wall and so reduce the width to be spanned by the main arch-braces. The greatest of roofs built on this system is that of Westminster Hall (below), made by Hugh Herland in 1394–1400 for Richard II. (76)

'Bell Harry' Tower, the central lantern of Canterbury, rides proudly over the Cathedral (right). Built in 1493–1505 by John Wastell, who had worked previously at Peterborough and King's College, Cambridge, it completed the building begun in 1379 by another architect of genius, Henry Yevele. Yevele had worked on several royal castles and on the nave of Westminster Abbey before he designed the new nave of Canterbury (below right). By the 14th century it becomes possible to follow the careers of most leading master masons. (77, 78)

The last invention of English Gothic was the pendant vault, a feat of virtuosity that seems to defy the laws of gravity. Henry VII's Chapel at Westminster Abbey (below) was designed by Robert and William Vertue and built between 1503 and 1519. (79)

Most perfect of English west fronts is arguably that of Beverley (below). Built within a few years (about 1400) to one consistent design, it displays all the force and dignity inherent in the Perpendicular style. (80)

The range of late Gothic

is so wide that it is difficult to point to any single feature shared by all buildings falling within the same period. The brick Cathedral of Albi (right) even looks distinctly un-Gothic. It was built between 1282 and 1390 in a country still ravaged by the Albigensian Wars and still bitterly hostile to the Roman Church. It is a fortress against heresy; there is a single entrance, no openings at ground level and in the massive west tower arrow-slits instead of windows. (81)

'So great and of such a kind' was the Cathedral of Seville to be, 'that those who see it finished shall think we were mad.' That was in 1401; it was finished in 1506, the largest church in the world. This view from the south (below) shows the triple flying buttresses of the nave, the transept front and the Capella Real, added in 1551–75. (82)

Flanders followed the French lead, with minor variations. Her most ambitious buildings, like her commercial prosperity, belong to the later period of the Middle Ages. The Cathedral of St Bavon at Ghent (right) was begun in 1274 but the tower, the last part, was not complete until 1533. It formerly had a spire. (84)

The tangled story of Milan Cathedral can still be read in the minutes of the church-council. It was begun on a huge scale in 1387 but the authorities were not content to trust the work to a single man. Endless conferences were held; master masons were invited from all over Europe; architects were appointed, found wanting, and dismissed; the building dragged on for generations and was still unfinished in the 19th century. Its low, spreading proportions are Italian, but all its details, such as the east end with its riot of flamboyant tracery (below), are of the north. (83)

Bruges, a few miles from Ghent, was one of the richest trading centres of Europe in the later Middle Ages. Its famous belfry is shown on p. 261. The town-hall (right), begun in 1376, is equally confident in its assertion of civic achievement—a confidence echoed in the Renaissance splendour of the 'Ancien Greffe' on its left. (85)

died not slowly but in a blaze of glory. Between about 1480 and 1550 many of the most magnificent buildings of any age were created, with a virtuosity and genius hardly equalled before or since.

Peter Parler began work on the triforium and vault of the choir of Prague Cathedral (above) in 1374. It displays all the originality of both the architect and the period—a glazed triforium, whose shafts seem to grow through the horizontal line of masonry into the mullions of the clerestory, and diagonal tabernacles where the windows meet the vaulting shafts. (87)

The play of light on the west front of Rouen (above) that so fascinated Monet is due to Roulland le Roux's rich design of 1509. The lower parts belong to the 13th-century church, upon which le Roux superimposed his filigree screen of ogee curves and nodding tracery canopies. (86)

'Rococo Gothic', an extraordinary style of intertwining ribs and playful fantasy, was evolved in Bohemia by Benedikt Ried. His Vladislav Hall (right) in the Castle of Prague, was designed in 1493. (88)

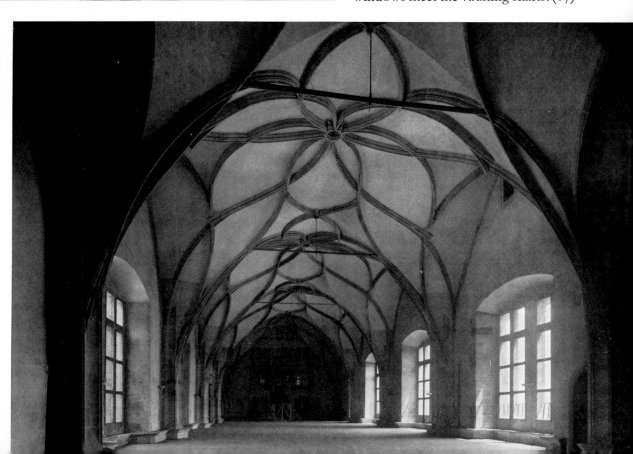

The ascending spirit of Gothic is nowhere more ardently expressed than in the high openwork spires of Germany. Among the earliest is that of Freiburg-im-Breisgau (below), begun about 1340. It was the model for many others. (89)

The highest cathedral in Christendom—Beauvais—dates from the mid-13th century, though altered and repaired later, and never carried further than the crossing. In 1499–1549 it was given its superb south transept front (above right) by Martin Chambiges of Paris, perhaps the peak of the *style flamboyant* in France. (90)

Vast in scale and unified in design, the interior of Seville Cathedral is one of the most notable in the world, rivalling the greatest triumphs of Gothic in France, England and Germany. It has double aisles, plus side chapels, so that the resulting plan is nearly square (an exterior view is shown in pl. 82). The shallow mouldings and small capitals may be compared with English Perpendicular, although the architect was probably French. (91)

Tter natus
est nobis et
filius datus
est nobis cuius imperium

super humerum eius et uo
cabitur nomen eius ma
gni consily angelus. ps
Cantate domino canti

A world of colour that once gave life and brilliance to mediaeval architecture has vanished for ever—a fact easy to forget. Gilded statues and screens, painted vaults, as well as stained glass and rich vestments all contributed to a consciously planned effect. This miniature from the *Très Riches Heures*, painted by Jean Colombe for Charles I of Savoy, shows the Christmas Mass in Charles's chapel at Chambéry. In the initial beneath is the Nativity, and in the floral decoration at the sides, the shepherds adoring. (92)

The Development of Architecture

JOHN HARVEY

The builders of Chartres. This drawing from a 13th-century window shows a master mason (left) checking a wall with his plumb-line; near him hang a plan, with four columns and a quatrefoil pier, and a triangular level. The other three men are stonecutters using various types of hammer, the one on the right wearing a glove on the chisel-holding hand. Squares lie on the ground. At the top are templates showing sections of mouldings and a pair of compasses. (1)

THE MIDDLE AGES exert a fascination over the modern mind largely because of their art which, in spite of tragic losses, survives in massive quantity. Like all art, that produced in Europe between the fall of Rome and the coming of the Renaissance is the concrete expression of an outlook which informed society. Art comprises the whole of man's works, the material outcome of his thought as expressed by his hands and through the tools of his invention. Within this total orbit art may be subdivided according to the senses to which it appeals, as poetry and music do to the ear; or classified in a hierarchy of purpose wherein the arts of merely practical concern rank below the fine arts regarded as an inessential luxury appealing to a faculty of highly educated appreciation. This latter distinction not only overlooks the essential character of fine art, but also obscures the fundamental unity of the skills involved in artistic production. While an artifact may have positive utility wholly divorced from aesthetic quality, the converse does not hold good: all true art, aesthetically speaking, rests upon a sound grasp of underlying craftmanship. It is due to the close identification between efficient craftsmanship and aesthetic perception during the Middle Ages that the art of the period has so intense an interest.

Discussion of an artistic culture requires that its origins must be fixed in place and time. Here we are concerned primarily with western Europe from Iceland and Ireland to Poland and Hungary, from Norway to Portugal and Italy: in fact the sum total of those lands whose religion was western Christianity owing allegiance to Rome. In time, the age as a whole intervened between the collapse of the western Roman Empire in the 5th century and the deliberate re-creation in the 15th of neo-Roman arts and techniques based upon surviving written texts and upon study of architectural and technical remains. Within this total period of a thousand years we must here discuss the second five hundred, for between the 5th century and the 10th stretched the Dark Ages of retrogression and resurgent savagery. In spite of their barbarism these early centuries were mysteriously shot through with glimpses of highly imaginative art and were alive with aspirations towards a future level of achievement.

'Building Big': A Fresh Concept

Beside the continuity of Byzantine art, the unending miracle of Chinese sensitivity and poise, or the precocious brilliance of Islam, all possessing long and augmented traditions of science and techniques, the contribution of north-western Europe between the years 400 and 900 must seem provincial at best. Admirable as may be individual works, some of them noble and even awe-inspiring relics of an age of simplicity, it would be vain to seek among the Franks, Goths, Anglo-Saxons and Scandinavians for any capacity for organization on the grand scale. The greatest cathedrals, monasteries or palaces are insignificant when compared with the ruins left by the Romans or even the earliest of the magnificent buildings of the resurgent 11th century. Whether or no we attach major historical significance to the millennial hypothesis—that men who believed in the end of the world at AD 1000 would devote scant attention to grandiose material projects—it is a fact that it was the 11th century that witnessed a profound change in outlook. Hitherto a collection of small units

thinking of local affairs, Europe was suddenly transformed. Tiny principalities gave way before the concept of nationality and political unification took the place of empty theories such as that of the Bretwalda (or sovereign of Britain). The geographical insularity of Britain may in this way have been responsible for the emergence of the nation-state elsewhere. What is certain is that by the 11th century notions of co-ordination, not only political but also economic and technical, were current and were beginning to give rise to the possibility of grand constructions emulating one another and leading to ever greater and more noble scale.

The question of scale is of the utmost importance since mere size involves a high degree of constructional organization. Even the largest buildings of Carolingian times, such as the Palace and Chapel of Charlemagne at Aachen (792–805), had roofs of relatively small span. No outstanding competence in the designing of centering or scaffolding was called for; the details of architectural design were either closely copied from Roman or Byzantine work or were extremely crude. The beginning of a new competence in design on a much larger scale can be seen from the very start of the 11th century. In churches this appears in St-Martin at Tours (c.1000–50), St-Bénigne at Dijon (1001–18) and in the other grandiose churches built through the century and culminating in Santiago de Compostela begun about 1075, and the new church of the monastery of Cluny started 1088 and finished in 1121. In secular buildings the capacity to build on a notable scale is shown by the Imperial Hall at Goslar (c. 1040–50) measuring internally some 145 feet by 45 and, to a far greater degree, by the great hall of William Rufus at Westminster, built in 1097–99 and measuring 238 by 68 feet, the largest room in Europe for well over a century. It will bear comparison even with the central hall of the Basilica of Constantine at Rome (AD 312), which measured some 265 by 83 feet.

p 29 (34)
p 47 (12)
p 104–5 (76)

A revolution was in progress, or rather a series of revolutions. The first stage is marked by the desire to build on a large scale, even if crudely, and most of the constructional experts involved seem to have come from Italy. In the case of St-Bénigne at Dijon we actually know that the work was directed by the Italian William of Volpiano (near Turin in Piedmont), who brought Italian masters. The second stage, far more concerned with niceties of design and capable of even larger buildings, occupied the second half of the century. About the year 1100 this second stage was itself overtaken by a third wave of still greater accomplishment. The achievements of the later Middle Ages are due to the new skills brought by the leaders of this threefold revolution of the 11th century.

It is certain that the new energy infused into western art came from outside the area of north-western Europe. Even during the

Dark Ages there had been occasional glimpses of higher aesthetic quality or technical capacity, usually to be connected with the arrival in some western country of clerics or artists from the Near East, and both Syrian and Armenian influences have been traced in Visigothic, British and Irish art. In the earlier period, however, the number of such contacts was slight and their effects minimal. The events of the 11th century show that much more direct contacts, affecting considerable numbers of persons, must have been involved. Consideration of historical and geographical factors suggests several main lines of influence.

So far as concerns Britain there is little evidence for the onset of major building in the early part of the 11th century, but the rebuilding of devastated churches and monasteries under Canute, the son of a Polish princess, may reflect some Byzantine influences brought by the overland route. Rather more direct contacts between northern Europe and the civilized lands of the Mediterranean followed the conquest of southern Italy and Sicily by the Normans in the generation after 1042. Perhaps even more fruitful, as a source of skilled craftsmen, was the siege and capture of Barbastro in the north-east of Spain in 1064. An army of Normans and Frenchmen, with the blessing of the Pope and under the command of William VIII, Duke of Aquitaine, took many Moorish prisoners, sending several thousand into France, 1500 to Rome and 7000 to Constantinople. Singers, musicians and other artists are stated to have been among the number, and presumably also the Moorish corps of engineers which had defended Barbastro. It seems probable that the spoils of war included a substantial number of craftsmen who possessed a degree of technical skill hitherto unknown north of the Alps and Pyrenees.

Such contacts between Normans and Saracens go far towards explaining the ambitious architectural programme which became manifest in northern France and in England shortly before, and in the generation succeeding, the Norman Conquest of 1066. Fully developed Romanesque (in England, Norman) architecture includes much work of small scale: the little village churches and the rare stone houses of merchants or Jews. The very large number of such small buildings, however, implies a considerable force of skilled men, while the relatively few buildings on a grand scale must have tested to the utmost the capacity for organization available in that age.

The Palatine abbey of Durham (1093–1140), the new cathedral and priory of St Swithun at Winchester (1079–1120), and above all such a gigantic church and monastery as that of Bury St Edmunds (1081–c.1130), well exemplify the new ability to think and to build big. The royal and noble patrons and distinguished clerics shared with the master masons who worked for them this capacity to envisage grandiose concepts; and it was the masons who developed the practical organization and techniques involved in their realization. With few exceptions the great Romanesque buildings erected in England were larger than their counterparts in France or elsewhere on the continent of Europe. This was probably due to the 'colonial' aspect of Norman power in England. Whereas France was already well supplied with churches and monasteries, England came as a virgin field for architectural expansion and experiment. Even the greatest of the Saxon minsters were small, and the colleges of priests or abbeys of unreformed Benedictines must have seemed fit only for demolition and total replacement. The extent of the resulting campaign of reconstruction in early Norman England placed the country in the forefront of an architectural revolution comparable in character only to the Industrial Revolution eight centuries later.

Labour and Transport

The political unification of England under the Norman kings and the subordination of the feudal system in England to the power of the Crown made it possible to raise large funds for building. Yet even assured finances could not of themselves have enabled a visionary programme to become effective. The masters responsible had to be able, not merely to plan and design suitable buildings, structurally stable and aesthetically pleasing to their clients,

The late 11th century marks a change not only in architectural style but also in the scale on which builders and patrons were prepared to think. Churches were vaster than at any time since the Early Christian period, and with far bolder technical features. The planning of whole complexes of buildings, such as monasteries and palaces, also became more grandiose. At Bury St Edmunds, shown here, a new programme of building began in 1081. The church itself (A) was over 500 feet long (longer than most cathedrals) and the other buildings were equally ambitious. The cloister (B), chapter-house (C), refectory (D), dormitory (E) and Abbot's palace (F) dated from the early 12th century. Farm-buildings belonging to the abbey's large estates were grouped round the Great Court (G). Other notable features were: the two gate-towers (H), which still stand; the great hall (J); the fish-ponds, called 'the Crankles' (K); and the infirmary (L). The two churches of St James (M), now the cathedral, and St Mary (N) are later additions. To the south of the abbey church was the cemetery (O) with the charnel house (P), and across the river lay the large vineyard (Q) of the monks. (2)

100   0   100   500 FT.

0   50   100   150 M.

Sites of the chief architectural monuments of the 12th century. The choice of places, in this and the other maps of this chapter, is inevitably selective. Important work could be found in progress in most large towns at any time during the Middle Ages. (3)

but also to organize the provision of great gangs of men and the acquisition and transport of vast quantities of materials. The extent to which Caen stone, already quarried on a large scale in Normandy and within easy reach of water carriage, was imported for use in England is one of the factors which indicate the dependence of the early generations of our Romanesque builders upon headquarters overseas.

During the late 11th century, in England and on the Continent, the difficulty of attracting a sufficient number of skilled craftsmen to a building site, possibly remote, must have been very great. It is not at all clear, in fact, how the greater jobs were manned. Later in the Middle Ages the royal power of impressment was freely used, not only by the Crown, but by other building owners who paid for licences to make use of this prerogative. It is known that by the 13th and 14th century it was normal for men to be recruited even from very distant parts of the country. In 1233 carpenters taken at Reading were sent to Painscastle in Radnorshire, about 120 miles off, and were allowed journey money of 1s 4d each. Certainly there must, even in earlier times, have been ways and means of encouraging, or even forcing, men possessed of the needed skills to converge upon the major sites.

Transport of materials made great demands, not only on the funds available, but also upon the logistic ability of the masters. All communications were slow, and every stage of the operations had in consequence to be worked out well in advance. Yet we find, not only that very large amounts of stone were imported from Caen, but that stone at many quarries was worked to shape before transport, on a basis of patterns drawn on parchment or canvas and sent in advance. Since land transport was excessively

costly, much ingenuity was expended in working out feasible routes for water carriage. The stone for Bury, some of it from Caen and some from Barnack in Northamptonshire, was taken by boat to points within about ten miles of the abbey, by the sea and up the Gipping in one case, and through Fenland waterways to the Little Ouse in the other. When Abingdon Abbey was rebuilt soon after 1100, the great timbers for roof-beams and rafters were brought from Shrewsbury in six wains drawn by twelve oxen each, and the journey is recorded as having taken six or seven weeks coming and going. Since the return journey is about 220 miles, this implies a rate of progress of only five miles a day, a clear indication of the state of the roads. That such journeys were not merely possible, but must have been frequent, shows the ingenuity and determination of the men who organized them.

The earlier Norman masons were not yet fully competent to design the large structures which they were attempting. A considerable number of their great towers fell down and, in spite of some attempts to attribute such catastrophes to divine vengeance or satanic interference, there were contemporary chroniclers shrewd enough to suspect inadequacy of craftmanship or poor foundations. It must, also, be remembered that for a generation or more after the Conquest the English labour force was largely composed of Saxons unused to large-scale operations. Their employment produced in many instances the phenomenon of the 'Saxon overlap', when buildings obviously erected under Norman auspices show Saxon characteristics in detail. It was not to be expected that with such a mixed force of men, with very few masters of really outstanding ability, the vast campaign of works should be carried out without some collapsing. It was only

Builders of the mid-13th century, at work on the abbey of St Albans. Two men turn a windlass which raises masonry in a basket to the top of the wall; two more, with double-axes, cut a foliated capital (left) and a block of ashlar. Above them, standing on the wall they are building (there is no scaffolding), one man tests for horizontal with a plumb-level, while another sets a stone block. Note the ladder made from a single beam; in surviving examples the rungs are long pegs driven through holes. (4)

as time went on that the burning of lime was perfected to produce adequate mortar, and the roughly shaped small stones of early work gave place to exquisitely true blocks of ashlar. It is the ability to produce really fine worked ashlar that characterizes the onset of the late Norman period at the opening of the 12th century.

The Origins of Gothic

Within a few years of 1100, and certainly no later than 1110, this fine masonry had reached England. Not only were the stones better cut, but they were of larger size, implying the existence of improved cranes and hoists. The mortar joints were now very fine, so that a chronicler commented upon Bishop Roger's buildings at Old Sarum, begun in 1102, that the stones were so accurately set that the joints were not seen and the whole work might be thought to be cut out of a single rock. Certainly this remarkable improvement in methods must indicate a fresh importation of skills from the East and this applies not merely to England but to all western Europe at this time. It can hardly be a coincidence that the great campaign known as the First Crusade had just taken place. Since chronology is here essential to a grasp of the historical possibilities, the main dates must be recapitulated. The Crusade was opened by an appeal from Pope Urban II, launched on 27th November, 1095. Large bodies of troops were gathered and moved eastwards across Europe, converging upon Constantinople by the end of 1096. During the summer of 1097 Nicaea was captured and the Turks defeated in Anatolia; next year Antioch was taken and a still more remote 'western' principality founded at Edessa. The Crusade was crowned with success on 15th July, 1099, when Jerusalem fell after a six weeks' siege.

The new Eastern dominions of the Franks, as the Western Crusaders were called, were defended by an extensive chain of castles which called forth the fullest resources of the military engineers and masons. There is no doubt that many developments in fortification took place as a result of the experience gained on the Crusades and especially through the opportunities for examining Byzantine, Armenian and Saracenic defences and interrogating local craftsmen. It may be supposed that returning Frankish engineers from 1099 onwards would have come back equipped with fresh knowledge of structural expedients, and that a proportion of Eastern prisoners of outstanding capacity were brought back to the West. At least one such prisoner, 'Lalys', built Neath Abbey and is said to have been architect to Henry I. Nor did the matter end there, for it is only from Eastern sources that the Western architects can have acquired the pointed arch which was to become the symbol and chief mark of the Gothic

style. To this extent it must be accepted that Sir Christopher Wren was right in supposing, some three centuries ago, that the origins of the Gothic style were to be found in the Eastern buildings seen by the crusaders. Whether or no the invention of the ribbed cross-vault is likewise Eastern, (and vault-ribs of a relevant kind were certainly built in Persia and in Armenia before 1100) it is at Durham Cathedral that it was first seen in the West, so far as exhaustive investigations can show. The first stone of the church at Durham was laid on 11th August, 1093, and the wooden centering of the vaults is known to have been removed only just in time for the translation of the body of St Cuthbert on 4th September, 1104. It is a very strange coincidence, if indeed it be a coincidence at all, that the first known ribbed vault in the West should have been built within the five years that succeeded the taking of Jerusalem.

p 88–8
(21)

The precise date at which the Eastern pointed arch is first evidenced in Western Europe is a matter of controversy. It is generally accepted as an original feature of the arcades of the great church of Cluny, begun in 1088 and finished as far as the transepts by 1100. Professor Kenneth J. Conant regards the source of these arches as the Benedictine monastery church of Monte Cassino, rebuilt in 1066–71, by craftsmen some of whom were from Amalfi, a commercial republic with trading stations in the Near East and as far away as Baghdad. What is quite certain is that such pointed arches, on a grand scale, formed part of the design of Autun Cathedral, built in 1120–32, and that they were linked with the cross-rib vault in the narthex of the abbey of St-Denis, built for Abbot Suger before 1140. From then onwards Gothic style existed.

p 93
(40)

p 92
(31)

Dimension and Design

Apart from the technical skill to cut stone to true shapes, to lay foundations, to work out adequate scaffolding and temporary supports for arches, vaults and roofs, the building masters must certainly have acquired a knowledge of principles of design. It is evident, partly from study of the buildings, partly from treatises written later, that this knowledge consisted quite largely in systems of proportion. The pupil architect was taught, by his father, uncle or master, certain methods of geometrical setting-out, and certain geometrical and numerical formulae. Basic to the

p 86-7
(12-15)

Part of the plaster tracing-floor above the north porch of Wells Cathedral, from a photographic survey by L. S. Colchester. Repeated use of the surface over a long period has produced a maze of lines, largely unintelligible, but the geometrical setting out of a number of architectural features can be seen. Another floor of similar character exists above the vestibule to the chapter-house of York Minster. (5)

'Wouldst thou draw a plan for a pinnacle after the mason's art, by regular geometry?' —one of the diagrams from Matthäus Roritzer's work on pinnacles, published in 1486. At the bottom is the basic plan (the diagonal of the inner square being equal to the sides of the outer); at the top the elevation with the mouldings added. Roritzer, like Rodrigo Gil and many others, came from a family that had included master masons for generations. He was cathedral architect at Regensburg, and his treatise doubtless records the traditional practices there. The methods illustrated, he confesses, are not his own invention but derive from 'old connoisseurs of the art' and particularly from 'the younkers of Prague,' i.e. the Parler family. (6)

Among the sparse documentary remains of the Gothic tradition, one of the most interesting is the text and drawings of the Spanish architect Rodrigo Gil de Hontañón (died 1577), which have survived as part of a later 'Compendio de Arquitectura' of 1681. Gil himself was not born until about 1500, but he came from a family in which the old tradition was strong. His father, Juan, had been master mason at the cathedrals of Salamanca and Segovia, and Rodrigo succeeded him on both projects, completing them in the original style. Two of his main preoccupations were with vaulting and with proportion. The stellar vault of this design seems to owe something to German influence, while the simple ratios on which the plan is based are indicated by numbers: the first bay from the choir is square (40 × 40), the other bays 30 × 40 and the aisle bays 30 × 20. Ratios and vaulting pattern are both very similar to those actually used by Gil at Segovia (7)

problems of the mediaeval mason was the setting-out of a correct right-angle upon the ground; and, as few laymen would then have known, the simplest method of doing this was and is to lay down, with pegs and cord, a triangle with sides measured as 3, 4 and 5. The knowledge of a number of such problems in practical geometry, series of numbers, and methods of subdivision, would provide the architect with the essentials of his skill or mistery.

The main secret of design, as practised in the late Romanesque and early Gothic periods, consisted in the application of a module, or standard dimension, in multiples, sub-multiples and combinations. The modular unit itself had to be settled in accordance with the particular standard of measurements of the place, either that of the building site or that of the master's origin. In many parts of Europe during the Dark Ages the Roman foot had remained as a standard of measurement, and according to this (0.295 metre, or about 11⅝ inches) some of the most important buildings were set out. At Cluny, for instance, Professor Conant has been able to demonstrate the use of a modular unit of five Roman feet (1.475 metres or 4 feet 10 1/16 inches). In some cases a change of unit can be demonstrated between works of different periods in the same building: at Cluny the earlier work had used a foot of greater length (0.34 metre or 13⅜ inches), while in England, certainly from the 12th century if not earlier, the standard was the royal foot still in use, equivalent to 0.305 metre and divided into 12 inches. The French *pied du roi* was longer (0.3248 metre or about 12¾ inches of the English measure). It can easily be seen that, even starting from a single system of modular geometry, individual results would differ, and that the differences would become extremely complex once the system began to be applied according to different standards of measurement. Hence it is that the very existence of such systems has been denied.

There have been many attempts to reconstruct the systems used for laying down the plan and erecting the elevation of a great mediaeval church, and these depend for the most part upon two documentary sources of late date. One of these is the commentary upon Vitruvius by the Italian editor Cesare Cesariano (1521), in which an account is given of disputes about the design of Milan Cathedral in 1386 between Italian, French and German masters, used to different systems of proportion. The two main systems were known as *ad quadratum*, based upon a square, and *ad triangulum* based on the equilateral triangle. Applied to the cross-section of a church, the system *ad triangulum* naturally resulted in a lower, more squat, proportion of height to width; it was this system which was regarded as normal by the Italian masters in the 14th century. The other document is far more

p 107 (83)

explicit: it consists in a manuscript *Compendium of Architecture* of 1681, written by Simón García, a Spanish architect of Salamanca. In his own work García luckily incorporated the rules of the Gothic builders which had come down to him in an earlier manuscript compiled by Rodrigo Gil de Hontañón. Rodrigo Gil, who was already at work in 1521 and died in 1577, was the last of a notable family of Spanish architects, responsible for several of the largest cathedrals. Similar principles to those derived from the Milan discussions of 1386 and the practice of Rodrigo Gil in the 16th century are also found in several German treatises of the 15th and 16th, among which the best known is Matthäus Roritzer's tractate on pinnacles, published in 1486, based on the system of squares inscribed diagonally within one another.

Much nonsense has been written on the subject of mediaeval art, and several baseless ideas have gained wide currency. Among these have been the notions that all art was produced by the clergy and more especially by monks; that it was produced spontaneously by anybody, untrained but with some instinctive capacity for design and construction; and that great architecture was produced entirely without drawings. None of these views has any real foundation in fact. Though men trained as artists or as building craftsmen might exceptionally enter religious orders as laybrothers, or become monks, it is clear that from the 11th century if not earlier, all architecture and most sculpture was produced by laymen with a training in craftsmanship, to which literacy might be added. That, on rare occasions, there was voluntary assistance from large crowds of laymen, anxious to further some religious project, is true; but no scrap of evidence has yet been found to suggest that these 'building bees' consisted of anything more than unskilled labourers. In regard to drawings, it is quite certain that no large building, such as a cathedral, with complex inter-relations between its parts, depending upon accurately shaped stones, could have been put up without at least the geometrical setting-out of its parts upon the ground. It is, in fact, very likely that the disappearance of most early constructional drawings is due to their having been traced on the ground or on a floor-slab of plaster made for the purpose. After use such drawings would be obliterated, though the plaster floors used for the purpose actually survive at Wells and York cathedrals, and an important one was in use at Strasbourg until the 18th century.

In England, very few drawings of a technical character earlier in date than the 16th century have survived, but even here there are some fragments. In France, Germany, Austria, Italy and Spain there are much larger numbers of highly finished constructional drawings and details, from the 13th, 14th and 15th centuries, many of them of outstanding excellence.

f 7

f 6

f 5

f 38

115

The sketchbook of the Picard master-mason Villard de Honnecourt is the most complete and best-known of all collections of mediaeval architectural drawings. He must have accumulated them for his own lodge between 1220 and 1235, travelling widely, probably working at some of the sites himself and taking a keen interest in everything that was useful or novel. This section through the choir-buttresses of Rheims was made while the building was still unfinished. Evidently Villard was only concerned to make rough notes, not to preserve an accurate record of what he saw. Parts of this sketch would have been impossible to build: e.g. the window on the right, of which we see the two shafts of the jamb in section, is taken so far up that there is no room left for the arch. Other drawings by Villard are reproduced on pp. 85 and 309. (8)

The Architect's Status

Naturally there is far more evidence concerning the architects of the later Middle Ages than for those of earlier centuries, and it might be that there had been a marked rise in status in the course of four or five centuries. What evidence there is, however, does not suggest this. Even before the Norman Conquest, the master mason Godwin Gretsyd, in charge at the building of Westminster Abbey for Edward the Confessor, was sufficiently well-to-do to be able to leave properties in Southampton to the Abbey and also, along with his wife Wendelburh, to be a benefactor of Hyde Abbey at Winchester. The Norman master Robert who designed St Albans Abbey and was said to excel all the masons of his time, could give 10s a year to the abbey funds, a sum which then (c. 1100) must have been equivalent to about £100 of the money of 1966. Later in the 12th century Richard of Wolveston, architect to Bishop Puiset of Durham, was not only famous as a building master, but carried about in his wallet a number of painted letters of great beauty, presumably illuminated initials. This odd fact, known to us from the account of a miracle attributed to a fragment of cloth from St Cuthbert's body, placed by Master Richard along with the paintings, helps to fill out the picture of a literate and sophisticated professional man, rather than one of the rude artisans of popular imagination.

For the later Middle Ages there are detailed financial records which show what high rates of pay the greater architects could command, and the distances they were called to give advice. While it is impossible to translate mediaeval monetary values precisely into modern terms, it is not difficult to get a general idea of relative scales of pay. The masters of architectural status were paid three to four times as much as fully skilled craftsmen in their own trade. Whereas a mason or carpenter of the second half of the 14th century, after the Black Death, was paid wages roughly equivalent to £12 a week nowadays, a William Wynford, a Hugh Herland or a Henry Yevele would earn £3,000 a year and upwards in salary and allowances, apart from substantial profits as a contractor or maker of tombs and monuments. In the late 13th century Edward I's great military engineer, James of St George, was paid something like £6,000 a year, and other outstanding masters about £2,000. The French mason, Eudes de Montreuil, was getting rather more than this in the same period.

p 85 (8)
f 8
p 309

Among all the drawings of a technical character which survive, the most precious are those which form the album (so-called) of a Picard master, Villard de Honnecourt, now preserved in the Bibliothèque Nationale at Paris. Two main views have been held as to the purpose of Honnecourt's album: that it was simply the sketch-book of a mediaeval architect, filled with notes of buildings, details, and constructional devices that interested him or took his fancy; or that it was a compilation made with didactic intent for the use of a permanent building organization such as the mason's lodge of a cathedral. The modern study by Hahnloser has shown, as conclusively as is possible without direct evidence, that the latter explanation is correct. Not only are many of the drawings highly finished to a degree most unlikely in a sketch-book, but they are accompanied by lengthy written explanations. Furthermore, there are additions by later hands, at least two in addition to Honnecourt himself, and these imply continuity of use for technical purposes, rather than the mere handing down of a family possession. Again, many leaves have been cut out of the book, apparently at an early date, and this would suggest that these sections contained material regarded as valuable by some mediaeval artist who detached them to carry with him for use. That the album was in fact a sort of manuscript technical encyclopaedia of the building trades is made even more probable by the fact that many documentary references occur in mediaeval wills and other records to the existence of books of designs in the possession of master craftsmen.

The inscriptions by Honnecourt reveal still more: that he was literate and could write a very fine hand, and that he knew at least some Latin, as well as French. This is, of course, inherently likely, since mediaeval architects attached to cathedrals and the greater monasteries were in close touch with the important schools taught by the secular clergy or the monks, or by schoolmasters retained by them. Thus the building master's sons could easily obtain some book education before serving as assistants or apprentices to their fathers. That the sons of building masters were as acceptable socially as those of modern architects at the best schools is shown by the fact that among the earliest scholars of Winchester College were sons of the master mason, William Wynford, and of the master carpenter, Hugh Herland. Richard Bertie, son of the master mason of Winchester Cathedral, was admitted to Corpus Christi College, Oxford, in 1534 at the age of 16, and after a brilliant career married the widowed Duchess of Suffolk and founded one of the greatest families in the English peerage. The educational evidence agrees with that for the relatively high social position of the mediaeval architect, who was commonly entertained at the high table of colleges and monastic houses, and ranked among the esquires of the royal household. Sometimes portraits of architects were put in places of honour in the building, as the stained glass figures of Wynford and Herland in the chapel of Winchester College, or the bust of Peter Parler in the choir of Prague Cathedral.

f 39

It was Eudes de Montreuil, in 1248–54, who accompanied St Louis on crusade and worked at Jaffa and in Cyprus, while in 1287 Etienne de Bonneuil went from Paris to Uppsala in northern Sweden as master mason of the cathedral, taking with him a number of assistants. All through the Middle Ages there is evidence of the employment of foreign architects and artists, and of extensive journeys undertaken, sometimes in search of materials, sometimes to inspect existing buildings relevant to a new design. Many consultations are on record, when architects from great distances were brought together to solve difficult technical problems. Twelve architects, some coming from distances of well over 100 miles, assembled at Gerona in Spain to give advice in 1416 on the best design for the nave, and in central Europe the masons of the Empire were organized on a continental scale, and travelled up to 250 miles to attend periodical congresses of their craft. The rapid spread of stylistic changes is thus not difficult to explain.

p 100 (65) f 16

Apart from the false picture of mediaeval building methods that has grown up, more general ideas of life in the period are often inadequate. This is largely due to the 19th-century notion of continuous progress: it is well known from many sources that European home conditions in the 17th and 18th centuries were highly insanitary, and that the roads were mostly in a deplorable condition, making travel difficult and slow; hence it was assumed that the state of affairs in the Middle Ages had been much worse. This was a fallacy, for it has been established that the greater cities of the Gothic period did much to establish paved streets, water supply, public sanitation and municipal hygiene. Travel, on roads adequate for riding horses and mules, was not unduly difficult and was far more frequent and extensive than has been supposed. It need not be cause for amazement, then, to learn that designs for buildings were carried far and wide and across frontiers, and that even in an age without

p 84 (2)

1200

1300

1400

1520-50

1575

A selection of English masons' marks. Those of c.1520–50 are from Kentish quarries, the rest from Kenilworth Castle, Warwickshire. Masons carved their own mark to show responsibility for work done. The same or similar marks passed from father to son, but were subject to change within the lodge to avoid duplication. There is no way of connecting these marks with named masons but they can prove contemporaneity of work. (9)

printing or any form of technical news-sheets, architects could be well-informed. There were compensating factors, such as the absence of artistic copyright. The great designs for major buildings, drawn out on skins of parchment, such as can still be seen at Strasbourg and Vienna, could be and were copied, and used as the models for other works at a distance. Thus the perforated masonry spires of Burgos Cathedral in Spain, designed in 1442 by the German master Hans from Cologne (Juan de Colonia), were based upon the drawings for the western steeples of Cologne: not actually built until 1880, when the work was completed from the original designs, which had in the meantime been lost and later rediscovered.

Two social institutions in particular led to extensive travel: pilgrimage, which induced very many persons to spend long periods on journeys to Rome, to Jerusalem, to Santiago de Compostela or, to take an English example, to Canterbury; and wander-years, when a young craftsman just out of his apprenticeship would spend three years on jobs at a distance from his place of training, and often in foreign countries. Many of the names of foreign craftsmen preserved in account rolls are doubtless those of young men on their wanderings, and it must not be overlooked that even more foreigners were employed than the names would suggest, for in all countries names tended to become naturalized, as Hans von Köln in Spain became Juan de Colonia. Very frequently it is now impossible to distinguish the foreigners with any certainty.

Instead of thinking of Europe in the Gothic age as a patchwork quilt made up of the separate kingdoms and principalities, and divided by almost insurmountable barriers, we should imagine it as a relatively united and unified world in which, even in times of war, there was much travel and a general awareness of what was happening in Christendom as a whole. Nor was Christendom itself the limit of Western culture, for not only did science depend very largely upon retranslations of ancient authors made from Arabic versions, but a great deal of the mechanical invention of the period was brought from the Far East and ultimately from China. The contacts between Western Christians and Muslims, in Spain, in Sicily, and in the Levant, and the trade-route opened up across Asia by the friars and Marco Polo, were vital to the continued flow of ideas.

It can hardly be a mere coincidence that the technical revolution which ushered in the Gothic period in architecture was contemporary with the introduction to the West of Euclid's *Elements* in

translation by Adelard of Bath. Adelard travelled in Spain, Italy, and through North Africa and Asia Minor, lived for a time in Sicily, and had returned to England by 1130, when he was receiving a pension from Henry I. His translations and treatises, based on the works of classical and Arabian philosophers, formed the foundation of modern science, and were soon reinforced by the productions of the school of translators of Toledo, whence versions of Aristotle made from the Arabic were issuing about 1150. Thus it is that a new art coincided with a new outlook and a phase of renewed learning. The Gothic cathedrals expressed in concrete form far more than their Carolingian or Romanesque predecessors.

One of the profound changes which most clearly separates the quality of Gothic art from the Romanesque is an emphasis upon individuality. It is true that some degree of individual quality in design can be recognized at all periods, yet in certain cultures such as the Byzantine it was subordinated to strict adherence to rules and formulae. This implies that in the Byzantine world, as to a lesser degree in the Romanesque period in western Europe, ancient tradition was recognized as something on a higher level than what could be attained by modern man on his own. A startling reversal of outlook comes in with the Gothic style: no canonical rules bound the new art within a straitjacket, and the masters exhibited their powers of invention to the full, though borrowing ideas from one another. Instead of slowly running down, propelled by the stored momentum of a former Golden Age, art began to be activated from within and to gather speed as it took on a form radically different from anything hitherto seen. The responsible masters, furthermore, were recognized as persons of outstanding distinction, and during the 12th century signatures of individual artists abound. We cannot now identify the earliest generation of Gothic designers by name, but the separate styles of many men have been recognized.

Mason's Marks

Perhaps only a sculptor, but possibly also an architect, was the first great individualist in 12th-century art, the Gislebertus who signed the tympanum of the western portal of St Lazarus at Autun. Gislebert, as has been shown by Professor George Zarnecki, worked at Vézelay as well as Autun, and had probably trained on the works at Cluny; his *floruit* can be put at c.1115–40, the very moment when Gothic elements (such as the sharply pointed arcades of Autun) make their first appearance in the West. Among the craftsmen who worked on the Royal Portal of the west front of Chartres Cathedral, in about 1145–50, was a *Rogerus artifex* who likewise signed his work, and who had very likely worked previously on Abbot Suger's church at St-Denis. From its opening years, the Gothic period was an age, not of anonymity, but of sharply defined and emphasized identity.

A particular sign of identity, parallel to that afforded by heraldry among the knightly class but without social significance, was the mason's mark. Found from remote antiquity down to modern times, the banker-marks or personal signs indicating that a particular mason cut a specific stone are of frequent occurrence in the Gothic period. Such marks are quite distinct from the position-marks, generally numerals of some kind, cut upon stones prepared at the quarry to enable them to be erected according to a diagram, course by course. The banker-mark indicates individual responsibility for work done, and is most often found where very numerous masons, strangers to one another and to the master in charge, were brought together to carry out some large operation. Some marks, and especially those of the late Romanesque and Transitional periods, were very simple, and must have been allotted again and again to gangs of men. At a given job marks of this simple kind, crosses and stars, were enough to distinguish the output of one man from that of another; but duplication of a mark must have been frequent, and have led to confusion. Later it seems that there was some degree of official control among masons, for in 1844 members of the British Archaeological Association were told by one of the elder masons at Canterbury Cathedral that his own mark had belonged to his father and grandfather before him, and that 'his grandfather had it from the lodge'. It was also stated that when a stranger joins in work with other men, one of whom has a mark similar to his, the 'foreigner' 'has to apply

p 84
(4, 5)
p 100
(63)
p 101
(68)

p 28, 29
(30–33)
p 66, 67

p 284 (5)

p 91 (30)

p 182 (6)

f 9

to his lodge for a fresh mark', but on leaving that set of workmen may resume his former sign. This evidence of traditional usage is important, and helps to explain the observed facts. In many cases it appears that marks similar but not identical (that is, 'differenced' like heraldic charges) were adopted by members of the same family or by pupils of a master. Very few marks, however, can be attached to the names of their users, and no written register of marks seems to have survived from the Middle Ages.

p 86 (14)

There is not much evidence to suggest that the masons' 'lodge' of the Middle Ages had any of the esoteric significance attached to the lodges of modern speculative Freemasonry. The lodge was a workshop and shelter, and might be a permanent building in which there was a floor-slab of plaster for setting out the details of the work, as well as a drawing office provided with trestle tables or drawing boards of some kind. Administratively, the 'lodge' was also a courthouse and the body of men assembled in it, under the control of the master mason, maintained discipline and upheld the regulations of the masons' craft. These are known from manuscripts which have come down from the 14th and 15th centuries, setting forth a traditional history of the mason's craft as well as the series of regulations known as the Articles and Points of Masonry. It is of interest that the traditional history, containing both mythical statements as to the earliest origins of the craft in Old Testament times, and the attribution of geometry to Euclid, can be traced back, as regards some of its elements, to the first quarter of the 12th century. This is what would be expected on the supposition that the beginning of the system of building organization was in fact the introduction of Gothic elements into western Europe.

p 83 (1)
p 85 (10)

Apart from the reference to Euclid and the equation of geometry with the mason's craft, the manuscripts state that the rise of masonry was due to 'great lords' children freely begotten' and forbid a master to take any apprentice born of bond blood. Even allowing for exaggeration, there can be no doubt that mediaeval masons enjoyed a relatively high social status, and that this tended towards the creation of an architectural profession, whose members were regarded as practising a liberal art rather than a base skill. High status was also implied by the mediaeval iconography of God the Father as Creator, designing the Universe with a pair of compasses: the concept of 'the Great Architect of the Universe' goes back far beyond the modern expression of the idea.

In various forms there was highly developed organization of the mason's craft in Europe. Throughout the Empire, and indeed beyond it, there existed a widespread jurisdiction under the control of the Master of the Strasbourg Lodge, with subordinate regions directed from Berne, Cologne, and Vienna, which extended its rule over the whole of Hungary as well as the Austrian duchies. There is positive evidence that congresses were held in the late 14th and 15th centuries, attended by representative masters from an area nearly 500 miles across. In such circumstances new fashions in architecture were rapidly carried over wide distances, and the revolutionary art of the Parler family, for instance, spread over the whole of central Europe within a century.

p 84
(2-5)

In France the mastery over the masons had been the subject of a royal grant before 1268, and in England the king's master mason certainly exerted considerable influence on style, even though he had no formal control over masons throughout the country. There were local assemblies of masons of some kind, and according to the early masonic constitutions these were presided over by civic officials, the sheriffs of counties or the mayors of towns. In 1305 Walter of Hereford, one of the chief masters of Edward I, was granted the continuance of his right to hold his 'free Court' over the workmen at Caernarvon Castle, with the fines for breaches of contracts made by the subordinate craftsmen. Though the direct evidence is scanty, it is sufficient to prove that mediaeval masons did not work in any anarchistic isolation.

p 140
(13)

The Birth of Gothic

The development of architecture through the period may be divided into three main phases. First, at the opening of the 12th century, came the elements of Gothic style and their gradual elaboration over a period of rather more than a century. Soon after the year 1200 there was a fully co-ordinated Gothic art particularly marked by the invention of windows with bar-tracery, probably first used by Jean d'Orbais at Rheims Cathedral during the generation following 1211, when the east end was begun. A century of classic poise followed, in which an international architecture reached its peak and produced perfected forms of cathedral, castle and palace, enriched with painting, stained glass, patterned tiles and figure sculptures. In third place came the segregation of national styles, corresponding in some measure to political divisions. True to her insular position, England led the way in this latest Gothic epoch, followed by Germany and by the kingdoms of the Peninsula. France remained, until almost the close of the Middle Ages, conservatively attached to the earlier international aesthetic, and only slowly incorporated into its tradition the highly enriched style of late or Flamboyant Gothic which, inspired by the ogee curves adopted in England near the end of the 13th century, became characteristic of building in Flanders and the Low Countries and was thence carried into Spain.

The characteristics of the Gothic style in Italy differ widely from those found elsewhere. Beginning at the south, influenced as it was by Byzantine and Saracenic factors, style in Sicily was so untypical that it cannot be considered here. In southern Italy true Gothic was an alien style, a direct importation of French or Spanish forms, while in central Italy around Rome and throughout the Papal States it might be said that Gothic never existed. Only in three northern provinces, Tuscany, Lombardy and Venice, were there genuinely Gothic styles, and their aesthetic qualities differed greatly from the norm accepted elsewhere in Europe. For this reason not much of the Italian architecture of the Middle Ages belongs to the main stream of artistic development. Where Gothic in general was tall and aspiring, that of Italy was low and spacious. Profoundly permeated by the survival of Roman forms of antiquity, Italian art could never acquiesce in the extension of length or height, the sharpness, the angularity of mediaeval buildings. The dome, usually rejected elsewhere, was accepted; external colour largely took the place of the play of light and shade upon mouldings. Only in Venetian Gothic did moulding and tracery play a full and rich part.

p 102-3
(69-74)

p 102
(70)

p 103
(72-74)

We have seen that the first sparks of the Gothic spirit, coming from the East, reached eastern France early in the 12th century, and that related constructional ideas had already reached England earlier still. Before 1150 architecture in a style recognizably Gothic in its elements existed at St-Denis, close to Paris; at Chartres Chathedral fifty miles away; and also in the Crusaders' church of the Holy Sepulchre at Jerusalem, over two thousand miles off at the far end of the Mediterranean. This architecture, consistently pointed in its arches and designed for ribbed vaults, may be contrasted with the essentially Romanesque and round-arched work hitherto current. As a complete church just beyond the point where Gothic as a style had begun, Sens Cathedral, built between 1135 and 1160, is of outstanding interest. It has further importance as the presumed place of origin of William of Sens, the French master brought to England to design the new choir of Canterbury Cathedral, begun by him in 1175-78 and continued, in more advanced style, by his assistant William the Englishman, from 1179 to 1184.

p 93 (40)
p 91
(29,30)

p 92 (32)

f 11

The early Gothic of the Cistercian Order, deprived by strict rule of adventitious decoration, can be seen at Pontigny (c. 1140–1210), and even better at Alcobaça in Portugal, where the great church of 1158-1223 survives entire. In Spain too, at the Old Cathedral of Salamanca, can be seen the remarkably successful achievement of a new aesthetic within a generation or little more of the arrival of the first elements of the new style. On a magnificent scale, in France itself, is the cathedral of Laon, begun soon after the middle of the 12th century and mostly built by 1205, though its east end was rebuilt and its towers never finished. The spreading wave of the new style reached England after the chaos of Stephen's reign had given place, in 1154, to the vigorous government of the Angevin Henry II. Within the next twenty years the elements of Gothic began to be seen in the western bays of the nave at Worcester, and in the aisleless nave of Ripon built for Archbishop Roger of York towards the end of his

p 57 (51)
p 56 (49)

p 85
(8, 9)

The choir of Le Mans Cathedral, seen in axonometric projection (i.e. as if looking up through the floor, so that both plan and elevation are seen together). Le Mans was begun in 1217 to a design closely modelled on Bourges (see p. 94), with tall piers and double aisles. But as building went on the architects incorporated ideas from Amiens and the nave of St-Denis, also in course of construction at the same time. The choir was finished in 1254 and the rebuilding went no further. The Romanesque nave still remains, in strong contrast to the Gothic east end. (10)

long episcopate (1154–81) and perhaps still later, under the mason Master Arthur, who flourished about 1190. To some degree under the influence of work done for the Cistercian Order these first attempts at insular Gothic remained transitional in character.

Romanesque elements were first completely abandoned at Wells Cathedral, designed in or soon after 1175 and largely built by 1192. Entirely distinct from earlier work in France, and from *f 12* the French style of Canterbury, the style of Wells preserves nothing of Norman solidity and massing, while exquisitely graceful carvings enrich capitals and bosses. At Wells a purely new aesthetic had made its appearance and scored its great triumph, before spreading through western England and South Wales, and across to the zone of English occupation in Ireland, *f 13* where Dublin had been taken in 1170. At Lincoln Cathedral also, where the choir and transepts were built in 1192–1200, there was a great advance beyond the Canterbury stage of work, and individual idiosyncrasies can be seen in the wall arcading and the strange ribbed vaults.

England, for the thirty-five years of Henry II's reign the centre of the strongest political organism of the West, had begun to achieve that mercantile hegemony of the western seas which she was to maintain for more than seven centuries. In research too England was entering upon a new era of primacy. In France itself the highest level of contemporary scholarship and culture was attained by John of Salisbury (c. 1115–80), an Englishman of Saxon descent (as Adelard of Bath had been), who became Bishop of Chartres. The life of such churchmen-courtiers was spent largely in travel and in the greater palaces of the kings and *p 104–5* princes of their time. Among such palaces Westminster is the *(76)* chief survivor, in respect of its great hall, and England can show too

the notable keeps built for Henry II at Newcastle-upon-Tyne (1171–77) and Dover (1180–91), by the engineer Maurice. Still greater was the castle built for Richard Coeur-de-Lion at Château-Gaillard in Normandy in 1197–98.

It was not only in England that the new tendency to eliminate Romanesque solidity and to reduce supports to slender dimensions took root. This modern trend is well seen in the ambulatory of Ávila Cathedral in Spain, built between 1160 and 1200. On the other hand, some greater churches retained the transitional style, harking back to Romanesque models which seem to peep through a Gothic veneer, and such a church, noble but conservative, is the old cathedral of Lérida in Catalonia, not built until 1203–78. A conservative adherence to much of the older style remained characteristic in France, where some degree of subservience to the Roman orders of architecture can long be noted, even in the new Chartres Cathedral begun after 1194. Still weighty and classical, Notre-Dame in Paris, begun in 1163, and the rebuilt Chartres lead on towards the more purely Gothic but still conservative Rheims (1211–90) and Amiens (1220–88). In the meantime a far more original solution of the problem of cathedral design had emerged at Bourges, begun in c. 1192. The architect of Bourges, while *p 94 (45)* adhering to the essential plan of Sens and Paris, broke away from *f 14* traditional treatment for the first time in France, and flung upwards immensely tall pillars surrounded by slender shafts. Though *p 95 (46)* this has the effect of reducing the triforium story to somewhat crushed proportions, the effect of soaring height appearing actually to be forcing itself towards heaven had been achieved. Of all the great cathedrals of the earliest true Gothic, Bourges is both the most original and the most successful in its internal effect. It was complete in essentials by 1225, and was followed by two others

Comparative plans of Gothic cathedrals, all drawn to the same scale. Approximate building dates are given for the main parts.

Canterbury: choir by William of Sens 1175–78 and continued at the east end by William the Englishman 1179–84; nave, 1379–1405, and cloister, 1379–1414, by Henry Yevele. (11)

Wells: choir, crossing and nave 1175–1260; Lady Chapel and chapter-house 1295–1319; west front completed 1365–1435 (see p. 99). (12)

Lincoln: choir, crossing and nave 1192–1253; Angel Choir 1256–80 (see p. 98). Both Canterbury and Lincoln illustrate the English predilection for extreme length and the characteristic double transepts. (13)

Bourges: whole church, except for parts of the west front, 1192–1266 (see p. 95). In marked contrast to the typical English plan, Bourges eliminates transepts altogether. (14)

50	0	50	100	150 FT.	
10	0	10	20	30	40 M

Gerona: east end 1312–47; nave 1416–1604. The change in plan between the two building periods at Gerona results in the dramatic contrast seen on p. 100. (16)

Vienna: choir 1304–40; nave 1340 onwards; net vault 1446. The tower is over the south transept. (15)

Toledo: choir; 1226–38; crossing finished by 1300; nave by 1400. (17)

Seville: whole cathedral (apart from Muslim tower of 1184–98) 1400–1498; Capilla Real 1551–75. The biggest in area of all Gothic cathedrals, see p. 106. (18)

Chief architectural sites of the 13th century. (19)

The first traces of this search for unity in bay design are seen in a church still largely Romanesque in character: the new choir of St-Remi at Rheims, built in the 1170s, with low arcades, a tall tribune, and a stunted triforium incorporated into the clerestory. No such four-storey work occurs in England, but within a few years the nave of St David's Cathedral in Wales similarly incorporated a triforium of small arches within a round-arched clerestory. The style of the Gothic features at St David's is clearly derived from Wells, not from France, and it was masons from Wells or the Bristol area who must have designed Christ Church Cathedral in Dublin. There, in the nave begun about 1213, was a fully Gothic design in which a triforium and a clerestory of adequate heights were integrated and given their full proportional value in the bay. The same scheme appeared in England at Llanthony Priory soon afterwards and at Pershore Abbey choir between 1223 and 1239; then at Southwell Minster in the period 1234–50. It is noteworthy that the strictly Gothic development of this unifying factor in design took place entirely within the West of England school, the least subject to direct influence from France and in fact showing virtually no details of French style.

In France itself, however, parallel development was taking place under the great king's mason Pierre de Montreuil, possibly the father of the Eudes de Montreuil already mentioned. In the rebuilding of St-Denis from 1231, clerestory and triforium were linked by vertical shafting and tall shafts detached from the wall were used by Pierre de Montreuil in such a way as to give an illusion of movement. This idea was exploited on the south-west tower of Coutances Cathedral, and later became the key-note of the extraordinary front at Strasbourg. Such exploitation of vertical members was one of the main features of mature Gothic, and was to lead in England to the invention of what is known as the Perpendicular style, the most individual and recognizable of all the national styles of late Gothic.

The 'Classic' Century

Before the coming of Perpendicular in England and of *Sondergotik*, its German derivative, another century was to elapse. It was in this hundred years, from the first third of the 13th century onwards, that the great culmination of the 'classical' Gothic style took place. In England, where the true Gothic had been ushered in at Wells, slender verticality reached a peak in the Lady Chapel of Salisbury Cathedral (1220–25). The rest of the cathedral followed without a break and was completed, except for the central tower and spire, by 1266. The nave of Lincoln Cathedral, where patterned vaulting of a perfected type appears for the first time, was built between 1220 and 1237, and its design was almost immediately adopted in the new presbytery at Ely, built between 1234 and 1250. A later phase of 13th-century English style, influenced to some extent by French models, begins with King Henry III's rebuilding of Westminster Abbey from 1245, and appears at Lincoln in the noble Angel Choir of 1256–80.

Developments on the Continent included the building of Siena Cathedral in Italy, in the half-century after 1226, and the start of work, in 1227, of the Metropolitan cathedral of Spain at Toledo. Though inspired by French models and perhaps laid out by a French master, the Martin mentioned by several documents, Toledo Cathedral initiated a Spanish type of greater church. Far less high than the French models, it shows the Peninsular tendency to spread in area and to proliferate in side chapels. On the other hand, León Cathedral is almost wholly French in character and was largely built between 1255 and 1277, when the master Enrique de Burgos died. He may well have come from France before 1235, when he had taken up the work of the cathedral there, already begun in 1221. Both at Burgos and at León, Enrique (Henri?) was succeeded by a Spanish master, Juan Pérez. As with the English Henry of Reyns (Rheims?), who worked for Henry III from 1243 at Windsor, Westminster and York, we have here an instance of the architect-mason who had control over jobs in widely separated places. Such men were a commonplace by the 1260s, when the Dominican friar Nicholas de Biard preached a sermon now famous in the annals of art history. Bishops, said de Biard, were like those master masons who, wearing gloves and holding a measuring-rod, say to others: 'Cut it for me this way',

p 92 (33)
f 10
p 93 (41)

which had learned its lesson: Le Mans, built in 1217–54, and Coutances in Normandy, built in the generation from about 1220 to 1250. Coutances, a cathedral strangely neglected by the historians of art, is probably the purest example of the early maturity of Gothic style, and has for its central lantern the noblest tower ever built. The massing and external composition of Coutances are superb, and it shares with the unfinished Le Mans the distinction, in its own period, of having been manifestly designed for architectonic effect, without as well as within.

French designs of the earlier 13th century include the cathedral of Meaux and that of Troyes, begun in 1208; further to the east lay Metz, where the nave of the cathedral was started in 1239–60 though not completed until 1348. The ambitious choir of Beauvais, probably designed by Eudes de Montreuil, the master who accompanied St Louis on crusade, was put up in 1247–72, but the vaults, the highest ever built (158 feet), collapsed in 1284 and restoration lasted another forty years, under a new master, Guillaume de Roy. The fall of Beauvais must have been a landmark in the progress of mediaeval masoncraft, empiric as it was: so notable a failure must have served as a valuable though costly lesson. The general design of Beauvais was echoed at Cologne, where the first stone was laid in 1248, only one year later. At Cologne the vaults rise to 150 feet, and the whole project was eventually completed, though late in the 19th century. It is at Cologne that we see best the intentions of the architecture of St Louis and his age.

The first Gothic cathedrals had accepted the general character of Romanesque internal design: the division into three heights, of arcade, triforium, and clerestory. Characteristic of the 13th century was the attempt to reorganize this pattern to produce greater unity of effect. One early way of trying to achieve unity was to include the triforium in a tall arcade, as was done in the nave of St Frideswide's, Oxford, between 1158 and 1180. A similar design is found at Glastonbury Abbey, but its awkwardness must have been apparent, and future efforts were directed towards the incorporation of the triforium in the clerestory, and the linking of the horizontal stages by continuous vertical members. Both in France and England this search for unity was proceeding in the late 12th and early 13th centuries.

p 98
(57, 58)
p 92 (34)

p 92 (35)

p 98 (59)
p 103
(72)
f 17

doing no labour yet getting higher pay. In another discourse he challenged those prelates who worked by word alone, like the chief masters then usual at great buildings, who ordain by word, rarely or never set their hands to the work, and are paid more than anyone else.

By this time we know the names of a large proportion of the great architects responsible for the outstanding churches, castles and royal palaces of Europe. Salisbury was begun by Nicholas of Ely; the nave of Wells completed by Adam Lock (who died in 1229) and its glorious west front carried out by Thomas Norreys and the sculptor Simon; at Durham the eastern Chapel of Nine Altars was built by Richard Farnham from 1242; Master Sampson was engaged at Ely between 1240 and 1274; the architect of Lichfield was one Thomas at the time the transepts were built and the chapter-house designed, in 1220–50; at Lincoln and at Worcester the works were controlled by the great master Alexander, who succeeded at Lincoln to one Michael, and was in his turn replaced by Simon of Thirsk, who built the Angel Choir. At Cologne the original architect of 1248, a man obviously very well-informed as to French work at Amiens and Beauvais, was Master Gerhard. His contemporary in France, Jean des Champs, trained on the building of the Sainte Chapelle at Paris, went south to start a new cathedral at Clermont-Ferrand in 1248, and thus opened a fresh chapter in the history of French Gothic style.

In the south of France the character of the greater churches had hitherto differed greatly from the northern style of Normandy, Paris and Champagne. Wide churches of a single span, or of hall type, with aisles of equal height, and sometimes buttressed by ranges of side chapels, were normal in the whole of the southern regions bordering on the Mediterranean and in the centre of the country. Starting with Clermont-Ferrand and pushing on to Limoges (begun in 1273), to Narbonne and the choir of Toulouse, both started in 1272, and to Rodez, whose cathedral was begun

five years later, Jean des Champs carried the new wave of design to the limits of the country. Meanwhile, in the north, still further advances in style were being made in the transepts of Amiens (c. 1270–88) and the splendid west front of Rheims, built by Bernard de Soissons between about 1255 and 1290. In what was then western Germany, the designs for Strasbourg were being made, and its west front begun in 1276. Though greatly influenced by French precedents, all the Strasbourg masters were Germans: Rudolf the elder, who was building the south transept in the 1230s and the nave between 1250 and his death in 1276; Erwin von Steinbach, who built the front to the top of the great rose window in 1276–1318; and his sons and nephews who completed the towers by 1365. The northern steeple, added later in the period of *Sondergotik*, was likewise carried out by Germans, Ulrich von Ensingen who built the octagon (1399–1419) and Johann Hültz, who finished the spire in 1439.

Diverging Styles

By the last decade of the 13th century a great turning-point had been reached. Gothic style had until that time been entirely dominated by the inventions of masters who either worked in France or had their origins there. To this there is a partial exception in the early Gothic of the English West Country school, sharply independent of the French introductions at Canterbury, Chichester or Lincoln. It must be remembered too that there were two utterly different ruling styles within France itself: that of the north, too commonly regarded as the only 'Gothic', and the very different and more spacious style of the south and west, with related works in Italy, in eastern Spain and, occasionally, in England, as at the Temple Church choir in London finished in 1239. French masters travelled to England and across Europe; to northern Scandinavia and to southern Italy; to Spain in the west and to Cyprus and Palestine in the east. Villard de Honnecourt's

p 96 (50)
p 97 (55)

99 (61)
98 (59)
f 21

The great complex of Westminster Abbey and Palace goes back to pre-Conquest times. Edward the Confessor's Abbey was rebuilt by Henry III. East end (a) and transepts (b) date from 1245–69; nave (c) from 1377–1539. Henry VII's Chapel (d) was added about 1503–19. The monastic layout, of various dates, included: the cloister (e), chapter-house (f), abbot's lodging (g), refectory (h), dormitory (j) with its latrines (k), infirmary cloister (l), with its own chapel (m), and the now-vanished sacristy (n). St Margaret's church (o) was built in 1488–1523. The Palace was a rambling collection of buildings clustered round Westminster Hall (p), which was flanked on the north by exchequer buildings. To the east lay St Stephen's Cloister (q) and Chapel (r); then to the south the White Hall (s), Painted Chamber (t) and Queen's Chambers (v). A wall surrounded the Palace, with the Jewel Tower (w) and Great Gateway (x) at the two west corners. Close to the eastern side ran the Thames, reached by a landing stage (y). In the north wall is the famous clock-tower (1365–67), the first really public time-piece in England. (20)

0 100 150 200 FT

0 10 20 30 40 50 M

The choir of Narbonne was begun in 1272 but little was done before the arrival of Jean Deschamps in 1286. Although basically in the 'classic' style of Amiens and Rheims, Narbonne displays certain innovations which show that the conventions were by no means rigid. Work here continued until 1319. (21)

known journeys took him from St-Quentin in Picardy to Laon and Rheims, to Lausanne in Switzerland and across Austria to Hungary and back.

England, which in Norman times had excelled France itself in the number and scale of its churches and castles, built for the energetic dynasty of the Conqueror, had descended into political anarchy by the time that early Gothic was making its appearance. After fifty years in which England was a leading power, another political eclipse set in under King John, whose loss of Normandy in 1204 led to a long period of French ascendancy. Hence, for much of the 13th century, English architectural design took second place to developments in France, while it was the renewed domination of the West by Edward I (1272–1307) that saw England once more able to forge ahead and to take the lead, this time decisively, not only for herself but in respect of the course to be taken by architecture over most of Europe for the next two hundred years. As at the opening of the Romanesque and Gothic

periods, a new age of development began with the arrival of fresh ideas brought from the East. During the 13th century the appalling menace of the Mongol hordes had swept westward and then receded, to be replaced by at first uneasy and then relieved relations between the West and the immense and peaceful dominions of the Great Khan. Once more the products of Oriental invention were brought to Europe by merchants and returning travellers. The Mongols, broad-minded pagans, were seen as a field of missionary activity and as allies against the Muslims.

The western dominions of the Mongols, centred in Persia, were ruled by a viceroy called the *ilkhan*, and Arghun, *ilkhan* from 1284 until 1291, cultivated relations with the Christian states and sent embassies to the West, including one which reached London in 1289. Edward I sent a return mission to Persia under Sir Geoffrey Langley, who had been on crusade with him in 1270–74, and this mission went by way of Constantinople and Trebizond to Tabriz in 1292, returning in the following year. In that same

Section through the choir of Bristol Cathedral. The aisles are practically the same height as the centre (i.e. a 'hall-church' design, much commoner in Western France and Germany than in England) and the thrust of the main vault is carried across the aisles on masonry bridges, producing the complicated interpenetration of spaces shown on p. 92, pl. 37. The twisting ribs of the vault, the restless tracery of the east window and the concave curves of the 'star recesses' all contribute to the same effect. Remembering the innovations of St Mary Redcliffe (figs. 23, 24) and the spectacular skeleton vault of the vestibule to the Berkeley Chapel (p. 92, pl. 36), it is clear that in the first half of the 14th century Bristol was in the vanguard of architectural development in Europe. (22)

year, 1293, Christian missionaries from Italy reached China, and in 1295 Marco Polo with his father and uncle returned safely to Venice from Peking. That such contacts with the East actually affected western buildings is shown by the instance of the great hall of the Palazzo della Ragione at Padua, designed by Frate Giovanni, an Austin friar, in 1306. He had travelled widely in Europe and Asia and 'brought back plans and drawings of all the buildings he had seen'. Among his drawings was one of the roof of 'a great palace in India beyond the sea', which Brother Giovanni used as his model in designing the enormous timber roof at Padua, which covers an area of 240 by 84 feet.

The embassy of Sir Geoffrey de Langley included a certain *Robertus sculptor*, who may well have been another artist equipped with a sketchbook. Certain it is that during the last years of the 13th century new motives in pattern appear in England, and closely resemble Persian diaperwork. The ogee arch, formed of S-curves, was also exploited in England before 1300, and was probably used still earlier in Venice. That a form so characteristic of later Gothic should be found in western Europe at first precisely in Venice and in England strongly supports the derivation of the motive from those Oriental contacts which were common to both mercantile societies. The unusual north doorway of the porch of St Mary Redcliffe at Bristol, paralleled in the West only by the related polygonal openings in Bristol Cathedral and at Berkeley Castle, and dating from not later than the first quarter of the 14th century, is the most notable instance in the whole of western Europe of the impact of Oriental ideas before the arrival of the Portuguese Manueline style (1495–1521) incorporating motives from the Indies. At Bristol the Redcliffe porch is itself a hexagon in plan, echoing the dominant polygon found in the new style of diapered pattern, and also the plan of the Eleanor Cross at Waltham, built in 1291–94.

The possibilities of the ogee curve in unifying the dissociated circles of geometrical tracery patterns were soon realized, and a widespread use of 'reticulated' tracery in windows and as decoration was the result. This style had a vogue of some fifty years in England before it was driven out by the advance of the Perpendicular style, but it was taken up on the Continent and, in France and Flanders, was still further developed into the twisted and writhing shapes described as *flamboyant*. To this extent the later course of the Gothic style in Europe, even in France itself, was determined by events in England. In England, however, a change of a profoundly different kind was shortly to take place, the invention of the Perpendicular style. This, though like all other styles based upon and influenced by its forerunners, must be regarded as a specifically new creation, produced about 1330 by William Ramsey, a master mason from a Norwich family who was in time to be the king's chief mason south of Trent, from 1336 until he died in London during the Black Death of 1349.

The English Contribution

Perpendicular made its first appearance in or very soon after 1330. The simplicity and even starkness of the new style, its rigid verticals and horizontals, have often been attributed to poverty and lack of skill subsequent to the Black Death of 1348–49, when so many of the older generation of artists died. It is now quite certain that no such causal connection could have existed, for the essential features of the new style were in being quite fifteen years before the pestilence. The earliest signs of Perpendicular motives are related to reticulated pattern, which comes to be laterally compressed so that each reticulation tends to develop, instead of continuous curves, straight vertical sides. This process in design is seen first in works with which William Ramsey was associated, the south cloister of Norwich Cathedral designed about 1324, and the new cloister and chapter-house for St Paul's Cathedral in London begun by him in 1332. On a grand scale the motive appears in the south window of the transept of Gloucester Cathedral. The transept, built in c. 1331–36, had not otherwise employed this specific motive, which seems to be a stylistic afterthought, to be dated not earlier than c. 1335.

Whence, at this time, could ideas have reached England that would so far tend away from the main line of Gothic progress? Again, it seems likely that the inspiration came from the East.

Margin references:
f 23
96 (52)
f 24
96 (49)
96 (50)
f 25–32
96 (51)
f 26
f 29
f 30

Plan and view of the north porch of St Mary Redcliffe, Bristol. Built c.1320–30, its design is unusual in several respects. The hexagonal plan is a symptom of a new feeling for space, characteristic of the Decorated style (Ely octagon was planned at the same time); the vault inside is also hexagonal but is not placed in line with the walls—an angle of the vault meets a side of the wall, and vice versa. The strange profile of the doorway is almost certainly due to Eastern contacts. More familiar Decorated motifs are the 'nodding' ogees under the gables and the swarming naturalistic foliage. (23, 24)

10 ... 0 ... 10 ... 20 FT
0 ... 5 ... M.

The evolution of the Perpendicular style. The reduction of Curvilinear tracery to straight hexagons is foreshadowed in Islamic architecture, such as the tomb of Mustafa Pasha in Cairo (25). Travellers from Europe are known to have visited the the Muslim states at this time: a Robert 'sculptor' went to Turkey and Persia in 1292 and two Franciscans, one of them an artist, to Cairo and Palestine in 1323. Some of these travellers may well have brought back sketchbooks.

One of the key figures in the development of the new style is William Ramsey of Norwich. His Curvilinear tracery in the south cloister of the cathedral (26)—see also p. 96—contains the germ of Perpendicular. In 1322–36, the new choir of Ely (27) shows a similar trend, and the arches are placed within rectangular frames. The Lady Chapel (28) introduces vertical mouldings rising to the top of the frame, (in this case rising from the tops of two ogees and penetrating the larger ogee above them), giving the wall a panelled treatment. In 1332 Ramsey was working in London on a new chapter-house and cloister (29) for St Paul's, and used straight vertical lines even more emphatically. The three windows at the bottom of the page show the final fulfilment of these promises. The south transept window of Gloucester (30) was built about 1335. Although the main lines of the tracery are curved the rectilinear treatment of the St Paul's cloister appears at the top, where the shapes are almost regular hexagons. The east window of Wells (c. 1335–39) (31) uses the same idea in a modified way, while in the great east window of Gloucester (after 1337; probably after 1351) it is completely assured (32). The style perfected here remained essentially unchanged in England until the Renaissance.

Mihrab wall from the tomb of Mustafa Pasha, Cairo. 1269–73. (25)

South cloister of Norwich Cathedral, by William Ramsey. c. 1324. (26)

Choir of Ely Cathedral. 1322–36. (27)

Lady Chapel, Ely Cathedral. c. 1330. (28)

Cloister of Old St Paul's, by William Ramsey. Designed 1332. (29)

East window of Wells Cathedral. c. 1335–39. (30)

South transept window of Gloucester Cathedral. c. 1335. (31)

East window of Gloucester Cathedral. c. 1351. (32)

Something very closely akin to the earliest 'squeezed hexagons' of Perpendicular tracery is found in Muslim buildings in Egypt dating from the early 13th to the early 14th century. Associated with other features of Perpendicular character, such as vertical members running up to cut the curve of an arch, these forms are

f 25 found in Cairo in the Mausoleum of Mustafa Pasha (1269–73). That pilgrims, including artists, were visiting Egypt within the relevant period is shown by the itinerary of Simon Simeon and Hugh the Illuminator, Franciscans from Ireland who went to the Holy Land in 1323. It is not without interest that the unique manuscript of this narrative first belonged to Simon Bozoun, prior of Norwich in 1344–52, and though such a travel-book could not itself have influenced the course of art, it may be significant that documents of this kind were collected at major cathedral monasteries like Norwich.

The English Perpendicular style was never adopted outside its own country, apart from a few buildings designed by English architects in Scotland, Ireland and Calais. Two slightly earlier developments were, however, exported. One of these was the 'babewyne' or grotesque animal carved or painted, apparently an English speciality of the first generation of the 14th century. Where such grotesques are found abroad, they seem usually to be the work of travelling English artists, as in the case of Santes Creus in Catalonia, where the remarkable series of carvings in the cloister was made in 1332–41 by an English mason called 'Reinard Fonoll' (Reginald Fenell?). Fonoll's works in Spain are completely English in style and fully confirm the statement in the records that he was from England; what is more, he arrived in Spain about 1321, and immediately practised in a style that would have been up-to-date at home. It is astonishing to find similar babewyneries engraved in metal at Mosul in Iraq by 1333, the date of the 'April bowl' preserved at Konya, a gift to the mother-house of the Whirling Dervishes. Possibly another English artist, captured when on pilgrimage, executed the work while a prisoner of war.

A more important part was played by English inventions in vaulting. The original ribbed vault, characteristic of the first Gothic buildings, had consisted of a single pair of diagonal ribs, crossing each other at the centre of the bay. In France this form of vault was retained until near the close of the Middle Ages, though alongside other forms, some of which had a regional derivation outside the area of the main stream of Gothic style. Thus the domical vaults of western France, originating in the Angevin dominions, differed not only in their centre rising high above the lateral and transverse arches limiting the bay, but in having intermediate ribs. These additional ribs ran along the vault and across it at right angles, making angles of 45° on plan with the main diagonal ribs and thus splitting up the vault-surface into eight sectors. Further subsidiary ribs were added later, by the opening of the 13th century.

It seems certain that English architects, aesthetically attracted by the patterns formed by such a multiplicity of ribs, deliberately adopted them for the sake of pattern. At Lincoln by the end of the 12th century the choir vault had a longitudinal rib along the ridge, and this feature was adopted at Worcester by 1224 and was thereafter a mark of English influence. Additional (tierceron) ribs begin

2 (34) with the Lincoln nave vault designed about 1225–30 and soon
2 (35) afterwards appeared in the south transept at Lichfield and the presbytery of Ely. Already English enrichment of vault surfaces had gone far beyond what was customary abroad, but early in the 14th century it underwent a further development. Vaults deliberately designed to form patterns were being produced before 1320.

The patterns can be classified under two main headings: the star-vault, in which additional short ribs were introduced between the main ribs to produce star shapes; and the net-vault, in which the ribs of the vault itself were interrupted so as to form lozenges and triangles, often breaking the continuity of the ridge-ribs and transverse ribs. The earliest star-vault known seems to be that in the crypt of St Stephen's Chapel in Westminster Palace, built about 1320, while net-vaults were used in the extraordinary hall-choir of

f 22 Bristol, begun about 1311. Later in the 14th century came the exclusively English fan-vault perhaps first in the chapter-house
p 104 at Hereford, now ruined, and then in the cloisters of Gloucester,
(75) about 1370.

Cross-section of the choir of Prague Cathedral. It was begun in 1344 under a French architect Mathieu d'Arras, who had worked previously at Avignon. After his death in 1352 it was continued by Peter Parler who, in the side chapels and upper parts, introduced new ideas in his own characteristic style. A view of the triforium and clerestory is shown on p.108. (33)

0   10   20 FT.
0   5 M

A fourth English peculiarity in vaulting was the skeleton-vault, in which the vault itself with its attached ribs was supported upon a separate series of detached ribs comparable to the frame of an umbrella. First found on a very small scale in the miniature Easter Sepulchre in Lincoln Cathedral, built about 1300, such flying-ribs appear only a few years later in the vestibule to the Berkeley *p 92 (36)* Chapel at Bristol, and on a large scale in the choir vault of St Mary's, Warwick, dateable to 1381–91. Both the net-vault and the skeleton-vault were copied by German masters of the 14th century, and became integral parts of the new style of Continental practice carried across central Europe by the architects of the Parler dynasty. The masterwork of this school was to have been the cathedral of Prague in Bohemia, begun in French style by Mathieu d'Arras in 1344–52, and then continued under Peter *f 33* Parler. The great south front of 1396–1420 contains a porch with skeleton-ribs and the details in many respects indicate their derivation from English practice.

Achievements of Gothic Maturity

During the later Middle Ages a certain few monuments of grand scale and quality dominated the scene and were widely imitated. Imitation was doubtless in part unconscious, but was largely due to a deliberate practice of copying. Patrons wished their own building to be modelled on some existing work which they could inspect, but they wished their own to go one better. This constant emulation led to continuous refinements upon a limited number of basic designs. It was during the 14th century that the great models were set up. For central Europe, apart from the immense influence exerted by Cologne and by Strasbourg there was a more southern centre at Freiburg-im-Breisgau, where the church steeple was built c.1310–50. This fine tower formed the basis of many designs throughout southern Germany and Switzerland. The ambulatory of Freiburg (1354–60), designed by Hans Parler, the brother of Peter, was another epoch-making work in its region, and showed characteristics which were parallel to those of English Perpendicular, though without its detail. Another kind of German church, a hall comparable to the choir of Bristol Cathedral but with very tall windows (like those of the Lady Chapel at Lichfield) and moulded piers and arches without capitals, is the Wiesenkirche at Soest in Westphalia (1331–76), by Johann Schendeler.

In Spain the 14th century saw much activity, especially in the kingdom of Aragon and Catalonia. Barcelona Cathedral was begun in 1298 and the transept completed by 1317; in the next 12 years the chevet was built under the great master Jaime Fabre, who was probably responsible also for the impressive cathedral at Palma in Majorca and for the great parish church of Sta María del Mar at Barcelona (1329–83). At Gerona work began in 1312 at the east end under a mason named Enrique, but the notable design for the church as a whole, with its nave of a single span, belongs to Jacques Favran of Narbonne, who was in charge from 1320 to 1347. The nave was not in fact built until after 1416, when an architectural conference had been held, attended by twelve masters from places as distant as Narbonne, Urgel, Tarragona and Tortosa. The old cathedral, La Seo, at Saragossa was rebuilt between 1316 and 1412, and important works were in progress at Valencia in 1330–60. But two of the most exquisite gems of small-scale design are the little cathedrals of Orihuela (1305–55), and Tortosa (1345–1441), begun by Benito Dalguayre.

In France, where the 14th century brought civil discord and then chronic war with England, the architectural leadership of the West was lost. Yet a substantial amount of important work continued,

notably the building of the old royal palace of the Louvre, begun in 1362 under Raymond du Temple, one of the greatest of French architects and founder of a dynasty. Throughout the century, and until the end of the Middle Ages, the most significant continuous centre of building activity was the abbey of St-Ouen at Rouen, where the choir was built in 1319–39, perhaps to the design of Jean Camelin. Many details of St-Ouen served as pace-setters for the last two centuries of Gothic style, and show for how long the capital of Normandy retained its artistic vigour.

It may be said of the second half of the 14th century that it witnessed the climax of European art. The search of the artists for an underlying unity was rewarded, in the best works, with success. The sense of strain, so marked in earlier work, is no longer noted, and the greater buildings breathe a spirit of confidence and demonstrate the supremacy of achievement of which their authors were capable. Not only had individual buildings acquired artistic unity, but every part and detail was so subtly proportioned to the whole, and to human scale, that it gives the impression of a work of nature rather than of human striving. A quality of glory—not secular pomp, nor elaboration of enrichment—informs the greatest architecture and the attendant carvings, paintings, embroideries and other minor arts which joined together as if in some orchestral symphony.

This quality, itself perhaps of Eastern inspiration, is marked in the buildings of Venice that so aroused the enthusiasm of John Ruskin. The work which could be carried out for the patrician patrons of a city-state unique in history, endowed with continuity of tradition, direct links with Byzantium and with the centres of world activity such as Cairo, and enormous wealth, enabled secular architecture to show to advantage. Elsewhere it is mainly in the churches that we must seek for the finest flights of Gothic enterprise; but in Venice it is the dwelling, the mansion, the palace that take the palm. The magnificent water front of the Doge's Palace was begun in 1343 by Pietro Baseggio, and finished in 1404, thus spanning the period of two generations which marked the culmination of this refined yet rich, splendid and vigorous art.

The origin of the national English style, Perpendicular, has already been described; but something more must be said of the

Chief architectural sites of the 14th century. It will be seen that by this time there was Gothic activity over the whole of Europe except for the Balkans and Russia, where the Eastern Orthodox Church maintained the Byzantine style. (34)

The choir of Gloucester Cathedral, showing how the Norman structure was faced, in the mid-14th century, with a grid of Perpendicular tracery, completed by a huge new east window and lierne vault. It is here that the new style—beginning probably in London—finds its first mature expression. The tracery grid obscures the old division into arcade, gallery and clerestory, and the effect is to make the whole chancel into one great room. Behind the grid, in the aisles and triforium gallery, the Norman work is untouched. (35)

amazing outburst of art which accompanied the resurgence of England as a great European power. Unusual and even exotic themes, such as the octagon of Ely Cathedral, made their appearance during the first half of the century. There, the immense timber vault and lantern of 1328–40 were the work of William Hurley, one of the greatest of English carpenters, brought from London to design and supervise the works. Edward III completed and embellished the royal chapel of St Stephen at Westminster, and surrounded himself with architects and artists of the highest standing. Later in the century there came a second crop of noble works, largely the product of these royal artists or of their provincial pupils and associates. The grandiose state apartments of Kenilworth Castle, built for Edward's son John of Gaunt between 1372 and 1395, set a new trend in fashion, and the cathedrals and greater churches vied with one another to build and rebuild in the latest style. So at Canterbury the nave begun in 1379 was designed by the king's mason Henry Yevele, while that of Winchester, transformed for William of Wykeham from 1394, was the work of Yevele's colleague William Wynford, who had already designed Wykeham's two educational buildings, New College at Oxford and Winchester College, and was also architect to Wells Cathedral, where he designed the western towers. Yevele and the carpenter Hugh Herland renewed the great hall at Westminster in 1394–1400 where Herland's oak roof remains as the greatest single work of art of the whole of the European Middle Ages. No such combined achievement in the fields of mechanics and aesthetics remains elsewhere, nor is there any evidence for such a feat having ever existed. This amazing work owes its existence to the

99 (60)

p 186 (17)
99 (61)

p 104 (76)

taste and cultural energy of the King, Richard II, for whom the contemporary Wilton Diptych was painted, while Geoffrey Chaucer wrote his Canterbury Tales.

p 287 (15)

Though the new roof of Westminster Hall was the most remarkable work of its kind ever carried out, England had no monopoly of great halls, and had few civic buildings of notable size. Among the few worthy of mention is the London Guildhall, 153 feet long with a span of 49 feet, built in 1411–46 by the mason John Croxton. Comparison is interesting with Barcelona, another of the great maritime capitals of western Europe, where the Hall of the Hundred was built between 1373 and 1402. Just as the London Guildhall was a reduced version of the king's hall at Westminster, so this municipal chamber at Barcelona was a reduction in scale of the king of Aragon's Tinell in the Royal Palace, built in 1359–70 by Guillem Carbonell. The kingdom of Aragon produced many noble public buildings, including Exchanges in Barcelona (1380–92), in Valencia (1482–98) and at Palma in the island of Majorca (1426–48), the last a distinguished design by Guillermo Sagrera, who had been architect of Perpignan Cathedral in 1416 and later moved to Naples, where from 1450 onwards he was rebuilding the Castel Nuovo. Barcelona still possesses another remarkable building in the Hospital de la Santa Cruz, used until quite recently as a hospital but now the Central Library of Catalonia; its original buildings of 1401–15 remain structurally complete.

p 100 (64)

p 261 (47)

The later 14th century and the first years of the 15th century saw much activity on major building works. At all the main centres of Europe the Gothic style was producing much of its most

p 105
(80)
p 85 (7)

p 85 (6)

p 96 (52)

p 106
(82)
p 109
(91)
f 18

distinguished output. In England the west front of Beverley Minster (c.1390–1420) excelled almost everything previously done at the cathedrals. In 1392 the great western tower of Ulm on the Danube was started, though operations dragged on for just a century before leaving the work unfinished until modern times. As at Cologne and Strasbourg a succession of architects was responsible: Ulrich von Ensingen was the original designer, while the upper stage of the tower, built in 1474–92, was the work of Matthäus Böblinger, whose designs for the spire survived to permit ultimate completion. The steeple of St Stephen in Vienna, begun in 1399, was built with advice from Wenzel Parler, son of the great Peter, and completed in 1433 by Hans von Prachatitz, Peter Parler's pupil.

In Portugal the period was enriched by the noble monastery of Batalha, commemorating the battle in which independence was won. It was founded in 1387 and the first architect was Affonso Domingues, who built most of the church and began the cloisters before his death in 1402. Several features at Batalha are strongly reminiscent of English Gothic, and there is no doubt that the alliance between England and Portugal extended beyond the political field. In Spain the great undertaking of the 15th century was the construction of Seville Cathedral, the largest Gothic cathedral in the world and planned deliberately to be 'so great and of such a kind that those who see it finished shall think we are mad', as one of the Chapter said during consideration of the designs. The conclusion of the deliberations was expressed in a report that 'a new church shall be made so good that there shall be none its equal'. Seville is the great summation of Peninsular Gothic, borrowing ideas from Toledo, from Barcelona and from northern France. It seems probable that the architect was an expatriate Norman known in Spain as Carlín, but whose name was really Charles Gaultier, from Rouen. Likenesses of detail to the late 14th-century works in the Norman capital suggest that this must have been in fact the training-ground of the Seville designer.

Soon after the opening of the 15th century the political complexion of Europe changed for the worse. The Lancastrian usurpation of 1399 had set a bad tone in England, and was soon follow-

ed in Bohemia by the Hussite wars of religion. France was to be ravaged by the renewed outbreak of the Hundred Years' War. Though many great building works were in progress, some had to be suspended for long periods, as was the nave of Westminster Abbey; while Prague Cathedral was simply abandoned half-finished until the mid-19th century. Some churches of considerable importance were built in outlying areas of Gothic Europe, as in northern Germany, Scandinavia and the Baltic region. In central and southern Germany several parish churches of very large scale belong to the middle of the century: St Georg in Dinkelsbühl, built in 1448–92 by Nicolaus Eseler; the choir of St Lorenz in Nuremberg (1445–72) by Konrad Roritzer; and the brick Frauen-kirche in Munich (1468–88), designed by Jörg Ganghofer. In Hungary, St Elizabeth's Cathedral in Kassa belongs to the hundred years 1380–1480, while St Maurice at Olomouc (Olmütz) in Moravia is a hall-church spanning the years 1412–91.

p 101
(67)

The Rekindling Fire

Towards the end of the century, however, a new breath of energy swept across the scene. The embers of Gothic art were rekindled into a final blaze of glory which enriched every European country apart from the determinedly classical Italy. It would be impossible even to enumerate within a small compass the major churches alone, and only a selection of the most outstanding works can be mentioned. Between about 1480 and 1550 or even later, many of the most truly magnificent buildings of all time were erected, in England, in Flanders and the Netherlands, in Germany, Bohemia and Poland, and in Spain and Portugal. And while these greater monuments of church art were in progress, it must not be overlooked that castles, palaces, mansions, universities, colleges, guildhalls and other public and private secular buildings also formed part of the great and rich harvest.

At this time the dominance had passed to Flanders, or at least to the powerful Dukes of Burgundy who held sway over a great area of eastern France, geographically speaking, as well as over the whole of modern Belgium, Holland and Luxembourg, together with adjacent parts of north-eastern France. Within their dominions a rich style, based on that of late 14th-century France, but more

Chief architectural sites of the 15th century. The explosive energy of earlier centuries shows little sign of slackening, in spite of political and economic recession. (36)

Chief architectural sites of the 16th century. The retreat of Gothic to the north and west before the withering blast of the Renaissance from Italy can be clearly seen; but the intense vitality of Gothic is still marked, since this map reflects the activity of only fifty not of a hundred years. (37) ▶

opulent and at times overburdened with enrichment, came into being. At the giant cathedral of Antwerp, which had been started in 1352, the west front was built in 1422–74, and then the enormous tower of Rombaut Keldermans and Dominique de Waghemakere, finished in 1518. At Ghent the nave and tower of St Bavon were built between 1461 and 1533, while at Malines the outstanding feature is the vast but never quite finished tower begun in 1452 by Andries Keldermans, and continued by his son Antoon. In Holland the main influence came from Utrecht Cathedral whose tower of 1321–82 by Jan van Henegouwen was the model for several others, among them that of Breda (1468–1509). The great Dutch church of the end of the Middle Ages was the cathedral at 'sHertogenbosch, where the choir had been built in 1419–39. But the nave and the famous sculptures belong to the period 1478–1529, mainly under the direction of Alard van Hameel.

p 107
(84)

Flemish masters travelled to Spain and to England, and much of the vivid panash of late Gothic is undoubtedly due to them. They were not the only migrant influences, however, for as we have seen the western steeples at Burgos are due to a German mason from Cologne, and the later works completing the cathedral were designed by his son Simón and grandson Francisco de Colonia. Simón de Colonia built the chapel of Sta Ana (1477–82) and the pinnacled chapel of the Constable (1482–94) at the east end; while the central lantern, completing the composition of the whole building, was put up in 1540–68 under his son Francisco. Elsewhere in Spain the same architects were at work: Simón de Colonia began the cathedral at Astorga in 1471, to be continued between 1530 and 1559 by Rodrigo Gil de Hontañón. At Plasencia a vast new cathedral was started in 1498 by Enrique de Egas, to be continued under Francisco de Colonia and Juan de Álava in 1513–37. But the two greatest works of the last Gothic age in Spain were the new cathedrals of Salamanca, begun in 1512, and Segovia (1522), both by Juan Gil de Hontañón and continued by his son Rodrigo. In Portugal the two grand works were the convent of Thomar (1492–1513) by João de Castilho, who also completed the Jeronimos at Belém, begun in 1500. Possibly even more remarkable, as an example of the strange sculptural style named

p 100
(62)

Drawing for one bay of the screen round Bishop Fox's Chantry in Winchester Cathedral, probably by Thomas Bartu. Bartu (or Berty), born about 1485, was in charge of the Perpendicular remodelling of the eastern parts of Winchester. Still essentially a late Gothic master mason, he experimented with Italian Renaissance ornament in some of his later works (he died in 1555), though he relied on foreign workmen for the details. Below: Bartu's signature on a lease of 1543. (38, 39)

after King Manuel I (1495–1521), are the unfinished chapels at the east end of Batalha, begun in 1503–09 by Matheus Fernandes, one of the greatest examples of invention in architecture and a glory not only of Portugal but of Europe.

Architects of outstanding genius sprang up in all quarters. In Moravia the magnificent church of St James at Brno (Brünn), in course of construction from 1480 to 1552, owes most to Anton Pilgram, master from 1495 to 1515; while in Bohemia an extra-ordinary style of rococo Gothic, with curving vault-ribs and spacious vistas, was created by Benedikt Ried. Ried, author of the Vladislav Hall in Prague Castle (1493–1503) and the nave of St Barbara at Kutná Hora (c. 1540), may be considered the last Gothic genius of central Europe. Meanwhile there had been an Indian summer of Gothic art throughout the whole of the Baltic region and a Polish *flamboyant* style appears in the church of St Anne at Vilna (1516), and in the Jagellonian Library (1492–97) at Cracow, with cellular ribless vaults, found earlier in eastern Spain, and in this period also in Bohemia.

p 108 (88)

Returning to France, where the *flamboyant* style and enriched detail had at last taken root, we find notable architects once more at work. Several cathedrals were adding new fronts in the latest style, and the last of the great cathedral churches was begun at Auch by Jean Chesneau in 1489. St-Wulfran at Abbeville (1488–1539), St-Nicolas-du-Port in Lorraine (1494–1530) by Simon Moyset, and the church of St-Jacques-de-la-Boucherie in Paris, of which the noble tower survives (1509–23), by Jean de Felin, must stand for the greater churches. Secular building is exemplified by

William Vertue's amazing vault to Henry VII's Chapel, Westminster Abbey. One of the last glories of English Gothic (it dates from about 1515), this roof looks back to such 15th-century pendant vaults as that of the Divinity School at Oxford (see p. 186), but surpasses them all in daring and brilliance. Structurally the vault rests on strong transverse arches, of which the bottom parts are free-standing so that one looks through them, and the upper concealed above the fretted ribs in the centre. The pendants are really part of the transverse arches but they seem to hang unsupported from the intricate panelling behind and in front of them. The effect from below is seen on p. 105. (40)

the Palais de Justice of Rouen, designed by Roger Ango and Roulland le Roux (1499–1526). Le Roux also designed the central west front of Rouen Cathedral (1509–14), while his greatest rival, Martin Chambiges of Paris, was responsible for transeptal fronts at Sens (1494), Beauvais (1499) and the main front of Troyes (1502–31). It may have been Chambiges who inspired the last daydream of French Gothic: an immense steeple rising to 502 feet in height, over the crossing of Beauvais. The work was done by Jean Vast, son of an elder Jean Vast who worked under Chambiges; the spire was finished in 1569, but collapsed four years later. Vast lived to complete the necessary repairs to the church below, but the steeple was never rebuilt. The fire of Gothic aspiration had at last died down.

p 108 (86)

p 109 (90)

For a final glimpse of the style whose elements first appeared together at Durham about 1100, we return to England. The 'white robe of churches' of an earlier period was renewed once more in the terrific outburst of architectural exuberance which swept the country between the return from exile of Edward IV in 1471, and the dissolution of the last monasteries by Henry VIII in 1540. Among the host of masons and carpenters employed, a few stand out as men of profound genius. Such were John Wastell, designer of the great Bell Harry tower of Canterbury Cathedral (1493–1505) and of the eastern chapels of Peterborough Cathedral, under whom the magnificent chapel of King's College at Cambridge was completed (1508–15). The brothers Robert and William Vertue were the king's chief masons to Henry VII and Henry VIII, and jointly designed the new Bath Abbey of 1501–39, and Henry VII's Chapel at Westminster (1503–19). William Vertue also designed Corpus Christi College, Oxford (1512–18) and completed St George's Chapel at Windsor, of which he designed the west front (c. 1500–27). Along with William Vertue, who died in 1527, and his colleague Henry Redman, one of Cardinal Wolsey's architects, there worked the great carpenter Humphrey Coke, whose roof over the hall of Christ Church, Oxford, is the last triumph of English Gothic carpentry.

p 105 (77)

p 105 (79) f 40

Gothic had had its day: its complex systems of proportion made no appeal to the dilettanti of a new age, intoxicated with notions of Roman grandeur and suffering from an overdose of simplified Vitruvius. The will-of-the-wisp of spurious antiquity lured wealthy patrons away from those architects still learned in tradition, and substituted foreign patternbooks for the parchment skins and plaster tracing-floors which had displayed the living art of five hundred years. Religious fanaticism and material self-interest concluded an unholy alliance to destroy the outmoded art, and the great buildings became too often mere stone quarries from which pillaged materials might be drawn. Yet in spite of the enormous scale of destruction, starting in the middle of the 16th century and continuing for four hundred years until the present time, enough of the Gothic stones is left to bear witness. In sheer bulk of material shifted, in area covered, in space enveloped, it is evident that the Gothic age was pre-eminent among all the cultural epochs known, through recorded history and about the globe. This was the outcome of profound religious inspiration, however misguided it may sometimes have been. It is hard to justify the Crusades as an expression of the Christian spirit; but we must accept that among their consequences was the origin of the greatest art the world has yet seen. And in remembering the crusaders we may think also of their corps of engineers, recruited from among the most skilled artists and craftsmen then to be found in the West: sharing the danger and heat of the day, but still finding time and energy to make note of beautiful details or strange skills. To those that came back, bearing this harvest with them, we owe the greater and enduring harvest of the glorious world of Gothic art.

IV KINGS AND CASTLES

Court Life in Peace and War

CHRISTOPHER HOHLER

There were fair turrets fashioned between, with many loopholes well devised to shut fast. Gawain had never seen a better barbican. Further in he saw the hall rising high, with towers all about, whose pinnacles rose high aloft, with carven tops cunningly wrought. On the tower roofs his eye picked out many white chimneys that gleamed like chalk cliffs in the sunlight. And there were so many pinnacles, gaily painted, scattered about everywhere and climbing one above another among the embrasures of the castle, that it looked as though it were cut out of paper.'

SIR GAWAIN AND THE GREEN KNIGHT

The order of mediaeval society

was rigid and confining, but it varied from country to country and had a logic of its own. Problems of security and economics, in a period of almost constant, if small-scale, warfare, led to the evolution of feudalism, which was firmly established by the beginning, and well on the way to disintegration by the end, of what we call the Middle Ages. Society was generally divided into those who were free and those who were serfs, and these two classes were bound to each other by regulations, loyalties and mutual obligations sanctioned by tradition, the law, or both. The serfs who cultivated the land of their lord paid, by their labour, for military protection and life-long tenure, which was ownership in all but title. The lord, in his turn, was bound by mutual obligation to a higher noble; the highest rank of nobility was that of baron, and he, like those below him, was a vassal bound by similar allegiances to the highest of all, the king, who derived his financial and military support from the lords who held their properties in fief from him. All classes of this lay hierarchy, low and high alike, were required to fulfil certain military duties, but the true mediaeval warriors, who formed a class somewhat apart, were the mounted and armoured soldiers, the knights.

The dwelling of the landowner, whether baron or king, developed because he was regularly on duty or on his guard, into a domestic fortification, and the simple early towers and enclosures were improved upon until they became the elaborate and often highly original castles of the 12th to 14th centuries.

Military considerations demanded a castle large enough to house a substantial body of knights and their horses, and to store the food, provender and equipment they would need for period of weeks or months in case of siege; and some castles contained all the offices of community life within their walls. The primary consideration in their design and construction was defence, but they were also planned for peace-time habitation and included living-quarters appropriate to the owner's wealth and station.

In the later and more sophisticated age of castles, when their opportunities for display and splendour held an interest equal to, if not greater than, their military function, the French King, Charles VI, and his brothers the ducs de Berry and d'Orléans, commissioned or had rebuilt a great number, many of which, however, have been destroyed by the accidents of time. The duc de Berry's castle at Saumur is represented as it was in the late 14th century in one of the illuminations painted by the Limbourg brothers for the *Très Riches Heures* (opposite). It has the typical French round corner towers, machicolated battlements from which stones could be dropped on the attackers and the iron grills over the lower windows. The gateway, in the foreground, has a drawbridge evidently in working order. The oddly-shaped building to its left is the castle kitchen (compare the monastic kitchen on p. 52). Saumur was clearly capable of resolute defence, yet, with its crested battlements and tall gilt weather vanes, it might almost be the fairy-tale castle described in *Sir Gawain and the Green Knight*. (1)

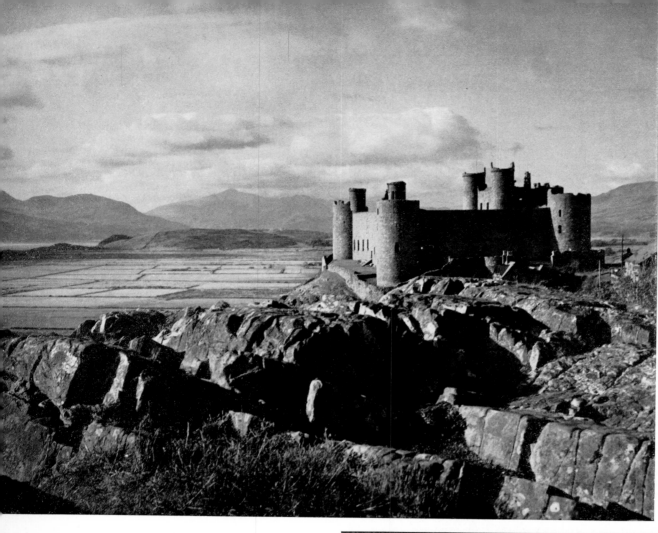

A great variety of forms can still be seen in the substantial remains of mediaeval castles. Harlech (left), grim and commanding on a rocky eminence in Wales, was one of a chain of stout fortresses built in the late 13th century, with the aid of architects from Savoy, during the reign of Edward I, after he had conquered North Wales. Approximately square in shape, with a system of double defence works, Harlech was very nearly impregnable. (2)

Gravensteen at Ghent (below), which dates from the late 12th century, was the residence of the Counts of Flanders. John of Gaunt was born here in 1340. This historic and dramatic castle, particularly famous for the Great Hall of the rectangular keep that rises in the centre, is surrounded by an unusually wide moat. (3)

Eltz on the Moselle (above) rises tall in a romantic setting of mountain and forest. Begun in the 12th century, this castle still belongs to descendants of the family that lived in it originally. (4)

Castel del Monte in Apulia (left), built in 1240, was one of several castles constructed in southern Italy for the Hohenstaufen Emperor, Frederick II. Characterized by its careful symmetry, as a perfect octagon with uniform towers, Castel del Monte was conceived as an imperial hunting residence rather than as a bastion of defence. The impulse of its architect was aesthetic and totally non-functional. A particularly interesting detail is the doorway, typical of classicizing trends in 13th-century building. (5)

The stronghold of Loches (below) in France shows an 11th-century rectangular keep, or *donjon*, within a high defensive wall. The keeled bastion in the foreground is characteristically French. This was one of the royal residences of Charles VII in the 15th century. (6)

Vincennes, just outside Paris, was Charles V's favourite castle and most of it was built in the 1360s during his reign. The square *donjon* with its round corner turrets (above) is the dominating feature of the castle, which admirably combined residential and military functions. (7)

The splendour of castles when they were newly-built and in active use can still be seen in contemporary paintings. The early 15th-century miniature (below) shows the Earl of Salisbury arriving at Conway Castle. Its distinctive feature, the bent rectangular hall, is the blue-roofed building within the walls. (8)

A French castle under siege: Mortagne (right), ▶ on the Gironde near Bordeaux, held by the English, was besieged at the end of 1377 by Owen of Wales, a soldier in French service. He is the man on the right of this 15th-century manuscript illustration with a dart in his breast, killed through the treachery of a countryman, John Lambe. The castle, surrounded by a moat, held out for more than six months. (10)

Poitiers and Vincennes (opposite, below) appear in the *Très Riches Heures* as backgrounds to peaceful activities such as sheep-shearing, reaping and the hunt. The triangular shape of the Lower Castle of Poitiers (there was also an Upper) is rare, though not unique, in castle-design, and may have been dictated by its site, a wedge of land between the Clain and Boivre rivers. The original castle of about 1200 was reconstructed by the duc de Berry in the 1370s. The towers of Vincennes (see pl. 7) were connected by a curtain-wall, hidden by the trees in the painting. (11, 12)

An Italian hill-fort in the desolate area south of Siena appears in the background of this fresco by the 14th-century Tuscan artist, Simone Martini (below). Guidoriccio da Fogliano, *capitano della guerra* on horseback, put down a brief rebellion against that city: hence the depiction of encampments and the catapult behind the castle wall. (9)

The ground-plans of castles

and their development are clarified by aerial photography. **Caernarvon Castle** (below) is the irregularly shaped enclosure on the left. Its walls are continuous with those of the borough founded at the same time. **Caerlaverock,** on the Scottish border (below, centre), was conceived on a triangular plan, like Poitiers (see pl. 11), and was protected by two ditches. **Beaumaris,** in Anglesey (bottom), one of several Welsh castles built for Edward I by Master James of St George, is one of the most extreme examples of symmetrical planning. The basic castle is a virtual square, with round towers at the corners and identical gatehouse blocks at the centres of two of the walls. This whole structure is surrounded by a lower skirting wall. Attackers could be fired at with crossbows, slings and catapults from the towers and the parapet of the inner wall, as these were higher than the skirt. (13, 14, 15)

Bodiam in Sussex (above) is a 14th-century castle built not by a king or nobleman, but by a knight, Sir Edward Dalyngrygg, enriched by ransoms obtained during the wars. Though planned in accordance with sound military principles, it is really an old soldier's dream-house and could never have played a significant part in a late 14th-century war. (16)

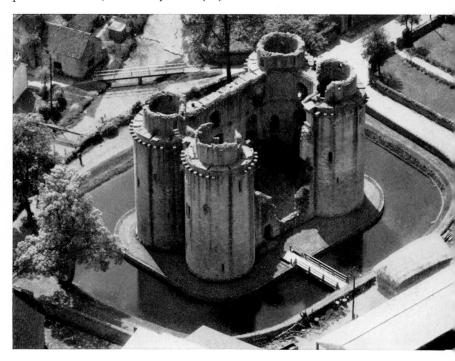

Nunney in Somerset (above) is another 'castle' built by an affluent knight, Sir John Delamare. Though it had towers and a moat, and all the appearance of an authentic castle, it was rather small to have accommodated a mounted garrison and had slight military significance. It is, indeed, little more than a handsomely fortified manor-house. (17)

Warkworth in Northumberland (right) is remarkable for the keep built about 1400 within an earlier enclosure. It is basically in the shape of a Greek cross with the corners filled in, the rooms being fitted into this complex shape with extreme ingenuity. Its principal feature was a Great Hall 41 feet long and two storeys high. (18)

Chepstow (above), at the mouth of the Wye in Monmouthshire, was laid out around the gigantic hall-keep as a military base for the conquest of South Wales in the 11th century. The 13th-century outer walls replace earlier palisades making full use of the lie of the land. In times of siege it could be provisioned by boat from the river. (19)

The Tower of London (below), the concentric castle *par excellence*, developed around the beautifully proportioned Norman keep in the centre; the walls and round towers went up in the 13th century, and the other buildings came later. The king had no residence in the City of London, but a royal garrison in the Tower could effectively assert his authority. (20)

Knighthood

was a military rank, independent of feudal land-tenure, of which the nearest modern equivalent is probably pilot-officer. It could originally be conferred by any responsible superior officer, baron, prince or king. By the 14th century it was in practice conferred by kings alone. In England it became obligatory for all above a certain level of income from land to become knights, but few of these were 'strenuous', i.e. genuine soldiers. Elsewhere it seems that all who were socially and financially entitled went through the motions of being 'strenuous knights', to the detriment of military efficiency. But a mystique of knighthood was built up by French poets and this was influential beyond the borders of France. In the course of the 13th century, if not before, all knights adopted distinctive devices, more or less hereditary, which they displayed on their shields, pennons or banners, and clothing. In the later Middle Ages these were supplemented in war by badges to show which leader the knight was serving under. At jousts they were often purely romantic, concealing rather than announcing the wearers' identity. A very remarkable shield of this kind (right), probably never actually used, shows a knight kneeling before his lady. *Vous ou la mort* reads the scroll: hence death in the background. (21)

Sir Geoffrey Luttrell (below), a knight of Lincolnshire in the early 14th century, is shown in full array, in this illumination from the Luttrell Psalter. He is being seen off by his wife and daughter-in-law. (22)

Girding with the sword was the essential ceremony of knighting, but how far the presence of a priest was required is difficult to discover. Top: *Coment Viviens fu fais chevalier*, from a manuscript of the *Chansons* concerning Guillaume d'Orange. Above: the knight receives his sword from the king in a miniature from a late 14th-century manuscript. (23, 24)

'I am the symbol of an armed knight ▶ of Prato . . . Look upon the face of your subject people.' The manuscript (right) is a 14th-century address by the people of Prato to their protector, Robert of Anjou, King of Naples. The 'chief' (top portion of the knight's shield) stands for Naples. (25)

fecit

Clausa iubet qp sic in equo rex stem imo sessor
Militis armati signum sum namqp professor
Rutensis referemqp suam sic stando figuram
Indulge fidei subiecte respice puram
Mentem deflebam tibi semper ubiqp paratam
Nam dno michi te dnum qz re fore gratam
Esse meum noscas in preiunctis quia cerno
Rex quia virtutes sequeris nuqz tua sperno
Iussa pretor dignare preces audire precantis
Sponte tibi vero fidei celo famulantis
Prex mea tibi matre preces cu supplicia mente
Porrigo pro Roma genitrce mea mo ffente
Nuc eget ipsa parens tutela nuceqp senatus
Sensato senio rex cuius tu trabeatus
Quondam consul amor quia stans urbe Senator
Te rogat ut culpe ne crescat fis medicator
Indiget ipsa tui presenti conditione ✠

Supplico puate qui regia carmina audit
Hec tua que trudit inimica pro breuitate
Exaudire uelis que possit nomine prati
Ut tibi sint grati iuuentes rex pie celis
Gloria lausqp deo tibi rex decus inde paritur
Et tantiqp detur eximie spes magna tropheo
Res faciendi seu uerbor sato labore
Iusta salus hore qua poscitur ut mala semi
Nuc patrare putent si formido uideatur
Ipsa necis dantur sic prelia dum fore mitet
Uel quasi re mira contingere qp meditant
Unde retardantur ne figant uulnera dira
Esca completa sedabit bella uetusta
Cumqp uia iusta reddet comota quieta
Non fiunt facile que non in pace petuntur
Donaqp planguntur senio qui iam iuuenile
Tempus uidebat rex dapsilis ~ pius esto
Ut facias presto tuus ut pater ipse solebat

✠ Cum manet ancipiti mentis luctantis agone
Si uirtute tua quam sperat pace fruetur
Confidas felix qp te fortuna sequetur
Scilicet ipsa dei que gra prospera reges
Sublimat fiuat letatur condere leges
Sic ego spero quidem timor hinc orietur in orbe
Mqp discedes longe tu pessime morbe
Plene doli ductum te falso putasse pudebit
Et qp qui sequitur tua pessima nota dolebit :·

Tournaments

were a form of entertainment, sports event and essay of arms. A French invention, they were always most popular in that country, though they also had a vogue in England, where they were controlled by licence and at certain times banned altogether. To start with, tournaments were a tough and realistic imitation of battle, involving on occasion as many as 3,000 mounted knights; by the 14th century, however, they had become more ritualistic exercises of chivalry bound by rules, jousts between two knights only, engaged in a test of strength and endurance. At a 15th-century French tournament, as depicted in the *Livre des Tournois du Roi René*, the knights' banners and helms were exhibited before the fight (above). The knights are at the left, their squires holding up the pennants inside the counter; the four men in the foreground are constables, and ladies of the court appear on the right. The helms, as distinctive as the banners, bear personal devices of identification, such as animals' heads, antlers, a miniature knight with shield, a basket of flowers (on the floor), etc. These helm decorations can be seen again in the mêlée (right) which marked the start of the event. The heralds blow their trumpets; the knights meet in an enclosure overlooked by the enthusiastic lords and ladies; the standard-bearers make off on the right. By the end of a day's fighting, before a champion emerged, the arena might well look like a battlefield. (26, 28)

The joust was more courtly and demanded more skill; chances of serious injury were much less. The pageantry of the contestants' parade is seen in the 15th-century illumination of the Jousts of St Ingilbert, made famous by Froissart, in which three French knights vied with 36 foreign challengers for one week. (27)

The hunt was the normal outdoor pastime of the mediaeval nobility, and is often represented in such hangings as the Hardwick tapestry (above). Here the end of the hunt is shown; the hind's belly has been cut open and chunks of bread are soaked in the blood to satisfy the hounds, while the gentry look on. Alongside a lady is hawking. (29)

◄ **Fold out**

147

Inside the castle the great contrast in furnishing with more modern times lies in the complete absence of the chest of drawers and its derivatives, the rarity of chairs, and the absence of pictures hanging on walls. For colour, even more than today, the main resource was textiles. Wall-hangings were much in use; they were regularly carried along with other appurtenances from one castle to another by the royal or noble household. A hall in the comte de Foix's castle at Orthez, capital of Béarn, is shown in an illumination from Froissart's *Chroniques de France et d'Angleterre* (left). Jean Froissart (c.1337–c.1404) spent from November 1388 to February 1389 in Orthez, and is himself seen before the Count, while the page behind carries the book Froissart is presenting. The arms of Béarn are suspended from the ceiling. Below: the King of Portugal, centre, and John of Gaunt, Duke of Lancaster, on the King's right, dine together on the border between Portugal and Galicia. Two noblemen, an archbishop and three bishops make up the rest of the company. The table is plain; the bishops sit on a bench. On the left servants bring the food through a hatch from the kitchen. The wall-hangings and tiled floor provide the only colour and variety in the room. (30, 31)

The Queen of France, Isabel of Bavaria, wife of Charles VI, is seen in her chamber (above). Kneeling before her is Christine de Pisan, presenting a book of her poems. Except for the carpet and chair, all the upholstery and hangings are decorated with the arms of France and Bavaria; the roof has a coved ceiling of wainscot and painted beams. Christine, native of Pisa (c.1364–c.1430), is one of the few women of the period who achieved professional success. (32)

Private chapels naturally formed a part of palaces and noble households. In a 15th-century miniature from the *Traité sur l'oraison dominicale* (right), Philip the Good, Duke of Burgundy, is shown at Mass. He is the figure in black, wearing the order of the Golden Fleece, kneeling within a private oratory. His coat of arms is woven into the rug in front of the altar. (33)

149

The precious contents of castle halls and chapels have been mostly dispersed and lost. The most complete of the royal inventories to have survived is a later copy of that of Charles V; the frontispiece (left) contains his portrait, not, however, contemporary. (34)

A miniature walled city in gilt copper crowns this German goblet of the late 15th century. Even the legs are made in the form of gates and battlements. (36)

The sceptre of Charles V (below), partially restored, was in the treasury of the Abbey of St-Denis. Of gold and silver-gilt, it is topped by a statue of Charlemagne enthroned. (35)

La Sainte Chapelle in Paris is an important example of royal private chapels (see p. 14). St Louis, before leaving for his first Crusade, commissioned this building to house the precious Crown of Thorns he had bought from the Emperor of Constantinople. Finished in 1249, it initiated a form that became common to royal chapels in consisting of two levels: the lower chapel (bottom), whose precise function is uncertain, supported the upper chapel (right), which was thus level with the state apartments. La Sainte Chapelle, which Louis decorated with an opulence he abstained from in his personal life, is particularly notable for its profusion of stained-glass windows. (37,38)

The ivory Virgin (above), added in the 14th century to the treasure of La Sainte Chapelle, is remarkable for the gay, untroubled expression of both Mother and Child. (39)

This splendid Virgin in silver-gilt (left) was given to the Abbey of St-Denis in 1339 by Jeanne d'Evreux, widow of Charles IV; it exemplifies the royal taste for luxurious display in religious objects and is of a period when gold came to be preferred to ivory. The base, divided into fourteen panels, tells the story of the Passion in enamel. The fleur-de-lys in the Virgin's hand was a reliquary containing *Des cheveus Notre Dame*, according to an inscription. (40)

The 'Little Gold Horse' of Altötting (the *Goldene Rössel*) (right) was a New Year present from Isabel of Bavaria to her husband Charles VI in 1404. The Madonna sits with the Child under a canopy of jewelled flowers, and two angels hold a crown over her head. At her feet sit the two St Johns—the Baptist (with lamb) and Evangelist (with chalice). In front of this group, the King, wearing a green cloak covered with fleurs-de-lys, is shown on his knees, while a page in blue holds his helmet. A groom in the same livery stands at the bottom tending the 'little horse' itself, which is made of pure gold but enamelled white. This marvel of the goldsmith's craft shows the great distance such decorative objects had moved from their purely religious function. (41)

True likenesses of kings and queens in the early Middle Ages are impossible to find, for royal portraits were primarily images of kingship. In the 14th century, however, genuine portraiture becomes common. Charles V of France (1337–80), a strong and resourceful monarch, appears as St Louis (detail, left) about 1375. This realistic statue, together with one of his wife, Jeanne de Bourbon, were carved for the portal of the Chapelle des Quinze-vingts, a hospital for the blind in Paris, founded by St Louis. Below: a miniature from *Les Grandes Chroniques de France* shows the coronation of Jeanne de Bourbon in 1364; among the peers on the left is Marguerite, comtesse d'Artois. The Queen appears again in a detail from the late 14th-century 'Parement de Narbonne' (bottom), an altar frontal of silk painted in Indian ink, which was made for Lenten use in the King's chapel and which came to light in Narbonne. (42, 43, 44)

Edward III of England, a contemporary of Charles V, with whom he and his sons were generally at war, is shown on a 14th-century seal, seated imperially on his throne with orb in hand. Seals of this kind were of great significance during the period, for such pendant wax-impressions attested the authenticity of official and legal documents. (45)

King John II of France, 'Jean le Bon' (1319–64), was defeated by the English at Poitiers in September 1356 and taken as prisoner to England where he lived for many years and died. Among his retinue in this relatively luxurious captivity was the French artist Girart d'Orléans; it is believed that he painted this portrait (above), the only remaining leaf of a polyptych which, according to Charles V's inventory, was in the Hôtel St-Pol. (46)

155

Glittering symbols of power, both ecclesiastical and temporal: crowns, orbs, sceptres and rings—all of precious metals and encrusted with gems—remain in various national treasuries as reminders of the mediaeval sense of the sacredness of monarchy. The crown shown here may originally have belonged to Richard II's queen, Anne of Bohemia. But it can first be traced with certainty in 1402 when Princess Blanche, the ten-year-old daughter of Henry IV of England, went to Cologne to marry the Elector Ludwig III, Prince Palatine. It was a political match—the Elector had to strengthen his position against the other princes of Germany and Henry, in his turn, wanted to prevent him from allying Germany with France. Blanche gave her husband a son, Rupert, 'the Englishman', and died of fever at the age of 17. The crown passed into the Treasury of the Palatinate. By a strange chance, it came once more into brief contact with the royal house of England in the 17th century, when Elizabeth, Charles I's sister, took it from Cologne to Prague. She was the wife of the Elector Frederick, 'the Winter King' of Bohemia, defeated by the imperial armies at the Battle of the White Mountain in 1620. By 1764 it had arrived in the Bavarian Treasury and has remained at Munich ever since.

Eleven sections ending in jewelled leaf-shapes are fitted together in a circle (which can be expanded or made smaller by adding or removing intermediate panels). The metal is solid gold, the gems diamonds (some false), balas rubies, emeralds, sapphires and pearls. (47)

Court Life in Peace and War

CHRISTOPHER HOHLER

Goslar, an imperial palace going back to the mid-11th century, was remodelled after a collapse in 1132, acquiring the central loggia and great staircase at one end. The lower hall was used in winter; the upper ('aula regia'), with its large window arcades, in summer. On the left is the octagonal chapel of St Ulrich. Although walled, Goslar was never a real fortress.(1)

THERE ARE FEW PLACES in Europe where the remains of some mediaeval castle are not within easy reach. The castle may indeed be intact and, as at Dover, have been in unbroken military occupation since it was founded, or, as at Churberg, still be inhabited by descendants of the men who built it. But it is more likely to be in ruins or more or less dilapidated, since the distinctive features of castles have made them equally inconvenient as barracks or as houses for many centuries; and their survival has been due, as much as anything else, to the solidity of their construction.
Whether they stand, like Castel del Monte, alone in the wilderness, p 137 (5) or, like the extraordinary castles of Chauvigny, grouped together in some little town, these empty buildings and broken walls never fail to evoke romantic sentiments in the most matter-of-fact minds. The world which brought them into being genuinely was, all romanticism apart, utterly different from anything to which we are accustomed; and their builders meant them to be beautiful and splendid. Beautiful and splendid they have remained, even in their decay; though it is difficult to remember, as one looks at the grimy mass of the Tower of London, that p 141 (20) there was a time when Henry III could order the rainwater-spouts to be lengthened, so that the water should not make ugly marks on the gleaming whiteness of its newly limewashed walls.

A Safe Stronghold

The building of defences round towns and round the citadels of towns is in no way peculiar to the Middle Ages. It was sound and common military practice down from misty ages of prehistory to a century ago, and Sebastopol differed from Jericho principally in being much more difficult to take. Mediaeval walled towns and citadels have their distinctive features; but in general they take their place in a long and continuous history. The peculiar contribution of the Middle Ages was the fortified country house.

The form this took varied enormously with date and place, with the kind of man who owned it and his wealth; and by no means all houses provided with some sort of fortification would have been called castles when they were built, or deserve the name now. The Middle Ages had a variety of names for different kinds of fortified house, but the only distinction formally drawn depended on whether the buildings or their enclosing wall had or had not a wall-walk and battlements. A house could thus be surrounded by a moat or palisade, or both, and not come within the definition at all; and the definition actually covers a number of houses such as Tretower Court which are not really castles either. The essential point, nevertheless, is that the houses of mediaeval landowners were normally provided with some means of defence, whereas those of Roman landowners were not fortified at all.

The conditions under which this change took place were a breakdown of public authority, but it was by no means a necessary consequence. Public disorder was no less in Scandinavia than anywhere else; but the home of a Viking chieftain was unfortified, and early Scandinavian history is punctuated by descriptions of men waiting for their rivals to get drunk along with their bodyguard and then burning the hall over their heads. It does, of course, strike one as odd that, in several centuries of this sort of thing, no one thought it worthwhile to take a few precautions.

Probably to do so would have been regarded as despicable cowardice and have made the leader lose the confidence of his men. But in other regions of Europe a less sporting attitude to war becomes apparent during the 10th century. The castle of Fulk Nerra of Anjou at Langeais, built in 992, is really no more than an enormous hall, on the first floor as French halls usually are. It was once set in an enclosure which has mostly vanished and does not seem to have been very formidable. But the hall, being built of stone, could not simply be set ablaze.

A stone hall in itself does not, of course, constitute a castle: Boothby Pagnell manor house is a manor house, and the palace at Goslar is a palace. And incidentally, in view of what has just *f 1* been said, it is remarkable how few habitations of this precise kind seem in fact to have been built of stone in the Middle Ages. But Langeais and, a century after Langeais, the keep of Chepstow p 141 are clearly castles, since their size and solidity (and history) all go (19) to show that they were built with a positive military intent; and both were always meant to be combined with defensible, though less substantial, enclosures. They nevertheless illustrate a particular approach to the idea of a castle, one apparently distinctive of north-western France, in which the principal defensive feature of the castle is the hall. This idea was in due course exported to England, Sicily and the Crusading States; but most mediaeval fortification develops, on the contrary, from the basic idea of the tower.

A tall slender tower, assuming there is no artillery able to knock it down, can, owing to its small perimeter, be adequately defended by a few men, and at the same time provide considerable accommodation for stores, treasure and non-combatants. Strategically it is not much use, but if there is a possibility of relief arriving, or of attacking forces not thinking it worthwhile to stay and besiege it, it is the ideal refuge. Such towers accordingly form the original nucleus of an immense number of castles in southern France, Germany and Italy and (as the familiar Round Towers) were constructed in most Irish monasteries. They were also once prominent adjuncts of the dwellings of the rich in a great many Italian towns. In the later Middle Ages they appear, in conjunction with less substantial constructions, at the centre of quite unassuming properties along the Scottish border and in southern Sweden. But for their use in this way in northern and north-western Europe at an early date there seems at the moment no evidence beyond the casual remark of Suger, the 12th-century p 26 (26) abbot of St-Denis, that Henry I of England had got into his own hands or destroyed not only every castle but nearly every tower in Normandy. The early towers that we know of from this part of the world regularly form part of motte-and-bailey castles, earthworks combining a banked and ditched enclosure with a conical mound. It has normally been taken that the bank and

157

A knight receives the accolade on the field of battle, from a romance of Sir Lancelot, 14th century. Such occasions, though more frequent in the pages of courtly fiction than in reality, were in fact a part of aristocratic life. The Black Prince was received into knighthood after distinguishing himself at the Battle of Crécy. (2)

mound were intended to carry a palisade and a low wooden tower, but two mounds recently excavated have proved to have been thrown up against the bases of towers, one wooden, the other of stone, which had already been constructed. It cannot be shown that either tower was erected before the motte-and-bailey was thought of, but it may be so; in which case it is possible that small isolated towers were once to be found in north-west Europe much as in other areas. The motte-and-bailey itself seems to be a purely military device, related to short-term considerations, and not, in its earth and timber form, regarded as a sensible kind of residence or even permanent fortification. It is in any case manifestly not the germ from which the castle grew in Europe as a whole, for castles are mentioned in Italy as early as anywhere else, though earth and timber are not there the natural materials; moreover, motte-and-bailey is not even the normal type of earth and timber castle over wide areas of the Continent.

A tower is not in itself a castle, any more than a stone hall is. For it is of the essence of a castle that it should be able to accommodate a sufficient number of men and horses for its garrison to be in a position to affect the course of a war. It is the matter of the horses which makes the defensible enclosure essential to the concept of a castle, and it is the matter of the garrison that makes the term fundamentally inapplicable to the home of a mere knight. But at this point it is necessary to consider the society of the time when these various constructions came into being.

The arming of a knight: he receives sword, spurs, helmet and shield while musicians play in the background. This scene illustrates the story of Troy, the knight being Pyrrhus; but its details are of the late 14th century when it was painted. (3)

The Rise of the Knights

The military organization of the Carolingian Empire (and of the English Heptarchy) had proved quite incapable of dealing with a succession of invaders, Saracen, Danish, Norman and Hungarian, who arrived suddenly on horseback or by sea. In the course of the ensuing wars and civil wars it had become clear that if defence were to be effective it must be under local control and that the essential military figure was the armoured cavalryman, the knight. The art of fighting on horseback seems to have been greatly developed in France and Germany at this time. The English at Hastings in 1066, who dismounted to fight, and the Danes at Fotevik in 1134, opposing on foot a body of mounted German mercenaries, came to disaster through their failure to keep abreast of military developments. But the knight was a specialist, who had to be trained and kept in practice. By the year 1000 this had resulted in much of the soil of Europe being divided into little estates, each providing sufficient clear rent for a knight to support his family, devote his time to administration and military training and, as need arose, join in actual war under some hereditary captain in the neighbourhood whose 'man' he was. The pressure to make the whole of this structure of military landowning hereditary was irresistible, because the knight was liable to be killed young and there was no equally certain means of ensuring a pension for his widow and orphans. This was recognized on all hands, and anyone disinherited by his overlord without good and clear reason could go into rebellion confident of widespread and warm support. The resultant pattern of land-holding, however, made no provision for the younger sons of military families. A good many had to go into the Church where they were technically celibate. The extent to which this was done can be well seen in the case of the Limousin nobleman Ebles III, Viscount of Ventadour. Of his eight sons one succeeded him as viscount, while of the others two were successively abbots of Tulle, one was a canon of Maguelonne, two were canons of Limoges one was dean of Mauriac and only one remained a layman. Those who did not go into the Church formed a class of landless knights hanging around the courts of the nobility, unable to marry unless and until the accidents of mortality and the favour of their overlord secured them the hand of the widow or heiress of one of their better-endowed colleagues. Manual labour and trade were out of the question for them, reasonably paid ecclesiastical posts could not always be had for the asking, and the evidence suggests that the nobility, at least, often therefore deliberately limited the size of their legitimate families. Yet it does not appear that there was ever any shortage of members of the knightly class.

Meanwhile, with so many families divided between the military and ecclesiastical professions, mutual influence was inevitable. On the clerical side, though priests were not supposed to bear arms, it was not extraordinary for them to do so in the 11th century; and Suger describes with manifest pride the part taken (as a sapper) by a local parish priest in the storming of the wooden castle of Le Puiset by the forces of Louis VI of France in 1111. By this time, however, such activities were probably going out of fashion and the most striking subsequent illustrations come from countries on the fringes of Latin Christendom. No fewer than five Danish bishops fell at Fotevik in 1134; and at Mohi in 1241 both the Hungarian archbishops were among the five prelates slain. In the last case it might have been supposed that the clergy were present in a purely spiritual capacity; the Tartars would hardly have bothered to distinguish. But actually the chronicler describes how the archbishop of Kálocsa, furious at the inaction of his king, led his own knights in a charge against the enemy and galloped them straight into a bog. On the military side the fusion went much deeper. The positive encouragement of war against the Infidel, which began to become general Church policy after the capture and holding to ransom of St Maiol, abbot of Cluny, by Saracen robbers in 972, opened the eyes of the West to the possibility of careers in the colonies for those whose prospects at home were dim. The Scandinavians had thought in these terms for centuries, and it was in fact Normans who were to the forefront in the conquest of Sicily and the establishment of the Crusading States, having already, without religious excuse, expelled the Byzantine government from southern Italy and, under Roussel de Bailleul,

Map showing the sites mentioned in this chapter. (4)

made an attempt to take control of Asia Minor. Subjects of the French Crown, however, who were not Normans, leaped at the idea when it received religious sanction, and took prominent parts, not only in the first three Oriental Crusades, but in the *Reconquista* in Spain. German colonial wars against the Slavs similarly became Crusades; and at the end of the 12th century, when it was decided that heretics called for the same treatment as heathens, the Crusading concept was used by the northern against the southern French, and by the members of the Fourth Crusade against the Byzantine Empire. These developments, while only offering palliatives to the pressure of population at home, made it easier for the king of France at least to control his kingdom. They had the further effect of giving experience in the handling of larger armies; and they undoubtedly brought about that union of Christianity and warfare which gives their characteristic colour to the last five mediaeval centuries. Elaborate ceremonies for girding the knight with his sword 'for the defence of widows and orphans and the furtherance of justice' were devised, honorific knightly orders with their own special chapels and staff of clergy came into being, and it is with hardly a twinge of surprise that one learns that Henry V attended three masses before leading his troops to the siege of Caen in 1417; that one finds the apparatus for lowering the portcullis to block the wall-walk placed behind the altar of a chapel in Marten's tower in Chepstow Castle; or reads engraved on the armour of a 14th-century Vogt, von Matsch, at Churberg the words, several

f 2, 3
p 142
(23, 24)

times repeated, 'But he, passing through the midst of them, went his way', words originally used by St Luke with reference to Christ himself. The Vogts were, of course, closely associated with the Church, their title, which they preferred to that of count, relating to their position as protectors of the abbey of Marienberg. They took their office, which was profitable, very seriously; and Vogt Ulrich in 1304 earned undying renown by killing Abbot Hermann of Marienberg for having the impertinence to appeal against his particular brand of protection to that of the Count of Tyrol.

This military-ecclesiastical fusion came, as far as the Church was concerned, gradually and with intermittent hesitations about the path which was being trodden. We still have a tariff of the penances to be performed before reconciliation by those who, having fought at Hastings under a banner blessed by the Pope, might have had the misfortune to commit some deadly sin there, such as homicide. The indulgence for taking part in the First Crusade was markedly more realistic, and the establishment of the Knights Templars recognized as members of the clergy men whose primary task was warfare. Still, throughout the 12th century, councils repeatedly condemned the tournament; and no one in 1200 could possibly have envisaged that a day would come when a king would enrol his tournament-team as a knightly order, using a lady's garter as a badge, in close association with the refoundation of a collegiate church, under the special patronage of St George.

The joust grew in aristocratic favour in the 14th century, after the 'mêlée' or tournament came to be considered too dangerous. Jousting was a sport, a military exercise, a test of skill and a social occasion, often described in *minute detail by the chroniclers. Single combat could take place with a variety of weapons, on horseback or on foot, generally ending only with heavy bruises and the surrender (as right) of one of the combatants. (5, 6)*

Chivalry as a Career

p 144–6
(26, 28)
Tournaments were invented by Geoffroy de Preuilly, who died in 1066, and were taken up in France with great and lasting enthusiasm. The only difference between a tournament, as at first conceived, and a battle was that the object was to capture opponents, not to kill them; but there was no question of single combat or blunted weapons, and a number of important people did get killed. The captured participant lost his horse and armour to his captor and, if he was known to have means, had to pay a ransom as well. We are extremely fortunate in having in the *Chanson de Guillaume le Maréchal* the biography of the Anglo-French tournament champion of the mid-12th century, written apparently by his herald immediately after his death in 1219. William Marshall was the penniless younger son of a militarily distinguished but otherwise not very prominent baron. He was attached by his father to the court of the Connétable de Tancarville in Normandy, and there is a touching and illuminating (though not quite accurate) account of the difficulties in which he found himself in his early days when his horse got killed and he had not the money to buy another. However, he was able to borrow the most unmanageable horse in the Connétable's stable and, by repeatedly capturing rich opponents in tournaments, he soon set himself on his own feet. On his deathbed it was represented to him that the Church held this to be robbery, and that he ought to make restitution either to his victims or to the Church. He declined.

Meanwhile, the eldest son of Henry II of England decided to take up tournaments, a course which (even if he avoided getting killed) promised to be very expensive indeed in ransoms, unless he also avoided capture. Maintaining a team of knights to take part in the various meetings put a heavy enough strain on the allowance his father was prepared to make him; but his father very wisely put him in William Marshall's charge, and William was in fact able to rescue the Young King on several occasions when disaster seemed imminent. The Young King's sporting proclivities won him the fulsome approval of nearly every agency of publicity known to the 12th century, while William's prowess secured him the friendship of great men whom otherwise he would scarcely have known. As a result he was in due course given the hand of the heiress of a moderate-sized lordship in Lancashire. With admirable prudence he refrained from actually marrying her, and was therefore free a year later to accept the offer of the heiress of Richard de Clare. She brought him most of South Wales with the castles of Chepstow and Pembroke, half the honour of Crendon, and the kingdom of Leinster in Ireland. The Lancashire lady was passed on to somebody else.

But not all younger sons who did not go into the Church could mark up successes of this order and, failing luck in tournaments, were liable to try putting pressure on their elder brothers. The only younger son of Ebles III of Ventadour who did not go into the Church tried this course, and the troubadour Bertran de Born quarrelled with his brother Constantine with whom, until he got

him out, he had to share the family castle of Hautfort. He preferred, however, proper war in which he could plunder merchants with impunity; and in the course of the 12th century war itself took on much of the aspect of a tournament since so many of the participants were interested in ransoms. As a result war became much less dangerous for the knight, and tournaments, by repercussion, too dangerous. By the 14th century they were almost completely displaced by the joust, which was single combat with foul blows barred; and improvements in the design of armour ensured that this could hardly have worse consequences than heavy bruising. It called, nevertheless, for great physical strength and remarkable control of the horse, and the Jousts of St Ingilbert in 1389 deserve the immortality Froissart has given them. The Sire de Boucicault and two companions challenged the knighthood of England, a large party came over to Calais, and for four successive days the three Frenchmen took turns against no fewer than thirty-six successive Englishmen, Hainaulters and Bohemians, without one of the French being unseated. This was a serious sporting event for men, England and France being momentarily not at war; whereas the kind of meeting envisaged by 13th-century romantic poets included large-scale entertainment by some host and the presence of a great many ladies. The most informative poems are probably *Flamenca* (written in *langue d'oc*) and *Guillaume de Dôle* (in northern French), two delicious works, akin to the modern novel, and including among their secondary characters a large number who bear the names of real people. While the picture they give is much too good to be true, it is clearly intended to be a recognizable reflection of high life. *Flamenca* turns on the King of France sporting a favour, given him by his hostess, in a joust, as a result of which the Queen gets jealous and makes the host jealous. *Guillaume de Dôle* is about a romantic marriage between a German Emperor and the daughter of a Walloon nobleman. The heroine of the second poem, who is eminently virtuous, is introduced to the reader sitting with her mother in the chamber embroidering church vestments, and both the ladies sing *chansons de toile* to please the Emperor's messenger. Flamenca, however, (whose husband clearly deserves more sympathy than the poet accords him) manages to make an assignment with an admirer during Mass on Sunday, being at other times rightly locked in a tower; she then meets him in a private bath in the thermal establishment at Bourbon l'Archambault into which he has made an underground passage, and where she has persuaded her husband she needs to go for her health. The great social events in these stories are always tournaments, described with great minuteness, both as to the prowess of the combatants and the detail of their dress, and as to the nature of the feast and the poems sung by the *jongleurs*. Social life in England, where licences for tournaments were nearly always refused or cancelled by the king in the 12th and 13th centuries, must have been very dull; and much of the popularity of Edward III in the 14th century is certainly due to the fact that he enjoyed organizing them.

f 5, 6

p 144
(27)

As to the romantic ladies, they are a vision of the later 12th century. If one turns to poems, the core of which belongs to an earlier age, the picture is different. The heroine, so far as there is one, of *Raoul de Cambrai*, is a young woman who tells a man held prisoner by her father that she means to speak to her father about him; would he sooner she said that he wanted to marry her, or that it was time he was executed? In *Girart de Roussillon* a damsel from the village is part of the furniture of any visitor's bedroom. Both these very splendid poems (as we have them) have, however, been supplemented by romantic additions at the beginning or end; for by the late 12th century André the Chaplain, in his manual on Love, is laying down that making love to peasant women is really unbecoming to a gentleman, while his noble ladies, assumed to be already married, are to engage in formal badinage and would clearly never operate by threat. Those favourite themes of later 12th- and 13th-century verse, the seduction of shepherdesses (in spite of André's disapproval) and the tactful and anonymous adoration of married ladies, are manifestly related to a world where courts were full of hefty young men whose future depended entirely on waiting till they could marry an heiress. On top of this has been imposed an elaborate code of good manners.

There are times when one wonders whether 12th-century good manners were not a French secret weapon devised to torment the Germans. John of Salisbury relates with manifest glee how Roger II of Sicily welcomed all kinds of foreigners to his court except Germans 'on account of their extreme barbarousness':

which under the circumstances must be taken as the view of the French, the Italians and the Anglo-Normans. But it is difficult to see how any 'barbarousness' could exceed that of the heroes of *Raoul de Cambrai* and *Girart de Roussillon*, so that the French themselves cannot have supposed they had sloughed off the quality long before.

The manners were probably taken over from the Saracens, with whom the French (in the Levant) and the Spaniards were in constant touch, since they take the form of elaborate regulations recalling nothing so much as those Traditions of the Prophet which relate to his behaviour in daily life. Fantastic rules, designed to keep outsiders out, make their literary début in the Anglo-Norman *Tristan*. To judge from its derivatives, this included the episode in which the hero on his way to Tintagel meets King Mark's huntsmen, and teaches them the correct way to break up and carry home a stag after the kill. He is then able to create a sensation by arriving with the procession complete with man at rear carrying a forked stick adorned with the animal's liver, etc. Why King Mark's huntsmen should have admiringly agreed to being told to do all this, instead of telling Tristan not to be a silly ass, does not emerge from the story; but, verisimilitude apart, the poet of course knew that half his audience would be listening to see if he had got it right, and the other half to memorize it all for future reference. This sort of thing got steadily worse and worse; manuals had to be put out, and by the end of the 15th century experts on Burgundian court etiquette could tell you the number of shelves for displaying gold plate permitted in the chamber of a woman in childbed according to whether she was an ordinary countess (three), the Duke's daughter-in-law (four) or the Duchess (five). And by the 14th century a German joke can turn on a social faux-pas in *The Half Pear* in the same sort of way as an Egyptian one in the equally unedifying *Steward's Tale* in the story of the Hunchback and the Tailor from the *Thousand and One Nights*.

Who Lived in Castles?

But to return to the knight and his home. This would not normally in England have been fortified at any date and would certainly not have been a castle. It seems doubtful whether it would have been fortified anywhere in Europe before the 13th century. In time of war a knight could expect to be fighting away from home, and he was in no position to afford an elaborate kind of house or pay trained men to defend it. He might, however, find himself living in somebody else's castle as its hereditary castellan or as a member of its hereditary garrison. Hereditary garrisons of this kind seem unknown in England, the nearest approach being the holding of land by a serjeanty of castle-guard, for instance at Windsor, which meant no more than a brief turn of duty once a year or payment in lieu. This system was, of course, known on the Continent. The garrison of Carcassonne was theoretically supplied *f 23–25* in this way down to the 18th century; but both France and Germany can show castles in which the several different families providing the hereditary garrison actually lived side by side within the walls. The famous and picturesque castle of Eltz on the Moselle *p 136 (4)* was occupied and garrisoned by five branches of the family named after it (to whom it still belongs) and was apparently always their own; but the castle of Salzburg (near Neustadt a. d. Saale and now

And at a knyght thenne wille begynne

knyght there was a worthy man
a   That fro the tyme that he first began

Chaucer's Knight, from the Canterbury Tales of about 1490. By Chaucer's time the ideals of chivalry were liable to receive the attentions of wits, though its values were still held in esteem. The knight 'loved chivalry, truth and honour, freedom and courtesy... He was a very perfect gentle knight.' (7)

in ruins) was held on behalf of the bishop of Würzburg, who built its walls late in the 12th century as a frontier defence, by a substantial number of different families who put up their own houses inside the walls. A well-known illustration of the same phenomenon in France was Vergy in Burgundy. There in the 12th century each of the families providing the garrison was known by the nickname, such as White, Green, or Fat, of the ancestor who first took on the duty, or from the position of its house, for instance, 'of the Gate'. But by the mid-13th century this arrangement was obsolete; the families once providing the garrison were living out on the estates attached to their ancient duties, taking their names from them (it sounded better to be called 'de Chazant' than 'le Gras') and selling their houses within the castle walls. The most famous French example is the Roman amphitheatre at Nîmes which had become the town citadel. Houses had been erected on the tiers of seats and the families occupying them, known collectively as the *chevaliers des Arènes*, and each responsible for the defence of its own sector, are prominent in the 12th-century history of the town. In the course of the 13th century they too lose their importance.

f 8

Roman buildings were adapted to a variety of uses during the Middle Ages. Circuses became public squares (e. g. at Lucca or the Piazza Navona in Rome); theatres a warren of houses (as the theatre of Marcellus still partially is); and mausolea citadels (the Castle Sant'Angelo). At Nîmes and Arles the amphitheatres assumed the appearance of small towns. That of Arles (above) was fortified in the Middle Ages, and the three towers of this engraving are the remains of this work. The houses built into the great masonry arcades gradually declined in status. By 1825 they were slums and were cleared away, the Roman arrangements being restored. (8)

Hereditary constables were similarly rare in England: but on the Continent, where there was no such clean break at the very beginning of castle-building as in England, they were quite common. By origin they were quite likely to be the family who owned the land on which the castle stood; or, in the Empire, to be former serfs of the Emperor or some prominent magnate who had been given an estate and told, or had helped, to build a castle on it. This last system produced a new nobility who for many generations could be trusted to be loyal to the family of the man who had established them, since they were bound to it by law, and were never quite regarded as equals by those whose families had been free as far back as memory or record went. It seems normally to have been people of this kind who were induced to live in fantastically inconvenient places, such as on pinnacles of rock in the Alps where the water had always to be drawn from a cistern, and it is generally thought that sites of this kind were not occupied much, if at all, before the 12th century. Certainly it is in the 12th century, and often quite late in it, that the existing buildings seem to have been begun, and that families begin to be called after the castles. But it is not necessarily a rule. Similar castles exist in France. Cabaret is one of the astonishing group of four castles called Lastours high in the mountains north of Carcassonne, and the first time a notable

is described as 'of Cabaret' is in 1086. But Cabaret itself is mentioned as a place already in the 6th century; and it is difficult to think why it should have been important, or even inhabited, at any date unless it was fortified. Castles of this kind seem to have been less formidable than they look; Greifenstein in the Tyrol, for instance, which looks utterly impregnable, was captured three times in the course of its history. And as they could normally hold only very small garrisons, they could normally be rendered harmless by building a small fort to cover the approach to them and manning it with a force of comparable size. But they could, nevertheless, be a very great nuisance for a considerable time in determined hands. During pauses in the Hundred Years' War the French government always had to deal with castles in the Massif Central which lay on their side of the truce line, but were held in the English interest by free-lance roughs; and, whenever possible, they bought them out. In any case, it was most often this kind of castle that had a hereditary castellan. Even Greifenstein had one, calling himself 'of Greifenstein', although the castle belonged to the Counts of Greifenstein who normally lived in some less inaccessible spot; and it is usually only in places like this that families who stood socially and financially on the lowest rung of the feudal ladder were the effective, though not technical, owners of castles. Other exceptions to the rule that mere knights would live in mere houses are provided by individuals who grew rich beyond their station from ransoms during the Hundred Years' War. Sir John Delamare and Sir Edward Dalyngrygg were thus enabled to build themselves the castles of Nunney and Bodiam respectively. Sir Edward in his application for a licence to crenellate said his castle would be useful in the event of a French invasion. This was manifest eyewash: what he needed was a house of a military character appropriate to his profession, and of a magnificence appropriate to his wealth; but he did at least build a castle. Nunney is no castle; it could not accommodate a single horse, and is merely a large tower-house, surrounded by a moat, of exceptionally inconvenient design for habitation.

p 140 (16)

p 140 (17)

The Castle-Builders

The erection and maintenance of true castles was thus normally the affair of the higher nobility, and more especially of kings; but it must be emphasized that these people, also, did not regularly live in castles. In the first place they were, during most of the Middle Ages, so ceaselessly on the move, campaigning or hunting or visiting their different estates or different parts of their king-

The flat Netherlands offer few opportunities for natural defence, and castles here were usually ring-forts—fortified walls enclosing a courtyard. The earliest was Leyden (c. 1150). Oostvorne (above) was later and more elaborate version, incorporating a substantial tower in the middle. (9)

Caerphilly Castle (1267–77), in South Wales, though not a royal castle, belongs to the same series as those built by Edward I. Castles were now strong enough to be able to resist most assaults, but were still vulnerable to siege and starvation. Caerphilly therefore is designed to provide outlets to the surrounding country for sorties and for bringing in supplies, without sacrificing security. This was effected by increasing the number of gates and posterns and by building outworks.

The castle stands on an island in a lake. On the east the approach is defended by a long barbican or screen-wall (a) with three gates (b), which also acted as a sluice controlling the level of water in the lake. The castle itself has two lines of walls (c, d), two gates (e), a sally-port (f) and several smaller posterns. On the western side is another defended island called the 'hornwork' (g) giving emergency access to the opposite shore. The strongpoint of Caerphilly was the eastern gateway, which contained living rooms and an oratory. The hall (h) was against the inner south wall. (10, 11)

100   0   100   200   300   400   500 FT.   50   0   50   100   150 M.

doms, that it would be difficult to say they lived anywhere at all. Nor were their wives any more stationary, as one may judge from where Edward III's children were born: three at Woodstock, two in the Tower of London, two at Windsor Castle, one at Waltham, one at Hatfield by Doncaster, one at King's Langley, one at Antwerp and one at Ghent. In the second place there was probably no period when they did not own and visit houses which were not castles. Woodstock and King's Langley, just named, in England, Vincennes before the 14th century in France, Goslar in Germany were all royal residences of a non-military kind. Crendon in Buckinghamshire was the principal seat of an earl and the administrative centre of a large fief in the 12th century, yet it never had a castle. Nor was it an Italian peculiarity for magnates to own town-houses, though the tall towers attached to such houses were common only in Italy. To take obvious examples, the Savoy Palace in London was built by Peter of Savoy, Earl of Richmond, in the 13th century and was occupied by John of Gaunt, Earl of Lancaster, in the 14th; and several charters of Raymon IV, Count of Toulouse, are dated from his 'stare' in St-Gilles. This was not originally fortified and the abbot of St-Gilles made a terrible fuss when towers, no doubt on the Italian model, were eventually added. From the standpoint of these men a castle was a military work of which the maintenance was expensive; it was not for them, as it was for Sir Edward Dalyngrygg, a matter of prestige to live in one. And Sir Edward was probably influenced by France where circumstances had made castles the normal homes of a much larger social group than in England.

The general pattern of castle-building, or more precisely castle-maintenance, was therefore governed by considerations of economy. Any effectively autonomous area, kingdom, duchy or whatever it may be, tends to have a few castles belonging to its ruler in the centre of the territory, primarily maintained as treasuries, prisons and dépôts, and a larger number round the perimeter to meet the danger of foreign attack. These last the ruler frequently

left in the hands of subordinates who would from self-interest keep them in repair without cost to him. This was the pattern in the English kingdom where castles on the borders (Caerphilly, Warkworth) or near the coast (Arundel, Framlingham) were usually baronial; of those in the interior, a few (Tower of London, Nottingham) were carefully maintained, whereas others built immediately after the Conquest to dominate the country (Oxford, Cambridge) tended to be left for years in a state of disrepair. England was, however, unusual among kingdoms in possessing a relatively tidy organization, divided into counties of roughly equal size, in each of which the king retained sufficient land and dues to pay a sheriff, a frequently changed official, to look after his interests, and where in each county town the castle, if any, and even if in disrepair, belonged to the king, not to the earl or the bishop, and was the centre of the sheriff's administration.

In France, however, with bribery to obtain support in the civil wars of the 9th and 10th centuries and the final change of dynasty in 986, the royal lands and revenues, as such, disappeared; and by 1000 the king had little more than an honorific title and the highly localized lands and revenues his family possessed by virtue of being Counts of Paris. Their great source of strength was the support of the Church. But they were only able to establish themselves as effective rulers by reconquering the rest of the country; and this they did not do till the 13th century through the defeat of John and Henry III of England, and the Albigensian Crusade. By that time there had been two centuries of castle-building which in Aquitaine and Languedoc had not even been under effective ducal control. It has been calculated that in Aquitaine there was a castle every eight miles or so, presumably because a four-mile radius proved to be the range at which an 11th-century garrison could join battle with an attacking force before it had done too much damage. The kind of warfare with which this pattern of castle-building was designed to contend consisted not so much in sieges as in ruining your opponent by killing his peasantry and

f 28–31
f 1

f 10, 11
p 140
(18)

A castle was not only a centre for offence and defence, it was also one of the principal residences of its owner, from which his estates in the area were administered. This diagram of Goodrich Castle, in Herefordshire, omits the purely military features in order to show the internal arrangements as they functioned in times of peace.

Goodrich was built for the de Valence family between 1300 and 1350. The castle stands on a cliff edge protected on the south and east (top of drawing) by a rock-cut ditch (D) and on the other side by the steepness of the cliff above the river Wye. It incorporated an older keep (B) but this had no place in the later domestic routine. The living rooms surround a central court (A) with a pentise or cloister connecting them. They were divided into four groups, each practically self-contained.

The Gatehouse: to enter one had to pass over a drawbridge, through the outer gate into the Barbican (X), across the great stone bridge and over a further drawbridge into the heavily defended gate passage (W) which finally led to the inner court. In a commanding position over the gatehouse, with control of the portcullis, was the lodging of the constable of the castle (T, U) and, beside the gate passage, the castle chapel (S) open to the court.

The State Rooms: the Great Hall (E) and State Chamber (F) with its own service and storage rooms (G, H) were reserved for state guests, who could be of royal rank, the whole suite being accessible by only one entrance from the inner court.

The Private Rooms: the Earl himself and his personal household lived in a similar suite of rooms (L, M) in the north-west tower. His hall (K) was also the court-hall and had an ante-room (N) in which suppliants could wait. Below were two rooms for the squires of the household (O, P), within easy reach of the stables (J) in the outer court by means of a postern door.

The Guest Rooms: the third hall of the castle (Q), along the east side, was communal; it could be entered from two directions and was connected to the south-east tower, where there were more rooms for guests (R). Beside the old keep was the great kitchen (C) connected to all parts of the castle by the pentise walk.

All the private rooms and state guest rooms were provided with fireplaces, and each had its own garderobe and wash-basin. (12)

THE GATEHOUSE
S. *The Castle Chapel*
T. *Constable's outer Chamber*
U. *Constable's inner Chamber*
W. *Gate passage*
X. *The Barbican*

Q. *Eastern Hall*
R. *Guest Rooms*

THE PRIVATE ROOMS
K. *Hall*
L. *Great Chamber*
M. *Inner Chamber*
N. *Ante-Room*
O. *Squires' Hall*
P. *Squires' Chamber*

burning their houses and crops; and if the duke or count was unable to stop private war of this kind, he could hardly stop his barons taking the necessary defensive measures. But the majority of these castles were not particularly formidable, for to build really strong fortresses would have been beyond their possessors' means; and superimposed on this pattern is another of stronger castles built by the dukes or their principal feudatories on the same general principles as in England. The Emperor on the other hand was in quite as strong a position as the king of England, though it is not clear how much land belonged to the crown as distinct from the family possessions of successive dynasties. But the 10th-century Emperors had made the mistake of assigning a great deal of their land to the Church on the assumption that they would always be able to appoint the bishops. When in the 11th

century their right to appoint was challenged, prolonged disturbances, culminating in the second half of the 13th century in a lengthy interregnum, brought the Empire in the 14th century to a state comparable to that of France at the end of the 10th. Germany, too, became covered with a forest of castles, which are usually correspondingly late, few going back much before 1200. The pattern seems to be much the same, the stronger ones being the seats of prominent feudatories (including bishops and the Teutonic Knights) or designed to protect their frontiers. From the 13th century there were also, however, what appear to be a number of imperial hunting-lodges. The best-known, Castel del Monte in Apulia, is not a military work; but there are powerful military-looking buildings in the south German forests whose sites can hardly have been chosen on military or administrative grounds.

p 137 (5)

A. *Inner Court*
B. *Keep*
C. *Kitchen*
D. *Ditch*

THE STATE ROOMS
E. *Great Hall*
F. *State Chamber*
G. *Service Rooms*
H. *Storage*

J. *The Stables*

In the countries so far mentioned there was usually reasonable stability over long periods during the Middle Ages, and a pattern can be seen. In Spain, Italy and Ireland this was not so, and the difficulties of sorting out the dates and builders of the innumerable castles and relating the structures to local and general history seem to have daunted researchers; but no doubt the pattern at any given time was much as in Germany or Aquitaine. On the other hand the countries on the eastern and northern periphery of Latin Christendom seem to conform more to the pattern found in England. Castles, as opposed to towers, are nearly always royal, occasionally episcopal, in Scandinavia: and they are relatively few. In Hungary they were built by the great feudatories, and sometimes by the king, after the Tartar invasions of the 13th century, as a precaution against another invasion of the same kind.

Patterns of Defence

As to the detail of the buildings themselves, it has been said that any castle must comprise a tower, a seigneurial habitation, and a fortified enclosing wall, though these may be combined in various ways. Thus the 'tower' may be the twin towers of the gatehouse which may have the seigneurial residence in its upper storey. The enclosure usually follows the lie of the land, unless the country is featureless, when it is normally rectangular. As time progresses, numerous refinements come to be introduced into the design of the defences of the more expensive types of castle, but it is permissible to be rather cynical about their military importance. Their presence may, of course, have improved the garrison's morale, and no doubt they figured prominently in the engineer's commendation of his own design: but granted certain preliminary points, the rest were most unlikely ever to be put to the test. The first requirement was that the walls should be solid enough to withstand the artillery of the time. This, between the 11th and the mid-14th centuries, consisted of a variety of giant slings and catapults for hurling stones, thereafter progressively more and more of cannon. The best masonry was, of course, Roman and the Triumphal Arch of Orange, the monument of Hadrian in Rome and the tomb of Cecilia Metella in the Campagna all formed the core of mediaeval citadels. The wall should if possible be built on rock so that it could not be undermined. Failing that, a water filled moat would prevent mining; but a determined besieger could usually divert the water and wet soil was liable to be a bad foundation. The walls of Calais were constantly subsiding. It must be possible to defend the base of the wall against sappers with picks. This could be achieved by building the wall with a broad glacis at the foot, as at Lucera; by building out the wall-walk on machicolations (or providing a projecting wall-walk of wood); by setting projecting bastions along the wall; or by a combination of all three. The gate should be proof against rushing by the enemy pursuing retreating members of the garrison after a sortie. This involved some system of double gates, usually achieved by building a barbican outside the main gate, so that those retreating and their pursuers could come into an area controlled by the garrison without actually entering the castle. It also involved the use of the portcullis closed by gravity, as well as doors which a garrison might not be able to shut against pressure from outside. Provided these matters were attended to, a castle could hardly be captured unless through treachery, failure of morale, or exhaustion of food, water or ammunition. Scaling an unbreached wall or even reaching the wall-top from a movable wooden tower was always extremely difficult and hazardous, unless the enceinte was too long for the garrison to defend properly in the face of simultaneous attacks at widely separated points by a numerous enemy. And it is clear that it made in practice no real difference whether bastions were rectangular, semicircular or brought to a point; whether the approach to the gate did or did not compel an enemy to turn his right side, not protected by a shield, towards the defences; whether the gatehouse was or was

f 13, 14

not provided with a mass of ingeniously placed arrow slits and holes for dropping projectiles from above. Such things, and also elaborate concentric defences, are designed to meet theoretical contingencies which in practice would never arise. Lagopesole, which has none of these frills, would have been just as impossible to storm in the Middle Ages as the Tower of London, which has all of them; and the chances of the Tower of London having at any time a garrison sufficiently numerous to take useful advantage of all the possibilities of covering fire which its concentric defences offered were as remote as an invader or rebel, with a large enough force to assault the Tower (or Lagopesole) from several sides at once under such circumstances, being fool enough to try.

p 141 (20)

In fact, however, garrisons were not of this order. On the occasion of sieges in the time of Henry II Crowmarsh castle was held by about 160 men, Chaumont by 135, Le Mans by 90. Odiham was held for a week against an invading French army in 1216 by three knights and ten serjeants. The standing force at Pembroke in 1252 was two mounted men-at-arms and ten foot soldiers, at Conway in 1284 thirty fencible men of whom only fifteen were professional soldiers, at Warkworth in 1319 twelve men-at-arms. The last relates to a vital fortress on the Scottish Border five years after Bannockburn; and Conway in 1284 was one of the principal castles designed to hold down a still imperfectly subdued North Wales. These figures suggest that when one finds truly concentric arrangements, as at Beaumaris or Rhuddlan, they were built with some such object as to provide, between the two enceintes, a ready-made entrenched camp for occasional occupation by elements of an army, rather than to add anything useful to the defences of the castle in the centre, already quite adequate as they stood. A great part of the function of any royal castle was to serve as a dépôt where stores, treasure and munitions could be effectively guarded by a small body of men.

p 140 (18)

p 138 (8)

p 140 (15)

The isolated tower or keep is, as already remarked, the kind of fortification which can be guarded by fewest men; and within the Empire it is almost always purely utilitarian. Everywhere its only door is on the first floor and approached by a drawbridge or wooden steps; the ground floor is always without windows, entered by a trap door, and in many cases used as a prison. The

The stronghold of Lucera, on a high plateau in southern Italy, was begun and possibly designed by the Emperor Frederick II about 1235. The square donjon tower (shown here in plan and in section) stood on a sloping base or 'glacis' (a), inside which a corridor (b) ran round all four sides, roofed with a half-barrel vault and containing nine arrow-slits on each side. Above the glacis the castle rose another two storeys, the upper one turning octagonal (c). Like Castel del Monte (see. p. 137) it was also a royal residence and was provided with finely decorated state rooms, filled by the sophisticated Emperor with antique statues and other works of art. Later in the 13th century, under Charles of Anjou, Lucera was enlarged by an irregular pentagon of outer walls and towers, mostly rectangular but in two cases (called 'the lion' and 'the lioness') circular (d, e). The main gateway (f) was in a re-entrant angle and strongly defended. (13, 14)

Castles placed strategically—and pictur-
esquely—on the heights above the middle
Rhine valley have tried to dominate the
great highway since the earliest times. The
central tower of the Marksburg (above)
is Romanesque, and the fortress round it
has grown up by slow successive additions.
This sketch shows it as it looked in the
15th century, when it belonged to the house
of Hesse. Basically, like many German
strongholds, it is simply a large house
and a free-standing tower surrounded by
a wall. The Marksburg is the only castle
on the Rhine that has escaped destruction.
(15)

height of the building gave it value as a lookout post, and it was
the obvious place to keep valuables. But the remnants of a garrison
shut up in a tower with its only door twenty feet above the
ground were out of the war unless relieved, and unlikely even
to be allowed to surrender on favourable terms. Exceptions to
all these rules are provided by those keeps, such as that of Flint
or the Tour Constance at Aigues-Mortes, which were surrounded
not merely by a wet moat, but by one linked to the sea. But,
presumably because their limited military value had become clear,
keeps from the 13th century are often omitted from the design
of castles altogether. They were, indeed, normally retained only for
the particular type of castle where the tower was also the seigneurial residence.

Peaceful Uses

The basis of all living accommodation in northern Europe in the
Middle Ages was the two-room suite of hall (with fireplace) and
chamber (with latrine). Both rooms could develop into groups
of rooms in a large house, storage and cooking being removed
from the hall into the buttery, pantry, kitchen, salsary, etc. opening
off its lower end, while the chamber could be extended by an
inner chamber, any number of closets, and a private oratory. But
large houses show an equally pronounced tendency to reduplicate
two-roomed suites, and it often looks, in two-storeyed arrangements, as if a hall and chamber for servants were provided on the
ground floor and the same accommodation for the master on the
floor above. Great men who expected to entertain visitors travelling with their own retinues had to be able to provide the same
sort of accommodation for them; and at Clarendon the king's
hall and chamber were in a different building from the queen's.
The same manifestly inconvenient arrangement seems to have prevailed in 13th-century French royal palaces; otherwise St Louis
and his Queen would not have found it unusually satisfactory to
live at Pontoise where, since their bedrooms were one above the
other and linked by a private stair, they could frustrate the
determined efforts of the Queen-Mother to interfere with their
married life. In the ordinary way, in the earlier part of the period,
visiting bachelors must have had to take their chance in attics; but
sets of small chambers for visitors and servants are to be found
in ambitious houses such as Haddon or Dartington Hall from the
late 14th century onwards. There appear to be distinct differences
of fashion between different countries, the arrangement with the

master's hall and chamber on the first floor being normal in France
and in English circles following French fashions. The normal English arrangement was to have a hall on the ground floor with its
appurtenant chamber on the first floor of a two-storey block at the
upper end; and this design was not wholly rejected even by the
Norman kings, as is evidenced by the gigantic hall of William   p 104
Rufus, still standing, though altered by Richard II, at Westminster.   (76)
The Germans on the other hand seem to have favoured an enormous hall on the second floor, with chambers on the first: such
at any rate is the design of the palace in the Wartburg in the 12th
century and in the Hradschin at Prague in the 15th; and it appears
in Norway, presumably under German influence, in the castles of
Bergen in the 13th century and Akershus early in the 14th. This
arrangement is not, however, specifically German since it is also
found in essentials in the 12th-century Sicilian-Norman palace of
the Zisa at Palermo. The provision of rooms specially designed for
particular uses seems, in any case, mainly a French and English
habit. In Italian buildings the rooms seem relatively small, more
numerous, and little differentiated; and it is much harder to
determine how, individually, they were meant to be used.

In a great many castles, including nearly all German ones, a
straightforward house of the usual local design is simply set
within the enclosure, or, more often, incorporated in the enclosure wall on the castle's least accessible side. The Wartburg is an
obvious example, the Marksburg above Braubach on the Rhine   f 15
another and the 'Norman House' at Christchurch (where the
enclosing wall has disappeared) a third. Very much more interesting from the standpoint of architectural design are the castles
where the residence is combined with the keep or with the
design of the castle as a whole.

The White Tower of the Tower of London is a fusion of the   p 141
gigantic stone hall with the military tower. It is the first of its   (20)
kind known, and may well have been the first of its kind built.
The main hall-chamber and chapel are all on the second floor
instead of the first, allowing for the unlighted basement proper
to towers as well as a service floor, and enabling reasonably large
windows to be provided in the main rooms which, at this height,
do not affect the defensive value of the building. Towers of this
group are distinguished by a heavy dividing wall down the middle,
which at London, on the main floor, separates the hall on one
side from the chamber and chapel on the other, and is further
intended to carry the inner slopes and dividing gutter of the pair

of gabled roofs, hidden behind the parapet, by which the building is covered. In smaller versions of the design the great chamber is placed above instead of alongside the hall, equivalent alterations are made in the staff quarters, and the cross wall is omitted. The inconvenience of having the great chamber on the fourth or fifth floor is obvious, and it is safe to conclude that such buildings were not put up by magnates, let alone kings, with a view to frequent occupation by themselves. It is indeed surprising to find this arrangement well on in the 14th century in the knight's p 140 'castle' at Nunney, mentioned above, which must have been built (17) to its owner's design.

Fearful Symmetry

The main factor operating here would seem to have been the marked predilection shown in the later Middle Ages for houses externally displaying a clean geometrical form. The history of this taste has not been written, indeed it has often (and absurdly) been attributed to 'the Renaissance', and one can only draw attention to a few monuments which appear to illustrate the trend. The rectangular castle with towers at the corners, which is ultimately a Roman form, appears in the mid-12th century in the citadel of f 24, 25 Carcassonne. It was freely employed in the south Italian castles of the Emperor Frederick II in the early 13th century, and later mediaeval examples are fairly common in most parts of Europe. It is, however, comparatively rare for the buildings within the walls to be set against them, with any regard for symmetry, before the 14th century. The idea of arranging buildings round a square

court had been accepted for monasteries since the St Gall plan of the early 9th century; but the earliest mediaeval houses set round regular courtyards I am aware of are those in the castles of Sherborne and Old Sarum, built by that remarkable man Roger, Bishop of Salisbury, in the first half of the 12th century. These houses are set within, not against, the castle walls; and the same arrangement was used in the second half of the century for the royal apartments in the Inner Bailey of Windsor Castle, as rebuilt by Henry II, and to some extent at the bishop of Winchester's castle of Wolvesey. Meanwhile more elaborate external volumes were being used for towers, such as the quatrefoil of Etampes or the buttressed cylinder of Conisborough. All the experiments f 16–22 belong to the French and English sphere, and precede the buildings of Frederick II, to which they must in some way relate. By no means all Frederick's castles, for instance Lagopesole, show a serious interest in symmetry; but those that do (Catania, the destroyed keep of Lucera, and Castel del Monte) carry it to great f 13, 14 lengths. It is indeed, difficult to see how the rooms within them were meant to be used. Requirements in this respect, as observed above, seem to have been different in Italy and in the north, where Frederick's designs, with their numerous identical rooms, or great mosque-like halls, would have been unacceptable; but these buildings must have been inconvenient even in Italy. The really important ones appear to be Castel del Monte and Lucera, p 137 (5) since they introduced the idea of the geometrically regular tower with a light-well.

English architects seem to have been brought to think more

The keep of Conisborough, an example of the tight functional planning that went into castle-building. It was built about 1170 by a half-brother of Henry II and consisted of a simple cylinder with six massive buttresses. Each floor contained one large circular room; staircases and subsidiary rooms were ingeniously fitted into the thickness of the wall and into the buttresses. Shown here are two vertical sections (one through the main building, the other, top, through the buttresses as well) and plans of the four principal floors.

The lowest storey (a) was a cellar, with a well below it, and could be entered only through a trap-door in the first floor. This was the only stone floor; all the others were wood. The entrance was at first-floor level (b) originally across a drawbridge; the present steps are modern. Neither of these storeys has any windows.

The second floor (c) contained the main hall of the castle, with a two-light window (d), fireplace (e) and latrine (f). The third floor (g) had two windows (h), a fireplace (j), latrine (k) and vaulted chapel (l) of two bays inside the buttress, with its own tiny sacristy (m).

The fourth floor (n) consisted of a circular gallery on the thickness of the main wall. Four of the buttresses at this level housed guardrooms (p), a dovecote (q) and an oven (r) (water was raised to this height from the well through holes in the other floors). In the two other buttresses were stairs leading to the roof (s) which had a defensive wall-walk. (16–22)

0 100 200 FT.

0 30 60 M.

10 5 0 10 20 30 40 50 FT.

0 5 10 15 M.

The most complete example today of a mediaeval fortified town is Carcassonne, in south-western France. Its present appearance is the result as much of the extensive restoration carried out in the 19th century as of the survival of the original fabric; and yet the total impression is probably not far from historical reality. Below is a plan of the city and (right) an old drawing of 1462, which shows the 'Cité' on its hill and the Lower Town (Basse Ville) in the foreground.

Parts of the walls of Carcassonne go back to the Visigothic period in the 6th century, but most of the inner wall, with the citadel, dates from the 11th and 12th centuries and the outer from the end of the 13th. The main gateway, the Narbonne Gate (a) is on the east side (not seen in the old drawing). It was guarded by two barbicans and had to be approached by way of a narrow oblique path between them. Ditches protect the walls on the north, south and east sides. On the west, projecting from the citadel, was an elaborate outwork going down by a steep walled path to a round barbican (b) near the bank of the river Aude. This enabled the garrison to make sorties in the direction of the river, and rendered the task of the besiegers even more difficult.

The barbican was demolished in the early 19th century, but it is clearly seen in the old drawing, and a reconstruction by Viollet-le-Duc is shown right. The citadel itself, in the background (c, on the plan), consisted of a courtyard with main rooms on the south and west and had a barbican (d), ditch and ramparts of its own.

Carcassonne played a leading rôle in the Albigensian Wars, falling to Simon de Montfort in August 1209. In 1262 a revolt led to the expulsion of several leading citizens who were, however, allowed to settle nearby and founded the Basse Ville. The Cathedral of Carcassonne, St-Nazaire (e), dates mostly from the 12th and 13th centuries. (23, 24, 25) systematically in these terms by the Savoyard, Master James of St George, who designed the Welsh castles of Edward I at the end of the 13th century. The emphasis in these, however, is still on p 136 (2) the exterior volume of the castle as a whole (Harlech, Beaumaris) p 140 (15) and only in the Inner Ward of Conway are there signs of an attempt to plan the domestic structures conveniently and at the same time in relation to both the outside wall and an interior court. Moreover the exterior form is always that of towers applied to a rectangle. Nevertheless, the seed had been sown. The Scottish p 140 (14) castle of Caerlaverock applied all these considerations to a triangular plan, while there are a number of ingeniously planned houses of the late 13th century, of which Broughton 'Castle' near Oxford is an outstanding example. In this a single building has been devised in which four separate private suites (with communicating accommodation for personal servants) all have separate access to, or windows looking into, the chapel, and separate access to a common great hall. The ability to design in three dimensions is already striking, but it becomes even more impressive when, as at Old Wardour, this kind of planning is fitted into a geometrical exterior. The 'keep' of Old Wardour is a regular pentagon in plan and has a light-well; and, starting with these formal limitations, the architect has fitted in the whole series of highly differentiated rooms, isolated from one another or communicating as required, which a century earlier would have formed half a dozen entirely separate buildings. There are a number of later structures of this kind, the most brilliant being p 140 (18) probably the keep of Warkworth, of which the basic plan is a Greek cross. How far these tendencies were also operative in France is difficult to judge since so many of the buildings which might have p 139 (11) enlightened us are gone, such as the Lower Castle of Poitiers, known from a miniature in Jean duc de Berry's *Très Riches Heures*, which had the triangular form of Caerlaverock. But on the whole buildings exhibiting the same preoccupations in France, such as f 37 the Louvre, seem to be rather rare and to belong to the reign of Charles V, while the obvious prototype for Edward III's (de- f 26 stroyed) cylindrical castle at Queenborough (begun 1361) is not in France but is the castle of Bellver built by James I, King of Majorca, about 1300. All these last belong, in any case, to the same family as the Inner Ward of Conway, that is to say, the outer walls of the courtyard-house are those of the castle proper. The designing of isolated towers as convenient late mediaeval houses seems to have been cultivated predominantly in England, though Charles V built himself a splendid example at Vincennes, and Vincennes is presumably the model for the few analogous Continental buildings such as the Danish royal castle of Hälsingborg (now in Sweden).

The circular castle was a logical step from the circular keep, and can still be seen in such 'shell-keeps' as Restormel, in Cornwall. Perhaps the most elaborate was at Queenborough, Kent, a royal castle built in 1361–77 under the supervision of William of Wykeham (also responsible for the palace in the upper ward of Windsor Castle). The outermost defence was a moat (a); next came a massive wall (b) surrounding the outer bailey (c), which was turfed and used for jousts. The castle proper (shaded) had six high towers and was entered by a gate (d) placed on the opposite side from the gate into the outer bailey (though there was a postern on this side) so that attackers had to pass half round the castle exposed to the fire of the garrison. (26)

The Royal Routine

The castles last discussed, though of formidable military strength, were, indeed, just as convenient for their royal or princely owners as their non-military residences; Edward III often lived at Queen- f 26 borough, and Charles V at Vincennes. They had, therefore, to be f 28–31 able to accommodate very large households, in which the purely military element did not predominate. Queenborough and Vincennes were near enough to London and Paris for no significant part of the administrative staff of the kingdoms to have to follow the king; but at Conway the extensive sanitary accommodation provided for the clerks of the Chancery, who were to be lodged outside the castle proper, forms a picturesque and much admired feature of the town wall. As for the life of their royal masters, the simplest way of getting a picture of its framework is to refer to the *Libro del Infante* of Juan Manuel, the nephew of Alfonso X the Learned of Castile, and a prominent figure in the politics of that kingdom in the first half of the 14th century. The advantage of his writings over others' is that he was himself an almost independent prince, not a cleric or a courtier. His programme for a king's day, not disturbed by urgent political matters, is as follows. The morning is to be occupied by attendance at Mass and Office, followed by military training. Dinner is to be taken in company with the king's entire suite, and is to be the occasion of singing and reading from the epics describing the exploits of the national heroes. The siesta and Vespers follow: then affairs of state of all kinds are to be attended to till nightfall. Lighter distractions are to follow supper; and the reading prescribed for sleepless nights is, once again, the histories of past heroes. The Infante also sets out a programme for a prince's education, which is to be the way he was himself brought up by his own mother, a princess of Savoy. The general framework of the day is as before. After early Mass on weekdays the boy is to be taught reading, writing, languages and, of course, history till dinner and again between the siesta and supper; except that on Mondays, Wednesdays and f 27 Fridays the morning is to be devoted to hunting, preferably in p 147 the mountains, and military exercise. On Sundays the boy has (29) only to be up in time for High Mass: the rest of the Sunday morning and the afternoon are to be devoted to riding and sport but not hunting; and there is to be no Sunday study.

This kind of programme had been long established: but it appears to have taken on particularly rigid forms through a wish to follow the example of St Louis of France, to which Juan Manuel specifically appeals. It seems, however, that in more northern countries official business normally preceded dinner instead of following the siesta. Henry I of England, particularly admired for the regular pattern of his life, dealt with public business before the canonical hour of Sext, i.e. midday, and 'the young men of his household did not attend him before dinner, nor the old ones after, except by his special wish'. Henry II of England, on the other hand, put his court to great inconvenience by the irregularity of his habits, and by his failure ever to decide beforehand how long he would remain in a given place or when and where he would move next. This was the more serious as in the 12th century kings were accompanied on their ceaseless travels by the entire machinery of administration and justice. At the battle of Fréteval in 1194 Philip Augustus of France, defeated by Richard I of England, managed to lose not merely the battle, but the archives of the Crown which had accompanied him. But the English archives had already acquired fixed homes in the Tower of London and Westminster Palace; and in the 13th century the French royal archives were permanently accommodated in the treasury built by St Louis on the north side of the Sainte Chapelle in his palace at Paris.

The physical forms taken by mediaeval administrative documents are entirely fascinating and marvellously inconvenient. Most transactions required the preparation of several parchments with pendant wax seal-impressions. These were liable to be held invalid if the seals got broken, as they constantly did; and St Louis was particularly commended for recognizing the validity of a document from which most of the seal was missing. Such documents were rolled up and stored in chests in which, of course, it was nearly impossible to find a particular one for reference without turning the whole chest out. And in the Tower of London, at

A king goes hawking: this frontispiece of a late 15th-century work on falconry shows the author (foreground) presenting his book, and some of the subjects treated in it. Top left: hooded birds being given medicine. To the right, training to come to the lure, and making the kill. In the right foreground a falconer with dogs feeds a hawk on his wrist. (27)

least, there was no organized system of identifying the chests, which were distinguished from one another by having painted on them such things as red quatrefoils or caricatures of eminent administrators. The documents issued each year by the English royal chancery were entered on long skins of parchment, sometimes on the back as well as the front, and all the skins used in a given year were sewn together end to end and rolled up. In order to refer to a writ sent out early in a year you have therefore to unroll the whole thing, which is liable to be fifty yards long and more. The pleadings in the Courts of Law are admittedly on skins joined together at one end only; but the skins are about six foot long and searching through a plea-roll involves ceaseless walking to and fro as you turn each skin over. It is not as if perfectly ordinary books were unknown to the officials concerned: they were used, for instance, for the day-to-day accounts of the Royal Wardrobe. But for accounting at the Exchequer the figures had to be transferred to rolls; and it is difficult to think how the roll ever came to be invented unless because it is stronger for carrying from place to place.

Castle Furniture

The furnishings of royal residences continued to be moved with the king for much longer than administrative records were; but it is possible to exaggerate the extent to which this was so in the 14th century when information is fairly full, and it will probably prove to have been exaggerated for the 13th century when the English royal accounts for that period have been properly examined. To fix ideas as to the contents of mediaeval castles it will, in any case, be best to consider a few individual inventories.

For the military aspect, one can hardly do better than refer to the store-check taken at Dover Castle in 1343 when the Earl of Huntingdon, outgoing Warden of the Cinque Ports, handed over to his successor, Sir Bartholomew Burghersh. It concerns only government property, listed room by room, including the bakehouse, brewhouse and forge. Anyone with recent experience of military hand-overs will notice a familiar ring about this one. A good many of the chapel vestments, stored in two chests, though clearly up to establishment, were 'rotted', 'useless' or 'valueless'; the candlesticks were bronze or iron; the processional cross was bronze. In the hall were five immovable tables, three movable ones (with one trestle short) and a number of benches. There was one five-branched candle bracket of iron, also an 'alms-tub' for left-overs, two ladders, and a barrel of sand for putting the shine on armour. The adjacent chamber contained nothing but a firescreen. The kitchen, where the fixtures are noted, contained nothing movable (apart from four dressers) but a bucket for hauling stones up into the keep, presumably in the wrong place. The bucket in the well-house was unserviceable. Someone had got at the mead, though it was stored in the keep, and for each cask the number of inches between the top of the fluid and the top of the vessel had to be noted. The only other object in the keep was a quern. The longest entry is for the armoury. Its contents included fifty bows dating from the time of the king's grandfather, twenty-two bascinets of ancient type covered with rotted leather, twenty-five rusty coats of mail, twenty-five decayed gauntlets of an antique model, a hundred and three round shields of which thirty-four were unserviceable, six buckets full of unserviceable arrows without feathers, and a hundred and eighteen lances of which eighteen lacked their heads. There were a few items which were serviceable, and no doubt incoming troops brought their own equipment. But Dover was one of the principal English fortresses on the Channel, and in 1343 England and France were at war.

Charles V at Home

For the other side of the picture, by far the most instructive inventory surviving is that of the most valuable possessions of Charles V of France, taken on his own orders in 1379–80. Its special interest is that it lists not merely the things in store in the castle of Melun but also, room by room, the things the king had out in the palaces in which he normally lived, primarily the Tower of Vincennes and the Louvre, but also his smaller houses near Paris, the Hôtel St-Pol, St-Germain-en-Laye and Beauté-sur-Marne. One is thus faced with items such as three walking sticks which had been made for the Queen Mother, all the late Queen's hats, and a little box containing bits of sheet gold damaged by fire. Actual furniture is not recorded, but a great many items are listed as the contents of particular chests and hutches. The most illuminating account is for Vincennes, since Vincennes still exists and can be visited; and it is therefore worth considering this splendid building in some detail first.

The castle of Vincennes forms an immense rectangle surrounded by a broad ditch and by walls punctuated by rectangular towers, once remarkable for their height. The Great Tower stands in the middle of one of the longer sides and forms, with its surrounding enclosure, a small separate castle of its own. It may have been begun by John II, the king captured at Poitiers, but substantially it is the work of Charles V himself. The Tower is square, of four storeys and an attic, with a cylindrical turret at each corner, to one of which, in neglect of symmetry, is attached an oblong projection to house the latrines. The Tower's own enclosure is square, embattled, concentric with it and surrounded by its own moat, which is crossed by a drawbridge. The apartments of the palace were partly in the Tower and partly set against the enclosure wall, those in the latter position including the hall, the chapel and the principal visitor's room called, presumably from its decoration, the Chambre aux Daims; and the King had a private study on the upper floor of the gatehouse. From this upper floor a second drawbridge led to the first-floor entrance of the Tower itself, opening into a lobby in the thickness of the wall. The lobby at its two ends opened into rooms in the two near turrets, one being a guardroom, the other the base of the Great Stair; and a door, not facing the main entrance and thus avoiding draughts, led from it forward into the Great Chamber. This had a vaulted

p 150 (34) p 154 (42)

f 28–31 p 137 (7) p 139 (12)

roof (the vault being, most exceptionally, wainscoted), a large fireplace, and subsidiary closets in the two far turrets, one with its latrine. The Great Stair led only to the next floor, which reproduced the arrangements of the floor below, the main room being the Upper Chamber, and the only difference that a private oratory was fitted in next to the latrine. The kitchens occupied the basement which must always, contrary to 12th-century practice, have been entered through a ground-floor doorway; and from the basement a narrow service stair in the thickness of the wall ran up four floors. The floor above the Upper Chamber was for the royal children and had closets, some with fireplaces, in all four turrets. The attic above was for the staff. The ingenuity of this design can hardly be sufficiently admired. In the last analysis it is simply the the familiar hall-and-chamber house, with a tower, set in an enclosure; but everything is on a generous scale (the chamber for instance has become two very large rooms with subsidiary closets), the requirements of privacy, security and convenience have been fully met, and the whole forms one composition, compact, geometrical and neatly interlocked.

Of its contents in 1379 the inventory lists first what was found in several chests, the yellow wooden box in the turret leading off the Great Chamber; and, in the Great Chamber itself, the square box with two lids in the window near the entrance, the large deep chest between the two doors, and the box, divided in two sections, which stood on brackets near the fireplace, while the dresser in the Great Chamber then contained the plate belonging to the Dauphin's establishment. In one closet opening off the Upper Chamber was a large chest of which the King kept the key, and in a window nearby a small box supported on iron brackets. All save one of these were linen-chests, 'linen' including a magnificent series of lengths of patterned silks and velvets, and there was another such chest in the garret over the Chambre aux Daims. The exception was the box, divided in two, in the Great Chamber, which was filled with particularly fine illuminated service books, mainly breviaries, the exquisite *Bréviaire de Belleville* among them. Besides these chests the inventory lists a mass of jewellery and bric-à-brac, without unfortunately specifying how it was stored or displayed. The pictures of interiors of about 1400 do not suggest a clear answer. There were about 700 miscellaneous objects listed, and most were of the kind that for the past couple of centuries would have been displayed in glass-fronted cupboards or stood about on chests of drawers, occasional tables and mantelpieces. None of these things existed in 1379 and there appears to have been only one dresser. The objects must, presumably, have been kept in closed cupboards, with a few choice pieces and the practical items such as candlesticks on top of the cupboards. 'Practical' is not quite the right word for the candlesticks; typical is 'a little image of a naked child in silver sitting on a gold chair holding a candlestick and a box' or 'a white sheep [presumably enamelled] standing on a silver-gilt base diapered with the arms of the King and Queen, with a little candlestick on its back.' The King seems to have kept in each of his sets of apartments a clock, a reading-desk, a table-lighter and an astrolabe. The lighters (flint and steel) are not further described, and should therefore have been more or less functional, though Charles' brother, Jean duc de Berry, had some in the form of his badge, the bear. Other remarkable items are a wax tablet for writing, in an enamelled silver case, and two sketching blocks, one with horn covers, in jewelled cases. These last were presumably like those surviving wooden sketchbooks, of which that attributed to Jacquemart de Hesdin is the best known.

The books the King had out were all in French (apart from service books) and were nearly all either devotional (including a French Bible which he always took with him) or concerned with astrology, hence no doubt the astrolabes; though the *Gouvernement des Princes* and the *Grandes Chroniques de France* were in his room at St-Germain-en-Laye. His library, to which scholars had access and which was in the Louvre, was, however, excellent; and it is possible he had taken a less restricted interest in its contents when he was younger. Paintings on panel were few and mostly set up in chapels. The paintings of the Annunciation and Baptism on the door of one of his private rooms at Melun, presumably not fixtures since they are listed, are the only exception, apart from

his one non-religious picture, a polyptych with portraits of himself, his uncle the Emperor Charles IV, his father, King John II, and Edward III of England. This was in one of his rooms in the Hôtel St-Pol, and it is generally supposed the surviving portrait of King John was one of its leaves. His figured tapestries, however, of which he had some thirty sets, were nearly all of secular subjects, frequently romances. What was evidently the largest single piece, depicting the wars of Judas Maccabaeus, was of Arras work and is described as covering the whole wall of the gallery at Beauté-sur-Marne; but is not stated where in 1379 the rest were hanging.

p 155 (46)

Kitchen and Wardrobe

What is entirely lacking from this inventory is the wooden furniture and the everyday equipment of such departments as the kitchen. Some indications on these matters can be deduced from textiles in store: bed-hangings for instance imply particular kinds of bed; but in general it is necessary to turn to other sources of information. In 1317, one learns, the French Queen took out of store in the Great Tower of the Louvre, besides some cloth and a reading-desk which had belonged to St Louis, two tables to eat at. Both were folding tables, of 'two and a half' and three pieces respectively, inlaid with small pieces of ebony and ivory; and a century later we have the bill for upholstering the chair on which the Queen (Isabel of Bavaria) sat to have her hair done. It was a folding chair, the wood painted scarlet and powdered with her arms and her and her husband's initials, with a scarlet velvet seat with flame-coloured silk fringes, fixed with gilt nails; and when it was in use she and her servant would have been hidden from curious eyes by a kind of tent, several of these figuring in the inventory of Charles V (her father-in-law). The matter of chairs is rather difficult, since it is certain that people sat on benches for meals, and otherwise normally on beds, chests and window-seats: there were always plenty of cushions. For princesses, however, and probably also for kings, two chairs were considered essential. This emerges from the details of what the English Wardrobe provided for Edward III's daughter, Princess Joan, when she set off in 1348 at the age of thirteen to marry Pedro the Cruel of Castile. She fell ill of the plague en route, poor child, and died somewhere near Bordeaux. But in the present connection the interest of the matter is that the list tells us precisely what equipment was thought necessary for an English princess, making a long journey with an appropriate retinue, who must have expected to have to occupy for short periods a succession of more or less empty houses in a manner befitting her rank. She took with her the complete furnishing of a chapel, two sets of hangings for a hall (one of worsted worked with popinjays, the other embroidered mainly with roses), the hangings for two beds, two chairs, one specifically for washing and the other for 'tiring' her hair, a suitable quantity of saddlery (including three ceremonial saddles), and the pots, pans, cutlery, etc., needed to equip a kitchen, pantry, buttery and spicery together with a supply of spice. The two chairs no doubt explain why in 1337 Edward III was provided from his wardrobe with two chairs, one decked with purple velvet, the other with leather, and at the same time the Princesses Isabel (aged 5) and Joan (aged 4) also each received two chairs, one covered with leather, the other with green and blue velvet. They are bedroom furniture to be used solely in connection with the dressing of hair.

p 155 (45)

It is rather sad that we have no list of the kitchen equipment at Vincennes, as Charles V's chef, Guillaume Tirel, nicknamed Taillevent, is an historical figure. His tombstone shows him in honorary dress as sergeant-at-arms, with his bascinet and mace, and his shield charged with three cooking-pots. His career can be followed from his entry, as kitchen-boy, into the service of Queen Jeanne d'Evreux in his teens, to his death in his eighties, as lately retired master of the royal kitchens in 1395. He wrote the first standard French cookery book, which enjoyed a truly phenomenal success. It was one of the first French books to be printed; and it went on being reprinted until 1604, thus having maintained its reputation for over two centuries. It would have been pleasant to know just how his kitchen was equipped; but in the basement of the Tower of Vincennes one can still see where he worked.

f 32

The inventory includes a list of Charles V's best robes (seven

The royal castle of Vincennes, as it appeared in the 17th century. (Du Cerceau, who made this engraving, has omitted other buildings, including the Sainte Chapelle, which stood within the walls and concentrated on the fortress). Probably begun by John II, it was substantially finished by Charles V about 40 years later. The principal entrance was on the right, over the bridge. The Great Tower, or donjon (see p. 137), over 150 feet high, with walls nine feet thick at the base, rises behind its own defences in the middle of the western side. A diagonal section is shown (below right). There were 'tourelles' at each corner, one of them containing the main staircase.

Left: The way into the Great Tower from the main court of the castle. This can be clearly followed in the old engraving. Passing through a gateway (a) one crossed a drawbridge (b) and arrived at another large fortified gate, the Chatelet (c), where Charles V had his private study (d). From here one entered the 'enceinte' of the donjon—a massive square enclosure standing on a sloping ramp—and so into the donjon itself at first floor level (e). (The ground-floor, f, was originally the kitchen). This floor was taken up by the Great Chamber (g), a splendid room covered with a quadripartite vault supported on a single pier in the centre. From this room the 'escalier d'honneur' ascends to the second storey (h), almost identical with the first. An oratory (j) opened off one corner. From here only the narrow service staircase (k) led to the upper storeys. (28–31)

173

the assistance of specially trained squirrel-hounds. In 1391 the Åbo agent of a single firm in Reval was able to deliver his employers as many as 200,000 skins. In the hope of maintaining this lucrative trade, the hunting season, anyhow limited to winter by considerations about the colour of the fur, was further limited by law, opening usually on October 13th and ending in some areas as early as February 2nd.

The Economics of Piety

The principal field for extravagant display was always the chapel. The overwhelming mass of the precious objects in Charles V's inventory (as in all similar French documents) had some religious *f 34* justification. It is not only the cupboards in chapels and oratories that are full of gold and jewelled statuettes of sacred personages and of reliquaries; they are also prominent among the objects listed under the ordinary rooms of the palaces, where they jostle with collars with gold buckles (for lapdogs), knives with jewelled handles, spoons and occasional forks. It is these objects which were out of store that bring us nearest to the heart of that very puzzling subject, 14th-century piety; and it is tiresome that it is in general impossible to distinguish what was out at the King's own wish from what had been taken out by the Queen who had only died in 1378. The discipline with the ivory handle and four gold chains was hers—it had her arms on it; and there were silver balls or diminutive reliquaries on chains with the inscription *Jesus autem transiens...* (as on the Churberg armour) at both Vincennes and the Hôtel St-Pol, which suggests that the King himself probably thought they had talismanic value. But perhaps his mother had

The tombstone of Taillevent (Guillaume Tirel), 'maistre des garnisons de cuisine du roy,' i.e. Charles V, and the author of the first, long-popular French cookery book. Taillevent died in about 1395; his tombstone shows him wearing his honorary dress as sergeant-at-arms, but the emblem on his shield is three cooking-pots. (32)

six-piece suits furred with ermine, seven three-piece suits furred with miniver, and sixteen parts of suits also furred with miniver, besides cloaks and mantles), but his everyday clothes are specifically omitted. This is a pity, as 14th-century kings were always ordering new suits, and it would be interesting to see how many at a given moment were still wearable. Edward III, for example, had sixteen new suits (all but two six-piece, furred with miniver) in the course of 1348, besides placing a long series of orders for tournament clothes and armour. Clothes were one of the great extravagances of the time. Members of the English royal family had their own appointed tailor from a very tender age, Princess Margaret for instance before she was two. Princess Joan's trousseau is duly detailed; she took with her eight full sets of robes besides the two she was to wear on her wedding day, and half a dozen less formal ensembles. Amusingly, we have also details of the trousseau of Blanche de Bourbon, who was sent off from the French court to marry Pedro the Cruel in her turn, four years after Princess Joan's death. She had a miserable time. However, what is immediately relevant is that she took only five sets of robes in addition to those for her wedding day, and only four less formal ensembles; but, to judge from the expressions used, there was more fashionable variety in their cut. In her case we have very full details of the fur used. The principal item was, as usual, miniver, the fur from the belly of the (European) grey squirrel, of which in this one trousseau no fewer than 11,794 skins were used. They only cost eighteen deniers each, but £900 of 14th-century money is a substantial figure. As all members of all royal families used miniver at this sort of rate all the time, the massacre of animals in the north every year was gigantic. The animal was hunted in the forests of Sweden and Finland with snares, traps and blunted arrows, with

The royal gold cup of England and France (above) was probably made in Paris about 1380 for the duc de Berry. He gave it to Charles VI, whose father, Charles V, had been born on St Agnes Day, and who made something of a cult of this saint. The coloured enamel decoration accordingly shows scenes from the life of St Agnes. On the lid she is offered a jewel box, her sister standing beside her; on the bowl two of her posthumous miracles— a lame man approaches her tomb on crutches and a princess, suffering from leprosy, lies on it. On the stem are the symbols of St Matthew and St John. The later history of the cup was chequered. In 1434 it was brought to England and became part of the royal treasure. James I gave it to a Spanish diplomat who presented it to a convent. The convent sold it in 1883 and it found its way back to the British Museum in London. (33)

The Sainte Chapelle in Paris was built by St Louis in the 13th century as a shrine for the Crown of Thorns and other relics of the Passion which he had acquired from Syria and Constantinople. Over the centuries many more accumulated; this engraving shows some of the most celebrated shortly before the Revolution, all of course housed in precious reliquaries: (a) the Crown of Thorns; (b) Christ's swaddling clothes; (c) row of objects connected with the Crucifixion—Christ's bonds, the sponge, the reed, a vial of His blood; (d) a fragment of the True Cross; (e) the tip of the Holy Lance; (f) a flask containing some of the Virgin's milk; (g) Moses' rod; and (h) the top of John the Baptist's head. (34)

made him wear one when a child. The statues and groups in precious metals included some which descended from Jeanne d'Evreux, widow of the last king but two, who had died in 1370; and if they resembled the exquisite Virgin (still extant) which she gave to St-Denis, their suitability for devotional use need not be questioned. But then one finds a silver-gilt image of St Agnes sitting on a white sheep (her emblem), and a silver tree with twelve branches from which hung disks containing relics. One wonders just what was thought of them at the time; as, of course, one wonders as one stands before the only surviving relic-tree I know: that in the Imperial Treasury at Vienna, which was a present to an Empress from a 17th-century pope.

In any case, all mediaeval rulers had chapels attached to their castles and palaces: only the Emperor Frederick II and his sons seem to have thought them superfluous. Indeed, most important castles had at least two, like the Tower of London, one being the oratory of the royal apartments, the other primarily the garrison church. Vincennes had three when the Sainte Chapelle in the outer ward had been built. The Dover inventory should provide a sufficient corrective to any illusions that splendour or even decency were necessary attributes of divine service in the chapel of a royal castle in an alleged 'age of faith'. But in a chapel the king was at all likely to attend, decency was of course assured. One chapel, at least, in each of the palaces of Charles V where inventories were taken, had the minimum necessary equipment for Mass in the best materials and good order; but any king travelling took the furnishing of a chapel with him. Castle chapels were very often two-storeyed or, more precisely, had a gallery, the type being traceable back in the West as far as Charlemagne's palace chapel at Aachen. There has been much discussion about the significance

of this arrangement, but it appears to be purely practical. The upper storey, as for instance in St John's chapel in the Tower of London, is on a level with the royal apartments, thus allowing the royal family to attend the service conducted by the priest in the lower chapel without having to go downstairs, bother about security, be polite to the outdoor staff or otherwise discompose themselves. The extreme form of this system will be found in the baronial castle at Broughton, where there is no gallery but the chambers of two separate suites simply have windows looking into the chapel, set high in its wall. If there is an altar in it, an upper chapel can be used as a private chapel independently of the ground floor; but in the Sainte Chapelle at Paris, and St Stephen's in Westminster Palace, there are two superimposed chapels which do not communicate with one another. This arrangement has probably nothing to do with the galleried chapel. Both at Paris and at Westminster the lower chapel is little more than an undercroft and, in the absence of specific texts, we do not know how or how often it was meant to be used. It serves, however, to bring the upper, now main, chapel level with some semi-public rooms; and at Westminster this upper chapel was itself provided with a royal pew in a gallery at the west end.

The staffing of such chapels varied enormously. At the bottom end of the scale we have certainly to envisage many baronial chaplains as unfortunate hangers-on whose relation to their masters was that of the Rev. Mr Supple to Squire Western; and kings had small groups of chaplains who travelled with them and whose status, though one hopes they were better treated, was much the same. But major royal castles, such as Conway, carried a permanent chaplain on the establishment, and really important chapels, Aachen, the Sainte Chapelle at Paris, St George's at Windsor,

p 152 (40)

p 149 (33)

p 151 (37, 38)

p 138 (8)

The clasp of St Louis (Louis IX), part of the royal treasure of France; a chased silver plate with fleur-de-lys picked out in amethysts, emeralds, garnets and sapphires. Although called after St Louis (and sometimes ascribed in mediaeval inventories to Charlemagne) it is more likely to be of 14th-century date. It held together the royal mantle at coronations and great ceremonies. (35)

were endowed collegiate churches with their own dean and canons. Such collegiate churches existed also in baronial castles, for instance Vergy where the stalls of the church of St-Denis were regularly filled by the clerical sons of the hereditary knights. In the course of the 14th century, with the great development of polyphony, the staffs of collegiate churches in princely castles seem more and more to have been selected for their musical ability. A considerable number of the known English composers of the 15th century were at some date canons of St George's, Windsor, or St Stephen's, Westminster; and the attitude of kings is illustrated by the well-known anecdote of Henry VIII listening to a chorister of Wolsey's with a particularly fine voice and then demanding that the boy be transferred from the Cardinal's chapel to his own.

How splendid the furnishing of these chapels could be one can learn from such documents as Charles V's inventory, though it is probable that the French royal chapels were exceptionally well looked after. Inventories of St George's, Windsor, seem to include a disproportionate number of reliquaries with a pinnacle or two missing or angels with only one wing. The principal items are vestments and plate, and lists of both are melancholy reading, since so little survives from which their appearance can be envisaged. Charles V's collection of vestments (of which the best, as remarked, were all in store) are mostly in sets, or 'chapels' which included altar hangings matching the robes of the officiants, classified according to colour, white, red, blue and black being best represented. By comparison with other inventories this shows a marked preference for plain silks or velvets embroidered, as against patterned silks; and this type of vestment can hardly be illustrated from anything surviving except the famous set with the leopards of England which probably began as a horse-trapper before being taken into ecclesiastical use. For Lent there were two white chapels painted in grisaille; the famous *Parement de Narbonne* with its portrait of Charles V and his Queen is probably the actual dossal from the second set listed, painted by Girart d'Orléans, the King's favourite painter. He had, among numerous copes, only one of *opus Anglicanum*, given him by his brother the Duke of Anjou. There were painted wooden polytychs in place in both the chapel and the private oratory at Vincennes and in most of the other chapels he visited; to envisage what they can have been like we have only the Carrand and Wilton diptychs to help us. For the plate one turns inevitably to the *Goldene Rössel* at Altötting, though the kneeling prince embodied in its composition is Charles V's son, and the art of enamelling curved surfaces does not seem to have been mastered to the point where an object like the horse itself could have been produced before Charles V's death. Nevertheless, in its intricacy of conception the Rössel had been foreshadowed by 1379 when the collection at Melun included a large silver-gilt image of Our Lady in a cave, surrounded by little angels with St John the Evangelist on one side and St Agnes on the other, and with three angels holding a crown with the divine Lamb above it on the top.

The passion for ecclesiastical jewellery of this kind seems to have been a distinctive mania of the French royal house during the 14th century. The innumerable jewelled images in precious metal (Charles V owned about 200 gold or silver-gilt statues of Our Lady alone, besides plenty more in ivory and wood) served no very obvious purpose once they had been made; for most of their existence, they lay locked away in chests to be turned at length into coin. The *Goldene Rössel*, in the perfection of its technique and the multiplicity of its appeal has some claim to be the

p 154 (44)

p 287 (15)

p 153 (41)

The King of Majorca's wardrobe: this miniature from the Household Ordinances of James II of Majorca (1337) affords a glimpse behind the ceremonial scenes. The palace is probably Bellver, at Palma, built by James I, its elegant circular plan reflected in the circular coffered hall on the left. The officer with the sword, giving orders, is the King's Chamberlain. One man works on a robe lying on a table; a second seems to be shaking out a bag to put it in. In the background is a huge chest and more folded clothing hanging over a rail. (36)

King Philip II built the Louvre, in Paris, as a royal residence and as part of the defences of the city. It stood originally outside the city wall, at a point considered most vulnerable to attack. In the 14th century the city expanded and took in the Louvre, which was itself added to by various rulers and finally pulled down in the 16th century when the present palace was begun. This reconstruction by Viollet-le-Duc shows it as it was during the reign of Charles V. The moated central tower, the donjon, (a fortress within a fortress), remained from the time of Philip. Immensely strong, modelled probably on the Keep of Coucy, it served as the king's treasury and state-prison. Within the old 13th-century walls Charles V built more palatial apartments in a later style, connected to the donjon on one side by an ornate gallery. The Louvre with its outbuildings formed a self-contained community, almost every trade and craft having quarters within it. (37)

most splendid object in the world; and, if they wish, thousands now can go and look at it. But it could never have come into being if for several generations numerous members of one very rich family had not gone on demanding from the Parisian goldsmiths objects of precisely the same kind, made of the most expensive possible materials, with the one requirement that the new one should be more exquisite than that delivered to some brother or cousin the year before; objects which only a select few would ever see, and which themselves would soon be outshone by something better. The *Rössel* was the Queen's New Year present to the King in 1404 and the analogy to be found in the place held by Fabergé's jewellery in Russian court life is obvious and instructive. The passionate connoisseurship implied is illustrated by the survival into Charles V's inventory of six pieces of plate which had once belonged to Enguerrand de Marigny and had presumably been confiscated when he was judicially murdered in 1315. In the interval King John's ransom had had to be paid and Charles is known to have sent most of his own plate to the mint as a contribution to the cost of the war in 1369. Enguerrand's silver can hardly have escaped except because it was particularly beautiful.

English royal inventories create a different impression. There
f 33 is plenty of plate for the table (as there is in France) and plenty of
useful altar plate, including suitable reliquaries for significant relics. But the little statues, and the elaborate confections designed
to hold some insignificant splinter of bone, are on the whole absent.

The life of a king throughout the last five mediaeval centuries
was always fairly dangerous. Three kings of England were murdered, two fell in battle, two French kings were captured on the
battlefield, one Emperor was murdered. Five kings of Scotland
fell in battle and two were murdered, and other countries can tell
a similar tale. The sanctity of the royal person was a dubious and
unreliable concept, voiced principally by flatterers; but there was
a general desire to know who, at any given moment, was the legitimate king. The Church, turning to biblical precedent, held this
to be settled, on a basis of primogeniture, by anointing and crowning. The biblical precedents were however, uncertain, as was pointed out in Norway by that wonderful character King Sverre, who
had been a priest in his time; and primogeniture was introduced
after he had won the civil war, not before. In any case, some monarchies remained elective, there was frequently no legitimate male
heir, and in cases of dispute different bishops might crown and
anoint different kings. Attempts were made to settle difficulties
of the last kind by demanding crowning with the right crown,
as in the Empire and Hungary, or anointing with the right oil
as in France and England. Regulations of this kind, however,
fell before political facts. Robert the Bruce was successfully
crowned at Scone, although the mystic Stone had been removed

to Westminster. Nevertheless there was value in the traditional *p 14 (3)*
forms; even Sverre had himself crowned, though all the bishops
concerned found themselves excommunicated as soon as the Pope
heard of it. Accordingly most countries of Europe in the course
of the Middle Ages acquired traditional regalia. Where they have *p 156*
survived they are intensely interesting, and there is fascination in *(47)*
reading through the lists of those, such as the English, which no
longer exist, at least in their mediaeval form. All traditions of this *f 35*
kind have, of course, a beginning; and the robes and crowns
which came to be considered essential to a proper coronation
were in their time chosen from among many. Charles V owned
fifty-five crowns and circlets, and any royal house will own, or
have owned, a comparable store. The 'correct' ones were regularly those used (or thought to have been used) by some forebear
who had been sainted, Charlemagne, St Stephen of Hungary,
good King Wenceslas, Edward the Confessor; and the resistance
of objects with this double consecration to the assaults of time
has usually been strong, since it has required both a religious and
a political upheaval to remove their usefulness. To their association with kings who were saints we owe the almost miraculous
survival of splendid embroideries of the 11th century, the mantle
of St Stephen of Hungary, and the mantles given by St Henry
the Emperor to Bamberg cathedral; to its association with the
regalia of the Empire the magnificent mantle of Roger II of Sicily.
They are curious memorials, in their beauty and sanctity, of a
world equally typified by the fragments of the skin of Richard of
Pudlicote, executed for burgling the treasury of Edward I, still
nailed to the door of the room at Westminster where he broke in.

V THE SUM OF KNOWLEDGE

Universities and Learning

RICHARD HUNT

'We are dwarfs mounted on the shoulders of giants,

so that we can see more and further than they; yet not

by virtue of the keenness of our eyesight,

nor through the tallness of our stature, but because we

are raised and borne aloft upon that giant mass.'

BERNARD OF CHARTRES,
CHANCELLOR OF CHARTRES CATHEDRAL

The organization of learning

did not effectively develop in Europe until the 12th century, a period sometimes called 'the Mediaeval Renaissance'. Until then, education was a function of monasteries and cathedrals, its quality dependent on the personality and ability of individual teachers. Many factors made possible the rise of a new system of education, culminating in universities: freedom from attack by external enemies, the recovery of a more orderly form of government, economic expansion, and the growth of towns. The animating force was simple—a desire for knowledge. Men were aware that the Greeks and Arabs had treasures of knowledge which were not available to them at home. They set out to discover the treasure and make it accessible by translations into Latin, their natural medium of exact and learned expression. At the same time they created new institutional forms in self-governing universities and encouraged learning in the religious orders, and so ensured the transmission of the knowledge they had won.

The greatest figure in this intellectual reawakening was St Thomas Aquinas (1225–74). Son of an Italian nobleman, he received his early education at the Benedictine Abbey of Monte Cassino and the University of Naples; in 1244 he became a Dominican friar. A student of theology at Paris and Cologne, St Thomas devoted his life to teaching and writing, producing a large body of work which had a profound influence on European thought for many centuries beyond his own. His most important contribution to Christian theology, particularly in his vast but unfinished masterpiece, the *Summa theologica*, was the recon-

ciliation of Aristotelian philosophy with the teachings of Christ.

In the 14th-century fresco in Sta Maria Novella in Florence, 'The Triumph of St Thomas', attributed to Andrea da Firenze, St Thomas is shown, enthroned, as the focus of an allegory on learning (detail, opposite). Above his head are the four cardinal virtues (Prudence, Temperance, Fortitude and Justice) and the three theological virtues (Faith, Hope and Charity). In his hands he displays the Wisdom of Solomon: the passage begins, 'I prayed, and understanding was given me'. The great Muslim philosopher, Averroës, and the heresiarchs, Sabellius and Arius, are at his feet, and flanking him are the Evangelists and prophets: on the left, St John the Evangelist; far right, a bearded Moses holding the Tablets of the Law. The row of women at the bottom of the fresco are personifications of the theological sciences and the Liberal Arts (seven of each in the full work). The four on the right (left to right) are Arithmetic, Geometry, Astronomy and Music. The men seated on the tier in front of them represent those who are supposed to have discovered or invented these arts: Pythagoras, Euclid, Ptolemy and Tubalcain. According to Vasari, the men sitting below the theological sciences on the left are not particular individuals but symbols of man's various estates and positions: pope, emperor, king, cardinal, duke, bishop and marquis.

The fresco as a whole provides a comprehensive scheme of mediaeval learning: its roots, its aims and its complete identification with Christianity. (1)

The 'masters' of the Middle Ages, who attracted scholars from all parts of the Continent, formed the nucleus round which the idea of universities grew. Peter Abailard (1079–1152), shown with his mistress Héloïse (top left), was the great and famous teacher of Paris. Robert Grosseteste, Bishop of Lincoln (c. 1175–1253) (top right), was a teacher at Oxford and first Chancellor of the University. A mentor and associate of St Thomas Aquinas, St Albertus Magnus (1206–80) (above), was a Swabian who became a Dominican while studying at Padua. He wrote on virtually every scientific, theological and philosophical subject. St Bonaventure (1221–74) (below) was an Italian Franciscan who became famous as a teacher at Paris. (2-5)

Renewed interest in science, based on Greek, Arabic and Jewish sources, was one of the significant trends in mediaeval learning. Among the greatest mathematicians and mechanicians of the period was Nicole Oresme (c. 1323–82), who was born near Caen and studied in Paris, where he was a member, and later Master, of the Collège de Navarre. From 1377 to his death he was Bishop of Lisieux. Right: Oresme is shown with his armillary sphere, a mediaeval mechanical device used for teaching astronomy and for plotting celestial longitude and latitude. Above: Oresme presents his French translation of Aristotle's *Ethics* to his patron, Charles V. (7, 8)

Using compass and square, Richard of Wallingford, Abbot of St Albans (c. 1292–1336) is constructing a scientific instrument, probably an astrolabe (above). On the left hangs a quadrant. His abbatial symbols, the crosier and mitre, are also represented. (9)

The clerk, the astronomer and the mathematician are shown making their calculations (right). The astronomer holds an astrolabe of which we see the back. Pivoted at the centre is an alidade, a sighting rule to measure the angular elevation of a heavenly body. (10)

(a)

(b)

(c)

(d)

(e)

(f)

(g)

(h)

Aspects of student life are illustrated in a 14th-century manuscript of the College of Ave Maria in Paris. Left: (a) Each week one boy, called the hebdomadary, was chosen to perform certain functions; one of these was to light a lamp every evening before the statue of the Blessed Virgin in the College chapel. The founder had ordered that a number of poor people should be supported by the College; after celebration of Mass on certain feast days, each of them received a quart of wine. (b) The students were required to say the Matins and Vespers of Our Lady daily, and to set a candle before the altar. The hebdomadary was instructed to sweep out the chapel every Saturday. (c) Another weekly ceremony was the accounting made by the incumbent hebdomadary of the library books, chained and unchained, to his successor. Six students are shown lined up for an inspection, called *ostensio*. (d) The first boy awake had to ring the bell and say the Ave Maria. Another task of the hebdomadary was to feed the goldfinches, the most cherished bird in mediaeval France. (e) Ten poor women supported by the College are shown sitting in a row; some are spinning, others appear to be having a friendly talk. (f) The poor men living on the College's charity carry the tools of their trade: among them can be identified a shoemaker, a tailor, a mason, a wine-seller, a butcher, a carpenter, and a smith. (g) On great feast days the students enacted a representation of the founder and the Blessed Virgin. The kneeling boy in a white cloak is taking the part of the Virgin, while the seated boy with the crown symbolizes the founder. In front of the Virgin were set out a piece of bread, half a piece of meat, a pint of wine and a bowl of soup; these were to be distributed to the poor women. (h) Eight students in their grey clerical dress are shown in procession towards the statue of the Holy Virgin. Each student receives the blessing of the Holy Infant. (11, 12)

A university classroom in 14th-century Germany (right, above) included students who were by no means all young men. A scene of a teacher with boys (right, below) is meant to represent, in mediaeval terms, Aristotle teaching the boy Alexander. In a classroom at the University of Paris, Amaury de Bène, a theologian who died about 1206–7, lectures to four student clerics (centre). Amaury's theological teachings were condemned by the university and Pope Innocent III.

The birching of an offending schoolboy or student in the Middle Ages (far right) was obviously not an unusual event. (13–16)

Laurencius de Voltolina pinxit

A truly mediaeval and European phenomenon was the rise of the universities, beginning in the 13th century. The growth of intellectual activity and the increasing concentration of clerical students and scholars round certain groups of teachers eventually resulted in official sanction by pope and king. Paris was the first to receive legal recognition as a self-governing corporation; Oxford achieved this status a few years later.

An early patron of Oxford was William of Wykeham, Bishop of Winchester, who founded New College (1380–86). A manuscript illustration shows the College in the 15th century (left, below). William and tonsured students are seen in the foreground; behind them are the College chapel, hall and other buildings. The universities, as opposed to the colleges, did not usually have buildings of their own until the 15th century; the Divinity School at Oxford (left), was built by Richard Winchcombe between 1426 and 1488. (17, 18)

Cambridge University had its origin in 1209, when a number of Oxford students and masters migrated thither. An impression of the first Cambridge seal of about 1261 (above) shows the chancellor seated between the two proctors. The River Cam, with an arched bridge crossing it, is represented below them. (19)

At Cracow the quadrangle of the Collegium Maius was reconstructed in 1494 after a fire. (20)

Bologna, from the early 12th century, was Europe's leading law school, out of which one of the first mediaeval universities grew. The professors of law were men of international standing, and the most highly paid in Europe. The splendid tombs of some of them still survive. Above: the tomb of Guittone Sinibaldi, called Cino da Pistoia (1272–1337), in the cathedral of Pistoia. A classroom with professor and students appears at the bottom in bas-relief. (21)

The independence of universities was strongly supported by royal power in conflict with civic authorities. The stone carving below is from the tomb of Pierre Gougis, an Austin friar studying in Paris, who was killed in 1440. His three assailants (on the right) were condemned to a heavy fine and to make a humble apology on their knees to the University authorities in the porch of St Mathurin. On the left is the chancellor preceded by two bedels, and behind him other masters. (22)

The study of medicine, starting on the foundation of Greek and Arabic writings, was the special discipline of the school at Salerno in Italy, which had its greatest influence during the 12th and 13th centuries. Below: a mediaeval pharmacy in a miniature from the French translation of Roger of Salerno's *Chirurgia*, c.1300. (23)

The trained physician of the Middle Ages relied mainly on traditional methods of diagnosis and cure: auscultation, blood-letting, potions, and the like. A consultation at the patient's bedside is seen in a 14th-century miniature (above). One of the doctors is inspecting a specimen of urine. In the miniature below, from an early 14th-century French chronicle, doctors are administering medicine to a king who, according to the text, 'drank so many kinds of potions and powders... it was a marvel the way he endured it.' (24, 25)

The blessings of surgery: these six scenes are also from the manuscript of Roger of Salerno's famous work. They illustrate: (top row) the use of hot water to soften broken ribs, the removal of an arrow and a lance from the chest, cutting open the chest and abdomen; (bottom row) a wound in the lungs, an operation on the intestines, and a man suffering from 'phlegmatic abscess'. (26)

Making a will: a 14th-century legal manuscript from Bologna contains this vignette of a dying man, attended by priest and family, dictating his last testament to a notary. (27)

Handwritten books

could only be produced in small numbers and at enormous expense. Yet large collections did exist, mainly in monasteries. Among the most significant results of the traffic in books was the entry into Europe of Arabic science and philosophy and the gradual percolation of this knowledge into the vernaculars. Below: Jean de Vignay sits in a well-stocked library translating the *Miroir Historial* from Latin into French; assistants bring him books from the shelves. (28)

The precious volumes

were normally kept either lying flat, resting on sloping shelves or, if the collection were small, in book-chests, some of which still survive in cathedral libraries. This detail (left) from the *Tucher Altar* at Nuremberg shows a scholar's shelves in the 15th century, with leather-bound volumes, spectacles, ink bottle and sealed letters. Simon, Abbot of St Albans (below), who founded the abbey library, sits reading at his book-chest. (29, 30)

Knowledge of plants and their medicinal uses was handed down in Greek, Latin and Arabic sources. Here are shown a Latin herbal of the 12th century (right), and an Arabic one dated 1328. The plants are couch grass, sword lily and rosemary in the Latin, couch grass and catchfly in the Arabic. (31, 32)

Textbooks multiplied, spreading education and strengthening the professions. The frontispiece (left) of a 14th-century legal work shows the author, Joannes Andreae, in four scenes of his life. From left to right: in his office, presenting his book to the pope, teaching in a law-school, and apparently helping to sell copies of his book in a shop. The first and last miniatures include book-chests convertible into seats, cupboards with folding doors and circular revolving stands. (33, 34)

In a university library the books were kept chained on sloping desks. This illumination from Freiburg shows the university statutes chained outside the door. (35)

The figures of the constellations go back beyond the Greeks. They were known in the Middle Ages from late antique Roman copies, and in translations of the work of Al-Sûfî, from which this illustration comes (right). It is a copy executed in South Italy or Sicily about the middle of the 13th century. Hercules has been made to look like an Arab, with his club turned into a scimitar. The stars that make up the constellation are represented by dots of varying size to indicate relative magnitude. They are marked in Arabic numerals, then beginning to be used in the West. (37)

Dental instruments (above) from the work on surgery by the Arab writer Abu'l-Qāsim, known in the West as Albucasis. The illustrations in the original were taken over in the translation. This is from a late 13th-century Italian copy. (36)

A library in use is depicted in a French translation of Boethius' *De consolatione philosophiae*, a 6th-century work that was widely read in the Middle Ages. The sloping desks were normal library furniture in the later Middle Ages. They were required because many texts were produced in folio size, a practice that was continued by the early printers. The subject of the picture on the wall is Philosophy offering consolation to Boethius. (38)

A Dominican friar, Vincent de Beauvais, is shown writing in his private study (below). The type of desk he uses is fairly common in 15th-century illustrations; the pipe-like apparatus supporting it could be used as a swivel. The weighted strings hanging over the top of the desk keep his book flat. The instrument on the chest in the background appears to be a magnifying-glass. (39)

Universities and Learning

RICHARD HUNT

SCHOLARSHIP AND LEARNING in the Middle Ages from the 12th to the 15th century were more closely bound up with schools and universities than at any other period of European history. One of the outstanding achievements of these centuries was the creation of corporations, of legal working institutions that made possible the pursuit of learned activities within a framework that ensured continuity.

The Idea of a University

The most active centres of learning at the end of the 11th century, except in law and medicine, were in France. They were the schools which were a part of the cathedral establishment. The cathedral schools at Laon, Chartres, Orléans and Paris, to name the most important, became schools of more than local repute. At first it was the reputation of a famous master which drew students from far and wide. If he migrated, many students might follow him: the classic example is the career of Peter Abailard. But by the second half of the 12th century the schools at Paris had drawn ahead. Teachers multiplied there and began to organize themselves. Legal recognition was received from both king and pope in the early years of the 13th century, and a primitive body of statutes was drawn up by the papal legate, Robert de Courçon, in 1215. Paris had become a university in all but name. For the word *universitas* means a corporation of any kind, and it was not until much later in the Middle Ages that the word by itself came to denote a place of higher learning. The inscription on the corporate seal of the University of Paris was: 'The seal of the university of masters and scholars at Paris'. Paris became the most important centre for the study of the arts and of theology in Europe, but also had faculties of canon law and medicine. The study of civil law was forbidden by Pope Honorius III in 1214. The largest faculty was that of arts and its head, the rector, became eventually the chief officer of the University.

In Italy the status of the cathedral schools is less clear. The two most important schools had no connection with a cathedral. They were at Bologna for law and at Salerno for medicine. Both of them drew students from all over Europe. The rise of Bologna can be traced to the recovery of Justinian's *Digest*. The earliest teacher was Irnerius (*fl.* 1100–30), and from then onwards there was a succession of teachers in civil law. Side by side went the growth of a more systematic study of the law of the church, canon law. The work of Gratian, the *Concordia discordantium canonum*, more shortly known as the *Decretum*, which came to be recognized as part of the law of the church, was completed about 1130. The stages by which the school of Bologna became a university are hard to follow. The charter of the Emperor Frederick I in 1158, in which he takes under his protection scholars who 'travel for the sake of study', does not mention Bologna. It seems that the law students, especially those from outside Italy, formed themselves into 'universities' or gilds for mutual protection and self-government, and chose 'rectors'. The professors were excluded from these gilds. In the course of the 13th century the 'universities' were reduced to two, the Italians (*cismontani*) and the foreigners (*ultramontani*). They exercised considerable power over the professors. One consequence was that the faculties of arts and medicine had a separate organization. There was no faculty of theology until 1364.

p 182 (2)

f 1

p 188, 9
(23–7)
p 187
(21)

p 188, 9
(23–6)
f 12

'*The seal of the corporation of masters and scholars at Paris.*' *When Paris University received legal recognition in the 13th century, 'universitas' meant a corporation of any kind, not necessarily connected with education. Here the Virgin and Child are flanked by St Catherine of Alexandria and St Nicholas, with scholars reading beneath.* (1)

The school of Salerno was a medical school only, and it never developed into a full university. During the 12th and early 13th century it was the chief medical school in Europe. It was here that the study of Greek and Arabic medicine was begun. In the 11th century Constantine the African had translated a large number of medical works by Greek and Arabic writers. It was at Salerno that a selection of works including the *Aphorisms* of Hippocrates, the *Isagoge* of Johannitius, the *Tegni* of Galen, Philaretus *On the Pulse*, and others were formed into a corpus known as the *ars medicinae*, which formed the basis of medical teaching in the medical faculties of the later universities.

The spread of universities began before they were fully organized, and first to England, where there were cathedral schools on the French model, but of more local fame. The most flourishing in the late 12th century was at Lincoln. There were also schools in other towns, notably Oxford and Northampton. Here it was Oxford which drew ahead and achieved legal recognition only a few years later than Paris, which was its model.

In these early days, when there was no elaborate equipment, endowments or buildings, it was easy for the masters and students to move if they fell out with the authorities of the town. The early history of universities is punctuated by violent quarrels between town and gown. The difficulties of accommodating a large influx of strangers, and young ones at that, were great. The most powerful weapon in the hands of the university authorities was to strike, or in mediaeval terms to order a cessation of lectures, a right which was solemnly allowed at Paris by a papal bull in 1231. These 'cessations' of study sometimes resulted in permanent new foundations. Such were the cessations at Oxford in 1209 and at Bologna in 1222 which led to the foundation of universities at Cambridge and Padua. But the growing esteem in which universities were held made it natural that deliberate steps would be taken to plan new foundations. The earliest was the foundation of a university at Naples by the Emperor Frederick II in 1224, in order to train men under his control in opposition to Bologna. The next was the foundation at Toulouse in 1229 under the auspices of Pope Gregory IX to propagate sound doctrine in the face of the Albigensian heresy. The salaries of fourteen professors were to be paid for ten years by Count Raymond VII of Toulouse. Henceforward all universities were founded by secular authorities, whether princes or cities, in conjunction with the papacy. In Spain one university was established in each kingdom in the course of the 13th century: Valladolid in Castile, Salamanca in León, Lérida in Aragon; in Portugal, at Lisbon (moved to Coimbra in 1308-9). They were chiefly modelled on Bologna. The expansion in the 13th century took place in France and Italy. It is surprising that no universities were founded in Germany or further east. The first central European university was founded at Prague by the Emperor Charles IV in 1347. It was followed later

p 186
(19)

The schools of Paris began in the shadow of Notre-Dame on the Ile de la Cité, but soon spread to the Left Bank, still called the 'Quartier Latin'. By 1500 there were about seventy colleges, some very small, mostly in this neighbourhood. Above is part of a plan of Paris made in the mid-16th century. Ave Maria College, of which the daily routine has been illustrated on p. 184, is arrowed, slightly to the left of the church of St-Etienne. The Collège de Navarre is on the extreme left and Boncourt just inside the city wall to the north. (2)

p 184
(13) in the 14th century by Vienna, and then by the German universities: Heidelberg, Cologne, Erfurt, Würzburg, Leipzig and Rostock. In Poland, Cracow was effectively founded in 1397. At the other end of Europe three universities in Scotland were founded in the 15th century: St Andrew's, Glasgow and Aberdeen, all three founded by bishops with royal and papal approval.

The force of the university movement is nowhere better seen than in its effects on the religious orders. Not only were the new orders—the Franciscans and Dominicans—swept into it, but the older orders felt its effects. Even the Cistercians, who had been so long hostile to intellectual pursuits, had by the middle of the 13th century a college in Paris, ironically called the Collège St Bernard, to which monks of the order studying theology were sent. The Austin Friars and the Carmelites, who came into prominence in the latter part of the 13th century, had an elaborate system of schools by which a promising boy could proceed from the study of grammar to logic, philosophy and theology.

Students and Studies

The mediaeval universities in their heyday had no elaborate administrative machinery, hardly any buildings of their own, and no great endowments. Such endowments as there were were mainly in the hands of colleges, which are found in Paris before the end of the 12th century. In 1180 Josce, a London vintner, on his return from a pilgrimage to Jerusalem, bought a room in the Hôtel Dieu to be appropriated for the lodging of eighteen scholar-clerks. Later they acquired a house of their own, and as the *Collège des dix-huit* it remained in existence until the French Revolution. On a much larger scale was the college founded by the almoner of St Louis, Robert de Sorbon, in 1257. Originally designed for sixteen students of theology who were already masters of arts, it was afterwards enlarged by other benefactions to thirty-six. Later, in the 14th century, it became the home of the theological faculty. About seventy other colleges had been founded by 1500 but these two institutions display the two main types: the one intended for poor students, the other making it possible for graduates to work for their long courses in theology and canon law.

f 2
p 184
(11, 12)

p 186
(17) Colleges on the Parisian model were founded in Oxford and Cambridge from the later 13th century onwards. They had greater autonomy in managing their own affairs than their Parisian

194

counterparts, and their dominance over the central university from the 16th to the 19th century makes it difficult to appreciate their relative insignificance before the later 15th century; but it has been said by a modern historian of Oxford that down to 1450 if all the colleges had been swept away it would have made no great difference to the university.

By the time of the foundation of German universities the existence of colleges could be looked upon as an integral part of a university. Consequently, in many of them, colleges were part of the original scheme; they were used as a means of ensuring a sufficient number of salaried teachers. Thus at Erfurt the town built the *Collegium maius* for masters of arts, which comprised a lecture hall and accommodation for eight masters and a number of students (*bursarii*).

Outside England the mediaeval colleges have disappeared. The Spanish college at Bologna alone is still in existence, but its mediaeval buildings have been replaced. The colleges at Salamanca were rebuilt in the 17th century. Only the buildings of the Jagellónski college, Cracow, survive from the 15th century.

p 186
(20)

It was not until the 15th century that universities generally had buildings of their own. At Paris the congregations of the masters were held in the church of St-Julien-le-Pauvre and later in the Mathurine Convent, where the university seal-chest was also kept. At Oxford the church of St Mary's, still called the university church, was used for the same purpose. The lecture-rooms were hired by the masters, and to guard against a shortage the university was able to insist that a school once let for university purposes should be let for no other. In the later 14th century the English-German nation at Paris began to have schools of its own. In 1415 the Faculty of Decrees, that is of canon law, built two schools in the Clos Bruneau; the block of stone with the title of one of them is still in existence. At Oxford the canon law schools had belonged to the university since 1279, but the splendid Divinity School was not begun until 1426 and was not completed until 1488. Again outside Oxford and Cambridge hardly any university buildings have survived. The outstanding exception is the *salle des thèses* at Orléans.

f 3

p 186
(18)

The early universities were open to all free men without restriction. Paris was notable for the welcome which it gave to men from all parts of Europe. The three greatest theologians who taught there in the 13th century, St Thomas Aquinas, St Albertus Magnus and St Bonaventure, came from Italy and Germany. All the archbishops of Canterbury in the same century, except Boniface of Savoy, a relative of King Henry III, had studied there, and four of them, Stephen Langton, Robert Kilwardby, John Pecham and Robert Winchelsey, had also been notable teachers. Three of the greatest masters in the Arts were Siger from Brabant, Boethius from Sweden and Martin from Denmark. The list could be continued into the 14th century. It was the rise of national sentiment

p 180 (
p 182
(4, 5)

Scole secūde facultatis decretorum

'Scole secunde facultatis decretorum'—the inscription from one of the two schools of canon law built in 1415 in the Clos Bruneau in Paris. (3)

NORWAY
SWEDEN
Uppsala 1470
DENMARK • Copenhagen 1478
SCOTLAND
Aberdeen 1494
St.Andrews 1413
Glasgow 1451
IRELAND
ENGLAND
Cambridge c.1209
Oxford c.1170
Rostock 1419
HOLY
Greifswald 1428
POLAND
NETHERLANDS
Louvain 1425 Trier 1454 • Cologne 1388 Erfurt 1379 • Leipzig 1409
Caen 1432 Paris c.1150 ROMAN
(Sorbonne 1257) Mainz 1476 Würzburg 1402 • Prague 1347 • Cracow 1397
Orléans before Heidelberg 1389 BOHEMIA
Angers c.1229 1231 Tübingen 1476 • Ingolstadt 1459
Nantes 1460 Bourges 1464 • Freiburg 1455 Vienna 1365
Poitiers 1431 Basel 1459 EMPIRE • Pozsony (Pressburg) 1465
FRANCE • Besançon 1485 Buda 1389 •
Dôle 1422 • Vercelli 1228 Vicenza 1204 HUNGARY
Bordeaux 1441 Turin 1405 • Pavia 1361 Treviso 1318 • Pécs (Fünfkirchen) 1367
Cahors 1332 Valence 1452 Grenoble 1339 Piacenza 1248 Padua 1222
Toulouse 1229 Orange 1365 Avignon 1305 Ferrara 1391
Palencia 1212 Huesca 1359 Aix 1409 Reggio 1188 Bologna late 12th Cent.
Coimbra 1308 Valladolid c.1250 Montpellier late 12th Cent. Pisa 1343 Florence 1349
Lisbon Saragossa 1474 Lérida 1300 Siena Arezzo 1215
1290 Salamanca Sigüenza 1489 1246 Perugia 1308
PORTUGAL before 1230 Perpignan 1349 Rome
Alcalá 1499 Barcelona 1450 (Curia Romana 1244
CASTILE ARAGON Valencia 1500 Majorca Studium Urbis 1303)
Seville 1254 Palma Naples 1224 • Salerno 1231
1483
SICILY • Catania 1444

0 _____ 400 mls.
0 _____ 600 kms.

The universities of Europe during the Middle Ages, with the dates of their foundation. In some cases these can be slightly misleading, since the schools often existed long before any official recognition. The University of Paris, for instance, was flourishing in the mid-12th century, but was not recognized as a legal corporation by the Pope until 1211, and did not receive its statutes until 1215. Salerno's medical school was famous in the 11th century; Frederick II reconstituted it in 1231, but in fact it never enjoyed full university status. At Bologna, Frederick Barbarossa conferred certain privileges on the students in 1158, but it did not become a university until the end of the century. (4)

of which the foundation of German universities was one expression, capped by the disarray caused by the schism in the Church at the end of the 14th century, which greatly restricted freedom of movement.

What brought these men to the universities? Broadly speaking it was to prepare themselves for a career in church or state. Very few indeed stayed in the university as permanent teachers. After 'determining' as master of arts a man was bound to stay on to lecture for at least two years, a period which was termed his 'necessary regency'. After that he went on to make his career. To take an example, Geoffrey of Aspale studied at Oxford, and as master of arts lectured for several years. His commentaries on some of the books of the natural philosophy of Aristotle have survived. Then he entered the service of Gilbert de Clare, Earl of Gloucester,

and from him passed to the service of the wife of King Edward I, Queen Eleanor, whose chancellor he became. When he died in 1287, he held at least fifteen livings. If a man wished to become a civilian or canon lawyer or a doctor of theology, he had to stay on for a further period at the university. The longest course was that in theology, for which fifteen or sixteen years were required on top of the arts course of five or six years. Many theologians were members of religious orders which provided for their support. One of the purposes of the foundation of colleges was to maintain secular theologians in their long course. These men were the successful. There were, no doubt, always many who fell by the wayside. A rhyming verse was long current at Oxford: *'Oxonium veniunt multi, redeunt quoque stulti'* ('Many come to Oxford and return home none the wiser').

A page from a 12th-century copy of Boethius's 'De Musica'. Top left is Boethius himself; the other figures are philosophers who influenced him in his work on music—Pythagoras, Plato and Nicomachus. (5)

Seven Liberal Arts

p 180(1)
f 9   The framework of the studies in the cathedral schools was the seven liberal arts, a cycle canonized in the Carolingian age: the *trivium* comprising grammar, rhetoric and logic, and the *quadrivium* comprising arithmetic, geometry, music and astronomy. The books available for the study of these subjects were few: Priscian

f 6   and Donatus for grammar; the *Rhetorica ad Herennium* and Cicero's *De inventione* for rhetoric; the *Isagoge* of Porphyry, the *Categories* and *De interpretatione* of Aristotle with Boethius' commentaries, and the logical texts of Boethius for logic; the treatises by or

f 5   ascribed to Boethius for arithmetic, geometry and music. For astronomy there was even less. The nearest approach to a text was the eighth book of Martianus Capella on the marriage of Philology and Mercury. The first satisfactory astronomical text was the *De sphaera* of Johannes de Sacro Bosco (early 13th century). To these texts we must add Macrobius' Commentary on the *Dream of Scipio*, Calcidius' partial translation and commen-

f 7   tary on the *Timaeus* of Plato and Boethius' *De consolatione philosophiae*. There is no curriculum in which these books are laid down, but there is evidence from which their use can be inferred. William of Conches, the most influential teacher of the arts in the 12th century, has left commentaries on Priscian, on Macrobius, on

p 192   the *Timaeus* and on Boethius' *De consolatione*. By his references
(38)   from one to another it is clear that they formed for him a kind of

p 182   corpus. Peter Abailard in the earliest version of his *Theologia*,
(2)   known as the *Theologia Summi boni*, uses these texts as his sources for showing how pagan philosophers were in possession of some Christian truth. In addition he gives a single quotation from the Latin poet Lucan. An extensive use of the poets would have been out of place in his book, but this single quotation and the more numerous ones which are found in his *History of his troubles* illustrate the way in which a familiarity with Virgil, Horace (especially *Satires*, *Epistles* and *Ars poetica*), Ovid, Juvenal, Persius and

196

Statius was expected of an educated man in the 12th century. The occasional quotations and echoes in St Bernard, who turned his back on such worldly accomplishments, show how much a part of a young man's education such a knowledge was. By comparison the Latin prose writers were less widely studied. Acquaintance with Sallust's *Catiline* and *Jugurtha*, Cicero's *De amicitia*, *De senectute* and *Paradoxa*, and some Seneca was common; but the philosophical writings of Cicero were hardly read and the rediscovery of Seneca's *Dialogues* was not made until the middle of the 13th century.

In theology the basic book was the Bible, around which grew a vast apparatus. The standard commentary, which came to be known as the common or ordinary gloss, was the work of the masters of the 12th century, beginning with Anselm of Laon (d. 1117). The same masters began to make collections of 'sentences' on the chief topics of theology. By the middle of the century (1154–57) Peter Lombard was able to compose his *Liber sententiarum* which superseded all earlier collections and was used as a text-book throughout the rest of the Middle Ages. About a decade later Petrus Comestor wrote his admirable *Historia scolastica*, which was quickly accepted as the standard work on biblical history. In civil law the new starting point, as we have seen, was the rediscovery about 1070 of Justinian's *Digest*. The standard apparatus was the work of Accursius (1228). For the law of the church, canon law, Gratian, a Camaldolese monk at Bologna, had compiled his *Concordia discordantium canonum*. The standard apparatus to it was the work of Bartholomew of Brescia (c. 1250).

In giving his book the title of a harmony of dissonant canons or rules (a canon is the term for an ecclesiastical law), Gratian was proclaiming a new programme. There had been many earlier collections of ecclesiastical canons, and attempts had been made to organize them systematically. Gratian's aim was so to arrange the material that apparent contradictions of the heterogeneous mass could be harmonized and resolved. Peter Lombard in his *Liber sententiarum* pursued a similar aim. The three text-books were a remarkable achievement. The judgment of Rashdall, the historian of mediaeval universities, on the work of Gratian, can be applied to all three: 'great text-books, which, appearing just at the right time and in the right place, take the world by storm'. The *Historia scolastica* has received less attention from modern scholars than the

Rhetoric giving instruction—an elaborate allegorical initial from the 'Rhetorica ad Herennium'. The stalk of the tree divides into the three main parts of Rhetoric—'Causa', 'Oratio' and 'Materia', while the leaves symbolize the sub-divisions of each part. The whole system is taken from Cicero's 'De inventione'. (6)

Plato and Socrates as the 13th century saw them. Plato was known to the Middle Ages only through a part of the 'Timaeus', an uncharacteristic dialogue, and two others. In this drawing by Matthew Paris, Socrates seems to be taking down Plato's words, instead of, as we should expect, the other way round. (7)

The classics of Latin literature were copied and re-copied in the monastic scriptoria of the Middle Ages, and most of those which have come down to us owe their survival to this process. This illustration from a mid-12th century manuscript of Terence's 'Woman of Andros' was copied from a Carolingian version which in turn went back to a manuscript of the 4th or 5th century. In the scene shown here (Act I, Scene I) preparations are being made for a wedding. (8)

other two, but in his skill in selecting and arranging his sources, and in relating biblical to secular history Petrus Comestor deserves a place with the other two. Later mediaeval legend made the three men brothers.

Whatever the subject, the method of teaching was the same. The master read out the text and commented on it. The students, or some of them, took notes. Quite early in the 12th century the demand grew for a reliable version of the master's lecture. Many of the commentaries of the masters of the later 12th and 13th centuries contain traces of having originated as a report of a lecture. In the middle of the text one comes on phrases like 'the master says so and so', or 'then the students catcalled, and the master says: "I will only say this, You are tired."' Often the master revised the report before it was issued. Sometimes more than one independent report of the same course was in circulation, as those of St Bonaventure's *Collationes in hexameron*, which were delivered in Paris in 1273.

The other exercise, which in various forms came to dominate academic life, was the disputation. The subjects for disputation, whether in grammar, logic, theology or law, arose out of questions raised in the lectures or text-books. To begin with there was no separation between lecture and disputation. The master posed and resolved the question. By the last quarter of the 12th century the discussion of 'questions' had become an independent exercise. Later careful rules were laid down. The disputation became the academic exercise *par excellence*: 'determining' a question was the crowning act of a bachelor's career by which he became a master.

Furthermore the technique of disputation spread into written works, and in the later 13th century came to dominate exposition. For example, the *Summa theologica* of St Thomas Aquinas is built up out of a series of articles. In each article the arguments for and against are marshalled in the form of syllogisms. The reply, which forms the body of the article, is then given. Finally any difficulties remaining in the arguments against are disposed of. It was a rigorous method, and at its best one of great power, but it lacked any literary grace. In the hands of lesser men the divisions and distinctions, which could be prolonged endlessly, led to aridity. It was against a debased and mechanical form of disputing that the humanists of the 15th century protested. Their protests, couched in terms of mockery and scorn, have coloured our estimation of the system even at its best.

All the lectures and disputations, as well as the written works based on them, were in Latin. Mediaeval Latin, no less than mediaeval dialectic, was attacked and ridiculed by the humanists who returned to earlier classical models. The decay in our own day of the Renaissance tradition of classical teaching has made it possible to treat mediaeval Latin on its own merits, and to recognize that it was a living language. In the hands of St Bernard it became a splendid instrument for the expression of new thoughts and feelings; in the hands of St Thomas Aquinas it reached a new precision in the exposition of abstract thought.

What strikes one most forcibly in the 12th-century curriculum is the paucity of material which was available for the study of the liberal arts. Logic alone could be seriously studied in depth. Consequently there was a concentration on logic which underlay all higher education. It had a prestige which it is hard to recapture. When Henry I was entertaining Pope Callixtus II in 1119 the high point of the entertainment was a disputation by two young nobles, the sons of the Count of Meulan. This form of entertainment outlasted the Middle Ages. When Queen Elizabeth I visited Oxford in 1566 the University arranged for the performance of a disputation. Logic seemed to be the key to the understanding of all problems, even though its application to the problems of theology gave rise to much heart-searching.

Light from the Greek and Arab World

Apart from logic whole tracts of philosophy—metaphysical, moral and natural—were virtually unrepresented. But there were those who knew that the Greeks and Arabs had much more than was available in the West: the remedy was to seek out their works and to translate them into Latin. The translators were adventurous individuals, working on their own initiative. The translation of the Koran by the Englishman, Robert of Ketton, at the expense of Peter the Venerable, is an exception. It is therefore astonishing to find how much had been recovered by the end of the 12th century. A great number of translations had been made of astronomical, astrological, mathematical, medical and philosophical works. The names of the translators known to us show their varied places of origin: James of Venice, Adelard of Bath, Plato of Tivoli, Burgundio of Pisa, Robert of Ketton, Hermann of Carinthia, Dominicus Gondisalvi (Gundisalinus), Gerard of Cremona. For the last named, who died in Toledo in 1187, we have a list of his translations drawn up by his pupils, which runs to seventy-one works. They include Euclid's *Elements*, Ptolemy's *Almagest*, Avicenna's *Canon*, Aristotle's *Posterior Analytics* and many works by or ascribed to Hippocrates and Galen. His method of translation was to employ the services of an interpreter. The name of one Mozarabic interpreter, Galippus, has come down to us. In an age when there were no Arabic-Latin dictionaries or grammars, it was the only way to discover the meaning of a

p 190–1 (31, 32, 36, 37) *f* 10

f 10

Philosophy, the mother of learning, with her seven daughters, the seven Liberal Arts. This small illuminated initial comes from a 13th-century manuscript of Aristotle's 'Metaphysics' with the commentary of Averroës. By this date more reliable translations of Aristotle were being made direct from the Greek instead of by way of Arabic versions. The commentaries of the Arabic philosophers Avicenna and Averroës, however, continued to be influential. (9)

rare word or to understand a difficult passage. The position of the translators has been compared with that of the Sanskrit scholars in the early 19th century, who had to call on the services of a pundit before they could understand the texts. In the early days there was a considerable amount of overlapping effort. Before Gerard's time, or contemporaneously with him, Euclid had been translated from the Greek by Adelard of Bath; Ptolemy's *Almagest* by an anonymous translator in Sicily who was in close touch with the currents of thought in the French schools; the *Posterior Analytics* by James of Venice.

To make translations was one stage. Their use and assimilation was a more arduous task. The slow rate of assimilation is seen not only in the works on natural science, but even in logic. We have already seen that only two books of Aristotle's *Organon* were studied in the schools in the early 12th century. The recovery and assimilation of the rest were not completed until the first half of the 13th century. Boethius had almost certainly translated the whole *Organon*, but it was not until the second decade of the 12th century that we begin to find some knowledge of it in the writings of Peter Abailard, Thierry of Chartres and a few others. Boethius' translation of the *Posterior Analytics* was lost, and was replaced by that of James of Venice. The first books of the 'new logic' which were incorporated in the curriculum were the *Sophistici Elenchi* and the *Topics*, both of which provided a fuller treatment of matters useful in disputation. They seem to have been in general circulation by the third quarter of the century. The first commentaries on the *Posterior* and *Prior Analytics* which received more p 182 (3) than local recognition were written by Robert Grosseteste and Robert Kilwardby.

There is another factor in the slowness of assimilation. The method of translation was intentionally literal. The texts were rendered word for word. Many Greek terms were simply transliterated because there was no exact Latin equivalent. Aristotle is difficult enough in Greek, but when turned into a Latin which follows Greek constructions his meaning becomes even more difficult to absorb.

The Emergence of Aristotle

The works of Aristotle on metaphysics and natural philosophy were too remote from current ways of thought to be assimilated without more preparation. But the works of Arabic philosophers, the *Metaphysics* of Avicenna and Algazel and the anonymous *Liber de causis*, evoked a quicker response. Their authors had written under strong neo-Platonic influences as had some of the Fathers, notably Augustine. From the end of the 12th century or the beginning of the 13th we have some short works in which an attempt was made to combine Christian ideas with those of the Arabic philosophers. Over a wide field this created no difficulties, but when questions of the nature of God, of the creation, of the nature of the soul were drawn into discussion, the danger to the faith was great. It is no surprise that in 1210 we meet with the first official condemnation of books produced in the University of Paris. The condemned books, written by Amaury of Bène and p 184 (15) David of Dinant have only survived in fragments, and the sources and bearing of their doctrines cannot be determined with any certainty. But there have survived one or two other works from this period which allow us to see what confusion might arise. One of them is a *Liber de causis primis et secundis* which is largely composed of extracts from Augustine, Avicenna, Johannes Scotus Erigena and Gilbert de la Porrée. Avicenna has the lion's share. The zeal of the unknown writer had outrun his discretion. In the same year and again in 1215 the masters of arts at Paris were forbidden to lecture on the metaphysical and physical books of Aristotle. The effect of the decrees was limited because they did not forbid theologians to study the works in private, and because they did not apply to universities other than Paris. John of Garland in his manifesto for the new University of Toulouse makes one of its attractions the opportunity of hearing lectures on the books of Aristotle which were forbidden at Paris. The masters at Oxford were not deterred from lecturing on them. The commentaries of Adam of Buckfield (Buckingfold in Northumberland) on the *Metaphysics*, *De anima* and the physical works except the *De* f 9 *animalibus*, which summed up the work of a generation of teachers, circulated widely outside England. By the middle of the 13th century lectures were being given on these texts at Paris. An immense effort was made to render Aristotle intelligible. It was seen that current translations were not always adequate. New or improved translations were made with the help of manuscripts brought from Greece, for example, by the Flemish Dominican, William of Moerbeke. He was in the habit of noting in the colo-

Interest in scientific subjects increased as more Greek and Arabic texts were made available in Latin translation. This drawing by Matthew Paris from the 'Liber experimentarius' of Bernardus Silvestris shows Euclid (left) holding a 'sphaera' and looking through a 'dioptra'. (The dioptra was not a telescope; it was simply a hollow tube to cut out extraneous light and to measure, by means of sliding plates inside, the angle and apparent diameter of heavenly bodies.) Beside him sits Hermann of Carinthia, the mediaeval translator of several Arabic works on astronomy, holding an astrolabe. (10)

To the mediaeval mind all knowledge formed a harmony—hence the way (alien to modern thinking) by which facts were chosen and interpreted according to theological systems rather then collected empirically for their own sake. In this pen drawing of about 1200, Harmony is personified in the figure of Air (AER), which, like the soul, 'embraces everything between heaven and earth'. He is controlling the four winds, and in the three segments of the cosmic circle are medallions of the nine muses beneath Arion (literature), Orpheus (music) and Pythagoras (the sciences). (11)

phon of his translations the places where he worked: Nicaea in Asia Minor, Thebes and Corinth in Greece, Viterbo and Orvieto in Italy. This improvement is reflected in the manuscripts containing the translations of Aristotle's works on natural philosophy (*libri naturales*). After the middle of the 13th century the older versions from the Arabic are replaced by new ones from the Greek, and the older translations from the Greek appear in a revised form.

The effect of the new knowledge on the curricula was correspondingly slow. In the Parisian statutes of 1215, apart from the old and new logic, only a part of the *Ethics* is added; but by 1255 lectures are prescribed on the *Metaphysics*, *Physics*, *De anima*, *De caelo et mundo* and a range of the books on natural philosophy. Aristotle, the whole Aristotle, had arrived: he was the philosopher *par excellence*. The greatest theologian of the age, St Thomas Aquinas, was able to absorb and transform the teaching of Aristotle. His fellow Dominican, St Albertus Magnus, was no less eager to embrace the new knowledge. More conservative theologians were not prepared to follow them. The position was complicated because the masters of arts, whose duty it was to lecture on the Aristotelian texts, seemed to some to be taking up positions dangerous to faith. The result was an explosion. On March 7th, 1277, Stephen Tempier, Bishop of Paris, condemned 219 propositions as erroneous. The two masters of arts most directly concerned, Siger of Brabant and Boethius of Sweden, fled to Italy and disappear from sight. But the range of propositions condemned was very wide. Doctrines taught by St Thomas Aquinas

were censured. He quickly found defenders, not only from among the members of his own order. It soon became possible and respectable to adopt the positions taken up by St Thomas. He was canonized in 1325. More surprisingly Siger of Brabant was placed by Dante in Paradise.

Authority and Observation

The work of enquiry and speculation continued. New fields were opened up. The masters at Paris gave increasing attention to the principles of mathematics and the natural sciences. A generation ago, when the great French scholar Pierre Duhem first explored these forgotten and forbiddingly technical works, he thought that he had discovered the 'precursors of Galileo'. Further explorations and a better understanding of the texts have led to a less dramatic conclusion. These men 'inaugurated a new mathematical approach which gained momentum as it spread from Oxford to continental universities, to Galileo, to Newton and the highly complex physics of our own day'.

Since these masters had gone so far, it may well be asked why they did not go further, and in particular why they did not turn to the verification of their speculations by observation and experiment. This is not a question to which a positive answer can ever be given, but there are two considerations which may help us to approach it. Firstly, if we open a work of St Thomas Aquinas we are confronted at every turn by the reference to authorities, 'As Augustine says', 'As it is found in Aristotle' or 'in the Philosopher'; if we open a medical work, we find constant reference to

fungul de nare sic inciditur

Medical knowledge came largely from Greek and Arabic sources. This drawing, from a 12th-century treatise, shows treatment of a nasal affliction—'Fungus de nase sic inciditur.' ('Thus polypus is cut out of the nose.') (12)

Hippocrates and Galen. They were the authoritative, the 'authentic' writers whose opinions could not be contradicted. If they appeared to be wrong or inconsistent, an explanation must be found or the inconsistency reconciled. Now mediaeval thinkers knew that authorities must not be taken without any criticism. Adelard of Bath coined the well-known phrase that an authority (in the concrete sense) had a wax nose that could be turned this p 182 (2) way and that. Peter Abailard in the verses of advice which he wrote for his son warned him to care for what is said, not who said it. Nevertheless respect for ancient authorities was a basic attitude, and it was a reasonable one in a period when Western Europeans had so much to learn from them. A good illustration is the collection of *materia medica* made by Simon of Genoa in the late 13th century, which he called the *Key of Healing*. His task was to collect and collate existing authorities, though he did have recourse to a wise old woman in the mountains of Crete. He was

extraordinarily thorough in his search for the literature of the subject, Greek and Arabic (in translation) and Latin. He has preserved for us extracts from works which have since been lost, for example the only known fragments of a translation of the leading Greek ophthalmologist, Demosthenes. He patiently collated the different equivalents in the sources for the names of medicinal plants. There was little room for observation. On the other hand, it would be misleading to give the impression that mediaeval writers did not observe things with their own eyes. Even so unscientific a writer as Gerald of Wales has many interesting observations on birds and beasts in his *Topography of Ireland*. On an entirely different level are the many original observations in the scientific works of Albertus Magnus. But it is a long step from making observations to the formulation of a theoretical basis of experimentation, and the climate, where authorities counted for so much, did not favour it.

A second factor is the predominance of logic in mediaeval thought. From logic to mathematics is a more natural step than to physical or biological sciences. Thus considerable attention was paid to optics which led to a correct understanding of the phenomenon of the rainbow. It was in optics that that remarkable *f 14* genius, Roger Bacon, had solid achievements to his credit.

Actual experiments were confined to alchemy which is, scientifically speaking, a blind alley. Roger Bacon did speculate about 'unheard of engines', of machines for navigation without rowers, of flying machines, of machines for walking in the sea and rivers, *f 13* even to the bottom, without danger to life or limb. But he thought that such machines had been made in antiquity and in his own times. He confesses that he had never seen a flying machine nor met anyone who had, but he says that he knew an expert who had thought out a way to make one. Such half-fabulous reflections may be regarded as faint pointers to the future. We have become so much accustomed to rapid scientific and technological change that we are apt to forget how slow the early steps must have been.

Mediaeval Libraries

It is time to turn to a consideration of the way the scholars and p 190, 1 thinkers obtained their books. There had been no bookshops in (28–35) the West for six centuries. Hence libraries were all-important, and the greatest part since the Carolingian revival had been played by libraries in monasteries. Monastic libraries continued to play an important part, but it was a gradually diminishing one. In the 12th century, with the creation of new orders and the founding of hundreds of new monasteries, many new monastic libraries were built up. The core of their collections was a stock of patristic texts, especially the works of the four Fathers, Augustine, Ambrose, Jerome and Gregory. To these came to be added the works of 12th-century writers such as St Bernard and Hugh of St Victor, and the glossed texts of the books of the Bible. Hundreds of such volumes have survived in the libraries of France, Belgium, Germany, Austria, Switzerland and England. They are even still to be found in the places where they were written, as at Admont or St Gall or Durham.

The orders of friars followed suit in the 13th century. Friars needed not only to have a convent library, but to make provision for their members assigned to study. A convent sending a student to Paris to study was bound to provide him with the basic texts, including a Bible and Peter Lombard's *Liber sententiarum*. The friars were not allowed to own books; they were assigned to their use. Much time was taken up in general chapters in laying down rules for the disposal of books on the decease of a friar.

There were no university libraries in our sense of the term till late in the Middle Ages. The nature of the instruction did not call for a large supply of books. The master could own those which he needed for his teaching. If he needed others he might hope to borrow them. A council at Paris in 1212 impressed on monasteries their duty to lend books as one of the chief works of mercy. There has survived in the binding of a manuscript from the College of the Sorbonne a fragmentary catalogue of books in the libraries of Ste-Geneviève and St-Germain-des-Prés, which is conjectured to be the remains of a collection of catalogues of the monasteries in Paris, an early type of union catalogue. Some libraries in Paris received bequests specifically earmarked for the use of poor stu-

The Greeks and Romans, once their achievements began to be appreciated in the 13th century, were credited with even greater marvels than were actually true. Roger Bacon believed that they had constructed flying machines; and in the histories of Alexander the Great it was recorded that he made a glass barrel and descended to the bottom of the sea to study the fishes. 'Alas', wrote Alexander Neckam (1157–1217), an assiduous collector of scientific knowledge, 'he did not leave us his observations.' (13)

The science of optics—perhaps because it is closer to pure geometry than other branches of physics and biology—fascinated the later Middle Ages. This diagram of the eye, from the work of Roger Bacon (c. 1214–94) is completely scientific in its method. 'I shall draw therefore', he wrote, 'a figure in which all these matters are made clear as far as possible on a surface, though the full demonstration would require a body fashioned like the eye in all the particulars aforesaid. The eye of a cow, pig or other animal can be used for illustration, if anyone wishes to experiment.' Light from an object (the straight line at the top) is shown entering the eye and being refracted. (14)

dents. Gervase of St Augustine's, Canterbury, gave to St Victor his glossed books of the Bible, his *Sentences* and his *Historia scolastica* for the use of poor clerks studying theology 'as long as they last'. A similar gift was made to Notre-Dame de Paris by Stephen, archdeacon of Canterbury. It was the colleges which built up the first university libraries. The earliest and the most important was that of the College of the Sorbonne. Robert de Sorbon was one of those founders who had the gift of interesting their friends. His own donation of books was considerable (at least sixty-seven volumes), but it was outshone by that of Gerard of Abbeville which comprised about 300 volumes, of which 118 are still preserved in the Bibliothèque Nationale at Paris. The earliest surviving catalogue, dated 1290, shows that the library contained 1,017 volumes, and the next, dated 1338, 1,722.

This was a very large collection. The catalogue of Christchurch, Canterbury, in the time of Prior Henry of Estry (1284-1331), has 1,831 entries, the papal library at Avignon at the beginning of the Great Schism 2,102. In his will Gerard of Abbe-

ville had left his books not only for the use of the members of the Sorbonne but for other secular masters. The religious were excluded 'because they are well provided for'. By 1338 a division of the books had been worked out. The library was in two parts: in the 'great' library of 330 volumes, which was a reference collection, the books were chained to the desks; in the 'small' library of 1,090 volumes the books were available for lending. This arrangement was widely followed. It is found in the Oxford college libraries of the 14th and 15th centuries. At Merton College there is a list of 250 theological books (drawn up about 1350), of which thirty-one are marked 'in the library'. It is found also in the libraries of the friars. The Franciscan convent at Assisi in 1381 had 181 volumes in the chained library and 537 in the 'secret' or lending library. The Carmelite convent at Florence in 1391 had 113 and 618.

Books were expensive. It has been said that if a fellow of Merton College at Oxford in the 14th century 'could have spent all his allowance of 50s a year in kind on books, he could have bought a dozen cheap texts or indulged in two stately folios'. A few people did, however, contrive to make considerable collections, and there were probably more than we know of. We have, for example, a casual reference in an English lawsuit of 1221 to tolls levied on carts by the villagers of Wychbald in Worcestershire. The jurors said that they detained two carts which carried the books of Richard, the rural dean of Worcester; but unfortunately it was no concern of the law to tell us what the books were. The earliest list we have of the collection of an individual is that of the fifty-six volumes which Pope Celestine III (d. 1144) bequeathed to the cathedral at Città di Castello. It is a list mainly of standard theological books, but a more personal touch is given by the presence of two works of Peter Abailard under whom the Pope had studied. Considerably larger (113 volumes) was the collection which Philippe d'Harcourt, Bishop of Bayeux (1142-64), gave to the monastery of Bec. It is remarkable for the relatively large number of Latin classical prose writers with not a single poet. Of the same order of size were the libraries of Cardinal Guala Bicchieri (d. 1227) and of Bernard II, Archbishop of Santiago de Compostela (1224-37). At least twice as large was the library collected by Richard of Fournival, chancellor of Amiens in the middle of the 13th century. This was a systematic collection which its owner described in his *Biblionomia*. His description is set in the frame of a garden in which the youth of Amiens are invited to walk. The books on each subject are arranged on lecterns set up in three parterres. A letter of the

One of the earliest publishers' lists of books for sale. It advertises titles available from Peter Schöffer of Mainz, in 1469: 'Those wishing to buy for themselves the books on the list below, which have been carefully corrected and printed in this fount at Mainz and well set out, should come to the place written below' (an inn called 'Zum Wilden Mann', probably at Nuremberg). The first two items on the list are 'A beautiful Bible on parchment' and 'The Secunde secundae of St Thomas Aquinas'. (15)

alphabet is assigned to each subject and the volumes in it distinguished by different varieties and colours of the letter. Twelve volumes are assigned to each subject. In spite of its fanciful framework this was a real library, strong in Latin classical writers, both prose and poetry, in philosophical and scientific works translated from Greek and Arabic, and in the chief writers of the 12th century. If Richard really intended to establish a library in Amiens, he seems to have been frustrated, but a considerable part of the collection came into the hands of Gerard of Abbeville, a fellow member of the cathedral chapter of Amiens; it was absorbed into that which he bequeathed to the College of the Sorbonne.

The Written Word

Monastic libraries had been built up chiefly by writing books in the monastery itself; and for the greater part of the 12th century monasteries were the main centres of book production. The actual scribes were often professionals, about whose training and careers we know nothing. Where did Faricius, Abbot of Abingdon (1100-17), find six scribes whom he set to copying books for the library, while the monks wrote service books? Occasionally we find monks or canons working side by side with professionals. In a group of manuscripts from the Augustinian abbey of Cirencester the names are given of the canons who wrote them. They were assisted by a professional named Ralf of Pulleham whose hand is judged by a modern critic to have been 'much superior to theirs'. Whether produced by members of the communities or by professionals, the books were of a high standard. They are spacious, the script is clear, the abbreviation of words is kept within narrow bounds. The decoration is lively and varied. The products of the rising universities stand in clear contrast. The script is smaller and more compressed, far more abbreviation is allowed. The decoration is standardized. These books are rarely dated, and still more rarely signed, but the centres of production were probably in the towns. A certain Guiot, who copied a collection of the romances of Chrétien de Troyes some time after 1213, tells us that he had his premises in front of the church of Notre-Dame-du-Val at Provins, one of the Champagne fair towns. The witness lists of charters drawn up in Oxford give us the names of scribes, illuminators, and parchment makers who lived in the neighbourhood of the Church of St Mary.

The change in type of books went hand in hand with the rise of the new script, which we call Gothic. The bows of the letters instead of being rounded are angular. It was a script capable of being written in many sizes from the formal text hand used in large-scale service books down to the tiny script used to write on the very thin but opaque parchment of the pocket-sized Bibles which began to be produced in considerable numbers in the second quarter of the 13th century. One of the causes of the change of style was the desire to fit more matter into a smaller space. It became possible to compress into one volume works which would have filled three or four. An example is the manuscript belonging p 182 (3) to Robert Grosseteste which contains in one volume Augustine's *De civitate dei* and Gregory the Great's *Moralia in Job*, now in the Bodleian Library at Oxford. It shows well how such books were used for intensive study. Grosseteste and his friend Adam Marsh, the Franciscan, had conceived a vast plan of making a theological subject index to the books available to them. They devised a

collection of some 400 signs—mathematical symbols, letters of the Greek alphabet, conventional designs. They entered these signs in the margins of their books (in the Bodleian manuscript they are in Grosseteste's hand) and collected up the references for the passages in an index arranged according to the signs, part of which has survived prefixed to a Bible in the Bibliothèque Municipale at Lyons. Cumbrous as the system was, it continued to be used by some English Franciscans in the late 13th century.

It is not known how early Paris and Bologna became important centres of book production, but by the middle of the 13th century the university in each place had taken steps to regulate the book trade. The stationers who performed the functions of booksellers and publishers were under its control. The system was f 15 basically very simple. The stationer held a copy of a book *(exemplar)* unbound in quires or pieces *(pecie)*, and hired it out to a scribe piece by piece to copy. The stationer was bound to display in his shop a list of the *exemplaria* which it held, with the number of pieces which it contained and with the official price for hiring the pieces. A commission of masters *(peciarii)* was appointed by the university to supervise the work of the stationer and to watch over the correctness of the *exemplar*. Lists of *exemplaria* from Paris in 1275 and 1304 have survived. The scribes were in the habit of noting in the margins of the copies which they made the numbers of the *pecie*, and in this way it is easy to identify a book copied under the system. A certain number of the *exemplaria* have survived: Père Destrez, to whom we owe our knowledge of the working of the system, has identified eighty-two of them in the course of examining some 7,000 manuscripts. They can be recognized by their tired look. The parchment shows signs of having been folded in two, the margins are full of marks which a scribe made to show the point he had reached. It was an ingenious system, but the dispersal of the quires among a variety of scribes had obvious disadvantages. A scribe might easily lose or damage one of the *pecie*. According to the regulations the *peciarii* were to supervise replacements, but it not infrequently happened that the replacement was made from an inferior copy. In spite of its defects the system worked for more than a century. It is found not only at Paris and Bologna, but at Oxford, Naples, Padua and other Italian universities.

The *pecia* system probably ceased to be used because it no longer answered a need. Mediaeval books written on parchment had a much longer life than a modern book printed on paper. The basic texts of instruction remained in use. Hence there was available a stock of texts which were passed on from generation to generation. To give an example, the pocket Bibles already mentioned, of which hundreds survive, ceased to be produced after the early 14th century. The most likely explanation is that a sufficient number was available to meet the demand for them.

The ending of the *pecia* system did not, of course, mean that the production of new books came to an end. The manuscripts written in the 14th and 15th centuries now in our libraries far outnumber those written in the earlier centuries.

The books of the Middle Ages are the most enduring visible legacy of its flowering. Despite the losses caused by revolutions and wars and periodical neglect, they have survived in their thousands, authentic witnesses, not doctored by the restorer's hand.

VI KING DEATH

Mortality, Judgment and Remembrance

T.S.R. BOASE

'All these ceremonies concerning the dead, the care of the burial, the fashions of the sepulchres, the pomps of the funerals, are rather solaces to the living than furtherances to the dead...

The family of that rich gorgeous glutton prepared him a sumptuous funeral unto the eyes of men: but one far more sumptuous did the ministering angels prepare for the poor ulcered beggar in the sight of God; they bore him not unto any sepulchre of marble but placed him in the bosom of Abraham.'

ST AUGUSTINE'S 'CITY OF GOD', BOOK I, CHAPTER XI

'Into Thy hands, O Lord,

I commend my spirit. You have redeemed me, O Lord, Thou God of truth.' Every man and woman of the Middle Ages hoped to die with Christ's words on their lips. The moment of death was of supreme concern, for upon their spiritual state then depended their happiness or misery for the whole of eternity. It is no paradox to say that life was a preparation for death. And reasonably so: the constant reminders of the end, the skulls, cadavers, Dooms and devils which surrounded them and which may seem obsessive to us, were considerations of prudence. Death might be horrible, but it was nothing compared to the torments that threatened if its coming were forgotten.

The immediacy of that terror and that hope still burn in many mediaeval works of art. The illumination reproduced here from the Rohan Book of Hours was painted in the first quarter of the 15th century; its subject is no less than the fate of Man. The dying Christian commits his soul—symbolized by a tiny naked figure—to God. A devil, always on the watch, has seized it. But God grants salvation; St Michael hurls himself to the rescue, sword in hand, and other angels of the heavenly host, almost invisible in the blue background, attack the devil with spears.

God (speaking in French, one notes, though the dying man uses the Latin of the Psalms) promises the sinner: 'Do penance for thy sins, and thou shalt be with me on the Day of Judgment.' The warm colours of the earth and the mantle throw into dramatic contrast the pallor of the naked body, gaunt and rigid in its last agony. (1)

Death's kingdom was the whole earth, and human life, with its ambitions and struggles, was only a macabre dance that led to the grave. In the later Middle Ages this perennial concern with death took on a fanciful, almost sardonic, tone. At masques men dressed as skeletons and danced with figures representing the various grades of society. A fresco at La Chaise-Dieu, France (right), displays such a scene.

It had its origin in a 13th-century poem of the *Three Living and the Three Dead*. Three rich young men out hunting meet with three skeletons or, as in the version shown here, come suddenly upon three open coffins in which lie corpses in progressive stages of decomposition. They draw back in horror; but an old hermit appears and tells them that the three bodies are—themselves! On the wall of the Cemetery, the *Campo Santo*, of Pisa (below) a fresco combines this story with the familiar motifs of *memento mori* and the vanity of earthly pleasures. (2, 3)

Death triumphant: draped in a shroud, death carries off his prey (top)—an illumination made for Mary of Burgundy and completed after she had been killed in a hunting accident in 1482. Above and below: two miniatures from a Book of Hours of Philip the Fair—death and the lady, and a strangely moving fantasy of a naked corpse lying like an effigy on its own tomb. (4, 5, 6)

The grim truth

that a man might at any moment be snatched suddenly from life or stricken with intolerable pain could neither be ignored nor concealed. Death was everywhere. It was public and brutal in a way that we associate only with times of disaster or the horrors of war.

Execution by the sword: Aymerigot Marcel, a *condottiere* who terrorized the Auvergne in the 14th century, was arrested by the vicomte de Meaux, brought to Paris, pilloried and beheaded (left); his body was cut into four pieces and nailed over the gates of the city. (7)

Plague: Pope Gregory the Great leads a procession to pray for the cessation of the plague in 590; cardinals, monks, a hermit and laymen follow him . . . but a monk falls dying even as they pass along (a miniature of the late 15th century). Bubonic plague had reached Europe in 1348 and killed a third of the population. (8)

Slaughter in battle: mediaeval weapons, especially when armour protected the vital parts, maimed more often than they killed outright. This scene from the 13th century (right) shows knights in chain-mail and helmets. Their arms include heavy swords—for hacking, not piercing—mace, battle-axe, arrows and a catapult for hurling rocks. (9)

Surgery was a desperate expedient, with certain pain and doubtful success. Many medical textbooks survive from the Middle Ages describing surgical treatment. This drawing (above) dates from the early 12th century and demonstrates the cautery of the temples; in the lower half an assistant heats the instruments. (10)

Burial of plague victims at Tournai in the year when the disease was ravaging Europe, 1349. Here there has still been time to make coffins. As mortality increased the dead were simply carried away in carts and buried in mass graves. No cure was ever found. In Erfurt the next year 12,000 corpses were thrown into open pits. (11)

A **mourning cortège** followed the departed to the grave and prayed for his soul. Left: preparing and shrouding the body, while the widow sits apart. Below left: mourners from the tomb of Louis de France (see pl. 28); they represent those who were present at the funeral, including the sons of Henry III of England. Bottom: a daughter of the comtesse de Joigny (late 13th century) gazing sadly down, one hand in the band of her cloak. She wears a travelling dress. These 'weepers', small figures placed along the sides of mediaeval tombs, remind us of ancient grief. (12, 13, 14)

Eight hooded figures, their heads bent in grief, their faces hidden, carry the body of Philippe Pot, Grand Seneschal of Burgundy, to the tomb. The group, life-size, forms one of the most dramatic of mediaeval monuments. Philippe Pot died in 1493 and was buried in the abbey of Cîteaux. (15)

Funeral mass—the solemn Office of the Dead—was moving and impressive, especially when the expression of private grief and faith was combined with the symbolic pageantry of the state. This miniature shows the funeral procession of Charles VI of France, *le Bien-aimé*, with Paris in the background. On the coffin lies a wax effigy arrayed with all the attributes of power. The mourners wear black, except for the members of the Parliament of Paris; they are dressed in scarlet, according to the protocol that 'the King never dies'. Charles died on October 21st, 1422, and lies with his ancestors in the royal abbey of St-Denis. (16)

'Give them eternal rest' — *Requiem aeternam dona eis* — the words of the Requiem Mass from a Book of Hours of the mid-15th century. The miniature of a funeral which accompanies it is painted with engaging realism — the choristers cheerful and indifferent, the draped coffin, and the mourners following in genuine grief. In the foreground a gravedigger unearths bones from previous burials. Books of Hours, rich in such illustrations, were collections of psalms, hymns and liturgical texts made for the private devotions of lay people. (17)

During the Requiem the coffin stood in the nave or choir of the church surrounded by mourners. In this miniature it is surmounted by an elaborate wooden framework, the 'herse', to which candles are fitted. (18)

213

Sir Richard Beauchamp, Earl of Warwick, died in 1439 and was buried in the chapel built in accordance with his will in the church of St Mary at Warwick. It was among the most splendid of English chantry-chapels and has survived almost complete.

'I will that when it liketh to God that my soul depart out of this world, . . . there be made a chapel of Our Lady, well, fair and goodly built, within the middle of which chapel I will that my tomb be made . . .'

Everything was done as he ordered; the tomb (right) is of Purbeck marble, with angels and mourners along the sides. The Earl's effigy (above) lies upon it under an arched metal herse. His surgeon helped the sculptor with the likeness. (19, 20)

Edward the Black Prince (left), eldest son of Edward III, won his spurs commanding the right wing at Crécy at the age of 16; but he died before his father and never reigned. His effigy in Canterbury Cathedral is expressive rather of the soldier than of the man; over the tomb were hung his sword, bronze gauntlets, wooden shield, helmet and velvet coat embroidered with the arms of France and England. (21)

Edward III of England reigned for fifty years (1327–77), a period of peace at home and—generally—successful wars abroad. His tomb portrait (right) was probably based on a death-mask, though the schematic treatment of hair and beard gives it an added dignity and power. (24)

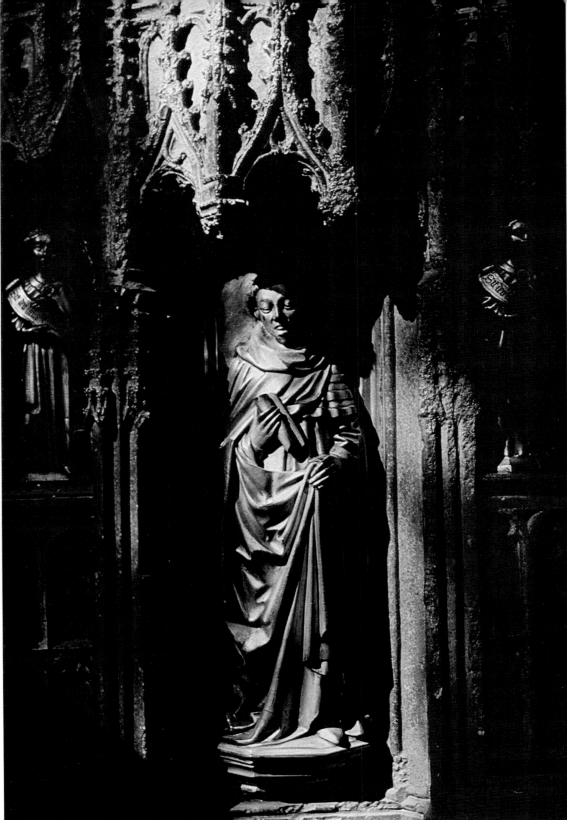

Where the open eyes of the Earl's effigy are fixed, in the centre of the vault, is the small figure of the Virgin as Queen of Heaven. She stands on a crescent moon, crowned with a diadem of pearls, and holding the orb and sceptre. The whole of the Beauchamp Chapel was planned as a unified theological *schema*. Right: one of the gilt copper 'weepers' at the side of the tomb. Their downcast eyes and heavy drapery show the influence of Burgundian art. (22, 23)

To be remembered after death is a constant and universal ambition, and the image that a man chooses to leave behind him is often strangely revealing not only of the way he accepts death but of his ruling passion during life. Archbishop Siegfried III of Eppstein was concerned that posterity should not forget the power he wielded in imperial politics. His gravestone (left), dating from 1249, shows him crowning two minor emperors who owed their thrones to his influence—Heinrich of Raspe and William of Holland. They are represented appropriately smaller in scale than the archbishop who is at the same time trampling on a lion and a dragon. As often with tomb sculpture of this period, the effigy is a compromise between a recumbent and a standing figure. (25)

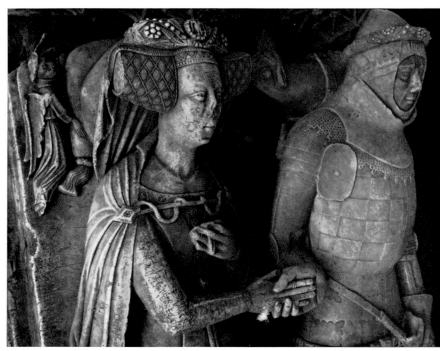

Hand in hand, Sir Ralph Greene (died 1417) and his wife quietly wait for the Last Day. Their pet dogs lie at their feet; angels hold the lady's pillow. (26)

Fiercely scowling, a knight in chain mail and surcoat lies frozen in the act of drawing his sword on a tomb at Dorchester, Oxfordshire. It is an amazing combination of energy and repose. Death has not ended the fierce challenge to which the nameless warrior dedicated his life. (27)

Serene faith is reflected in the figure of Louis de France—son of St Louis—who died in 1260 and was buried in the abbey of Royaumont. The face marks a new departure in sculpture, being evidently a realistic portrait. Within a few years the faces of tomb effigies were being modelled from death-masks. (28)

An ambitious duke and a devout bishop are each commemorated by attributes that characterize their lives. Henry the Lion, Duke of Brunswick (far left), holds a model of Brunswick Cathedral and a sword. Evrard de Fouilloy (left), builder of the present Amiens Cathedral, flanked by censing angels and acolytes with candles, raises his hand in blessing. (29, 30)

217

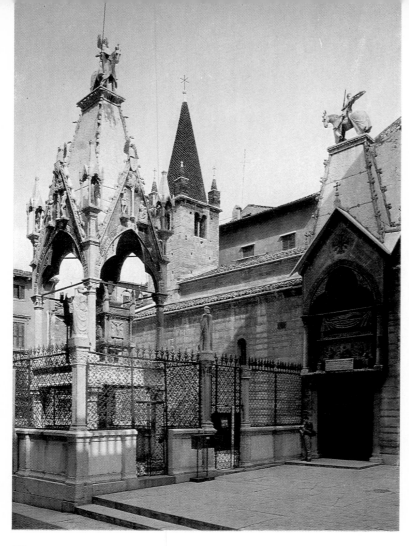

Kings and princes were as splendidly housed in death as in life. Above: the tombs of the Scaliger family, rulers of Verona in the later Middle Ages. Over the church-door is the proud equestrian monument of Can Grande della Scala (died 1329), and left the sarcophagus and canopy of Mastino II (died 1351). (31)

◀ **The murdered Edward II** of England (left), unofficially canonized by his son and successor, became the centre of a flourishing pilgrimage. Beneath a forest of nodding arches, cusps and battlements lies the alabaster effigy, one of the masterpieces of English sculpture. (32)

A dazzling climax of lavish tomb building was reached by the Dukes of Burgundy in the late 14th century. Philippe le Hardi had his tomb begun in 1383, twenty years before his death. The effigy is of alabaster, with the face and hands painted; the angels at his head have wings of gilt bronze. Around the base of the tomb, weaving in and out of the intricate Gothic arches and vaults, walks a procession of mourners robed in heavy mantles and carved with astonishing naturalism by Claus Sluter and Claus de Werve. Two thousand men of the Burgundian Court and Church followed the Duke to his grave in 1404. (33)

Beneath the stately tomb lay the decomposing corpse, a sombre truth upon which the later Middle Ages dwelt with peculiar fascination. Above: the calm effigy of the Duchess of Suffolk at Ewelme, Oxfordshire. Behind the tracery panels (impossible to photograph) lies another carving, of her dead body reproduced in grisly detail. Below: Jacques Germain of Dijon, wrapped in his shroud (compare pl. 12), and (bottom), Canon Parkhouse of Exeter, the skin stretched tight over skull, bone and muscle.

Right: Cardinal Lagrange, died 1402. In his will he ordered that his body be 'boned', the skeleton to be buried at Avignon, the flesh at Amiens. (34–37)

Physical horror can go no further. Left: toads attack the face of François de Sarra (died 1360, but the tomb c. 1400) and huge worms writhe over and into his naked limbs. Above: Louis XII and his queen lie together at St-Denis, the stitches of the embalmers reproduced with gruesome realism. (38, 39)

A good life made possible (though it did not guarantee) a pious death, and had for practical purposes been reduced to the few simple principles known as the Seven Acts of Mercy. The miniatures on this page are from a 14th-century Catalan version of the *Breviari d'Amor*, a Provençal poem of about 1280. From left to right: Admonishing the sinner; Visiting the sick; Feeding the hungry and giving drink to the thirsty; Visiting the prisoner; (below) Sheltering the homeless; Burying the dead; and Clothing the naked. In the final picture is the pious man's reward, his soul redeemed and taken up to Paradise. (40–43)

Angels carried the soul from earth to Heaven, where God received it, sitting enthroned among cherubim. Theologians might offer refined interpretation of these truths but for most of the people, no doubt, it was the simplest image that made the strongest impression. One of the panels from an altarpiece painted about 1480 (right) shows the soul of St Bertin lifted visibly into the sky over the roof of the abbey church dedicated to him at St-Omer. (45)

Michael the Archangel brings a napkin full of souls to Christ. This severely schematic yet very tender painting is from a Psalter made in the mid-12th century for a nunnery at Shaftesbury, Dorset. The hieratic, almost Byzantine, figure of Christ gazes out frontally, but the angel, standing on snail-like rolls of cloud, is typically graceful and linear; note the way in which one of his wings goes right through the ornamental border of the page. (44)

After death – the Judgment: 'For the trumpet shall sound, and the dead shall be raised'; 'for the hour is coming when all who are in the grave will hear his voice and come forth'. Below: the Resurrection from the west front of Orvieto Cathedral. It was St Augustine's theory that the dead would all be resurrected at the age of thirty-three because that was Christ's age at the time of the crucifixion, and consequently the most perfect. This relief dates from about 1320, but already shows many features that were to characterize the Renaissance. The tombs from which the dead arise are classical sarcophagi. (48)

'Thou art weighed in the balance'. The image of the angel weighing men's souls goes back to the Book of Daniel. At Bourges (left) the human soul is in the right-hand scale. A devil, like a toad, clings to it and tries to pull it down, but the bowl on the other side, which contains Christ's redeeming blood, weighs heavier. (46)

'He was carried away by angels into Abraham's bosom . . .' and so from the story of Dives and Lazarus (see p. 21) Abraham's bosom became a symbol for Paradise. In this detail from the tympanum at Conques (right) Abraham is flanked by figures under arches, probably the Apostles who 'shall sit upon twelve thrones judging the twelve tribes of Israel'. Above them is the Resurrection of the dead on the Last Day. (47)

DI ELI GAVDIA VICTIS GLORIA PAX REQVIES PERPET WSQ DIES ✠

ES PIETATIS AMILI SIC STANT GAVDE ES SECVRI NIL ME TVENTES

ANS MVTETIS NISI MORES VDICIVM DVRVM VOBIS S CITO

'And then shall they see the Son of Man coming in a cloud with power and great glory .... And he shall send his angels with a great sound of the trumpet and they shall gather his elect from the four winds, from one end of heaven to the other.

'And he will separate them one from another, as a shepherd divideth his sheep from the goats; and he shall set the sheep on his right hand but the goats on the left. Then shall the King say to them on his right hand, Come, O blessed of my Father, inherit the kingdom prepared for you from the foundation of the world .... Then shall he say also unto them on the left hand, Depart from me, ye cursed, into everlasting fire, prepared for the devil and his angels ... And these shall go away into everlasting punishment.'

The accounts of the Day of Judgment given in the Gospels were expanded by the thinkers, poets and artists of the Middle Ages into a vast iconography of doom which must have been fixed indelibly in every heart.

The miniature on the left accompanies part of the Requiem Mass—*Dies illa, dies ire* ('O day, the day of wrath'). This text became the basis for one of the most famous of mediaeval poems, the *Dies Irae* of Thomas of Celano (about 1220), written in rhyming triplets and later incorporated into the Requiem. (49)

'So shall it be at the end of the world: the angels shall come forth and sever the wicked from among the just, and shall cast them into a furnace of fire; there shall be wailing and gnashing of teeth.' The Apocalypse speaks of sinners being 'thrown alive into the lake of fire that burns with brimstone', and the mediaeval church added new refinements of its own. This detail (fold-out) is from a Last Judgment painted by Stefan Lochner about 1430. In the centre the damned are dragged forward in chains; upper right, a miser vomits up his gold; and on the extreme right a terrified group, including a king, a bishop, a cardinal and even a pope, is pulled into the deepest abyss. (50)

'Here is Hell and the angel who closes the gate', reads the simple and direct inscription (right) in old French over this dreadful vision of Hell-mouth: *Ici est enfers e li angels ki enferme les portes*. It was painted in England in the mid-12th century. (51)

Fold out

Fantasies of death

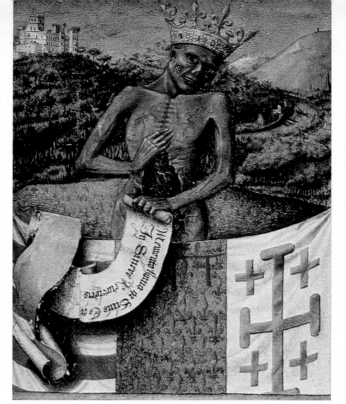

multiplied in the plague years, the bizarre product of strained imaginations. Only in this way, perhaps, could the nightmare of reality be assimilated and faced. The crowned corpse (right), already a mass of corruption, was added to an earlier manuscript about 1435. The tripartite banner is that of King René of Anjou, and the picture may actually have been painted by him. (52)

'**And I looked** and behold a pale horse: and his name that sat on him was Death.' The Triumph of Death from a former hospital in Palermo (below) was painted around 1445, but the artist is unknown. The horse still has its flowing mane and tail and vestiges of flesh still cling to its body (the tongue and gums are intact, the rest of the head an eyeless skull). Death shoots his arrows not at those who wait for him—the poor, the maimed and the old, huddled on the left—but at those in the flower of youth and happiness, dressed in gay clothes and listening to music by a fountain. Under the horse's hooves lie those already stricken—lords, ladies, bishops, popes and friars. (53)

Mortality, Judgment and Remembrance

T.S.R. BOASE

DEATH WAS A GRIM BUSINESS in the Middle Ages. With no alleviation of pain, no dulling of the horrors of surgery, the *acerbitas mortis*, the bitterness of death, was very real. 'For two hours he lay as though unconscious and half dead; then I came and saw the father sweating in anguish, the pallor of his face flushed, his eyes filled with tears, the ball of his nostrils twitching, his lips bitten by his teeth. I said to a brother, "Of a truth the lord abbot now suffers much, for those changes in his members are signs of great pain." But he, gazing on me fondly—for he was so sweet—said, "Yes, my son, yes, yes, just as you say, I am greatly vexed by the agonies of this sickness; by the will of the Lord Jesus there will soon be an end to all this trouble".' It was to be for some two weeks in the Christmastide of 1166 that Ailred of Rievaulx lay in this final agony. These pious deathbeds were fortified by the acceptance of pain as an offering to God, but at the same time rendered more terrible in their details by the heroic desire for expiation. St Hugh of Lincoln, perspiring profusely in mortal fever, calling on God to hasten his rest, would still not throw off his cowl and hardly allowed his attendants to remove his hair shirt, though caked and hardened with sweat. Diagnosis was empirical and uncertain. Amaury of Jerusalem, against the advice of the Syrian doctors, ordered his Latin physicians to give him a purgative remedy when smitten by severe fever and dysentery. 'They administered medicine which produced the desired result easily and seemed to give him some relief. But before he could take nourishment to strengthen his body which had been weakened by the violent remedy, the usual fever returned and he yielded to his fate.' Eastern medical skill, as William of Tyre implies in the above quotation, was in advance of Western, and was gradually penetrating the European techniques, which the more advanced Arabs despised. Thabit, a Lebanese doctor, told Ousama ibn Munkidh how the Franks brought him a knight with an abscess in his leg, which he poulticed till it opened and began to heal. Then one of their own physicians intervened, saying, 'This man knows nothing about the treatment required', and asked the knight whether he preferred to live with one leg or die with two. The latter opted for life with one, and another knight was summoned with a sharp axe, who struck the leg a severe blow but failed to sever it. He dealt another blow, upon which the marrow of the leg burst out and the patient at once expired. 'I was looking on', said Thabit. A manuscript in Vienna of the second half of the

Medicine made some advances during the Middle Ages but could do little to alleviate pain and the horrors of disease. In this drawing (from a late 12th-century account of the conquests of the Emperor Henry VI) William of Sicily is treated by his doctor (left) and his astrologer (right)—equally respectable remedies and, one imagines, equally efficacious. Both doctor and astrologer are obviously Arabs. (2)

14th century, an Arabic treatise on surgery translated by Gerard of Cremona at Toledo in the 12th century, is illustrated by grisly little pictures of an Arab doctor operating on his naked and unanaesthetized patients. Undoubtedly pain was a constant preoccupation from which we, whatever our new barbarities and dangers, are reassuringly relieved by medical progress.

p 209
(10)

Death in Battle

A sword stroke or spear thrust in battle might bring a speedier death, but even here the hacking blows of mediaeval warfare, where armour protected the more vital parts, were likely to cause wounds that were mutilating rather than fatal. Freeman's famous account of the death of Harold at Hastings, compiled though it is from writers of varying authority, gives a picture of defeat in battle that can be paralleled, if less eloquently, from many sources. 'At last another arrow, more charged with destiny than its fellows, went still more truly to its mark. Falling like a bolt from heaven, it pierced the King's right eye; he clutched convulsively at the weapon, he broke off the shaft, his axe dropped from his hand, and he sank in agony at the foot of the Standard. . . . But Harold, though disabled, still breathed; four knights rushed upon him and despatched him with various wounds. . . . One thrust pierced through the shield of the dying King and stabbed him in the breast; another assailant finished the work by striking off his head with his sword. But even this vengeance was not enough. A third pierced the dead body and scattered about the entrails; the fourth, coming, it would seem, too late for any more efficient share in the deed, cut off the King's leg as he lay dead.' The Bayeux Tapestry shows (though other interpretations of the scene are possible) Harold pierced by the arrow, and the mutilation of his body, while below Norman soldiers pillage the conquered dead. In his account of a battle of a much later date, that of Bannockburn, John Barbour, writing about 1375, describes how Robert the Bruce slew Sir Henry de Bohun:

p 209
(9)

> And he, that in his sterapis stude,
> With ax that wes both hard and gude
> With so gret mayn raucht him a dynt,
> That nothir hat no helme mycht stynt,
> The hevy dusche that he him gave,
> That he the hed till harnys clave.
> The hand-ax-schaft ruschit in twa,
> And he doune till the erd gan ga
> All flatlyngis, for him falit mycht;
> This wes the first strak of the ficht.

A 15th-century French manuscript shows the Battle of Hastings in the contemporary costumes of the artist's time but with much the same carnage as in the embroidery of four hundred years before. The brutality of warfare lives in many illuminations, whether they

Accidental death: Matthew Paris (mid-13th century) relates how Gilbert Marshall was thrown from his horse when the reins broke; how his foot caught in the stirrup and how he was dragged to death. (1)

The frontispiece of the 'Liber Vitae' of New Minster, Winchester. At the top, St Peter opens the gates of the New Jerusalem; in the centre the saved and the damned are separated; at the bottom the key is turned upon those lost forever. (3)

purport to represent the battle of Gilboa or the death of Hector. And apart from the give and take of warfare there was the ferocity of justice, for treason and other crimes great or petty; and little clemency for captives in battle or for those who incurred tyrannical displeasure. An illustration to Froissart's Chronicle shows the execution of Aymerigot Marcel, the robber baron, whose only joy was 'to ride forth at adventure, when all the country trembled, for all was his going or coming', and now in the painting he kneels in his shirt, his hands bound, his eyes hooded, awaiting the sword stroke, while all round the scaffold windows are filled by a gay and interested crowd.

p 208 (7)

'A Heavy Judgment Awaits You'

Beyond the pangs of dissolution lay threats of greater torment and the over-shadowing dread of the Last Judgment, that day of whose coming no man knew, when the blessed would be received into Paradise and the wicked pass to everlasting damnation. In the *Liber Vitae* of New Minster, Winchester (c. 1016–20),

f 3

there is a vivid realization of the theme: in the centre a very youthful St Peter drives off with his keys a devil who tries to seize a soul; beside St Peter stands the recording angel with his book; beyond, a man and woman, pathetically clasping hands, are in the grip of a clawed devil; below is Hell's mouth, into which a devil propels struggling souls, while an angel locks the door upon them; above, St Peter flings open the gate of Paradise and beckons to a procession of the saved that stretches on to the opposite page, while within the New Jerusalem, shown as a walled city, the elect receive the beatific vision of Christ in Majesty. In the 12th century this became a great and dominant theme of Western art. Here was a matter of deepest import to both craftsmen and onlookers, an unknowable but not unimaginable mystery, to which forms of lasting significance were being given. It was a public and general art of communication, such as is hardly found in contemporary art today.

The normal Byzantine rendering of the Last Judgment, as shown for instance in the mosaic on the west wall of Torcello (12th century), begins at the top with Christ releasing Adam from Limbo; in the second row is Christ in Majesty, between the Virgin and the Baptist, and seated rows of apostles and the elect; below Christ's feet are burning wheels from which issues a fiery stream that flows down into Hell; in the third row is an empty throne on which lies the book of life with Adam and Eve kneeling before it, while on either side angels with trumpets drive off the beast and the woman mounted on the beast, scenes that combine the vision of Daniel with the Apocalypse; in the fourth row are the angel with the scales, the Virgin in supplication, and on one side those who are saved, on the other the damned driven down into Hell. The West developed a more concrete visual formula, less involved with the books of Daniel and Revelations, though the latter in illustrated Apocalypses had a long visual tradition of its own. The Resurrection of the Dead, not shown at Torcello, has much prominence. In the *Perikopenbuch* of Henry II at Munich (between 1002 and 1014), one page is devoted to the dead clambering, fully clad, out of their tombs, while four angels sound the last trump and at the corners the four winds, shown as horned heads, blow out a great storm; on the opposite page angels lead the blessed up a flight of steps to Christ, seated between the Apostles; in the right-hand corner, as through a crevasse in the steps, the damned are dragged down into Hell where the devil lies chained. No torments are shown. It is still, as is to be expected in an Ottonian manuscript, some way from the final Western version.

f 5

This can be seen fully developed in the tympanum at Conques, not securely dated but most probably of the 1130s, an early and masterly realization of the subject. Christ in Majesty is seated in an aureole; above, held by flying angels, is a great cross; on His right hand are the souls in the joys of Paradise, to His left is the mouth of Hell and the bottomless pit; below His feet the dead rise from their tombs and finally, on the lowest register, an angel separates the just and unjust, the former being led towards a row of seated figures, framed in arches, the latter being thrust down into a second Hell's mouth. Here is a full programme of the after-life, dealing not only with the Last Judgment, but with the intermediate period before that great and terrible day. The wicked at death are thrust forthwith into Hell, still recognizable by worldly attributes: a knight who falls from his horse, a usurer with his bag hung about his neck. For them the resurrection of the body and the judgment will only bring intensification of suffering. Below the tympanum runs in Latin the threatening warning: 'Sinners, if you do not mend your ways, know that a heavy judgment awaits you.' But for the righteous there is a period of rest and refreshment before the Day of the Lord will bring the full revelation of the Beatific Vision. Central amongst the seated figures in the colonnade is a venerable man with his arms round two smaller figures, who seem to hold flowers in their hands. He is the patriarch Abraham.

f 4

p 225 (47)

In the obscure unknown beyond the grave, one certainty, as it seemed, was illuminated by the Gospel story of Dives and Lazarus in the sixteenth chapter of St Luke. 'And it came to pass that the beggar died, and that he was carried away by the angels into Abraham's bosom: and the rich man also died and was buried. And in Hades he lifted up his eyes, being in torments, and seeth

The Last Judgment, the 'Doom', was the theme for some of the grandest and most terrifying works of art of the Middle Ages. It was displayed above the principal entrances to the churches, over the chancel-arches or, in fresco, glass or mosaic, on the huge west walls.

In the tympanum of Conques (above) its message is spelled out in words adapted from the Latin Vulgate. The scroll in Christ's right hand reads: 'Come, ye blessed of my Father, inherit the kingdom prepared for you'; in his left: 'Depart from me, ye cursed.' The rest of the lettering is in four main bands. Above the blessed: 'The assembly of the saints is blessed in Christ the judge.' Above the damned: 'It is thus that wicked men are plunged into Hell.' Below Christ's feet: 'Thus is given to the elect, united in the joys of Heaven, glory, peace, repose and everlasting day. The wicked are tormented by pains, burnt in fire and tremble and groan perpetually among the demons.' On the sloping roof above the blessed: 'The pure, the peacemakers, the friends of piety thus stand rejoicing secure and fearing nothing.' Above the damned: 'Thieves, liars, false, lustful and avaricious men are thus condemned with the wicked.' Along the bottom: 'O sinners, if you do not amend, know that a heavy judgment awaits you.'

At Torcello (right) the whole west wall is devoted to the same subject, treated this time according to Byzantine tradition. It is divided into five levels. First: Christ releases Adam from Limbo. Second: Christ in majesty between the Virgin and John the Baptist. Third: the Book of Life with Adam and Eve kneeling in adoration. Fourth: the weighing of souls, with the elect on one side, the damned on the other. And fifth: Heaven, with the souls in Abraham's bosom, and Hell, with souls roasted in a stream of fire which issues from below Christ's feet. (4, 5)

Abraham afar off, and Lazarus in his bosom.' The Vulgate punctuates it even more forcibly, *et sepultus est in inferno*, 'and was buried in Hell'. It was a description that was early welcomed. Tertullian in his *Adversus Marcion*, written about 207, formulates the view that 'there is a spatial concept that may be called Abraham's bosom for receiving the souls of all peoples ... which, though not celestial, is above the lower regions, to provide refreshment (*refrigerium*) to the souls of the just until the consummation of all things in the general resurrection'. The early sacramentaries in the prayers for the dead take up the same theme, praying that 'the soul of this your servant may be brought by the hands of your holy angels to the bosom of your friend the patriarch Abraham and may be raised again on the last day of the great judgment'. It was not, however, till the Romanesque period that this became a common visual image in Western art, though there were earlier Byzantine prototypes for it, and Abraham holding a soul in his bosom appears in the lowest row of the Torcello mosaic.

p 20 (19) At Moissac (1125–30) the scene of Dives' feast is shown with the dogs licking the sores of the dying Lazarus, while an angel carries off his soul, which is then seen wrapped in a fold of Abraham's cloak; on Abraham's right a seated, bearded figure points to a scroll; this is possibly another patriarch, but the scroll suggests that it is St Luke, who gives Gospel authority to the scene depicted; below, devils carry off the rich man's soul, as he dies recumbent on an elaborate couch, mourned by his wife. His punishment in Hell is then shown in gruesome detail. This is a direct transcript of the parable which, if derived from some Byzantine source, has been re-thought in Romanesque

The weighing of the soul—good deeds against bad, guardian angel against devil—finds vivid representation in art. On this altar frontal from Catalonia the soul is saved (in spite of the cheating demons who push down the scales) and safely delivered to St Peter at the gates of Paradise. (7)

stylistic terms. At Lincoln, in the mid-12th century, the scene has become more generalized, and Abraham, unfortunately a much damaged figure, now holds three souls in his lap while angels bring others to him. On the west front of St-Trophîme at Arles the Last Judgment is depicted on the jambs and lintels of the porch, with Christ in Majesty on the tympanum. Here angels bring souls to the three patriarchs, Abraham, Isaac and Jacob, a rare interpretation; but Arles is full of unusual details, such as the door of Paradise closing in the face of the damned, who cover their eyes with their hands before this awful sight. At Autun, where the cathedral is dedicated to St Lazarus, there is some conflation of the two bearers of the name. On the tympanum of the north doorway, now destroyed, was depicted the resurrection of Lazarus of Bethany; on a still surviving capital of the doorway Lazarus the beggar, whose sores gave this combined saintliness efficacy against leprosy, is shown at the rich man's threshold and then in Abraham's bosom, averting his gaze from the pleading Dives. At Toulouse on a capital in St-Sernin, at Ávila in the church of S. Vicente, the same story is repeated, and a complete list of its occurrences would be a long one.

In illumination it is an equally popular subject. A necrology of the abbey of Obermünster in Bavaria shows angels bringing souls to Abraham, while below him are the Tree of Life and the rivers of Paradise. The Psalter of St Louis, of the mid-13th century, shows the patriarch holding souls, with Hell below him. Throughout western Europe it was a dominant theme, and the accepted symbol for the intermediate state of bliss to which the souls of the righteous are borne upon death. 'When a man dies', says the Life of St Hugh of Lincoln, 'he is led to the joy of Paradise or is snatched away to the horror of Tartarus, and there will he be; since between Abraham's bosom and Hell a great abyss is fixed.' 'That rest', wrote Aquinas, 'which is given men after death is called the bosom of Abraham.' In the Last Judgments of Laon, St-Denis, Chartres and Notre-Dame at Paris, Abraham and the souls are shown on a voussoir on the right hand of Christ; at Amiens Abraham, unusually, is standing, holding up three souls in the lap of his cloak; in the tympana themselves are the terrible events of the Last Day, and on the left-hand voussoirs the damned are hurled through a gaping mouth into the perpetual horrors of Hell. At Bamberg, similarly, Abraham is a voussoir figure, while on the tympanum the elect rejoice in Paradise or howl in Hell with disconcertingly similar grimaces. At Rheims, on the other **f 8** hand, Abraham figures on the lowest band of the tympanum where there is a singularly beautiful representation of the angels approaching him, while on the opposite side the wicked, fully clad in their distinguishing robes, are led to the cauldron of Hell. Above,

The pious death of Abbot Lambert. His soul, a small naked figure, is carried aloft to Christ by angels, their hands covered, according to early Christian imagery, with cloths. In the half-circles are Almsgiving and Patience, the Virgin (holding a model of the church built by the Abbot) and St Bertin. (6)

On a tomb-slab at Ely, possibly that of Bishop Nigel (1133–69), the dead man's soul is shown on its way to Heaven in the care of St Michael. (9)

The Last Judgment tympanum at Rheims (above) was carved over a century after that of Conques, but the message and most of the iconography remain the same. Christ the judge is again the apex of the composition. Beneath him the dead rise from their graves—nude figures of surprising naturalism. At the next level are the blessed seated on thrones and the damned (almost destroyed), while at the bottom saved souls are being brought to Abraham's bosom and those condemned dragged by devils to the cauldron of Hell. On the soffit of the arch the theme is continued with rows of seated angels, some of them sounding the trumpets of the Last Day. (8)

the elect sit on one side, on the other naked souls are in torment; then comes the resurrection of the dead and above it the Virgin and St John kneel in intercession. This seems to be a reasoned statement to be read from the lowest row upwards. At death the elect are in repose (Abraham's bosom), the wicked are in Hell. At the Last Judgment these dispositions will not be wholly changed, but with restored bodies the elect will enter into a new phase of felicity, the damned of hopeless agony.

At Bourges the resurrection occupies the lintel. Above it is depicted the weighing of souls: on one side the elect, admitted by St Peter, are entering an edicule where Abraham sits; on the other side souls are in torment. At a higher level, angels hover above the elect with crowns, the final reward of the blessed. Here the stages of salvation seem less clearly marked, and the intermediate nature of the place of 'solace' more indeterminate. The Bourges tympanum dates probably from about 1280 to 1290.

p 224
(46)

Slightly later, the very beautiful tympanum of the west doorway at St-Urbain of Troyes sets the Last Judgment in an elegant tracery scheme reminiscent of a window, an almost playful treatment which reduces the terrors of Hell to a very subordinate place in the pattern, and makes the seated Abraham serve as the main symbol of Paradise. Here, as at Bourges, it is no intermediate state, but follows on the resurrection of the dead, which occupies the lintel. At Rampillon (Seine-et-Marne) in the midst of a very realistic resurrection, where a man yawns sleepily as he emerges, Abraham, a highly classical figure, has the souls playing round as well as sitting on his knees.

The Fate of the Soul

By the 14th century, however, views as to the after-life were losing some of the certainties of earlier times. In the 12th century, whatever theories were expressed by theologians, the idea of Purgatory seems to have been little considered. The souls of the righteous were carried directly to Abraham's bosom or even, as on the page of a Boulogne manuscript showing the death of Abbot Lambert in 1125, into the presence of Christ. 'He surrendered his spotless spirit into the hands of his Father, and was at rest in Christ', wrote Walter Daniel of the death of Abbot Ailred of Rievaulx. In the scene of the martyrdom of Stephen on the west front of St-Trophîme at Arles an angel draws his soul up to God: 'and they stoned Stephen calling upon the Lord, and saying, "Lord Jesus, receive my spirit".' In the late 12th-century roll of the Life of St Guthlac the saint is shown lying dead while an angel

f 6

Many small country churches must have had such horrifying pictures of the Doom as this at Chaldon in Surrey. It is 17 feet long and over 11 feet high, and is based on an Eastern idea, the 'Ladder of Salvation'. The bottom half comprises Hell, the upper Heaven. On the lower right is the Tree of Life with the serpent—the source of all the punishment depicted. To the left a usurer, with money-bags round his waist, is being tormented and vomits up his gold. On either side couples, representing Lust, are embracing. Above them two devils hold a long beam like a saw—the 'bridge of spikes', an ordeal again of Eastern origin. On the other side of the ladder more sinners are being crammed into a cauldron. In the upper part are the familiar scenes of the weighing of souls and the Harrowing of Hell. (10)

p 223
(44)
f 9
carries his soul aloft; in a Shaftesbury psalter an angel stands with souls gathered in his arms, bringing them to Christ; on a tomb at Ely, possibly that of Bishop Nigel (1133–69), a great angel with spread wings holds the soul of the deceased in a napkin; on a Templar's tomb in Zamora two angels perform the same task; and it was a popular scene for the altarpieces and wooden frontals of mediaeval Spain. On the shutters of a retable painted about 1459 for the abbey church of St-Bertin at St-Omer, the painter (generally, though on inadequate grounds, thought to be Simon Marmion) showed the soul of St Bertin being carried by two angels, above the roof-top of the church, to God the Father seated in a halo of cherubim.

f 7
p 223
(45)

Such were pious deathbeds. The soul of the sinner, of whom Dives was the type, was snatched down to Hell by clawing demons, as shown on the terrifying slab at York or on a capital at Vézelay, among other examples. There is in these representations a certain dramatic contrast between the pleasures of this life and the torments of the next. The powerful and wealthy were to have the reward of their arrogance and worldliness, the poor and patient were to find in the next world recompense for their miseries in this. Hugo Candidus of Peterborough, writing in the mid-12th century, put it in its crudest form: 'For the wicked in this life enjoy delight and tranquillity so that in this life they may reap the reward for any good, however small, they have done, but in the life to come they may find no rest. But the righteous shall endure in this world all their woes, so that they may rest in peace in the life hereafter.' Hugo, writing in the reign of Stephen when it seemed God slept, was looking out on the troubled world around him from the devoted life of the monastery, but this was the theme also of innumerable sermons, particularly when the mendicant friars brought a new vigour to popular denunciation. 'At the day of Judgment', to quote but one example, from an English friar, Nicole Bozon, 'the simple folk will be exalted for their good deeds and the haughty abased for their pride. Then God will do as the mender of old clothes, who turns the lappet to the front, and what was uppermost downwards.' This could be dangerous, revolutionary stuff, and it is not surprising that itinerant preachers were often associated with peasant risings; but more generally it may have had an opiate effect, redeeming present misery by hopes of future bliss. For either reason the death of Lazarus remained a popular tale which survived the Reformation and was, on the painted hangings that were the decoration of the poorer houses, familiar to Shakespeare's Falstaff whose recruits were 'as ragged as Lazarus in the painted cloth, where the glutton's dogs licked his sores'.

'What Other Place is there?'

The pious went to Abraham's bosom, the wicked to the cauldron of Hell. But then as now the ordinary man was neither outstandingly virtuous nor thoroughly bad; the Last Judgment must to many have appeared a very real weighing of souls, the outcome of which was no foregone conclusion. If the elect and the damned each had their place of waiting for that Judgment, what happened to those in between these states? To the early Fathers the millennium was not long distant, and the mediate period therefore one of short duration, whose nature they were content to leave imprecise. With St Augustine the doctrine of purifying and expiatory pain between death and judgment was established. Whether all pass through Purgatory or only those who have inadequately atoned on earth remained something of an open question. Augustine himself wrote of his dead friend Nebridius: 'Now he lives in Abraham's bosom. Whatsoever that state be, which is signified by that bosom, there lives Nebridius my sweet friend . . . for what other place is there for such a soul?' Writing in the early 12th century, Honorius of Autun held that purgation could, wholly or partially, be accomplished in this world by self-inflicted fasts and penances, by loss of worldly goods, by want of food and clothing or by the bitterness of death itself. After death there would be purgation by the heat of fire or the rigour of cold or by some other punishments, the least of which would be greater than anything imaginable in this life, but in these purifying torments angels and saints would appear to those suffering them and there would be hope of salvation.

St Bernard is more explicit: there are three regions, Hell where there is no redemption, Purgatory where there is hope, and Paradise where there is the Beatific Vision. To the middle path of Purgatory the generality of mankind is committed by its humanity: 'I will go there and I will see the great vision, how the Father leaves his sons in the hand of the tormentor that they may be glorified, not to kill, but to purge'. This was a doctrine that received steady confirmation from writers such as Vincent of Beauvais and St Thomas Aquinas, and in 1274 at the Council of Lyons, where Pope Gregory X was striving, in the interests of the crusading kingdom, to achieve some unity with the Eastern Church, Purgatory and the efficacy of prayers for the dead were included in an agreed profession of faith. The extent, however, to which penance on earth and blamelessness of life could, as it were, by-pass Purgatory and bring the soul at once to bliss remained something of an open question. In 1331 Pope John XXII alarmed theological circles by a series of sermons in which he preached that none, however worthy, could enjoy the Beatific Vision before the Last Judgment. This was held to threaten the validity of intercession by the saints, and was formally contradicted by his successor, Benedict XII, in 1336. By now the doctrine of the Treasury of Merits, the infinite merits of Christ and the accumulated virtues of saints and martyrs, whose resources could be administered by the Church, was widely held as a means of salvation, and anything that questioned its efficacy in reducing the period of purgation roused much popular resistance. Indulgences, by which part of the temporal penance, due to sin even after repentance and absolution, was remitted, could be earned by joining a crusade, making a pilgrimage to a particular shrine, or building a church; eventually they could simply be bought. As penance on earth might lessen purgatorial suffering, these substitute penances were matters of great moment, and popular shrines or papal agents had a vested interest in them. The high imagination of Dante could invest Purgatory with deep spiritual significance. Mystics such as Juliana of Norwich could desire 'full sight of Hell and Purgatory', and meditate upon 'the medicines by which the soul is saved'; but more generally it was torment rather than spiritual progress that was emphasized. Lurid legends circulated: Peter of Branham tells how a certain chaplain walking in the countryside suddenly met his dead father riding with his concubine, who carried her child that had died without baptism. The father had confessed his sins and repented, else he would now have been in Hell, whereas he was in Purgatory, where there was the consolation of hope; *in inferno nulla est consolatio*. The chaplain then saw a vision of Purgatory: flames and sulphur on one side, frost and terrible cold on the other, filled with figures whose various garments and states of nudity distinguished the various sins and degrees of repentance before death. Outside Italy, where Dante's *Commedia* found some visual realizations, there was, however, little attempt to represent Purgatory in painting or sculpture. Imagination seemed to have been exhausted by the effort of embodying Hell. In the church of Chaldon in Surrey a fresco, of about 1200, represents a ladder with souls upon it, some climbing, some falling from it, which may have some Purgatorial implications. On the splendid monument erected in St-Denis by Louis IX to King Dagobert, a relief behind the recumbent effigy retails a legend, the meaning of which is explained by Guillaume de Nangis, who knew well this carving in his own monastery. St Denis on the death of Dagobert commanded a hermit, John, to pray for the king's soul; in a vision the hermit saw the soul of Dagobert in a boat tormented by demons, but St Denis, St Maurice and St Martin appeared and rescued him, carrying him aloft in a cloth to Abraham's bosom—or so says Guillaume though the figure in the very apex of the arch might well be God the Father. This is a clear statement of the validity of the invocation of saints, but it was commissioned by a king, himself a saint, and cannot be taken as representative of widespread opinion. Another striking illustration of the doctrine comes appropriately from Avignon, securely dated by a detailed contract to 1453, the painting of the Coronation of the Virgin by Enguerrand Quarton. In the centre, the Trinity crown the Virgin, their wide-spreading cloaks forming a great circular pattern. On either side, much smaller in scale, are groups of the

p 324
(15)

f 10

f 11

p 288
(17)

The image of 'Abraham's bosom' as the place of rest for the elect comes originally from the story of Dives and Lazarus. It was interpreted quite literally and occurs over and over again in pictures and sculpture. On the topmost pinnacle of the Percy tomb, at Beverley in Yorkshire, the soul kneels in prayer, and it is hard to tell whether Abraham or God the Father is intended. (12)

elect. On a hill below, between very generalized representations of Rome and Jerusalem, a monk kneels before the crucifix. At the very foot an angel releases souls from the flames of Purgatory, and a devil drives others into the torments of Hell. In 1439, at the Council of Florence, Purgatory had received further affirmation in the discussions with the Orthodox Church, and this Avignon altarpiece may be taken as a visual statement of the revived doctrinal interest. In keeping with this new emphasis is the gradual disappearance in visual art of the figure of Abraham. On the topmost pinnacle of the tomb of Lady Eleanor Percy (d. 1328) at Beverley a bearded figure holds a little naked soul kneeling in prayer in the lap of his garment, and this is more likely the figure of God than the intermediate resting place in the patriarch's bosom. In the great 15th-century representations of the Last Day, such as Stefan Lochner's wonderful mingling of tenderness and brutality, Abraham seldom appears. He retained, however, his place in the liturgy and was long a familiar name in popular speech. When in Shakespeare's *Richard II* Bolingbroke hears the news of Thomas Mowbray's death, he says, with a certain flippancy, as though using an outdated formula:

f 12

p 227-8
(50)

> Sweet peace conduct his sweet soul to the bosom
> Of good old Abraham.

Even more clearly cynical is Richard III's comment on the murdered princes, 'The sons of Edward sleep in Abraham's bosom.' There is more feeling, more survival of traditional belief, despite some verbal confusion, in mine hostess's account of Falstaff's end: 'Nay, sure, he's not in hell, he's in Arthur's bosom, if ever man went to Arthur's bosom.'

Prayers for the Dead

With Purgatory a more accepted concept, prayers for the dead received proportionately more urgency. Pious founders of religious houses, hospitals, and almshouses, benefactors of cathedrals or parish churches, expected that intercession should be regularly made for their spiritual welfare both before and after death. Later, colleges were added to the list, and here, if masses have been discontinued, the frequent mention of *fundator noster* in bidding prayers and graces has proved a very lasting commemoration. Some of these foundations were corporate rather than personal in their purpose. Archbishop Chichele in 1438 founded All Souls College for the offering of prayers for the souls of Henry V, King of England and France; of Thomas, Duke of Clarence; and of other nobles and faithful subjects who died in the French wars, and the statutes stressed the obligation of prayer on his 'poor and indigent scholars' over that of study. Above the doorway a relief showed the Resurrection of the Dead at the Last Day, or so it is interpreted in the restored version made in 1826; it is possible

The invocation of saints as protectors in the after-life presupposed some intermediate stage between death and judgment, though Purgatory itself is only rarely portrayed in art. This detail from Louis IX's monument to King Dagobert recalls the legend of Charon. The King is being rowed in a boat by demons when St Denis, St Maurice and St Martin appear and rescue him from their clutches. (11)

that it may have been a rare example of souls in Purgatory. Chichele himself was buried in the choir of Canterbury Cathedral and to this day the College cares for the upkeep of the tomb.

Confraternities banded together to ensure their spiritual welfare. The Gild of the Holy Cross was already in existence at Stratford-upon-Avon by 1269, and today its group of buildings provides a wonderfully complete reminder of mediaeval activities. It employed chaplains, usually four in number, to say masses for the souls of its members, living or dead, both in the gild chapel and at altars supported by the gild in the parish church. That church itself was served by a collegiate body, founded by John de Stratford, Bishop of Winchester, who added to the church in 1331 a chapel of St Thomas the Martyr where masses were to be celebrated for himself and his relatives. The gild came to have many other functions—a school, almshouses, property-owning in the town, upkeep of the bridge over the Avon—but its prime commitment remained unchanged. Over the chancel arch of its chapel can still be seen the painting of the Doom.

For smaller grants, obits could be obtained, that is, a mass on the anniversary of the donor's death, either for a limited number of years or in perpetuity. The wealthier members of the community might endow a special priest for more frequent services, founding a chantry or trust for this purpose, and in some cases building a small canopied chapel round the tomb for the saying of the necessary offices. England is particularly rich in surviving examples and nowhere can they be better studied than in Winchester Cathedral. Six bishops, Edington, Wykeham, Beaufort, Waynflete, Fox and Gardiner, a line stretching from 1345 to 1555, have their chantries here, vying with one another in their dignity, and illustrating stylistic changes over a period of two hundred years. Wykeham's chantry in one of the bays of the nave masks the archway in which it is set and thereby achieves a sense of soaring height compared with the open bays on either side; within lies the effigy and at his feet are three praying monks, sometimes more romantically interpreted as the master builders. Beaufort's chantry in the retro-choir, canopied by a forest of pinnacles, is Gothic art at its most elaborate. Waynflete's is neighbour to it, more delicate and less domineering in design. The effigy, holding his heart between his folded hands, gazes up at an intricate canopy in the centre of which an angel displays his shield with the lilies that passed from him to the colleges of Eton and Magdalen. Henry V, whom Chichele had commemorated at All Souls, had his own chantry chapel in Westminster Abbey, for which he left detailed instructions in his will with provision for 'every day three masses to be sungen in a fair chapel over his sepulchre'. The chapel is in the unusual form of a bridge spanning the ambulatory, and the sculpture includes many heraldic devices, the scene of Henry's coronation, and the King mounted and arrayed for battle. It was the first royal chantry in the Abbey, but was to have a greater successor, the chapel built by Henry VII to replace the 13th-century lady chapel. It is the climax of Perpendicular Gothic, that peculiarly English style, but the tomb that it enclosed was by the Florentine, Pietro Torrigiano, the first great Renaissance work in England. Splendid as Henry's memorial is, it lacks the clarity and directness of statement, the effortless sincerity, that can be found in the tomb chapel ordered in his will by Richard Beauchamp, Earl of Warwick, who died in 1439: 'A noble knight as was well proved in his joustying at Mantua, and at the General Council at Constance... and in the Wars of France'. 'I will that when it liketh to God that my soul depart out of this world, my body be entered within the Church Collegiate of Our Lady in Warwick, where I will, that in such a place as I have devised, which is known well, there be made a Chapel of our Lady well, fair and goodly built, within the middle of which Chapel I will, that my Tomb be made—Also I will that there be said every day, during the World, in the aforesaid Chapel, that (with the Grace of God) shall be thus new made, three masses whereof one every day of Our Lady God's Mother, with Note [or requiem] after, and as the Ordinal of Salisbury doth assign.' On a tomb chest of alabaster, surrounded by bronze angels and cloaked mourners, lies the effigy of the Earl in plate armour, his hands not folded but slightly apart, his eyes fixed on the Virgin as she appears carved on a panel in the eastern bay of the roof. The figure was cast by William

p 14 (5)

p 105 (79)

p 326 (24)

p 214, 5 (19, 20 22, 23)

Austen and probably designed by John Massingham, 'Kerver, Citizen of London', as he is described in the very detailed contract. The features are composed in broad smooth planes that echo those of the armour; the hands are carefully veined, perhaps on the advice of Roger Webbe, the Barber-Surgeon, whose name also appears in the contract. In its stylized simplification, the effigy has something of the certainty that came so easily to Florentine artists. Over it rises a metal framework, or herse, upon which a black pall could be draped for the celebration of funeral masses. The reredos of the chapel, now replaced, for it drew the fury of Puritan iconoclasts, contained the Annunciation, and in the east window, now only fragmentary, the Earl knelt before his patron saints. In the window arch is a series of carvings, fortunately well preserved, again of angels in their hierarchies, with God the Father at the centre of the arch; in the lowest niches are St Barbara, St Mary Magdalen, St Catherine and St Margaret. In the side windows was more stained glass, of which a choir of singing angels survives. On the west wall the Last Judgment was painted by 'John Brentwood, Citizen and Steyner of London'. The chapel as a whole is a full and detailed scheme of the after-life, and the careful differentiation of the angelic hierarchies shows skilled theological knowledge. Even with its many losses, it remains one of the most satisfying renderings of 15th-century hopes of immortality.

p 215 (22)

'Death's Cold Embrace'

Behind the religious dictates concerning salvation, memorials to the dead had other and more mundane purposes, and in particular the preservation of the deceased's repute and achievements. When in 1560 Elizabeth issued a royal proclamation against the defacing of monuments, it was to prevent the 'extinguishing of the honorable and good memory of sundry vertuous and noble persons deceased', and 'not to nourish any kinde of superstition'. This repeated the safeguarding clause in the act of 1550 against superstitious books and images, by which any 'image or picture set or graven upon any tomb in any church, chapel or churchyard only for a monument of any king, prince, nobleman or other dead person' was specifically excepted from destruction, thereby no doubt doing much to preserve our heritage of tomb sculpture. Here is the great breach in the uses of sepulchral exhortation. The 'phantasing vain opinions of purgatory and masses satisfactory to be done for them departed' had in England been condemned, and even prayers for the dead were viewed with suspicion. Tomb inscriptions no longer invoke orisons for the departed soul, but inscribe and praise mortal fame:

> Here lies within death's cold embrace
> A lovely darling youth
> Replete with every social grace
> Of Virtue and of Truth.

The glance is backward now, and does not search 'the undiscovered country'. Such commendations, the cult of fame and the precept of example, were of course fully accepted in the Middle Ages, even if subordinated to more speculative aims. The virtues of great men, William of Malmesbury had written in a dedicatory letter to his *Gesta Regum Anglorum*, were not only praiseworthy in themselves, but commendable in that they drew the admiration of others. Tombs had always set out something of the deeds and functions of the man. The earliest mediaeval effigies, mainly ecclesiastical, show with some care the vestments that distinguish the office of the deceased. The stone slab of a bishop in Exeter cathedral, dating almost certainly from the last quarter of the 12th century, is in very flat relief, set in a niche as though the transposition of a standing figure to a recumbent attitude. The bishop raises his right hand in blessing and holds his crozier with his left; he is shown, that is to say, in his most important living act; but under his feet is a dragon which he treads upon and transfixes with his crozier's point, and in the spandrels of the niche are two censing angels. The memorial is both symbolic of good triumphing over evil and also, through the angels, expresses a hope of salvation. There may well be in these episcopal effigies the further intention of preserving for their church the blessing of a notable incumbent of the office. In deeper relief and with much more

f 13

p 217 (30) life-like reality, the funeral slab of Bishop Evrard de Fouilloy (d. 1222) at Amiens shows the same gesture, the same trampled dragon and censing angels as the Exeter plaque, but adds two small acolytes holding candles. It is cast in bronze, a rare survival of the memorials in metal. Many of them, such as the plaque of Geoffrey of Anjou, were enamelled. This must have been the most splendid form of 12th-century commemoration, though most vulnerable to the rapacity of the iconoclasts, whose rage in France, unlike England, was particularly directed against royal and aristocratic representations. Evrard de Fouilloy is particularly praised in an inscription as the founder of the new cathedral. Obligations towards benefactors is another and important element in the cult of the dead, and one which opened the churches as places of burial to lay patrons, whereas earlier convention had given something of a monopoly in such sepulture to ecclesiastics.

p 216 (25) In the cathedral at Mainz, a wonderful repository of tomb sculpture, Archbishop Siegfried III of Eppstein (d. 1249), a genial, complacent figure, crowns Heinrich of Raspe and William of Holland, neither of them ever securely seated on the Imperial throne. Though engaged in this activity and trampling upon a lion and dragon, the Archbishop still has a cushion behind his head and his staff lies on his body without any contact with the ground; the two emperors, much smaller figures, have consoles on which to stand. It is an uneasy compromise between recumbency and activity. By the middle of the 15th century Archbishop John of Nassau (d. 1439) stands firmly in a niche, and all reference to the prostration of death has gone. In the same cathedral, however, some sixty years later, Bernhard of Breydenbach, whose account of his travels to Jerusalem will always perpetuate his memory, lies with his head on a pillow, though framed in a niche, his alb falling in folds between his legs which are clearly shown beneath the thinness of the stuff, his hands crossed, a chalice upon his breast, realistic in every detail of his prone position, but even here the eyes are open. There was a strange reluctance in the North, as opposed to its full acceptance in Italy, to simulate the complete repose of death.

For the layman new motifs were needed. The effigy of William Longespée in Salisbury Cathedral (c.1230–40), the work of the skilled carvers concentrated in the West Country for the façade of Wells Cathedral, holds his shield, on which the heraldic device, originally coloured, must have been highly decorative, over his left side; instead of the frontal glance of the blessing bishops his head is half-turned, giving a new rhythm to the design. It was a rhythm that was to be infinitely developed. By the end of p 216 (27) the 13th century, the unknown knight at Dorchester, fiercely scowling, draws his sword from its sheath, while his limbs twist in agitation as though struggling to rise from the ground on which he lies. It is a marvellous design, curiously modern in its contrasts of solid and void; it is also a perpetuation of the active life, not an aspiration towards divine peace. There is much imagination in the search for suitable actions for these recumbent figures. At Fontevrault Eleanor of Aquitaine reads from an open book, or so late 19th-century restorers interpreted a damaged remnant that in photographs seems less certainly identifiable; and in the cathedral at Lisbon Maria Vilalobos holds a book where the *Ave Maria* is legibly inscribed, while round her feet three small dogs crunch the remains of a mangled chicken. At Brunswick, p 217 (29) on a tomb made most probably about 1240, Henry the Lion holds a model of the cathedral in which he is buried. Here,

in the disturbed crinkles of the drapery, the strongly marked features, the pressure of the head upon the cushions, there is a new realism, a psychological interpretation of character if not an attempt at actual likeness. Beside him his wife Matilda folds her hands in prayer, a gesture that was gradually to supersede all others as that appropriate for effigies. Almost contemporaneously with the work at Brunswick, Louis IX of France showed on the tomb of his eldest son in the Cistercian Abbey of Royaumont (now in St-Denis) the young man gazing upwards, one knee p 217 (28) slightly raised as though alive, with his hands joined in prayer. At his feet, instead of a dragon, is a small dog, possibly heraldic but a companionable beast. Around the sarcophagus is the funeral cor- p 210 (13) tège, carrying the prince's bier, a cortège in which the sons of Henry III of England assisted. Here is perpetuated the funeral pomp, the mourning for the lost heir, but above all it is the symbol of continuing prayer that is emphasized, the folded hands after the man himself has become inanimate, the permanent example stimulating the prayers of others for the welfare of his soul. A long chain of these praying figures lie on tombs throughout Christendom and survived the Reformation in many Northern countries, a severe and reticent contrast to the dramatic ecstacy and gran- p 214 (19) diose poses that prevailed with baroque art. The Earl of Warwick's hands, not quite closed as his eyes gaze on the Virgin in glory, are as fine as any interpretation of this motif.

The mourners round the tomb of the young Prince Louis were likewise to have many successors. They introduce a human touch, the sense of personal loss, the family bond. The tomb of the comtesse de Joigny at St-Jean at Joigny, dating from the end of the 13th century, has in the arcades of the sarcophagus her four children, dressed in the fashions of the time. One of the daughters, as she gazes mournfully downwards, links one hand through the p 210 (14) band of her cloak and gathers its folds in with the other. On one end of the tomb is a curious carving of a young man clinging to the branches of a tree while two dragons gnaw at the foot of its trunk. It is a scene from the legend, very popular at the time with no awareness of its Eastern Buddhist source, of Barlaam and Joasaph, and here it symbolizes the insecurity of life and the heedlessness with which its dangers are constantly disregarded. It is a new element of fantasy in these carved meditations on mortality. There were to be many variants on these personal touches. At Bodenham in Herefordshire a lady has a child sheltering in the folds of her dress. The tomb at Elford in Staffordshire of the boy, John Stanley, shows him holding the tennis ball with which in 1470 he was accidentally killed. At Lowick, North- amptonshire, Ralph Greene (d. 1417) and his wife touchingly hold p 216 (26) hands; the contract for the tomb, dated two years before Ralph's death, exists and specifically orders that this handclasp should be shown. At Howden in East Yorkshire the niches round the sarcophagus of a recumbent knight are filled with minstrels. But these are relatively unusual details. The noble processions that surround the Warwick tomb and the great sepulchres of the Dukes p 219 (33) of Burgundy or the free-standing figures that support the bier of Philippe Pot are mourners, relatives and retainers, not individually p 211 (15) differentiated in their cloaks and hoods, but elements in a pan- oply of grief and departing pomp, testimonies of family and status that with all the accompanying heraldic display establish the lineage and prestige of the defunct, ensuring, as it was phrased in Queen Elizabeth's proclamation, that 'the true understanding of divers Families in this Realme (who have descended of the bloud of the same persons deceased)' shall be not 'so darkened, as the true course of their inheritance may be hereafter interrupted'.

Panoply of the Tomb

The finest craftsmanship and the most lavish expenditure were reserved for the shrines that contained relics of the saints. Their costly materials rendered them immediate objects of pillage in the English Reformation and the French Revolution. The 'degar- nishing' of the shrine of St Thomas at Canterbury provided several cartloads of jewels and precious metals for Henry VIII. Germany can boast Peter Vischer's superb shrine of St Sebaldus p 327 at Nuremberg, completed between 1508 and 1519, but it is in (27) Italy that the most elaborate shrines have survived, and of these the Arca of St Dominic at Bologna set an early and influential

Tomb-slab of a Bishop of Exeter, possibly Bartholomew (died 1184). He raises his right hand in blessing and with the staff in his left transfixes a dragon at his feet. (13)

example. The work of Niccolò Pisano and his school, it was composed of a sarcophagus supported on caryatids. The body of the saint was transferred to it in 1267, by which date the sarcophagus must have been completed. In the relationship between the reliefs, corner and central figures, and supporting caryatids it is much influenced by the great Italian pulpits, but in the shrine a pinnacled canopy was probably always intended, though delays in carrying it out were such that the final figures came from the hand of the young Michelangelo, and Renaissance garlands take the place of Gothic ornament. Between 1335 and 1339 Giovanni di Balduccio created the shrine of St Peter Martyr in the church of S. Eustorgio in Milan, where the sarcophagus has a sloping roof surmounted by a three-gabled tabernacle with the Virgin and Child between St Dominic and St Peter Martyr; the commission for the work specifies that it should be 'similar in every respect to that of our father St Dominic'. More elaborate, including a full-scale recumbent effigy, ninety-five statuettes and fifty reliefs, is the Arca of St Augustine at Pavia, made by Lombard carvers probably between 1350 and 1362. These richly carved, free-standing monuments were not without their effect on secular tombs. The tomb of Bernabò Visconti (d. 1385) is composed of a sarcophagus supported on pillars and surmounted by a large equestrian statue by Bonino da Campione, carved from one great block of marble and completed during Bernabò's lifetime. Bonino also was responsible for the tomb of Cansignorio della Scala at Verona with its double tier of pinnacled niches, once more topped by an equestrian figure. The earliest, and certainly the most genial, of these mounted warriors was Cangrande della Scala, whose tomb was placed above the doorway of Sta Maria Antica in Verona, but in such a way that its upper storey and its rider were free-standing. Most Italian tombs are, unlike the shrines, placed against church walls, but they share with the shrines the Gothic gabled canopy, the sarcophagus and the supporting caryatids or pillars. The tomb of Robert of Anjou in Sta Chiara in Naples, partially destroyed in the Second World War, was one of the most lavish examples of the style, and included, as well as three representations of the king, figures of all the Neapolitan royal family. Free-standing chest tombs with recumbent effigies, normal north of the Alps, were rare in Italy; and the reassembled tomb of Ilaria del Caretto, that for Ruskin 'altered the course of my life', and whose effigy might pass for the diluted essence of all those figures that lie on Gothic tomb-chests, probably lacks a superstructure of a more Italian and, in all likelihood, distracting kind. Ilaria lies with her eyes

p 218
(31)

f 14

Some of the most spectacular Gothic tombs were made in Italy, a tradition that survived into the Renaissance. The tomb of Marie de Valois, one of the ruling Angevin dynasty of Naples, dates from about 1333. Her effigy lies on a sarcophagus behind curtains being drawn back by angels. The whole composition is framed by a high crocketed gable. (14)

closed in death. Beneath the horsemen of the Scaliger tombs lie effigies of the dead. Popes and cardinals sleep their last sleep soundly under Gothic as under Renaissance canopies: Robert of Naples, surrounded by virtues and relatives, enthroned in the highest niche, is still an old and wearied corpse. But if there is a quiet realism about the Italian approach, realism of a grimmer nature was to be found in the North in the later Middle Ages.

The Grim Reality

On one of the most beautiful Gothic tombs in England, that of the Duchess of Suffolk at Ewelme, the Duchess lies in prayer, her finely-drawn, aging features almost certainly a portrait; above is a choir of angels while on the sarcophagus other angels hold armorial shields; but below, through a tracery panel, can be seen a decomposing corpse, carved with infinite detail despite the obscurity of its position, stretched on its shroud, the long hair still falling from the skull. The Duchess died in 1475. She was a granddaughter of the poet Chaucer, and was twice married; her second husband, William de la Pole, the supposed lover of Margaret of Anjou, was murdered in 1450. She had had reason to think upon the mutabilities of life. More and more, the physical side of death was gripping men's imaginations. Beyond wars and violence, plague had always been the most dread adversary, but the Black Death of the 14th century had been unprecedented in the scale of mortality and an inescapable warning of how speedily men might be called to their account. 'Having to begin our treatise by recounting the extermination of the human race... my mind is stupefied as it applies itself to write the sentence that divine justice in its great pity sent on mankind, worthy by corruption of sin of the final judgment.' Thus wrote Matteo Villani when he undertook to continue the chronicle of his brother, dead of the plague in 1348. It was a new and abiding terror in men's minds, a judgment that implied their sinfulness and therefore the threat of Hell. When the Limbourg brothers painted in the early 15th century the *Très Riches Heures*, they drew in much detail the scene of Pope Gregory the Great staying the plague in Rome, leading the procession through the town in 590, the year of his election to the papacy, when on the summit of Hadrian's mausoleum the archangel Michael appeared, sheathing his sword in sign that the time of trial was over. Already in another work they, or painters of their school, had drawn the same scene, and closely following it, a procession of penitents, scourging themselves as they went, so that, by pain suffered willingly on earth, the rigours of Purgatory could be lessened.

p 220
(34)

p 209
(11)

p 17
(10, 1)

p 208
(8)

> Since for the Death remeid is none
> Best is that we for Death dispone
> After our death that live may we
> *Timor Mortis conturbat me.*

Much earlier than Dunbar the tomb of the Black Prince at Canterbury, dead while the memory of the Black Death was still vivid in England, was inscribed with a metrical exhortation in French, thus Englished by John Weever:

> Such as thou art, sometime was I,
> Such as I am, such shalt thou be.
> I little thought on th'oure of death,
> So long as I enjoyed breath.

> But now a caitife poore am I,
> Deepe in the ground, lo here I lie,
> My beautie great is all quite gone,
> My flesh is wasted to the bone.

Beneath the recumbent effigies in their robes lie the skeletons, with little of the grisly details of decomposition spared, under the elaborate tracery of Bishop Richard Fleming's chantry at Lincoln (c. 1430), or that of Bishop Thomas Beckingham at Wells (1465), or, a hundred years later, on the tomb of William Parkhouse at Exeter. At Tewkesbury the tomb of John Wakeman (d. 1549), who adroitly succeeded in being the last abbot of Tewkesbury and the first Bishop of Gloucester, shows a mouse, snakes and snails preying upon the corpse. In France there was the same lingering on decay. In the Museum at Laon is the sculptured

p 220
(36)

'The Three Living and the Three Dead'—a variant of the 'Memento mori' theme that runs through so much of mediaeval art and thought—originated in a French 13th-century poem and became widespread in wall-paintings and miniatures. This one is from the Lisle Psalter, an early 14th-century English manuscript. The horror of the subject (note the worms in the belly of the first corpse) almost disappears in the delicacy of the drawing. (15)

cadaver of Guillaume de Harcigny (d. 1393), physician of Charles VI; in the Musée Calvet at Avignon is that of Cardinal Jean de Lagrange (d. 1402), Bishop of Avignon and a great patron of the arts; another cardinal, Pierre d'Ailly (d. 1412), is similarly shown at Cambrai. Even in the magnificent elaboration of the tombs of Philibert-le-Beau and Margaret of Austria at the church of Brou naked, half-shrouded bodies, though not yet marred by putrefaction, lie under the royally-clothed effigies. The corpses of Louis XII and Anne of Brittany, beneath their kneeling figures, have not yet decomposed, but along their bellies can be seen the stitches of the embalmers. As late as 1544 René de Chalons, mortally wounded, ordered that he should be shown on his tomb 'as he would be three years after his death' and Ligier Richier carved a standing skeleton, stretching up his hand, holding his heart, to heaven. Here appetite for repulsion is almost sated, and by then this cult of the charnel house was on the wane, though the cadaver that lies beneath the effigy of Robert Cecil, 1st Earl of Salisbury, in Maximilian Colt's stately Renaissance tomb at Hatfield, is as uncompromising as any of its predecessors. On the whole, however, the 17th century preferred the decency of shrouded figures to too accurate renderings of corruption.

Dance of Death

One of the strangest manifestations of this morbid interest had been the Dance of Death. It originated in a late 13th-century poem, *Le Dit des trois morts et des trois vifs*, a subject carved on the façade of the church of the Innocents in Paris at the orders of Jean de Berry, a man much concerned with death to judge by the elaborate arrangements for his own burial chapel. The same theme recurs on one of the pages of the *Très Riches Heures*. It spread rapidly throughout Europe, penetrating even Italy, where such macabre thoughts (the word macabre itself first appeared in France c. 1376) were less congenial, and was painted, with many additional details, on the walls of the Campo Santo in Pisa. In England it can still be seen on the walls of village churches, such as Widford in Oxfordshire; and in the pages of manuscripts such as the Lisle Psalter, as early as the first quarter of the 14th century. There is a naive but vigorous rendering of it, typical of the hold it had on popular art, in the church of Skiby in Denmark. The Dance of Death itself was sometimes performed as a masque, as for instance at Paris in 1422 and at Bruges in 1449, when men dressed as skeletons danced with figures representing the various grades of society; and a great wall painting

'La Grant Danse Macabre', one of the early printed books (published at Lyons in 1499) provides an interesting extension of the normal setting for the appearance of Death in the scenes of everyday life. Here Death carries off the printers and the bookseller themselves. In the later years of the Middle Ages, after the coming of bubonic plague in 1348, Europe lived under the threat of disaster comparable with the fear of the atomic bomb in our own times. (16)

of it decorated the cloister of the Holy Innocents in Paris, above rows of charnel houses where actual bones were exposed, a dismal décor which did not prevent these cloisters from being p 206 one of the popular rendezvous of Paris. The wall paintings at (2) La Chaise-Dieu and at Kermaria Nesquit in Brittany are the best surviving representations of the subject. Woodcuts gave even wider circulation to the theme, such as those of Guyot Marchant published in 1485 or the far greater series by Holbein. Villon and other poets share in this obsession.

> *La mort le fait fremir, pallir,*
> *Le nez courber, les vaines tendre*
> *Le col enfler, la chair mollir*
> *Joinctes et nerfs croistre et estendre.*

('Death makes him shudder and grow pale, his nose curve, his veins stretch, his neck swell, his flesh soften, his joints and tendons grow and strain.')

It is a strange preoccupation with putrefaction. The Church had preached the transience of mortal things, but there was in the 15th century in northern Europe a morbid indulgence in disgust which answered some need now hard to understand. The earlier Middle Ages had their fill of the horrors of damnation, and gradually the image lost its potency. The mind must in the end have developed resistance to such gruesome forebodings, and if it was still too dangerous to question orthodox teaching, there must have been many who rejected its crudity and substituted for its

South of the Alps there was, as has been said, less brooding on mortality; and even the Day of Judgment, until Signorelli's and Michelangelo's frescoes, is handled with far less conviction than in the great tympana of north-west Europe. On the east end of the Arena chapel in Padua, Giotto's Hell, with its small, insect-like figures, has none of the solid reality that he gives to his procession of the elect. On the façade of Orvieto Cathedral the rising dead p 224 and the newly-clad blessed have a sensitive nobility that distracts (48) the eye from the less skilful torments of the damned. A hundred years later, Fra Angelico (or some pupil working on his design) is much more entranced by the joys of his heavenly garden than awestruck by the various circles of Hell. There were of course popular movements and excesses in Italy as elsewhere, but the clear, clean sanity of Renaissance art is on the whole untroubled by the ferocity of northern nightmares. It is all the more striking, therefore, when we find in one of the great key pieces of *quattrocento* genius a direct example of Gothic moralizing. In Masaccio's fresco in Sta Maria Novella in Florence, God the Father supports the crucified Christ, between the Virgin and St John and two kneeling donors; behind him stretches the famous perspective of a chapel roof, the fullest realization hitherto achieved of the new scientific approach to representation; but below, painted most accurately, lies a skeleton in a tomb, with the inscription, *Io fu ga quel che voi siete e quel che son voi aco sarete* ('I was that which you are and what I am that will you be'). It is the very phrase of the Black Prince's tomb in Canterbury.

Two scenes from English manuscripts showing the shroud in which the body was wrapped. Left: the raising of Lazarus from the Winchester Psalter. Right: the burial of Judas Maccabaeus from the Winchester Bible. Willing helpers raise the slab from Lazarus' coffin: mourners lower Judas Maccabaeus into his. (17, 18)

detailed realism the less immediate awesomeness of the unknown. A more luxurious and sophisticated society concentrated on the p 207 physical corruption of their being. In a Book of Hours made for (4) Mary of Burgundy and her husband, Maximilian, and probably only completed after her death in 1482, one page shows a terrible skeleton, his shroud falling from him, brandishing a spear and carrying a coffin. On another page three skeletons pursue a hunting party of a lady and two men, a version of *Les trois vifs*, but here surely with a reference to the hunting accident in which Mary lost her life. The scene has been copied in a later Book of Hours with opposite it an elaborate funeral procession, and in the borders skulls in niches, a motif also taken from the Master of Mary of Burgundy and one that was visible in actuality in many places such as the cloisters of the Innocents in Paris. In a painting in a Book of Hours of the use of Bourges, from the second half of the 15th century, skulls are shown displayed in a gallery above a portico, in front of which death spears a young nobleman; below is depicted a graveyard.

The Body's Sepulchre

Burial was in the ground or in vaults. The body was wrapped in a shroud, knotted at head and feet. In many cases it was laid directly in the grave, but from an early date stone, wooden or lead chests were employed. In representations of the raising of Lazarus, where for a time there was some dispute with the Eastern traditions of emergence from a cave, the lid of the tomb-chest is generally being prised open by workmen, as in the well-known Chichester relief. The Gospels of Pembroke College, Cambridge, probably to be dated about 1125–35, shows Lazarus *f 17* coming forth from a tomb cut in the rock. The burial of Judas *f 18* Maccabaeus from the Winchester Bible, where the shrouded corpse is being placed in a coffin, may be taken as an example of the common 12th-century procedure, at least for men of note. In a splendid page from the York Psalter (c.1170) in the Hunterian Library at Glasgow, the Virgin is shown completely swathed in grave-cloths, while the angels carrying her aloft from her stone tomb draw back the outer shroud as a means to support this corporeal assumption. Here was another theme, much debated from the second half of the 12th century onwards, which provided many instances of burial illustration. From a later date a page from the Book of Hours of Philip the Good shows a more domestic scene, p 210 the interior of a bedchamber with the corpse being swathed (12) while the widow sits mourning. The tomb of Jacques Germain (d. 1424), a bourgeois of Cluny, in the museum at Dijon shows p 220 him completely covered by a voluminous shroud. (35)

Much importance was attached to the place of burial. Where land and status were so closely linked, it was natural to seek a grave in one's own territory, there to await the final resurrection. But this very desire caused a conflict. The corpses of great men dying far from their homes were sometimes dismembered, the flesh cleaned from the bones by boiling and the latter brought back to the native soil, while the other remains were buried at the place of death. Sometimes also the heart was buried separately from the body, as for instance was that of Aylmer de Valence (d. 1261) in its shrine at Winchester. Here no doubt the wish to have some relic of a great man or benefactor played some part, but the theologians looked askance at this partition, which in an age so accustomed to visual representations of figures rising from their tombs raised obvious problems. Pope Boniface VIII felt it a sufficient abuse to require legislation against it. Embalming was also practised, but required skilled practitioners, and prolonged transits of the corpse could lead to ugly happenings. When Henry I of England died at Lyons-la-Forêt, near Rouen, in 1135,

Handbooks on 'How to Die' ('Ars moriendi') were best-sellers in the Middle Ages, when the soul's state at the moment of death was thought to determine its future in the after-life. This plate from a block-book of about 1450 illustrates the sin (and the folly) of Impatience. The dying man, tempted by a devil, has overturned the table and is kicking the doctor from his side. This series of woodcuts is based upon (or possibly provided the source for) a more famous series of engravings by the Master E.S. (19)

his entrails, brains and eyes were buried at Rouen and the body was embalmed in order to be taken to Reading, the abbey that Henry had founded 'for the salvation of his soul'. Such was the state of the body, however, when the embalming was carried out, that the surgeon died of an infection, 'the last of many', says the chronicler, 'whom Henry destroyed'. The body was carried to Caen, sewn in a bull's hide, and laid before the tomb of the Conqueror, where despite all precautions its noisome state was still apparent. It was well, Roger of Wendover remarks, that it was in the cold of winter that, some four weeks later, it finally reached Reading. In the margin of one manuscript is written: 'Note the vileness of human flesh. It gives cause for humility.' (Food easily turned bad in those unhygienic days and was a frequent cause of death, more real than the poisons often suspected at the time. The 'surfeit of lampreys' that precipitated Henry's death was no doubt dangerously inedible. It was after eating stale fish that the notorious Fulk de Bréauté was found 'dead, black, stinking and intestate'.)

Funeral masses were occasions of great solemnity and are often shown on the appropriate pages of breviaries. The coffin covered by a great black cloth stood in the centre of the nave surrounded by mourners in black cloaks. Above it, for those of great estate, was an elaborate framework of wood or metal fitted with prickets for candles, which recalled the teeth of a harrow and so was known as the 'herse'. When in 1503 in Rhodes, Pierre d'Aubusson, the Grand Master, died and the coffin stood in the church of St John, there were on one side his vestments as a cardinal, on the other the hacked and battered armour he had worn in the defence of the island. On a Spanish tomb of the early 14th century from the monastery of Las Avellanas, now in the Cloisters, New York, the soul of the defunct, Armengol VII, Count of Urgel, is being carried aloft by angels, while on a long carved relief the funeral mass is shown in progress. Funeral processions were also occasions of considerable display. In royal or episcopal funerals the corpse might be carried exposed in robes of office on a bier, but more often it was already in a coffin with a wax or wooden effigy lying upon the lid; more normally the coffin was draped in the pall, which varied from a plain black cloth, marked with a cross, to costly fabrics of velvet embroidered with cloth of gold. The pall used in commemoration services for

p 213 (18)

p 212 (16)

Henry VII in the University Church is still preserved in the Ashmolean Museum at Oxford, and is a very splendid piece of work. A page in the Hours of Amadée de Saluces from the second half of the 15th century, nicely distinguishes the heedlessness of the choristers preceding the bier and the grief of the mourners following. Below, a gravedigger throws out a skull with his spade, as though it might well be Yorick's. A strange and moving
p 207 (6) painting in a Book of Hours belonging to Philip the Fair while Archduke of Austria, illustrating the Vespers of the Dead, shows a naked corpse stretched on a tomb chest in a church with mourners sitting below, a fantasy rather than an actual event. In two
p 207 (5) roundels on the border, skeletons seize a knight and a lady. It is curiously evocative of the emotions of the time.

The Art of Dying

In the business of dying it was all important to make a good end. On one of the bells in St Andrew's, Yetminster (Dorset), cast in 1608, is inscribed:

> I sound to bid the sick repent
> In hope of life when breath is spent.

Illuminations and woodcuts stressed the importance of deathbed repentance that, even at the last moment, might save the sinner from Hell and reduce the period of Purgatory. Numbed as the mind must have been by the too frequent harping on horrors, when death was at hand they must have taken on a new reality.
p 205 (1) On a splendid page of the Rohan Book of Hours (1418–25) a naked corpse lies amongst skulls and bones; from his mouth comes a scroll: 'Into Thy hands, O Lord, I commend my spirit. You have redeemed me, O Lord, thou God of truth.' Above, a devil has seized his soul, but is being attacked by the Archangel Michael. From the clouds an immense figure of God looks down, bearing a sword, but answering: 'Do penance for thy sins, and thou shalt be with me in the judgment'. In a volume of French ascetic treatises in the Bavarian State Library in Munich an illustration to *La Science de bien Mourir* shows a singularly repulsive devil and an angel struggling over a man's deathbed. A work known in many versions was the *Ars moriendi* to which was often added another treatise, the *Stimulus timoris Dei ad bene moriendum*. The Master known by the initials E. S. made for the *Ars moriendi* a series of engravings that were widely reproduced, and vividly showed contrasting scenes: on one page the devils surround the sick bed and eagerly point to scenes of fornication, murder and robbery; while on the opposite page St Peter with his cock, St Mary Magdalen, the penitent thief and the converted St Paul testify to the efficacy of repentance. Another pair of
f 19 scenes show the sick man kicking the doctor and overturning a bedside table, while opposite are the patient martyrs and the suffering Christ. In the Grimani Breviary, in the Marciana Library in Venice, there is a very detailed deathbed scene. Last unction is being administered, while in the background two physicians hold a conclave and notaries draw up the will; in the curtains of the great bed an angel drives off a devil. Below is a vigorous rendering of the Trois Morts, skeletons fighting with three horsemen. 'Why dost thou not provide for thyself', wrote Thomas à Kempis, 'against the day of doom, when no man shall be excused nor defended by another, but every man's burden shall be enough for himself. Now thy labour is fruitful, thy weeping acceptable, thy mourning audible, thy suffering is satisfactory and purgatory . . . Better it is to cut away and purge thy sins and thy vices here, than to reserve them to be purged in time coming . . . Be now busy and sorrowing for thy sins, that thou mayest stand safe in the day of judgment with blissful men.'

More crudely it was thought that death itself might be postponed by good intentions. When the Empress Matilda lay grievously ill after the difficult birth of her son, the future Henry II, 'the prudent matron', we are told, 'distributed her treasures to widows, orphans and the poor and so escaped the peril of death'. But the wise man practised virtue throughout his life. An early 15th-century Catalan text, the *Breviari d'Amor*, has a page with scenes of the Works of Charity leading up to a very peaceful and p 222 (40–43) pious deathbed, with the soul almost too complacently elevated by angels in a napkin.

The Reformation brought a cleavage in the European view of mortality. Protestantism was eventually in some of its branches to evolve theories of predestined damnation as terrifying as any mediaeval doom, but at first it weakened, with its denial of Purgatory, the certainties of the after-life, and its iconoclasm destroyed the visual exactitudes which had dismayed the Catholic world. The after-life never again was to be so generally accepted a concept; death ceased to be so clearly a stage in an inevitable progress. Shakespeare, as so often, shows us in Claudio's speech the new uncertainties, the preoccupation with decay and, at the same time, the lingering hold of the old beliefs:

> Ay, but to die, and go we know not where;
> To lie in cold obstruction and to rot;
> This sensible warm motion to become
> A kneaded clod; and the delighted spirit
> To bathe in fiery floods, or to reside
> In thrilling region of thick-ribbed ice;
> To be imprison'd in the viewless winds,
> And blown with restless violence round about
> The pendent world; or to be worse than worst
> Of those that lawless and incertain thought
> Imagine howling: 'tis too horrible.

The mouldering bodies carved below the tombs have their verbal equivalent in 'to lie in cold obstruction and to rot'; 'the fiery floods' and 'thick-ribbed ice' are the familiar extremes of mediaeval Purgatory, the suffering in which the soul delights because of its justice and the hope of redemption (Protestant commentators have made heavy going of the epithet delighted), and 'worse than worst' the howling hopelessness of Hell. *Measure for Measure* is Shakespeare's most Catholic play; but the *via media* was in England already softening the impact. The age of epitaphs extolling a man's virtues and charities was at hand, a boastfulness which the Middle Ages, with all their pomp, would never have allowed. There was room too for more personal lamentation. On Roubiliac's monument of 1761 in Westminster Abbey to Lady Elizabeth Nightingale, a shrouded skeleton emerges from a vault, a successor to many late mediaeval fantasies, but, above, the sinister visitor is repelled by a gesture of the husband, who supports the dying lady. It is an affirmation of human affection in revolt against death, not a reminder of the dust to which we must all come. Mediaeval memorials are, with some few exceptions, lacking in tenderness, but they never lapse into sentimentality. They confront the predicament of mortality in varied ways, at times with an excessive panoply of display, but never without a basic resignation to a divine purpose, whose justice stood beyond question. Unfortunately for Christendom, this justice was given visual form in terms of Heaven and Hell, represented with such genius that they long dominated all thoughts of the life to come. Mediaeval Hell may have been at times a useful deterrent; it was certainly the grossest incident in the debasement of things spiritual to anthropomorphic crudities.

VII CURRENTS OF TRADE

Industry, Merchants and Money

DONALD KING

'In the name of God and of profit'

*Inscription on the first page of the ledgers of Francesco Datini,
merchant of Prato*

Across the map of mediaeval Europe

lay a tight web of trade-routes, the arteries of commerce and exchange. They bound together cities, principalities and kingdoms, linking them even with the infidel world of Islam and the alien, exotic East. Few historical processes have had a more decisive effect on the future than this steady commercial expansion which took place from the 12th century onwards. By stimulating industry and technology, by requiring new financial systems and new codes of international agreement, it was to change—finally to help destroy—the whole political and ideological framework of feudal society.

The Hanseatic League (*Hanse* means 'company') epitomized the new values. It was a federation of towns based purely on mercantile interests, and by the 14th century it was strong enough to assert those interests in the face of any other authority that could oppose it. It controlled the trade of northern Europe from England to Germany and from Stockholm to the Alps. From its centre among the 'free' cities of the Empire (Danzig, Lübeck, Cologne, Hamburg), it grew to comprise 160 towns and to have semi-independent branches in England, the Netherlands, Poland and even Russia. The League's power was exercised not by force but almost entirely through the economic weapons of boycott and blockade.

The illustration opposite is from a 15th-century manuscript of the laws of Hamburg. The port is filled with ships of all sorts and sizes—ocean-going vessels, yawls and rowing-boats. On the left, the town crane leans over the water unloading barrels; on the right sit the customs officers to claim their dues, while the quayside is busy with burghers, merchants and seamen. (1)

Hard toil on land and sea was still the lot of three-quarters of the people. Most regions were self-supporting; imports were luxuries. The fishermen with their nets (below) come from an English Psalter of the early 14th century. Scotch salmon was even then an expensive delicacy, but salted herrings from Dutch and Baltic waters appeared on tables all over Europe.

The 15th-century scene on the right is a composite image of the farmer's year—planting apple-trees, gathering the apples, cutting up the dead wood for fuel. In the foreground wheat is sown and harvested; a man sharpens his sickle. (2, 3)

Bee-keeping provided not only wax for candles but also honey, and honey—fermented—provided mead, an intoxicating drink popular in northern Europe where the vine did not flourish. Sugar was scarce; it had to be imported from the Near East. Honey was actually exported from Europe to Islamic countries. The manuscript illumination (right), showing the hives and beating of gongs to prevent swarming, is a late 15th-century illustration to Virgil's *Georgics*. (4)

The sower (below) from the Luttrell Psalter combines realism with a touch of humour. A dog chases away one bird from the newly scattered seed, but another is gorging itself at the sack. (5)

Treading the vintage (above) and bringing in the corn harvest (below)—two big events of the mediaeval year. Bottom: a 14th-century windmill, a comparatively recent invention: they were hardly known in England before the 13th century. (8, 9, 10)

'**The dairymaid** (above) ought to be faithful and of good repute, and keep herself clean', according to a 13th-century writer on husbandry. Below: the mule bringing corn to a water-mill is from the same manuscript, a Bestiary of about 1200. (6, 7)

Sheep-shearing: the sheep's legs are bound and it is laid on a cloth so as not to lose any of the wool. Shears remained unchanged in design for many centuries. The wool trade was among the richest of mediaeval Europe, with England the chief exporter. (11)

The magnificent cloth
of the later Middle Ages is an achievement that has never been surpassed. (The white robes worn by the Pope are still made from English wool.) Little of this most perishable of the arts has survived, but in tapestries and manuscript illuminations we can still see some reflection of its splendour. Left: a richly dressed couple from a tapestry made in France in the late 15th century. Below: dyers at work, the colours heated in a huge vat. (12, 13)

Silkworms were not bred on a large scale in Europe until the 14th century. In this miniature (below) the worms are collected from mulberry bushes and the silk threads unwound from the cocoons are prepared for weaving. (14)

Spinning and weaving: the raw flax (above, right foreground) is pulled into sections, carded and placed on the end of a distaff held under the left arm. From this the 'spinster' draws the fibres with her left hand, twisting them into thread with her right, aided by the rotary movement of the spindle. In the background the threads are woven on a hand loom. (15)

The sumptuous material is cut into a robe ornamented with gold and jewels (centre). Above right: craftsmen at work on embroidered hangings, about 1400. Below: one of the masterpieces of tapestry-weaving, a panel from the Angers Apocalypse. It was designed by a leading Parisian painter, Jean de Bondolf; this section shows the Sounding of the Second Trumpet. (16, 17, 18)

Industrial enterprise,

though still on a comparatively small scale, continued to expand throughout the Middle Ages, and the status of the skilled artisan to improve. The group on the right—a meeting of workmen in the 15th century—includes master carpenters and masons.

Iron was smelted in most countries; smiths (as their name still testifies) were universal. The 14th-century blacksmith's shop (above) shows the furnace with bellows, hammers and pincers; two men beat the hot metal bar into shape.

Below: carpenters shown at work, c. 1430—a clear picture of mediaeval tools and their uses: iron nails to hold the planks to the roof; wooden pegs for the framework; a plane (unusually large by modern standards); drills, axes, saws and (lying unused in the foreground) a brace and bit almost exactly the same as it would be today. (19, 20, 21)

Coopers, men of another craft that has ▶ become a surname, made the casks and barrels in which wines and all other liquids were transported. It was a skilled technique, since the casks had to be completely airtight and often capable of withstanding considerable pressure from inside. The upright curved staves were of oak bent into shape by heating or steaming, the truss-hoops of iron. This relief (by Antelami, 12th century), shows the final tight adjustment of the cask before the vintage. (23)

Glass-blowing needed training and skill, and tended to be the speciality of certain districts. This drawing (right) from Bohemia shows the raw material, sand, being dug; the furnace and glass-blowers and, on the left, the finished vessels being examined and packed. (22)

An iron-miner, with pick, candle and hod, from the Forest of Dean, England. This region has produced iron since Roman times, but it never rivalled the Continental iron-fields. The figure is part of a monumental brass and dates from 1463. (24)

Devotion, decoration and display created a demand for works of art, though the men of the Middle Ages would not so have described them. All the objects on this page are of kinds that must have been widely distributed through the channels of European trade. The plate below shows, from left to right: an enamel reliquary from Limoges, 13th century; a glazed earthenware drug pot from Florence, mid-15th century; a gilt-bronze ewer in the shape of a monster, made in the Meuse area, mid-12th century; an ivory statuette of the Virgin and Child, from Paris, early 14th century; and a glazed earthenware jar from Valencia, Spain, mid-15th century. The cloth forming the background is Italian silk velvet, brocaded with silver-gilt thread. (25)

Enamelled glass came from Syria, where glass-making had been practised since Roman times. This example (mid-13th century) was brought to Europe soon after it was made, and still has the tooled leather case, which was made for it in the 14th century. It was regarded as a talisman by the English family to whom it belonged and has long been known as 'The Luck of Edenhall'. (26)

English alabaster carvings were shipped to many parts of Europe, and exported pieces have often survived longer than those left at home. This superb figure dates from the early 15th century, and still retains much of its original colouring. It represents St Michael weighing souls; the Virgin influences the issue by tilting the scales with her rosary, but part of the carving is lost at this side. (27)

255

The busy roads and rivers of mediaeval Europe carried a surprising density of traffic. Crowds went on pilgrimages (Chaucer's Wife of Bath had been to Jerusalem three times); churchmen travelled incessantly for conferences or on legal business; many craftsmen were itinerant. For the rich, travel could be luxurious. Above: a 14th-century carriage with slung suspension. Behind it is Matthew Paris's map of the route from London to Dover, made in about 1250. Below: travellers of the highest rank, from the Luttrell Psalter. (28, 29, 30)

Across a bridge in Paris in the 14th century go a pilgrim and men dragging a wine-cask on a trolley; on the river, boats unload a cargo of coal. (31)

◀ **The stately ship** of Jacques Coeur of Bourges (left) symbolizes his wealth and ambition. The late 14th-century manuscript (above) shows a mediaeval use of the compass. (32, 33)

Shipwreck and robbery, amongst other hazards, menaced the traveller. Above: a storm at sea, from a 15th-century Italian manuscript. Below: money rather than life being surrendered to a highwayman. (34, 35)

The proud new class of merchants eventually joined the nobility as patrons of the artist. From the 15th century portraits of businessmen become increasingly common. Giovanni Arnolfini (below) came from Lucca, in Italy, but lived in the great northern trading centre of Bruges, where Jan van Eyck painted his wedding portrait. (36)

Tommaso Portinari of Florence (left) joined the Medici bank in 1439 and spent all his working life as its agent in Flanders. His portrait is part of the altarpiece by Hugo van der Goes that he sent back to his native city. (37)

Francesco Datini (above) was the son of a tavern-keeper in Prato, Italy. After over 30 years at Avignon, then the seat of the popes, he returned to Prato in 1383 a rich man. Eventually his great trading empire included branches and agencies throughout western Europe and the Near East. (38)

Niccolò, Matteo and Marco Polo (seen, above, setting off from Venice in 1271) stayed in China for 17 years, becoming valued diplomatic agents of Kublai Khan. (39)

Georg Gisze, native of the Hanseatic city of Danzig, merchant of the Steelyard in the City of London. Born in 1497, Gisze came to London as a member of the Hanse in 1522. Holbein's great portrait of him shows him in his office, with seal, inkstand, quill and box of money. On the shelf behind are scales and another seal; the ornate metal box holds sealing thread. Even the business letters in the rack are painted so meticulously that we can read who they are from: 'Thomas Bandz', 'Georg of Basel', 'Hans Stolten'. The letter he is in the act of opening is from his brother, addressed to himself at '*lunden in engelant*'. (40)

Civic pride went hand in hand with the growth of the new bourgeois class. An aristocracy of trade began to overtake the aristocracy of birth.

Complex local rules governed transport and payment. Above: a detail from a stained-glass window at Tournai, showing the town weights, and some bales and barrels signed with merchants' marks. (41)

English wool merchants made huge fortunes in the 15th century, fortunes to which such Cotswold houses as that of William Grevel at Chipping Campden, with its Perpendicular panelling (above), bear witness. (42)

Thomas Paycocke (died 1461) of Coggeshall in Essex was a butcher turned sheep-farmer. His sons and grandsons became rich cloth-merchants, building this fine Tudor house with carved front. (43)

The house of Jacques Coeur is the most splendid of all the mediaeval merchants' houses. Built in the mid-15th century, it presents an elaborately decorated façade (left) leading into a yet more lavish courtyard. Even the fire-places have lively sculptured figures in traceried niches (above). Jacques Coeur was not long allowed to enjoy it. In 1451 he was arrested on trumped-up charges; all his property was confiscated and he was condemned to pay the equivalent of £ 1,000,000 in modern currency. (44, 45)

England: Poultry Cross, at Salisbury, is the only survivor of the city's four market-crosses. It is hexagonal, and its ogee ribs support a canopy that originally held statues. (48)

Germany still abounds in mediaeval town-halls. Many of her leading cities were self-governing to an extent that was impossible in France or England. The picturesque *Rathaus* of Alsfeld (below) was built about 1500. (49)

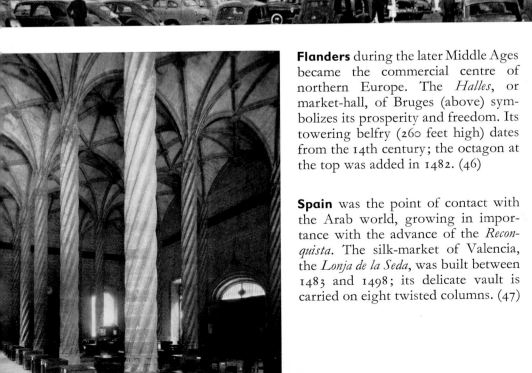

Flanders during the later Middle Ages became the commercial centre of northern Europe. The *Halles*, or market-hall, of Bruges (above) symbolizes its prosperity and freedom. Its towering belfry (260 feet high) dates from the 14th century; the octagon at the top was added in 1482. (46)

Spain was the point of contact with the Arab world, growing in importance with the advance of the *Reconquista*. The silk-market of Valencia, the *Lonja de la Seda*, was built between 1483 and 1498; its delicate vault is carried on eight twisted columns. (47)

From every land

merchants, craftsmen and buyers gathered at the great international fairs. The six fairs of Champagne at one time dominated the
trade of Europe. There were also national fairs, those of England
being at Northampton, St Ives, Boston and Winchester, and fairs
for special commodities like the book-fair at Frankfurt.

Many originated as religious festivals. The fair of Lendit, held
near Paris, of which two illustrations are shown here (above
centre and above right) began in this way. In 1109 the Cathedral
of Notre Dame acquired a piece of the True Cross, which was
shown to the people once a year, on the second Wednesday of
June. The place chosen was a large open space between Montmartre and St-Denis (the Latin *indictum* [assembly] became *l'endit*
and so *Lendit*). Traders were soon attracted by the vast numbers
of pilgrims, although the Procession of the relic and Benediction
still formed the centre of the occasion. The miniature (above right)
shows the Bishop of Paris blessing the people, with the booths and
shops of the merchants all round. Above centre: dealers in shoes
and hose, gold vessels, and clothing. (51, 52)

Shopping and celebrating, three scenes of urban life in France
and Italy. Left: a paved street with shops—a tailor's (the assistant
sits cross-legged), furrier's, barber's and druggist's. Right: stalls
in a covered market, with a shoemaker (being paid), a cloth
merchant (note the bright rolls of material in the cupboard
and money on the tray) and two dealers in gold-plate and silverware. Far right: a tavern in Genoa. In the cellar, barrels of red
and white wine; in the upper room guests carousing and apparently—extreme right—suffering for it. (53, 54, 55)

Money –
the most essential tool of trade—took an endless variety of forms. Weights and measures were not standardized and exchange was complicated. Above: an English 'noble' of about 1350; the king is Edward III. Right: money-changers, a stained-glass window at Le Mans (1240). The balance, for weighing coins, appears also in the drawing of a century earlier (below) showing royal officers receiving taxes. (56, 57, 58)

Financial business was largely in the hands of the Jews, to whom the Church's condemnation of usury did not apply. A 14th-century miniature (above) shows moneylenders at Genoa. The table is piled with coins; amounts are entered in a ledger, while at the back are the various objects in pawn. With contract law still in its infancy, business disputes were often referred to private arbitration, as in this 15th-century illustration (above right). At the top the deal is agreed; underneath, in the presence of the same witnesses, the affair is settled and the money involved peaceably divided. (59, 60)

Gold currency from Europe and beyond: (*a*) French *écu*, 1380–1422. This is the coin lying uppermost in the famous picture by Quentin Massys (below), which gives a fascinating close-up of the money-changer at work. (*b*) Arabic *dinar*, 697–8. (*c*) English noble, 1346–51; the obverse of this coin is the one shown opposite, top left. (*d*) Florentine florin, c. 1300. (*e*) a Byzantine *nomisma*, 1042–55, (*f*) Venetian ducat, 1280–89. (61, 62)

Banking grew up in Italy during the later Middle Ages partly because the currency of the Italian mercantile cities was among the most stable in Europe. Florence, Venice, Siena and Genoa were the leaders. The two scenes shown here (left) were probably painted in Genoa: above, the bank's counting-house and coffers; below, customers and account-books. (63)

Mediaeval professions were 'closed shops': it was necessary to belong to a gild in order to practise them. To qualify as a master-craftsman a man frequently had to serve an apprentice-ship of seven years, give evidence of his skill, and pay a fee to the gild he wished to join. In this illustration (above) from a 15th-century manu-script, a mason and a carpenter pro-duce their 'master-pieces' before the gild-warden. (64)

Industries, Merchants and Money

DONALD KING

Fish and vegetables in 15th-century Florence: a woodcut of a market scene in which various trades are represented. Two women sit spinning thread; another, between them, carries an assortment of garden produce; while at the stall on the right fish are being weighed in a scale with a sliding weight, a type still used for the same purpose today. (1)

THE AIM OF INDUSTRY is to convert things of lesser utility and value into things of greater utility and value, by the application of labour and skill. The aim of trade is to convey things from persons or places where they are of lesser utility and value to persons or places where they are of greater utility and value. The two activities are interdependent, for trade supplies industry with its prime materials and also disposes of its finished products. Indeed, they may be regarded as the static and the mobile aspects of a single activity, that of providing humanity with its material requisites. Perhaps industry is more fundamental than trade, since it is possible to conceive a way of life from which trade is absent and each family group, by its own industrial efforts, produces its own food, its own clothing, its own shelter, its own tools, furniture, and all other utensils. But so primitive a society has hardly been known in Europe in historical times and is far removed from the highly diversified and complex commercial activity of the European Middle Ages.

Food . . .

f 1

*248,49
(2–10)*

It is true that many of the inhabitants of mediaeval Europe devoted the greater part of their industrial effort to the production of food for their own consumption, an activity to which trade could contribute comparatively little. But small farmers and great landowners alike aimed at producing a surplus, which they could sell in order to buy the foodstuffs and the other commodities and specialized services which they could not easily provide for themselves. Towns existed primarily to provide the facilities for this buying and selling, and the specialized traders and craftsmen demanded by the surrounding countryside.

Apart from the innumerable primary producers, the business of food and drink employed other specialists in very large numbers all over Europe—butchers, fishmongers, millers, bakers, brewers, vintners, taverners and many more. Indeed, there can be no doubt that the industries of food and drink, taken as a whole, were incomparably larger than any other group, although most of the producers worked on a small scale, and most of the trade was over the short distance between the countryside and the market town. Yet there were always certain foodstuffs which could only be obtained from more distant places, while certain kinds of community—a capital city such as Avignon in the 14th century, a city of traders such as Venice, a manufacturing area such as Flanders, a country of restricted agriculture such as Norway, a region of specialized agriculture such as the wine-growing districts of Gascony—were forced to import even some of their essential foodstuffs from far afield.

Fortunately, there were certain areas which generally had a surplus of grain for export. Northern France and western Germany supplied Flanders and the Netherlands. England sent wheat to Scandinavia, to Gascony and occasionally even to Italy. Great quantities of rye and other grain were shipped from eastern Germany and Poland to Flanders, Norway and other western countries. Russian grain was shipped west by way of the Baltic and the Black Sea. Rice was exported from Spain and the Levant.

In most areas meat, poultry and eggs were abundant enough to meet normal demands. They were also difficult to preserve and transport, and they figured comparatively little in international trade, though bacon, for example, was exported from eastern England and Germany. Livestock was sometimes shipped, but generally for purposes other than slaughter. Oxen exported from Poland on the hoof were probably draught animals; sheep shipped to and from England were probably for breeding; fine horses and hawks, exported from various parts of Europe, were always in demand among noblemen, while for their ladies the Italian galleys carried exotic pets, such as apes, marmosets and parrots, together with parrot seed. More profitable than these trifles was human freight—pilgrims, merchants and other voluntary passengers, and the slaves shipped by Italian merchants from the Slav lands to Islamic ports.

Dairy products were of some importance in international trade; butter, for example, was exported from Poland, Scandinavia, Holland and England, and English cheese was exported across the Channel in considerable quantities. Much more important was the trade in fish, which were caught all round the coasts of Europe and conveyed to the most remote inland regions. Fish and fish-oil were the principal exports of Norway and Iceland. Fish from the Black Sea was exported to Mediterranean countries. The salt herrings exported from the Dutch fishing-grounds and those of the Baltic (especially round Skania, now southern Sweden) were a significant source of food for large areas of Europe, while for more refined palates there was a limited trade in such fishy delicacies as Scotch salmon and Russian caviare.

Salt was a commodity of very great importance, not merely as flavouring, but also as the principal means of curing fish and preserving meat for winter use. It was produced by evaporation of sea-water at many points round the coast of Europe, and inland deposits and brine-springs were also exploited. In the broad land-mass of eastern Europe, however, there was a chronic deficiency of salt, and great quantities were shipped eastwards to the ports of the Baltic and the Black Sea. The principal exporting area was the Atlantic coast of France, with its great natural salt-pans, especially in the bay of Bourgneuf near the mouth of the Loire, whence Hanseatic fleets sailed annually with cargoes of salt for the Baltic ports.

The mediaeval taste for highly spiced foods made the trade in pepper and other culinary spices, such as cinnamon, cloves, galanga, ginger, mace and nutmeg, a very profitable one, even though the price of these products was inflated by the heavy transport costs incurred in conveying them from the East Indies to the Levantine ports where they were acquired by European merchants. Many medicinal products used in mediaeval Europe —aloes, cassia, camphor, rhubarb, senna, zedoary—and many perfumes and aromatics—ambergris, balm, incense, musk, myrrh, rosewater—were likewise Asian products, imported from Levantine ports. Europe produced comparatively little in these classes, but licorice was exported from Spain, and mastic was exported from Chios to Islamic countries. A large proportion of the sugar consumed in Europe was imported from the Near East. Honey, on the other hand, was exported to Islamic countries from Europe, where it was very generally produced; Russia, Spain and Portugal were among the principal exporters of honey, as well as of wax.

f 1 Fresh vegetables and fruit were generally obtainable locally and formed only a small item in international trade. Nevertheless, England, for example, imported cabbages, garlic, onions and onion seed from France and the Low Countries, and pippins from Normandy. Oranges, lemons, pomegranates and various fruit preserves were exported in small quantities from Spain and Portugal. But far more important than these was the trade in dried fruits—currants from the eastern Mediterranean, raisins, dates and figs from North Africa, Spain and Portugal. From the same areas came almonds, which were used in astonishingly large quantities in mediaeval cooking. Olive oil was an important commodity in Mediterranean trade and was exported from Spain, North Africa, Italy and Greece.

Ale and beer were brewed and drunk in vast quantities in northern Europe; the standard allowance of ale for a monk was one or sometimes two gallons per day. Beer made with hops, at first a speciality of Germany and the Low Countries, only gradually displaced the traditional ale in England. Small amounts of gin were exported from Holland. But by far the largest part of the international trade in beverages was concerned with wine, with France and Germany as the main exporters and England as a principal importer. There was a lively trade in Rhenish wine, in wines of Portugal, Spain and Italy, and in the sweet wines—romney and malmsey—of Greece and the Greek Islands.

... and Clothing

After food and drink, man's most compelling need is that of
p 250 clothing, and it is not surprising that the trade and industry of
(12) textiles during the Middle Ages were second in importance only to those of foodstuffs. Indeed, the textile industry was by far the most important manufacturing industry of the Middle Ages, partly owing to the scale of the demand, partly owing to the complexity of the processes involved. Each of the four principal textile materials, wool and linen, cotton and silk, required, when delivered in the raw state from the primary producer, a lengthy preparation to convert it into thread. Natural impurities had first to be removed and cleansed away; by various processes, differing according to the material, individual fibres had to be arranged
p 251 more or less parallel to one another; finally the fibres of wool,
(15) linen and cotton were spun into thread by hand or spinning-wheel, while silk threads were made in water-powered throwing mills. The thread was dyed, sometimes before, sometimes after,
p 250 being woven into cloth. The craft of the dyer demanded great
(13) skill and knowledge of the properties of the dyestuffs and mordants which, by their chemical interaction, fixed the colours in the material. The weaver wove the cloth on the loom, one of the most complex machines in use in the Middle Ages, especially the type known as the draw-loom, which was used to produce automatic repetitions of a pattern in silk and linen textiles. After weaving, various other treatments were necessary to remove faults and otherwise improve the cloth. In the case of woollen cloths, these finishing processes were particularly elaborate, including washing and felting by trampling in troughs or with water-powered fulling mills, drying and stretching on tenter-frames, raising the nap by brushing with teasles (the heads of a kind of thistle), and shearing the nap level. The multiplicity of operations and the high cost of the necessary materials and machines favoured the development of the cloth industry on capitalist lines, with wealthy *entrepreneurs* sometimes financing and controlling all the stages of production from the purchase of the raw textile fibre to the wholesale marketing of the finished cloth. In effect, these powerful industrialists operated a factory system, even though most of the hired craftsmen performed their tasks in their own dwellings.

Sheep were raised for wool, and woollen cloth was woven in many parts of Europe; but the principal sheep-raising areas were Spain, central France and England. In England, sheep-raising was

Timber was grown all over Europe, and most regions had enough to satisfy ordinary needs. But softwoods or unusually large beams were imported from eastern Europe and Scandinavia. Here staves (note the triangular section of the piece on the ground) are being loaded on to a cart in France. (2)

the main source of income for many monasteries and other great
landowners. The superb quality of English wool was renowned p 249
throughout Europe and in the Islamic world, and for a long (11)
period raw wool was by far the most valuable English export, *f 3*
supplying the main centres of European wool-weaving in p 260
Flanders, northern France and Italy, especially Florence; by the (42, 43)
14th century, however, England's own developing cloth industry was absorbing most of the material and exports of cloth rapidly overtook those of raw wool. Flax-growing and linen-weaving were also widely practised, the principal areas being northern France, the Low Countries and central and eastern Europe; the finest linen cloth was woven at Rheims. Large quantities of woollen and linen cloths were exported from the main manufacturing areas to all parts of Europe, while those shipped to Near Eastern ports constituted some of Europe's most valuable exports to the Islamic world.

On the other hand, silk cloths were being imported to Europe from Islam all through the earlier Middle Ages and it was not until the 14th or 15th century that the Italian silk-weaving industry at Lucca, Florence, Venice and Genoa, seconded by various Spanish centres, was in a position to supply the bulk of the European demand. Even then, silkworm culture in Europe was quite p 250
insufficient and the industry remained dependent on massive (14)
imports of raw silk from Asia. Raw cotton and cotton cloth were also imported from the East. Certain important dyestuffs, particularly the red dyes, kermes and lac, and the blue dye, indigo, were likewise obtained from Asia, as was also the best alum, an important mordant for dyeing. The principal dyestuffs produced in Europe were the red dyes, kermes (exported from Spain and Portugal), madder (from Flanders) and archil (from Norway); the yellow dye, weld; and the blue dye, woad (from Picardy, Languedoc and elsewhere). Among other products important for textile-processing, potash was shipped from Baltic ports, oil and soap from Spain and elsewhere, and teasles from Flanders.

Besides the main branches of the textile trade and industry, there were many associated branches, such as those of the tailors, hatters, cappers, knitters and many others. Sail cloth was exported from Spain, and hemp ropes and cables from the Baltic. Figured tapestry wall-hangings of wool and fine embroideries in silk and gold thread were made in various countries; the former were exported chiefly from Flanders and northern France, while for the latter England had an international reputation. Patterned pile carpets were produced in Spain, North Africa and the Near East.

Feathers for mattresses and cushions were exported from Germany. Furs, much used for lining winter clothing, came from Scandinavia and eastern Europe, and were one of the European commodities exported to the Islamic world; rabbit skins were among the products of Spain. Spain and Portugal were also well known for the high quality of their leather, while in all countries the dressing of animal skins by tanning with a decoction of oak bark, or tawing with oil and alum, were important crafts, supplying many other craftsmen—shoemakers, glovers, girdlers, saddlers, bottlemakers and so on. Another related craft was that of converting sheep-skins into parchment, though this was rapidly being displaced in the later Middle Ages by the making of paper from rags.

Many parts of 15th-century England owed their prosperity to the woollen industry, and the great Perpendicular churches built by the merchants ('wool churches') still testify to their pride and their piety. On this brass from Northleach in Gloucestershire, William Midwinter (died 1501) is shown with his feet resting on a sheep and a wellfilled woolpack bearing his merchant's mark. In a letter dated May 1480, the merchant Richard Cely writes to his son George, at Calais: 'By the grace of God I am a-busied for to ship this foresaid 29 sarplers (a measure of wool), the which I bought of William Midwinter of Northleach 26 sarplers, the which is fair wool, as the wool packer Will Breton saith to me . . . .' (3)

Ironworkers of the 14th century. Fires burn in the centre, and on each side the metal is worked on an anvil and bench (4)

Timber, Stone and Coal

Next after food and clothing came the need for houses and other buildings, giving employment not only to skilled masons but also to innumerable carpenters, daubers, plasterers, thatchers, tilers, masons, and many more.

The basic materials of building and furnishing were available p 252 in all countries. Nevertheless, western Europe, particularly the (20) most densely populated areas, suffered from a shortage of soft wood and tall timber, which had to be supplied from the coni- f 2 ferous forests of eastern Europe and Scandinavia; from these sources there was a continuous westward flow of logs, boards, wainscots, rafters, masts and spars. Along with these, England imported large quantities of bowstaves from Baltic ports and it has been suggested that the bows carried by the English archers at Crécy and Agincourt may have been cut on the Carpathian mountains. The forests of eastern Europe were also the main sources of tar, pitch, and potash. The Islamic Near East likewise sought to supply its chronic local deficiency of timber by imports from Europe.

Most countries quarried sufficient stone for their own needs and this, though often carried on coasting vessels and on inland waterways, was only rarely shipped overseas. South-east England, lacking building stone of good quality, imported a good deal of oolitic limestone from the quarries of Caen. Stone sculptures were sometimes shipped over considerable distances; for example, Tournai fonts to England in the 12th century and Nottingham alabasters to France in the 15th. Bricks and tiles were made in many places, but Flanders and Holland exported them in considerable quantities. Earthenware vessels were likewise made in all countries, but there was an export trade in Dutch pottery and in the decorative wares of Spain and Italy; examples of decorative Oriental wares also reached Europe, but were comparatively rare. The situation in the manufacture of window glass and glassware p 253 was similar; plain glass was made in many areas, but the Low (22) Countries, northern France and other regions exported glass, and there was a luxury market for the decorative glassware of Venice and the Near East.

Lastly, there were the mining and the metallurgical industries. Although the commonest domestic fuels of the Middle Ages were wood and charcoal (with a little peat), coal was coming more and more into use in manufacturing industries. Northern England was a principal exporter and much coal was shipped from Newcastle to Germany, the Low Countries and France; coal was also mined in many places on the continent, the Liège coalfield being the most productive. Some ironstone was mined, and iron smelted, f 4 in most countries; the principal exporting areas were Sweden and p 253 northern Spain, and there were important centres in Germany, (24) Austria and other parts of central Europe. The main sources of copper were in Sweden, Germany, Austria and Hungary, those of zinc in Germany and Austria, of lead in Germany and England, of tin in south-west England, and of mercury in Spain and at the head of the Adriatic. Germany, with its wealth of metallic ores, was the leader of Europe in mining and metallurgical techniques and was renowned for its iron and steel products, especially swords, guns, and armour; the armaments industry of Liège was also important, while the armour of Milan had a European reputation. Blacksmithing and other iron-working techniques were p 252 practised everywhere. Pewter-ware, made from an alloy of tin (19) and lead, was an English speciality. Brass-ware, made from an alloy of copper and zinc, was chiefly made in Germany and the

Low Countries, notably at Dinant on the Meuse. Bronze, an alloy of copper and tin, was used in many countries for casting bells, statuary and cannon. The Islamic Near East suffered from a shortage of common metals and imported them from Europe whenever possible. Silver and small quantities of gold were extracted from the ores of Germany, Austria, Bohemia and Hungary. European gold supplies were occasionally augmented by Islamic gold coinage and Senegalese gold, received in exchange for exports to the Near East and North Africa, but the metal remained rare in comparison with silver. Goldsmiths, who were active in all countries, were apt to enjoy an influence exceeding that of other craftsmen, thanks to the value of their materials and their intimate contacts with kings and noblemen. Precious stones and pearls were imported from the East; the fresh-water pearls of northern rivers were greatly appreciated. Of the semi-precious materials, amber came from the Baltic and coral from North Africa and south Italy; both materials were exported to Asia as well as to European countries. East African ivory, imported from the Levant, was carved in many European countries; the workshops of Paris were the most distinguished. Enamelling on metal was also practised in many places, though none surpassed the reputation of Limoges.

Cologne joined the Hanseatic League in 1201, by which time she was already so rich and powerful that she immediately became one of the three leaders of the federation. Her greatness was founded upon trade; she dealt particularly in wine and herrings, manufactured cloth and was famous for metalwork. In this woodcut, printed at Cologne in 1474, the river wall encloses the church of St Martin and the choir of the unfinished cathedral, with the crane which remained there for centuries and became so familiar a landmark in the city. (5)

Patterns of International Commerce

Farming of various kinds was the universal industry of mediaeval Europe. There were, however, some areas of relatively dense population, mainly engaged in manufacture, chiefly of textiles, but also of metalwork and ceramics. One of these areas, consisting at first of the Low Countries and north-eastern France, later enlarged its boundaries to include north-western Germany and south-eastern England; the overspill into England of skilled craftsmen of every kind from adjacent parts of the Continent was a remarkable phenomenon of the later Middle Ages. A second manufacturing area comprised the northern part of Italy. Between these two main areas other, more scattered, manufacturing towns developed during the later Middle Ages in southern Germany, Switzerland, southern France and the Mediterranean coast of Spain. The manufacturing areas were surrounded by a less populous zone, comprising much of the rest of Europe, which was principally occupied with agriculture and the extraction of minerals. From this zone the manufacturing areas received, by way of trade, part of their food supplies and some of the raw materials for their industries, exporting their manufactured goods in return. To the north and east of this zone lay thinly-populated areas which exchanged their fish, furs and forest products against grain, wine and manufactured goods. To the south and east lay the Islamic world, supplying silk, spices and other luxury commodities in exchange for woollen and linen cloth, metals, farm and forest products, furs and slaves.

f 9 A glance at the map will show that the region of Tuscany and northern Italy was particularly well placed to profit from this pattern of international trade. In the heart of Europe, at the hub of the ancient network of Roman roads, this area commanded not only its own products, but those of a vast European hinterland;

in the centre of the Mediterranean, with convenient sea-lanes running east, south and west, it dominated trade with the Islamic world, Greece and the Black Sea. It formed a kind of two-way funnel, transmitting and exchanging the European products which converged on it from the north, and the Mediterranean, African and Asiatic products which converged from south and east. Italian merchants established colonies, dépôts and branches in all parts of this large trading area to ensure a smooth flow of trade in both directions, and they played a leading role in the external trade of countries such as France, England and Flanders. Not content with the financial success of the transit trade, Italian *entrepreneurs* sought to cut costs and boost profits by themselves producing some of the goods most in demand. Thus they developed a great woollen industry, reducing the need to import woollen cloth from the north, and a great silk industry, reducing the need to import silk stuffs from the Islamic world. Metallurgical, ceramic and glass industries were likewise developed. Small wonder that northern Italy was one of the most prosperous and culturally advanced areas of the world in the 14th and 15th centuries, and that Italians were the bankers of Europe—a historical fact which is still echoed by the name Lombard Street in the City of London.

Another trading area which enjoyed some of the geographical advantages of northern Italy was that of southern France and eastern Spain, but it was less well placed in relation both to the European hinterland and to the Islamic trade and never achieved a comparable level of prosperity. A third important trading area was that covered by the Hanseatic League of north German and Netherland towns, which controlled the exports of the hinterlands of north and east Germany, north Russia and Scandinavia. These were shipped westwards in exchange for the products of western and southern Europe and those of the Islamic East, the latter obtainable at Bruges, the main northern terminal of Italian trade. Like the Italians, the Hanseatic towns established dépôts and branches in alien lands, the most important being those of Novgorod, Bergen, Bruges and London. *f 5* p 246 (1)

This pattern of international trade, effective throughout the later Middle Ages, was to be utterly destroyed by the opening of the Cape route to the Indies and the discovery and exploitation of America. Northern Italy, which had been the centre of the old pattern, was marginal in the new system which now emerged, and her commerce and prosperity declined. From the 16th to the 19th century it was the countries fronting the Atlantic—Portugal, Spain, France, Holland, Britain—all of them peripheral to the old system, which found themselves most favourably placed between the European hinterland and the major markets overseas.

Market Towns and the Great Fairs

Mediaeval towns were tiny by modern standards. Few exceeded 10,000 inhabitants and not many had more than 5,000. Most towns were small centres in which the inhabitants of the surrounding countryside disposed of their surplus production in exchange for products of the town's own industry, or those which arrived there from other regions. The town served to collect the surplus of its own area and pass it on to other areas, while at the same time receiving parts of the surplus of other areas and distributing them to its own area. Just as a small town served as a collecting point and distributing centre for its surrounding countryside, so a large town served many small ones or a whole country. Thus London, with about 40,000 inhabitants, was the main collecting point for English products and the main distributing centre for imports arriving in England from overseas. In the heavily industrialized Low Countries, Bruges, Brussels and Ghent were of about this size or larger, while in Italy the great trading and industrial cities of Bologna, Florence, Genoa, Milan, Naples and Venice all had between about 50,000 and 100,000 inhabitants.

Country-dwellers could supply most of their own requirements in food and other commodities and it was not difficult for the inhabitants of small towns to raise a good deal of their own food. At the same time the demands of the average mediaeval household for industrially produced clothing, furniture and other utensils was comparatively small. Thus the process of buying and selling was much less continuous than it has since become, and for most purposes it was found convenient to concentrate it in a once-weekly market, though larger towns might have more frequent markets, as well as permanent shops. The right to hold a market was generally granted by royal licence and the market tolls collected from the traders could be an important source of revenue for the nobleman, or the ecclesiastical or civic authority possessing this right.

p 262
(50–52)
Just as the weekly market was convenient for a great deal of local trade, so the annual, or sometimes twice-yearly, fair, of several weeks' duration was a favoured channel for trade over longer distances. The right to hold these was also granted by royal licence and the tolls, rents of booths and other dues were often of great value. There were four great fairs in England in the 13th century—at Northampton, St Ives, Boston and Winchester—as well as a number of lesser ones, and fairs of this kind were held throughout western Europe. All were overshadowed, however, in the 12th and 13th centuries, by the six great fairs of Champagne, at Lagny, Bar-sur-Aube, Provins (twice-yearly) and Troyes (twice-yearly). Here the merchants of Italy sold the produce which they carried from the Mediterranean and Islamic lands, and here they bought the produce of northern Europe, above all woollen cloth, in order to carry it back with them to the south. For a time at least the great Champagne fairs formed the pivot of the whole system of international trade.

In the later Middle Ages, as a result of changes in the political situation and in the international wool trade, the fairs of Champagne lost their importance. Indeed, the importance of fairs in general, and of many markets also, tended to decline as the great merchants of the towns took a firmer grip on the administration of all trading activities and sought to eliminate those markets and fairs which remained under aristocratic or ecclesiastical control and thus escaped their jurisdiction. More and more business passed through established channels in the towns and substantial commercial houses engaging in the long-distance trade tended to open dépôts or branches, or at least to acquire a local representative, in the towns with which they were particularly concerned.

Alien merchants, though often able to ingratiate themselves with royal or other administrations by personal services or diplomatic pressures, were always exposed to the jealousy, restrictive practices and occasional physical violence of the local merchants and populace. It was often found safer and more convenient for all concerned if alien merchants and their goods were concentrated in a single building or group of buildings which, particularly in Islamic countries or in Russia, as in the Hanseatic station at Novgorod, had some of the characteristics of a fortress. In London the Hansards lived and had their warehouses in a complex of buildings round the Steelyard. The activities of alien merchants were further controlled by obliging them to deal through the agency of specified local merchants or through brokers appointed for this purpose.

p 259
(40)

Carriage by Land and Sea

Each town was at the centre of a web of local roads. A large town such as London was at the centre of a network of main roads, many of Roman origin. Indeed, the Roman road-system was preserved, at least in outline, throughout western Europe. Maintenance of the roads themselves, however, was haphazard and sporadic, and the condition of many was appalling, especially in winter. Although in many parts main roads were legally the 'king's highways', the Crown rarely initiated any extensive road-works except in conjunction with military operations. But it was nearly always in the interest of individuals or of municipal authorities to keep a road open, and if it threatened to become impassable some *ad hoc* means of raising funds for repair could generally be devised. Thus in the 14th century the municipality of Ghent contributed to the repair of a defective stretch of road in the neighbourhood of Paris, since the maintenance of French roads was of importance to the merchants of the town. Landowners and farmers had an interest in keeping roadside ditches scoured since traffic was liable to diverge from a flooded road on to land alongside. A great deal was also done by ecclesiastical and private charity, particularly in the construction and maintenance of causeways and bridges. A distinction between the fundamentally military character of the Roman road-system and the overwhelmingly civil and commercial use of mediaeval roads is sug-

Genoa and Venice struggled throughout the Middle Ages for the commercial leadership of Italy, a struggle from which Venice emerged supreme. Genoa – seen here, as it were, through her rival's eyes (a Venetian woodcut of 1486) – was organized on similar lines under a doge elected from the principal families. She maintained a powerful fleet, with trading agencies all over Europe and the Near East. (6)

gested by the fact that the Romans were often content with a ford where the Middle Ages preferred a bridge, if possible, a stone-built bridge. Many of these mediaeval stone bridges are still in use today. The importance of bridges in mediaeval communications is underlined by an occasion in the 14th century when the decay of bridges and causeways at Stratford-at-Bow led to higher prices and food shortages in the City of London. It was natural that special attention was given to the building and repair of such structures. Apart from private and corporate benefactions, a toll known as 'pontage' was sometimes levied on goods passing over a bridge, in order to pay for its maintenance, while in other cases, as in that of London Bridge, the rents of certain properties were allotted to the work of repair. Although road-maintenance in the Middle Ages was far from satisfactory or systematic, the European road-system as a whole was nevertheless kept in working order and some important additions were made to it, even in difficult country such as the Alps. The construction of a bridge over the Schöllenen gorge in the 13th century, opening the St Gotthard pass to pack-mules, and the construction of a road for wheeled traffic over the Septimer pass, in the 14th century, were significant improvements to the routes between Italy and the north.

Apart from the humbler chapmen or pedlars, hawking their f 8 packs of trinkets and haberdashery from village to village, few foot-passengers carried merchandise along the roads, except over very short distances. Pack-animals, chiefly horses, were com- f 7 mercially important, especially for local traffic between town and countryside or town and town. Owing to the relative smallness of their loads they were hardly suitable or economic for bulk traffic over long distances, except where roads were difficult or non-existent, as in the mountainous areas of Europe, or the desert areas of North Africa and Asia, where the camel caravan was the principal means of overland transport. In Europe generally, the vehicle most used for land transport was the cart, chiefly the four- p 256 wheeled cart drawn by horses (less often by oxen) in teams of from (28, 29) two to five beasts, or occasionally more if the load or the route demanded. Carts were available in great numbers. Farm carts could be hired cheaply for local traffic, and numerous professional carters operated along the main long-distance routes; in London, and doubtless in other large towns, there were even professional cart-brokers, acting as intermediaries between carters and merchants. In England carts could be expected to cover twenty to thirty miles per day at a cost of between 1d and 3½d per ton per mile.

Although such charges were fairly modest in proportion to the value of many types of goods, they were nevertheless considerably higher than the cost of water transport, since a single river-boat, and still more a sea-going ship, could easily carry loads which would have required dozens, if not hundreds, of carts. Hence water transport, if available, was usually preferred to land transport for bulk merchandise, and it is not surprising that nearly all important European towns were situated on sea-coasts or on navigable rivers. Many of the rivers of Europe—Garonne, Loire, Rhône, Saône, Seine, Somme, Oise, Scheldt, Meuse, Rhine, Main, Weser, Elbe, Vistula—were major routes of continental commerce and even quite tiny streams carried their quota of cargoes. Rivers were particularly important in English internal trade, offering easy routes from town to town and from inland areas to the sea. Large numbers of professional boatmen found employment along these river routes and considerable attention was given to maintenance works, such as dredging and embanking, and to preventing the obstruction of the channel by private installations, such as water-mills or fish-weirs.

Both roads and rivers were subject to tolls. Some of these were levied to defray the cost of necessary constructional or maintenance work along the route; others were imposed by local or national authorities as a means of raising general revenue. Tolls of the latter kind were less common in England than on the Continent, especially in France and Germany, where, besides the toll-stations on national frontiers, there were many others along all important roads and still more on the rivers. These tolls were certainly a burden and an impediment to trade; it has been calculated, for example, that in the 15th century toll charges on grain shipped 200 miles along the Seine represented over half the selling price—but they could not profitably be increased above the level which trade was capable of bearing. Moreover, thanks to the multiplicity of available routes, long-distance trade at least was generally in a position to abandon a route which grew too costly in favour of a cheaper alternative.

p 257
(32, 33)
The cheapest means of bulk transport was the sea-going ship. Mediaeval ships, though small by the standards of later periods, were nevertheless by far the largest and also the most economical bulk-carrying vehicles of their time. For example, the cost of shipping wool from London to Calais in the 15th century represented less than 2% of the value of the wool. Ships tended, indeed, to become steadily more efficient as their size increased; ships of several hundred tons capacity were not rare in the later Middle Ages. The introduction of the compass encouraged mariners to abandon devious coastal voyages in favour of more direct sea routes. From the early 14th century onwards Italian vessels, which in earlier times had rarely emerged from the Mediterranean, began to operate regular services to northern Europe, calling at Bruges, London, Southampton and other ports. Sea transport had the additional advantage of avoiding the innumerable tolls on continental road and river routes, while the various special charges

The main limiting factor on trade was the physical difficulty of transporting goods over long distances. The coastal waters and rivers bore the heaviest traffic. Otherwise it all had to be carried in carts or on the backs of horses. This pack-horse walked the roads of Germany in the 12th century. (7)

incurred at the terminal points of the voyage—harbour dues, cost of discharging into lighters, charges for use of the town crane, and the like—were comparatively modest. Customs duties levied by national authorities on certain types of merchandise were sometimes heavy, but this would apply to road and river transport as well as to sea routes. Among the highest of these duties were the English export duties on wool in the 14th and 15th centuries, amounting in all to about 20% of the value.

The Hazards: Piracy, Shipwreck and War

In the Middle Ages, as in all other periods, commerce was subject to many risks. In the first place, there were the ordinary commercial risks inherent in almost any operation of buying and selling goods over considerable distances. When the goods might be weeks or months on transit, and the merchant had no telegraph or telephone to inform him of price movements, his forecasts of demand might easily be falsified by changes in political or economic circumstances at the point of sale. There was always the risk that commercial rivals might be manipulating prices by such practices as 'forestalling' or intercepting goods before they reached the open market, and 'engrossing' or 'regrating'—making a corner in a commodity. There were, however, many laws and regulations designed to prevent this type of speculative interference with the normal processes of supply and demand.

The natural hazards of long-distance transport were great, especially by sea. Mediaeval ships, with their high, rounded hulls, must have rolled and pitched abominably and caused acute discomfort, if nothing worse, to merchants travelling with their goods. Frequently equipped only with a single square sail, they were unhandy, sluggish, and incapable of beating against the wind. They carried little or nothing in the way of maps, charts or navigational aids. Small wonder that wrecks were frequent. And even if the shipwrecked mariner or merchant was fortunate enough to reach the shore, records of ugly incidents around the coasts show that the local inhabitants were likely to show little mercy or respect for either his person or his goods. Against this, it must be remembered that the craft of shipbuilding and the art of navigation were steadily improving during the Middle Ages. Charts and compasses were increasingly used. Beacons were built at harbour-mouths. Codes of rules were drawn up which minimized mischances as far as was humanly possible. The respective responsibilities of merchants and shipmasters, both in emergencies and in normal circumstances, were codified; there were even regulations with regard to the storage of perishable goods on shipboard. Indeed, shipping traffic was in every way more regulated and more regular than might be imagined. For example, as early as 1312 there was a gild of ferry-ships at Dover, operating the Channel ferry in rotation, according to fixed tariffs. Again, at the beginning of the 16th century, the forty experienced pilots of the Gild of the Holy Trinity, Deptford, were working a rota-system to take ships up and down the Thames.

p 257
(34)

Besides the natural hazards of travel, there was a constant risk from human agencies. Merchants travelling in remote and alien countries, or in troubled areas, took due precautions, and were accompanied by armed escorts; but highway robbers were no respecters of peaceful times, or of their own countrymen. The robbers of 15th-century England were considered to surpass those of all other countries both in numbers and in boldness, and one contemporary writer goes so far as to regard their prowess as a proper source of national pride. While robbery on the roads was probably not more frequent then than it is today, piracy at sea was a graver problem. Mariners were often wild and lawless men, who, if they fell in with a weaker ship, particularly a foreigner, were by no means reluctant to take advantage of the situation. Doubtless Chaucer's Shipman was not untypical:

p 257
(35)

> Of nyce conscience took he no keep.
> If that he faught, and hadde the hyer hond,
> By water he sente hem hoom to every lond.

Apart from the motive of plunder, such actions were stimulated by political and commercial rivalries and—in the case of the Turkish and Barbary pirates who infested the Mediterranean—by religious hostility. They even tended to be perpetuated by pro-

A travelling pedlar of Germany displays his wares to the lady of the castle. Carrying her little dog, she seems tempted by an ornamental belt. (8)

cesses of law. In accordance with the mediaeval legal concept of collective responsibility, a merchant who had been robbed or defrauded by nationals of another country could obtain from his own authorities a grant of 'reprisals', by which other nationals of the offending country were officially mulcted of an equivalent value. Or, alternatively, he might be granted 'letters of marque' which entitled him to fit out a piratical expedition in order to capture an equivalent value from the shipping of the offending country. There were other avenues of redress through the law-courts and through diplomatic channels, but these were generally too lengthy and too costly to be of much practical use. It is not surprising that merchants with valuable cargoes preferred to sail on large, fast, well-armed ships, such as the Venetian galleys, or in convoys, such as the English convoys for wool and wine, or the Hanseatic fleets. Even these were inevitably vulnerable to a large, well-organized attack, as when a great Flemish, French and Spanish wine-fleet was captured by the Earl of Arundel in 1387, and again in 1449 when a Hanseatic fleet of a hundred ships was seized by an English squadron in the Channel.

These were acts of war, and war, then as now, was the greatest of all hazards to industry and trade. It blocked normal trade channels and overturned existing commodity values, raising some and depressing others. It ruined some merchants, and allowed others to amass enormous fortunes. But apart from the cataclysm of war, it may be doubted whether commerce was as hazardous as might be assumed from the surviving documents. Since these are, to a great extent, legal and official papers, they are apt to give special prominence to disaster, dishonesty, theft and violence, because these were departures from normal circumstances and conduct, which the law and the authorities were concerned as far as possible to rectify. Most commercial activity, then as now, consisted of comparatively humdrum operations, producing small but regular profits, and was probably not much more hazardous than similar activity today, except in so far as mediaeval life in general was shorter and more dangerous than modern life.

The Tools of Trade

In buying and selling, quantity-measurement is of great importance. The diversity of weights and measures used in the mediaeval world posed serious problems for the merchant, necessitating frequent recourse to conversion tables, since the measurements employed at the point of sale were often different from those at the point of purchase. Common measures of length such as the ell were apt to vary not only from country to country, but also from town to town, and there was an endless variety of local custom by which arbitrary values were attached to common numerical and quantitative terms—a few of these still survive, for exam-

ple in 'bakers' dozens' or 'long hundreds'. In addition, there were enormous variations in the sizes of manufactured goods. For example, almost every weaving centre made cloths which differed in both length and breadth from similar cloths produced in all other weaving centres, and moreover these measurements were apt to change from time to time. Though the situation was evidently chaotic, it was nevertheless controlled to some extent by local and national regulations. Thus all cloths of a particular quality produced in a particular weaving centre at any given time not only had identical measurements, but also contained precisely the same number of threads. Most towns maintained scales for public use, and the accuracy of weights and measures was checked from time to time by the authorities. National governments made repeated attempts to standardize weights and measures, which, though often frustrated by local conservatism, were not wholly without success.

There was also endless variety in the most essential of all tools of trade—money. Most countries had a number of different coins in circulation, both of gold and of silver, as well as of baser metals, and the relative values of gold and silver differed from country to country. The number of states and princes issuing coinage was considerable, and their coins differed greatly in degree of fineness; nor was the fineness necessarily stable, but varied from time to time. The international merchant had to be aware of the relative and changing values of numerous coins, but he naturally preferred to use those whose fineness was most stable and reliable. The weight of a coin was also subject to variation, both at the time of issue, and later, due to wear; hence a small pair of goldsmith's scales, for checking the weight, was a necessary part of a merchant's equipment. p 264, 5 (56–62)

Since travelling with large sums in coin was both inconvenient and dangerous, much business was done in the form of credit transactions. For instance, it was normal for the king's purchases at one of the four great English fairs to be paid for at the fair next following, and this principle of credit was widely adopted in most branches of trade and finance. Debts were often recorded on 'tallies', that is, short sticks cut with notches representing the sum, sealed by the parties, and split longitudinally so that each party retained one part; when the debt was eventually settled, it was the responsibility of the debtor to see that the tally was destroyed. Tallies similar in form but different in purpose were used by the royal exchequer to avoid cash payments. A merchant presenting his bill to the exchequer would receive, not cash, but one half of a tally which was, in effect, a cheque drawn on one of the official collectors of revenue, who had cash in hand, and would pay out the requisite sum on surrender of the tally; finally, the collector would return the tally to the exchequer as evidence that the debt was discharged. The 'letter of credit' was a useful device by which a person of known financial standing could provide for the expenses of others travelling on his behalf; addressed to merchants generally, it pledged the credit of the signatory to repay any loans, up to a specified sum, which might be made to the bearer. The 'bill of exchange' was a very important factor in international trade and finance, especially in the later Middle Ages when important firms had branches and agents in various parts of Europe. A merchant of Bruges, wishing to purchase goods in Florence, could make a payment to the Bruges branch of a Florentine firm and receive in return an order on the firm for a similar payment (less profits on the exchange); this order or bill of exchange he would send to his agent in Florence, who would present it to a Florentine firm, receive cash in return, and make the required purchase. In this way, the Bruges merchant obtained currency for his purchase in Florence, while at the same time the Bruges branch of the Florentine firm received local currency for possible purchases in Flanders, without any physical transfer of funds from one town to the other. Bills of exchange were also used, not only by merchants but also by other travellers, for the same purpose as modern traveller's cheques.

The negotiation of bills of exchange was one of the principal functions of mediaeval banking. Another was the provision of monetary loans. Here we encounter a moral question which long preoccupied the Christian Church. The Church, basing itself on the Scriptures, was suspicious of all profit which did not derive p 266 (63)

Map labels (geographical and commodity, as printed):

NORTH SEA · BALTIC SEA · ATLANTIC OCEAN · MEDITERRANEAN SEA

Bergen · RED DYE · IRON · COPPER · ROPE · FISH · FISH-OIL · PITCH · FURS · TIMBER · Stockholm · Narva · Reval · Pernau · Dorpat · Pskov · Novgorod · POTASH · Warberg · Wisby · Calmar · Hälsingborg · Roskild · Riga · Libau · GRAIN · AMBER · Kovno · TIMBER · Flensborg · Kiel · Hamburg · Lübeck · Rostock · Stralsund · Danzig · Königsberg · Marienburg · HONE · Bremen · Brandenburg · Berlin · Magdebrug · Frankfurt · Brunswick · Warburg · Thorn · FURS · BUTTER · OXEN · GRAIN · TIMBER · LINEN · Breslau · PITCH · TAR · Cracow · POTASH · SALMON · COAL · Newcastle · Durham · York · Hull · Boston · Worcester · Chipping Campden · Bristol · Northampton · WOOL · London · Thames · St Ives · TIN · Tiverton · Malmesbury · Salisbury · Bruges · Brussels · Rhine · Weser · Meuse · Cologne · SILVER ZINC · COPPER · WINE IRON LEAD · ARMAMENTS · BRASSWARE · Main · Elbe · SALT · Angers · Loire · Paris · Seine · WINE · Bourges · Saône · Augsburg · SILVER · IRON · COPPER · MERCURY · Dniester · Limoges · ENAMEL-WORK · Garonne · Rhône · WINE · Montpellier · Avignon · YELLOW & BLUE DYE · ARMOUR GLASS-WARE · Milan · Verona · Venice · Genoa · Bologna · Prato · Lucca · Pisa · Florence · Siena · Faenza · Po · Danube · IRON · CITRUS & DRIED FRUITS · Tagus · ALMONDS · LEATHER · WINE HONEY WAX · CARPETS · CERAMICS · MERCURY · OLIVE OIL · Ebro · Barcelona · Corsica · Rome · SILK · WOOLLEN CLOTH · CERAMICS · METALWORK · EMBROIDERY · Naples · Bari · OLIVE OIL · CORAL · Constantinople · Valencia · Majorca · Sardinia · ALMONDS · CURRANTS · Pho · Chios · Sm · MASTIC · OLIVE OIL · WINE · CARPETS DRIED FRUITS · CORAL ALMONDS OLIVE OIL · Tripoli · IVORY · Inset

---

from work. It tolerated profits arising from financial operations which might equally involve loss—such as venturing capital in commercial enterprises—and even profits arising from international exchange operations, but it condemned usury, or the charging of interest on capital lent without risk, as a mortal sin. For this reason, money-lending was largely the prerogative of Jews in the earlier Middle Ages. But the increasing concentration of capital in the hands of the great merchants, particularly Italians, and the constant demand for capital elsewhere, almost forced the merchants to undertake this class of business, though the contracts were generally drawn up in terms calculated to conceal their true nature. Eventually, however, ecclesiastical opinion on this subject was so far relaxed that the Franciscan order was issuing loans at 10% interest. Although many of the loans made by mediaeval merchants were theoretically without risk, some of them, and

especially loans to princes, were in practice very dangerous indeed. One of the most spectacular financial crashes in history, the bankruptcies of the two greatest Florentine houses—that of the Peruzzi in 1343, that of the Bardi in 1345—was largely due to the failure of Edward III to repay capital or interest on their enormous loans to him, and many of the mediaeval merchants who dabbled in royal financing found it in the long run a most unprofitable form of business.

Premium insurance was a useful facility which came into use in the 14th century, especially for shipments by sea; overland insurance and life insurance remained comparatively rare, though the sale of annuities was common. Premiums on shipments were high—up to as much as 18%—but varied greatly with the estimated risks of the voyage. In 1454, the premium paid on a shipment from Venice to Bruges by an ordinary small sailing vessel was 11%,

This map shows the chief trade-routes of the Middle Ages, with the most important products that were exported. The main manufacturing areas were south-east England, the Low Countries and northern France, and northern Italy. (9)

while for a cargo shipped from Sandwich to Venice on the fast, safe Venetian galleys the rate was only 3%. Mediaeval merchants, with their long tradition of venturing, rarely insured a cargo for more than half its value.

In general, merchants were not narrowly specialized, but engaged in various types of business, and dealt in many different commodities. For success it was essential to keep accurate office records. Calculations, which were by no means simple with the Roman numerals still generally in use, were facilitated by the use of counters on an abacus or counting board, ruled in columns representing different units of value; the results of the additions, subtractions, multiplications and divisions carried out on this device were then entered in some form of ledger. For the small trader this might be a quite simple diary of transactions, but for great firms with a number of branches and innumerable interests

elaborate book-keeping techniques, leading to the production of an accurate balance-sheet, were indispensable. The Medici bank required each of its branches to submit an annual balance-sheet and indeed Florentine firms were required by law to include a balance-sheet with their income-tax returns. Double-entry book-keeping was in use by Italian firms from the 14th century onwards, though it did not spread to other European countries until the 16th century, following the publication of Italian manuals on the subject. Another class of manual, which circulated in manuscript in the Italian merchant houses, gave details of commodities, prices, weights, measures, and other special features of the principal international markets of western Europe and the Near East. These books, of which the best known is the *Pratica della Mercatura*, compiled about 1340 by Francesco Pegolotti, one of the factors of the Bardi company, were invaluable in their day and are now a rich mine of information for the historian. But the real education of the merchant was derived, not from books, but from the school of experience.

A type of written communication which was indispensable for commercial operations was the business letter, used to place orders, to notify shipments, and to pass information on current sales, prices, foreign exchange rates, and future market prospects. Since there was no official postal service, groups of merchants with common interests generally organized their own, and there seems to have been a regular service of couriers carrying sealed mail bags between all the main centres of trade. For example the Catalan mail bag and its bearer left Bruges for Barcelona twice a month, and spent about three weeks on the journey.

The tangible relics of mediaeval industry and trade, now garnered into archives, museums and private collections, are astonishingly numerous. The documentary remains, comprising letters, bills of exchange, ledgers, contracts, insurance policies, tax-returns, gild-regulations, mercantile laws, mercantile handbooks, seamen's maps and charts, and an infinity of other papers, contain inexhaustible stores of detailed information. The archive of the firm of Francesco Datini alone, preserved almost in its entirety at Prato, contains several hundred thousand documents.

p 260 (41)   Among tools of trade, weights and capacity-measures survive in considerable numbers; they are generally of cast bronze and bear the coat-of-arms of the responsible local or national authority. Far commoner than these are coins, the most essential tools of all. Most good coin collections include examples of the coins used in p 265 (61, 62)   European trade, the Arabic *dinar*, Byzantine *nomisma*, Venetian ducat, Florentine florin, French *écu*, English noble, and many more. The coins are often of great historical interest and some of them, particularly the gold pieces, are beautifully designed, but these were not qualities which had much appeal for the mediaeval merchant; the coins which he most admired were those which, like the English silver penny, remained unchanged in appearance, in weight and in fineness from reign to reign, and from century to century.

Mutual Protection

The merchant could, and often did, operate single-handed on his own account, but in view of the hazards of travel, especially long-distance travel by sea, it was often deemed advisable to spread the risk—particularly in the period before the use of maritime insurance—by means of partnerships, which were generally valid for a single voyage. Investment and partnership agreements took many legal forms. They might be made among a number of partners who participated equally in a venture. Often they were agreements between investing partners, who contributed most of the finance and took a larger share of eventual profits, and travelling partners, who might risk some of their own capital, but whose principal contribution was their own commercial ability and zeal.

From the late 13th century onwards, as intermittent trading in fairs and the like gradually gave way to permanent trading in great mercantile towns, Italian merchants tended to group themselves in semi-permanent partnerships, or companies, and to set up permanent branches in the main foreign centres. At first these large enterprises were in the form of a single partnership, with the partners—often comprising several members of one family, who formed the nucleus of the association—generally resident in Italy, and the branches manned by employees. Later, after the Bardi-Peruzzi débâcle, a new type of organization was adopted, in which the company was composed of a series of autonomous partnerships, one for each branch; each branch remained under the control of the senior partners in Italy, but was often under the immediate direction of a resident junior partner. This, the organization adopted by the Medici and others, avoided the danger that a disaster affecting a single branch might bring about the collapse of the entire company.

Common interest, and the necessity of acting with corporate strength rather than individual weakness, led to the formation of many other types of trade association. The most widespread were p 266 (64)   the craft gilds, associations of all the master-craftsmen in a town who practised the same craft. Such gilds also had social and

religious functions, but their primary purpose was to regulate prices, quality and conditions of production, to settle disputes among members, and to represent the interests of the craft against all others. Besides the gilds of master-craftsmen, there were also societies of journeymen-workers, which pressed wage-demands on the masters and sometimes organized strikes, but this type of association was frequently forbidden and suppressed by the town authorities. In some ways analogous with the craft gilds were the associations of merchants trading in the same commodities, such as the Mercers and other companies of the City of London, or, with wider scope, the Merchant Staplers and the Merchant Adventurers, who dealt respectively with the export of English wool and English cloth. Sometimes, as in London, the various gilds and other associations engaged in bitter struggles for supremacy in the administration of their town; in other cases this supremacy was firmly in the hands of the Gild Merchant, an association of the principal traders and industrialists.

In some continental towns a number of prosperous families formed an urban patriciate which maintained its supremacy for generations, or even, as at Venice, for centuries. Occasionally, as the Medici did in Florence, a single family so far outstripped its competitors as to achieve hereditary supremacy for itself alone. Town authorities everywhere enjoyed considerable administrative *f 10* and juridical power. In England, for example, they administered in their own courts, which were distinct from the king's courts, a code of Merchant Law—concerned with questions of contract or debt—which was distinct from the Common Law.

The authorities of a great town exercised an economic and political power which could profoundly influence the policies of the national administration—witness the numerous conflicts between the king and the City of London. A number of the great Italian towns—Venice, Florence, Genoa and others—were nation-states in their own right, governed by merchant-oligarchies whose policies were directed to the achievement of maximum profits. Towns, like individuals, sometimes formed associations to promote their common interests. By far the most effective association of this type was the Hanseatic League, which, at the p 246 height of its power in the 15th century, comprised as many as (1) sixty-four north German and other towns, and for several centuries defended its predominant position in northern trade and its special privileges in foreign countries, including England, by astute diplomatic pressure and by successful wars.

Some Business Careers

The history of mediaeval industry and trade is full of interesting careers and personalities. Only a few of these can be briefly mentioned here, but they may perhaps convey some idea of the quality of commercial life in the Middle Ages.

Saewulf was an Anglo-Saxon merchant in the circle of Wulfstan, the saintly Bishop of Worcester, who tried to persuade him to enter the religious life. This he declined to do, but in 1102, some years after Wulfstan's death, he undertook a penitential pilgrimage to Jerusalem. His account of this gives an impression of the hazards of mediaeval sea-travel. Wrecked near Bari, he took ship again and spent thirteen weeks on the voyage to Jaffa; the day after he landed, a hurricane destroyed before his eyes twenty-three of the thirty great ships in the harbour. When he had worshipped at all the holy places, he re-embarked at Jaffa and spent four months, harassed by Mohammedan fleets and pirates, on the voyage to Constantinople. A few years later he was living as a monk at Malmesbury. The hazards of sea-voyages were not much diminished in 1506, when Sir Richard Guildford's secretary spent over four months, with many disasters and near-disasters, on the journey from Jaffa to Venice.

Godric of Finchale was the son of a poor farming family in Norfolk. An ambitious youth, he became a pedlar, at first in his own locality, but later extending his activity to more prosperous places further afield. After a few years, in association with other like-minded young men, he began to undertake short trading voyages, to Scotland, Flanders and Denmark. With some of his partners he bought a half-share of a merchant ship, and subsequently a quarter-share of another. He became wealthy, 'for he sold dear in one place the wares which he had bought elsewhere at a small price'. The perils of the sea made him an ardent worshipper of the saints. After sixteen years as a merchant, he went as a pilgrim to Jerusalem, returning by way of Compostela, and settled as a hermit at Finchale near Durham, where he lived many years in fasting, cold and prayer. He died in 1170 and was declared a saint.

Ansaldo Baialardo of Genoa was still a minor when, in 1156, he entered into a partnership for a coastal trading voyage to Provence, Montpellier and Catalonia; this voyage was entirely financed by the investing partner, while Baialardo contributed his labour and ability, for which he received one quarter of the eventual profits. All of this he invested in a second similar voyage undertaken by the same partnership. This too was profitable, and the same partnership undertook a third voyage, this time to Syria, Palestine and Egypt, with Baialardo now contributing about two-thirds of his accumulated capital. Again the enterprise was successful, so that by these three voyages, in the space of about three years, the investing partner had nearly trebled his invested capital, while Baialardo, who started with nothing, was on the way to becoming a wealthy man.

Romano Mairano was a Venetian who, from 1155, resided in Constantinople, where he owned a house, and organized short trading voyages to Smyrna and to Greek ports. By 1167, he owned two ships, on one of which he sailed as master, and was making longer trips, financed in part by loans from other Venetians, between Constantinople and Alexandria. In 1171, the Byzantine Emperor ordered the arrest of all Venetians in Constantinople; the only ones to escape were those who took refuge on Mairano's ship, which outsailed the pursuing Greek fleet. Thereafter, Mairano settled in Venice, but continued to make trading voyages to the Near East, carrying such cargoes as timber on the outward journey, and returning with pepper and alum. He retired from seafaring about 1192, when he was a little over sixty, leaving his ventures in the charge of his son, but evidently the latter did not long survive, for when Mairano died, soon after 1201, his only heir was his daughter, a nun, and her convent inherited all his property, together with his business papers.

Benedetto Zaccaria was born into a noble family of Genoa some time before 1240. A remarkably versatile man, he was the builder of a great commercial empire, as well as a subtle diplomat, a renowned naval commander, and a pirate. He speculated in foreign exchange, investments, real estate, and traded in spices, salt, grain, cloth and furs. From the Byzantine Emperor he received as fiefs the island of Chios, principal source of the valuable aromatic herb mastic, and the mines of Phocaea, one of the major suppliers of alum. He was one of the commanders of the Genoese fleet which destroyed the Pisans at Meloria in 1284, led the Castilian fleet that crushed the Moors at Marzamosa in 1291, and captured Tripoli in Syria. Among other diplomatic enterprises, Zaccaria planned and helped to execute an economic blockade of England, on behalf of Philip the Fair of France. He died in his palace at Genoa in 1307.

p 258 (39) The brothers Niccolò and Maffeo Polo were members of a noble family of Venice. Following a successful trading voyage to Constantinople, they decided to extend their operations to the Crimea and the capital of the north-western Tartars on the Volga. Their return route having been cut by a Tartar war, they pushed on to Bokhara, capital of the eastern Tartars, and after three years there proceeded to the capital of the Mongol emperor in China. The Emperor Kublai charged them with an embassy to the Pope, and they returned to Italy, after an absence of many years, in 1269. In 1271 they set off again on a return embassy to Kublai, accompanied this time by Niccolò's son Marco, a youth of about seventeen. Travelling overland as before, they reached Kublai's capital in 1275, and remained in the emperor's service for the next seventeen years. They then accompanied an embassy to Persia, which took two years over the sea-voyage from China to the Persian gulf, losing six hundred of its members by sickness. From Persia, the three Venetians returned to their native city in 1295. Venice was then at war with Genoa and the wealthy Polo family was called upon to equip a war-galley, which was under Marco's command when the Venetian fleet was defeated by the Genoese off Curzola in 1298. In prison at Genoa, Marco dictated an account of Asia which is perhaps the most

Commerce was regulated by a complex system of local and national rules. In this woodcut (1501) of the municipal court of Paris, the provost presides with other high officials at the back of the hall. Merchants' and burgesses' representatives are in the foreground, and behind them are the clerk and collector of dues. (10)

celebrated of all books of travel. He returned to Venice in 1299 and died there in 1324.

Sir William de la Pole, son of a merchant of Hull, was himself a merchant of the same town from 1319 onwards. He made a great fortune from the wool trade and other enterprises, and in the 1330s he advanced large sums of money to Edward III. In 1340 he was arrested and imprisoned for mismanagement of the royal finances, but the case against him was annulled by the parliament of 1344. About 1350 he founded a hospital outside Hull, which he later converted into a convent for nuns of the Order of St Clare. His daughters married into the noble families of Scrope and Neville and his son Michael became first Earl of Suffolk. Sir William de la Pole, who died in 1366, is noteworthy as the first English merchant to found a great noble house.

Francesco Datini was born about 1335, the son of a taverner of p 258 (38) Prato near Florence. Orphaned by the Black Death in 1348, he was only fifteen when he moved to Avignon, where he remained for the next thirty-two years. At the age of twenty-eight he set up a small company, contributing half the capital himself, and laid the foundations of his fortune by trading in armour, silks, woollens, embroidery, religious pictures and other commodities. When he returned to Prato in 1383 he was already a rich man, and his business continued to prosper. Eventually he controlled a large number of companies, financed wholly or chiefly by himself, which dealt in every aspect of banking, insurance, and trade; besides his headquarters at Prato, he had permanent branches at Avignon, Florence, Pisa, Genoa, Barcelona, Valencia and Majorca, as well as agents scattered throughout western Europe and the Near East. He was a hard man, who pursued temporal profit unrelentingly, but he was also anxious to lay up treasure in Heaven. On the first page of his ledgers were written the words, 'In the name of God and of profit'. When he died in 1410 ('it seemed to him very strange that he should have to die, and that his prayers should be of no avail') he bequeathed the bulk of his vast fortune to set up a charitable foundation in Prato.

p 260
(44, 45)
Jacques Coeur, the son of a rich merchant of Bourges, was born about 1395. The outset of his career was inauspicious. As a moneyer he was condemned for striking coins of less than the prescribed fineness. In 1432, returning from a voyage to Syria, he was wrecked on the coast of Corsica and robbed of all his possessions. But in the following years he built up an immense trading network, covering the Mediterranean from Alexandria to Barcelona and extending throughout France and neighbouring countries. He was also concerned with silk-weaving, dyeing, paper-making and mining. He became master of the royal mint and favourite of the King, carried out various diplomatic missions, was ennobled, and acquired vast estates. In 1449 and 1450 he made very large loans to the King. The following year he was thrown into prison on fanciful charges and condemned to forfeit his possessions. In 1454 he escaped and fled to Rome, where the Pope placed him in command of a small fleet to fight the Turks; after ravaging the coasts of Asia Minor, he died in Chios in 1456.

p 258
(37)
The histories of the great mercantile families of the later Middle Ages, such as the Medici of Florence or the Fugger of Augsburg, are far too complex to be touched on here, but something may perhaps be said of a junior member of one of these firms. The Florentine Tommaso Portinari joined the Medici bank in Flanders as a young office-boy in 1439 and remained there for the rest of his working career, apart from holidays and business visits to Italy. He became manager of the Bruges branch of the firm, but at the same time he was a personal friend of Charles the Bold, Duke of Burgundy, a member of his council and, in addition, a great patron of Flemish art. In 1469, Piero de' Medici, then head of the firm, warned him of the dangers of dealing with princes, but after Piero's death Portinari persuaded Lorenzo de' Medici to sanction very large loans to the Duke. As a result, when the Duke was killed at Nancy in 1477, the Bruges branch suffered severe financial losses, and it became necessary to wind it up in 1480.

p 260
(42)
p 260
(43)
f 3
Among English industrialists and merchants some of the best known are the great clothiers and wool-merchants of the later Middle Ages, men such as William Grevel of Chipping Campden, Thomas Spring of Lavenham and Thomas Paycocke of Coggeshall. The papers of the Cely and the Stonor families reveal the life of the wool-merchant in intimate detail, not only in its commercial but also in its human aspects. The letters of Thomas Betson among the Stonor correspondence, and especially one which he addressed to his young betrothed, then about thirteen, in 1476, are among the most delightful letters in the English language, affording a glimpse of a mediaeval merchant, not as an historical figure, but as an entirely natural and charming human being.

The Mediaeval Art Market

This is not the place to discuss the fine arts. Important works of painting and sculpture were always produced to order and did not normally pass through commercial channels, though the trade in art and antiquities did sometimes flourish around the great connoisseurs of the later Middle Ages, such as Jean, duc de Berry, just as the trade in religious relics had flourished around the pious princes and prelates of an earlier period. There was also a certain production of low-grade paintings for trade purposes, like the cheap religious pictures in which Datini dealt at Avignon, and this class of imagery moved decisively into the industrial sphere with the introduction of printing for religious pictures and playing-cards from the late 14th century onwards. Similarly, book-production and distribution became increasingly commercialized when manuscript was replaced by printing in the 15th century. The main centres of production for printed books and pictures were in Germany, Italy and the Low Countries.

p 255
(27)
A good deal of small sculpture was produced on a commercial scale. The most notable examples among stone-sculptures are the English alabaster religious figures and reliefs of the 14th and 15th centuries, which were in England largely destroyed at the Reformation, but which survive elsewhere. Small objects of ivory or bone were exquisitely carved with figure subjects: little religious figures, tiny folding altar-pieces with Biblical scenes in relief, and rosaries, all intended for private devotions. There are also dagger-hilts, gaming pieces for chess and draughts, boxes and caskets, combs, mirrorcases and other toilet requisites, with charming reliefs of courtly and romantic subjects. Such carvings were produced in many countries, but the main centres of production for international trade were France, particularly Paris, in the 13th and 14th centuries, and northern Italy in the 14th and 15th centuries. There was also a considerable commercial production of small objects, boxes, chests and other furnishings, carved in wood, furnished with reliefs in gesso, or ornamented with tracery in metalwork of various kinds.

p 254
(25)
Large-scale metalwork, decorated armour, and costly goldsmith's work were generally, like important sculpture and painting, made to order. A great deal of minor metalwork was produced for general sale and trade. There was a considerable international trade, for example, in arms and armour of ordinary qualities, from the main production centres in Germany and northern Italy. Germany, Lorraine and Flanders produced for export much minor metalwork in bronze and brass, of which many examples still survive—ewers, often in fanciful forms of men or monsters, dishes engraved or embossed with figure subjects, candlesticks and chandeliers. English churches contain a number of engraved sepulchral brasses imported from the Continent as well as many, even nobler, of home production. Engraved and damascened metalwork with Islamic ornament was imported to Europe from the Near East, and at the end of the Middle Ages was extensively imitated in northern Italy, especially at Venice and Milan. Enamelling on metal was practised in many centres, but from the 12th to the 14th century Limoges had an extensive export trade in *champlevé* enamels on copper, with figure subjects and armorial decoration; the numerous extant examples include boxes, bowls, candlesticks, a variety of ecclesiastical requisites, and even tombs, such as that of William of Valence in Westminster Abbey. Limoges lost its supremacy in the 14th century, when the *champlevé* technique was generally superseded by the exquisite effects of translucent enamels over reliefs in silver or gold, but regained it once more in the late 15th century with the advent of the less elaborate technique of painting enamels on copper. Goldsmiths and silversmiths were active in all countries; besides examples of specially commissioned plate, their smaller commercial products—spoons, rings, brooches, and other jewellery and trinkets—survive in considerable numbers. There was an international trade in gems, many of which came from Asia; the Polo family, for example, specialized in this.

Mediaeval bricks and plain tiles survive in great numbers, but are of no special interest. Decorated floor-tiles, likewise numerous, were made in many parts of northern Europe, with inlaid or relief patterns produced from stamps; the chapter house of Westminster Abbey still has its original floor of inlaid tiles. Near Eastern techniques of painting patterns on tin-glazed tiles were adopted in Spain and Italy, and examples were being exported at the end of the Middle Ages; the mayor's chapel at Bristol still has its 16th-century pavement of Spanish *cuenca* tiles. Lead-glazed earthenware vessels, sometimes with simple relief ornament, were made in many parts of Europe. More refined wares were sometimes imported from the East. A number of Far Eastern celadon and blue-and-white vessels have survived with European gold and silver mounts; Near Eastern vessels with painted lustre or polychrome ornament on white tin-glazed backgrounds are found encrusted in the façades of Italian churches. The Near Eastern techniques were adopted in the Hispano-Moresque lustreware of the 14th and 15th centuries, much of which was made in the neighbourhood of Valencia, and in the still more familiar Italian *maiolica*, made in Florence, Faenza and other towns from the 15th century onwards. Plain window glass, stained glass windows and simple glass vessels were made in a number of European centres, but vessels of glass with enamelled ornament were imported from the Near East until the 15th century, when Venetian production of fine enamelled glassware became important. A Syrian enamelled glass in the Victoria and Albert Museum is known to have been in England from an early date, and still has the tooled leather case which was made for it in mediaeval times. The production of such

p 254
(26)

containers and boxes, of incised and moulded leather (*cuir bouilli*), was another industrial art which was widespread in mediaeval Europe.

Woollen tapestry-hangings with armorial, scriptural or mythological subjects were made in many places, but the principal centres of the industry were Paris, in the 14th century, Arras and Tournai in the 15th century, and Brussels in the 16th century. The set of *Hunts* formerly at Hardwick Hall are examples of Flemish tapestries which have probably been in England since the 15th century, and the remnants of Henry VIII's vast collection of Flemish tapestries may still be seen at Hampton Court. Embroideries in silk and gold thread were made in many places; London, Florence, Venice and various Netherland towns are among the internationally celebrated centres. The larger and more costly pieces of embroidery, as of tapestry, were made to order, but smaller pieces, such as orphreys for ecclesiastical vestments, circulated in trade; embroidered orphreys from Lucca were among Datini's more valuable goods at Avignon. The European weaving industry was primarily concerned with plain, unpatterned woollen and linen cloths. Silk textiles, woven with repeating patterns on the draw-loom, were imported from far afield. Some were made in China. Others were woven in central Asia; the funerary garments found in the tomb of Can Grande della Scala, Lord of Verona, who died in 1329, were almost entirely composed of central Asian silks, while in the tomb of Duke Rudolf of Austria, who died in 1365, was a silk woven with the name of the Persian ruler Abu Said. Still more were imported from Byzantium, and from the Islamic states of the Near East and Spain. These silk textiles conveyed remote artistic influences to mediaeval Europe. The strange fauna of early Islamic silks, inherited, by way of Sassanian Persia, from ancient Mesopotamia, inspired the sculptors of Romanesque churches. Silks imported in the 14th century brought Chinese ornament to Europe. It was not until the late 14th or 15th century that the Italian silk industry, at Lucca, Florence, Genoa and Venice, was sufficiently strong to meet most of the European demand for patterned silks and to evolve a recognizably European style of woven ornament. At the end of the Middle Ages, Flemish linen weavers employed this ornamental style, together with armorial and pictorial subjects, in fine linen damask tablecloths and napkins, some of which were made for export to England. Another group of textiles which familiarized exotic Oriental motifs in European domestic settings were the woollen pile carpets, with patterns of animals and interlace imported from the Near East.

Commercial Patronage

Many mediaeval craftsmen, or heads of industrial workshops, were necessarily, from the very nature of their work, artists and designers. This was true, in varying degrees, of carvers, goldsmiths, potters and others. Some enterprises, such as those producing painted tiles, *maiolica* or enamelled glass, employed teams of journeymen painters. Others, such as those producing patterned silks and velvets, required specialist designers, who understood and were capable of influencing public taste for these fashionable wares, and were at the same time acquainted with the technical capabilities of machines such as the draw-loom. Workshops producing fine embroideries used designs supplied by professional painters, sometimes painters of the first rank; extant examples include pieces designed by Paolo Veneziano, Pollaiuolo, Botticelli and other leading artists of the 14th and 15th centuries. The same

p 251 (18)

is true of the tapestry workshops; the famous Apocalypse tapestries at Angers were designed by Jean de Bondolf, one of the leading painters of Paris, who planned them after careful consideration of earlier illustration of the same subjects in illuminated manuscripts.

This type of employment or patronage of artists was indispensable to the production of the industrial arts. Another type of patronage exercised by industrialists and merchants, the commissioning of buildings and other works for their own corporate or private use, reveals more of their character, as individuals and as a class. A comprehensive study of this type of patronage would extend to many volumes and cover almost every field of later mediaeval art, for, unlike the art of the earlier Middle Ages, which

p 147 (29)

The municipal seal of Ypres, one of the three great trading centres of Flanders during the 14th century (the other two being Bruges and Ghent). Prominent in the design is the famous Cloth Hall, begun in 1201 and completed about a century later. It was over 450 feet in length and survived intact until the First World War, when it was totally destroyed. (11)

was chiefly patronized by princes, by feudal nobles and by the ecclesiastical foundations which they endowed, art from the 13th and 14th century onwards was increasingly patronized by the mercantile class and paid for out of the profits of trade. This was pre-eminently true of Italian art, which was almost entirely produced for and financed by industrialists, merchants and bankers.

There was a tendency to mark the increased wealth and prestige of trade by the erection of fine commercial buildings, often more costly and elaborate than was necessary for their practical purpose. Handsome stone porticoes were built, to provide shelter in open market-places, sometimes as independent structures, as in the market-crosses at Chichester and Salisbury or the 14th-century *Loggie* at Bologna and Florence, and at other times incorporated in town halls and other public or private buildings, as in the market-square of Montpazier in the Dordogne, and in most of the other *villes neuves*. Sumptuous enclosed halls were also built for commercial purposes, such as the elegant 15th-century exchange at Valencia, with its slender twisted columns. The various gilds and associations of merchants built splendid meeting halls and warehouses, such as the Guildhalls of York and London, the *fondachi* of Venice, and those supreme expressions of commercial wealth and pride, the gigantic cloth-halls of Bruges and Ypres. To express their political power, as the governing bodies of great and prosperous towns, the merchant communities built with even greater pomp: witness the massive town-halls of Italy, the imposing town-halls of Germany, the ornate town-halls of Flanders, and the superb palaces of the great civic dignitaries, as in Florence, and, above all, the Doge's Palace in Venice. Many of these splendid buildings were decorated with fine sculptures and paintings, such as the frescoes of Simone Martini and Ambrogio Lorenzetti in the Palazzo Pubblico of Siena, and they were naturally equipped with an appropriate wealth of furnishings and plate.

p 261 (48)

p 261 (47)

f 11

p 261 (46)

p 261 (49)

p 103 (74)

p 18 (13)

p 293 (24)

Much of the ecclesiastical building of the later Middle Ages was also financed by merchants. This is obvious in the case of independent mercantile towns such as Florence and Venice, but it is equally true of the kingdoms of northern Europe. East Anglia, the Cotswolds and south-west England are full of churches built wholly or in part from the donations of wealthy merchants of wool or woollen cloth. On some of these churches are carved the merchant's personal mark, which was painted on his bales of merchandise, or, as at Tiverton, the ships which had brought him his fortune. The interior fittings of the churches, such as carved and painted screens, were likewise often the gift of merchants. So, too, were the paintings. Many of those in Italian churches were commissioned by merchants; for instance, in Florence, the fresco-cycles of Giotto in the chapels of the Bardi and Peruzzi families in Sta Croce, or that of Ghirlandaio in Sta Trinità, painted for Francesco Sassetti, general manager of the Medici bank. The gilds (themselves religious confraternities) often participated in religious functions as corporate bodies and many merchants also belonged to religious brotherhoods for prayer and mutual assistance. Among the monuments of this corporate religious activity are the richly decorated building in Florence known as Orsanmichele, and the sumptuously embroidered palls with which the livery companies of the City of London honoured the body of a deceased member at his funeral service. From the 14th century onwards, the tombs of merchants began to vie in splendour with those of princes, nobles and bishops and to proclaim in plain terms the dignity of the merchant's calling. Only the greatest merchants, however, allowed themselves the luxury of effigies. Most English merchants were content with monumental brasses, and merchants' wills not infrequently include the prudent injunction that their funerals should be modest, without undue expense.

p 103
(73)
The great merchants proclaimed their wealth and power not only in public buildings and in churches, but also in their private houses. Some of the town-houses of Italy were indeed palaces, sometimes exquisitely graceful, like the Palazzo Pisani or the Ca' d'Oro in Venice, sometimes severe and massive, like the Palazzo Medici or the Palazzo Pitti in Florence. There are also many fine

p 260
(42, 43)
town-houses on a much smaller scale in northern Europe, such as William Grevel's house at Chipping Campden or Thomas Paycocke's timbered house at Coggeshall. Some of the more successful merchants also acquired country estates and built country houses; Stokesay Castle, for example, was bought and enlarged by the wool merchant Lawrence of Ludlow, and the great hall of Penshurst was built by Sir John Poultney, four times Lord Mayor of London. Large and handsome though these northern European houses are, they lack the palatial style of the Italian examples. The

p 260
(44, 45)
notable exception to this is the splendid house of Jacques Coeur at Bourges, with its seven spiral staircases, and its wealth of internal and external sculpture, including the owner's proud device, *A vaillants coeurs rien impossible*. But such ostentation, permissible for the commercial oligarchs of Italy, was dangerous for the subject of a northern sovereign; Jacques Coeur had overreached himself, and was about to fall.

These great houses were furnished with every comfort and luxury, including hangings, pictures and plate. It is interesting to note in this connection how eclectic was the personal taste of the great merchants and bankers. The Medici palace in Florence was hung with Flemish tapestries; the Medici agents in Flanders were connoisseurs of Flemish painting. Hugo van der Goes painted a

p 258
(37)
great altar-piece, for Tommaso Portinari. Memlinc worked both for Portinari and for his colleague, Jacopo Tani; the altarpiece which he painted for Tani was despatched to Florence by sea, captured by a Hanseatic ship (Florence and the Hanse were at war), and carried off as booty to Danzig. An English example of such patronage of foreign artists is the triptych painted for the Bristol merchant, Paul Withypole, by the Venetian Antonio de Solario.

An interesting development in the history of painting is the appearance, from the 1430s onwards, of portraits of merchants. Independent portraits of earlier date (as distinct from portraits of donors in religious paintings) invariably represent persons of royal blood; now the merchant, too, wished to hang a record of his appearance in his own house. Italian merchants working in northern Europe were among the earliest clients for these portraits. One of the most fascinating examples is the marriage por-

p 258
(36)
trait by Jan van Eyck in the National Gallery, which shows Giovanni Arnolfini, a merchant of Lucca resident in Bruges, and his wife Giovanna Cenami, daughter of a Lucchese merchant living in Paris, standing in the bedroom of their home. But perhaps the finest of all these merchant-portraits of the late Middle Ages is

Holbein's portrait of Georg Gisze, a Hanseatic merchant from
p 259
(40)
Danzig. Gisze is shown in his London office, behind his office-table, which is covered with a Turkish rug; at his elbow is a bunch of flowers in a glass vase, and all about him, exquisitely painted, are the impedimenta of his profession—his money, scales, keys, business letters, writing materials, seals and ledgers. No king with his regalia could be more nobly portrayed.

The Merchant in Society

It would be idle to make far-reaching generalizations concerning the personal character of mediaeval merchants and industrialists. They included men of many types, some pleasant, such as Thomas Betson, some perhaps less pleasant, such as Francesco Datini. Yet the fact that they all passed their lives in the common pursuit of profit naturally produced certain general tendencies and effects. These men often drove hard bargains; many indulged in sharp practice; a few were ruthless criminals, guilty of piracy and murder. Most, however, were restrained from cynicism and materialism by a sincere and profound piety. Their worldly success, coupled with ecclesiastical condemnation of certain kinds of commercial profit, perhaps made them more than usually sensitive concerning the fate of their own immortal souls. But the striking feature of their piety is their sympathetic understanding of the needs of others. Symptomatic of this were their confraternities, devoted to prayer for their departed members and to practical assistance for the impoverished living. All this is abundantly clear in their wills, which include generous bequests for new communal buildings for their fellow-merchants, for schools, hospitals and almshouses, and for the relief of the poor. Men such as Datini and Richard Whittington, thrice Lord Mayor of London, gave deep thought to the disposal of their vast fortunes on sensible, business-like projects which would afford the maximum benefit to the community. The Whittington Hospital is still administered by the Mercers' Company of which he was a member.

Merchants and industrialists were necessarily open-minded and inventive, rather than conservative. The profit-motive led them to improve their products, to devise new technical processes, to deal in new commodities, to explore fresh markets in strange countries. In these ways they conferred a general benefit on mankind by increasing the comforts and commodities of life and, though they were not often men of learning, they extended the frontiers of human knowledge, particularly in the fields of manufacturing techniques, economics and geography. Although the pursuit of profit often led to bitter competition and sometimes to commercial wars, the habit of foreign travel gave many merchants a broader outlook and a tolerance of foreign ways. Marco Polo examined the civilization of the Far East with a cool, appraising eye, and did not fail to recognize that, in some respects, it was superior to that of Europe.

Merchants and craftsmen were the mobile element in a mainly static environment. Not only did they move from place to place, traversing the known world from end to end, but they also broke through the existing class-structure of society, undermining the established power-patterns of church and state with the aid of new powers—the power of capital and the power of civic authority. Naturally, they remained men of their own time. Thus some successful merchants concluded their careers by assimilating themselves into the older patterns: in the earlier Middle Ages by entering the cloister, and later by joining the ranks of the landed gentry. But they were also confident of their own emergent powers, and strong in the knowledge that even kings must depend upon them. This confidence they expressed in the greater dignity and refinement of their private lives and in the more than regal pomp of their civic ceremonies. Some of the more perceptive among them may perhaps have realized that they were marking out the future of mankind. For there can be no doubt that the society of post-mediaeval and modern times owes its greatest debt, and is most nearly akin, not to the princes, nobles and churchmen of the Middle Ages, but to the craftsmen, the bankers and the merchants.

VIII THE RISE OF THE ARTIST

The changing status of the Craftsman

ANDREW MARTINDALE

'Whoever will contribute both care and concern

is able to attain a capacity for all arts and skills . . .

What God has given man as an inheritance, let man strive

and work with all eagerness to attain.'

THEOPHILUS, 'CONCERNING THE VARIOUS ARTS'

Art has always been made by artists,

that is, by trained professionals who paint or carve or build for a living. That was as true in the Middle Ages as it is now. What has changed is the way in which the activity of the artist is understood and valued.

In the 13th century he was an artisan, on the same social and intellectual level as the armourer, the shipbuilder, the tailor or the cook. By the end of the 15th he was a man with a divine gift, or at least a man whose inspiration went beyond mere skill. The change was twofold. First his social status improved. As taste became more self-conscious, the outstanding craftsman was competed for by both secular and ecclesiastical patrons. He came to have an honoured place at court; he left the ranks of the interior decorators and furniture-makers and approached those of the poets and the scholars. But still his essential role had not changed; he was still the servant of his patron, doing exactly and only what he was told. The myth of the 'Great Artist' had not been born.

That came with the Renaissance, the product of the humanists' rediscovery of classical attitudes and of the enlightened patronage of men like the Medici and the 15th-century popes. Art was now seen as the unique expression of the artist's genius and the artist himself—the man, his personality, his private life—became of absorbing interest (as it still is). Consequently art since the Renaissance is named and documented, whereas that of the Middle Ages is mostly anonymous. But it is a change that concerns patrons, public and appreciation: it should not be read back into the art itself. A work of the 11th century is just as much the expression of one man's personality as a work of the 16th.

It is interesting to watch those artists who belong, as it were, to both worlds. The German sculptor Adam Krafft, for instance, was born about 1455–60 and died in 1508. Almost the whole of his life was spent in his native Nuremberg, apparently unremarked by the outside world. In the eyes of his contemporaries, and it seems in his own eyes, he was simply an honest, competent and successful workman. By a series of virtuoso works in the ela-

borate Late Gothic style of northern Europe, culminating in the huge Schreyer tomb in the church of St Sebald, Krafft had become accepted as Nuremberg's leading sculptor. In 1493 he was commissioned to make a Tabernacle for St Lorenz, and the original contract, between Krafft and his patron Hans Imhof the Elder, still survives. The Tabernacle, or *Sakramentshaus*, was to be a tall stone structure, rather like an openwork spire. The parts that could most easily be seen were to be made with particular care, the higher stages still skilfully and carefully but not so intricately, and the topmost part only as well as necessary. Krafft was to employ three assistants, who should not be put to any other work, and would be paid 700 guilders. The final account was settled on St Barbara's Day (December 4th), 1495 and Krafft received a bonus of 70 guilders.

The Tabernacle is over 60 feet high and stands on the north side of the choir, with the top leaning over to follow the bend of the vault. As stipulated in the contract, the upper parts are not carved with the same precision as the lower. At the base, supporting the whole structure, Krafft carved himself (opposite) and his assistants, in their working clothes and holding the tools of their trade.

So far Krafft would seem to be a typical mediaeval craftsman. Yet within 50 years he is being given the 'Renaissance' treatment. The public has become interested in him as a man, as a 'Great Artist'; his name is remembered, his works are sought after and admired. In 1547 Johann Neudörfer wrote his *Account of the most Eminent Artists and Craftsman who have lived in Nuremberg*, and we read: 'What a skilful, industrious and ingenious stonemason Master Adam was is shown by the Tabernacle in the church of St Lorenz, . . . under which he has first of all portrayed himself as though he were alive, and behind him his two assistants . . . He was just as ready to work with his left hand as with his right, but he had a marvellous way of always employing a coarse, strong peasant boy as his assistant . . .' (1)

The artist's status probably owed something to the belief that St Luke had been a painter and that Our Lady herself had sat to him for her portrait. The tradition goes back at least to the 6th century; there were in fact icons of the Virgin and Child which were attributed to him—one of them still exists in the church of Sta Maria Aracoeli in Rome. Naturally St Luke became the patron saint of artists and is often represented painting the Virgin's portrait. This miniature is Flemish and dates from the late 15th century; the palette, brush and manner of work have hardly changed. (2)

'Gislebertus made this' – '*Gislebertus hoc fecit*' is the laconic inscription beneath one of the greatest of mediaeval masterpieces, the tympanum of Autun Cathedral. It shows Christ in Judgment, with the damned being dragged to Hell on one side and the saved led to Heaven on the other. Gislebertus, or Gilbert, was a man with a dramatic and individual style—as definite a personality as any Renaissance artist. He must have worked at Autun for about ten years, 1125–35, carving not only this tympanum but also most of the capitals throughout the church. His reputation was clearly already very high for the bishop and chapter to have allowed his name to be placed in this very prominent position. It seems likely that he had worked at Cluny, possibly as one of the chief assistants of the master there. (5)

Legendary artists of mythology and those scarcely less legendary of Greece and Rome enjoyed lasting renown, although it was not until the Renaissance that artists themselves began to be proud of the fact. Left centre: Pygmalion, from a *Roman de la Rose* of about 1470: he kneels before the statue he has made – '*Comme Pygmalion requiert mercy a son ymage.*' Below left: a 15th-century illustration to Boccacio based on a passage in Pliny's *Natural History*: 'Jaia of Cyzicus, who never married, painted pictures with the brush at Rome, chiefly portraits of women ... and also a portrait of herself, done with a looking glass.' Both these miniatures, in spite of their fictional subjects, give realistic pictures of the mediaeval artists' materials. (3, 4)

Routine jobs for the artist included painting frescoes (above) and making incised tombs (below). A certain amount of work was also produced in monastic studios (bottom). (6,7,8)

Self-portraits indicate a new self-esteem. Top: Lorenzo Ghiberti (c. 1445) – still mediaeval in many ways, modern in others – 'I did not join in the chase after money but occupied myself with Art.' Above: Nicholas Gerhaert of Leyden (1467), from the former carved stalls of Strasbourg. (9,10)

Philip the Good, Duke of Burgundy (above) is presented with the *Chroniques de Hainault* by its 'publisher' Simon Nockart. Philip's young son stands beside him, while on the left is another outstanding patron (of Jan van Eyck among others), Chancellor Nicolas Rolin. The sovereign Duchy of Burgundy in the 15th century was the equal of any kingdom in Europe. Philip the Good (reigned 1419–67) won his nickname by his equable government and care for justice. He spent lavishly on the arts, encouraging not only painting but poetry and music also, and founded the University of Dôle. (11)

The patrons, royal, ecclesiastical or civic, exercised direct control over the artists. Major works were produced to order, to satisfy a specific demand. The bulk of it was paid for by churches or private individuals, but the higher the rank of the patron, the greater was his influence upon the arts.

The Emperor Charles IV (left) created a centre of patronage at his new capital of Prague. This panel is by the imperial court painter Theodoric (c. 1370). Charles built the Cathedral of Karlstein and founded the first Central European university. (12)

Charles V of France (above) receives an illuminated Bible from one of his courtiers, Jean de Vaudetar. The painter was Jean Bandol, *pictor regis* at a salary of 200 livres *per annum*. Charles wears the cap and gown of a Paris Master of Arts. (13)

Robert of Anjou (above) ruled the Kingdom of Naples for thirty-four years (1309–43) and was the patron of no less an artist than Giotto, with whom he is said to have been on terms of personal friendship. This portrait shows him in about 1340. (14)

Richard II (left) was one of the most cultured of English kings, a quality that exposed him to accusations of extravagance. This fine image from the Wilton Diptych was painted in England but the nationality of the artist is uncertain. (15)

Jean, duc de Berry, commissioned many splendid manuscripts, none more famous than the Limbourg brothers' *Très Riches Heures.* In this scene he sits, in fur cap and blue robe, surrounded by the luxury in which he delighted. (16)

'Contract for painting an altarpiece for Dominus Jean de Montignac, priest.' This fascinating document was discovered in 1810. The parties are Enguerrand Quarton, painter, and Jean de Montignac, a Carthusian priest at the Chartreuse of Villeneuve-lès-Avignon. The picture, now known as the 'Coronation of the Virgin', was for his own church and the date is April 25th, 1453.

The contract stipulates the subject matter in the most minute detail, and although the painter did retain some freedom of interpretation it is obvious that in cases like this (where the patron was a theologian with definite ideas of his own) little was left to the artist's initiative. What follows is an abridged version of the contract:

'There should be the form of Paradise, and in that Paradise should be the Holy Trinity, and there should not be any difference between the Father and the Son; and the Holy Ghost in the form of a dove; and Our Lady in front as it will seem best to Master Enguerrand; the Holy Trinity will place the crown on the head of Our Lady.

'At the side of Our Lady should be the Angel Gabriel, and on the other side St Michael. On the right side should be St Peter and St Paul with other apostles; on the other side, St John the Baptist with other patriarchs and prophets. [The names of the saints to be shown on each side are then listed.]

'On the side of the setting sun should be the church of St Peter of Rome, a part of the walls of Rome, the castle of St Angelo and a bridge over the Tiber; in the said city the church of the Holy Cross where St Gregory celebrated mass. Outside Rome, the Tiber will be shown entering the sea. On the other side of the sea, will be a part of Jerusalem; first the Mount of Olives, where will be the cross of Our Lord, and at the foot of that will be a praying Carthusian. On the right side, a church where the tomb of Our Lady is.

'On the second mountain will be Moses with his sheep, and Our Lord in the form of fire in the middle of a bush.

'On the right part will be Purgatory where the angels lead those joyous on seeing that they will go to Paradise. On the left side will be Hell. In Purgatory and Hell will be all the estates according to the judgment of Master Enguerrand.

'The said Master Enguerrand will show all his knowledge and skill in the Holy Trinity and in the Blessed Virgin Mary, and will be governed by his conscience.'

Quarton was given a year to finish his work and the fee was 120 florins. (17)

Sculptors' names have occasionally survived from inscriptions. Wiligelmo of Modena (c. 1100), whose relief of the Creation of Eve is shown below, describes himself without undue modesty as 'worthy of honours'. Signed works by Gislebertus of Autun (c. 1130) and Antelami of Parma (c. 1180) have already been seen on pp. 284 and 253. (18)

A Florentine workshop of the early 15th century (below): Nanni di Banco, who carved this panel for the church of Orsanmichele was born about 1384, became *capomaestro* at Florence Cathedral in 1414 and lived long enough to collaborate with Donatello and Brunelleschi. Renaissance style is already evident here. (19)

The 'St-Denis' of Burgundy was to be Philippe le Hardi's Chartreuse de Champmol, just outside Dijon. It was begun in 1383; successive dukes continued the work. The architect was Drouet de Dammartin, and a great artist, Claus Sluter, made the sculpture for the chapel and for the 'Calvary' in the cloister. This stood over a well, and was mounted on a high base (left) which is now almost all that survives. Here Sluter carved monumental figures of prophets which almost foreshadow Michelangelo. The three seen here are Zachariah, Daniel and Isaiah. (20)

To restore the ancient palace at Poitiers, burnt down by the English, Jean duc de Berry employed Guy de Dammartin, the brother of Drouet. At the end of the great hall Guy placed statues of the Duke and his Duchess Jeanne (above) a beautiful image of courtliness and grace. (21)

From Rome in 1308 to the Angevin court at Naples came the painter Pietro Cavallini. (Simone Martini of Siena followed him in about 1317 and Giotto of Florence in 1329.) Cavallini was given an annual salary and a house but seems to have had no official position. This head of St James is from his fresco at Sta Cecilia in Rome and was painted in about 1293. (22)

Among the painters working at Champmol was Henri Bellechose, nominally the Duke's *valet de chambre*. His 'Martyrdom of St Denis' (below) was originally commissioned from his predecessor Jean Malouel. It was finished in 1416. On the left Christ visits St Denis in prison and gives him the Last Sacrament; in the centre the Crucifixion; on the right his execution with two other martyrs. (23)

Republican Siena placed itself under the divine protection of the Virgin, thus combining democratic freedom with the loyal sentiments of a monarchy. In the main chamber of the Palazzo Pubblico the Commune decided to display the 'court' of the Virgin, the Maestà (opposite), with inscriptions dedicating the city to her, praying for her favour and setting forth the principles of the just state. (In the next room are Lorenzetti's Good and Bad Government frescoes; see p. 18.) To paint it they commissioned the young Sienese artist Simone Martini, then about 30 years old. The scheme of the picture was no doubt settled by the authorities. The Virgin, sitting on an elaborate Gothic throne and wearing a diadem, presents the Child Jesus to her own city of Siena. At her feet angels offer bowls of flowers while a host of saints surrounds her. (24)

Fold out ▶

The wings of the altarpiece closed over it (see inside fold-out), leaving a large blank surface exactly matching the main section in the centre. To paint this, and also to colour and gild the reliefs inside, the Duke sent the whole altar from Termonde to Ypres, to his favourite painter, Melchior Broederlam. It was finished in 1399, transported to Dijon and installed at Champmol. Broederlam's two panels were awkwardly shaped, and he had to fill them with four scenes—the Annunciation, Visitation, Presentation in the Temple and Flight into Egypt. The last two are shown here. A tower and a mountaintop occupy the upper spaces. The landscape scene especially marks a new step towards naturalism, with its receding distances and the earthy realism of the peasant St Joseph. (26)

For the altar of the Chartreuse de Champmol Philippe le Hardi went to a sculptor of Termonde, in Flanders. He had been impressed by two retables carved by Jacques de Baerze; now he commissioned him to make copies. Part of the best known is shown here. On each side of the main section, which consisted of the Adoration, the Passion and the Entombment in high relief, were hinged wings, each covering half of the centre-piece. This page and overleaf reproduces the right-hand wing. (The central section may be imagined occupying the two pages opposite; the left-hand wing would then require another fold-out meeting this one in the centre.) The saints are St Anthony, St Margaret, a royal saint, St Barbara and St Judoc. In 1391 the altarpiece was finished but for the colouring. (25)

'Master Honoré', the illuminator, lived in 1292 in Paris, in his own house in the Rue Erembourc-de-Brie; the ground-rent was one *denier* and he paid 10 *sous* in tax. Four years later, we learn from the records, he received 107 *livres* 10 *sous* from the King for a Breviary. At this time the copying and painting of manuscripts was ceasing to be a monastic monopoly and becoming a well-paid secular profession. For a really sumptuous book the talents of several artists would be required. This miniature (left) is from *La Somme le Roy*, a treatise on the Virtues and Vices produced in Honoré's studio for King Philip III of France in 1279. It shows four of the Virtues: Prudence (instructing three girls), Temperance (admonishing a girl about to accept a cup from a kneeling man), Fortitude (standing on the river Tigris) and Justice. (27)

'International Gothic' is the name given to a late phase of ▶ mediaeval painting from about 1350 to 1420. A common style spread across Europe, just as the artists themselves travelled, from Hungary to Spain and from Flanders to Italy. The colours of this international style are bright, the backgrounds dark and lush, men and women noble, and the general effect decorative and full of charm. Some of the best examples are at Avignon, where the popes lived during their exile from Rome. In 1343 Pope Clement VI commissioned Matteo Giovanetti of Viterbo to decorate part of his palace. The frescoes were continued by French artists whose work blends effortlessly with that of the Italians, like a rich tapestry. This detail (opposite) in the *Chambre du Cerf* shows two falconers in the forest. (30)

'Hugh the Painter' – *Hugo pictor* (above)—was the first manuscript painter, as distinct from a scribe like Eadwine of Canterbury (see p. 54) who executed both text and pictures, to have left his self-portrait. It comes from Jerome's Commentary on Isaiah and dates from about 1100. Hugo, in monk's habit, dips a pen into an inkhorn with one hand and in the other holds a knife to resharpen the quill when necessary. Above him is his name with the inscription, *Imago pictoris et illuminatoris huius operis.* (29)

Jacquemart de Hesdin or 'de Odin' was probably of Flemish origin. He worked for the duc de Berry both as a manuscript illuminator and as a decorator in his palace at Poitiers. This miniature (left) from the *Très Belles Heures* of Brussels (not to be confused with the *Très Riches Heures*) was probably painted about 1400. An inventory of 1402 calls the Hours '*très richement enluminées et ystoriées de la main de Jacquemart de Odin.*' The miniatures in the book, however, are by two different hands, and it has been suggested that this one is by André Beauneveu, who was also working for the Duke at about the same time. The Virgin sits on an elaborate Gothic throne while the Child writes on a scroll—His answer to the Duke's prayer, who kneels in supplication on the page facing it. (28)

Most of the sketchbooks that have survived from the Middle Ages were studio properties, pattern-books helpful as sources for the various commissions that the *atelier* might be given. Among the most interesting is one bearing the inscription *Johininus de Grassis designavit*. Giovannino de' Grassi was a painter, miniaturist, architect and sculptor who is known to have worked on Milan Cathedral (1380–91) and the Certosa di Pavia (1396) and to have died in 1398. He became the head of a busy studio, where the sketchbook was obviously kept, accumulating additional designs by later hands. It contains a variety of subjects—beautifully observed animals and birds (right), a fantastic alphabet of grotesques (bottom right) and studies for drapery. One of the most intriguing drawings is the group of dogs savaging a boar which is identical with the group in the Limbourg brothers' *Très Riches Heures* (see p. 139). It seems probable that neither is the original source of the design, but it does serve as an example of the way artists picked up whatever they found interesting and stored it away in their sketchbooks. (32–35)

Before a mediaeval fresco could be begun the design had to be sketched out on the wall in a reddish brown ochre called *sinopia*. This was then covered, a small area at a time, with wet plaster on which the fresco was painted. If the work is damaged or removed for restoration, the *sinopia* is revealed underneath. This one (above) underlies the head of the old hermit in the Pisa Triumph of Death, reproduced on p. 206. (31)

Animals and birds similar to those recorded in an English sketchbook of about 1400 (above) found their way on to embroidered copes in *opus Anglicanum* as well as into miniatures and wall-paintings. It was clearly an *atelier* book, used by men employed on different arts. The sketches are not life-studies (sometimes the animals are heraldic) but they have a lively realism. (36, 37)

The horse's head probably by Pisanello (below) already shows the sketchbook being used in the modern way—to make vivid, spontaneous transcripts from life to be worked up later into finished pictures. Pisanello (1395–1455), in many ways a typical International Gothic artist, is no longer content with a record of tried and accepted ideas. (38)

Polite society in a painter's studio at Ghent: this miniature pretends to illustrate the story of Zeuxis but every detail belongs to 15th-century Flanders where it was painted. Cicero gives the following version of the traditional tale in his *Rhetoric*: a town in southern Italy invited Zeuxis, the most famous painter in Greece, to paint a portrait of Helen, the perfection of human beauty. Needing a model, he was shown first the schildren (top), then the young women (top right). He chose five of the fairest, 'not being able to find all the physical charms he sought in one person', and combined the best points of each in a single surpassing image. (39)

The changing status of the Craftsman

ANDREW MARTINDALE

Paris, like other capital cities, had its colonies of artists and craftsmen, usually congregated in districts according to their trade. Here a goldsmith of the early 14th century is seen through his open door from the street, at work on a cup. In front of him, on a shelf, stands one already finished. (1)

IT IS USUAL to write the history of art as it were from the top downwards. If however, one wishes to build up a balanced picture of the artist in mediaeval society, one cannot ignore the lower echelons of those producing art. Before the 15th century there is no evidence for any of the *mystique* which has since grown up around the Great Artist. Good artists were almost certainly regarded as superior craftsmen in a particular occupation; and any investigation of the place of the artist in society must take this attitude as a starting point. The artist was in the first place a craftsman, working perhaps in some busy, cosmopolitan centre where any one craftsman had to live alongside many other people practising different crafts or trades. From this point of view, almost any large mediaeval town would serve as a point of departure; and if our choice falls on Paris, this is chiefly on account of the convenient documentation.

'Those Craftsmen Working with their Hands'

In 1323 the French scholar Jean de Jandun wrote a treatise in praise of Paris. One chapter is headed 'Concerning the Manual Artificers', and it represents an educated man listing, in rather elaborate Latin, those crafts which he felt were an ornament to the city:

'We have also thought to add something concerning those craftsmen working with their hands, if it will not displease the reader to consider them. Here indeed you will find the most ingenious makers of all sorts of image, whether contrived in sculpture or in painting or in relief. Here too you will see the most cunning constructors of instruments of war... Again, you will discover men preparing most diligently clothing and ornaments.

'We are not ashamed to mention here the makers of bread...

f 1 nor yet the fashioners of metal vessels... The more intently the parchment makers, scribes, illuminators and bookbinders devote themselves in the service of wisdom to the decoration of their works, the more copiously do the delightful fountains of knowledge flow forth from that most profound source of all good things.'

This is a strange and apparently disjointed list. It clearly did not appear inappropriate to Jandun that painters should be praised almost in the same breath as the Parisian bread-shops; nor that in this short chapter, those supplying books to the university should rub shoulders with the armament or clothing manufacturers.

This general picture of the artist as one craftsman among many can be elaborated into something far more precise from the Parisian taxation lists. The earliest surviving list, which dates from 1292 and is therefore not very long before Jandun's description, gives a much more detailed picture of the artist working in a community. The number of declared artists was small. In 1292 there were nearly 15,200 taxpayers in Paris. Of these, only 33 said they were 'painters'; 24 said they were 'image-makers' and 13 'illuminators'. Understandably, most tradesmen and craftsmen made their living by providing the necessities of life. Over 350 made shoes, over 350 were concerned in the making of clothing. There were 214 furriers; 104 made *pâtisseries* and sweetmeats; 157 kept eating-houses and taverns; 120 were grocers.

Against each person in these lists is written his assessment for tax. Most mediaeval taxation of this variety was levied on an agreed valuation of a man's movable goods so that, although the key to the exact significance of these figures may now be lost, the individual amounts, taken collectively, should provide a sort of comparative table of opulence (or at least of *signes extérieurs de richesse*).

As occupations went, painting and image-making did not apparently open up vistas of immense wealth. The richest Parisians were, of course, the Lombard bankers and financiers. Amongst those, the highest individual tax liability was 114 *livres* 10 *sous*. Amongst tradesmen and craftsmen the most highly taxed (and therefore the most well-to-do) were two potters (19*l* and 7*l* 10*s*), two merchants of precious and semi-precious stones (10*l* and 7*l* 10*s*), two mercers (16*l* and 8*l*), and a considerable number of others paying between 5*l* and 10*l* tax. Only one painter (called Nicholas) reached this class (6*l*). Only two painters and one image-maker paid more than 1*l* tax, the majority paid 10*s* or less. About only one of the listed artists is anything definite known—that is, Master Honoré, the manuscript illuminator. He was the most distinguished book illuminator in Paris of the time. Some of the books which he produced for the royal court still survive, and by any standards he was an artist of great skill and technical mastery. Master Honoré, however, paid only 10*s* tax, which means that, unless (possibly with royal consent) he was practising tax evasion on some scale (there is, incidentally, no reason to suppose this), the property on which the tax was assessed cannot have been worth an enormous amount. Master Honoré was probably comfortably off since he possessed a servant. But, to judge from this general scale of taxation, only the one painter Nicholas would probably have been thought rich.

Trades and crafts in mediaeval towns tended to congregate in communities. This, too, is illustrated by these lists, which were drawn up by parishes and streets. Most of those people in Paris concerned in book production, including the majority of the manuscript illuminators, lived on the south bank, in the vicinity *f 3* of the university. On the other hand most of the painters and image-makers lived on the north bank, particularly in the three parishes of St-Germain-l'Auxerrois, St-Leu and St-Eustache which were at that date on the north-west perimeter of the city. But in fact there was a sprinkling of these trades throughout the city on the north bank. The painter Nicholas lived apart in the parish of St-Jean-en-Grève—a parish, it may be noted, which also contained the wealthiest scribe and two of the wealthiest masons.

Professional Conduct

Most mediaeval trades and crafts were organized on a gild basis within each city. Painters and sculptors were no exception. Many of the gild ordinances survive and, since the general aims of these associations were similar, it is not surprising that these separate sets of ordinances should have features in common. By the 14th century the principle aims of a gild were to protect the local craftsmen from unreasonable outside competition, to protect the local craftsmen from each other and to safeguard the quality of work produced by the members. To these protective measures were sometimes added charitable ones: enjoining the visitation of the sick and indigent members by those more fortunate, and also ensuring that members' funerals should be well attended. This last provision was prompted as much by *esprit de corps* as by any finer feeling of grief. It would have been unfitting that a member should go to his grave unmourned and without ceremony. Sometimes *esprit de corps* prompted further measures. The ordinances of the painters' gild of Siena, for instance, went to extraordinary lengths to ensure that the annual service on the festival of St Luke (the patron saint of artists) should be properly attended by the whole body of painters and apprentices, each bearing a candle. The festival arrangements, it was decreed in 1355, were to be made at a general meeting held eight days previously. An amendment of 1357 added that non-attendance at this meeting was no excuse for not turning up for the festival. A further amendment of 1361 added that, in the event of absence from Siena, a painter still had to ensure the presence of a representative bearing a candle. An addition approved in 1367 instituted a special fine for those complaining against the arrangements for St Luke's feast, and a further addition approved in 1402 stated, in passing, that illness was no excuse for not being represented by a proxy. In an age in which actual appearances counted for so much, the heads of the gilds were, it seems, anxious that the painters should 'put up a good show' on the feast of their saint.

The various gild ordinances are also of interest because they provide information about what the artists did. It is at this point perhaps that the stature of an artist in the Middle Ages becomes particularly hard to understand, and it may be easiest to consider painting and sculpture separately.

The earliest ordinances (1283) of the London painters' gild contain only nine clauses. Of these, the first four (which are the only clauses relating to any specific type of work) are concerned with the painting of saddles. The first clause forbids the patching-up and painting of saddles which were unsound. This was perhaps the equivalent to respraying a defective motor-car which, while appearing to be new, might later fall to pieces at some crucial mo-

Among the tasks expected of an artist was the painting of saddles. St Eligius, the patron saint of goldsmiths, is here seen making the gold covering of a saddle. In the shop behind him his assistants are at work with bellows and anvil, while the men next to him are busy on a plaque and an incised cross. Samples of their wares lie with their tools on the counter. (2)

ment. What is important here, however, is that this may seem to confirm a suspicion in the reader's mind that this chapter has concerned itself too much with what he might call 'craftsmen' whereas it should be concerning itself with 'Artists'. It must therefore be made clear that it is virtually impossible to draw this distinction in the Middle Ages, at least in occupational terms. The most eminent painters are found executing commissions which, by present-day standards, might well seem to belong to the 'craft' side of the trade, rather than the 'art'. Melchior Broederlam of Ypres, the skilled and reputable painter of the Duke of Burgundy, was expected to paint standards and decorations as well as altarpieces. In 1386–87 he painted the Duchess's hearse and also the drapery and pavilions on the Duke's boat.

In 1390–91 Broederlam did in fact decorate two sets of jousting harness for Philippe le Hardi of Burgundy and throughout the Middle Ages the painter's calling was associated intimately with tasks which would today be judged menial. The painters' gild in London was for a long time considered an offshoot of the saddler's gild and the early crises about which anything is known all centred on the production of saddles. In Paris in the 13th century the gild regulations divided the painters into two groups: those whose primary task was painting saddles, and presumably horse-trappings generally; and those whose primary task was painting images. It is true that the distinction is not clear in the taxation lists already mentioned, although two painters lived actually in the *Selerie* and the second wealthiest painter in Paris lived just off the *Selerie* in the Rue St Jacques. But this confounding of what would now be called Art and applied art is a uniform feature of the Middle Ages.

Many regulations survive of which the purpose was specifically to prevent the painter from applying his art with intent to defraud. This has already been mentioned in connection with the London ordinances of 1283. A Florentine provision of 1335 sought to protect the quality of horse-armour. The 15th-century Painters' Statutes of Padua made similar reference to painted shields. The Venetian statutes of 1271 contained the general regulation that any vendor had to declare, on sale, whether his objects were new or old—that is, brand-new or refurbished; and the statutes were concerned much more with shields, helmets, chests and (perhaps surprisingly in Venice) saddles than with altarpieces. However, the trade in altarpieces did receive attention. Here the danger was not that the article would collapse, perhaps in the middle of a battle, but that the patron would be delivered something, the intrinsic value of which was less than had been paid for. The artist might have employed gold leaf of unusual thinness, carelessly applied, or an inferior blue in the place of lapis lazuli. In fact, patrons themselves sometimes tried to guard their own interests by specifying in the course of a written contract the materials which were to be used. Thus, in a contract for an altarpiece of 1320, the Bishop of Arezzo ordered specifically that the best gold leaf of the quality of 100 leaves to the florin and genuine azure ultramarine (lapis lazuli) should be employed.

Prospects of Success

An 'image-maker' might be a painter; he was more commonly a specialized kind of mason. A mason was basically someone who worked in stone. But the term covered a wide range of pursuits and an even wider range of skill; and already by 1300 separate trades were included within the wider term. In 1292, there were 104 declared masons in Paris; but clearly there was a wide discrepancy between the king's mason, who lived in the *Cité* and paid 6*l* tax and the majority who paid 5*s* or less. Some of these would have been little more than stone-cutters. They were in any case distinguished in the taxation lists from the quarriers and also from the *imagiers*, and the majority of them must have belonged to the building trade. The *imagiers* were the nearest approach to sculptors in the modern sense, producing individual works of greater or lesser quality. Claus Sluter, the famous sculptor of the Duke of Burgundy, was generally referred to as *imagier*. These image-makers were often further distinguished as *marbriers* (marble-workers) and *tombiers* (tomb-makers).

Understandably, less is heard of image-makers as an independent group, probably because of the constant tendency to be ab-

p 284 (2)

f 2

p 294,
(25, 26)

p 291
(20)
p 285 (7.

sorbed into the general mason's craft. It is true that the Parisian Statutes of 1391 for the image-carvers, sculptors, painters and illuminators are, in fact, very much concerned with carved images; but once again, it seems that it was the power of the painter to conceal basic faults in workmanship which was particularly feared. The preamble, in fact, opens by reciting how several poor churches in Paris had been deceived because those concerned with them, such as the churchwardens and others in charge, priests and many other good and devout people, who from devotion had ordered ornaments of paintings and images, knew nothing about these things. The general tenor of the regulations suggests that a number of images had been marketed which had later fallen to pieces, perhaps while being carried in procession.

All this serves to give some idea of the urban setting of the mediaeval artist; and it is essential to try to grasp its nature because practically every artist of any distinction served an apprenticeship in a setting of this kind. It may well be asked what goals were open to an ambitious artist anxious to establish a reputation in his town. The first point to make is that in repute the arts were not equal. There is no doubt that the positions which carried the greatest prestige were those of senior masons in charge of building works. These have been described in Chapter III, but the whole career of a senior master mason—the results (perhaps a royal chapel), the enormous financial and material responsibility and his engineering expertise—automatically placed him on a different plane from the other artists. The painter or sculptor might indeed become famous but one gets the impression that it was fame on a different scale and of a different kind. The ladder of success for a mason was reasonably clear since there were a large number of permanent salaried positions as 'surveyors to the fabric' of particular cathedrals or public buildings. But public recognition of this kind for a painter or image-maker was limited or non-existent. To begin with, no town council ever appears to have appointed an official image-maker or sculptor. This is reasonable on account of the architectural context of much mediaeval sculpture, which would automatically have brought it within the province of the surveyor, himself almost certainly a mason. The post at issue here is really that of 'official painter to

the town'—a post which did exist and which, it might be expected, would have complemented that of surveyor or master of the works. The fact that this did not happen deserves explanation since it throws further light on the position, status and prospects of a painter in the city.

Official posts were, in origin at least, intended to satisfy practical needs. Thus buildings needed constant inspection and surveyance; and they received indeed practical attention which was seldom lavished on paintings. Picture conservation was virtually non-existent. The Parisian painters' ordinances of 1391 contain the provision that wall-painters should erase well and truly the old colours of any previous scheme of decoration that they were over-painting—an observation that throws some light on the attitude to earlier work. It seldom seems to have been considered necessary that one man should be singled out and given a regular salary to execute new civic paintings, much less to look after old ones. Very occasionally it did happen, but even then in conditions of which nothing is known. In 1271, for instance, the town council of S. Gimignano voted that the commune should seek out a painter who was willing to remain permanently in the town, and provide him with a house and workshop 'in order that he may exercise his art'. Although this may seem, on the surface, a reasonable practical proposition, in fact the experience of other towns suggests that, in normal circumstances, such a step was completely unnecessary. It has already been shown that in 1292 Paris possessed a 'pool' of 33 painters of varying skill. Other towns must have been in comparable positions. As long as the level of the 'pool' was maintained, there was no need to single out one man as town painter. The artists were there, in residence, and municipal work was assigned to them as and when required. We know when any particular man gave extra satisfaction, simply because his name appears in the municipal accounts year after year. This happened in the case of Simone Martini at Siena (c. 1320–33) and equally in the case of an otherwise obscure painter at Ypres, Henri Mannin (c. 1311–30). The additional measures found necessary by the town council of S. Gimignano in order to attract one permanent resident artist are thus very hard to explain and certainly do not represent common practice.

Official Recognition

There was no practical necessity to change this state of affairs. Neither of the Lorenzetti brothers nor Simone Martini nor Henri Mannin were appointed to any official position. Yet this had important results. Almost without exception, honorific positions developed originally out of positions of responsibility instituted for practical reasons. The concept of an official painter to the town might have developed if the painter could first have joined the ranks of the town officials as a practical necessity. But until this step was taken (and there was no reason why it ever should have been taken) it was unlikely that the painters would ever secure an honorific position of their own. The case of Giotto illustrates the position in the 1330s. In 1334 he received from the city of Florence a final act of recognition in a successful attempt to get him to stay in the city. As the most eminent Florentine painter, he was made city architect.

This gives a most illuminating insight into the status of painters. It may well seem surprising that Giotto, today regarded as a founding-father of Italian painting, should not have received honour *as a painter*. But painting was regarded as one craft among many. Something has already been seen of the people and work with which the craft was associated. In modern terms, one might perhaps try to imagine a city council paying homage to a successful local shoe manufacturer. Few city councils nowadays would do this simply by emphasizing his craft unless the position of bootmaker to the mayor and aldermen already existed as an honourable one (which is unlikely). The important point is that some position or title has (and had) to be found which will associate the prospective holder with some form of eminence already existing. This seems to be what happened to Giotto. No position of city painter existed in Florence; and even had it occurred to the Florentine authorities to make Giotto city painter, this would merely have associated him more closely with the type of appointment already noted at S. Gimignano, which seems to have been one of desperation rather than honour. To make him city architect, however, was a very different proposition. Although, as far as we know, completely untrained as a mason, he was given as it were a commission into the ranks of the senior master masons; for they were the only mediaeval artist-craftsmen to achieve an international standing and eminence which Giotto had himself achieved *in spite of* the fact that he was only a painter.

The position of painter to the town does however make a sporadic appearance towards the end of the Middle Ages—so sporadic, indeed, that generalizations are almost impossible. In 1400, at Ypres, a painter named Jacques Cavael, who had worked on civic commissions satisfactorily for some years, petitioned that, in return for painting a current order of banners, banderoles and costume designs free, he might receive the title of town painter. His wish was granted and he was given permission to wear the robes of a town official. It is not clear whether a regular salary was attached to this position. Cavael had a successor in 1406 when a France van der Wichterne petitioned for and obtained the same office. From published records, the office seems then to have lapsed. The famous painter Roger van der Weyden held a similar post at Brussels in 1436. To him too was granted the right to wear the cloak of a town official. In his case, some sort of payment was received since the abolition of the post was discussed in connection with a series of economy measures. Roger also had a successor in the worthy but totally undistinguished Vrancke van der Stockte. Finally one may instance the official painters of the Venetian state towards the end of the 15th century, paid out of state funds and holding as a sinecure the official position of a broker at the *fondaco* of the German merchants.

One can do little more than conjecture about the motives behind the institution of these posts. It is striking that at Brussels, the post was considered at one stage a luxury which the town could hardly afford; and this idea of a luxury commodity may hold the key to the situation. For it seems likely that the positions originated not as practical necessities, nor yet with the idea of honouring particular artists, but with the idea of honouring the town itself by giving it an additional status symbol. The *peintre de la ville* was perhaps appointed in imitation of the *peintres du roi* or *peintres de monseigneur le duc* who appear more and more frequently during the course of the 14th century. Unfortunately, if this was so, the course of this particular development is still extremely obscure. But it does not seem that, as a general rule, a mediaeval painter (or figure-sculptor) would have expected formal recognition of his skill in his craft from his home town; nor would he normally have looked for any official position in his home town which he could ultimately hope to hold. As far as can be judged, the rewards that he sought for his skill were more direct ones; and his success would have been judged not by titles but by the standing of his patrons. In his immediate vicinity, this patronage would certainly have included civic commissions. In addition, however, there would have been commissions of corporations and religious confraternities. Finally, there would be commissions of private individuals. At the top of the scale of private patronage stood the court; and at this point the court becomes an immediate focus of attention. For the general status of painters—and other artists—as a class in society will certainly be illumined by the way in which those at this level were treated. The following section, therefore, will begin by examining the way in which artists were associated with a mediaeval court and the ways in which they were absorbed into its structure.

Royal Patrons

To be more precise, we should examine the relationship of artists to the royal household. Not every mediaeval monarch felt it necessary to keep artists in his immediate *entourage*, that is, his household. The kings of England are an example. Neither Henry III nor Richard II, two of the most cultured mediaeval kings, appears to have kept a painter or illuminator there. For instance, of the various painters who worked for Henry III the most eminent was probably Walter of Durham; but he was called king's serjeant and painter—not an office attached to the household. His salary by 1271 was derived from three separate sources, suggesting in itself an *ad hoc* arrangement to pay an office for which no regular Exchequer provision existed. Under Richard II, two painters called Prince acted successively as king's painter but it was not found necessary to give them any more specific appointment. They did not even receive a regular salary but were paid for piece-work through the office of the Great Wardrobe.

A similar state of affairs seems to be found in France c. 1300. Nothing definite is known about the artists employed by the 13th-century kings of France, and there is at least no sign of any special relationship to the royal court. Master Honoré, who has already been mentioned, may have produced books for the royal chapel but he does not appear to have had any official standing. In the first two decades of the next century, three *émigrés* Roman painters (including the reputable Filippo Rusuti) received pensions from the French treasury. They are styled variously *pictores regis* and *peintres nostre sire*, but, as with Walter of Durham in England, no closer association with the Crown is suggested. Another *émigré* Roman painter, Pietro Cavallini, was invited to the Angevin court at Naples in 1308. Again, although he was granted an annual salary and a house, no court status appears to have been assigned to him.

Perhaps, before proceeding further, something may be said about a mediaeval royal household—the organization to which, so far, artists have not apparently belonged. On enquiry, this will perhaps not appear particularly surprising. The royal household was primarily an administrative service which kept the king fed, clothed, mobile (when necessary) and (if one adds the normal establishment of fools and minstrels) amused. It was large and complicated and organized on typical civil service lines in departments. The duties and allowances of each member of each department were defined by household ordinances which were drawn from time to time as occasion demanded; and, scanning the personnel of these departments from the bedchamber to the stables, it is admittedly very difficult to imagine both the practical circumstances in which an artist could be brought on to the strength of the court and the department to which he would be attached, should this occur. For whatever section one chooses—bedchamber, butlery, hall or whatever—none seems quite fitted to take, as it might be, a working manuscript illuminator.

p 18 (13)
p 293 (24)
p 22, 24 (20, 22 24)
p 287 (15)
p 292 (22)

In Roman mythology Mercury was the messenger of the gods, the patron of travellers and the conductor of the dead to Hades. He was also the god of thieves and liars. Perhaps by extension from this he became the patron of orators and poets and finally (by way of astrological symbolism) of all artists. In the later Middle Ages craftsmen are called 'the children of Mercury'—as in this German block-book of about 1470 showing the influence of the various planets on the affairs of men. Mercury rules over potters, painters, goldsmiths, carpenters, masons, musicians, writers—and even clock-makers. (4)

However, between 1300 and 1315 this development did take place in the circle of the French royal family. In Naples at the Angevin court in 1310, a painter called Montano of Arezzo was received into the royal household *(inter familiares)*, and in Paris in 1313 in the household of Philip the Fair there was an illuminator called Maciot. Maciot was included in a court role under the general category of *valeti et alii hospitii* or *valeti et familia hospitii*; they were as a general rule the members of the royal household who were neither noble, clerical, knightly nor legal. It was a category that included the members of the chief household departments such as the kitchen and the stables already mentioned, and was the obvious grading for a supernumerary craftsman. In view of what has just been said, however, it is interesting that his position in the household was not further defined. We shall return to this point.

Membership of the *familia hospitii* is also implied by the other expression already mentioned—*familiaris*. It was in this classification that the celebrated Florentine artist Giotto was eventually placed when he visited Naples. The text of the royal order of 1330 confirming the appointment still exists and runs as follows:

'Freely do we associate in the community of our *familia* those approved by the uprightness of their ways and commended by their distinctive excellence. Sensible therefore that Master Giotto of Florence, painter, *familiaris* and our faithful servant, is sustained by prudent deeds and exercised in fruitful services, we willingly receive him as our *familiaris* and retain him in our household, that he may possess and enjoy those honours and privileges which other *familiares* possess, after taking the accustomed oath.'

p 287
(14)

This development was apparently not followed in England but echoes of it occur elsewhere in Europe. In 1367, at the imperial court of Prague, the painter Theodoric was styled in the course of an imperial grant 'beloved master . . . our painter and *familiaris*'.

p 286
(12)

As a part of the history of the rise of the artist, this development should have great importance; yet in many ways it raises nothing but questions. In the case of Maciot, for instance, he came in 1302 from the Counts of Artois to serve the French king. He was, however, given a house of his own in Paris; and although this was on the *Cité*, he had moved to the north bank by the time of the taxation roll of 1313 and had a house in the parish of St-Merri. This was the year of the court list in which he is mentioned.

At this point, an obvious problem emerges. Why could not Maciot, from his workshop in the parish of St-Merri on the north bank, supply the royal family with works as Honoré had done from the parish of St-Séverin on the south bank? Why was it necessary to place him on the establishment of the court among the *valeti et alii hospitii*? The same problem occurs in the case of Giotto. What different circumstances operated which made it necessary to make Giotto of Florence a *familiaris* when Cavallini of Rome had merely been given an annual salary and a house?

In view of Giotto's subsequent eminence, his appointment has generally received considerable notice. It is therefore necessary to disembarrass it of some of its reputed grandeur. In the first place, the language of his appointment, imposing in itself, seems nevertheless to have followed a civil service formula, since an almost identical form of words was used for the similar appointment of an otherwise unknown clerk in 1316. It is frequently pointed out that Petrarch was accorded the same distinction in 1341. At the other end of the scale, however, one has to remember the royal Neapolitan barber called Simonetto who in 1297–98 is also called *familiaris noster*. This single example makes it likely that Giotto at Naples was being granted an appointment similar to that of Maciot at Paris among the *valeti et familia hospitii*.

It is, incidentally, necessary to emphasize the distinction between general service to the king and service at court. Montano had already been working for the Angevin royal family; Giotto was first retained on a monthly salary without the title of *familiaris*. Moreover, Giotto's salary was increased in 1332, independently of his allowances as a court servant. Unfortunately nothing is known of the circumstances of the appointment of Maciot, although he was positively removed from the royal household in the ordinance of 1319. The main point here is that, from the start, membership of the royal *familia* seems to have been something extra enjoyed at the top of a professional career.

A Place at Court

It has already been suggested that there is no apparent obvious professional reason for drafting an illuminator or painter on to the strength of the court. The artists must have arrived at court because the king wanted them there. There is, indeed, only one solid reason for placing them on the strength of court personnel —namely, that they would have right of access to the court and it would consequently have been easier for a king to get at them, should they be required. Now, why *should* the king require them? Not surely to satisfy unpredictable peripatetic urges for art. High-quality manuscripts or panel painting are not produced in the make-shift surroundings of a royal progress from palace to palace. The only compelling reasons must have been found in personal links between artist and king which are now lost—links that need not necessarily have had anything to do with art at all.

The fact is, of course, that we are still in the prehistory of artistic personalities. We have to wait until the 16th century to have it recorded that Raphael or Leonardo had demeanours which were acceptable at court. However, there is one instance in the first half of the 14th century of a painter entertaining a king in a non-professional capacity. This happened in 1326, not in France but in England. In the Wardrobe accounts for this year the treasurer accounted for a gift of money paid to 'Jack of St Albans, painter of the King, who danced before the King on a table'. Jack of St Albans was not, apparently, a regular member of the household establishment. But it is sufficient to illustrate that kings could call upon unexpected resources for their entertainment. There is, however, no need for us to imagine Giotto in the undignified posture of dancing upon a table. In this connection, it is sufficient to remember Vasari's stories about Giotto's career at Naples. Vasari wrote in the mid-16th century. There are no grounds for supposing that this account is anything but apocryphal and it is usually dismissed out of hand. The social order had not, however, radically changed between 1330 and 1550 and, whoever invented these stories, they must represent, however faintly, something of the personal qualities which helped to transform the ordinary *pictor regis* into *familiaris*.

p 287 (14) '[Giotto's works] much pleased that king, by whom he was so greatly beloved that many times, while working, Giotto found himself entertained by the King in person, who took pleasure in seeing him at work and in hearing his discourse. And Giotto, who had ever some jest on his tongue and some witty repartee in readiness, would entertain him with his hand, in painting, and with pleasant discourse in his jesting. Wherefore, the King saying to him one day that he wished to make him the first man in Naples, Giotto answered, "And for that end am I lodged at the Porta Reale in order to be the first in Naples". Another time, the King saying to him, "Giotto, if I were you, now that it is hot, I should give over painting for a little", he answered, "And I, i'faith, if I were you" . . . Now the King having one day out of caprice besought him to paint his realm for him, Giotto, so it is said, painted for him an ass saddled, that had at its feet a new pack-saddle, and was sniffing at it and making semblance of

desiring it; and on both the old pack-saddle and the new one were the royal crown and the sceptre of sovereignty; wherefore Giotto, being asked by the King what such a picture signified, answered that such were his subjects and such a kingdom, wherein every day a new lord was desired.'

It seems to be the case that artists were only admitted to the household after serving the king for some period of time, which suggests, again, that the king's desire was for closer association as the result of previous experience. One cannot therefore help suspecting, as a result of all this, that Maciot may have been a brilliant personable young man, that Montano of Arezzo perhaps had an inexhaustible fund of wit and that Giotto really was a fascinating character. In fact, like Master Honoré and Pietro Cavallini, all these men were in the first instance brought to the royal notice as a result of success in their craft. Their presence in the household, however, seems unlikely to have had much to do with their talents as artists and may be taken to demonstrate that, unlike Master Honoré and Pietro Cavallini, they had personalities which were congenial to the princes whom they served. In these circumstances, the three Limbourg brothers who were taken into the household of the duc de Berry may be seen not only as superb manuscript illuminators but also as a sort of Netherlandish Bushy, Bagot and Green.

Such people have always been subject to a variety of pressures. It is not merely that they get called the 'caterpillars of the commonwealth'. Social considerations apart, painters were not easily assignable to any known administrative category—this problem has already been noted. Maciot, in fact, appears in a preliminary list of names, many of which have no occupation attached to indicate attachment to any particular household department; and there would normally be a tendency on the part of the king to collect extra people on top of the given establishment. It is, however, equally to be expected that there would be a strong administrative tendency to tidy these people away, either by expelling them from the court (not always possible) or by lodging them in an existing administrative 'pigeon-hole'.

The artists appear to have got both types of treatment. A laconic note in the French household ordinance of 1317 says 'That, Guy and Maciot the illuminator shall be removed', the full significance of which is now lost. The second course was adopted later in the century.

There was one royal painter called Girart d'Orléans who was employed by the king's works on and off from 1328 until 1350. Then suddenly, with the accession of John the Good, he was described as 'our beloved *familiaris* . . . painter and usher of our hall'. This is hardly an expected appointment. The 1318 Ordinance of Edward II of England makes it clear that the duties of these *ushers* were to keep order in the hall, to make sure that the place was decently appointed and to exclude gate-crashers. In terms of allowances, this position was not especially exalted and indeed it seems to have undergone a decline at the 14th-century French court. Girart in any case had a salary as a royal painter of 6s a day—far in excess of the cash allowances ever given to working ushers (2s per day in 1285; 1s 7 *deniers* in 1317; 9d in 1386) he was therefore being paid for a completely different job. He also had a house in Paris on the north bank by 1356. And, in all, it seems likely that the appointment must have been a purely nominal one. p 155 (46)

To make a painter usher of the hall may be unexpected. There was another position, however, which seems even stranger. This was the appointment of sergeant-at-arms. These men were the personal bodyguard of the king and were supposed to mount guard while he was at table or at Mass. They also rode as escort while he was travelling. Two men received this title. The painter, Jean Coste, having served the Crown at least since 1349 (with the title of *peintre du roy* since 1351), was suddenly referred to as *peintre et sergent d'armes du roy* in 1367. (This is the last surviving reference to him.) One other 14th-century master to receive this title was the master of the king's works at the Louvre, Raymond du Temple, according to a document of 1395. In the case of Jean Coste, at least, it is hard to take this appointment seriously —to imagine, in fact, a painter after over ten years' faithful service suddenly being chosen as a bodyguard. A more likely explanation

An artist mixing his paints, from an English 14th-century manuscript. The text discusses the etymology of the word colour, with appeals to the authority of Aristotle. (5)

is available, however. The sergeants-at-arms numbered 30 (at least in the ordinance of 1317), and it is likely that there would frequently have been vacancies in their numbers. When Charles V desired to have Jean Coste at court, it may only have been possible, administratively, to accommodate him as a sergeant. Everyday experience suggests that, whereas Charles would not have minded what his painter was called so long as he was at hand when required, the Master of the Household or the Master of the Chamber of Accounts would not have been happy until he could be labelled with some existing tag. There are no grounds for supposing that administrative 'regularization' is an invention of the 20th century.

A King's Painter

There was a third household position which eventually became far more commonly occupied by painters and other craftsmen.
p 155 (46)
It is interesting that, here at least, some sort of rational development can be demonstrated. It is connected with Girart d'Orléans, the painter whom we have already met nominally as an usher in the king's hall.

He was mentioned as usher once more in a document of 1355. In 1356 the French were defeated by the English at the battle of Poitiers and King John was taken prisoner to London. Girart d'Orléans went with him and during the course of the three years' captivity executed various small works. In these circumstances, his position as usher of the king's hall would have been meaningless, since the king's hall as an institution virtually ceased to exist in John's London quarters at the Savoy. In 1356 therefore Girart is found as 'servant of the chamber' and in 1359 as a 'valet of the chamber'—or, to use the normal French expression, *valet de chambre*.

Girart had therefore moved from the hall to the chamber. In the hierarchy of the household, the *valets de chambre* received allowances similar to the cooks or the furriers. They were almost certainly superior in prestige, however, since they were the personal attendants on the king. Their normal establishment included the king's tailor, his pharmacist and his barber. To illustrate the nature of this move in modern terms, one might therefore suggest that Girart d'Orléans was being promoted from titular 'N.C.O. in charge of the Men's Mess' to 'Commanding Officer's Batman'.

Moreover, in this particular case of Girart d'Orléans, it is possible to feel that he was, in some sense, a personal companion to the King. When King John of France was taken prisoner his court was necessarily reduced in number and the main departments were held in common with his son Philip, later Duke of Burgundy, who shared his father's captivity. All this can be deduced from such accounts as survive, and those accounts also

reveal who was in permanent attendance on the King. During the six months from December 1358 to June 1359, John had his previous freedom considerably restricted and he came under a surveillance closer than at any previous time, largely as the result of the contemporary political and military situation. Moreover, he was moved in April to Hertford Castle, and thence to Somerton Castle (Lincolnshire) in July and finally brought back to London (March 1360) where he was lodged in the Tower. Throughout this period he held together around him a court of sorts. During the six-month accounting period already mentioned, certain permanent office-holders appear, such as the *maistre de l'ostel*, the king's secretary, the royal chaplains (one of them the king's physician) and the clerks to the chapel. King John also had in attendance the royal fool and the king of the minstrels. Five *valets de chambre* are mentioned. None was a barber since John borrowed a barber from the retinue of his son. One was a tailor who was not in London in December but came over from France in March. Two further *valets de chambre* are mentioned who were *espiciers* (apothecaries). One came over from France in March and returned in May, the other was only appointed to the position in May. A further *valet de chambre*, whose occupation is not specified, left France in April. The only *valet de chambre* permanently in attendance on the King during this period was the painter Girart d'Orléans who apparently never left the court. During this period he executed a number of paintings for John and also constructed a *jeu d'échecs*, and these tasks may well be taken as symbols of his dual capacity. Not only was he a good painter; he was also personally companionable and (like the fool) had some sort of entertainment value.

The step of admitting a favourite craftsman to the royal chamber was in some ways expected, and it is admittedly obscure why Girart d'Orléans was made usher. It can only be suggested that the chamber establishment (which was small and fluctuated between about six and a dozen in numbers) was full at that point. But precedents were already to be found at the court of Edward II, who had a carpenter as a *valet de chambre*; and however much conservative opinion might grumble about the presence of these menials around the king, the establishment of the chamber was an obvious niche in which to lodge them.

Once the step had been taken of admitting an artist to the royal chamber, the precedent was set and the appointment became a frequent one. Girart d'Orléans was followed in 1364 by a painter Jehan d'Orléans, *valet de chambre*, who is likely to have been a relation. Jehan was followed by a François who was certainly his son and who succeeded in 1404 during the lifetime of his father. Jean Bandol, king's painter since 1368, was probably admitted to the household in 1378 or 1379. The royal dukes admitted to their chambers as valets numerous gifted artists, including Claus Sluter, Melchior Broederlam and the Limbourg brothers. In fact, by the close of the 14th century, the position of *valet de chambre* at a French court appears to have been a common appointment for any sort of craftsman or artist who might have taken a patron's fancy; for instance, goldsmiths, *tapissiers*, illuminators, embroiderers or musicians are all found in this post.
p 286 (13) p 291 (20) p 294, 5 (25, 26)

One cannot, I think, ignore at any time the personal aspect of the appointment. It is not merely that Jan van Eyck, *valet de chambre*, was sent on confidential missions by his master, the Duke of Burgundy, although this illustrates the point. But quite famous 14th-century artists are not recorded in any household position— for instance, André Beauneveu and Jacquemart de Hesdin. What is, however, completely obscure is the obligations incurred by accepting one of these posts. One cannot perhaps take the ushers and sergeants seriously; but were companionable artists ever required to do regular service in the chamber? The answer is not at the moment clear.
p 296 (28)

Risks and Rewards

The obligations of a king's painter (as opposed to *valet de chambre*) are more easily found. In 1374 Jean Bandol, already *pictor regis*, was granted an annual salary of 200 livres 'on this condition, that he shall be held to serve in all works of painting that the King shall command without other wages, either for himself or his servant'. The conditions of payment naturally varied between
p 286 (13)

Bandol who was paid about 13*s* a day 'all in' and Girart d'Orléans who was granted a salary of 6*s* a day in 1350 but was paid in addition for whatever work he executed. On top of this, patrons might often add presents of money, by way of encouragement. The main purpose of the patron was to retain a good craftsman for use at any required time. The same position presumably held good for Walter of Durham. Occasionally the restrictions were severe. A document of 1365 records how the painter Jean de Hasselt had been retained by Louis de Mâle, Count of Flanders, to work 'in our chapel at Ghent and elsewhere where it shall please us, without attending to any other work other than ours without our consent and permission'. Jan van Eyck's appointment of 1426 used a far less stringent formula; the Duke merely made the appointment 'in order that he (Jan) shall be obliged to work at painting for him (the Duke) as often as it shall please the Duke'. No explicit restraint was placed on outside commissions.

Houses were sometimes provided by patrons. François d'Orléans and his father were living in lodgings in the royal palace at
p 292 Paris in 1404. Henri Bellechose, *valet de chambre* and painter of
(23) the Duke of Burgundy, rented a house from the *Sainte Chapelle* at Dijon—probably obtained therefore at the instance of the Duke. Pol de Limbourg was presented with a house in Bourges by the duc de Berry. There does not seem to have been any definite rule. The prospects of these men also varied. The Lim-
p 287 bourg brothers seem to have prospered financially since Pol was
(16) able in 1415 to lend the duc de Berry 1,000 *écus*—a very large sum of money for a craftsman. Very occasionally attempts appear to have been made to better their families as in the case of Drouet de Dammartin. He was a master mason of the duc de Berry and in 1413 had sent his second son to study in Paris. His first son, however, followed the family craft and became a mason, but he in turn sent a second son to study law. An unusual if obscure distinction was conferred on another mason, Jean de Cambrai. In 1375 he was merely a 'hewer of free stone' at Cambrai. In 1397 he was a *valet de chambre* of the duc de Berry, living at Bourges. Finally, in 1403, he was formally called *esquire* in an order from Charles VI authorizing him to wear the collar of the *Geneste*.

The most obvious disadvantages of serving a prince were financial, for payment or repayment might be erratic. The largest
p 291 single item in the 1413 will of Drouet de Dammartin was a debt
(20, 21) from the duc de Berry of 2,000*l.* This was an extraordinarily large sum, equivalent to about ten to fourteen years' pay for a competent mason. Nothing, however, is known about the circumstances of the debt. The Limbourg brothers, in the loan already mentioned, had extracted a security from the Duke in the form of a ruby which covered the value of their loan three times over. But no mention of a security was made by Drouet. Lack of wages apparently reduced one illuminator of the Duke of Burgundy to poverty. A grant of 1459 by Philip the Good of Burgundy recites how Jehan de Pestimen had served the ducal family since his youth and had been a *valet de chambre* since 1418, serving the ducal court as long as he was able. Nevertheless, he had not been able to have the wages belonging to his office and now, at the age of about 68, he was reduced to begging. The Duke therefore granted him a pension of 30*l* a year. Pestimen had lived at Dijon since about 1432 and this probably explains his poverty. The Burgundian Duke seldom came to Dijon after about 1425 and the permanent establishment at Dijon suffered as a result, particularly where art was concerned. Supervision of the construction of the tombs in the ducal mausoleum at Champmol varied in character from laxity to mismanagement; and, apart from Pestimen, one other artist is
p 292 known to have suffered from absence of wages. This was Henri
(23) Bellechose, a painter who had received his official appointment at Dijon in 1415 but appears to have gone without pay from 1429 till his death sometime after 1440. There was no question of Duke Philip being merely uninterested in art because in the Netherlands he had during this period three other painters and *valets de chambre* including Jan van Eyck. The artists at Dijon, nominally attached to a court which was never there, were simply thrown on their own resources. According to Bellechose himself, he had been reduced by poverty to letting his wife run a market stall.

It is always assumed, of course, that artists, thrown on their own resources, can manage. But painting is partly a luxury and,

reflecting on the fantastic expenditure on luxuries by a court of the early 15th century, it is easy to see the extreme consequences of the removal of any court for those supplying the luxuries. One can only imagine that the mercers and furriers of Dijon were as sharply affected as the painters.

'Master of the Amusement Machines'

The work expected from court artists may well have been monotonous. Palace decoration often consisted in the repetition of formal patterns although full-scale history painting is sometimes mentioned. The demands of the age of chivalry on painters may well have seemed excessive. Hugh of Boulogne, painter, *valet de chambre*, colleague and contemporary of Jan van Eyck in the service of the Duke of Burgundy, seems constantly to have been involved in situations in which he and a band of subordinates had to work night and day to complete on time monstrous orders involving thousands of pennants and a great many escutcheons and banners. To end this survey of the position of the artist at court, therefore, something should be said about one of the more bizarre appointments about which anything is known. It was at the castle of Hesdin, which belonged in the 14th century to the Counts of Artois and passed at the end of the century to the Dukes of Burgundy; and the appointment was that of 'master of the amusement machines and of the painters'. The Counts of Artois had constructed in their castle at Hesdin a gallery of machines for the diversion of their guests and the amusement of the household. Something existed already in 1299 but unfortunately there is no full description until 1432. The machines, however, were constantly in need of repair and refurbishing throughout the 14th century and it seems likely that additions were made from time to time. As a gallery of diversions, they illustrate the somewhat Edwardian sense of humour of a mediaeval court. Most of the machines caused various forms of discomfort to anyone who had the misfortune to be invited to inspect them; most of the ensuing 'fun' depended on two classic standbys of slapstick humour, the jet of water and the bag of flour (or soot). Here are some of the devices which the painter at Hesdin was required to look after; the list represents the accumulated ingenuity of about 130 years; the result was an achievement reminiscent of Leonardo da Vinci and certainly worthy of him.

There was a general provision of machines for projecting water for the whole length of the gallery so that if it was required nobody in the gallery should escape being soaked. At one point there was a separate room painted with figures and histories, the ceiling decorated with gilded stars and other devices and having a large pendant key-stone adorned with figures dressed in imitation cloth of gold. This room must have been arresting to look at. Moreover, those entering were spoken to by a wooden figure of a hermit by the entrance. Above the ceiling was a machine for producing water like rain from the sky, and thunder, snow and lightning 'such as is seen in the sky'; and in the floor at one point was a trap down which those escaping from the 'rain' fell into a large sack where they were smothered in feathers. Various carved figures throughout the gallery projected water without warning at onlookers. Three jets near the entrance covered people who stopped in front of them with flour. There was an imitation window which, on being opened, revealed a figure who soaked the onlookers with water and closed the window again. On a table was an imitation book of ballads which smothered those who opened it with black (soot?) and also sprayed them with water when required. Alongside was a mirror where victims of the book were sent to look at themselves, only to be covered in flour again. Perhaps the masterpiece was a carved figure in the middle of the gallery which could be made to command in the voice of the Duke that all those in the gallery should leave immediately. Those taken in by this voice would rush towards an exit where they were assaulted, by large figures, on the head and shoulders and finally propelled across a bridge which precipitated them into water beneath. Those who were not taken in and stayed put were nevertheless drenched with water.

All this may seem to belong more properly to the by-ways of social history until one suddenly finds no less a person than Melchior Broederlam ordered to conduct a general overhaul of the

It was not thought unbecoming for a serious artist to apply himself to what we should regard as little more than toys. Villard de Honnecourt, in the mid-13th century, was as ready to make a joke-eagle that nodded its head as to design the choir of a cathedral.

At the top: 'How to make a saw saw by itself'. Here the chief component is a water-wheel with four radiating staves. The vertical saw is regularly pushed down by the staves of the upper wheel and pulled up again by the spring-pole.

Next is 'a cross-bow that cannot miss', and then on the left, 'how to make an angel point with his finger always to the sun'. An arrangement of ropes and pulleys moved by weights seems intended to rotate a vertical axis with a spike on the top. Some statues in the Middle Ages were in fact fixed to such movable axes, but it is hard to see how this could possibly keep time with the sun.

Then, on the right, 'a way to make the most powerful engine known for raising weights'. When turned, by means of a hand-spike at the base, the nut (at the bottom of the screw) will rise between grooves, lifting a heavy weight with it—probably a genuinely useful machine.

Lastly, lower left, 'How to make the eagle turn his head to the deacon during the reading of the Gospel'. The head is fixed to a pivot round which passes a string weighted at one end. When the other end is pulled the eagle will turn its head; when it is released, the weight restores it to its original position.

Bottom left: one more of Villard's 'jeux d'esprit': 'This is a contrivance that may be made in a drinking cup.' It consists of a bird which sits on top of a tower in the middle of a wine-cup, and when wine is poured in seems to drink it up. The mechanism is explained in the accompanying (modern) drawing. The cup is hollow at the base, and has a tube rising inside the tower to a point just below the rim of the cup. The bottom of the tower is perforated to allow wine to flow into it. When the level of the liquid rises in the cup it overflows inside the tower (unseen) into the hollow base. Air is forced up into the bird and out through its beak, producing a bubbling sound as if it were drinking. Villard's drawing is misleading since it shows the bird's beak considerably higher than the rim of the cup. (6, 7)

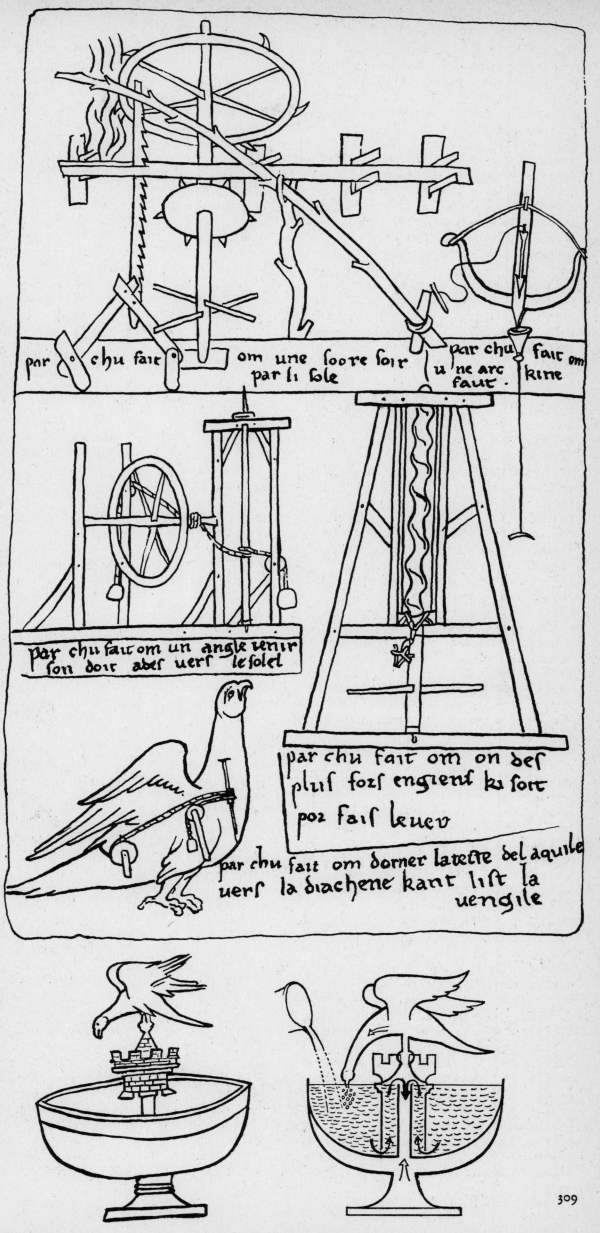

par d chu fait

om une soore soir par li sole

par chu fait om u ne arc faut kine

par chu fait om un angle venir son doir aber uers le solel

par chu fait om on des plus fors engiens ki soit por fair leuev

par chu fait om dorner la tette del aquile uers la diachene kant list la uengile

HILDEBERT

mensa hildebrt

One illuminator who has left his name to posterity is a certain Hildebertus, who worked on a text of St Augustine's 'De civitate Dei' in the 12th century. In this charming little scene he draws himself about to throw a sponge at a large mouse which is nibbling what seems to be a piece of cheese on his table, 'mensa Hildeberti'. His actual words are written in the book in front of him—'Pessime mus, saepe me provocas ad iram: ut te deus perdat': 'Wretched mouse, provoking me so often to anger; may God bring you to perdition.' In the foreground is his assistant Everwinus practising a design for an initial, the so-called 'clove curl'. (8)

machines in 1386. One would dearly like to have seen some of the devices after Broederlam had finished with them.

One might pass directly from this point to the question of the way in which mediaeval artists were treated by the society in which they lived and the general problem of the status attached to their craft. Before doing this, however, one particular group of artists must be considered. These were the men living in religious houses and under religious vows. Set apart from the strains of commercial and social competition, they demand for these very reasons to be considered apart from the others. At this point, too, it will be necessary to step back in time, since the greatest achievements of monastic artists belong to a period before the 14th century.

The Artist in the Cloister

The intention of this section is to deal generally with artists who belonged to some form of religious community and were bound by vows to some form of religious observance. While many of the artists were monks, it will be remembered that some, like Fra Angelico, belonged to a Mendicant Order. They have, however, this in common: in theory at least, their art was a part of their existence subordinate to the religious purpose to which their lives were dedicated.

Religious observance and art have never necessarily been incompatible. St Benedict, in the monastic Rule which ultimately became the basis of Western monasticism, foresaw the situation in which a monastery might admit craftsmen. Certain hours of the day were set aside for manual labour; and in Chapter 57 of the Rule, he wrote that craftsmen should be allowed, with the permission of the abbot, to practise their crafts. They should, however, not allow their skill to be a source of temptation to pride and anyone boasting was to be removed from his work until he had

p 62 (66)

humbled himself. If their work was to be sold outside the monastery, then those who sold it had to be scrupulous in the valuation and then to sell it slightly below its market price. Craftsmen or artificers were admittedly envisaged in general here. St Benedict probably had in mind carpenters or cobblers as much as people who would now be called artists. Nevertheless, his terms applied equally to the goldsmith or the illuminator.

These terms of admission for the artist may seem harsh or unrealistic, but, considering St Benedict's main purpose, rather the reverse is true. He was trying to set out the general conditions in which a community of men might serve God and seek out its own salvation. 'We must establish', he said, 'a school of the Lord's service; in founding which we hope to ordain nothing that is harsh or burdensome. But if, for good reason, for the amendment of evil habit and the preservation of charity, there be some strictness of discipline, do not be at once dismayed and run away from the way of salvation, of which the entrance must needs be narrow.' To find this way of salvation was the only purpose of a monk's life. However, St Benedict was humane enough to know the benefits of creative activity. Above all, it was a weapon against the 'enemy of the soul', idleness; it might also provide material necessities for the monastery. St Benedict's only concern was that at no point should the activity, whatever it was, become a source of sin, either to the creator or to those through whose hands the created products might later pass.

At this point the writings may be cited of a practising monastic artist who called himself Theophilus. He lived probably in the earlier part of the 12th century in north-west Germany; and he produced a treatise *Concerning the various arts* which recounted his entire experience as a craftsman. In the present context, it is interesting that three prefaces were written in the course of the treatise, all of which suggest at the very least that Theophilus was trying to put into practice the intentions behind St Benedict's words. Individual genius was not admitted by Theophilus. The artist was not seen as someone struggling to develop a personal gift but to rediscover an inheritance which was there for anyone to take. 'Whoever will contribute both care and concern is able to attain a capacity for all arts and skills as if by hereditary right.... What God has given man as an inheritance, let man strive and work with all eagerness to attain. When this has been attained, let no one glorify himself as if it were received of himself and not Another but let him humbly render thanks to God... Nor let him conceal what has been given in the cloak of envy or hide it in the closet of a grasping heart. But, repelling all vainglory, let him with a joyful heart and with simplicity dispense to all who seek.... I, an unworthy and frail mortal of little consequence, freely offer to all, who wish to learn with humility, what has freely been given me by the Divine condescension, which gives to all in abundance and holds it against no man'. Theophilus also urged his readers to study the useful arts particularly, because of the 'honour and advantage there is in eschewing idleness and in spurning laziness and sloth'. His work, in fact, reads at times almost like a gloss on the words of St Benedict.

One has little means of telling how widespread this attitude was amongst monastic artists. Numerous inscriptions survive in manuscripts in which the scribe says a few words about himself. Sometimes these are merely a pious self-recommendation:

> *Hunc librum solus monachus descripsit Amandus*
> *Pro quo perpetuae comprendat munera vitae.*
> (The monk Amandus alone wrote this book,
> for whom may it obtain the rewards of perpetual life.)
> (early 12th century)

Sometimes the writer, in a manner similar to Theophilus in his first preface, asks for the prayers of the reader.

> *Huius scriptori Willelmo sedulus oret*
> *Lector, opem reddat gaudia tuta Deus.*
> (May the zealous reader pray for the writer of this, William;
> May God grant [him] secure joys [and] help.)
> (early 13th century)

Against this type of sentiment, however, has to be set the occasional self-laudatory one. The most famous example is probably that of Eadwine who was a monk of Christchurch, Canterbury c. 1140. He left the following inscription round a picture of himself:

'I am the prince of writers; neither my fame nor my praise will die quickly; demand of my letters who I am.
The Letters: Fame proclaims you in your writing for ever, Eadwine, you who are to be seen here in the painting. The worthiness of this book demonstrates your excellence. O God, this book is given to you by him. Receive this acceptable gift.'
Only rarely is one given any detailed information about craftsmen in a religious community. The comparatively small amount of information does not, however, represent the tip of an artistic iceberg. There are no grounds for supposing that every monastery was a forcing-house of artistic activity. This appears perhaps more clearly when one examines the types of art most commonly associated with religious houses in general and monasteries in particular. The service of monks who were craftsmen was devoted in the first place to the supply of necessities. Since part of the monk's day was given over to reading, there was a permanent need for texts in the library. Thus, it was convenient that every monastery should have a *scriptorium* of its own. The church services required a certain amount of plate and utensils, and these too were sometimes made in the monastery. The church was often decorated with paintings and painted images which might be done by a monastic painter. At no time, however, was it essential that these activities should be carried out by the monks themselves. Everything depended upon circumstances, in particular on the most easily available sources of supply. Any monastery could and would buy from the secular world, should this be convenient, and from the 12th century onwards there is increasing evidence for the existence of secular craftsmen working in towns on a commercial basis.

The idea that art in the Middle Ages was produced exclusively by monks has long ago been abandoned, but it remains true that the monastic studios were often of vital importance. This frontispiece from a 12th-century manuscript of St Ambrose shows the painting of a shrine and (in the ten roundels) the production of a book, from the sharpening of the pen and the preparation of the parchment to the final binding. (9)

On the whole, stone sculpture was beyond the scope of monastic craftsmen, being too closely attached to the masons' craft which already in the 12th century was usually in the hands of professionals from the outside world. But book illumination, painting, and metal sculpture were certainly practised by monks. Theophilus makes this explicit. His first part is devoted to painting. The third part is devoted to metalwork and includes bell-founding. The second part, which deals with glass-painting and staining, adds a further category of art to the list. Furthermore, scattered references bear out the fact that professed monks could and did practise all these crafts.

Monastic 'Schools of Art'

The process by which art in any particular religious house developed, flourished and declined is for the most part still a matter of conjecture. Life in a wealthy house was in general congenial to the practice of art but it would certainly be wrong to see a 'monastic school' as an impersonal movement. So soon as evidence becomes available, any such 'school' appears to revolve around particular individuals, as in the case of Fra Angelico at the convent of San Marco in Florence. Throughout the Middle Ages, the sources provide only a sprinkling of names of such individuals, and frequently in the course of time their works have been destroyed so that their names alone remain. One may cite in the 12th century Master Hugo of Bury St Edmunds, praised by the Bury chronicler as a metal-smith and a manuscript illuminator. He may

p 54 (44)

f 9 f 10

p 62 (66)

have executed the so-called Bury Bible but any sculpture has vanished. Matthew Paris recounted the names of a group of four painters working at St Albans in the first half of the 13th century but no work can now definitely be assigned to them individually. Matthew Paris himself was said to be competent as a sculptor and goldsmith besides being a scribe and illuminator, but, once again, any sculpture has been lost.

It is unlikely that monasteries generated their own schools of art. Indeed it can occasionally be shown that artists were imported from outside, ready-trained. This might happen simply by transferring a trained artist from one monastery or convent to another; but equally, a convent sometimes recruited a fully-trained secular craftsman into its ranks. It is possible that Theophilus, already mentioned, had such a background since his phraseology is ambivalent in some places and is not entirely what one might expect *f 11* of a monk writing for other monks. Matthew Paris tells of the painter, Walter of Colchester, who was attracted into the monastery of St Albans by a monk already there called Ralph Gubiun; and, although he is not explicit, the inference is that Walter was a practising painter before becoming a monk. Paris also tells of a family of painters of whom the senior member William became a monk at St Albans. William had a brother Simon who was also his pupil; but since Simon never became a monk, William must have been proficient enough to train him before he himself entered the monastery. Finally, Simon had a son Richard, also a painter who, following in the steps of his uncle William, also became a monk. This particular group of three painters is interesting because, during the first part of the 13th century, they painted, according to Matthew Paris, altarpieces for all the altars in the abbey church. Had these altarpieces survived, one would have a 'school' of monastic painting which consisted, in fact, precisely of three men (one a layman); and although the position of Richard may be open to question, it is nevertheless likely that none of these three men was actually trained in the monastery.

It seems likely, on reflection, that in order to start a monastic 'school of art' some contact with the outside world was necessary, either with another monastery or with a secular workshop. Moreover, any abbot or sacrist interested in the production of church fittings and ornaments within his monastery, or in the continuation of such a tradition, would have faced a constant problem of recruitment. Theophilus' humble dictum, that anyone was 'able to attain a capacity for all arts and skills as if by hereditary right' provided that they devoted to them enough care and concern, may have had a limited validity; but the great manuscripts of the 12th and 13th centuries are clearly not the work of painstaking amateurs. It must always have been a problem to find prospective monks who were either promising artists or already proficient. It may not be fanciful therefore to see Walter of Colchester as something of a *coup* for Ralph Gubiun and the monastery of St Albans.

On the whole, however, it is extremely difficult to get a clear idea of the train of events by which the greater monastic artistic achievements came to be produced. Certainly wealth and importance played a part; but beyond this, the apparent reluctance of monastic chroniclers to interest themselves in art has robbed us of any detailed insight into the 'contingent and the unforeseen' which must certainly have played a large part. Even apart from this, the caprice of fortune has deprived us of large slices of evidence; widespread destruction of plate and glass and the almost total disappearance of certain major monastic libraries, like that of Westminster Abbey, make the broadest generalization fraught with danger.

The Personal Dimension

The anonymity of mediaeval art has been a frequent source of speculation and it has in general been contrasted with the highly personal achievements of the great artists of the Italian Renaissance. From this, a further familiar contrast has been reached between the Mediaeval Artist and the Renaissance Artist, the general tenor of which is that during the 15th and 16th centuries in Italy the artist in some way emerged as an individual. It is as if artists, as a species, underwent some fundamental change in response to the new humanist ideas current in 15th-century Florence and else-

The Church was probably the greatest patron of the arts during the Middle Ages, for decoration, for instruction or as part of the liturgy itself. In this late 14th-century miniature a goldsmith is working at a 'pyxis' with hammer and anvil. (10)

Matthew Paris (died 1259), monk of St Albans, was both author and artist, illustrating his own historical works. Only one of his drawings is signed—a Virgin and Child at whose feet the artist, 'Frater Mathias Parisiensis', is kneeling in adoration. But several other manuscripts can safely be attributed to him on grounds of style and he seems to have been the head of a large and influential 'atelier' at his own monastery. (11)

A mural painter of the early 13th century. The figure carrying a bunch of flowers in each hand was a conventional symbol for May in mediaeval calendars. It is probably a secular building which is being decorated, not a church. (12)

where in Italy. Whatever considerations may prompt it, the idea of the New Model Artist of the Renaissance should be subjected to critical examination. Not least, it is a concept which places mediaeval artists historically at a permanent disadvantage and makes them all too easily represent attributes the opposite of those of the supposed Renaissance Artist. Where he stands for individuality, his mediaeval forebear comes to embody anonymity; modernity is contrasted to archaism, progressiveness to retrogressiveness, and so on.

A comparison of the works themselves casts doubt on the supposition. The surviving works of Claus Sluter at the Chartreuse de Champmol represent the output of about a decade of his life. Is it possible to say that they are in some way a less 'individual' achievement than the works of Donatello when he was about the same age? This would mean divining some fundamental distinc- p 291 (20) tion separating Sluter's so-called *Puits de Moïse* from Donatello's figures on the Florentine Campanile. Similar comparisons spring to mind. Why should it be supposed that Gislebertus, the stupen- p 284 (5) p 285 (9) dous 12th-century sculptor of the cathedral of Autun, was less of an individual personality than Ghiberti?

There is, of course, a simple answer to this. As it happens we know a considerable amount about Ghiberti's personality be- cause historical record survives, whereas nothing is known about Gislebertus. The same is true about Donatello in contrast to Claus Sluter. However, this is a direct result of the Italian Renais- sance. Record was made because, at this time and place in history, art ceased to be merely a craft or a trade and became the object of intelligent interest to educated and articulate men.

It was remarked earlier that there is no evidence for any of the *mystique* of the Great Artist in the Middle Ages. There is, in fact, little evidence for an informed interest in the arts by non-artists at all. Nothing is, indeed, more striking than the apparent apathy towards art. Monastic writers practically never supply any form of objective comment on the careers of men who furnished their houses with illuminated books or enriched their churches with sculpture. Matthew Paris, himself an artist, took an interest in the decoration of his own monastery, St Albans, and (quite excep- tionally) provided a list of the works of one of the painters. Most mediaeval writers were content to do no more than to record a name here and there. Where artists are the subject of stories, the tone is not usually one of awed wonder. There is, for instance, the story (recorded in the 15th-century collection of Robert Capgrave) of the 12th-century painter who, commissioned to decorate the chapel of St Erconwald in St Paul's Cathedral, London, unwisely refused to stop work on St Erconwald's day and locked the en- trance against those who came to worship at the saint's shrine. It no longer seems strange to us that Michelangelo should have wanted to lock himself up in the Sistine Chapel while he was work- ing there. The legend, however, was not so kind to the London painter. For, 'while he was carefully laying out his colours, he was suddenly robbed of all strength and seized by a sudden afflic- tion so that he fell to the ground as if dead. When he had been thus tortured for a long time, behold the aforesaid bishop appear- ed, arrayed in episcopal robes and beat him sorely with his episco- pal staff, recounting his negligence that he should stubbornly have persisted in working on that day and should have shut the people out. This vision and beating the painter recounted to many people after he had recovered from that infirmity.' In fact, stories involving artists are very rare and seldom complimentary.

The development that has been described, by which artists entered the chamber of a king or duke in an official capacity, was really a very remarkable one. These men had in fact risen as high in mediaeval society as it was possible for a non-noble layman to go. Yet, if the reasons for this preferment were not primarily pro- fessional ones (as we have suggested), it is easy to see how this development had little, if any, immediate effect on the esteem in which art as an occupation was held. The non-professional aspect of the artists and *valets de chambre* seldom emerges into the light of history. We may see it in Jack of St Albans dancing on the table before Edward II (although Jack is not known to have been a ser- vant of the chamber). We may see it, too, in the joke-book present- ed by the Limbourg brothers as a New Year's present to the duc de Berry; and again in the confidential missions executed by Jan

Peter Vischer, sculptor of Nuremberg, was born in 1455 and died in 1529. Like Adam Krafft he stands between the Middle Ages and the Renaissance, many of his figures being closely modelled on the antique. His shrine of St Sebaldus is reproduced on p. 327; at one end of the base he included this portrait of himself wearing his leather apron and holding hammer and chisel. It is a typical mediaeval representation, quite un- touched by the more exalted view of the artist's role which was already widely accepted south of the Alps. (13)

van Eyck for the Duke of Burgundy. What is clear from the extremely slender evidence is that activity of this sort might advance the artist as a man but would not necessarily do much to advance the status of his occupation.

It took a long time to change this attitude to art and artists. The obstacles and prejudices involved are well illustrated in the *Courtier* of Castiglione. This book, planned in about 1508 and written and published during the following two decades, purports to record a series of conversations which took place at the court of Urbino in which the qualities of the ideal courtier were discussed. Its in- terest here lies in the fact that the status of the arts came in for consideration. The traditional prejudice against the arts is reiterated but Castiglione also shows how this prejudice was overcome. At one point, one of the speakers is made to put forward the idea that the courtier should know how to draw. 'Nor', he adds, 'are you to be surprised that I should suggest this quality which today may seem mechanical and hardly appropriate to a gentleman. Yet I remember having read that the ancients, especially throughout Greece, desired that noble children should be set to work at painting in the schools as a thing both wholesome, honest and necessary and this occupation was afforded a high place among the liberal arts. For it was forbidden by public order that it should be taught to slaves.' The ensuing conversation is extremely interesting because it indicates the terms on which polite society now talked about the arts. The rehabilitation depended almost exclusively on admiration for sentiments and actions recorded in antique texts, and it was largely by dwelling on these that courtly society was able to convince itself that there might be honour among artists.

Even so, the artist was not admitted to the society of gentlemen on the strength of his craft alone. His claim to attention was based fundamentally on the assumption that the complete artist possessed intellectual powers as well as technical skill. This claim was asserted explicitly at least twice in the course of the 15th century.

It is to be found in the writings of the Florentine sculptor
p 285 (9)
Ghiberti who, as a practising craftsman, also wrote three *commentarii* in imitation of antique precedent and thus claimed for himself a place as a scholar. It is to be found in reverse, so to speak, in the career of Leon Battista Alberti who, already a scholar, became profoundly interested in the theory and practice of art. It was perhaps Alberti as much as anyone who demonstrated that high intelligence, nobility and a close association with the arts were not necessarily incompatible. But it was Ghiberti who was the first writer to imitate the antique practice of recording details of art and artists of a past age. This particular contribution was in a sense a side-product of the whole revolution of attitude but it would be difficult to exaggerate its effects. For it was precisely the attitude that art and artists were subjects not merely worth discussing but also worth recording which led Italians to take the first steps towards the study of art history. Anecdotes, souvenirs and records of great artists were treasured in a way unparalleled in the history of Western Europe since classical antiquity. Almost instantly Italian art history acquired a personal dimension not found elsewhere in Europe, and it is in the first instance this which gives Italian 15th-century artists the appearance of being 'individuals'.

It was of course a prerequisite of this whole movement that antiquity should have had the compelling fascination that it acquired in 15th-century Italy, as polite fashion followed in the wake of humanist enthusiasm. The texts of Vitruvius and Pliny, upon which most of the new attitude to art was based, existed during the Middle Ages in monastic libraries, but few people can have bothered to read them. Only rarely does the name of an antique painter emerge, as when the 12th-century Gerald of Wales in one of his prefaces unexpectedly alludes to the Greek painter
p 300 (38)
Zeuxis. But it was first in 15th-century Italy that men were prepared to take the anecdotes of Pliny seriously and to comment, for instance, with approval and admiration, on the way in which Alexander was said to have treated his painter Apelles. It is this

sort of thing which was seriously discussed by Castiglione's courtiers in a way which one cannot imagine happening at the court of the duc de Berry. The new dignity acquired by the artists was to a large extent a dignity borrowed from antiquity.

The result of this whole movement is an increased awareness of the individual achievements of artists of the Italian Renaissance. Yet nobody seriously believes that Renaissance artists were alone in taking pride in their work and individuality. If proof were required to the contrary, one has only to consider the act of inscribing personal names on finished works. This practice was followed in Europe irregularly even during the Renaissance. But it can be traced back at least to the 12th century. It was a practice particularly common in Italy, but examples can be found north of the Alps. The main difference lies in the fact that the Italian inscriptions are often notably longer and openly self-laudatory. Gislebertus of Autun (c. 1130) was content to inscribe his *chef-d'œuvre*
p 290 (18)
with the words *Gislebertus hoc fecit*, whereas at Modena, a little earlier, the mason-sculptor Wiligelmo added to a dedicatory inscription the following Latin couplet:

> *Inter scultores quanto sis dignus onores*
> *Claret scultura nunc Wiligelme tua.*
> (Among sculptors, your work now shines forth, O Wiligelmo. How greatly are you worthy of honours!)

This type of inscription reached a climax in Tuscany in the second half of the 13th century on a series of pulpits carved by Niccolò Pisano and his son Giovanni. Their first effect now is to raise a smile to the lips, but they bring out clearly how much mediaeval artists could feel the individual merit of their creations and how greatly they cared about leaving permanent record of the creator's name.

It is even possible to sketch out the career of a mediaeval *uomo universale*—that is, an artist with the ability, much admired in the Renaissance, to practise in all three arts of painting, sculpture and architecture. Such a man seems to have been the Fleming André
p 296 (28)
Beauneveu. First mentioned as a sculptor at Valenciennes in 1361, he was paid for paintings in the town hall there in 1374. In 1364 he was working as a sculptor for Charles V of France, and by 1390 was in the employment of the duc de Berry, for whom he also executed miniature paintings. Apart from these duties he was also as a mason called in to advise on architectural problems at Valenciennes in 1363 and probably at Cambrai in 1378.

It would be misleading, therefore, to suppose that mediaeval artists were essentially different creatures from those of the Renaissance. Yet it is impossible to instil a personal role into most mediaeval art history because of the limitations of the sources. Much outstanding work is condemned to remain for all time anonymous; many artists who were eminent in their time are probably condemned to remain as mere names without known works; and motives and attitudes will remain a matter of reasonable conjecture. We can, for instance, conjecture that the painter who offended St Erconwald wished to lock himself in, undisturbed, for the same reasons as Michelangelo when he was working in the Sistine Chapel. But if, for many people, mediaeval studies appear to be dry and depersonalized, the fault lies in the records and not in the artists. In spite of such disadvantages, it is still possible to build up a picture of mediaeval artists as industrious, useful and, more especially, human members of the community.

IX THE FINAL HERITAGE

The End of the Middle Ages

JOAN EVANS

'Plus me plaist le sejour qu'ont basty mes ayeux,

Que des palais Romains le front audacieux:

> *Plus que le marbre dur me plaist l'ardoise fine,*

Plus mon Loyre Gaulois que le Tybre Latin,

Plus mon petit Lyré que le mont Palatin,

> *Et plus que l'air marin la doulceur Angevine.'*

'Mightier to me the house my fathers made

> *Than your audacious heads, O Halls of Rome;*

More than immortal marbles undecayed,

> *The thin sad slates that cover up my home;*

More than your Tiber is my Loire to me,

> *Than Palatine my little Lyré there;*

And more than all the winds of all the sea,

> *The quiet kindness of the Angevin air.'*

JOACHIM DU BELLAY   *translated by G. K. Chesterton*

Under the sign of the cross

stands the globe, the image of the Universe. The coronation orb is one of the oldest symbols of the Christian Empire, and no other piece of insignia more completely or more vividly represents the unity for which the mediaeval world was striving. It had its place in Byzantine ritual and from there was certainly copied by the revived Empire of the West under Charlemagne and his successors, although it is first expressly mentioned only in 1191 at the coronation of Henry VI.

The orb illustrated here was made at about this time and may possibly be this very one. It is a hollow sphere made of six golden plates soldered together and contains a filling of resin to prevent it from denting. The stones are amethysts, sapphires, garnets, emeralds and half-pearls, held together by filigree bands. The jewelled cross (Christ's cross radiant in victory) has points of resemblance to Byzantine imperial crosses, and the central sap-

phire is engraved with what seems to be a Byzantine monogram.

This unity, this stability, was the essence of mediaeval life. The balance of authority—religious and political—was such that the great majority of men knew their place in society and felt a security which became more tenuous in later ages until it vanished altogether. Through theology and moral teaching the Church ruled men's minds, and this domination was reflected in art. Through the kings and the Emperor, anointed by the Pope or his representatives, the Church ruled, or at least claimed to rule, the body politic. It was an extraordinarily consistent world. In some senses there was great variety, but it was variety within an agreed compass of ideas and attitudes. There could be no radical non-conformity. Poverty, ignorance, injustice, bigotry and pain there were in plenty, but it must have been difficult to feel alienated from society or from the Church as a whole. (1)

The life, loves and leisure of ordinary people are depicted only incidentally by mediaeval artists—in the details of religious paintings, in Books of Hours or the decoration of combs and mirrors. One of the rare paintings of the mid-15th century with a profane subject is that of an engaged couple (right) by the Master of Sterzing. This German pair, expensively dressed in the latest fashion, stand in an arbour of flowering fruit-trees; the details of costume and jewellery are carefully observed. (2)

In an orchard, a group of elegant Italian men and women enjoy a concert of music (below). The man in the centre, with a falcon on his wrist is Castruccio da Lucca; to the right of him a woman plucks a lute, while the man beyond her plays a stringed instrument. This scene of simple pleasures bears, however, a direful moral: it is a detail of *The Triumph of Death*, the great fresco in the Campo Santo at Pisa (see p. 206), and is meant to convey the unexpectedness of death. (3)

People of fashion and high degree are shown having a pause for refreshment during a hunt with falcons (above). The picture is a later copy of a mid-15th century subject; it still gives accurate renderings of contemporary dress, headgear and hairdressing. Right: at the other social extreme, shepherds and shepherdesses join hands in a country dance, with a walled town in the background. Far right: mummers, fantastically masked and costumed, were popular entertainers, performing folk-plays and providing music on feast-days. (4, 5, 6)

The crowded cities of the 14th and 15th centuries were created largely because of the rise of a middle class. These three details from larger paintings give an idea of the urban scene in Germany, Italy and Flanders. Above: Cologne—the choir of the Cathedral (unfinished, as it was for the whole of the Middle Ages) is on the right, the church of St Martin near the centre. Below: Florence, with the octagonal Baptistery in the middle, the tower of the Badia to its left, the Palazzo Vecchio behind and the unfinished Cathedral and Campanile on the right. Opposite: a Flemish town, possibly Tournai, through the window of St Joseph's workshop. The mousetraps allude to St Augustine's words: 'The cross of the Lord was the devil's mousetrap.' (7, 8, 9)

Dante Alighieri (1265–1321) dominates the literature of the Middle Ages. His great poem, *La Divina Commedia*, displays the whole universe, as it functions according to the divine law and through the power of divine love. In this 15th-century fresco he stands holding a book on which the opening lines are written. On the left is Hell and the mountain of Purgatory leading to Paradise; on the right, the city of Florence where Dante was born but from which, for most of his life, he was a political exile. (15)

Allegory was perhaps the most popular of all literary forms and its greatest achievement, the *Roman de la Rose*, was read all over Europe and had innumerable imitators. This scene from King René of Anjou's *Livre du Cœur d'Amour épris* shows *Cœur, Vif-Désir,* and *Largesse* embarking with *Fiance* and *Actente*. (17)

'Looking before and after', the Middle Ages often seem both to evoke ancient Rome and to foreshadow the Renaissance. Rome was the model of Empire. Frederick II (1212–50), in a deliberate revival of the past, fostered a 'neo-antique' style which had its effect on Niccolò Pisano. The head (below) from Frederick's Triumphal Arch at Capua could easily be mistaken for a Roman imperial bust. Bottom: a figure of the Virgin from Rheims Cathedral, c. 1220, also influenced by Roman sculpture. (18,19)

Dionysus transformed into God the Father: a figure from Niccolò Pisano's pulpit in the Baptistery at Pisa, carved in 1260. Niccolò may have worked at Capua and it is certain that he used Roman sarcophagi as models. (20)

Renaissance ideas entered France from Italy during the late 15th century. Jean Fouquet, court painter to Louis XI, portrays a classical background about 1460, long before such a building had actually appeared in France. (21)

Across the Channel the new style arrived still later, but a foretaste was provided by Torrigiano's tomb of Henry VII (right)—pure Florentine Renaissance in the midst of Gothic England. (24)

Renaissance motifs and structure that is still Gothic are combined in the styles of François I and of Tudor England. The Italian roundels at Hampton Court (left) clearly belong to the new age, yet they predate the Great Hall (right) which is typically Perpendicular. At about the same time the choir of St-Pierre at Caen (below) uses a lavish repertoire of Italianate forms side by side with flamboyant tracery, flying buttresses and gargoyles. (22, 23, 25)

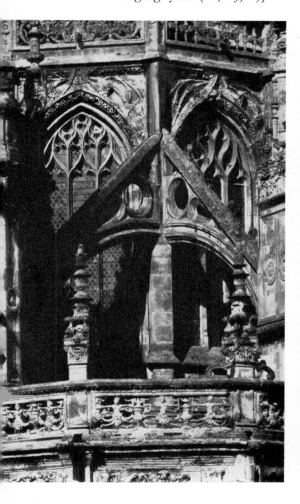

Germany was even slower to relinquish the old ways, and her 16th-century art is full of compromises. Conrad Meit of Worms, who made the tomb of Philibert-le-Beau at Brou in the 1530s, could produce classical nudes and winged *putti* in the most sophisticated Renaissance style; yet in the niches of the base he (or was it one of his French assistants?) carved graceful Gothic figures like this (right) representing a Virtue.

Far right: the shrine of St Sebald, Nuremberg. Thoroughly Gothic in overall design (it is carried on snails, a mediaeval symbol of resurrection), its smaller subsidiary figures on the base are wholly classical. (26, 27)

Cristofori faciem die quacumque tuens :·
Illa nempe die morte mala non moriens :· Millesimo cccc°
xxd° anno :·

The End of the Middle Ages

JOAN EVANS

Of all the women of the Middle Ages, real or imaginary, none is more alive than Chaucer's Wife of Bath—gross, earthy, pleasure-loving and tireless. 'She was a worthy woman all her life. Husbands at church door she had five, not counting other company in youth.' This woodcut is from Caxton's edition of about 1484. (1)

THE MIDDLE AGES achieved an extraordinarily coherent and integrated civilization. Had we knowledge and skill enough to recreate the pattern complete, we should have recovered a work of art as whole and as complex as the *Divina Commedia*. It was a civilization firmly based on Christianity. There were a certain number of heretics, who, because in the nature of things they were anti-social, were cruelly persecuted; it was not unreasonable to burn Savonarola in 1498. There were a number of Jews, who were tolerated or persecuted for political and economic reasons; a few Laodiceans and a handful of atheists. The range extended from a fanatic like St Bernard, a politician like Suger, a logician like Abailard and a philosopher like St Thomas Aquinas to a peasant who could hardly say his Paternoster; but all professed and called themselves Christians, and, in the crisis of the confessional, accepted the Christian ethic.

Our mental picture of the age—and, since the documents are difficult, the visible picture over-rides the documentation—emphasizes the fact. The towns appear with high-roofed houses sheltering round a great church like chickens under a hen; monasteries rise like affirmations of sanctity from the quiet countryside; colleges and universities base their day on the needs of prayer and the celebration of the Mass; and along the roads rise wayside crosses and shrines.

Every castle had its chapel, its chaplain and often its college of priests. The castle might have over its gateway a protecting figure of the Virgin and Child, or—as at La Ferté Milon—a sculpture of the Assumption, a divine image of feudal coronation. Even the heraldic splendours of hall and lists and battlefield had their origins in the Holy War of Crusade. The Orders of Chivalry were like communities of canons, though the knights might subsidize canons and bedesmen to fulfil their religious duties, as the Knights of the Garter did—and do—at Windsor. Even revenge had a chivalry of its own, for which it might have been difficult to find Christian authority, but which nonetheless was a part of the knightly conception of Christian duty.

◀ **The invention of printing,** more decisively than any other single event, marks the end of one era and the beginning of another. Before that there could be no real 'publication' in the modern sense, and the diffusion of knowledge was agonizingly slow.

The earliest form of mechanical duplication was by wooden blocks that included a picture (woodcut) and a text cut in the same block. The pages were bound together and are known as block-books. The St Christopher shown here belongs to this phase and is dated 1423 (the picture is tinted in watercolour). By about 1440 whole books without illustrations were being reproduced in this way and only the invention of movable type was needed for the art of printing to be born. That happened about ten years later, between 1451 and 1456. (28)

p 324 (15)

p 56 (47)
p 26 (26)
p 182 (2)
p 180 (1)

Death and Acceptance

Plague and murder, war and disease, made it impossible to forget the inevitability of Death; and Death, Resurrection, Judgment and Purgatory are the corner-stones of the Christian foundation on which the towering spire of Redemption could alone be based. Every illness had its protecting saint; every hospital was built round a chapel; and such hospitals were even in the late Middle Ages endowed with works of art that served to canalize the grief and patience of the dedicated nurses and the sufferers they tended. One of the finest Entombment groups in France—sculptured figures of the Virgin, the three Maries, John and Joseph of Arimathea round the dead body of Christ— is at the hospital at Tonnerre, given by a citizen in 1454. The Hermits of St-Antoine in the Vosges nursed men dying of horrible diseases, and it was for them that Matthias Grünewald painted that noble and horrifying picture of Christ, dead and suffering mortal corruption, against a sky black with despair. Each new patient was left before that picture, to study it at leisure and make what he could of it. Since out of suffering beauty may come, it is less strange that the bombardment of London revealed a dead Christ of the very end of the Middle Ages beneath the ruins of the chapel of the Mercers' Company.

p 322 (12)

p 323 (13)

Almost every church contained an altar or a chantry endowed for the saying of Masses for the repose of the soul of dead Christians. Death was everywhere, as it always is; but the Christian faith of the Middle Ages made it a part of life as it has rarely been.

In death the faithful departed might be equal, except for the spiritual audit of their lives; but in life no one cherished any illusion of equality. As the Middle Ages progressed the distinctions between rich and poor grew stronger, if those between noble and villein grew less cogent. It may have been that each man was more himself since he knew exactly where he stood in the social scheme. There is comradeship but no equality among Chaucer's pilgrims, but we accept their individualities as being natural and normal. The Catholic priesthood is always occupied with the individual, however dispassionately; the mediaeval conception of man was never generalized. Nothing, indeed, was generalized; individual bells, and jewels and cups and rings were given names—one might say pet-names—in the Middle Ages.

A Man's World

It was a man's world, as a Christian world is apt to be, for all the devotion owed and given to the Virgin and to the women saints. Fighting, administration, justice, learning, were all in men's hands. There were eminently capable lady abbesses, but, because they could not become part of a royal or ducal Civil Service as

Women and song: although the conventions of courtly love dominate the literature of the time, a more robust reality can often be perceived in letters or in unsophisticated woodcuts, such as this of the late 15th century. (2)

The Gothic Harvest

A flower blossoms, seeds and dies; and the time of its fruition depends on soil and aspect and weather. So it was with Gothic art. Its natural home in the Ile de France and Burgundy saw its first blooming; and all over France it lasted and burgeoned. In England—that at first had owed so much to France—there was another blossoming. The Curvilinear style, born at the very end of the 13th century and growing in splendour all through the 14th, stiffened into Perpendicular. Yet even here England gained much from the common market. William of Sens at Canterbury and the Savoyard castle architects of the Welsh marches contributed to the heritage of the West Country masons and the London carpenters who were as great in their craft as any architects we have ever had. p 136 (2)

In France Gothic continued after the fallow time during the dreadful years of war and plague, into a final *flamboyant* stage, first seen in the last quarter of the 15th century, that went on to the Art Nouveau splendour of Albi and Brou—the choir of Albi begun about 1500, Brou a great chantry church, between 1480 and 1504—a style in which the Gothic arch almost disappears, but in which there is nothing of the Renaissance unless it be the lushness of the draperies. p 327 (26)

Gothic art spread from Portugal to Jerusalem, from Cyprus to Norway, from the Polish borders to Ireland. Everywhere its dispersion depended on royal, ecclesiastical or monastic patronage, the patronage of an élite, and on the work of an élite of architects, masons and sculptors who had learned a tradition that ultimately went back to France.

France was indeed the centre of Gothic creation, in secular as in ecclesiastical work. The currents of power and patronage; the continuation of a Romanesque tradition so soundly based on construction that it was still fecund; the enrichment of life in the courts of France and Burgundy and in the religious foundations, that were a natural benefaction for great men who were proud of their descent from St Louis—all combined to form the splendid expression of a mature civilization. Ceremonial and ritual formed an elaborate fixed setting which provided space and time for men to think in. It was to modern eyes an age of formality, but it was a wonted formality that could be accepted without conscious thought. Even the almsmen had their dress and their doles and attended the Masses in their chapel from duty and right.

Nowadays we do not realize what art has lost from the lack of the direct patronage that it enjoyed in the Middle Ages: a patron who knew what he wanted and knew what he was going to do with it, and had the money to pay for it, and an artist infinitely skilled in his craft but also endowed with humility, could strike sparks from each other and create masterpieces. Art which is created to fulfil a direct function has an enormous advantage over the abstract doodlings of today, and the desultory patronage of those who occasionally buy at a Private View. Such patronage as that of the 14th and 15th centuries should, in the modern view, have stifled creation: in fact it stimulated it. The succession of splendidly illustrated Books of Hours painted for such princes as the duc de Berry, the duc d'Orléans, the Duke of Bedford and many other lesser men of no less taste, such as Etienne Chevalier, is as much a part of the history of art in Europe as the series of frescoes that men of their quality (if not always of their birth) commanded in Italy. Nor were the visual arts the only ones that flourished in the late Middle Ages, nor the only ones that continued the mediaeval tradition far into the 16th century. p 326 (21)

The Latin songs of the wandering scholars had been succeeded or accompanied by the lyrics of the troubadours and *trouvères*, which were echoed in most of the vernaculars of Europe; and all these lyrics were meant to be sung. The polyphony which appeared astonishingly early in the music of the Church in the first half of the 15th century developed into the *ars nova* of Machaut and Dunstable, which established a tradition that lasted far into the 16th century. With such music the poets' tradition of lyric lasted too; alongside the majestic and the classical, Ronsard remembers Villon, Joachim du Bellay the slate roofs of Angers. Italian composers might set Odes of Horace to music, but in England and France men still sang in the metres of the Middle Ages. f 3

an abbot could, they do not cut a great figure on the mediaeval stage. Héloïse is almost the only contemporary romantic heroine of the early Middle Ages, as Joan of Arc is of the later; the literary heroines, Iseult, Beatrice, and the rest, remain a little shadowy. p 182 (2)

> *La royne Blanche comme lis*
> *Qui chantoit a voix de seraine,*
> *Berte au grant pié, Bietris, Alis,*
> *Haremburgis qui tint le Maine,*
> *Et Jehanne la bonne Lorraine*
> *Qu' Englois brulerent a Rouan;*
> *Ou sont ilz, ou, Vierge Souvraine?*
> *Mais ou sont les neiges d'antan?*

Yet half the weight of the world was borne, as always, by women—women who gave birth to their children in the uncomfortable circumstances of cottage and castle, and even accompanying their husband on Crusade; women who held castles against the enemies of their absent husband and fulfilled, like abbesses, their feudal duties; women who hoed the fields and picked the grapes; women who as mothers and wives and servants and unenclosed religious tended the sick and taught the young; and a few women, like Christine de Pisan, who made a name for themselves as writers. The women of the Middle Ages tend to be anonymous, but they were not soft or sheltered; and occasionally —in Chaucer's *Canterbury Tales*, in the *Paston Letters*, in some accidentally surviving document—they come to life. p 149 (32) f 1

Women were chattels, at the disposal of their parents and guardians, in marriage as in all else. Courtly love—a romantic *amitié amoureuse*—proved the perfect counterpoise to a system that produced a rather surprising number of loyal and happy marriages, and inevitably a number of incompatible matings. Evidently men and women, married and unmarried, fell in love and coped with the situation as they best might, as they always do; evidently men found consolation outside the home as they have always done. In effect, the passions of the Middle Ages were human and are understandable at any date, if we remember the absence of divorce, the difficulty of annulment, and, for the knightly classes, the code of courtly love. The letters exchanged between Francesco di Marco Datini, the merchant of Prato, and his wife are (except in their formal language) dateless. Courtship in the days before the First World War was not very different from *Le Lai de l'Ombre*. p 258 (38)

Drama and Biography

The drama became one of the characteristic arts of the time: the first drama that owed nothing to Greece or Rome. The tropes of the Easter High Mass had grown into the liturgical drama in the monasteries and cathedrals, and its Latin had been translated into the vernacular, at first for the benefit of nuns whose knowledge of Latin was negligible. It had been an easy transition from the story of the Resurrection to the Nativity and stories of the childhood of Christ; and in the later Middle Ages the plays had grown, in England into cycles like the Chester mystery plays and in France into great communal performances that counted their players by hundreds and their audiences by thousands. Arnoul Gréban's vast and splendid *Mystère de la Passion* was created not long before 1452 for Notre-Dame de Paris, of which Gréban was for a time choir master. It brings to life all the iconography of a great cathedral: and, remarkably, it does not do this as a procession or a pageant—though its cast has 220 characters—but as a true drama. Like a Shakespearean play it has its low life and its comic relief, studied from the ways of ordinary men in the inns and by-roads of Paris. Gréban's *Mystère* is only one of many; every great city took pride in producing some such splendid play. Usually backed and financed and in part acted by members of the gilds, they stand, like some city churches, as artistic manifestations of civic pride. This source is still more evident in one of the few chronicle plays that have survived, the *Mystère du Siège d'Orléans*, that tells the story of an as yet uncanonized Joan of Arc. The secular action takes place on a lower stage; and above, there is a heavenly hierarchy like a formal picture; first St Aignan and St Euverte, the patron saints of the city of Orléans; then the Virgin; and, towering over all, Christ.

Such plays gave life and movement and speech to the interminable narratives of the sculptured portals and the painted windows of the churches, to which they owed their inspiration. If we are tempted to dismiss the idea that mediaeval art served to instruct *f 12* the illiterate as a romantic invention of the 19th century, Villon is there to show us that for him it was true. He makes his mother say:

> Femme je suis povrette et ancïenne,
> Qui riens ne sçay; oncques lettre ne lus
> Au moustier voy dont suis paroissienne
> Paradis paint, ou sont harpes et leus,
> Et ung enfer ou dampnez sont boullus:
> L'ung me fait paour, l'autre joye et liesse.

Even more specifically Eustache Mercadé, in a Mystery play before 1440, wrote:

> A plusieurs gens ont moult valu
> Qui n'entendent les escriptures,
> Exemples, histoires, pointures
> Faictes ès moustiers et palais,
> Ce sont les livres des gens lais.

Probably the cinema could claim to do as much for the illiterates of Africa and Asia.

It is easy, remembering such men as Cellini, to think of the Renaissance as the time when men appreciated the individual and the individual appreciated himself. (We forget that Villon hardly ever wrote about anyone but Villon.) In fact it was the Middle Ages that created the modern *genres* of biography and autobiography. Biography had its roots in the Latin lives of holy abbots, such as St Hugh of Cluny, written by men who knew them, composed in the hope of their canonization. Joinville's *Saint Louis* began with the same intention, but because it was written in French and because the writer and his subject were both secular and both gentlemen, the *genre* was subtly changed.

Already, indeed, the great adventure of Crusade had driven men like Villehardouin into contemporary military history. At the end of the Middle Ages the crusading theme came to a hysterically feminine end in the awful outpourings of Margery Kempe, from which the expense of parchment and the use of Latin would earlier have saved the world.

The troubadours—poets and minstrels exploiting almost for the first time the resources of the new European languages —began in Provence and soon carried the code of courtly love to Italy and France. In Germany they are known as 'Minnesänger' ('Minne' means courtly love); among the greatest was Walther von der Vogelweide (c.1170–c.1228), portrayed here in a collection of poems made for the Emperor Henry VI. Walther was a serious thinker, the originator of political verse in German and an active participant in the quarrels between Emperor and Pope. (3)

The monasteries had produced not only Lives of Saints but also Annals; and the *genre* merged with the half-pious stories of Crusade in the great Chronicles of the later Middle Ages. The noble and knightly classes were now literate; and while they might still enjoy the recital of *chansons de geste* could also appreciate the leisurely perusal of histories of events in which they and their parents had taken part. Such chronicles as Froissart's and Chastellain's presuppose such readership. In Froissart's case we can even see how he acquired his material and his audience. He was born at Valenciennes about 1337 and was attached for five years to the court of Philippa of Hainault in London, at a time when it was made more brilliant by the presence of the captive French King and of some sixty French prisoners and hostages. Here were 'sources' that only wanted to be listened to. With the existing chronicle of Jean le Bel, a canon of Liège, as a foundation, he could compile at leisure. When he left England for a canonry in his own country, he was free to travel to gain more material for his history in France, both from the sight of battlefields and from the conversation of knights returned from the wars.

p 148
(30)

The Latin literature of the monasteries and the universities was essentially ecclesiastical; but with the growth of a literate aristocracy in the later Middle Ages an increasing number of these Latin texts, especially those that a modern librarian would classify as scientific, were translated into the vernacular.

At the same time a new class of prose authors began to define itself: men who had usually taken orders and had a university training, and held some easy ecclesiastical post as a canon or a chantry priest to provide them with the equivalent of a research fellowship. Froissart and Alain Chartier are typical for France; Langland for England. Gréban was a Master of Arts of Paris and held a post in the choir school of Notre-Dame. Chaucer was, exceptionally, a civil servant; Villon a vagabond: but even he was brought up in the house of a kinsman who was a canon and a lecturer in the law schools of Paris.

Renaissance

'The Middle Ages ended with the coming of the Renaissance.' Popularizing historians sometimes write and speak as if this had been an event as definitive as the French Revolution or the First World War: 'and after it nothing was ever the same again'. In fact it was not an event but a reasonably slow and curiously insidious process, to which certain events contributed.

The discovery of America made remarkably little difference except to the geographers, the poets and the gold-importing monarchs of the Peninsula; the exploration of coastal Africa was nearly as important.

The fall of Constantinople in 1453 brought Greek scholars to Florence and Greek manuscripts to every Mediterranean port; it changed the destiny of Venice, and brought a sense of insecurity

The Gothic style in Italy appears more typically in sculpture than in architecture. The 'Arca' of St Peter Martyr at Milan by Giovanni di Balduccio (1339) makes lavish use of pointed arch and pinnacle. The eight caryatid figures are Justice, Temperance, Fortitude, Prudence, Faith, Hope, Charity and Obedience, and the reliefs on the sarcophagus (there are eight altogether) show the death of the saint, his canonization and his saving a ship at sea. (4)

style; and Niccolò Pisano had drawn inspiration from antique sarcophagi and had represented God the Father on the model of a figure of Dionysus supported by a satyr. Even at Rheims in the 13th century some statues are clearly modelled on Roman prototypes; and by 1402 the duc de Berry was buying Roman medals from a Florentine merchant.

p 326 (20)
p 326 (19)

Italy

Yet there is all the difference between a sound knowledge of classical texts and a mild interest in classical art and a humanism that—*ex hypothesi*—cannot be Christian. The problem was not faced, but ignored. Petrarch tried to take refuge in the past. 'The very sight of men of the present time wounds me sorely, whereas the memories, the deeds, the illustrious names of the ancients, give me joy, splendid and so inestimable that, if the world could know, it would be amazed that I should have so much pleasure in talking with the dead and so little with the living.'

Statues of the elder and younger Pliny were set like patron saints on the façade of the new cathedral at Como, and Leda and the Swan on the great doors of St Peter's. A new iconography made David the giant-killer a more interesting subject for sculpture than any Christian saint.

f 7

As Dr J. H. Plumb has wisely said, in the Middle Ages Italy never belonged wholly to Europe. Feudalism could not flourish in a civilization which had an essentially urban basis; the chief contribution of Italy to the Middle Ages was the contradiction of feudalism, banking. The vendetta belonged to the country, not to Christendom.

In Italy only the Cistercians and the Franciscans were at home in the Gothic style, and even the Cistercians in their great church at Chiaravalle outside Milan achieved an architecture that is far removed from the structural Gothic of the Order in its native Burgundy. 'Venetian Gothic' is as much Eastern as French; and the one Gothic church in Rome—Sta Maria sopra Minerva—seems an intruder.

to all eastern Europe; but it did not cause the Renaissance. Yet it marks, better than any other event, a watershed between two civilizations. Moorish Granada fell at the beginning of 1492; no subsequent war in Spain could be called a Crusade. The two events show a shift of the map of Christendom westwards, and another emphasis on the importance of Spain and Portugal, which is a mark of the Renaissance that is not always recognized.

The treasures of the libraries of Constantinople increased the European repertory of Greek texts, and encouraged the study of the language; but the classics were already familiar in the Middle Ages. The 'Renaissance' of the 11th and 12th centuries, headed by men such as Berengar of Tours, had to some extent been swamped in the dialectical theology of the 13th century; but in the 15th century men still believed that human reason was a reflection of the divine, and still read classical texts. Early in the century, in her *Epistle of Othea to Hector* (which Sir John Fastolf translated into English) Christine de Pisan uses classical figures, such as Perseus, Hercules and Bacchus, to symbolize the knightly virtues and the knightly temptations.

p 149 (32)

Charles d'Orléans, prisoner in England, passed the time in reading not only books of devotion, but also Boccaccio, Aristotle's *Politics*, Josephus, the *Ethics* of Nicole Oresme and St Augustine: an interesting list for a French prince in the years round 1430. Alain Chartier—admittedly a graduate and a priest—writing his *Espérance* in 1428, advises his readers to study Homer, Virgil, Livy, Demosthenes, Orosius, Justinian, Valerius Maximus and various other classical authors as well as the early mediaeval writers *qui ont travaillé à allonger leur brief aage par la notable et longue renommée de leurs escriptures*. He had not read them all himself though he does not admit it: certainly not Homer and Demosthenes; but he really did know his Sallust, Virgil, Horace and Seneca.

p 183 (7, 8)

What was more, he could see the romance of classical antiquity. In his *Quadriloge invectif*, written in 1422, he asks:

Où est Ninive la grant cité qui duroit trois journées de chemin? Qu'est devenue Babiloine, qui fut edifiée de matière artificieuse pour plus durer aux hommes, et maintenant est habitée de serpens? Que dira l'on ... de Ylion le chastel sans per, dont les portes furent d'ivoire et les colonnes d'argent: et maintenant à peine en reste le pié des fondemens, que les haulx buissons forcloent de la veue des hommes?

The Emperor Frederick II had had his great gate at Capua, built between 1233 and 1240, adorned with bas-reliefs of trophies and statues of the city, his ministers and himself, all in classical

p 326 (18)

Mediaeval iconography continues into the Renaissance, the innovations being chiefly stylistic. Series of signs of the Zodiac combined with Labours of the Months remained popular. Left: two panels from the west front of Amiens (early 13th century) representing the month of February. The sign is Pisces, the fish; the 'labour' is a man warming himself by the fire and cooking a fish. Right: the same month from the fountain at Perugia carved by Niccolò and Giovanni Pisano in 1278. The two motifs are now combined into one, and the fisherman is shown actually catching his fish (5, 6)

Like an alien style, Italian Gothic achieved its most beautiful manifestations in relatively small and relatively decorative and un-architectural work. There are any number of Italian churches that are not really Gothic in their construction but have beautiful Gothic doorways; any number of Italian tombs that are poems written in the Gothic idiom of arcade and pinnacle, whether they celebrate a saint, like that of St Peter Martyr in S. Eustorgio at Milan, or warriors like those of the Scala at Verona.

f 4
p 218
(31)

In Italy far too much architecture and art is commonly ascribed to the Renaissance that is in fact mediaeval. Buildings that contain no more classical embellishment than a simple colonnade, pictures in which the figures are draped in the angular folds of Gothic art rather than in the self-conscious draperies of the deliberate classicists, cannot reasonably be thought of as other than mediaeval. The traditional themes of mediaeval iconography, that provided the subjects for wall-paintings and altarpieces in noble and monastic chapels, and the larger illustrations in Books of Hours, were the slowest to receive the imprint of the Renaissance. Fra Angelico is still a mediaeval painter, in subject as in style; even Michelangelo's great *Pietà* in St Peter's is as much Gothic as Renaissance; its Renaissance quality lies rather in the beauty and youth of the Virgin than in the sculptural style of the whole composition.

p 62
(66)

Masaccio is still really an artist of the Middle Ages. There is nothing of the Renaissance in Giotto's Paduan frescoes; reduce them to miniatures, and they could adorn any book of devotion. A splendid and almost geometrical composition is not the prerogative only of Renaissance painters. Benozzo Gozzoli is as mediaeval as the illuminator of any royal Book of Hours, Pinturicchio has his mediaeval moments; but Botticelli is a man of the Renaissance, with his humanist's denial of material weight. The use of architectural backgrounds in classical style makes Piero della Francesca's *Flagellation* at Urbino a Renaissance picture, though he has not altogether forgotten the Middle Ages.

The sculptors were often no less traditional, especially in tomb figures; the carvings of the Labours of the Months on the fountain at Perugia, though set in a Renaissance framework, are clearly of the same lineage as the 13th-century sculpture of the same subject at Amiens.

f 5, 6

Donatello and Brunelleschi had to go to Rome to see what was left of antiquity; they returned, the one to recreate free-standing decorative sculpture, and the other to spread the ideas of Vitruvius in stern and splendidly proportioned buildings. The Strozzi and Rucellai palaces have nothing mediaeval about them.

Nature

The love of Nature, especially of the trees and the woods where man hunted, was a constant factor in the inspiration of mediaeval art, from the capitals of such cathedrals as Laon to the *selva oscura* of Dante and of the background of the Wilton Diptych. It inspired gold-work and tapestries and embroideries and illuminations: all the arts that made the austerity of castles beautiful. It was far from uncongenial to the classical style of the Renaissance; indeed it had Roman prototypes. Ghiberti's flower garlands on the north door of the Baptistery at Florence, cast in bronze in 1403, could vie with French sculpture in stone of an earlier date. Only on the east door, made thirty years later, are the rose-garlands broken by intrusive medallions and anthemia.

p 326
(24)

Torrigiano, when Henry VIII brought him to England in 1516 to make his royal father's tomb, used fruit, oak boughs and rose sprays more freely than the arabesque pilaster panels of the Renaissance. (Even the tomb figures do not deny the tradition of the Warwick effigy). Elizabethan decoration was often abundantly naturalistic, and in embroideries and tapestries the style lingered on through Stuart times. Milton is the first truly classical English poet, yet in *Lycidas* he numbers all the flowers of the garden and the countryside to make a garland for his dead hero. In France, too, naturalistic decoration survived, a little classicized and modernized by reminiscences of bucolics and pastorals, to achieve new triumphs in the age of Louis XIII.

Yet there was a clear and striking change, if one that it is not easy to define. In the Middle Ages an artist might almost accidentally display a naked human body in action, but it was not an essential part of art nor a theme for the display of virtuosity. (The

The great men of Greece and Rome were assimilated into the Christian universe without too much sense of strain. Virgil (on the strength of an ambiguous passage in the Eclogues) was received as a prophet of Christ; Erasmus felt tempted to pray to Socrates as to a saint; and in 1498 statues of the two Plinys were set up on the new façade of the Cathedral at Como. Above is Pliny the Younger. (7)

mediaeval artist was rarely a virtuoso.) The Christian belief in the Resurrection of the Body had forbidden dissection *post mortem* and the ban had affected not only the surgeon but also the sculptor. The surgeons of Bologna and the artist Leonardo da Vinci were the first to break the tabu; but none of them were men of the Middle Ages.

The humanists were prepared to begin from below, in scientific observation, if of a crude kind; the Christian philosophers of the Middle Ages (with the legendary exception of Roger Bacon) had begun from above, in a divine creation and a divine eschatology. Their *mystère* was like a mediaeval one, with God the Father, Christ and His Mother, and the saints in a hierarchy above the stage; the Italian humanists' stage-setting was on a simpler plan.

Patronage

Patronage still played a great part in the Renaissance, but it showed a greater respect for the artist: Francis I picked up the brush of Titian and gave asylum to Leonardo in his old age. In the Middle Ages the patron wanted something for a specific purpose in a specific place; with the Renaissance came the easel picture and the idea of 'Fine' art, detached from a specific purpose.

If the Middle Ages lingered on in Italy where the Renaissance was born, it is no matter of surprise that it should have been slow to depart in France. Yet the new style crept gradually in. Between 1445 and 1447 Fouquet visited Italy. Ten years later the miniatures he painted for the Book of Hours of Etienne Chevalier have

Two things were necessary for that revolution in the spread of knowledge which we associate with the Renaissance—the invention of printing and the manufacture of cheap paper. This woodcut of 1568 gives a clear idea of the early papermaker at work. In the background the raw material, rotted cotton and linen, is placed in a trough to be macerated by hammers operated by a water-wheel. It is then mixed with water in a vat (right foreground) and the 'vatman', using a shallow mould which he dips into the mixture, forms it into thin spongy sheets, shaking it as he does so to cross and mat the fibres. Then in the wooden screw-press behind him the sheets are pressed in piles of 144, separated by layers of felt, and the finished paper is hung up to dry. (8)

p 326
(21) Italianate marble architecture for their backgrounds. Italian artists came to France to practise in the new style. In 1461 a medal of Louis XI by Francesco Laurana was struck; and the artist stayed in France to make the tomb of Charles, comte du Maine, who died in 1473, in his city of Le Mans.

After the Burgundian defeat in 1477 the centre of French court life and art shifted to the Loire valley; by 1495 Italian artists were working there and inspiring the 'School of Amboise' to create a new half-Italianate style, sweet and gentle as good Loire wine. When Francis I brought in another generation of Italian artists, headed by Primaticcio, they naturalized the style of Giulio Romano in France; but this did not happen until about 1540 when the style was becoming old-fashioned in Italy. The great abbeys continued to commission work in the old style well into the 16th century. The Concordat of 1510, that gave papal permission to Francis I to nominate all abbots and many bishops, weakened the force of the tradition. Yet when Hector Sohier p 326
(23) between 1518 and 1545 built St-Pierre at Caen, he applied rich Renaissance decoration in Lombard style to a Gothic construction with buttresses, gargoyles and pinnacles. It seems that it may be fair to say that in France Gothic architecture is seriously enfeebled only with the Council of Trent in 1545. Such mediaeval survivals as may be found after that date *are* survivals.

By 1530 North Italian ornament was a commonplace in the art of the Low Countries; by 1535 Italian architects were employed at Landshut and at Prague.

The Middle Ages had witnessed a gradual local specialization in manufacture—tapestries at Arras, brass at Dinant, enamels at p 254
(25) Limoges, pottery at Faenza and Gubbio, cloth in England and Flanders, silks and brocades in the Italian cities and a hundred more that came near to causing an industrial revolution.

The Paper Revolution

Another minor industrial revolution had a particular impact on means of communication, literary and visual. Since even peasants had begun to wear a shirt between their skin and their outer clothing, there was a supply of linen rags; these began to be f 8 pulped for the manufacture of paper. Once paper was available it was possible to make notes, to exchange letters, to *communicate* without the expense and *expertise* of writing on parchment. Peter the Venerable and Héloïse had been able to correspond because as head of a monastic house each could command a *scriptorium* and parchment, but not many people found themselves so fortunately situated for letter-writing. With the later Middle Ages the use of paper made almost as much difference to human communication as the telephone has in the last eighty years. It is significant that our knowledge of late mediaeval family life is largely based on such collections as the Datini and the Paston letters, which could not, from the practical point of view, have been written earlier.

Paper was not a European invention. It had been widely used by the Arabs; its centre of manufacture seems to have been Damascus. It was made in Moorish Spain and Arab Sicily, and gradually crept into use in the parts of Europe—such as Venice—that were in touch with the East. By 1276 its manufacture was established in Italy at Fabriano near Ancona, and by the second half of the 14th century paper-mills were scattered all over the northern Italian states, and were soon rivalled by others in Germany set up with the help of Italian workmen. The first French water-mark is of 1348; in the 15th century the trade rapidly increased in France. In England it was introduced by way of the ports dealing with Spain and Gascony and Germany, and was in common use in the 15th century; its manufacture in Hertfordshire and Kent—still the great papermaking centres in this country—soon followed.

The only surviving wood-block of the 14th century is the 'Bois Protat' (so called because it belonged to M. Protat, the distinguished printer of Mâcon) which has an engraving of the Annunciation on one side and part of a Crucifixion on the other. The latter (a modern impression from it is shown above) shows the centurion saying, 'Truly this was the Son of God.' (9)

'*Manière criblée*' (*dotted style*) *came into use in the middle of the 15th century for prints and block-books intended for the common people: the rich went on collecting illuminated manuscripts even after the invention of printing. It was printed from metal plates and gives the effect of being riddled with small holes. This German example, with its simple patterns and naïve decorative borders, illustrates the considerable charm that it could achieve.* (*10*)

Printing: the Diffusion of Knowledge

Paper encouraged easy and ephemeral writing; but its real importance lay in the fact that it made printing a practical possibility. The Cistercians, in their desire to avoid the luxury of illuminated manuscripts, had used initials, stamped from movable blocks of boxwood, as early as the late 12th century, but the use had not been fruitful until paper came into common use and a good greasy printing ink had been invented. At first the whole page was printed at once from a single block and, perhaps because the larger part of the public were illiterate, pictures preceded printed words. *f 9* The *Bois Protat* with the Crucifixion and the Annunciation is the only surviving early wood-block from which such prints were made; it probably dates from between 1370 and 1380, and was significantly discovered at La-Ferté-sur-Grosne, the site of one of the great Cistercian abbeys of Burgundy. Yet its survival was a matter of chance, and scholars have argued for nearly a century about the place and date of the first use of such a block.

So far as dated or dateable engravings go, there is an engraving of the Virgin Mary in the Royal Library at Brussels that dates from 1418. In the early part of the 15th century blocks were produced all over Germany, Flanders, and Holland, with pictures usually accompanied by a text cut in the same block, or else on a separate page so that they could be bound together to form a block-book. All are devotional; some, like the St Christopher of 1423 in the John Rylands Library, had their apotropaic aspect too. p 328 (28) They flourished chiefly in the countries of northern Europe where the art of illumination was less developed than in Italy, France and England, and were oddly combined with the sale of indulgences, for which printed 'briefs' offered an obvious facility.

Rich men continued to order and to use Books of Hours with exquisite coloured illuminations, but *petits bourgeois* and villagers were glad to own single engravings of religious subjects printed on paper from wooden blocks. The only secular subjects in early

The new style of book illustration soon produced its own masterpieces; among the most popular and influential was Francesco Colonna's 'Hypnerotomachia Poliphili'. Colonna, a Dominican friar of Treviso, wrote his allegory in 1467, and it was printed by Aldus Manutius of Venice in 1499. The typeface that he used is still taken as a model ('Poliphilus') and the engravings were widely copied. The one shown here is a characteristic fantasy of antique ruins—fallen entablatures, broken arches, a palm-tree and an obelisk. (11)

French engravings are the Nine Worthies—a courtly subject that pageants had made familiar to citizens—and the Planets. The link with civic drama is made more evident by a French engraving of the Passion, of about 1490, with 215 personages, nearly as many as acted in Gréban's *Mystère de la Passion*.

f 10   The *criblé* technique, as of a target riddled with small holes, came into use in the middle of the 15th century; it was never used except for 'briefs' and books intended for humble people, and in its way prefigures 'folk art'. Not infrequently such plates were completed by a short inscription engraved on the same block as the picture. Indeed, the use of engraved blocks to print a text without illustrations was not uncommon in Germany and the Netherlands about 1440. Like the early pictorial block-books, they were all devotional, except for a treatise on reading fortunes from the hand and Donatus's *Grammar*.

It was a natural process to go on to movable types which could be used independently or combined with woodcuts in the mass production of books of devotion. The art of printing was born: the art that more than any other separates the Middle Ages from modern times.

The invention of movable types has long been disputed between Lourens Janzoon Coster of Haarlem and Johan Gutenberg of Mainz; at all events it seems to have occurred between 1451 and 1456. As with the block-books the earliest texts printed from movable types were indulgences; then followed whole books—Bibles, almanacs, Donatus, and a few devotional books, of which the *Speculum humanae salvationis* is typical. The first dated book—as opposed to 'briefs'—is a Psalter produced at Mainz in 1457.

Wooden types wore out rather quickly, and the transition to a metal fount seems to have been made in Holland before 1473

and perhaps before 1460. In 1458 Charles VII of France commissioned N. Jenson, one of the engravers of the Paris mint, to go to Mainz to study printing. In fact he went to Venice instead, but the choice of a man experienced in cutting metal dies suggests that he was sent to study the manufacture of metal types. Their use spread rapidly all through central Europe and beyond, nearly always by the work of emigrant Dutch and German printers. It reached Rome by 1467; Venice by 1469; and most of the north Italian towns between 1471 and 1474. London had a printing press in 1477, Oxford in 1478; even Edinburgh had a press by 1507, though Dublin did not until 1551. Music was first printed from type by Ulrich Hahn at Rome in 1476; and in 1525 Pierre Haultin of Paris invented type from which notes and staves could be printed simultaneously.

It is easy, but false, to suppose that books produced by such presses did much to spread the doctrines of humanism. That was the prerogative of an élite who, for the most part, depended on manuscripts. It is true that the first Italian books finely illustrated in Renaissance style—Francesco Colonna's *Hypnerotomachia Poli-* *f 11* *phili*, printed in 1499, and Ovid's *Metamorphoses* in the edition of 1497—had a considerable influence both in Italy and France. But, broadly speaking, what the printers did was to make the books of the Middle Ages more cheaply and more abundantly available. About 1480 Jean Molinet cited among the wonders of his day:

J'ay veu grant multitude
De livres imprimez
Pour tirer en estude
Povres mal argentez.
Par ces nouvelles modes
Aura maint escollier
Decret, bibles et codes,
Sans grant argent bailler.

Courtly historians like Froissart and Chastellain are known to us from illuminated manuscripts prepared for royal or noble use; but most of the French minor poets of the 15th century—and very good minor poets some of them were—are known to us from early printed books, mostly with wood-block engravings. Villon, a major poet, is represented in six manuscripts and two printed editions, of 1489 and 1501; Charles d'Orléans, a royal poet, and a few others who were attached to courts, naturally have their manuscripts written on vellum. Most oddly of all, the greatest mediaeval poem, Dante's *Divina Commedia*, does not exist in

François Villon, the most individual poet of the Middle Ages and one of its most fascinating personalities, from the 'Grand Testament' printed at Paris in 1489. Villon's life, violent and probably short, was lived in the Parisian underworld and the Parisian prisons. In his poetry mediaeval Paris comes to life. (12)

*Caxton's device, the initials W and C
with his trade-mark in between. Caxton,
the first English printer, learned the art
in Cologne and set up his press at Bruges,
before moving to Westminster in 1476. He
is known to have printed 102 books and
broadsheets, several of them written or
translated by himself. (13)*

*During the transition from Gothic to Ren-
aissance every art-form, from architecture
to book-production, went through a phase
in which the old and the new existed
together in uneasy combination. In this
title-page from a Bible of 1521, Gothic
elements (the black-letter title, the angels
beside the Virgin and Child) are juxta-
posed with novelties from Italy (the columns and other ornaments, the 'putti' and
the more modern capital letters). The central picture is in 'criblé' technique, and
includes the emblems of the printer,
Pierre Bailly of Lyons. (14)*

p 324
(16) manuscript but is known from printed editions published in 1472,
apparently both at Mantua and Foligno.

 The same perpetuation of mediaeval books can be seen in the
publications of the English presses. Caxton printed Chaucer,
Charles the Great and *Renaud de Montauban*, and in 1484 translated
and printed Ramon Lull's *Book of the Ordre of Chyualry* and
Christine de Pisan's *Fayt of Armes.*

 It was in the second stage of the Renaissance, when Protestantism had become nearly as important as classicism, that printing
played a part, and indeed a large part, in distributing the doctrines
of critics of Catholicism and reformers. Without printing there
could hardly have been a Reformation.

 Printing, too, created the modern idea of literary personalities.
In the Middle Ages, when a book, unless it were very brilliant or,
still better, very useful, only existed in two or three copies, it was
remarkably difficult to have a genuine literary success. Modern
authors and publishers will sympathize with Gerald of Wales,
who, when he had finished his great book on Ireland, took the
manuscript to Oxford, hired lodgings, and spent three days reading it aloud to three different audiences, whom he fed handsomely.
Only so could he hope to find a public. Erasmus's reputation
seems to some mediaevalists to stand too high; it was as much
based on printing as that of some men of our own time has been
on broadcasting and television.

It is natural that the art of engraving should have done much to spread the Italian style beyond Italy. Dürer, as an apprentice at Nuremberg, owned engravings by Pollaiuolo and Mantegna. Such title-pages as those abundantly produced at Paris and Lyons *f 14* and elsewhere, with a title in black letter capitals framed by vertical columns of Renaissance ornament like a candelabrum or a panel in Raphael's Vatican frescoes, were just what the provincial sculptor needed to provide him with a model for a Renaissance frame to a mediaeval relief, as they are on the choir screen at Chartres and on the stalls from Gaillon carved in 1509.

Roman Medallions

The Certosa at Pavia, and many other buildings in the ornate plateresque style of the early Renaissance, were adorned with medallions of human heads, usually in profile but sometimes full face, that were ultimately derived from Roman coins. Antonio Filarete used them on the hospital at Milan, and Caradosso at S. Satiro. Mantegna used them to fill odd corners of his frescoes in the Camera degli Sposi at Mantua.

The King of France, in the course of his successful invasion of Northern Italy, in 1494, saw and admired them at Pavia and elsewhere; and when he returned to his own country the next year with a retinue of Italian artists and forty tons weight of Italian works of art, Paganino reproduced them at Gaillon. By 1504 they appeared on the hospital of Santa Cruz at Toledo, and soon after on the Irish College at Salamanca.

It was not long before they were represented in engravings: in the editions of Petrarch's *Trionfi* published at Venice in 1500, 1523 and 1545, and again in various editions of Boccaccio. By 1517 they had reached the engraved pattern books of Enea Vico; ten years later they had crossed the Alps to appear in the pattern books of Lucas van Leyden. Their appearance outside Italy is indeed one of the tests of the importation of Renaissance style: at Hampton p 326 Court about 1521, on Bishop Fox's screen at Winchester (22) before 1528, at Haddon Hall about 1545, at Heidelberg in 1556. Occasionally, as at Bacon's Gorhambury, built between 1563 and 1571, they were importations ready-made from Italy; far more often they were local imitations. Wherever they appear they are an assertion of a classical taste.

Symptoms of Decline

A new civilization—and, within definite limits, the Renaissance became a new civilization—can come in only by force of arms unless the civilization it changes is decadent. The later Middle Ages were for many countries times of weakening catastrophes.

The seat of the Papacy was in dispute from 1309 until 1421, and the unifying power of a good pope was necessarily discounted when there were several claimants to the throne of St Peter. England and France wore themselves out in the Hundred Years' War and the Wars of the Roses; the employment of mercenaries changed the basis of feudalism, and in both countries a succession of politically weak kings gradually eroded the power of the monarchy. By contrast the 15th-century Italians remained rich and powerful. They could produce any number of patrons to whom money meant only the fulfilment of their will and the satisfaction of their fancy.

Everywhere, but especially in France and England, plague, pestilence and famine followed and accompanied war. The chronicler tells us that in 1339, when the Black Death raged in France, *la tierce partie du monde mourut.* The 15th century in France was *f 16* ruled by the idea of Death. Villon is obsessed with the idea of Death; and so, if to a lesser degree, are most of his contemporaries among the poets.

Et meure Paris ou Helaine,
Quiconques meurt, meurt a douleur
Telle qu'il pert vent et alaine;
Son fiel creve sur son cuer,
Puis sue, Dieu scet quelle sueur!
Et n'est qui de ses maux l'alege:
Car enfant n'a, frere ne seur,
Qui lors voulsist estre son plege.

La mort le fait fremir, pallir,
Le nez courber, les vaines tendre,
Le col enfler, la chair mollir,
Joinctes et nerfs croistre et estendre.
Corps femenin, qui tant es tendre,
Poly, souef, si precieux,
Te fauldra il ces maux attendre?

The existence of such an obsession with mortality inevitably weakens a nation's life. Because so many men's thoughts were set on death, the doctrine of purgatory and the possibility of buying indulgences to shorten its duration gained a new importance at a time when wars made the old way of saving one's soul by pilgrimage impossible: and such abuses weakened the Faith.

Even so, mediaeval ideas were slow to die. We have only to look at Wolsey's stair-case hall at Christ Church, the chapel screen of King's College, Cambridge, 1532-36, or Henry VIII's great Hall p 327 at Hampton Court, 1536, to see how strong the Gothic tradition (25) remained in England. Shute's digest of Serlio was not published until 1563, ten years after its author had returned from Italy. Not until Thomas Arundel, 1585-1640, had established his great collection of classical sculpture and Inigo Jones had studied in Rome did English architecture become truly classical.

Holbein's portraits of his English period are strangely and p 259 delightfully mediaeval; but for details of costume they would have (40) passed at the court of Burgundy. Dürer began, at least, as a mediaevalist; his noble woodcuts—for example the Apocalypse— are Gothic in drapery as in subject. The designs of the Seven *f 15* Candlesticks may be of the Renaissance but the spirit that informs the whole page is of the Middle Ages. His ideas of *Melancolia nobilis* and of the cavalier Death have a 15th-century quality about them.

Yet there was a weakness; a weakness which Europeans who have suffered in two great wars in a lifetime can understand. It made men in Germany and England ready to accept a destructive Reformation and laid France open to interminable wars of religion. Without question there was a decadence, and that decadence made it possible for a new civilization that was essentially Italian to spread over the rest of Europe.

Yet though the firm rule of the Church might seem to be weakened, the Renaissance made no real change in the Christian ideas of saintliness and of duty. Even Villon—the least conventional and dutiful of Christians, in whom some would see a precursor of the Renaissance—stops his sardonic *Testament* when the great bell of the Sorbonne sounds the Angelus:

Finablement, en escripvant,
Ce soir, seulet, estant en bonne
Dictant ces laiz et descripvant,
J'oïs la cloche de la Serbonne,
Qui tousjours a neuf heures sonne
Le salut que l'ange predit;
Si suspendis et mis cy bonne
Pour prier comme le cuer dit.

'*And I turned to see the voice that spake with me. And being turned,* ▶ *I saw seven golden candlesticks; and in the midst of the seven candlesticks, one like unto the Son of Man, clothed with a garment down to the foot, and girt about the paps with a golden girdle. His head and his hairs were white like wool, as white as snow; and his eyes were as a flame of fire; and his feet like unto fine brass, as if they burned in a furnace, and his voice as the sound of many waters. And he had in his right hand seven stars: and out of his mouth went a sharp two-edged sword: and his countenance was as the sun shineth in his strength.*' (*Revelations, I, 12–16.*) Dürer's superb interpretation of St John's vision—inspired yet literal, mystical yet precise—is thoroughly mediaeval in spirit, although such details as the candlesticks themselves are of the Renaissance. (15)

The Lingering Past

English literature was conservative. *Gammer Gurton's Needle*, the first English comedy, might well be staged in the manner of the marginal illustrations of a 14th-century East Anglian manuscript, and the tradition is continued in the knock-about farce of Shakespeare's early comedies. Shakespeare indeed is more mediaeval than the language of his greater speeches always allows us to realize. His chronicle plays are in the tradition of such dramas as the *Mystère du Siège d'Orléans*. Pierre Champion and R. L. Stevenson have pointed out how far the actual life of the poet-prince Charles d'Orléans prefigures the drama of Hamlet. The tragedy of *Hamlet* indeed, has much of the quality of a Gothic cathedral; it can only be appreciated in Latin countries at times when the classical tradition runs at the ebb. The mediaeval idea of courtly love is implicit in *Troilus and Cressida;* and Titania and Oberon and Puck are not of the Renaissance. Shakespeare's incidental lyrics remind us that snatches of 15th-century song were still being sung in the Warwickshire woods and villages, as they were long after his day.

Mercenary armies might have taken the place of feudal chivalry on the battlefield, but chivalric ideas survived in the code of education of well-born boys and in the splendours of the lists. Holinshed's accounts of the tournaments of the time of Henry VIII are completely mediaeval, unless it be in the elaborate and emblematic language of the jousters' mottoes. Bayard, the perfect knight, *sans peur et sans reproche*, lived in the 16th century, but he was judged perfect by the standards of an earlier day. The mediaeval 'point of honour' continued to be the basis of the code of a Spanish gentleman until long after the 17th century. Orders of Chivalry continued to be founded with all the trappings if not the ideals of the Middle Ages; it was not until James I sold his baronetcies that the mediaeval tradition ended in England.

Men have read the *Chanson de Roland*, Dante, Chaucer and the *Roman de la Rose* from the times they were written until to-day. In quiet Oxford colleges and French Benedictine houses, building in Gothic style went on in the 17th century until once again it received the approval of the fashionable *cognoscenti* of the 18th century and the religious revivalists of the 19th. Our tradition of biography goes back to the *Lives of the Saints* and to Joinville; our drama owes as much to the mystery and miracle plays and the crowded pageantry of the 15th century as it does to Euripides and Seneca. In England at least official ceremonial and civic pageantry are still mediaeval. The Middle Ages still form an essential if often unsuspected part of the civilization of our own times.

Freres humains qui après nous vives,
N'ayez les cueurs contre nous endurcis,
Car, se pitié de nous pouvrez avez,
Dieu en aura plustost de vous mercis.

Epitaphe dudit Villon
Freres humains qui apres no⁹ viues
Nayez les cueurs contre no⁹ endurcis
Car se pitie de no⁹ pouurez auez
Dieu en aura pluftoft de vous mercis
Vous nous voies cy ataches cinq fix
Quãt de la char q̃ trop auõs nourrie
Elle est pieca deuouree et pourrie
Et no⁹ les os deuenõs cẽdres ⁊ pouldre
De nostre mal perfonne ne sen rie
Mais pries dieu que tous nous veuil
le absouldre   g iiij.

In 1460 Villon was sentenced to death, to be providentially reprieved. Probably next year he wrote his 'Grand Testament' which contains his own epitaph as a hanged man, thus translated by Swinburne:

Men, brother men, that after us yet live,
Let not your hearts too hard against us be;
For if some pity of us poor men ye give,
The sooner God shall take of you pity.
Here we are five or six strung up, you see,
And here the flesh that all too well we fed,
Bit by bit eaten and rotten, rent and shred,
And we the bones grow dust and ash withal;
Let no man laugh at us discomforted,
But pray to God that he forgive us all.

Late in 1462 Villon was again arrested, again sentenced to death, again reprieved. He was banished from Paris and is never heard of again. Perhaps he did finally meet the end that he foresaw for himself. This woodcut, crude yet strangely in tune with Villon's words, decorates the edition of 1489. (16)

| | 1000 | 1010 | 1020 | 1030 | 1040 | 1050 | 1060 | 1070 | 1080 | 1090 | 1100 | 1110 | 1120 |

POPES
Leo IX (1048–54) · Nicholas II (1058–61) · Alexander II (1061–73) · Gregory VII (Hildebrand) (1073–85) · Urban II (1088–99) · Callixtus II (1119–24) · Paschal II (1099–1118)

HOLY ROMAN EMPERORS
Henry II (1002–24) · Henry III (1039–56) · Henry IV (1056–1106) · CIVIL WAR IN GERMANY · Henry V (1106–25)

KINGS OF FRANCE
Henry I (1031–60) Third of the Capetian dynasty · Philip I (1060–1108) · Louis VI (the Fat) (1108–37)

KINGS OF ENGLAND
Canute (1016–35) · Edward the Confessor (1042–66) · Harold (1066) · William I (1066–87) · William II (Rufus) (1087–1100) · Henry I (1100–35)

History

Danes invade England

Hungary becomes a kingdom under St Stephen

FIRST CRUSADE

Norman conquest of South Italy   Norman conquest of England

Jerusalem taken and Latin kingdom established there

Norman conquest of Sicily

1076–1122 WAR OF INVESTITURES

Emperor submits to Pope at Canossa

Rome sacked by Germans and Normans Pope flees

Conflict between Anselm and Henry I of England over investiture ends in compromise

Alfonso VI of Spain (1065–1109)

Henry I of England takes Normandy from his brother

The Cid takes Valencia from the Moors

Religion, Scholarship and Literature

St Peter Damian, monastic reformer, Bishop of Ostia

St Norbert founds Premonstratensian Order

St Nilus founds Grottaferrata Basilian monastery near Rome

Robert of La Chaise-Dieu hermit

Cistercian Order founded

Victorine Order founded

Civil law affected by Justinian's Digest

Templars founded

St Romuald founds Camaldolese Order

St John Gualbert founds Vallombrosan Order

Election of popes confined to cardinals by decree

St Bruno founds Carthusian Order

Orders of Fontevrault and Grandmont founded

William of Volpiano founds abbey of Bec

Abbot Odilo of Cluny

St Hugh Abbot of Cluny

Anselm Abbot of Bec First Cluniac house in England

Cluniac reform spreading in Spain

Anselm Archbishop of Canterbury

Peter Abailard establishes school at Paris

Augustinian Canons approved

Lanfranc Archbishop of Canterbury

St Bernard founds Clairvaux

Catharist heresy spreading in Western Europe

Hirsau follows Cluniac reforms Cluniac influence spreads under Popes Gregory VII and Urban II

St Bernard joins Cîteaux

Stephen Harding Abbot of Cîteaux

Controversy over transubstantiation between Berengar of Tours and Lanfranc

Irnerius teaching at Bologna

Adelard of Bath returns to England

Hospitallers established

Chanson de Roland

Art

Liber Vitae of New Minster, Winchester

Bayeux Tapestry   Stephen Harding's Bible

Perikopenbuch of Henry II of Germany

Theophilus' treatise Concerning the various arts

Hugo Pictor

Bernward, Bishop of Hildesheim, commissions silver crucifix and bronze doors for the church of St Michael

Gilt bronze chandelier made for St Michael's, Hildesheim

Wall-paintings of St-Savin-sur-Gartempe

Moïssac cloister sculpture

Capitals of Payerne Abbey

Cloister reliefs and capitals of S. Domingo, Silos

Wiligelmo's sculpture on the façade of Modena Cathedral

Capitals of crypt of Canterbury Cathedral

Puerta de las Platerías, Santiago de Compostela

Lintel of St-Genis-des-Fontaines

Carved portal of Cluny III

Capitals of Cluny III

Frescoes of Cluny III and Berzé-la-Ville

Architecture

St-Philibert, Tournus, under construction

La Trinité and St-Etienne at Caen founded

La Madeleine, Vézelay, begun

Autun Cathedral begun

St-Bénigne, Dijon, begun

Ste-Foy, Conques, begun

St-Sernin, Toulouse

St-Front, Périgueux, begun

St-Martin, Tours, begun

Cluny III begun; east end dedicated

Early rib-vault at Bayeux

Cluny III, nave vaulted

Westminster Abbey begun

White Tower, London

Winchester Cathedral begun   Old Sarum begun

Peterborough Cathedral begun

Bury St Edmunds Abbey begun   Westminster Hall

Ely Cathedral begun

St Albans Abbey begun   Old St Paul's begun

Durham Cathedral begun

St Mark's, Venice, begun

Church of Monte Cassino rebuilt   Norwich Cathedral begun

S. Pietro, Civate

Pisa Cathedral and Leaning Tower   S. Ambrogio, Milan

Santiago de Compostela begun

Worms Cathedral begun

Speyer Cathedral begun

Imperial Hall at Goslar

| 1000 | 1010 | 1020 | 1030 | 1040 | 1050 | 1060 | 1070 | 1080 | 1090 | 1100 | 1110 | 1120 |

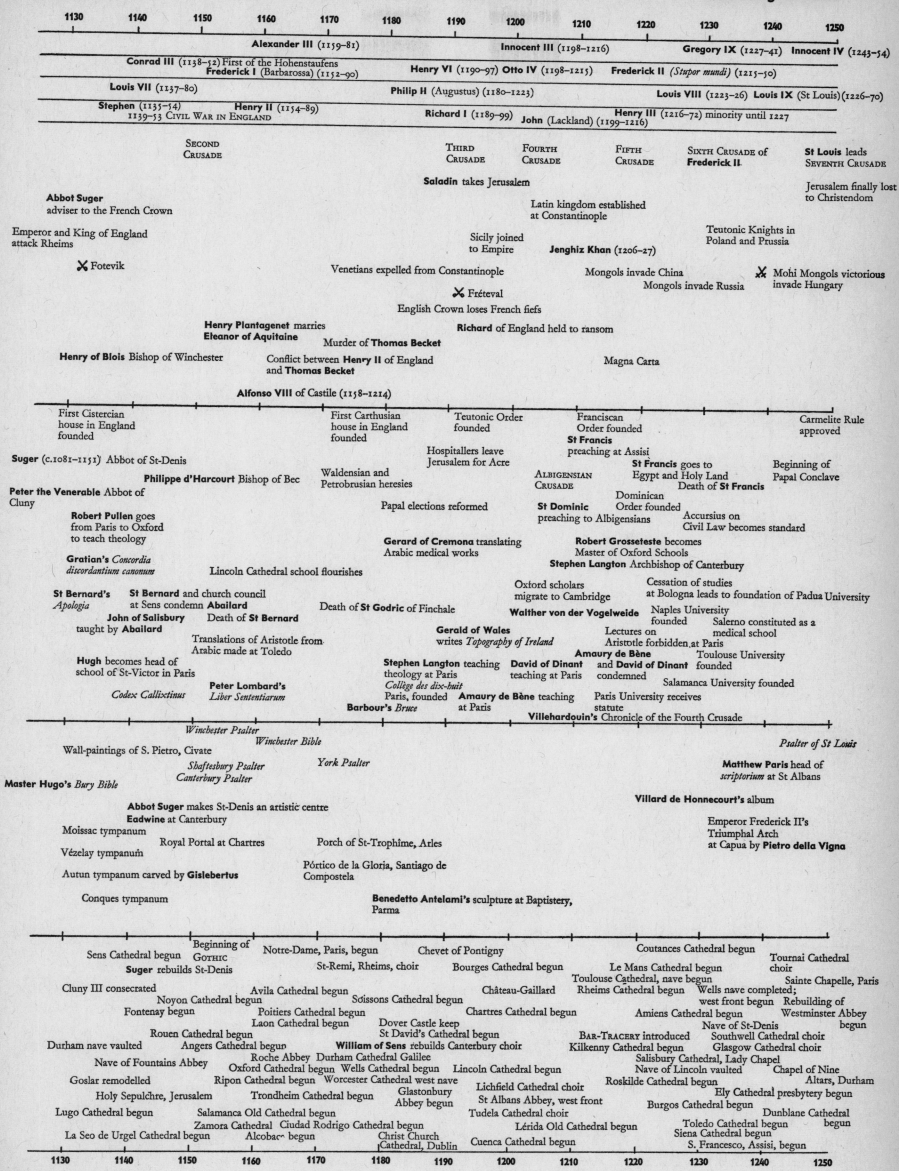

1130	1140	1150	1160	1170	1180	1190	1200	1210	1220	1230	1240	1250

Alexander III (1159–81) **Innocent III** (1198–1216) **Gregory IX** (1227–41) **Innocent IV** (1243–54)

Conrad III (1138–52) First of the Hohenstaufens **Henry VI** (1190–97) **Otto IV** (1198–1215) **Frederick II** (*Stupor mundi*) (1215–50)
Frederick I (Barbarossa) (1152–90)

Louis VII (1137–80) **Philip II** (Augustus) (1180–1223) **Louis VIII** (1223–26) **Louis IX** (St Louis) (1226–70)

Stephen (1135–54) **Henry II** (1154–89) **Richard I** (1189–99) **Henry III** (1216–72) minority until 1227
1139–53 CIVIL WAR IN ENGLAND **John** (Lackland) (1199–1216)

SECOND CRUSADE THIRD CRUSADE FOURTH CRUSADE FIFTH CRUSADE SIXTH CRUSADE of **Frederick II.** **St Louis** leads SEVENTH CRUSADE

Saladin takes Jerusalem Jerusalem finally lost to Christendom

Abbot Suger adviser to the French Crown Latin kingdom established at Constantinople

Emperor and King of England attack Rheims Sicily joined to Empire **Jenghiz Khan** (1206–27) Teutonic Knights in Poland and Prussia

✗ Fotevik Venetians expelled from Constantinople Mongols invade China ✗ Mohi Mongols victorious invade Hungary
Mongols invade Russia

✗ Fréteval
English Crown loses French fiefs

Henry Plantagenet marries **Eleanor of Aquitaine** **Richard** of England held to ransom
Murder of **Thomas Becket**

Henry of Blois Bishop of Winchester Conflict between **Henry II** of England and **Thomas Becket** Magna Carta

Alfonso VIII of Castile (1158–1214)

First Cistercian house in England founded First Carthusian house in England founded Teutonic Order founded Franciscan Order founded Carmelite Rule approved

Suger (c.1081–1151) Abbot of St-Denis Hospitallers leave Jerusalem for Acre **St Francis** preaching at Assisi

Philippe d'Harcourt Bishop of Bec Waldensian and Petrobrusian heresies ALBIGENSIAN CRUSADE **St Francis** goes to Egypt and Holy Land Beginning of Papal Conclave
Death of **St Francis**

Peter the Venerable Abbot of Cluny **St Dominic** preaching to Albigensians Dominican Order founded

Robert Pullen goes from Paris to Oxford to teach theology Papal elections reformed Accursius on Civil Law becomes standard

Gratian's *Concordia discordantium canonum* **Gerard of Cremona** translating Arabic medical works **Robert Grosseteste** becomes Master of Oxford Schools

Lincoln Cathedral school flourishes **Stephen Langton** Archbishop of Canterbury

St Bernard's *Apologia* **St Bernard** and church council at Sens condemn **Abailard** Oxford scholars migrate to Cambridge Cessation of studies at Bologna leads to foundation of Padua University

John of Salisbury taught by **Abailard** Death of **St Bernard** Death of **St Godric** of Finchale **Walther von der Vogelweide** Naples University founded Salerno constituted as a medical school

Translations of Aristotle from Arabic made at Toledo **Gerald of Wales** writes *Topography of Ireland* Lectures on Aristotle forbidden at Paris

Hugh becomes head of school of St-Victor in Paris **Stephen Langton** teaching theology at Paris **David of Dinant** teaching at Paris **Amaury de Bène** and **David of Dinant** condemned Toulouse University founded

Codex Callixtinus **Peter Lombard's** *Liber Sententiarum* *Collège des dix-huit* Paris, founded Salamanca University founded

Barbour's *Bruce* **Amaury de Bène** teaching at Paris Paris University receives statute

Villehardouin's Chronicle of the Fourth Crusade

Winchester Psalter
Wall-paintings of S. Pietro, Civate *Winchester Bible* *Psalter of St Louis*

Shaftesbury Psalter *York Psalter* **Matthew Paris** head of *scriptorium* at St Albans
Canterbury Psalter

Master Hugo's *Bury Bible*

Villard de Honnecourt's album

Abbot Suger makes St-Denis an artistic centre Emperor Frederick II's Triumphal Arch at Capua by **Pietro della Vigna**
Eadwine at Canterbury
Moissac tympanum Royal Portal at Chartres Porch of St-Trophîme, Arles

Vézelay tympanum

Autun tympanum carved by **Gislebertus** Pórtico de la Gloria, Santiago de Compostela

Conques tympanum **Benedetto Antelami's** sculpture at Baptistery, Parma

Beginning of GOTHIC Coutances Cathedral begun

Sens Cathedral begun Notre-Dame, Paris, begun Chevet of Pontigny Tournai Cathedral choir

Suger rebuilds St-Denis St-Remi, Rheims, choir Le Mans Cathedral begun
Bourges Cathedral begun Toulouse Cathedral, nave begun Sainte Chapelle, Paris

Cluny III consecrated Avila Cathedral begun Château-Gaillard Rheims Cathedral begun Wells nave completed;
Noyon Cathedral begun Soissons Cathedral begun west front begun Rebuilding of
Fontenay begun Poitiers Cathedral begun Chartres Cathedral begun Amiens Cathedral begun Westminster Abbey
Laon Cathedral begun Dover Castle keep Nave of St-Denis begun

Rouen Cathedral begun St David's Cathedral begun BAR-TRACERY introduced Southwell Cathedral choir
Durham nave vaulted Angers Cathedral begun **William of Sens** rebuilds Canterbury choir Kilkenny Cathedral begun Glasgow Cathedral choir

Nave of Fountains Abbey Roche Abbey Durham Cathedral Galilee Salisbury Cathedral, Lady Chapel
Oxford Cathedral begun Wells Cathedral begun Lincoln Cathedral begun Nave of Lincoln vaulted Chapel of Nine

Goslar remodelled Ripon Cathedral begun Worcester Cathedral west nave Roskilde Cathedral begun Altars, Durham
Lichfield Cathedral choir Ely Cathedral presbytery begun
Holy Sepulchre, Jerusalem Trondheim Cathedral begun Glastonbury St Albans Abbey, west front Burgos Cathedral begun
Abbey begun

Lugo Cathedral begun Salamanca Old Cathedral begun Tudela Cathedral choir Dunblane Cathedral
Zamora Cathedral Ciudad Rodrigo Cathedral begun Lérida Old Cathedral begun Toledo Cathedral begun begun
La Seo de Urgel Cathedral begun Alcobaça begun Christ Church Siena Cathedral begun
Cathedral, Dublin Cuenca Cathedral begun S. Francesco, Assisi, begun

1130	1140	1150	1160	1170	1180	1190	1200	1210	1220	1230	1240	1250

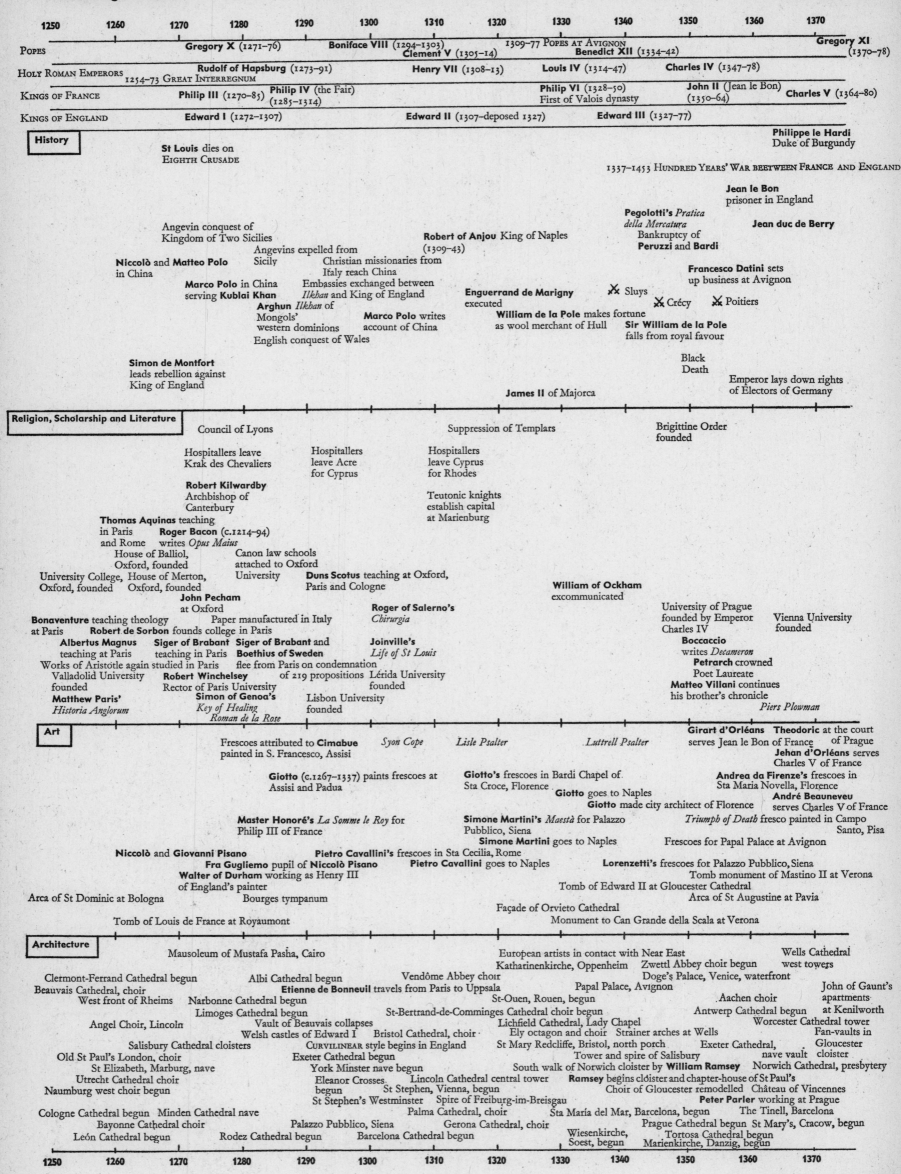

| 1250 | 1260 | 1270 | 1280 | 1290 | 1300 | 1310 | 1320 | 1330 | 1340 | 1350 | 1360 | 1370 |

POPES Gregory X (1271–76) Boniface VIII (1294–1303) Clement V (1305–14) 1309–77 Popes at Avignon Benedict XII (1334–42) Gregory XI (1370–78)

HOLY ROMAN EMPERORS Rudolf of Hapsburg (1273–91) 1254–73 Great Interregnum Henry VII (1308–13) Louis IV (1314–47) Charles IV (1347–78)

KINGS OF FRANCE Philip III (1270–85) Philip IV (the Fair) (1285–1314) Philip VI (1328–50) First of Valois dynasty John II (Jean le Bon) (1350–64) Charles V (1364–80)

KINGS OF ENGLAND Edward I (1272–1307) Edward II (1307–deposed 1327) Edward III (1327–77)

History

Philippe le Hardi Duke of Burgundy

St Louis dies on EIGHTH CRUSADE

1337–1453 HUNDRED YEARS' WAR BETWEEN FRANCE AND ENGLAND

Jean le Bon prisoner in England

Angevin conquest of Kingdom of Two Sicilies
Angevins expelled from Sicily
Robert of Anjou King of Naples (1309–43)
Pegolotti's *Pratica della Mercatura* Bankruptcy of Peruzzi and Bardi
Jean duc de Berry

Niccolò and Matteo Polo in China
Christian missionaries from Italy reach China
Francesco Datini sets up business at Avignon

Marco Polo in China serving Kublai Khan
Embassies exchanged between Ilkhan and King of England
Enguerrand de Marigny executed
✕ Sluys
✕ Crécy   ✕ Poitiers

Arghun Ilkhan of Mongols' western dominions
Marco Polo writes account of China
William de la Pole makes fortune as wool merchant of Hull
Sir William de la Pole falls from royal favour

English conquest of Wales

Simon de Montfort leads rebellion against King of England
Black Death
Emperor lays down rights of Electors of Germany

James II of Majorca

Religion, Scholarship and Literature

Council of Lyons
Suppression of Templars
Brigittine Order founded

Hospitallers leave Krak des Chevaliers
Hospitallers leave Acre for Cyprus
Hospitallers leave Cyprus for Rhodes

Robert Kilwardby Archbishop of Canterbury
Teutonic knights establish capital at Marienburg

Thomas Aquinas teaching in Paris and Rome
Roger Bacon (c.1214–94) writes *Opus Maius*

House of Balliol, Oxford, founded
Canon law schools attached to Oxford University

University College, Oxford, founded
House of Merton, Oxford, founded
Duns Scotus teaching at Oxford, Paris and Cologne
William of Ockham excommunicated

John Pecham at Oxford
Roger of Salerno's *Chirurgia*
University of Prague founded by Emperor Charles IV
Vienna University founded

Bonaventure teaching theology at Paris
Robert de Sorbon founds college in Paris
Paper manufactured in Italy
Boccaccio writes *Decameron*

Albertus Magnus teaching at Paris
Siger of Brabant teaching in Paris
Siger of Brabant and Boethius of Sweden flee from Paris on condemnation of 219 propositions
Joinville's *Life of St Louis*
Petrarch crowned Poet Laureate

Works of Aristotle again studied in Paris
Lérida University founded
Matteo Villani continues his brother's chronicle

Valladolid University founded
Robert Winchelsey Rector of Paris University

Matthew Paris' *Historia Anglorum*
Simon of Genoa's *Key of Healing*
Lisbon University founded
Roman de la Rose
Piers Plowman

Art

Frescoes attributed to Cimabue painted in S. Francesco, Assisi
Syon Cope
Lisle Psalter
Luttrell Psalter
Girart d'Orléans serves Jean le Bon of France
Theodoric at the court of Prague

Jehan d'Orléans serves Charles V of France

Giotto (c.1267–1337) paints frescoes at Assisi and Padua
Giotto's frescoes in Bardi Chapel of Sta Croce, Florence
Andrea da Firenze's frescoes in Sta Maria Novella, Florence

Giotto goes to Naples
André Beauneveu serves Charles V of France

Giotto made city architect of Florence

Master Honoré's *La Somme le Roy* for Philip III of France
Simone Martini's *Maestà* for Palazzo Pubblico, Siena
Triumph of Death fresco painted in Campo Santo, Pisa

Simone Martini goes to Naples
Frescoes for Papal Palace at Avignon

Niccolò and Giovanni Pisano
Pietro Cavallini's frescoes in Sta Cecilia, Rome
Lorenzetti's frescoes for Palazzo Pubblico, Siena

Fra Guglielmo pupil of Niccolò Pisano
Pietro Cavallini goes to Naples
Tomb monument of Mastino II at Verona

Walter of Durham working as Henry III of England's painter
Tomb of Edward II at Gloucester Cathedral
Arca of St Augustine at Pavia

Arca of St Dominic at Bologna
Bourges tympanum
Façade of Orvieto Cathedral

Tomb of Louis de France at Royaumont
Monument to Can Grande della Scala at Verona

Architecture

Mausoleum of Mustafa Pasha, Cairo
European artists in contact with Near East
Katharinenkirche, Oppenheim
Zwettl Abbey choir begun
Wells Cathedral west towers

Clermont-Ferrand Cathedral begun
Albi Cathedral begun
Vendôme Abbey choir
Papal Palace, Avignon
Doge's Palace, Venice, waterfront
John of Gaunt's apartments at Kenilworth

Beauvais Cathedral, choir
Etienne de Bonneuil travels from Paris to Uppsala
St-Ouen, Rouen
Aachen choir

West front of Rheims
Narbonne Cathedral begun
St-Bertrand-de-Comminges Cathedral choir begun
Antwerp Cathedral begun
Worcester Cathedral tower

Angel Choir, Lincoln
Limoges Cathedral begun
Lichfield Cathedral, Lady Chapel
Fan-vaults in Gloucester cloister

Vault of Beauvais collapses
Ely octagon and choir
Strainer arches at Wells
Exeter Cathedral, nave vault

Salisbury Cathedral cloisters
Welsh castles of Edward I
Bristol Cathedral, choir
St Mary Redcliffe, Bristol, north porch

Old St Paul's London, choir
CURVILINEAR style begins in England
Tower and spire of Salisbury
Norwich Cathedral, presbytery

St Elizabeth, Marburg, nave
Exeter Cathedral begun
South walk of Norwich cloister by William Ramsey

Utrecht Cathedral choir
York Minster nave begun
Lincoln Cathedral central tower
Ramsey begins cloister and chapter-house of St Paul's

Naumburg west choir begun
Eleanor Crosses begun
St Stephen, Vienna, begun
Choir of Gloucester remodelled
Château of Vincennes

St Stephen's Westminster
Spire of Freiburg-im-Breisgau
Peter Parler working at Prague

Cologne Cathedral begun
Minden Cathedral nave
Palma Cathedral, choir
Sta María del Mar, Barcelona
Prague Cathedral begun
St Mary's, Cracow, begun

Bayonne Cathedral choir
Palazzo Pubblico, Siena
Gerona Cathedral, choir
The Tinell, Barcelona

León Cathedral begun
Rodez Cathedral begun
Barcelona Cathedral begun
Wiesenkirche, Soest, begun
Tortosa Cathedral begun
Marienkirche, Danzig, begun

| 1250 | 1260 | 1270 | 1280 | 1290 | 1300 | 1310 | 1320 | 1330 | 1340 | 1350 | 1360 | 1370 |

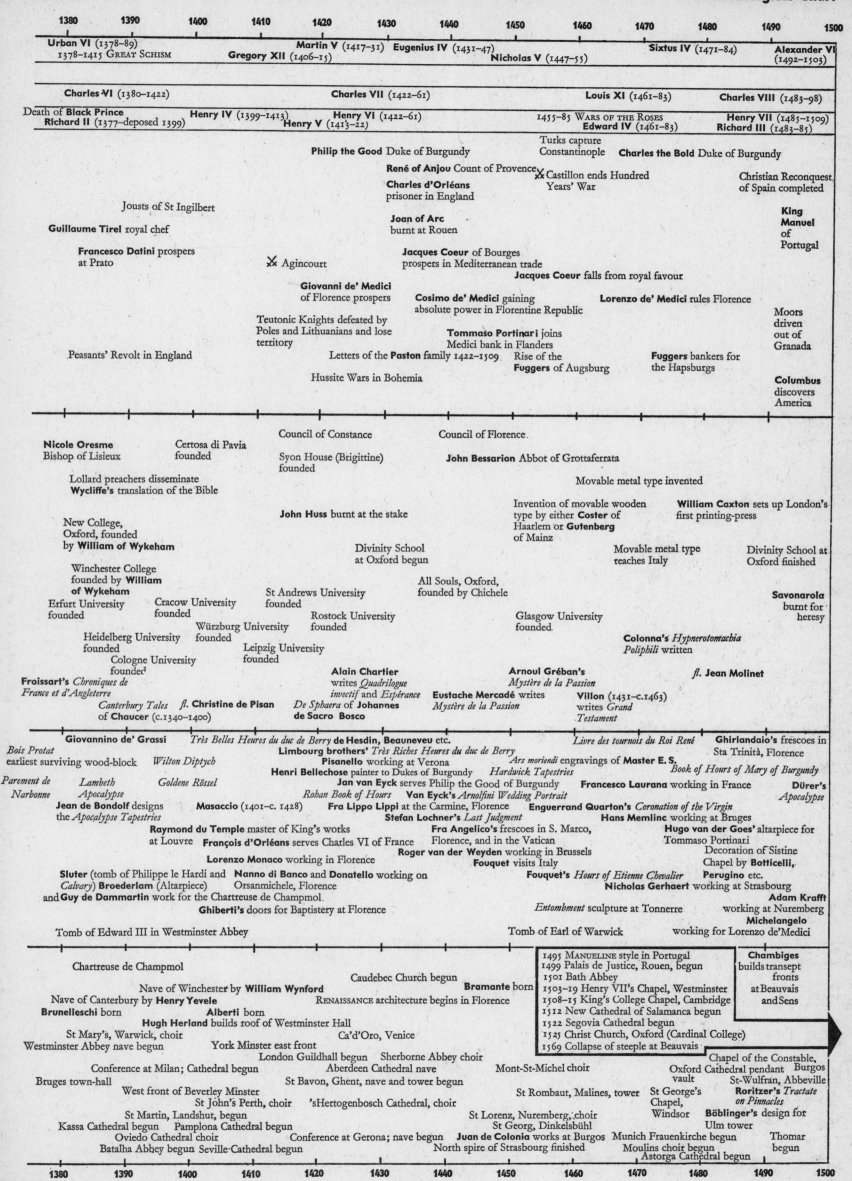

1380   1390   1400   1410   1420   1430   1440   1450   1460   1470   1480   1490   1500

Urban VI (1378–89)
1378–1415 GREAT SCHISM
Gregory XII (1406–15)   **Martin V** (1417–31)   **Eugenius IV** (1431–47)   **Nicholas V** (1447–55)   **Sixtus IV** (1471–84)   **Alexander VI** (1492–1503)

Charles VI (1380–1422)   **Charles VII** (1422–61)   **Louis XI** (1461–83)   **Charles VIII** (1483–98)

Death of **Black Prince**
Richard II (1377–deposed 1399)   **Henry IV** (1399–1413)   **Henry V** (1413–22)   **Henry VI** (1422–61)   1455–85 WARS OF THE ROSES   **Edward IV** (1461–83)   **Henry VII** (1485–1509)   **Richard III** (1483–85)

Philip the Good Duke of Burgundy   Turks capture Constantinople   **Charles the Bold** Duke of Burgundy

René of Anjou Count of Provence
Charles d'Orléans prisoner in England   Castillon ends Hundred Years' War   Christian Reconquest of Spain completed

Jousts of St Ingilbert
Joan of Arc burnt at Rouen   **King Manuel of Portugal**

Guillaume Tirel royal chef

Francesco Datini prospers at Prato   **Jacques Coeur** of Bourges prospers in Mediterranean trade
Agincourt   **Jacques Coeur** falls from royal favour

Giovanni de' Medici of Florence prospers   **Cosimo de' Medici** gaining absolute power in Florentine Republic   **Lorenzo de' Medici** rules Florence

Teutonic Knights defeated by Poles and Lithuanians and lose territory   **Tommaso Portinari** joins Medici bank in Flanders   Moors driven out of Granada

Peasants' Revolt in England   Letters of the **Paston** family 1422–1509   Rise of the **Fuggers** of Augsburg   **Fuggers** bankers for the Hapsburgs

Hussite Wars in Bohemia   **Columbus** discovers America

Nicole Oresme Bishop of Lisieux   Certosa di Pavia founded   Council of Constance   Council of Florence

Syon House (Brigittine) founded   **John Bessarion** Abbot of Grottaferrata

Lollard preachers disseminate **Wycliffe's** translation of the Bible   Movable metal type invented

New College, Oxford, founded by **William of Wykeham**   **John Huss** burnt at the stake   Invention of movable wooden type by either **Coster** of Haarlem or **Gutenberg** of Mainz   **William Caxton** sets up London's first printing-press

Winchester College founded by **William of Wykeham**   Divinity School at Oxford begun   Movable metal type teaches Italy   Divinity School at Oxford finished

Erfurt University founded   Cracow University founded   St Andrews University founded   All Souls, Oxford, founded by Chichele   **Savonarola** burnt for heresy

Heidelberg University founded   Würzburg University founded   Rostock University founded   Glasgow University founded   **Colonna's** *Hypnerotomachia Poliphili* written

Cologne University founded   Leipzig University founded

Froissart's *Chroniques de France et d'Angleterre*   **Alain Chartier** writes *Quadrilogue invectif* and *Espérance*   **Arnoul Gréban's** *Mystère de la Passion*   *fl.* **Jean Molinet**

Canterbury Tales of **Chaucer** (c.1340–1400)   *fl.* **Christine de Pisan**   *De Sphaera* of **Johannes de Sacro Bosco**   **Eustache Mercadé** writes *Mystère de la Passion*   **Villon** (1431–c.1463) writes *Grand Testament*

Giovannino de' Grassi   *Très Belles Heures du duc de Berry* de Hesdin, Beauneveu etc.   *Livre des tournois du Roi René*   **Ghirlandaio's** frescoes in Sta Trinità, Florence

Bois Protat earliest surviving wood-block   **Limbourg brothers'** *Très Riches Heures du duc de Berry*
Wilton Diptych   **Pisanello** working at Verona   *Ars moriendi* engravings of **Master E.S.**   *Book of Hours of Mary of Burgundy*

Parement de Narbonne   Lambeth Apocalypse   *Goldene Rössel*   **Henri Bellechose** painter to Dukes of Burgundy   *Hardwick Tapestries*   **Dürer's** *Apocalypse*

Rohan Book of Hours   **Jan van Eyck** serves Philip the Good of Burgundy   **Francesco Laurana** working in France

Jean de Bondolf designs the *Apocalypse Tapestries*   **Masaccio** (1401–c. 1428)   **Fra Lippo Lippi** at the Carmine, Florence   Van Eyck's *Arnolfini Wedding Portrait*   **Enguerrand Quarton's** *Coronation of the Virgin*

Raymond du Temple master of King's works at Louvre   **Stefan Lochner's** *Last Judgment*   **Fra Angelico's** frescoes in S. Marco, Florence, and in the Vatican   **Hans Memlinc** working at Bruges

François d'Orléans serves Charles VI of France   **Roger van der Weyden** working in Brussels   **Hugo van der Goes'** altarpiece for Tommaso Portinari

Lorenzo Monaco working in Florence   **Fouquet** visits Italy   Decoration of Sistine Chapel by **Botticelli**

Sluter (tomb of Philippe le Hardi and *Calvary*) **Broederlam** (Altarpiece) and **Guy de Dammartin** work for the Chartreuse de Champmol   **Nanno di Banco** and **Donatello** working on Orsanmichele, Florence   Fouquet's *Hours of Etienne Chevalier*   **Nicholas Gerhaert** working at Strasbourg   **Perugino** etc.

Ghiberti's doors for Baptistery at Florence   *Entombment* sculpture at Tonnerre   **Adam Krafft** working at Nuremberg

Tomb of Edward III in Westminster Abbey   Tomb of Earl of Warwick   **Michelangelo** working for Lorenzo de' Medici

1495 MANUELINE style in Portugal
1499 Palais de Justice, Rouen, begun
1501 Bath Abbey
1503–19 Henry VII's Chapel, Westminster
1508–15 King's College Chapel, Cambridge
1512 New Cathedral of Salamanca begun
1522 Segovia Cathedral begun
1525 Christ Church, Oxford (Cardinal College)
1569 Collapse of steeple at Beauvais

Chambiges builds transept fronts at Beauvais and Sens

Chartreuse de Champmol   Caudebec Church begun   **Bramante** born

Nave of Winchester by **William Wynford**
Nave of Canterbury by **Henry Yevele**   RENAISSANCE architecture begins in Florence

Brunelleschi born   **Alberti** born
Hugh Herland builds roof of Westminster Hall

St Mary's, Warwick, choir   Ca'd'Oro, Venice
Westminster Abbey nave begun   York Minster east front   London Guildhall begun   Sherborne Abbey choir   Chapel of the Constable, Burgos   Oxford Cathedral pendant vault

Conference at Milan; Cathedral begun   Aberdeen Cathedral nave   Mont-St-Michel choir   St-Wulfran, Abbeville

Bruges town-hall   St Bavon, Ghent, nave and tower begun   St Rombaut, Malines, tower   St George's Chapel, Windsor   **Roritzer's** *Tractate on Pinnacles*

West front of Beverley Minster   'sHertogenbosch Cathedral, choir   St Lorenz, Nuremberg, choir   **Böblinger's** design for Ulm tower

St John's, Perth, choir
St Martin, Landshut, begun   St Georg, Dinkelsbühl
Kassa Cathedral begun   Pamplona Cathedral begun   **Juan de Colonia** works at Burgos   Munich Frauenkirche begun   Thomar begun

Oviedo Cathedral choir   Conference at Gerona; nave begun   Moulins choir begun
Batalha Abbey begun   Seville Cathedral begun   North spire of Strasbourg finished   Astorga Cathedral begun

1380   1390   1400   1410   1420   1430   1440   1450   1460   1470   1480   1490   1500

Select Bibliography

ACKERMAN, P. 'Recently identified designers of Gothic tapestries', *Art Bulletin*, IX, 1926, p. 142

ADHÉMAR, J. *Influences antiques dans l'art du moyen âge français* (London, 1939)

ANTHONY, E. W. *Romanesque Frescoes* (Princeton, 1951)

AUBERT, M. *French Sculpture at the beginning of the Gothic Period, 1140–1225* (Florence & Paris, 1929)
L'Architecture cistercienne en France 2 vols (Paris, 1943)
La Sculpture française au moyen-âge (Paris, 1947)

AUBERT, M., SCHMOLL, J. A. and HOFSTÄTTER, H. H. *Le gothique à son apogée* (Paris, 1964)
English trs. *High Gothic Art* (London, 1964)

BECKWITH, J. *Early Mediaeval Art* (London, 1964)

BENESCH, O. *Art of the Renaissance in Northern Europe* (Cambridge, Mass., 1945; London 1965)

BLOCH, M. L. B. *Feudal Society* trs. by L. A. Manyon (London, 1961)

BLUM, A. *Les Origines de la gravure en France* (Paris & Brussels, 1921)

BOASE, T. S. R. *English Art, 1100–1216* (Oxford, 1953)

BRAUN, H. S. *The English Castle* (London, 1936)

BRÉHIER, L. *Le Style roman* (Paris, 1941)

BRIEGER, P. H. *English Art 1216–1307* (Oxford 1957)

BROWN, R. A. *English Medieval Castles* (London, 1954; revised ed. *English Castles*, London, 1962)

BROWNE, E. G. *Arabian medicine* (Cambridge, 1921)

BRUNET, A., PARÉ, G. and TREMBLAY, P. *La Renaissance du XIIe siècle* (Paris & Ottawa, 1933)

CAGNAT, R. *Le Château espagnol du Moyen Âge* (Madrid, 1949)

CALLUS, D. A. P. (ed.) *Robert Grossesteste, Scholar and Bishop.* (Oxford, 1955)

CARTELLIERI, O. *The Court of Burgundy* trs. by M. Letts (London, 1929)

CARUS-WILSON, E. M. *Medieval Merchant Venturers* (London, 1954)

CHAMPEAUX, A. de and GAUCHERY, P. *Les Travaux d'art exécutés pour Jean de France, duc de Berry* (Paris, 1894)

CHENU, M. D. *Introduction à l'étude de Saint Thomas d'Aquin* (Montreal & Paris, 1950)

CLAPHAM, A. W. *Romanesque Architecture in Western Europe* (Oxford, 1936)

CLAPHAM, J. H., POWER, E. E. and POSTAN, M. M. E. *The Cambridge Economic History of Europe*, Vols I–III (Cambridge, 1941–63)

CLARK, J. M. *The Dance of Death in the Middle Ages and the Renaissance* (Glasgow, 1950)

CLASEN, K. H. *Die mittelalterliche Kunst im Gebiete des Deutschordensstaates Preussen*, Vol I, *Die Burgbauten* (Königsberg, 1928)

COHEN, G. *Le Théâtre en France au Moyen Âge* 2 vols (Paris, 1928–31)

COLOMBIER, P. du *Les Chantiers des cathédrales* (Paris, 1953)

COLVIN, H. M., BROWN, R. A. and TAYLOR, A. J. *The History of the King's Works*, Part I, *The Middle Ages* 2 vols (London, 1963)

CONANT, K. J. *Carolingian and Romanesque Architecture 800 to 1200* (Harmondsworth, 1959)

COOK, G. H. *Mediaeval Chantries and Chantry Chapels* (London, 1963)

COULTON, G. G. *Five Centuries of Religion* 4 vols (Cambridge, 1923–50)

COURAJOD, L. C. J. *Leçons professées à l'Ecole du Louvre 1887–1896* 3 vols (Paris, 1899)

COX, G. T. *Jehan Foucquet, native of Tours* (London, 1931)

CRANAGE, D. H. S. *The Home of the Monk* (Cambridge, 1926; 3rd ed., 1934)

CROSSLEY, F. H. *English Church Monuments, AD 1150–1550* (London, 1921)

CURTIUS, E. R. *European Literature and the Latin Middle Ages* trs. by W. R. Trask (London, 1953)

DAVIS, N. (ed.) *Paston Letters* (Oxford, 1958)

DECKER, H. *L'Italie gothique* (Paris, 1964)

DEHAISNES, C. C. A. *Documents et extraits divers concernant l'histoire de l'art dans la Flandre, l'Artois et le Hainaut avant le XVe siècle* (Lille, 1886)
Histoire de l'art dans la Flandre, l'Artois et le Hainaut avant le XVe siècle (Lille, 1886)

DELISLE, L. V. *Recherches sur la librairie de Charles V* (Paris, 1907)

DENHOLM-YOUNG, N. *History and Heraldry, 1254 to 1310* (Oxford, 1965)

DENIFLE, H. S. *La Désolation des églises, monastères et hôpitaux en France pendant la guerre de cent ans* 2 vols (Paris, 1897,99)

DENNY, D. 'The Trinity in Enguerrand Quarton's Coronation of the Virgin', *Art Bulletin*, XV, 1963, pp. 48–52

DESCHAMPS, P. *French Sculpture of the Romanesque Period, Eleventh and Twelfth Centuries* (Florence & Paris, 1930)

DESTREZ, J. A. *La Pecia dans les manuscrits universitaires du XIIIe et du XIVe siècle* (Paris, 1935)

DUBRUCK, E. *The Theme of Death in French Poetry of the Middle Ages and the Renaissance* (The Hague, 1964)

ESCHAPASSE, M. *L'Architecture bénédictine en Europe* (Paris, 1963)

EVANS, Joan *Life in Medieval France* (London, 1925; revised ed., 1957)
Monastic Life at Cluny, 910–1157 (London, 1931)
Art in Mediaeval France 987–1498 (London & New York, 1948)
The Romanesque Architecture of the Order of Cluny (Cambridge, 1938)
English Art 1307–1461 (Oxford, 1949)
Cluniac Art of the Romanesque Period (Cambridge, 1950)

FAGNIEZ, G. *Documents relatifs à l'histoire de l'industrie et du commerce en France* (Paris, 1898)

FARAL, E. *La Vie quotidienne au temps de Saint Louis* (Paris, 1956)

FOCILLON, H. *Art d'Occident: le moyen âge roman et gothique* (Paris, 1938) English trs. *The Art of the West in the Middle Ages* 2 vols (London, 1963)

FOSSA, F. *Le Château historique de Vincennes à travers les âges* (Paris, 1908)

FRANKL, P. *Gothic Architecture* (Harmondsworth, 1962)

FRIEDLÄNDER, M. J. *Early Netherlandish Painting from Van Eyck to Bruegel* English ed. (London, 1956)

GARDNER, A. *Medieval Sculpture in France* (Cambridge, 1931)

GAY, V. *Glossaire archéologique du Moyen Age et de la Renaissance* 2 vols (Paris 1882–1928)

GAYE, G. *Carteggio Inedito, etc.* Vol. II for the 1355 Statutes of the Sienese painters (Florence, 1840)

GÉRAUD, P. H. J. F. *Paris sous Philippe-le-Bel* (Paris, 1837)

GILSON, E. H. *History of Christian Philosophy in the Middle Ages* (London, 1955)

GIMPEL, J. *The Cathedral Builders* (London & New York, 1961)

GODEFROY, T. *Le Cérémonial français* 2 vols (Paris, 1649)

GRABAR, A. N. and NORDENFALK, C. *Early Medieval Painting from the Fourth to the Eleventh Century* trs. by S. Gilbert (Lausanne, 1957)
Romanesque Painting from the Eleventh to the Thirteenth Century trs. by S. Gilbert (Lausanne, 1958)

GRIMSCHITZ, B. *Hanns Puchspaum* (Vienna, 1947)

GRIVOT, D. and ZARNECKI, G. *Gislebertus. Sculptor of Autun* (London, 1961)

GRUNDMANN, H. *Vom Ursprung der Universität im Mittelalter* (Berlin, 1957)

GUIFFREY, J. *Inventaires de Jean, Duc de Berry (1401–1416)* 2 vols (Paris, 1894–96)

HAHN, H. *Die frühe Kirchenbaukunst der Zisterzienser* (Berlin, 1957)

HAHNLOSER, H. R. *Villard de Honnecourt* (Vienna, 1935)

HARVEY, A. *The Castles and Walled Towns of England* (London, 1925)

HARVEY, J. H. *Henry Yevele, c. 1320 to 1400. The life of an English architect* 2nd ed. (London, 1946)
Gothic England. A survey of national culture, 1300–1550 2nd ed. (London, 1948)
The Gothic World, 1100–1600. A survey of architecture and art (London, 1950)
The Cathedrals of Spain (London, 1957)
English Cathedrals revised paperback ed. (London, 1961)

HASELOFF, A. E. G. *Die Bauten der Hohenstaufen in Unteritalien* (Leipzig, 1920)

HASKINS, C. H. *The Normans in European History* (Harvard, 1915; London & New York, 1916)
The Renaissance of the Twelfth Century (Cambridge, Mass., 1927)
Studies in the History of Mediaeval Science 2nd ed. (Cambridge, Mass., 1927)

HEER, F. *The Medieval World* trs. by J. Sondheimer (London, 1962)

HEMPEL, E. *Geschichte der deutschen Baukunst* (Munich, 1949)

HEYD, W. von *Histoire du commerce du Levant au moyen-âge* (Leipzig, 1885–86)

HOLT, E. *A Documentary History of Art*, Vol. I (New York, 1957)

HUIZINGA, J. *The Waning of the Middle Ages* trs. by F. Hopman (London, 1924)

IRSAY, S. d' *Histoires des universités françaises et étrangères des origines à nos jours* 2 vols (Paris, 1933–35)

JEUNEAU, E. *La Philosophie médiévale* (Paris, 1963)

JOPE, E. M. (ed.) *Studies in Building History* (London, 1961)

JUVENAL DES URSINS, J. *Histoire de Charles VI, Roy de France* (Paris, 1653)

KERN, F. *Kingship and Law in the Middle Ages* trs. by S. B. Chrimes, 2 vols (Oxford, 1939)

KERVYN DE LETTENHOVE, H. *La Toison d'Or* (Brussels, 1907)

KINGSFORD, C. L. *The Stonor Letters and Papers, 1290–1483* (London, 1919)

KNOWLES, D. *The Religious Orders in England* 3 vols (Cambridge, 1948–59)
The Monastic Order in England 2nd ed. (Cambridge, 1963)
The Historian and Character and other essays (Cambridge, 1963)

KOECHLIN, R. *Les Ivoires gothiques français* 2 vols (Paris, 1924)

KRAUTHEIMER, R. *Die Kirchen der Bettelorden in Deutschland* (Cologne, 1925)

KUTTNER, S. G. *Harmony from dissonance, an interpretation of medieval canon law* (Latrobe, 1960)

LABORDE, L. de *Les Ducs de Bourgogne. Etudes sur les lettres, les arts et l'industrie pendant le XVᵉ siècle* 3 vols (Paris 1849–52)

LA CURNE DE SAINT PALAYE, J. de *Mémoires sur l'ancienne chevalerie* 2nd ed., 3 vols (Paris 1781)

LAMBERT, E. *L'Architecture des Templiers* (Paris, 1955)

LASTEYRIE DU SAILLANT, R. de *L'Architecture religieuse en France à l'époque gothique* ed. M. Aubert, 2 vols (Paris, 1926)
L'Architecture religieuse en France à l'époque romane 2nd ed. (Paris, 1929)

LAWN, B. *The Salernitan Questions. An introduction to the history of medieval and Renaissance problem literature* (Oxford, 1963)

LEBER, J., SALGUES, J. B. and COHEN, J. *Collection des meilleurs dissertations, notices et traités particuliers relatifs à l'histoire de France*, Vol 19, p. 451, for the 1391 Statutes of Parisian sculptors and painters (Paris, 1826–38)

LEMAÎTRE, H. *Châteaux en France* (Paris, 1948)

LEROUX DE LINCY, A., and TISSERAND, L. M. *Paris et ses historiens aux XIVᵉ et XVᵉ siècles* for Jean de Jandun, *Tractatus de Laudibus Parisiis*, 1323 (Paris, 1867)

LETHABY, W. R. *Mediaeval Art from the peace of the Church to the eve of the Renaissance 312–1350* (London & New York, 1904; revised ed. D. Talbot Rice, London, 1949)
Westminster Abbey and the Kings' Craftsmen (London, 1906)
Westminster Abbey Re-examined (London, 1925)

LEWIS, C. S. *The Discarded Image. An introduction to medieval and renaissance literature* (Cambridge, 1964)

LIPSON, E. *The Economic History of England*, Vol. I, *The Middle Ages*, 12th ed. (London, 1959)

LONGHI, L. F. de *L'Architettura delle chiese cisterciensi italiane* (Milan, 1958)

LOPEZ, R. S. and RAYMOND, I. W. *Medieval Trade in the Mediterranean World* (London & New York, 1955)

MÂLE, E. *L'Art religieux de la fin du moyen âge en France* 2nd ed. (Paris, 1922)
L'Art religieux du XIIIᵉ siècle en France 6th ed. (Paris, 1925)
L'Art religieux du XIIᵉ siècle en France 3rd ed. (Paris, 1938)

MATT, L. von and HAUSER, W. *St Francis of Assisi. A pictorial biography* trs. by S. Bullough (London, 1956)

MOES, E. W. and SLUYTERMAN, K. *Nederlandsche Kasteelen en hun historie*, Vols I–III (Amsterdam, 1911–15)

MORTET, V. *Recueil de textes relatifs à l'histoire de l'architecture et à la condition des architectes en France, au moyen âge, XIᵉ–XIIᵉ siècles* 2 vols (Paris, 1911–29)

MUSPER, H. T. *Der Holzschnitt in fünf Jahrhunderten* (Stuttgart, 1964)

O'NEIL, B. H. St. J. *Castles* (London, 1953)

ORIGO, I. M. *The Merchant of Prato, Francesco di Marco Datini* (London & New York, 1957; revised ed., Harmondsworth, 1963)

OURSEL, C. *La Miniature du XIIᵉ siècle à l'abbaye de Cîteaux* (Dijon, 1926)
L'Art roman de Bourgogne (Dijon & Boston, 1928)

OWST, G. R. *Literature and Pulpit in Medieval England* 2nd ed. (Oxford, 1961)

PAINTER, S. *Mediaeval Society* (Ithaca, 1951)

PANOFSKY, E. *Abbot Suger on the Abbey Church of St-Denis and its Art Treasures* (Princeton & London, 1946)
Tomb Sculpture. Its changing aspects from Ancient Egypt to Bernini (London, 1964)

PARKER, J. H. and TURNER, T. H. *Some account of the Domestic Architecture in England from the Conquest to the end of the thirteenth century* (Oxford, 1851 etc.)

PEGOLOTTI, F. B. *La Pratica della Mercatura*, ed A. Evans (Cambridge, Mass., 1936)

PIRENNE, H. *Les Villes du moyen âge* (Brussels, 1927) English trs. *Medieval Cities* (Princeton, 1925)
Histoire économique de l'Occident médiéval (Bruges, 1951) English trs. *Economic and Social History of Medieval Europe* (London, 1936)

PORTER, A. K. *Medieval Architecture: its origins and development* 2 vols (New York & London, 1909)
Romanesque Sculpture of the Pilgrimage Roads 10 vols (Boston, 1923)

POWER, E. *The Wool Trade in English Mediaeval History* (Oxford, 1941)

POWICKE, F. M. *The Medieval Books of Merton College* (Oxford, 1931)

PROST, B. *Inventaires mobiliers et extraits des comptes des ducs de Bourgogne de la maison de Valois 1363–1477* 2 vols (Paris, 1902–13)

PUIG I CADAFALCH, J. *La Géographie et les origines du premier art roman* (Paris, 1935)

RASHDALL, H. *The Universities of Europe in the Middle Ages* new ed. by F. M. Powicke and A. B. Emden, 3 vols (Oxford, 1936)

RENOUARD, Y. *Les Hommes d'affaires italiens du moyen âge* (Paris, 1949)

RICKERT, M. *Painting in Britain: the Middle Ages* (Harmondsworth, 1954)

RING, G. *A century of French painting 1400–1500* (London, 1949)

ROMANINI, A. M. *L'architettura gotica in Lombardia* (Milan, 1964)

ROOVER, R. de *The Medici Bank: its organization, management, operations and decline* (London & New York, 1948)

ROSENFELD, H. *Der mittelalterliche Totentanz* (Münster & Cologne, 1954)

RUNCIMAN, J. C. S. *A History of the Crusades* 3 vols (Cambridge, 1951–4)

SABATIER, P. *Life of St Francis of Assisi* trs. by L. S. Houghton (London, 1894)

SACKUR, E. *Die Cluniacenser* 2 vols (Halle, 1892–4)

SALMI, M. *Italian Miniatures* (London, 1957)

SALZMAN, L. F. *English Industries of the Middle Ages* 2nd ed. (Oxford, 1923)
English Trade in the Middle Ages (Oxford, 1931)
Building in England down to 1540 (Oxford, 1952)

SAPORI, A. *Le Marchand italien au moyen âge* (Paris, 1952)

SCHMITZ, Dom P. *Histoire de l'Ordre de Saint Benoît* 7 vols (Gembloux, 1942–56)

SCHULTZ, A. *Das höfische Leben zur Zeit der Minnesinger* 2nd ed., 2 vols (Leipzig, 1889)

SHERLEY-PRICE, L. S. *Francis of Assisi. His life and writings as recorded by his contemporaries* (London, 1959)

SMALLEY, B. *The Study of the Bible in the Middle Ages* 2nd ed. (Oxford, 1952)

SMITH, A. L. *Church and State in the Middle Ages* (Oxford, 1913)

SOUTHERN, R. W. *The Making of the Middle Ages* (London, 1953)

STEIN, H. *Les Architectes des cathédrales gothiques* (Paris, 1909)

STONE, L. *Sculpture in Britain: the Middle Ages* (Harmondsworth, 1955)

STREET, G. E. *Some Account of Gothic Architecture in Spain* 2nd ed. (London, 1869)

SUGER, *Vie de Louis VI le Gros* ed. and trs. into French by H. Waquet (Paris, 1929)

SWARTWOUT, R. E. *The Monastic Craftsman* (Cambridge, 1932)

TIERNEY, B. *Medieval Poor Law* (Berkeley & Los Angeles, 1959)

TOY, S. *A History of fortification from 3000 BC to AD 1700* (London, 1955)

TUULSE, A. *Verzeichnis österreichischer Burgen und Schlösser* (Vienna, 1955)
Castles of the Western World trs. by R. P. Girdwood (London, 1959)

ULLMANN, W. *The Growth of Papal Government in the Middle Ages* (London, 1955)

VASARI, G. *Le Vite de' più eccellenti Architetti, Pittori, et Scultori Italiani da Cimabue insino a tempi nostri* ed A. Venturi (Florence, 1896)
The Lives of the Painters, Sculptors and Architects, trs. by A. B. Hinds, 4 vols (London, Toronto, New York, 1927)

VIOLLET-LE-DUC, E. E. *Dictionnaire raisonné de l'architecture française du XIᵉ au XVᵉ siècle* 10 vols (Paris, 1854–69)
Dictionnaire raisonné du mobilier français de l'époque carlovingienne à la Renaissance 6 vols (Paris, 1854–75)
Military Architecture trs. by M. Macdermott, 3rd ed. (Oxford & London, 1907)

VITRY, P. *Michel Colombe et la sculpture française de son temps* (Paris, 1901)

WAGNER, A. R. *Heralds and Heraldry in the Middle Ages* 2nd ed. (London, 1956)

WEBB, G. F. *Architecture in Britain: the Middle Ages* (Harmondsworth, 1956)

WEISHEIPL, J. A. *The Development of Physical Theory in the Middle Ages* (London & New York, 1959)

WILMART, Dom A. *Auteurs spirituels et textes dévots du moyen âge latin* (Paris, 1932)

WULF, M. de *Histoire de la philosophie médiévale* 6th ed.; Vol I, pp. 64–80, Vol II, pp. 25–28, for sections by A. Pelzer (Louvain, 1934–36)

YOUNG, K. *The drama of the Medieval Church* 2 vols (Oxford, 1933)

List and Sources of Illustrations

The page on which an illustration appears is shown by the first set of numerals, its plate or figure number by the second. Sources of photographs are given in italic.

Contributing artists indicated by abbreviations are as follows: RCD R.C. Donovan, WAD W.A. Dodd, IMK Ian Mackenzie Kerr, RdeS Rosalind de Senneville, JS John Stengelhofen, MW Martin Weaver, JDW Jon D. Wilsher, JW John Woodcock.

I Introduction

11 Woodcut showing an Emperor on horseback; German, c.1470

13 1. Miniature from a *Coronation Order*, the coronation ceremony (enlarged); ?French, early 14th C. MS 20, fol.68r. *By permission of the Master and Fellows of Corpus Christi College, Cambridge*

14 2. Detail of miniature from *La estoire de Seint Aedward le rei*, the coronation of Edward the Confessor; English, mid-13th C. MS Ee.3.59, fol.9r. *Cambridge University Library*
3. Coronation chair made for Edward I, containing the stone of Scone; 1300. Westminster Abbey, London. Photo *Thames and Hudson Archives*
4. Detail of calendar miniature from the *Très Riches Heures du duc de Berry*, the Ile de la Cité (June); by the Limbourg brothers, 1413–16. MS 65, fol.6v. Musée Condé, Chantilly. Photo *Giraudon*
5. London: shrine and royal tombs in the Chapel of Edward the Confessor, Westminster Abbey, London; 13th to 15th C. Photo *National Monuments Record*

15 6. Miniature from the *Codex Manesse*, Henry VI; Zürich, early 14th C. Fol.6r. *Universitätsbibliothek, Heidelberg*
7. Miniatures from the *Chronicle* of John of Worcester, the nightmares of Henry I (enlarged); English, mid-12th C. MS 157, pp.382 (top and centre) and 383 (bottom). *By permission of the Master and Fellows of Corpus Christi College, Oxford*

16–17 8. Detail of *The Allegory of the Dominican Order*, fresco by Andrea di Buonaiuto (da Firenze), the Church Militant; 1355. Spanish Chapel, Sta Maria Novella, Florence. Photo *Scala*
9. Detail of miniature from the *Decretals* of Boniface VIII, Pope Boniface presiding over the Sacred College; Italian, 14th C. MS Add. 23923, fol.2r. *Trustees of the British Museum*
10. Miniature from the *Cronaca Villani*, election of Pope John XXII; Italian, second half of 14th C. MS Chigi L.viii.296, fol. 214v. *Biblioteca Apostolica Vaticana*
11. Miniature from the *Cronaca Villani*, coronation of Pope Clement VI in the presence of King Philip of France, King Charles of Valois, and barons; Italian, second half of 14th C. MS Chigi L.viii.296, fol.186v. *Biblioteca Apostolica Vaticana*

18–19 12. Detail of *Good Government*, fresco by Ambrogio Lorenzetti, personifications of Siena and the Virtues; 1337–39. Palazzo Pubblico, Siena. Photo *Scala*
13. Detail of *Good Government*, fresco by Ambrogio Lorenzetti, street scene in Siena; 1337–39. Palazzo Pubblico, Siena. Photo *Scala*

20–21 14. Miniature from a cycle of *Lives of the Saints*, St Martin and the beggar; English, c.1280. MS 370, fol.5v. *Reproduced by permission of the Syndics of the Fitzwilliam Museum, Cambridge*
15. St-Parize-le-Châtel, Nièvre: detail of capital in the crypt, Avarice; 11th C. Photo *Auguste Allemand*
16. Detail of miniature from Jean de Vignay's translation of Vincent de Beauvais' *Miroir Historial*, diseased beggars (enlarged); French, 14th C. MS 5080, fol.373r. Bibliothèque de l'Arsenal, Paris. Photo *Giraudon*
17. Marginal figure from a *Pontifical*, leprous beggar-woman; English, 14th C. MS Lansdowne 451, fol.123r. *Trustees of the British Museum*
18. Miniature from the *Grandes Heures du duc de Berry*, St Peter leading the Duke into Heaven; French, 1409. MS lat.919, fol.96r. *Bibliothèque Nationale, Paris*
19. Moissac, Tarn-et-Garonne: relief on left jamb of the porch of St-Pierre, Dives and Lazarus; c. 1125–30. Photo *Archives Photographiques*

22 20. Fresco by Giotto in the Upper Church of S. Francesco, Assisi, *The Dream of Innocent III*; end 13th C. Photo *Scala*

23 21. Detail of *The Madonna of St Francis*, fresco by Cimabue, head of St Francis; late 13th C., subsequently retouched. Lower Church of S. Francesco, Assisi. Photo *Marzari*

24 22. Fresco by Giotto in the Bardi Chapel of Sta Croce, Florence, *St Francis before the Sultan*; 1317–23. Photo *Scala*
23. Fresco by Giotto in the Upper Church of S. Francesco, Assisi, *St Clare mourning St Francis*; end 13th C. Photo *Marzari*
24. Assisi: exterior of S. Damiano, from the west; early 13th C. Photo *Mansell-Alinari*

25 25. Detail of a diptych leaf, *The Mass of St Giles*; Flemish, by the Master of St Giles, c.1495. *By courtesy of the Trustees of the National Gallery, London.* Photo *John Webb*

26 26. St-Denis, near Paris: detail of stained glass window in the abbey, showing Abbot Suger (prostrate at the feet of the Virgin); mid-12th C., reset in the 14th C. window of the Life of the Virgin. Photo *Jean Roubier*
27. Sardonyx chalice mounted in gold, made for Abbot Suger; from St-Denis, c.1140. *National Gallery of Art, Washington, D.C. Widener Collection*
28. Roman porphyry vase with gold mount in the shape of an eagle, made for Abbot Suger; from St-Denis, mount c.1140. Louvre, Paris. Photo *Connaissance des Arts*

27 29. Miniature from the *Sarum Breviary*, Holy Relics Day (enlarged); French, 1424–35. MS lat.17294, fol.497r. *Bibliothèque Nationale, Paris*

28–29 30. Silos, Burgos: relief in the cloister of S. Domingo, Christ on the road to Emmaus dressed as a pilgrim to Santiago de Compostela; late 11th C. Photo *G. Zarnecki*
31. Marginal scene from the *Hours of the Duchess of Burgundy*, return of pilgrims from Compostela; French, 15th C. MS 76, fol.9r. Musée Condé, Chantilly. Photo *Giraudon*
32. Panel of an altarpiece by Friedrich Herlin, Compostela pilgrims at a meal; mid-15th C. St Jakobs, Rothenburg ob der Tauber, Bavaria. Photo *Bayerisches Landesamt für Denkmalpflege*
33. Painted stone statue of St James of Compostela as a pilgrim; from Semur-en-Auxois, Côte-d'Or, late 15th C. Louvre, Paris
34. Santiago de Compostela: west end of Cathedral nave; early 12th C. Photo *Mas*
35. Santiago de Compostela: tympanum in the Cathedral showing St James as Slayer of Moors; second half of 12th C., later reset. Photo *Mas*
36. Estella, Navarra: capital on the 'Palace of the Dukes of Granada', showing the legendary combat between Roland and the Moorish giant Ferragut; second half of 12th C. Photo *Mas*

30 37. Miniature from the *Descriptio Terrae Sanctae* of Burchardus Theutonicus, the siege of Jerusalem; Italian, late 13th C. MS 74, fol.13v. *Biblioteca del Seminario, Padua*
38. Miniature from the *Chroniques de France ou de Saint Denis*, St Louis leaving on the Seventh Crusade (enlarged); French, early 14th C. MS Roy.16.G.VI, fol.404v. *Trustees of the British Museum*

31 1. Marginal illustration from the *Taymouth Hours*, St Francis cutting out his habit; English, c.1325. MS Yates Thompson 13, fol.180v. British Museum.

32 2. Detail of drawing from *La estoire de Seint Aedward le rei*, King Edward the Confessor bearing a cripple on his back; English, mid-13th C. MS Ee.3.59, fol.17r. Cambridge University Library.

33 3. Marginal drawing from the *Topographia Hibernica* of Gerald of Wales, a cripple; English, end 12th C. MS Roy. 13. B. VIII, fol. 30v. British Museum

35 4. Miniature from the *Actes du Procès de Robert d'Artois*, King Philip the Fair with his council; French, 1322. MS fr.18437, fol.2r. Bibliothèque Nationale, Paris.

37 5. Gilt copper plaque decorated with champlevé enamel, showing Henry of Blois, Bishop of Winchester, kneeling and holding what is probably a reliquary; English (Winchester), c.1120–30. British Museum. IMK

II The Monastic World

41 Initial from St Gregory's *Moralia in Job*, a Cistercian monk reaping; French (Cîteaux), 1111. MS 170, fol.75v. Bibliothèque de Dijon. IMK

43 1. Page from St Gregory's *Life of St Benedict*, scenes from the life and legend of Benedict (enlarged); Italian (Monte Cassino), 11th C. Cod. Vat. lat.1202, fol.80r. *Biblioteca Apostolica Vaticana*

44–45 2. S.Pedro de Roda, Gerona: nave vault of the Benedictine abbey church; early 11th C. Photo *YAN*
3. Tournus, Saône-et-Loire: vaulting of the nave and aisle of St-Philibert (Benedictine); early 11th C. Photo *Jean Roubier*

4. Civate, Como: interior of the nave of S. Pietro (Benedictine), showing a wall-painting of the triumph of St Michael over the Devil; church 1040, painting first half of 12th C. Photo *Jean Roubier*
5. St-Benoît-sur-Loire (Fleury), Loiret: choir of the Benedictine abbey church, from the ambulatory; end 11th C. Photo *Archives Photographiques*
6. Milan: atrium and façade of S. Ambrogio (Benedictine); c.1100. Photo *Anderson*
7. Paray-le-Monial, Saône-et-Loire: interior of the Cluniac abbey church, looking east; first half of 12th C. Photo *Jean Roubier*

46–47 8. Miniature from the *Book of Offices and Chronicon Cluniacense* of St-Martin-des-Champs in Paris (Cluniac), dedication of the third abbey church of Cluny (enlarged); late 12th C. MS lat.17716, fol.91r. *Bibliothèque Nationale, Paris*
9. Capital from the abbey of Cluny, Saône-et-Loire, showing the third tone of plainsong; c. 1095. Musée Ochier, Cluny. Photo *Véronèse*
10. Capital from the abbey of Cluny, Saône-et-Loire, showing the first tone of plainsong; c. 1095. Musée Ochier, Cluny. Photo *Véronèse*
11. Berzé-la-Ville, Saône-et-Loire: fresco in the apse of the Cluniac grange, showing Christ in Majesty; early 12th C. Photo *Thames and Hudson Archives*
12. Cluny, Saône-et-Loire: southwestern transept and crossing tower; 1088–1135. Photo *Véronèse*

48 13. Silos, Burgos: capital in the cloister of S.Domingo (Benedictine), showing harpies; late 11th C. Photo *YAN*
14. Payerne, Switzerland: capital in the Cluniac priory church showing St Peter and Christ; c.1080. Photo *G. Zarnecki*
15. Canterbury: capital in the crypt of the Cathedral (Benedictine), showing a lion; c.1120. Photo *G. Zarnecki*
16. St-Genis-des-Fontaines, Pyrénées-Orientales: carved lintel on the façade of the Benedictine abbey church; 1020–21. Photo *Mas*
17. Silos, Burgos: capital in the cloister of S.Domingo (Benedictine), showing monsters and scrolls; late 11th C. Photo *G. Zarnecki*

49 18. Gilt bronze chandelier in St Michael's, Hildesheim (Benedictine); c.1070. *From an old photograph*
19. Reconstruction drawing of gilt bronze candlestick, now destroyed, from the Abbey of St-Remi at Rheims; 12th C. From M. A. Lenoir, *Architecture monastique*
20. Foot of gilt bronze candlestick from the Benedictine abbey of St-Remi at Rheims; 12th C. Musée des Beaux-Arts, Rheims. *From an old photograph*

50 21–24. Marginal roundels from a *Book of Hours*, showing Carmelite, Franciscan and Dominican friars and Benedictine monks; French, c.1470. MS lat.1176, fol.132r. Bibliothèque Nationale, Paris. From *The Horizon History of Christianity*
25. Miniature from the *Psalter of Henry VI*, friars in choir (enlarged); French, c.1430. MS Cotton Dom.A.XVII, fol.122v. *Trustees of the British Museum*
26. Roundel from a *Bible moralisée* drawing a parallel to Mark IX: 19 ff. (Christ casting out a demon), showing a man entering the monastic life and thus casting out his own evil spirit; French, late 13th C. MS Harl.1527, fol.33r. *Trustees of the British Museum*

51 27. Leaf from the *Polyptych of the Blessed Umiltà* by Pietro Loren-

1059–71, capital c.1120. Photo *Dr Harald Busch*

17. Durham: capital in the crypt chapel of the castle; c.1075. Photo *Courtauld Institute of Art, University of London*

18. Königslutter, Niedersachsen: capital in the cloister of the cathedral; c.1150–70. Photo *Lala Aufsberg*

19. Vienne: capital showing Samson and the lion, in St-André-le-Bas; c.1152. Photo *Archives Photographiques*

20. Bayeux, Manche: vault of the north-west tower of the Cathedral; c.1075. Photo *A. F. Kersting*

21. Durham: nave vault of the Cathedral; begun 1128, finished by 1133. Photo *Courtauld Institute of Art, University of London*

22. Canterbury: groin-vaulted crypt of the Cathedral; 1096–1107. Photo *Courtauld Institute of Art, University of London*

23. Iffley, Oxfordshire: detail of west door of St Mary's; c.1180. Photo *National Monuments Record*

24. Arles, Bouches-du-Rhône: west portal of St-Trophime; c.1170–80. Photo *Giraudon*

25. Saintes, Charente-Maritime: detail of west door of the Abbaye-aux-Dames; 1119–34. Photo *Archives Photographiques*

90 26. Pisa: general view of the Baptistery, Cathedral, and Campanile; 1063–1272. Photo *A. F. Kersting*

27. Worms: west front of the Cathedral; early 13th C. Photo *Dr Helmut Hell, by courtesy of Burkhard-Verlag Ernst Heyer, Essen*

28. Conques, Aveyron: aerial view of Ste-Foy from the north-east; c.1100–30. Photo *Scala*

91 29. Gloucester: nave of the Cathedral, from the south aisle; c.1120–60. Photo *A. F. Kersting*

30. Vézelay, Yonne: interior of La Madeleine, looking, east; nave c.1104–32, choir 1170–1201. Photo *Dr Wolfgang Salchow, by courtesy of Burkhard-Verlag Ernst Heyer, Essen*

92 31. St-Denis, near Paris: narthex vault in the abbey; c.1135–40. Photo *Archives Photographiques*

32. Sens, Yonne: sexpartite vault of the Cathedral nave; mid-12th C. Photo *A. F. Kersting*

33. Le Mans, Sarthe: quadripartite choir vault and radiating apse vault of the Cathedral; 1217–54. Photo *Marburg*

34. Lincoln: ridge-rib and tierceron vault of the Cathedral nave; c.1225–40. Photo *Marburg*

35. Ely: octagon and presbytery vaults of the Cathedral, the latter a star vault of tiercerons and liernes; 1328–40. Photo *Martin Hürlimann*

36. Bristol: skeleton vault of the Berkeley Chapel vestibule, in the Cathedral; c.1311–40. Photo *National Monuments Record*

37. Bristol: vault of south choir aisle in the Cathedral; c.1311–40. Photo *Reece Winston*

38. Langenstein, near Kassel: skeleton vault in the choir of the village church; late Gothic, c.1500. Photo *Marburg*

39. Schwäbisch Hall: net vault in St Michael's; second half of 15th C. Photo *Eugen Kusch*

93 40. Autun, Saône-et-Loire: nave arcade in St-Lazare; 1120–32. Photo *Jean Roubier*

41. Coutances, Manche: exterior of the Cathedral from the east; c.1220–50. Photo *Jean Roubier*

42. Chartres: flying buttresses of the Cathedral nave; lower ones c.1200, upper c.1220. Photo *Martin Hürlimann*

43. Amiens: flying buttresses of the Cathedral choir; c.1258. Photo *Jean Roubier*

94 44. Bourges, Cher: detail of stained glass window in the Cathedral given by the masons, showing building and the story of Dives and Lazarus; c.1220. Photo *Scala*

45. Bourges, Cher: detail of west front of the Cathedral; 13th to late 14th C., north porch and tower rebuilt 1508–40. Photo *Scala*

95 46. Bourges, Cher: interior of east end of the Cathedral; c.1192–1225. Photo *Scala*

96 47. Assisi: wheel window in the west front of S. Rufino; early 13th C. Photo *Lala Aufsberg*

48. Chartres: rose window in the west front of the Cathedral; designed c.1196. Photo *Martin Hürlimann*

49. Lincoln: the 'Bishop's Eye', rose window in the south transept front of the Cathedral; c.1330. Photo *Courtauld Institute of Art, University of London*

50. Amiens: rose window (surrounded by a wheel of fortune), in the south transept front of the Cathedral; c.1500. Photo *Jeiter*

51. Norwich: bay in south walk of the Cathedral cloister; by William Ramsey, c.1324. Photo *Jarrolds*

52. Batalha, Portugal: bay in the Royal Cloister of the abbey; begun 1387, tracery c.1500–10. Photo *Courtauld Institute of Art, University of London*

97 53. Caen, Calvados: west front of La Trinité (Abbaye-aux-Dames); c.1100. Photo *Jean Roubier*

54. Paris: west front of Notre-Dame; 1202–25, towers completed by c.1250. Photo *Martin Hürlimann*

55. Rheims: west front of the Cathedral; by Bernard de Soissons, c.1255–90, towers left unfinished in 1427. Photo *Martin Hürlimann*

56. Amiens: west front of the Cathedral; c.1220–36, towers above the level of the rose window later (north tower finished c.1420). Photo *Martin Hürlimann*

98 57. Salisbury: exterior of the Cathedral from the south-east; by Nicholas of Ely, c.1220–60, tower by Richard of Farleigh, begun 1334. Photo *Edwin Smith*

58. Salisbury: interior of Cathedral choir, looking east to the Lady Chapel; by Nicholas of Ely, c.1225. Photo *A. F. Kersting*

59. Lincoln: interior of the Angel Choir of the Cathedral; by Simon of Thirsk, 1256–80. Photo *A. F. Kersting*

99 60. Ely: interior of the wooden octagon over the crossing in the Cathedral; by William Hurley, 1328–40. Photo *A. F. Kersting*

61. Wells, Somerset: west front of the Cathedral; lower part by Thomas Norreys, 1230–60, towers designed after 1365 by William Wynford. Photo *A. F. Kersting*

100 62. Burgos: vault of the Chapel of the Constable, in the Cathedral; by Simón de Colonia, 1482–94. Photo *Mas*

63. Burgos: exterior of the Cathedral from the south-west; 1222–1568, spires 1442–58 by Juan de Colonia. Photo *A. F. Kersting*

64. Barcelona: interior of the Tinell hall in the Royal Palace; by Guillem Carbonell, 1359–70. Photo *Mas*

65. Gerona: interior of the Cathedral looking east; choir begun 1312, nave begun 1416. Photo *Mas*

101 66. Brunswick: north choir aisles of the Cathedral; c.1469. Photo *Marburg*

67. Munich: exterior of the Frauenkirche from the south-east; designed by Jörg Ganghofer, 1468–88. Photo *H. Schmidt-Glassner*

68. Cologne: exterior of the Cathedral from the north-west; designed c.1250, completed 1880. Photo *Helga Schmidt-Glassner*

102 69. Siena: façade of the Palazzo Pubblico; 1289–1309. Photo *Scala*

70. Venice: interior of SS. Giovanni e Paolo, looking east; begun 1260. Photo *Scala*

71. Pisa: exterior of Sta Maria della Spina from the south-west; 1230–1323. Photo *Scala*

103 72. Siena: west front of the Cathedral; begun by Giovanni Pisano, 1284–1300, upper parts completed 1369–80. Photo *Feature-Pix*

73. Venice: canal façade of the Ca' d'Oro; 1421–30. Photo *Scala*

74. Venice: the Doge's Palace; begun 1343 by Pietro Baseggio, finished 1404. Photo *Scala*

104–5 75. Gloucester: fan vaulting in the Cathedral cloister; c.1370. Photo *Edwin Smith*

76. London: interior of Westminster Hall; begun 1097 and altered several times, roof 1394–1400 by Hugh Herland. Photo *Country Life*

77. Canterbury: 'Bell Harry' tower, over the Cathedral crossing; by John Wastell, 1493–1505. Photo *Martin Hürlimann*

78. Canterbury: nave of the Cathedral, from the north aisle; by Henry Yevele, begun 1379. Photo *National Monuments Record*

79. London: pendant fan vaulting of Henry VII's Chapel, in Westminster Abbey; by Robert and William Vertue, 1503–19. Photo *Edwin Smith*

80. Beverley, Yorkshire: west front of the Minster; c.1390–1420. Photo *National Monuments Record*

106 81. Albi, Tarn: exterior of the Cathedral from the south; 1282–1390. Photo *A. F. Kersting*

82. Seville: exterior of the Cathedral from the south; 1401–1575, and later. Photo *A. F. Kersting*

107 83. Milan: exterior of the Cathedral from the east; begun 1387. Photo *F. A. Mella*

84. Ghent: exterior of the Cathedral of St Bavon; 1274–1533. Photo *Scala*

85. Bruges: façade of the townhall; begun 1376. Photo *Feature-Pix*

108 86. Rouen: central façade of the Cathedral; 13th C., new façade 1509–14 by Roulland le Roux Photo *Archives Photographiques*

87. Prague: triforium and clerestory of the Cathedral; by Peter Parler, late 14th C. Photo *Helga Schmidt-Glassner*

88. Prague: interior of Vladislav Hall, in the Castle; by Benedikt Ried, 1493, rebuilt 1502–3 after collapse. Photo *Helga Schmidt-Glassner*

109 89. Freiburg-im-Breisgau: interior of the spire of the Cathedral; c.1340. Photo *H. Schmidt-Glassner*

90. Beauvais, Oise: south transept front of the Cathedral; by Martin Chambiges, 1499–1549. Photo *Jeiter*

91. Seville: interior of the Cathedral nave, at the crossing; 1402–32. Photo *A. F. Kersting*

110 92. Miniature from the *Très Riches Heures du duc de Berry*, the Christmas Mass (enlarged); by Jean Colombe, 1488–90. MS 65, fol.158r. Musée Condé, Chantilly. Photo *Giraudon*

111 1. Chartres: detail of the masons' window, showing a master mason and stone-cutters; 13th C. From Didron, *Annales Archéologiques* (vol.II), 1847

112 2. Bury St Edmunds, Suffolk: plan of the abbey. After A. B. Whittingham, Archaeological Journal, CVIII, 1962

113 3. Map showing sites of the major architectural monuments of Europe and the Middle East in the 12th C. JW

114 4. Detail of drawing from the *Lives of the two Offas*, masons building St Albans Abbey; English (style of Matthew Paris), 14th C. MS Cotton Nero D.1, fol.23v. British Museum. IMK

5. Wells, Somerset: masons' drawings on the tracing-floor of the Cathedral. JOHN HARVEY, *from photographs by L. S. Colchester*

115 6. Sketches by Matthäus Roritzer from his *On the Ordination of Pinnacles;* plan and elevation of a pinnacle; German, 1486

7. Design for a vaulted church by Rodrigo Gil de Hontañón, from Simón García's *Compendium of Architecture;* Gil's design is of the first half of the 16th C., García's book of 1681. Biblioteca Nacional, Madrid

116 8. Drawing by Villard de Honnecourt from his album, section through the choir buttresses of Rheims Cathedral; French, c.1235. MS fr. 19093 fol.32v. Bibliothèque Nationale, Paris

117 9. Selection of banker-marks of mediaeval English masons. JOHN HARVEY

119 10. Le Mans, Sarthe: axonometric projection through the choir of the Cathedral; 1217–54. JS

120 11. Canterbury: plan of the Cathedral. MW

12. Wells, Somerset: plan of the Cathedral. WAD

13. Lincoln: plan of the Cathedral. RCD

14. Bourges, Cher: plan of the Cathedral. MW

121 15. Vienna: plan of St Stephen's Cathedral. RCD

16. Gerona: plan of the Cathedral. LORNA PAULL

17. Toledo: plan of the Cathedral. JS

18. Seville: plan of the Cathedral. WAD

122 19. Map showing sites of the major architectural monuments of Western Europe in the 13th C. JW

123 20. London: plan of Westminster Palace and Abbey. MW, after *The History of the King's Works* (Pt. I), 1963, and *Royal Commission on Historical Monuments (West London)*, 1925

124 21. Narbonne, Pyrénées-Orientales: section through the choir of the Cathedral. MW *after H. Nodet*

22. Bristol: section through the choir of the Cathedral, with the Berkeley Chapel on the right. MW

125 23. Bristol: north doorway of the north porch of St Mary Redcliffe. JS

24. Bristol: plan of the north porch of St Mary Redcliffe. JS

126 25. Cairo: detail of mihrab (prayer-niche) wall in the Tomb of Mustafa Pasha. IMK, after Creswell, *The Muslim Architecture of Egypt*, Vol. II

26. Norwich: tracery in a bay of the south walk of the Cathedral cloister. JOHN HARVEY

27. Ely: detail of a bay in the Cathedral choir. JOHN HARVEY

28. Ely: detail of wall of the Cathedral Lady Chapel. JOHN HARVEY

29. London: tracery in a bay of the cloister of Old St Paul's. JOHN HARVEY, after archaeological evidence and an engraving by Wenceslas Hollar

30. Gloucester: south transept window of the Cathedral. MW

31. Wells, Somerset: east window of the Cathedral. JOHN HARVEY

32. Gloucester: east window of the Cathedral. MW

the author (enlarged); English, late 14th C. MS Roy.6.E.V, fol.6r. *Trustees of the British Museum*

4. Detail of fresco by Tommaso da Modena in the chapter-house of S. Niccolò, Treviso, showing St Albertus Magnus; c. 1350. Photo *Mansell-Alinari*

5. Detail of fresco by Fra Angelico in the chapel of Nicholas V in the Vatican, St Bonaventure; c. 1450. Photo *Mansell-Anderson*

6. Chartres: detail of south door of the Royal Portal, showing Music and Grammar with Pythagoras and Donatus; mid-12th C. Photo *Marburg*

183 7. Detail of miniature from Nicole Oresme's translation of the *Ethics* of Aristotle, Charles V receiving the MS from Oresme; French, c.1376. MS 9505, fol.2v. *Bibliothèque Royale de Belgique, Brussels*

8. Miniature from Nicole Oresme's translation of Aristotle's *De coelo et mundo*, Oresme with his armillary sphere (enlarged); French, 14th C. MS fr.565, fol.1r. Bibliothèque Nationale, Paris. Photo *Presses Universitaires de France*

9. Detail of miniature from the *Gesta abbatum monasterii S. Albani*, Richard of Wallingford with scientific instruments; English, 14th C. MS Cotton Claud. E.IV (pt.1), fol.201r. *Trustees of the British Museum*

10. Detail of miniature from the *Psalter of St Louis and Blanche of Castille*, the clerk, the astronomer, and the mathematician (enlarged); French (from the Sainte Chapelle, Paris), 13th C. MS 1186, fol.1v. Bibliothèque de l'Arsenal, Paris. *Bibliothèque Nationale, Paris*

184-85 11, 12. Two pages of miniatures from the *Ordonnances de l' Hôtel du Roy* showing scenes of student life at Ave Maria College, Paris; French, 14th C. Archives Nationales, Paris. Photo *Giraudon*

13. Miniature from a compend of Aristotle's *Nicomachean Ethics* by Frater Henricus de Allemania, a university lecture (enlarged); German, 14th C. Staatliche Museen, Berlin. Photo *Georg Westermann Verlag*

14. Detail of miniature from *Le livre et la vraye hystoire du bon roy Alixandre*, Aristotle teaching the boy Alexander; French, early 15th C. MS Roy.20.B.XX, fol.10v. *Trustees of the British Museum*

15. Detail of miniature from the *Chroniques de France ou de Saint Denis*, Amaury de Bène teaching at Paris; French, early 14th C. MS Roy.16.G.VI, fol.368v. *Trustees of the British Museum*

16. Initial from the *Omne bonum* of Jacobus, boy being birched; English, mid-14th C. MS Roy.6.E. VI, fol.214r. *Trustees of the British Museum*

186 17. Oxford: interior of the Divinity School; by Richard Winchcombe, 1426-88. Photo *National Monuments Record*

18. Miniature from the *Chandler MS*, master and scholars of New College, Oxford; English, c.1460. MS 288, fol.3v. *By permission of the Warden and Fellows of New College, Oxford*

19. First seal of Cambridge University, showing the Chancellor and Proctors; c. 1261. From an impression in the Fitzwilliam Museum, Cambridge, *reproduced by permission of the Syndics of the Fitzwilliam Museum, Cambridge*

20. Cracow: quadrangle of the Collegium Maius; rebuilt in 1494. Photo *J. Krieger*

187 21. Detail of tomb-relief of Guittone Sinibaldi (Cino da Pistoia), in Pistoia Cathedral; c.1360. Photo *Mansell-Alinari*

22. Relief from the tomb of Pierre Gougis, apology being made to the University of Paris; 1440. Ecole des Beaux-Arts, Paris. Photo *Giraudon*

188 23. Miniature from a French translation of Roger of Salerno's *Chirurgia*, an apothecary's shop (enlarged); French, c.1300. MS Sloane 1977, fol.49v. *Trustees of the British Museum*

24. Miniature from the *Chroniques de France*, John, Duke of Normandy, with doctors examining a specimen of urine; French, end 14th C. MS Roy.20.C.VII, fol.78v. *Trustees of the British Museum*

25. Miniature from the *Chroniques de France ou de Saint Denis*, doctors administering medicine to Louis le Gros with a spoon; French, early 14th C. MS Roy.16.G.VI, fol.310v. *Trustees of the British Museum*

189 26. Detail of miniature from a French translation of Roger of Salerno's *Chirurgia*, scenes illustrating the treatment of wounds (enlarged); French, c.1300. MS Sloane 1977, fol.7r. *Trustees of the British Museum*

27. Miniature from a volume of the Bologna glossators' edition of the *Corpus iuris civilis*, dying man dictating his will (enlarged); Italian (Bologna), first half of 14th C. The text of this MS was copied by the *pecia* method. MS Adv. 10.1.4. (vol. i), fol.37v. National Library of Scotland, Edinburgh (on deposit from the Advocates' Library). *Reproduced by permission of the Faculty of Advocates, Edinburgh*

190 28. Miniature from Jean de Vignay's translation of Vincent de Beauvais' *Miroir Historial*, the translator at work; French, 15th C. MS Reg. Lat. 538, fol.1r. *Biblioteca Apostolica Vaticana*

29. Detail of the *Tucher Altar* in the Frauenkirche, Nuremberg, showing St Augustine's bookshelves; German, 15th C. Photo *Germanisches Nationalmuseum, Nuremberg*

30. Miniature from the *Gesta abbatum monasterii S. Albani*, showing Simon, Abbot of St Albans, seated at his book-chest; English, 14th C. MS Cotton Claud. E.IV (pt. 1), fol.124r. *Trustees of the British Museum*

31. Page from a *Herbal* of Dioscorides illustrating catchfly and couch grass; Arabic, 1328. MS Arab.d.138, fol.102r. *Curators of the Bodleian Library, Oxford*

32. Page from a Latin *Herbal* of Apuleius Plato illustrating couch grass, sword lily, and rosemary; end 11th–early 12th C. MS Ashm. 1431, fol.21r. *Curators of the Bodleian Library, Oxford*

191 33, 34 Details of miniature from Joannes Andreae's *Novella super Sexto*, the author writing, teaching, presenting his book to the Pope and selling books; Italian, 14th C. MS 620, fol.1r. Bibliothèque Municipale Classée, Cambrai. Photo *Studio M. Delcroix*

35. Miniature from the *Statuta Collegii Sapientiae*, a library with chained statute book; German, c. 1500. Fol.53v. *Universitätsbibliothek, Freiburg-im-Breisgau*

36. Detail of page from the surgical treatise of Albucasis, showing dental instruments; Italian, mid-14th C. MS e.Mus.19, fol.144r. *Curators of the Bodleian Library, Oxford*

37. Star-figure from a Latin translation of the *Astronomy* of Al-Sûfî, the constellation Hercules; Italian, mid-13th C. MS 1036, fol.6v. *Bibliothèque de l'Arsenal, Paris*

192 38. Miniature from Boethius' *De consolatione philosophiae*, the author

in a library; Flemish, 1476. MS Harl.4335, fol.1r. *Trustees of the British Museum*

39. Miniature from Jean de Vignay's translation of Vincent de Beauvais' *Miroir Historial*, Vincent in his study (enlarged); Flemish, late 15th C. MS Roy.14.E.I (vol.I), fol.3r. *Trustees of the British Museum*

193 1. Seal of the University of Paris; 13th C. After an impression in the Archives Nationales, Paris. RDES

194 2. Detail of map of Paris by Truschet and Hoyau known as the *Plan de Bâle*, showing the university quarter; 1550–52. Bibliothèque de la Ville, Basle

3. Inscription on a stone formerly built into the second school in the faculty of Canon Law of the University of Paris, which stood in the Clos Bruneau; 1415. Musée Carnavalet, Paris. RDES

195 4. Map showing the universities of Europe up to 1490. After Rashdall. JW

196 5. Page from Boethius' *De musica*, Boethius with Pythagoras, Plato, and Nicomachus; English (Canterbury), second quarter of 12th C. MS Ii.3.12. Cambridge University Library.

6. Initial from a MS containing the *Rhetorica ad Herennium* and Cicero's *De inventione*, allegory of Rhetoric giving instruction; ?French or English early 14th C. MS Burney 275, fol. 143r. British Museum. IMK

197 7. Drawing by Matthew Paris from the *Liber experimentarius* of Bernardus Silvestris, Plato and Socrates; English, mid-13th C. MS Ashmole 304, fol.31v. Bodleian Library, Oxford. RDES

8. Drawing from a copy of Terence's *Comedies*, preparations for a wedding (*The Woman of Andros*, Act I, sc. i); English (St Albans), mid-12th C. MS Auct. F.2.13, fol.4v. Bodleian Library, Oxford. RDES

198 9. Initial from a copy of the *Metaphysics* of Aristotle with commentary by Averroës, Philosophy with the seven Liberal Arts; English, second half of 13th C. MS 269. Merton College, Oxford. RDES

10. Drawing by Matthew Paris from the *Liber experimentarius* of Bernardus Silvestris, Euclid and Hermannus; English, mid-13th C. MS Ashmole 304, fol.2v. Bodleian Library, Oxford. RDES

199 11. Pen drawing from the so-called 'False Decretals', showing Air with personifications of the arts and the muses; c.1200. MS 672. Bibliothèque Municipale, Rheims.

200 12. Drawing from a medical treatise in Latin, prefixed to the *Herbarium* of Apuleius Plato, showing treatment for a nasal polyp; Franco-Flemish (Meuse region), third quarter of 12th C. MS Harl.1585, fol.9v. British Museum. RDES

13. Miniature from the *Romance of Alexander*, Alexander lowered into the sea in his diving bell; ?French, late 13th C. MS 11040, fol.70v. Bibliothèque Royale de Belgique, Brussels. RDES

201 14. Drawing from Bacon's *Optics*, diagram of the eye; English, late 13th C. MS Roy. 7.F.VIII. fol.54v. British Museum

15. Printed list issued by the printer Peter Schöffer of Mainz, stating books to be sold (probably in Nuremberg); 1469–70. Staatsbibliothek, Munich

VI King Death

203 Detail of woodcut from Geiler von Kaisersperg's *Sermones*, a skeleton archer; German, 1514

205 1. Miniature from the *Rohan Book of Hours*, the dead man before God; French, early 15th C. MS lat.9471, fol.159r. *Bibliothèque Nationale, Paris*

206-7 2. La Chaise-Dieu, Haute-Loire: section of wall-painting in the abbey church, the Dance of Death; c.1460. Photo *Archives Photographiques*

3. Detail of *The Triumph of Death*, fresco attributed to Francesco Traini, showing the Three Living and the Three Dead with the hermit St Macarius; c.1350. Campo Santo, Pisa. Photo *Mansell-Alinari*

4. Miniature from the *Hours of Mary of Burgundy*, Death carrying a coffin and spear (enlarged); Flemish, c.1477–82. MS 78B12, fol.221r. Kupferstichkabinett, Berlin. Photo *Walter Steinkopf*

5. Marginal scene from the *Hours of Philippe le Bel*, Death and the Lady (enlarged); Flemish, late 15th C. MS Add.17280, fol.271r. *Trustees of the British Museum*

6. Detail of miniature from the *Hours of Philippe le Bel*, naked corpse and mourners (enlarged); Flemish, late 15th C. MS Add. 17280, fol. 271r. *Trustees of the British Museum*

208-9 7. Detail of miniature from Froissart's *Chronicles*, the execution of Aymerigot Marcel; French, 15th C. MS Harl.4379, fol.64r. *Trustees of the British Museum*

8. Marginal scene from the *Très Riches Heures du duc de Berry*, procession against the plague in Rome in 590 (enlarged); by Jean Colombe, 1488–90. MS 65, fol.71v. Musée Condé Chantilly. Photo *Giraudon*

9. Miniature from an *Old Testament*, battle between the Jews and Philistines (enlarged); French c.1240. In 1507 the MS was presented by Cardinal Maciejowski of Poland to Shah Abbas I of Persia, who had the miniatures captioned in Persian. MS 638, fol.23v. *The Pierpont Morgan Library, New York*

10. Miniature from a collection of short pieces on medicine and astronomy, showing a surgical operation; English, early 12th C. MS Hunter 100, fol.119r. *By permission of the Dean and Chapter of Durham Cathedral*

11. Miniature from the *Annales* of Gilles le Muisit, burial of plague-victims at Tournai in 1349; Flemish, 1352. MS 13076–7, fol. 24v. *Bibliothèque Royale de Belgique, Brussels*

210-11 12. Miniature from the *Hours of Philippe le Bon*, preparation of the corpse; Flemish, mid-15th C. MS 76.F.2, fol.169r. *Koninklijke Bibliotheek, The Hague*

13. Stone mourners on the base of the tomb of Louis de France, from the Abbey of Royaumont, Seine-et-Oise; c.1260. Abbey of St-Denis, near Paris. Photo *Marburg*

14. Stone mourner on the base of the tomb of Adelaïs de Champagne, formerly in the Abbey of Dilo, Yonne, representing her daughter; the tomb was built c.1290 to honour the Countess (d.1187) as founder of the Abbey. St-Jean, Joigny, Yonne. Photo *Archives Photographiques*

15. Stone funeral monument of Philippe Pot, from the Abbey of Cîteaux, Côte-d'Or; c. 1493. Louvre, Paris. Photo *Archives Photographiques*

212 16. Miniature from the *Chroniques de Charles VII*, funeral procession of Charles VI; French, 15th C. MS fr.2691, fol.11r. *Bibliothèque Nationale, Paris*

213 17. Miniature from a *Book of Hours*, funeral procession and beginning of the Office of the

VII Currents of Trade

254-55 25. Group of goods imported into England: enamel reliquary from Limoges, 13th C.; earthenware drug-jar from Florence, mid-15th C.; gilt-bronze ewer from the Meuse area, mid-12th C.; ivory statuette of the Virgin and Child from Paris, early 14th C.; earthenware jar from Valencia, mid-15th C.; brocaded silk velvet from Italy, mid-15th C. Victoria and Albert Museum, London. Photo *John Webb*

26. Syrian enamelled glass known as the 'Luck of Edenhall'; mid-13th C. *Victoria and Albert Museum, London*

27. Alabaster carving of St Michael; English (Nottingham), early 15th C. Victoria and Albert Museum, London. Photo *John Webb*

256-57 28. Detail of miniature showing a carriage and horses; 14th C. MS Rh.15, fol.54r. *Graphische Sammlung der Zentralbibliothek, Zürich*

29. Detail of road map in Matthew Paris' *Historia Anglorum*, London–Dover; English, 1250–59. MS Roy.14.C.VII, fol.2r. *Trustees o the British Museum*

30. Marginal scene from the *Luttrell Psalter*, carriage and horses; English, c.1335–40. MS Add.42130, fol.181v. *Trustees of the British Museum*

31. Detail of miniature from the *Life of St Denis*, showing the bridges of Paris with a pilgrim and the transportation of wine and coal; French, 1317. MS fr.2091–2, fol.1r. *Bibliothèque Nationale, Paris*

32. Bourges, Cher: carving of a ship, from a lintel in the House of Jacques Coeur; 1442–53. Photo *Archives Photographiques*

33. Miniature from the *Livre des merveilles*, ships in the Indian Ocean; French, late 14th C. MS fr.2810, fol.188v. *Bibliothèque Nationale, Paris*

34. Detail of miniature from the works of Virgil, shipwreck; Italian, 15th C. MS Ricc.492, fol.63r. Biblioteca Riccardiana, Florence. Photo *Scala*

35. Detail of miniature from *La estoire de seint Aedward le rei*, a traveller being robbed; English, mid-13th C. MS Ee.3.59, fol.4r. *Cambridge University Library*

258 36. Detail of The 'Marriage of Giovanni Arnolfini and Giovanna Cenami' by Jan van Eyck; 1434. By courtesy of the Trustees of the National Gallery, London. Photo *Eileen Tweedy*

37. Detail of *The Adoration of the Shepherds*, from the Portinari Altarpiece by Hugo van der Goes, showing Tommaso Portinari; c.1476–78. Uffizi, Florence. Photo *Scala*

38. Detail of altarpiece for the Casa del Ceppo dei Poveri di Francesco di Marco, Francesco Datini and four *Buonomini* of Prato; 1453. Galleria Comunale, Prato. Photo *Scala*

39. Miniature from the *Livre des merveilles*, the three Polos leaving Venice; French, late 14th C. MS fr.2810, fol.4r. *Bibliothèque Nationale, Paris*

259 40. Portrait of the merchant Georg Gisze, by Hans Holbein the Younger; 1532. *Gemäldegalerie, Staatliche Museen, Berlin-Dahlem*

260 41. Detail from stained glass window in Tournai Cathedral, barrel with merchant's mark; early 16th C. Photo *A.C.L.*

42. Chipping Camden, Gloucestershire: Grevel's House; 14th–16th C. Photo *National Monuments Record*

43. Great Coggeshall, Essex: Paycocke's House; c.1500. Photo *National Monuments Record*

44. Bourges, Cher: eastern façade

of the House of Jacques Coeur; 1442–53. Photo *Edition des Monuments Historiques*

45. Bourges, Cher: detail of carving over a fireplace in the House of Jacques Coeur; 1442–53. Photo *Edition des Monuments Historiques*

261 46. Bruges: Cloth Hall; 14th–15th C. Photo *Martin Hürlimann*

47. Valencia: interior of the Lonja de la Seda (Silk Exchange); 1483–98. Photo *Mas*

48. Salisbury: the Poultry Cross; 15th C. with later additions. Photo *National Monuments Record*

49. Alsfeld, Oberhessen: the Rathaus; c.1500. Photo *Martin Hürlimann*

262-63 50. Miniature from the town laws of Hamburg, the cattle-market; German, 1497. Staatsarchiv, Hamburg. Photo *Georg Westermann Verlag*

51. Miniature from the *Grandes Chroniques de France*, the Lendit Fair at St-Denis (enlarged); French 14th C. Musée Goya, Castres. Photo *Giraudon*

52. Miniature from the *Pontificale Senonense*, the Bishop of Paris blessing the Lendit Fair; French, 1395–1426. MS lat.962, fol.264r. *Bibliothèque Nationale, Paris*

53. Detail of miniature from *Le Gouvernement des Princes*, street of shops; French, late 15th C. MS 5062, fol.149v. Bibliothèque de l'Arsenal, Paris. Photo *Giraudon*

54. Miniature from the *Ethics* of Aristotle, shops in a covered market (enlarged); French, 15th C. MS I,2(927), fol.145r. Bibliothèque de la Ville, Rouen. Photo *Giraudon*

55. Miniature from *De septem vitiis*, tavern scene; Italian, late 14th C. MS Add.27695, fol.14r. *Trustees of the British Museum*

264 56. Obverse of an English noble; 1346–51. British Museum. Photo *John Webb*

57. Detail of stained-glass window of the Miracles of the Virgin in Le Mans Cathedral, money-changers; c.1240. Photo *Archives Photographiques*

58. Detail of drawing from the *Canterbury Psalter*, royal officers receiving taxes; English (Canterbury), c.1148–49. MS R.17.1, fol.230r. *By permission of the Master and Fellows of Trinity College, Cambridge*

59. Miniature from *De septem vitiis*, moneylenders (enlarged); Italian, late 14th C. MS Add.27695, fol.7v. *Trustees of the British Museum*

60. Miniature from *Les Faits et les Dis des Romains et des autres gens*, a French translation of Valerius Maximus, settling a business dispute; French, c.1475 MS Harl.4375, fol.135v. *Trustees of the British Museum*

265 61. Gold currency: (a) French *écu*, 1380–1422; (b) Arabic *dinar*, 697–8; (c) English noble, 1346–51; (d) Florentine *florin*, c.1300; (e) Byzantine *nomisma*, 1042–55; (f) Venetian *ducat*, 1280–89. British Museum. Photo *John Webb*

62. Detail of *The Moneylender and his Wife* by Quentin Massys; 1514. Louvre, Paris. Photo *Giraudon*

266 63. Miniature from *De septem vitiis*, banking scenes (enlarged); Italian, late 14th C. MS Add.27695, fol.8r. *Trustees of the British Museum*

64. Miniature from the *Livre des proprietez des choses*, mason and carpenter with master behind them; Flemish, 1482. MS Roy.15.E.II, fol.265r. *Trustees of the British Museum*

267 1. Woodcut from the *Contrasto di Carnesciale e la Quaresima*, market scene; Italian (Florence), n.d., probably late 15th C.

268 2. Woodcut from the *Ordonnances de la Prevosté des Marchands et Echevinage de la Ville de Paris*, timber-haulers; French (Paris), 1500–1

269 3. Rubbing of the monumental brass of the wool-merchant William Midwinter (d. 1501), in the church of St Peter and St Paul, Northleach, Gloucestershire; early 16th C. JDW

4. Marginal illustration from the *Romance of Alexander*, blacksmiths at work; Franco-Flemish, c.1340. MS Bodl.264, fol.84r. Bodleian Library, Oxford. JDW

270 5. Woodcut from the *Fasciculus Temporum*, view of Cologne; German (printed at Cologne by Ther Hoernen), 1474

271 6. Woodcut from the *Supplementum Chronicarum*, view of Genoa; Italian (printed at Venice by Bernardinus Benalius), 1486

272 7. Drawing from the *Hortus deliciarum* of Herrade of Landsberg, two packhorses with their driver; German, 1165–75. MS formerly in Strasbourg, destroyed in the 19th C. JDW

273 8. Miniature from the *Codex Manesse*, a travelling pedlar with his wares; Zürich, early 14th C. Fol. 64r. Universitätsbibliothek, Heidelberg. JDW

274-75 9. Map showing trade routes and commercial centres during the Middle Ages

277 10. Woodcut from the *Ordonnances de la Prevosté des Marchands et Echevinage de la Ville de Paris*, administrators of Parisian commerce; French (Paris), 1500–1

279 11. Impression of the municipal seal of Ypres; late 13th–early 14th C. IMK

VIII The Rise of the Artist

281 Marginal sketch from Jerome's *Commentary on Isaiah*, self-portrait of the illuminator Hugo; Anglo-Norman, c.1100. MS Bodl.717, fol.287v. Bodleian Library, Oxford. IMK

283 1. Presumed self-portrait of Adam Krafft, from the Tabernacle in St Lorenz, Nuremberg; 1493–95. Photo *Peter Cannon Brookes*

284-85 2. Miniature from a *Book of Hours*, St Luke painting; Flemish, end 15th C. MS Add.35313, fol.12v. *Trustees of the British Museum*

3. Miniature from the *Roman de la Rose*, Pygmalion and Galatea; French, c.1470. MS Douce 195, fol.149v. *Curators of the Bodleian Library, Oxford*

4. Miniature from the *Livre des femmes nobles et renommées*, a French translation of Boccaccio, Marcia (Pliny's Jaia) painting her portrait in a mirror; French, early 15th C. MS Roy.16.G.V, fol.100v. *Trustees of the British Museum*

5. Autun, Saône-et-Loire: detail of the tympanum of St-Lazare, showing Gislebertus' signature at the feet of Christ; c.1130. From *Gislebertus, Sculptor of Autun*, Trianon Press, photo *Franceschi*

6. Miniature from a *Bible historiale*, decorators at work painting walls and statues ('the building of Solomon's house'); French, early 15th C. MS 394, fol.145r. *The Pierpont Morgan Library, New York*

7. Miniature from the *Roman du Saint-Graal*, monumental masons with a patroness; French, early 14th C. MS Add.10292, fol.55v. *Trustees of the British Museum*

8. Miniature from the *Lambeth Apocalypse*, Benedictine monk painting a statuette of the Virgin and Child, presumed self-portrait of the illuminator; English, third quarter of 13th C. MS 209, fol.2v. Lambeth Palace Library, London. Photo *John Freeman*

9. Self-portrait of Lorenzo Ghiberti, on the bronze east door of the Baptistery at Florence; c.1445. Photo *Mansell-Alinari*

10. Self-portrait of the sculptor Nicholas Gerhaert, fragment found during excavations at Strasbourg Cathedral, probably from the old carved stalls; 1467. Frauenhaus, Strasbourg, Bas-Rhin. Photo *Martin Hürlimann*

286 11. Miniature from Jacques de Guise's *Chroniques de Hainault*, Philip the Good receiving the MS from Simon Nockart; Flemish, 1448. MS 9242, fol.1r. *Bibliothèque Royale de Belgique, Brussels*

12. Detail of the *Ex-voto of Bishop Očko of Vlašim* attributed to Master Theodoric, the Emperor Charles IV; c.1370. *Narodni Galerie, Prague*

13. Miniature inserted in the *Bible of Charles V*, showing the presentation of the MS to Charles V by Jean de Vaudetar; miniature by Jean Bandol (Jean de Bruges), 1372. MS 10B23, frontispiece. Rijksmuseum Meermanno-Westreenianum, The Hague. Photo *A. Frequin*

287 14. Miniature from an *Address* by the town of Prato to Robert of Anjou, portrait of Robert of Anjou, King of Naples; Italian, c.1335–40. MS Roy.6.E.IX, fol.10v. *Trustees of the British Museum*

15. Detail of the *Wilton Diptych*, Richard II (kneeling at the feet of St John the Baptist and the Virgin); French School, c.1395. By courtesy of the Trustees of the National Gallery, London. Photo *Eileen Tweedy*

16. Detail of calendar miniature from the *Très Riches Heures du duc de Berry*, the Duke at table (January, enlarged); by the Limbourg brothers, 1413–16. MS 65, fol.1v. Musée Condé, Chantilly. Photo *Giraudon*

288-89 17. *The Coronation of the Virgin*, by Enguerrand Quarton; 1453–54. Made for the church of the Chartreuse du Val-de-Bénédiction at Villeneuve-lès-Avignon, Vaucluse, now in the Hospice Civil. Photo *Giraudon*

290-91 18. Modena: detail of relief by Wiligelmo on the façade of the Cathedral, the creation of Eve and the Fall; c.1099–1106. Photo *Cav. Uff. U. Orlandini*

19. Detail of relief by Nanni di Banco on the niche of the statues of the SS. Quattro Coronati, showing sculptors at work; early 15th C. Orsanmichele, Florence. The SS. Quattro Coronati were patron saints of wood- and stone-carvers. Photo *Mansell-Alinari*

20. The *Puits de Moïse*, base of the now-destroyed Calvary by Claus Sluter in the cloister of the Chartreuse de Champmol, near Dijon, Côte-d'Or; c.1402. Photo *Giraudon*

21. Poitiers, Haute-Vienne: statue of Jeanne duchesse de Berry attributed to Guy de Dammartin, from the fireplace in the Great Hall of the Palace of the Dukes of Berry; c.1385. Photo *Giraudon*

292 22. Rome: detail of fresco by Pietro Cavallini in Sta Cecilia, head of St James; c.1293. Photo *Scala*

23. *The Martyrdom of St Denis*, by Henri Bellechose; 1416. Louvre, Paris. Photo *Giraudon*

293 24. Detail of the *Maestà*, fresco by Simone Martini, enthroned Virgin and Child with saints; 1315. Palazzo Pubblico, Siena. Photo *Scala*

294 25. Right-hand wing of the *Champmol Altarpiece* (open), carved by Jacques de Baerze and gilded by Melchior Broederlam; made for the Chartreuse de Champmol

IX The Final Heritage

Page numbers in *italics* indicate illustrations